W9-CFZ-180

Phillips and Duncan's

MARKETING
Principles and methods

Seventh edition

PHILLIPS AND DUNCAN'S

MARKETING
Principles and methods

by

JAMES M. CARMAN   *University of California, Berkeley*

and

KENNETH P. UHL   *University of Illinois at Urbana-Champaign*

1973
RICHARD D. IRWIN, INC.   *Homewood, Illinois   60430*
IRWIN-DORSEY LIMITED   *Georgetown, Ontario*

Seventh Edition

First Printing, February 1973

ISBN 0-256-00416-1
Library of Congress Catalog Card No. 72–86625
Printed in the United States of America

To—
Evelyn Minard Phillips
Elizabeth Peairs Duncan
Carol Kohlruss Carman
Eleanor Lock Uhl

Preface

Managers in all areas of responsibility must recognize that their obligations and opportunities focus on the management of change. Success in our society is dependent on recognition and reaction to the rapidly changing environment. This is particularly true in marketing, since the market is the major contact point of organizations with their environments. Furthermore, the pace of change currently confronting marketing management has never been greater. Consequently, marketing, more than any other activity, provides an interesting, exciting, and rewarding field of study and work.

The approach used in this seventh edition of *Marketing: Principles and Methods* is to furnish an analytical framework for studying and understanding the marketing system. In our judgment, any book on basic marketing—because of the wide scope of the field—should include a description of the marketing system. Even more important, however, is the provision of a logical framework that enables the reader to understand and, hopefully, to predict when, how, and why change occurs within this system. Development of this analytical and logical framework is the most important change in this edition. We are convinced that such an approach, emphasizing the marketing system and the environmental forces in our economy and our society, is preferable in the basic marketing course to the strictly "managerial" approach.

But other changes have also been made. Among these are the incorporation of theoretical concepts from the behavioral sciences and a sharpening of the discussion of economic theory and economic analysis to facilitate the understanding of marketing processes. Parenthetically, it should be noted that much of this analysis suggests that the formal logic of mathematics might be developed to advantage. But no attempt is made to reduce marketing principles and methods to mathematical terms and formulas. Moreover, readers are not assumed to have backgrounds in either psychology or economics.

This volume is designed to introduce the reader to marketing through the logic of systems analysis in a readable and inquiring style. The book challenges the reader to appraise critically both the organization and the operation of our marketing system. It also identifies significant changes in the broad environment of the system that are continuously forcing innovations. And greater emphasis is placed on the information that must be collected, analyzed, and interpreted in order to change and improve the marketing system.

This text, like the previous editions, has been written for the basic marketing course, whether offered in the business school or the more general arts and science college. It should also prove of interest and value to the general reader and especially to the businessman who desires a broad picture of the structure and functions of marketing systems.

With this edition, the book adds two authors. This doubling of input has resulted in an influx of new ideas. It should come as no surprise, therefore, that this revision is very substantial.

There are, however, many features of the book which the new authors have not changed. First, we have tried to keep the organization logical and obvious. Second, we have aimed at language which is clear and direct and student-oriented. Third, we have kept this a basic book that is intended for the beginning student. Fourth, and perhaps most important, we have kept the book comprehensive—more comprehensive than any other book available in the field.

Fifth, most of the fundamental marketing concepts continue to be discussed in more than one context, thus aiding the reader to better understand and retain ideas presented in the description of system structure.

The organization pattern of this edition remains essentially the same as that of its predecessor, reflecting the approach and treatment which has proved pedagogically sound. There has been a reduction and a reallocation of space along with the introduction of new material. This seventh edition has been reduced to 25 chapters.

Part I offers an overview of the marketing task and an introduction to the marketing system. The basic systems analysis approach of description of the environment, structure, functions, institutions, and coordination is introduced. Also, Part I illustrates that marketing extends beyond businesses to not-for-profit and other types of organizations.

The chapters in Part II are concerned with the environment of the consumer products and services market. They cover consumer behavior, the dimensions of the consumer market, and the important subject of an informed and active consumer as a participant in the marketing process.

Part III in concerned with retailing, while Part IV is focused on wholesaling. In Part V, the focus changes to the marketing of industrial goods.

Part VI is completely new. One chapter is devoted to the marketing of services and one chapter discusses global marketing. These two topics have become so significant in the last few years that they virtually demanded explicit exposition.

Part VII turns to the managerial aspects of marketing. This edition retains the notion that managerial topics should be approached from the viewpoint of the managers of all types of marketing institutions, *not just manufacturers*. However, the managerial material has been extensively revised. For example, both information systems and marketing research are discussed and new treatments of promotion, pricing, product, and channel management have been provided.

Part VIII is new in content but not in spirit. The book continues to place great emphasis on the role of competition as the driving force in the system. Chapter 24 analyzes the role of competitive behavior in the system while Chapter 25 focuses on the role of government in regulating competition and marketing activities.

Despite the reduction in length, some present and prospective adopters of our textbook may still consider it too comprehensive to meet the time limitations imposed by university and college calendars. In such cases we suggest that instructors consider reducing the assigned reading by omitting Chapters 8, 9, 11, and 13. This may be done without loss of continuity. When such action is taken, it is recommended that Chapter 14 on "Agricultural Marketing" be used as a summary for the entire course since it contains a relatively complete elaboration of our marketing system.

Many teachers, businessmen, and students have made valuable suggestions which have contributed to the success this textbook has enjoyed. To attempt a listing would surely fail from lack of completeness. For this inspiration and assistance, the authors are deeply grateful. A special debt of gratitude is owed to the reviewers of the manuscript of this edition—each of whom did a particularly careful job and made substantial improvements. It is our hope that all readers will feel free to offer suggestions and comments on the seventh edition.

Charles F. Phillips and Delbert J. Duncan did not actively participate in preparing this edition although Professor Duncan did provide considerable source materials and general counsel, which were invaluable. More important, much of the strength of the seventh edition lies in the intellectual contributions which the original authors made in the first six editions. The junior authors feel a sincere dedication to maintain, in future editions, the high standard of excellence that has resulted in wide acceptance and recognition of this teaching instrument as a tradition in the marketing area.

January 1973   JAMES M. CARMAN
                                                        KENNETH P. UHL

Contents

Part II
The environment of the market for consumers' products and services

Part III
The retailing system

tan area. Expenses of retailers: *Influence of sales volume. Influence of population. Influence of kind of merchandise.* The risk of failure in retailing. Some current trends in the retailing system: *Change in the retailing system.*

Part IV
The wholesaling system for consumer products and services

country based. Foreign country "production." Channels within foreign markets. Why do companies make foreign investments? Environment for global marketing: *International monetary payments. National and international controls and restrictions.*

Part VII
Policies and practices within marketing organizations

Marketing research and information systems compared: *Marketing research shortcomings. An overview: Marketing information systems.* Objectives of marketing information systems. Overview of information needs: *Continually collected versus special-problem information. Internal versus external information. Buyers' versus sellers' information.* Major parts of marketing information systems: *Current-awareness subsystem. In-depth crisis subsystem. Incidental information subsystem.* Operating procedures: *Identify and define the situation and problems. Formulate hypotheses. Plan the research design. Collect and tabulate the data. Analyze and interpret the data. Communicate the findings. Follow up.* Data collection: *Construct data. Secondary data. Primary data. Gathering primary information.* Commercial information suppliers: *Types of commercial information. Other commercial services.* The future of information systems.

Product innovation: Nature and significance: *Product. Market. Product life cycles. The marketing mix. Incentives and responsibility for product innovation.* Product-line policies: *Planning for growth. Product development and introduction by manufacturers. Developing a marketing plan. Product management by manufacturers. Product management by middlemen.* Brand policy: *Meaning and types of brands. Advantages and disadvantages of branding for buyers. Benefits of branding for sellers. Branding by middlemen.* Other product policy decisions: *Packaging and labeling. Warranty. Postsale service.*

Selecting the type of channel members: *Analyzing the product. Examining the firm itself. Investigating the market and competition. Reviewing existing channels of distribution. Using more than one channel structure. Appraising sales, costs, risks, and profits. Securing customers' and middlemen's opinions. Determining the cooperation expected from the channel members. Planning the forms of assistance to channel members.* Selecting the number of each type of outlet to use: *Intensive distribution. Selective distribution. Exclusive distribution. Franchising.* Controlling and evaluating channels.

The physical distribution system: *Measures of performance. Components of the system —opportunities for conflict. Systems control.* Inventory management: *Reasons for inventory.* Warehouse location: *Plant location considerations. Warehouse operation considerations.* Public storage facilities: *Developments in public warehousing. Regulation of storage facilities. Storage costs.* Transportation facilities: *Railroads. Inland waterways. Motor transportation. Pipelines. Air transport. Express. Transportation rates.*

Promotion: What is it? *Components of promotion. A promotional system. Promotion by both sellers and buyers.* The communication process: *Selection of messages and media. Communication and promotion.* Relationship of promotion to buyer behavior. Promotion decisions: *Identify target market segments. Choose messages and determine competitive positioning. Select a media mix. Amount to spend on promotion.* Personal selling: *Importance of personal selling. Variety of personal selling jobs. Basic principles of personal selling. Management of the sales force.* Telephone selling.

Part VIII
Coordination of the marketing system

Appendixes

Indexes

Part I The marketing system

Marketing is exciting and fast-moving—it is a "now" subject. It will tickle your imagination and creative instincts. The marketing system is also vast and can be very confusing. To catch the excitement, we must first find an analytical framework in which to cast the system. Rather than slowly building the system one block at a time as we go through the book, therefore, a detail-free perspective of marketing systems is provided by the first three chapters.

We are all participants in the marketing system. Yet as ultimate consumers, most of us see it from only one point of view, which can cause distortions and misconceptions. The first chapter will explore some of these misconceptions of the marketing system, the true nature of the system, and its significance. The discussion is not limited to the United States but extends to numerous types of economic systems.

Chapter 2 focuses more explicitly on marketing systems: the problem of evaluating their performance, the functions performed by the system, and an introduction to some marketing institutions.

The final chapter of Part I provides an overview of the channel structure of the marketing system. This vertical structure provides much of the competitive uniqueness of marketing and is the aspect of the system which is most often overlooked. The chapter focuses on the development of this channel structure, some principles concerning the efficiency of alternative channel structures, and the nature of conflict and its resolution within channels of distribution.

You should gain from Part I a rather complete overview of the total marketing system. This will facilitate your learning by helping you fit the various topics into the framework.

1

1 Nature and significance of marketing systems

The primary objective of all living organisms is survival. Man is no exception; he must be protected against nature and against himself. While man must be wary of those things in nature, such as earthquakes, that can cause him physical harm, today he is more concerned with learning how to organize in such a way as to make optimum use of the scarce resources nature has provided. Thus men must protect themselves or their organizations against others who seek to destroy them in order to obtain more of the world's resources.

OBJECTIVE OF MARKETING SYSTEMS

One of the organizational devices man has developed to help solve the problems of allocation of resources is called a market or, more usefully, a group of organizations organized into a marketing system. **The primary objective of any marketing system is to allocate scarce resources efficiently and in such a way as to satisfy to the greatest extent possible the needs of man.**

You are embarking on the study of marketing systems, about which you may have some doubts. When you consider our urban or rural slums, you may wonder just how efficient a mechanism for resource allocation our system is. In view of the myriad advertisements for cigarette brands which "may be dangerous to your health" and appear to differ only in length and color of package, you may wonder just how exciting an adventure this will be.

Does not marketing sell unwanted encyclopedias, cause people to spend more on cigarettes than on education, lead physicians to prescribe branded drugs instead of cheaper generic equivalents, and force unwanted fashion changes on men, women, and children? Does it not cause the poor to pay more for goods and services and deny them adequate medical attention and other necessities? Does it not lead people to buy Texaco, Phillips 66, Bayer, St. Joseph, Budweiser, Schlitz, Crest, Colgate, Right Guard, or Dial, even though less expensive equivalent brands are available? Are these reasonable charges? Is advertising misleading, deceptive, repugnant, and not very helpful?

Finally, what about the price paid for this book, for shoes, for a new car; did not the dealer or retailer get at least 20 percent, or maybe even 40 or 50 percent, more than he paid for the goods? Could not the prices have been reduced by buying direct or through student bookstores or bypassing retailers or dealers in some other way?

So, what about marketing—can it really be a meaningful field of study and adventure? Is the central concern of marketing in truth the satisfaction of human needs? Answers to these two questions do not come easily and cannot be found in a few pages, but you should have a good basis for answering them when you finish reading this book. Our purpose is not to defend, to glorify, or for that matter, to castigate marketing. Rather it is to help readers learn about marketing systems—their objectives, environment, resources, components, and management—and to develop comprehensive insights into the subject. Only when these have been mastered can responses to these and many other questions relevant to marketing be formulated.

MARKETING MISCONCEPTIONS

Marketing is a subject a lot of people think they know a lot about. Look at Figure 1–1; some of the statements are true and some are false. Which do you think are true?

As consumers, all of us are active participants in the marketing system. Many hold the opinion that "marketing is just common sense." We "know" that when an advertisement fails to please us, it is ineffective. A store should not be out of the

FIGURE 1–1
Self test: Marketing misconceptions (some of the statements are true, some are false. What misconceptions do you start with?)*

Statement	True	False
1. Marketing is a part of economics.		
2. Advertising is a waste of money.		
3. Middlemen are necessary.		
4. Marketing forces fashion changes.		
5. Advertisements that fail to please are ineffective.		
6. Sellers who sell direct can sell for less.		
7. The primary objective of marketing is to efficiently allocate scarce resources.		
8. Marketing is unnecessary for not-for-profit organizations.		
9. Marketing for services and products is vastly different.		
10. Socialistic economies need marketing.		
11. As much is spent for marketing as for production in the United States.		
12. Middlemen can be bypassed, their activities cannot.		
13. Marketing could regulate itself if government would let it.		
14. The best way to sell products is through low prices.		
15. Marketing is little more than a parasite on society.		

* The answers are to be found as you learn about marketing.

Marketing: Principles and methods

products we want. Middlemen are unnecessary, and the seller who sells direct can sell for less money. If products are offered at lower prices in nicer stores and with more liberal credit terms, many more units can be sold. This is all "common sense" to many consumers, and if it is not, they possess an "uncommon" sense of marketing.

The truths about the above statements are that the offending advertisements may make consumers remember the product and its benefits, which may be one of the reasons they buy the product. Or, the ad may not be for them, but it may be effective on truly prospective customers. No store tries to stock all the goods that may be wanted by all customers. Instead, most stores try to serve a segment of the market in a manner that will encourage customer loyalty. "Buy direct and save" is a typical appeal to common sense, but unfortunately the direct seller normally has higher marketing costs than the channel employing middlemen. And to cap the common-sense discussion, prices can be too low as well as too high, and credit terms and other services are often too liberal rather than too conservative.

The moral of these examples is that your common sense and intuition about marketing should not be trusted until you have a thorough understanding of the marketing system.

Marketing and economics

Marketing is not a stepson of economics. The study of economics can be separated into macroeconomics, in which emphasis is on national and world economies and the major contributing factors are levels of consumption, investment, and imports and exports, and microeconomics, which focuses on individual firms and competitive structures and the factors of prices, quantities, and various concepts of consumer preferences. Such activities as advertising and personal selling are typically examined only as persuasion that may influence the demand for products.

One wit, in trying to explain the relationship between marketing and economics, said, "Marketing is a study of those topics that in the study of microeconomics are assumed away." A knowledge of many disciplines is useful to the student of marketing, but an understanding of basic economics will help provide the theory and analysis upon which much of marketing is based.

1. Marketing, like economics, can be divided into macro and micro units. Macromarketing is concerned with the structure of total marketing systems, the processes of structural change within a system, and its environment, component institutions, and control. Micromarketing considers the component institutions of a system—their functions, goals, measures of performance, and management.
2. Marketing is concerned with how and why consumers' needs are formed and changed. Economics assumes these, and hence demand functions are given.
3. Marketing is concerned with the process of new-product specification and development. Economics assumes products are given.
4. Marketing is most often concerned with understanding the workings of oligopolistic markets—those with few sellers and many buyers. This is the market structure that is least developed in economics.
5. Marketing is concerned with the geographic distribution of sellers and buyers and its effect on competition within the same trading area and between areas. Economics usually assumes "spaceless" markets.

6. Marketing is concerned with analysis of market operations in the absence of perfect information. The usual economic assumption of pure competition is that buyers and sellers are supplied perfect information at no cost.

It would be possible to go on for some time telling what marketing "ain't," and, for that matter, readers will continue to discover what it is not. However, this is the appropriate place to turn to what marketing is.

WHAT IS MARKETING?

Marketing is selling, advertising, buying, retailing, wholesaling, and a whole lot of other things. Marketing is distribution, and sometimes it is merely what housewives do when they go to a grocery store or what farmers do when they sell hogs.

In ancient times, man discovered that a primary way to conserve scarce resources was with a division of labor. Specialization of labor requires trade; when people produce more of some products and services than they can use, they seek to exchange them for needed goods and services that others have available. Thus trade and marketing activities arise to facilitate the exchange of goods and services, and they also influence what will be produced and exchanged. This is the essence of marketing and the marketing system—to allocate scarce resources efficiently in such a way as to satisfy the needs of man to the greatest extent possible.

Marketing includes the market activities of *communication* and *exchange*. It includes the searching activities of prospective sellers and buyers as they attempt to find the kinds of products and services they want and that are wanted by others and also includes the facilitating activities, such as *financing, storing,* and *transporting.* Thus marketing reaches far beyond the activity of exchange. It is concerned with the activities and decisions of prospective buyers and sellers and encompasses the plans and actions of many firms and persons who facilitate exchange but are neither buyer nor seller in the specific transaction. Buying as well as selling activities are included as part of its concern with determining what will be sold and bought. Marketing, however, does not include the physical transformation of goods into products or services—that is production.

Marketing: The creation of utility

Use of the word *production* calls for a definition of marketing in terms frequently encountered in beginning economics courses. The resource-allocation problem is often couched in terms of *conceiving of what* goods and services to produce, *how* to produce them, and *for whom* to produce them in order to maximize the utility (satisfaction) of the individuals in the society. Economists typically identify four types of utility: *form, place, time,* and *possession.* From these concepts the definition of marketing can be derived.

Both marketing and production are responsible for the creation of *form* utility. Marketing is concerned with anticipating what goods to produce. Production is concerned with how to produce them and the actual production process.

Marketing is concerned with for whom the goods and services are produced and consequently creates place, time, and possession utility by transporting them to the right places, storing them until they are needed by buyers, and selling them through promotion and exchange to buyers. Thus, as illustrated in Figure 1–2, only market-

FIGURE 1–2
Creation of utility

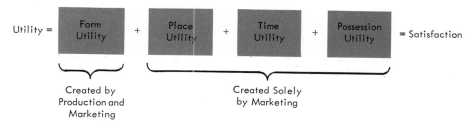

ing is responsible for the creation of place, time, and possession utility. These ideas have been brought together into a one-sentence definition of marketing:

Marketing is the process in a society by which the demand structure for products and services is anticipated or enlarged and satisfied through the conception, promotion, exchange, and physical distribution of such goods and services.

Or, as stated elsewhere, "When so viewed as a composite process, marketing is clearly a subject of much broader scope than the compilation of functions or managed activities commonly identified as marketing responsibilities in individual companies."[1] The emphasis is placed on the systems within a society that perform processes leading to the efficient allocation of resources.

THE MARKETING CONCEPT

Up to this point, the mettle, or spirit, of marketing that is important in business enterprises today has not been considered. It may seem strange to think of marketing as having a particular temperament or fervor. But many firms and organizations do possess (or are possessed by) a view or mode of operation which, in recent years, has become known as *the marketing concept.*

In the simplest of terms, the marketing concept means that an enterprise views its products and services as the adaptation of their resources, processes, and marketing activities to the characteristics and wants of prospective buyers. Enterprises operating under this concept have no less profit orientation than other firms; in fact, they may have more.[2] The success of a firm in a free enterprise economy is dependent on its ability to make sales, and more sales can be gained through less marketing efforts when wanted goods are produced. Consequently, firms pervaded by the marketing concept devote extensive attention to the marketplace, attempting to interpret and foresee its wants. They take their marching orders, confusing as they may be, from the market.

Management must find answers to such questions as: What products do the customers really want? What marketing policies and procedures will give customers those products in the manner most satisfactory from their points of view? How can

---

[1] The Marketing Faculty of The Ohio State University, "Statement of the Philosophy of Marketing," May 1964, p. 2.

[2] See M. L. Bell and C. W. Emory, "The Faltering Marketing Concept," *Journal of Marketing,* 35 (October 1971), pp. 37–42.

the firm reasonably meet the customers' wishes and still achieve its profit goals? The firm operating according to this concept

does not, in general, develop products in its labs and then determine how they might be marketed. It ordinarily *begins* with extensive customer testing and other marketing research, proceeds from there to develop some concept of a marketing opportunity, including even some notions about advertising campaigns; and only then does it turn to the labs for products that might meet these specifications.[3]

Traditional concept of business enterprise

The more traditional concept of business enterprise has emphasized physical and production activities and the accompanying financial structure and requirements. Marketing has been simply a way to dispose of the output of the firm. If adequate sales could be made, the firm could profit on its manufacturing activities. Manufacturing and production have been the essence of the business. Sales activities have been viewed as necessary evils, and marketing managers have usually been sales managers, regardless of their actual titles. They have not been part of top management and, accordingly, have not helped decide what products and services should be produced.

In recent years it has become increasingly difficult for firms operating under the traditional business enterprise concept to survive. A glance at the pages of a consumer magazine from 1950 or even 1960 (*Life, Look, Saturday Evening Post*) will show many brands that are now dead or way back in the pack—Ipana toothpaste, Lucky Strike cigarettes, Elgin watches, Harley Davidson motorcycles, and Stetson hats. Many magazines themselves have suffered the same fate—the *Saturday Evening Post, Look,* and *Colliers,* once popular weekly magazines, are no longer published. They failed to adapt to the ever-changing demands of the market and retained the traditional business enterprise concept instead of moving to the marketing concept.

The marketing concept: Not all new, not only an organization

The term *marketing concept* is relatively new and, indeed, for many enterprises its adoption in practice has resulted in major changes in operations.[4] This is particularly true for large organizations in which most top managers either did not have, or lost, frequent close contact with the ultimate consumers of their firms' products and services.

However, many enterprises employed a marketing concept mode of operation long before the term became popular. Early writings about retailing and wholesaling stressed that managers were purchasing agents for their customers, that their success would depend upon their customers' success and satisfaction, and that "goods well bought were half sold." Certainly not all, but many retailers, wholesalers, and even some manufacturers in years past owed their success to practice of the marketing concept.

It should also be emphasized that the marketing concept is not a unique organizational structure. It is a philosophy, in which marketing becomes more prominent throughout the organization and there are accompanying changes in the organizational structure. The essence of the marketing concept is shown in Figure 1–3.

---

[3] T. A. Wise, "Bristol-Myers' Hard Sell," *Fortune,* 75 (February 1967), p. 120.

[4] See H. C. Barksdale and B. Darden, "Marketers' Attitudes toward the Marketing Concept," *Journal of Marketing,* 35 (October 1971), pp. 29–36; and C. P. McNamera, "The Present Status of the Marketing Concept," *Journal of Marketing,* 36 (January 1972), pp. 50–57.

FIGURE 1–3
The marketing concept

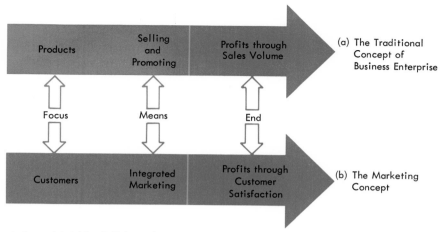

Products	Selling and Promoting	Profits through Sales Volume	(a) The Traditional Concept of Business Enterprise
Focus	Means	End	
Customers	Integrated Marketing	Profits through Customer Satisfaction	(b) The Marketing Concept

Source: Adapted from P. Kotler, *Marketing Management: Analysis, Planning and Control,* 1967.

AN ILLUSTRATION OF A MARKETING SYSTEM

An illustration of some of the many activities and institutions involved in or facilitating marketing of a product (a trail bike, for example), should help clarify and reinforce the preceding discussion. Marketing tasks interact with many others (within and outside the firm) to market products and services effectively.

The starting point is the purchase of a trail bike for $300 by a consumer. The consumer has written a check to the dealer (retailer) for $100 and signed an installment contract calling for 12 monthly payments of $20 each. As he rides away, the retailer realizes his bike inventory is getting low and he has no bikes on order. He estimates (forecasts) how many of each model he is likely to sell in the next 30–45 days. He examines his supply of bike accessories and replacement parts and prepares a list of needed items and their costs. He also notes that he needs more brochures describing the bikes.

The retailer mails the order to the wholesaler (distributor) on his way to the bank and the newspaper advertising office. The banker agrees to loan the dealer an additional $5,000 for five months but suggests that for the next season he should consider selling his installment contracts (loans to customers) to the bank instead of carrying them himself. At the newspaper office, the retailer reexamines the advertisements he had agreed to run and signs the advertising contract with the newspaper. The manufacturer is to pay one half the cost of the advertisements and to furnish the advertising materials.

The distributor (wholesaler) receives the order, checks his inventory of each item, and investigates the dealer's credit rating. He assembles the order and notifies a trucking company to make a pickup. A shipping document and invoice (bill) are prepared, and copies are sent to the retailer. The bill indicates that full payment must be made within 30 days.

Not all orders are so routine. Some dealers, because of poor credit ratings, must

1 / Nature and significance of marketing systems

enclose a check with their orders. Often items are out of stock and must be back-ordered. Some dealers simply call in their orders, and others stop in the office while their truck is being loaded with the merchandise.

The distributor, meanwhile, is in the process of developing marketing plans for his winter selling season. He has decided to drop the line of snowmobiles he carried the past winter and take on a new make, because he believes the replacement line is superior and he can get a better price on it, particularly if he buys at least 2,000 units. The manufacturer's salesman indicated his company would go 50–50 on all co-operative dealer advertising and would provide $50,000 of "umbrella" advertising (coverage over a number of geographic markets) in his territory. The manufacturer has also agreed to provide 15 man-days of dealer development support and will "floor plan" (require payment only when units are sold) his line from November through March.

The distributor plans to meet with a man from his advertising agency to rough out advertising plans after a marketing consultant has helped him determine the amount of dollars that should be spent on advertising and personal selling. By April 15th, the fall snowmobile marketing plans must be completed.

The manufacturer of trail bikes will complete the production of the last batch of this year's bikes in June. For the past year he has been working on bike redesign and improvement. Many sources of ideas have been utilized, including a survey of trail bike owners and numerous suggestions from distributors and dealers, particularly in terms of the mechanical problems they have encountered. This information was collected by a marketing consulting firm hired by the director of marketing information. And, of course, the manufacturer has bought units of all competitive bikes, tested and retested them, stripped them down and reassembled them. The new design is now ready, and the marketing and financing plans are being prepared.

The marketing vice president is developing a sales forecast and has roughed out the sales program in terms of salesman deployment; dealer development assistance; selection, termination, and replacement of distributors; and a cooperative advertising program. The advertising manager has an agency working on the advertising program and is scheduled to review their proposal for copy, media, and dollar expenditures. He has had proposals from three other agencies, but has decided to give the current one another chance.

The purchasing agent (buyer for the manufacturer) is particularly busy because several of the new units call for Japanese-built engines and he still has to secure second sources of supply for about half of the new parts. The manufacturer's representative for the engine company has been in the plant many times and on several occasions brought one or more engineers. Shipping schedules and credit arrangements still need finalizing. A local bank's international department has been most helpful with this.

Meanwhile, the vice president of finance has completed negotiations with three banks for a one-year $30,000,000 loan. This will permit the manufacturer to sponsor the "floor plan" for their trail bikes and to expand their inventory of bikes and parts sufficiently to use public warehouses in five sections of the country.

This illustration of marketing and its linkage with other activities could be developed in terms of other products, services, activities, and institutions. It also could be expanded to consider the various suppliers of parts to manufacturers as well as the eventual resale of the used trail bikes.

The marketing of all products and services involves hundreds of activities and institutions that fit together in a multiplicity of ways in order to provide satisfaction of human needs. This complex of constituent parts, viewed as a total set of interacting facets operating in an environment, is a marketing system.

SIGNIFICANCE OF MARKETING SYSTEMS

How significant—how important—are marketing systems? There are many facets to this question. How important are marketing systems to individual consumers, as a source of employment, to individual enterprises and other organizations, and to society? Some consideration of these and related questions can be provided here. However, they should be the subject of continuing inquiry long after this book has been put aside.

Importance to consumers

Would consumers (ultimate buyers) be better off without marketing systems? Although you are only a few pages into this book, the answer should be surfacing. How many individuals have the talents and time to be a weaver, physician, teacher, lawyer, farmer, soldier, and carpenter, and still handle all of their other wants? Without marketing systems, all individuals or household units would need to be self-sufficient—there would be no specialization and exchange. We would all be kept busy trying to subsist.

Because of past economic progress, the average American has a high income and considerable leisure time. We can often decide whether we want to secure a product directly from a seller or to have it delivered directly to our door through the marketing system. Some consumers are willing to pay for such services and others would prefer to keep their money and perform them themselves. One reason the marketing system is important to consumers is because it provides the opportunity to make alternative choices and hence maximizes total utility or well-being.

An indication of a healthy marketing system is that alternatives are available. There are full-service firms that offer credit, delivery, extensive help in buying, and complete product-line assortments; at the same time, there are competing firms that do not offer such services. In Chicago, for example, Marshall Field and Company and Carson, Pirie, Scott and Company are both full-service department stores. In contrast, Polk Brothers, a discount store, carries far less complete product assortments, offers no free credit, provides far less buying help, and has locations that are less convenient to most buyers. In general, Polk's prices are lower because they provide fewer services. Similar examples could be given for wholesalers and manufacturers.

The marketing system will generally offer alternatives for which there is sufficient demand to make them profitable and will withdraw those for which there is too little demand. Because perfect information or complete mobility of resources is seldom available, some alternatives are not offered as soon as they should be or in the correct form and place, and others persist beyond the time when the market demands them. This topic is discussed in more depth in Part VIII. The marketing system is of great importance to consumers in that it is responsive to most of their demands.

Importance of marketing systems to individual firms

The importance of marketing systems to individual firms was suggested above in contrasting the marketing concept with the more traditional concept of business enterprise. Peter Drucker (a management consultant and professor) made the point even more emphatically many years ago before marketing was considered appropriate for not-for-profit organizations:

Marketing is the distinguishing, the unique function of the busine●s. . . . Any organization that fulfills itself through marketing a product or a service, is a business. Any organization in which marketing is either absent or incidental is not a business and should not be run as if it were one.[5]

Some enterprises (retailers and wholesalers) are virtually all marketing because they create place, time, and possession utility but alter form only slightly, if at all. In many others (those operating under the marketing concept), marketing systems play a central, if not dominant, role—and their managements know it. As you learn about marketing, you should continually inquire how marketing systems are important to individual organizations.

Significance of marketing systems to societies

Marketing systems are a substantial part of all economic activity—including the use of resources—in all countries. Over 38 percent of all enterprises in the United States (not including farms) are in the retail or wholesale business. If sellers of services are included, the percentage increases to nearly 60 percent. Almost all other enterprises also engage in marketing to a significant extent.[6]

The volume of goods handled by marketing institutions of all types has increased tremendously since emergence from the depression of the 1930s. Much of this increase when measured in dollars may be attributed, of course, to the sharp rise in the price level. The total sales of wholesale establishments, which were reported by the Bureau of the Census as less than $55 billion in 1939, amounted to more than $459 billion in 1967.[7] Similarly, sales of retail stores increased from $42 billion in 1939 to over $351 billion in 1969.[8] When adjusted for price level changes, this represents real growth of over three times in each sector.

Labor force in marketing. In 1970, there were almost 71 million persons 16 years of age and older in the nonagricultural civilian labor force in the United States.[9] Although it is impossible with existing data to determine exactly how many of these were engaged in various marketing activities, about 15 million people, or over 21 percent, were employed in retail and wholesale establishments,[10] which generated approximately 15 percent of the nation's total national income.[11]

If we add to this percentage an estimate for the selling forces employed by manufacturers and for those engaged in transportation, communication, and other public utilities—about 6 percent in all—the picture is still incomplete. Many of those in financial marketing activities are not included in the calculation, such as employees of commercial banks and government employees in divisions lending to marketing cooperatives and private businessmen. Clerical workers associated with the production of large amounts of marketing information are omitted because data concerning them are lacking. Even some people directly engaged in the sale of goods are omit-

---

[5] P. Drucker, *The Practice of Management* (New York: Harper & Row Publishers Inc., 1954), pp. 37–38.

[6] U.S. Bureau of the Census, *1967 Census of Business, County Business Patterns: United States Summary,* 1968 (Washington, D.C.: Government Printing Office, 1971).

[7] U.S. Bureau of the Census, *1967 Census of Business* (Washington, D.C.: Government Printing Office, 1971).

[8] U.S. Bureau of the Census, *Monthly Retail Trade Report* (Washington, D.C.: Government Printing Office, 1971).

[9] U.S. Bureau of Labor Statistics, *Employment and Earnings* (Washington, D.C.: Government Printing Office, 1971).

[10] Ibid., p. 218.

[11] U.S. Office of Business Economics, *Survey of Current Business* (Washington, D.C.: Government Printing Office, 1971).

ted—for example, those in part-time selling at roadside stands, at auctions, and from house to house; and the 109,000 people engaged in providing advertising services have also not been counted. A conservative estimate is that one out of every four persons gainfully employed is, in some manner, engaged in marketing.

More affluence, more marketing. In the United States, there has been a marked increase in the proportion of the total population engaged in marketing activities since the Civil War. Between 1870 and 1950 the number engaged in producing goods increased by less than three times, but in retail and wholesale trades the advance was more than twelvefold.[12]

The situation in the United States is not unique. Lee Preston has pointed out that there is a relationship between a country's gross domestic product on a per-person (capita) basis and commercial employment. As a country becomes wealthier, marketing absorbs relatively more resources. Figure 1–4 indicates the contrast between four affluent "born free" countries—Australia, Canada, New Zealand, and the United States—and some less affluent ones.[13]

The more affluent a country becomes, the greater the number of goods and services that need marketing, and often these are ones that require proportionally greater marketing efforts. Electric can openers, life insurance, and high-fashion shoes require more marketing efforts than do staple foods and raw materials. Further, the

FIGURE 1–4
Relationship of gross domestic product per capita and percentage of commercial employment in the total labor force (C/LF ratio)

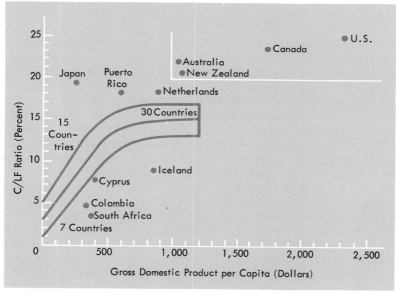

Source: L. E. Preston, "The Commercial Sector and Economic Development," in R. Moyer and S. C. Hollander (eds.), *Markets and Marketing in Developing Economies* (Homewood, Ill.: Richard D. Irwin, Inc., 1968).

---

[12] H. Barger, *Distribution's Place in the American Economy since 1869* (Princeton, N.J.: Princeton University Press, 1955), Table 1, pp. 4–5.

[13] L. E. Preston, "The Commercial Sector and Economic Development," in R. Moyer and S. C. Hollander (eds.), *Markets and Marketing in Developing Economies* (Homewood, Ill.: Richard D. Irwin, Inc., 1968).

more affluent the society, the more consumers want more marketing done for them. They perform fewer marketing functions themselves while paying sellers to provide them.

Marketing is important whether measured in terms of employment or other uses of resources, and whether viewed from the standpoint of individual businesses or individual consumers. And marketing is as important in other countries as it is in the United States.

MARKETING SYSTEMS IN NOT-FOR-PROFIT ORGANIZATIONS

Marketing and marketing systems extend beyond profit-seeking business enterprises. Their concepts are particularly useful to not-for-profit organizations that are seeking: (1) donations of money (2) acceptance of sets of beliefs, or (3) votes from large communities of people. Organizations like the Boy Scouts of America, the American Red Cross, the American Cancer Society, the Lutheran Church of America, the Sierra Club, and the Democratic National Party can and do make extensive use of marketing principles and methods.

Marketing is not useful for such organizations only at the national level. Numerous local organizations also do much marketing, and not merely to sell cookies or raise funds. The more common "commodities" offered by not-for-profit organizations are health, memberships, political candidates, issues, and religious and other beliefs. These items—like the products and services bought from for-profit organizations—are "bought" for the satisfactions (i.e., for the utilities) they promise or provide.

The major distinction—profit

One major distinction between not-for-profit and profit-seeking organizations is reflected in marketing systems. That, of course, is the matter of profit. The not-for-profit organization engages in marketing, in general, in order to help reach a distinct nonprofit goal, which is what the organization usually offers to prospects (customers). The Church of Jesus Christ of Latter Day Saints, for example, is reluctant to alter its offering (set of beliefs) to make it more acceptable (marketable) to more people. They have a product to sell, and their goal is to sell that product to as many people as possible. Other organizations may alter their beliefs to make them more acceptable to potential customers. A political party's philosophy may be somewhat alterable, and "reformed" religious sects such as the Reorganized Church of Jesus Christ of the Latter Day Saints have modified their beliefs. However, if the product is a set of beliefs, massive product changes seldom occur.

The same cannot be said about for-profit organizations if they follow the marketing concept. They will discontinue one product line and start another or switch from one market to another if they see a way to enhance profits. The Maytag Company's goal is not to produce washing machines or dishwashers any more than Textron is interested in a corporate goal of producing ballpoint pens, snowmobiles, or any other specific product or service. Any of these items can be spun off in short order if more profitable alternatives appear to exist.

The product fixation (what they have to offer) among not-for-profit organizations does somewhat alter the marketing methods and systems they employ. Like profit-seeking enterprises, however, not-for-profit organizations are concerned with the process by which the demand structure for their goods and services is anticipated or enlarged and satisfied through the conception, promotion, exchange and distribution of such goods and services. Marketing systems, as they are discussed in the ensuing pages, are not meant to be limited to business enterprises.[14]

APPROACHES TO THE STUDY OF MARKETING SYSTEMS

There are numerous ways to view most things. Spectators watching a football game from high in a pressbox overlooking the 50-yard line get a far different view from those watching from the first row behind the goalpost. And each different position, or viewpoint, provides a somewhat different view of the proceedings. Marketing systems also can be observed from different vantage points, each of which is likely to result in different perceptions, questions, and explanations. While all of the explanations should basically be in agreement—at least as to the final score of the game—some views offer better vantage points for some phases of the activity than do others.

Several major viewpoints have been employed for viewing and learning about marketing systems. These are usually designated as the commodity, functional, managerial, and institutional approaches. Societal, historical, and behavioral approaches have also been attempted but, to date, these have not become popular with students or teachers.[15]

Commodity

The commodity or industrial organization approach involves a study of how particular goods move from points of production to industrial and ultimate consumers. This process and the organizations engaged in it must be described for each commodity. A large number of such studies are necessary before generalizations will emerge from which a good picture of the field of marketing can be drawn.

Functional

The functional approach to marketing is through the classification and study of specialized activities or functions—such as selling, storing, and financing—involved in transferring products and services to consumers. By a careful investigation of how each of these activities or functions is performed, together with an analysis of the cost and problems involved, an understanding of marketing can be obtained.

Managerial

The managerial approach views marketing through the minds of marketing managers and focuses on the decisions they must make. Typically, marketing is viewed as consisting of controllable variables such as a firm's products, place (channels of distribution), price, and promotion, plus uncontrollable or environmental variables like competition, demand, and society. This approach, while a useful one, has placed too much emphasis on the marketing problems of manufacturers, to the detriment of other aspects of the marketing system.

---

[14] See *Journal of Marketing,* 35 (July 1971) for a further discussion and illustrations of marketing applied to fund raising, birth control, and health services.

[15] D. A. Revzan. *Perspectives for Research in Marketing: Seven Essays* (Berkeley: Institute of Business and Economic Research, University of California, 1965), pp. 41–54.

Institutional

The fourth major approach to the study of marketing—the institutional approach—considers the structural and geographic organization of marketing functions through the activities of manufacturers, wholesalers, retailers, and facilitating agencies such as transportation companies and advertising agencies that, together with many other institutions, make up the marketing system. In its most elaborate form, the institutional approach comes closest to the systems approach used in this book.

Total system approach

The major elements in marketing systems can best be understood if the key features of all four approaches are utilized. Consequently, all of them are used in this text, in what we refer to in Figure 1–5 as the total system approach. The concepts of this approach are developed in the following pages.

FIGURE 1–5
Approaches to the study of marketing

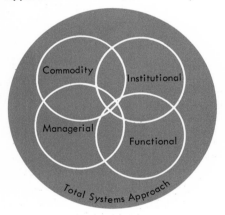

MARKETING SYSTEMS

Marketing scholars identified and studied marketing systems long before systems analysis became formalized. Since the end of World War II management scientists and electrical engineers have implemented a methodology for the study of systems to the point of being able to train men as "systems engineers." The details of this methodology involve highly mathematical theories concerned with utility, uncertainty, signals, communication, and control. While the applicability of most of these theories to marketing has not been proven, the introductory concepts of systems analysis do provide a useful framework with which to study marketing, and used in this book to describe the marketing system. Time will tell whether it will permit marketing scholars to apply the more formal aspects of systems analysis to their discipline.

Definition of a system

A system is a set of regularly interacting or independent groups coordinated in such a way as to form a unified whole and organized so as to accomplish a set of goals.

One must believe in God or some other supernatural order to acknowledge that such patterns as the solar and ecological systems have goals. Man's systems, however, are designed as the handiwork of his mind to achieve specific goals.

A system can contain within its structure a number of component parts or institutions, each of which is a system (or subsystem) within its own right. For example, the human body is a system which includes a respiratory system, a circulatory system, and a nervous system. At another level, a group of individuals may comprise a system known as a firm.

In marketing we are concerned with groups of consumers and with the group of individuals comprising a firm. Within that firm we are concerned with information systems, accounting systems, and distribution systems, among others. Firms can be collected into competitive systems, and all the institutions engaged in marketing can be studied as *the* marketing system, which itself is a part of the total economic and social system.

The boundaries we establish for a system are somewhat artificial. Systems usually are a part of a larger system which has an influence that sometimes is strong enough to determine how they perform. A system designed for travel to the moon may perform one way in the earth's atmospheric conditions and quite differently in space.

Why is it useful to study marketing as a system?

Studying marketing as a system not only provides a logical and intuitive framework in which to organize thoughts, but, more important, it facilitates analysis so that normative decisions and evaluations (i.e., not necessarily the way things are, but the way they should be) can be made. The systems approach yields the following benefits:

1. It helps determine which arrangement of components will produce the greatest consumer satisfaction at least cost.
2. It suggests which arrangement of components is most efficient.
3. It helps determine how the marketing system influences social, political, and ecological systems and vice versa. The true cost of a system must include the costs it creates in both the systems with which it connects and the one in which it is embedded.
4. By facilitating the study of structural change, it helps the pursuit of dynamic goals and optima rather than simply static ones.
5. It helps the marketing manager make decisions regarding his firm.

System specification

There are six basic specifications you should look for as you study marketing systems (Figure 1–6). Description of a system should specify:

1. The system's goals.
2. The performance measures for the total system.
3. The system's environment, which often acts as a constraint.
4. The resources of the system.
5. The components of the system, their structure, functions, goals, and measures of performance.
6. The management and control of the system.[16]

---

[16] C. W. Churchman, *The Systems Approach* (New York: Delacorte Press, 1968), pp. 29–30.

FIGURE 1–6
System Specification

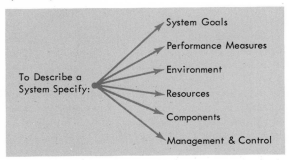

Goals. The system's purposes for being, or its goals, are often illusive. An oft-cited example is profit maximization as the objective of the business firm, which may prove to be inaccurate. As C. West Churchman notes, "The management scientist's test of the objectives [or goals] of a system is the determination of whether the system will knowingly sacrifice other goals in order to attain the objective."[17] For the marketing system as a whole, even the statement of the goals of the system at the beginning of this chapter is the subject of some debate. To understand a system, its *true* goals must be known.

Measures of performance. To know how well a system performs (to give a "grade" to a system), it is necessary to have measures of how well the system is doing in reaching its goals. Only with such measures does systems analysis become operational. The construction of performance measures for marketing systems is often complex (as we shall see in Chapter 2). It involves consideration of:

1. The dynamic efficiency with which the system perceives and anticipates changes, over time, in the needs and wants of consumers and of the other systems to which it relates.
2. The maximization of alternative goods and services which are available to final users.
3. The static efficiency of the system—that is, the quantity (or value) of output divided by the quantity (or value) of the inputs to the system at one point in time.
4. The quality of these outputs.

Environment. The environment of the system is the set of conditions in the host system that are affected by but are not under the control of the marketing system per se. In part, these act as constraints on the system. Examples are technology—the state of science of transforming inputs into outputs—and government foreign policy, which may act to constrain certain international marketing activities. The U.S. government significantly constrained trade with China, Russia, and Eastern Europe for over 20 years.

Resources. These are the inputs to the system. They include money, man-hours, and equipment. Resources, as opposed to the environment, are the things the system can change and use to its own advantage.[18]

[17] Ibid., p. 31.
[18] Ibid., p. 37.

Components. Only through separation of the system into components or parts can the analyst get the information and understanding he needs to determine whether the marketing system is operating properly and what he should do to change it. Each component or part of the system should be analyzed in terms of its (1) marketing functions, (2) component structure, (3) goals, and (4) measures of performance.

Marketing functions are the activities performed by the component institutions and subsystems which are necessary for the performance of the marketing system. The need to study these functions, which are described in detail in the next chapter, has been well stated by David A. Revzan:

> The analysis of functions not only calls attention to the basic nature of each group of activities and the component elements thereof, but to their interrelationship as well, and to the costs inherent in their performance. It is a basic assumption of such analysis in the present framework that forms of marketing organization and systems may change, and that the relative importance of the different sets of functions may be affected by changing conditions, but that the basic function, as such, must be always present in any kind of marketing system.[19]

The *component structure* means both the organization of activities within each component and the organization of the marketing functions among the manufacturing, wholesaling, retailing, and facilitating institutions within marketing systems.

The *goals* of the individual components—e.g., manufacturers, advertising agencies, and retailers—need to be studied in order to understand when component institutions seeking to achieve their own individual goals can provide a mechanism for achieving the goals of the total system (society) and when such pursuit of individual goals may run into conflict with achievement of the goals of the system.

Measures of performance of individual components (e.g., discount stores, mail order houses) must be studied to judge the success of these institutions.

Management and control of the system. Within an individual institution, people organize themselves and consciously cooperate as a subsystem to achieve the institution's goals. But how is the total marketing system in the United States managed and controlled? A detailed answer is suggested in Part VIII, but to facilitate the study of the marketing system, a brief answer is that it is controlled by the constraints placed upon it by its environment. That is, the market provides the control required for the marketing system to achieve its goals—if market mechanisms operate and if consumers have both freedom of choice and the information they require.

This self-controlling feedback mechanism which causes the system to tend toward dynamic equilibrium is a concept which was discussed in biology and economics long before it was discovered by systems analysts, but it is a central feature in systems theory. This natural tendency of the market system, or any system, to restore itself to a course aimed at achieving its goals is called *homeostasis*. It operates through a series of controls (like thermostats) called homeostats which, in marketing, are manifested mainly in the price system. While the system is constantly undergoing change, these homeostats constrain it from reacting violently. Thus the marketing system tends to operate toward optimal efficiency under conditions which are naturally destabilizing.

For example, a city may have a shortage of two-bedroom apartments. Realizing this, owners will raise the rent on such apartments, and the increased return will motivate them and others to build additional two-bedroom apartments. As supply increases relative to demand, prices are likely to decline, and building activity will subside. In fact, some overbuilding is quite likely to occur.

---

[19] D. A. Revzan, *Perspectives for Research in Marketing: Seven Essays*, p. 11.

1 / Nature and significance of marketing systems

MARKETING SYSTEMS IN THE ENVIRONMENT OF OTHER ECONOMIC SYSTEMS

Marketing systems are not the same in all countries and under all types of economic systems. All do not use a market mechanism to allocate resources. To better understand *marketing* systems in the United States—and in international markets (Chapter 16)—it is essential to be familiar with the major differences among *economic* systems of other societies.

The central economic problem is the struggle for existence which is necessitated by scarcity. Over the years, man has found only three basic arrangements for managing this problem. An economy can be operated basically as indicated in Figure 1–7, by tradition, by command, or by the marketplace.

Tradition-based system

The hallmark of a tradition-based economy is that its present-day answers to the scarcity problems are largely the solutions of the past. Tradition dominates in determining who does what, where, and when. For example, in an economy like India's, sons are farmers if their fathers were farmers; they raise virtually the same crops and in the same location and sell their surpluses in the same markets in the traditional ways. Sons and families throughout the economy both produce and consume in much the same patterns as their fathers and their families. The patterns of allocation of scarce resources become quite rigid—beliefs, customs, and laws dominate over rethinking of current economic situations. Change in the tradition-bound economy comes slowly compared to change in economic systems that champion innovation.

Tradition bias in the United States? The U.S. economy is by no means free of the tradition bias. Even today, it is very helpful for a student who wants to become a physician to have a mother or father who is one. This is true of bricklaying, plumbing, and many other professions—and it is not just a matter of genes; it has more to do with entry "rights" and upbringing. Furthermore, how many children of college

FIGURE 1–7
Alternative economic systems

Marketing: Principles and methods

professors or white-collar workers would elect to be garbage haulers, junk dealers, or laborers?

The allocation of human resources into various productive activities in the United States is firmly influenced by tradition. The same is true of consumption patterns. The homes and communities in which children grow to adulthood have a lot to do with their likes and dislikes, particularly as they settle into their own life styles after college age. Neither the United States nor any other economy is completely free of allocation of scarce resources by tradition.

Command-based system

The (autocratic) controlled countries of the world—such as the U.S.S.R., Haiti, Saudi Arabia—tend toward command-based economies, in which most decisions as to what goods and services will be produced, who will do what, and who will have access to the output are made by the government. The autocratic leadership, for example, can decide to build a new capital city or to invest in highways, airports, hospitals, or armies. It can channel the resources of the nation into whatever it thinks is most appropriate. Tradition may be disrupted throughout the nation as the government conscripts or attracts workers and other resources into its sponsored projects. The voice of the marketplace is relatively weak in such an economy. Consumers may want more rice and meat, but the government may direct resources instead toward the production of wheat and milk or steel and fertilizer.

Command bias in the United States? In considering whether the United States economy is free of the command bias, a brief digression is helpful. First, one should not assume all products and services provided by the public sector (governments) are the results of command decisions. Decisions to build such things as public schools, hospitals, or sewer and water systems are often made directly by the vote of the population involved on the separate issues, with the price tags attached (approval or rejection of bond issues).

Some public-sector allocation decision, however, are less directly influenced by the people in that they are made by elected officials. These officials can be impeached, but more practically, they can be turned out of office at the next election. Unfortunately, officials seek reelection based on more than an individual decision and, furthermore, candidates who are more representative may not be available for election. There is more command economy influence as: (1) more allocative decisions are placed in the hands of elected and appointed government, (2) elected and appointed officials serve long terms without reelection or reappointment, (3) barriers block easy entrance to elective offices (e.g., high costs of campaigning and extensive political patronage to office holders), (4) economic (monopoly) power widens so that government feels required to make resource-allocation decisions, (5) government is allowed to persuade instead of being persuaded by its constituents (voters), and (6) government becomes less public (and can hide more of its criteria for decisions, its actual decisions, and those responsible for decisions).

In the United States, many government decisions (and not only at the national level) do not reflect the sentiments of the marketplace. Decisions to commit massive resources to warfare, welfare, space exploration, and highway construction, for example, may not reflect the allocation decisions which would be made if we individually could specify how our individual taxes would be spent or even if all decisions were made through majority rule in a popular ballot.

1 / Nature and significance of marketing systems

Marketplace system

In a *pure* marketplace economy, the allocation of scarce resources is directed by the wants of individual consumers. Through their decisions, consumers are very important—they are sovereign. When they do not want a product or service or they find it priced too high, it goes unsold. In turn, the resources used to produce it remain unpaid and eventually get reallocated to some other use.

A very helpful definition of a pure market economy has been written by Karl Polanyi:

A market economy is an economic system controlled, regulated, and directed by markets alone; order in the production and distribution of goods is entrusted to this self-regulating mechanism. An economy of this kind derives from the expectation that human beings behave in such a way as to achieve the maximum money gains. It assumes markets in which the supply of goods (including services) available at a definite price will equal the demand at that price. It assumes the presence of money, which functions as purchasing power in the hands of its owners. Production will then be controlled by prices, for the profits of those who direct production will depend upon them; the distribution of the goods also will depend upon prices, for prices form incomes, and it is with the help of these incomes that the goods produced are distributed amongst the members of society. Under these assumptions order in the production and distribution of goods is ensured by price alone.[20]

Marketplace bias in the United States? Although the marketplace economy predominates, the economy in the United States reflects all three types of economic systems. It has been described as a *marketing economy,* because the prevailing mode of competition is monopolistic competition (not perfect competition) and because governmental control (command system) and tradition are intermingled with the marketplace system.

Government is forced to inject itself into market operations at various times to exercise control. This need is particularly acute when component institutions develop power to control parts of the market system or consumers are denied the information they require to make free choices in the marketplace. Conflicts between institutions develop, and the homeostasis quality (the stabilizing influence) of the market is less effective.

A major problem in U.S. society today is to determine just when such control from the environment is required and the form it should take. A change in structure of the system or its components might be preferable to governmental replacement of the market mechanism as the control device. Hopefully, the reader will obtain enough understanding of the marketing system from this book to form some reasoned opinions on the answer to this problem.

An overview of the marketing system in the United States is provided in the next two chapters. Part II, which includes a discussion of buyer behavior, is concerned with the environment for the marketing of consumer products and services. Part III deals with the retailing components of the system, Part IV with the wholesaling components, Part V with marketing systems for industrial products, Part VI with marketing systems in the special fields of services and international marketing, and Part VII with the policies and practices within marketing institutions. Finally, Part VIII takes a more detailed look at the mechanisms—both government and competition—that coordinate the marketing system.

---

[20] K. Polanyi, *The Great Transformation* (Boston: The Beacon Press, 1957), pp. 68–69. Paperback edition; originally published in 1944.

Marketing: Principles and methods

SUMMARY

The purpose of this chapter has been to introduce the nature and significance of various marketing systems. While you should be able to answer the questions at the end of this chapter, your study should lead to many other questions about marketing for which you should seek answers both in this book and as you continue to interact with marketing systems.

There are many complaints about marketing systems. Some are legitimate, but some, if not many, have arisen simply out of naïveté or out of the frustrations of living. We are all a part of the marketing system; it is a major component of our social and economic system. The reader should be sure he understands the system before he attempts to judge it.

Marketing is the process in a society by which the demand structure for products and services is anticipated or enlarged and satisfied through the conception, promotion, exchange, and physical distribution of such products and services. A systems approach is used to facilitate understanding of the components, their structures, and their functions. It also provides evaluation of the effectiveness of alternative marketing systems and aid in the understanding and evaluation of changes that take place in them through time.

A description of the marketing system requires consideration of goals, measures of performance, environment, resources, structure, and functions and controls.

Business enterprises are understandably concerned with marketing, but its use by not-for-profit organizations has frequently been overlooked. Readers could ask: "Are not marketing systems applicable to more than business firms?" in regard to topics throughout the book. Marketing will prove to be meaningful and useful to those who work with and for not-for-profit organizations, whether part or full time.

Finally, the reader should ask questions about marketing systems as they relate to individuals, to businesses and other types of organizations, to competitive and cooperative groupings of organizations, and to societies. We attempt to raise many questions to help you learn, but we cannot raise all those that you, with your unique experiences and perspective, should ask. This book should be of considerable help in formulating answers to many of these questions. However, we know it does not answer all of our own questions, and there is no way it can help you answer all of yours. But, then, we do not want you to stop asking and answering questions about marketing. As you gain additional knowledge about marketing, you should raise numerous additional questions. This is a part of learning; one measure of intellectual growth is the questions you ask—they are even more important than the answers you give. We want you to be students of marketing for a long time to come.

REVIEW AND DISCUSSION QUESTIONS

1. What is the primary objective of the marketing system in the United States?
2. What are the important differences between marketing and economics?
3. In your own words, explain what is meant by marketing.
4. The marketing concept emphasizes customer satisfaction and company profit objectives. Explain how these two are compatible.

5. What, if anything, is wrong with the traditional business enterprise concept in contrast to the marketing concept?

6. Explain the differences which would be present in your pattern and style of living if there were no marketing system in the United States.

7. "The best marketing system contains the least marketing." Do you agree or disagree with the statement? Explain your answer.

8. Does the twelvefold increase in the number of people engaged in retail and wholesale trades from 1870 to 1950, while production workers increased by only threefold, indicate there is growing waste and inefficiencies in marketing? Explain the change.

9. Compare and contrast the use of marketing in for-profit and not-for-profit organizations.

10. Explain the four major approaches to the study of marketing and discuss the relative merits of each. What other approaches can you suggest and defend?

11. Why is it useful to study marketing as a system?

12. Describe the system (using appropriate system specifications) used to market one of the following products in the United States: automobiles, beer, toothpaste, magazines, motorcycles.

13. Is a marketplace type of economic system inherently superior to a traditional or command type of economic system? Explain.

SUPPLEMENTARY READINGS

Bliss, P. C. *Marketing and the Behavioral Sciences.* 2d ed. Boston: Allyn & Bacon, Inc., 1967. The editor presents a collection of readings from the fields of economics, psychology, and sociology which are of value to the marketing student.

Churchman, C. W. *The Systems Approach.* New York: Delacorte Press, 1968. A modern, nonmathematical introduction to systems analysis.

Cox, R. (in association with **Goodman, C. S., and Fichandler, T. C.**) *Distribution in a High-Level Economy.* Englewood Cliffs, N.J.: Prentice-Hall, Inc., 1965. Professor Cox and his associates consider two basic questions: (1) How important a role does marketing play in our economy? (2) How effectively is the marketing task performed?

Cox, R.; Alderson, W.; and Shapiro, S. J. (eds.) *Theory in Marketing: Second Series.* Homewood, Ill.: Richard D. Irwin, Inc., 1964. While this volume of essays suggests that marketing is making "some progress toward that *sine qua non* of effective theory—the formulation of verifiable hypotheses" (p. 1), it clearly indicates that "we are far from having formulated a body of theory as impressive as that achieved by the theoretical economists and, even more importantly, by the theoretical physicists" (p. 13).

Kelley, E. J., and Lazer, W. (eds.) *Managerial Marketing: Perspectives and Viewpoints.* 3d ed. Homewood, Ill.: Richard D. Irwin, Inc., 1967. Recognizing advances in marketing literature, the authors have assembled materials in such areas as the marketing concept, external environments of marketing systems, the consumer, techniques of decision making, the marketing mix, and international marketing. The interdisciplinary aspects of marketing are emphasized especially on pp. 671–724.

Lavidge, R. J., and Holloway, R. J. *Marketing and Society.* Homewood, Ill.: Richard D. Irwin, Inc., 1969. Primary attention is devoted to articles that suggest how marketing contributes or can contribute to society as well as to societal issues.

Narver, J. C. and Savitt, R. *The Marketing Economy: An Analytical Approach.* New York: Holt, Rinehart Winston, Inc., 1971. An introductory textbook which is not managerial in its approach and is rigorous in concepts, definitions, relationships, and methods of analysis.

Preston, L. E. *Markets and Marketing, An Orientation.* Glenview, Ill.: Scott, Foresman & Co., 1970. Intended to provide an orientation, not a comprehensive description, for understanding the character and role of marketing activity in the economy and the firm, this book is solid and compact.

Preston, L. E. (ed.) *Social Issues in Marketing.* Glenview, Ill.: Scott, Foresman & Co., 1967. In this collection of readings, preceded by an introduction and supplemented with notes, emphasis is placed on three areas of social relevance in marketing: efficiency, fair competition, and consumer welfare.

Revzan, D. A. *Perspectives for Research in Marketing: Seven Essays.* Berkeley: Institute of Business and Economic Research, University of California, 1965. The first two essays in this short volume present the most accurate definition of the "institutional approach" to marketing available.

Schwartz, G. (ed.) *Science in Marketing.* New York: John Wiley & Sons, Inc., 1965. Eighteen marketing scholars have cooperated to produce this volume on the role of science in marketing.

2 *Marketing systems: Functions and institutions*

As people visiting a city for the first time consult a map to determine where items of interest are located and how to get from one place to another or consult a picture before they start to assemble a jigsaw puzzle, students beginning study of a subject can benefit from a preliminary overview. The purpose of this and the following chapter is to provide such an overview of the marketing system in terms of measures of performance, the process of equalizing supply and demand, marketing functions, institutions, and channel structures. Some of the views will be very brief at this point, since the functions, institutions, and channels are examined in detail in later chapters.

MEASURES OF PERFORMANCE

The primary goal of the marketing system, as observed in Chapter 1, is to allocate scarce resources efficiently in such a way as to maximize the satisfaction of man. There are no direct measures of performance to provide easy answers to the question of how well the marketing system accomplishes this purpose in the United States. Therefore, we will consider a set of objectives that, while not complete, does approach the primary goal and affords some measures of performance. These goals are discussed in the following pages under the headings of static efficiency, dynamic efficiency, and the quality of life. The reader not familiar with accounting may want to read Appendix A at this point.

Static efficiency

One measure of a marketing system's effectiveness is that it performs its functions efficiently at any one point in time (hence, static efficiency). Because it is concerned with output compared to input, a measure of efficiency is simply output divided by input. Performance, by this measure, improves as this ratio increases (i.e., as output exceeds inputs by more and more). Such an efficiency measure can be applied to the entire system, one subsystem (e.g., the marketing system for trail bikes), or alternative channels of distribution.

Inputs. The inputs to the system are the resources employed by the system or subsystem during the appropriate time period, as measured by their costs:

1. The cost of *labor* employed.
2. The economic cost of *entrepreneurship* (accountants might estimate this as the proprietor's "fair" salary or corporate dividends).
3. The cost of maintaining the *environment* (this could include taxes and contributions).
4. The cost of *capital* employed as rent, interest, and depreciation.

All of these inputs are difficult to measure. However, when good accounting data are available, only one problem causes really severe measurement difficulty—that of identifying and separating the marketing costs from the other costs incurred by producers. Marketing costs typically are immersed and intermixed with all others, such as the salaries of top management, who contribute to both marketing and production.

Outputs—the concept of value added. The measurement of the output of a marketing system cannot be simply the value of the products sold. The value of production, finance, and other nonmarketing activities is also included in this figure.

A more appropriate output measure is the *value added* by marketing. For measurement purposes, this term, as shown in Figure 2–1, may be defined as the value of sales, minus the cost of goods sold, minus the cost of purchased services such as utilities and legal and financial assistance.

In 1963, the last year for which figures are readily available, the value added by wholesale trade in the United States was $37.5 billion and by retail trade, $63.1 billion.[1] For that same year, the *total sales* of the wholesale sector were $358.4 billion, compared to only $244.2 billion in retailing.[2] Total wholesale sales were greater than total retail sales because, at the wholesale level, goods may be resold several times,

FIGURE 2–1

Method of calculating value added by marketing

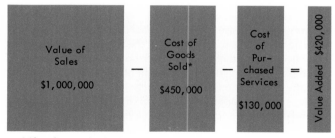

Value of Sales $1,000,000 — Cost of Goods Sold* $450,000 — Cost of Purchased Services $130,000 = Value Added $420,000

* After adjustment for changes in inventory value.

[1] U.S. Office of Business Economics, "Input-Output Structure of the U.S. Economy, 1963," *Supplement to Survey of Current Business,* 1969, Vol. 1.

[2] U.S. Bureau of the Census, *1963 Census of Business* (Washington, D.C.: Government Printing Office, 1963).

whereas a retail sale only occurs once.[3] Also, wholesale sales included sales to industrial users. However, all of these wholesale flows added less value to the product than that added in retailing.

It may be more meaningful to look at value added in relative terms. If we add the value added by wholesale and retail trades and express this amount as a percentage of retail sales, the result is a very crude estimate of the percentage of the end user's dollar which goes for the creation of marketing (excluding form) utility. This estimate is that about 42 cents of every dollar went for marketing in 1963.[4] Figure 2–2 illustrates this fact.

A major shortcoming of the "value-added" concept and the related measure of output is that they are not very useful in calculating efficiency (defined as output divided by input). This is true because the total marketing inputs are defined so as to be almost equal to total marketing outputs and not very different from gross margin. Moreover, the value-added approach fails to account adequately for the marketing activities of manufacturers.

FIGURE 2–2
Division of a $1 retail purchase (1963)

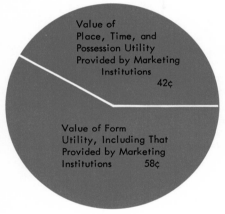

Value of
Place, Time, and
Possession Utility
Provided by Marketing
Institutions
42¢

Value of Form
Utility, Including That
Provided by Marketing
Institutions   58¢

Use of static efficiency.   The measure of static efficiency does not imply that greater efficiency is the same as a lower spread between the producer's selling price and the ultimate buyer's price or, in other words, fewer dollars for middlemen. In the United States, for example, if the middleman's margin on bicycles is $25, compared to $12.50 in India, this does not mean the Indian system is twice as efficient or even as efficient as the American system. This is true for two reasons. First, if markets are performing effectively, it is socially desirable for sellers to increase their marketing inputs (and associated costs) if such increases add to their profits. If consum-

---

[3] One authority estimates that the *Census of Business* in 1963 understated the gross volume of wholesale transactions by about 74 percent. See D. A. Revzan, *The Marketing Significance of Geographical Variations in Wholesale/Retail Sales Ratios, Part II* (Berkeley: Institute of Business and Economic Research, University of California, 1967), pp. 2–8.

[4] R. Cox, *Distribution in a High-Level Economy* (Englewood Cliffs, N.J.: Prentice-Hall, Inc., 1965), p. 148.

Marketing: Principles and methods

ers demand more marketing services, then sellers should increase the services they provide.

Second, decreased marketing costs may be more than offset by increased production costs. This is most likely to occur where decreased sales result from the decreased marketing activities and costs and there are relatively high fixed costs of production that must be spread over fewer units. An Indian, for instance, may pay the equivalent of $120 for his bicycle, whereas the American may pay only $75.

The value-added concept, although not very useful in measuring efficiency, at least helps in this understanding by shifting the emphasis in measuring marketing activity from the *costs* of marketing to the *contributions* of marketing. It also provides an excellent measure of output.

Dynamic efficiency

Two of the unique characteristics of Americans and their culture are the exaltation of growth and the tolerance for change. Within the private investment and consumption sectors of the economy, the most important force in keeping the process of growth and change vibrant is the American marketing system. Indeed, we have defined marketing as the process in a society by which the demand structure is anticipated or enlarged.

Consequently, any measure of performance that ignores the dynamic (growth) objectives of the system is inadequate and unsatisfactory. Social critics and even some economists are prone to overlook growth measures of performance simply because good measures are difficult to find. None of those we suggest are readily available, but it is possible to construct useful ones. Three are discussed here: aggregate growth, progressiveness, and the availability of alternatives.

Aggregate growth. It has been said that marketing is "the delivery of a standard of living." If this is true, then a measure of marketing performance could include such things as the rate of growth of real disposable personal income or real personal consumption expenditures per capita.

At an earlier time in our history, these measures would have been quite satisfactory by themselves. But today, government expenditures, world trade, and corporate investment also have tremendous impact on aggregate growth. In addition, there are those who argue that marketing has built personal consumption expenditures principally through consumer debt financing and, because this cannot be maintained, our growth machine is built on a "house of cards." Complete discussion of such issues is reserved for a later chapter.

Progressiveness. How innovative are firms in their efforts to anticipate demand? How willing are they to take risks in practicing the "marketing concept"? Some crude measures are available to answer these questions. One is simply the level of expenditures for research and development. Another is to guage the success of research and development activity by counting the number of new product introductions.

In addition to *willingness* to be progressive, however, there should be interest in the *efficiency* of innovative efforts. One measure of innovative efficiency on which marketers are often criticized is the very small percent of new consumer products and services that survives.

Availability of alternatives. If marketing is successful in anticipating demand, consumers should have a large number of form, time, and place utility "bundles" from which to choose. Since man's wants seem to be insatiable and since we are unique individuals, the marketing system should constantly be providing new combinations of utility bundles to see if there are enough customers for them to be marketed profitably. It is this constant probing for changes in taste which leads to individual and aggregate growth in satisfaction or in economic wealth.

If marketing managers are doing their jobs efficiently, the economic waste associated with introducing unprofitable products to the market should be minimized.

We should also have measures of performance which guard against mistakes of the other kind—opportunities in which products and services should have been introduced but were not. Would antipollution and safety devices on automobiles have been commercially successful before they were introduced by government edict? Could U.S. automobile producers have profitably offered an economy car before they did? Is an extended-life, low-energy-consumption light bulb producible at a price that would cause consumers to buy them in large numbers? Systematic measures of inefficiencies of this type are not easy to construct.

Poor measures of performance. In a market economy such as ours, economists and government antitrust lawyers have often observed only static performance when they need dynamic measures. They have fallen into this trap because of their traditional dependence on the static economic model of perfect competition and because good measures of dynamic efficiency were not available. The marketing system is frequently subject to undue criticism only because inappropriate performance measurements are used. This problem will be discussed in more detail in the last chapters of this text.

The quality of life

In considering a system for which maximization of individual satisfaction is the goal, it may seem contradictory to suggest that it may not be increasing the general good. Criticisms of the marketing system that are of this nature seem to relate to its impact on the quality of life. The measurement of quality in any context is not an easy matter, and the measurement of the impact of the marketing system on the quality of life has defied quantification. It may even be that marketing has no effect on quality measures. About the best that can be accomplished is to mention the symptoms of poor quality often attributed to marketing. Few tests exist of what is cause and what is effect.

One charge, eloquently made by John Kenneth Galbraith, is that marketing is creating "wants" that are not the right ones.[5] Perhaps we ought to be investing more resources in the public sector aimed at improving the quality of life—for example, we should spend less on trail bikes and more on reforestation of the trails on which they are used. According to this charge, the system misallocates because marketing pressures are more efficient in altering our tastes and life styles than are pleas for public works that will result in higher taxes.

In attempting to measure marketing performance on such a basis, it is necessary to consider at least the following three questions. First, should the tastes of one person or group be valued more than those of another simply because they acquire their tastes from a different cultural environment? Second, if our democratic processes really work, will not public resource allocations eventually follow the dictates of the public? For example, when consumers are willing to pay more for an automobile in order to reduce exhaust pollution, will they elect officials who will support such

---

5 J. K. Galbraith, *The Affluent Society* (Boston: Houghton Mifflin Co., 1958).

programs? Third, to what extent do such personal allocation decisions reflect greater trust in private economic decisions than in resource allocation decisions made in the public sector?

Another charge is that marketing, particularly advertising, glorifies sex and violence. Sellers deny this charge, stating that they use advertising that sells, and, if consumers respond to appeals aimed at their sexual desires, the advertiser is doing no more than recognizing a felt need. Moreover, advertisers do not select program, movie, and magazine content; networks, film studios, and publishers produce what sells. What is cause and what is effect?

A third charge made against the marketing system is that it reduces the quality of life by increasing the aspiration levels of disadvantaged groups, resulting in frustration when they are unable to fulfill these wants. It is not made clear by such critics whether some groups are disadvantaged because of the marketing system or some other defect in society, nor is it clear whether attempts should be made to bring such groups into the mainstream of society or to reduce their frustration by deemphasizing marketing efforts.

While simple answers to these complex questions will not be found in this book, we hope it will provide you with a way of analyzing these issues and encourage you to search for better answers.

Room for improvement

Many marketing tasks are labor-intensive (require much labor), but some of these activities can be transferred from the seller to the buyer. For example, in supermarkets buyers pick out their own goods and transport them home; full-service grocery stores will perform these activities for their customers. Productivity gains in such situations are difficult to achieve. There is general agreement that "while efficiency in marketing has increased over the last century, it has lagged behind other sectors of the economy."[6]

There are more problems in measuring and improving the performance of the system than those outlined here. For example, marketing has been a haven for the small businessman. Ease of entry, particularly into retailing, is thought to be important in maintaining competition and the American free enterprise system. Yet, small businesses are often inefficient and have high failure rates. Should bigness be encouraged in the name of efficiency?

Because of the role marketing plays in the delivery of a standard of living, it is important that all paths which may lead to better performance in marketing be followed—even though this performance is difficult to measure. Greater efficiency in marketing may be necessary for an individual company, simply to ensure its continued existence. In your study of marketing, keep in mind this question: How can a better performance of the marketing task be brought about in the particular area under study?

THE PROCESS OF MATCHING SUPPLY AND DEMAND

Discrepancy of assortments

Consumers want products and services for the perceived satisfactions they can supply. They will buy a broad assortment of products and services close to the times

---

[6] R. Cox, *Distribution in a High-Level Economy*, p. 197.

FIGURE 2–3

Discrepancy of assortments

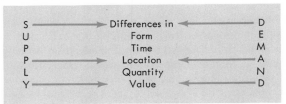

```
S  ——————————▶  Differences in  ◀——————————  D
U                    Form                        E
P                    Time                        M
P  ——————————▶      Location      ◀——————————  A
L                  Quantity                      N
Y  ——————————▶       Value       ◀——————————  D
```

they want to use them and close to where they live. In contrast, producers such as processors, miners, and manufacturers are concerned with the technology of production, preferring to produce the products and services for which they have the know-how, equipment, labor, and distribution facilities. They generally favor long runs and large quantities and find production more economical in a few rather than many locations. In situations such as mining, fishing, and farming, production is limited by the location of material sources, climate and soil, or alternative-use considerations.

The differences in the assortments desired by consumers contrasted with those that arise from production, processing, and mining are aptly called the *discrepancy of assortments.*[7] These differences or gaps are outlined in Figure 2–3.

Economics of production encourage the output of relatively *large quantities* of nearly *alike* products and services in a limited number of locations and in a brief time in order to minimize the combined cost of input resources. Economics of consumption, on the other hand, encourage the somewhat regular purchase of a wide assortment of small quantities of products and services in a great variety of locations. This results in a gap or discrepancy between the economics of production and consumption. The marketing task is to efficiently remove or equalize this gap.

Discrepancy in assortments, which provides the *need* for marketing, is not unique to marketing type economies. It exists in all types—traditional, command, and marketplace. A question arises, then, as to what marketing systems must do to compromise the discrepancy in assortments.

The equalization process

Activities necessary to bring supply and demand together, regardless of the type of economy, are (1) sorting out, (2) assembly, (3) allocation, and (4) assorting.[8]

Sorting out. A definite set of criteria must be established by which the heterogeneous supply (dissimilar items) can be graded into homogeneous groups or classifications. This sorting-out activity, and the need for it, can be quickly grasped in considering the marketing of apples or other agricultural products. Classifications for apples must be established before they can be graded, based on such measurable criteria as size, skin color, firmness, and the extent of skin blemish. The classification must be such that the sorted-out groups better fit the wants of consumers or facilitate either further processing or the marketing activities of physical handling, storing, or shipping. Soft and badly blemished apples may be sorted out for processing into cider or vinegar

---

[7] W. Alderson, *Marketing Behavior and Executive Action* (Homewood, Ill.: Richard D. Irwin, Inc., 1957), p. 216.

[8] Ibid., pp. 202–11.

or for distribution in the local market for animal food. Other apples may be sorted out by size and color. Smaller, poorly colored apples cannot command the price of bigger, brighter ones and cannot bear as heavy handling, shipping, and storing costs, so they may be shipped in bulk to processors, while the best-looking ones are shipped to more distant markets to be sold as fancy eating apples.

Sorting out also pertains to processed and manufactured products. Crude oil, which is of limited use to consumers, is processed into various useful products ranging from gas vapors to heavy-grade greases.

A manufacturer engages in sorting out even as supposedly like units are assembled. Every product that comes off an assembly line is inspected to see that it meets minimum specifications. Those that fail are culled out for repair, sold as seconds, or scrapping, depending on their condition. If the assembly operation has resulted in a run of dissimilar items (black and brown shoes), the items may be sorted out and the like items (color, size, and so forth) stored together. In many assembly operations, most of the sorting out occurs through the selection of parts to be assembled.

Sorting out also pertains to services. For example, health services of physicians and dentists or repair services of auto mechanics or plumbers vary immensely both in type and quality of service from supplies to supplier or even from any one supplier. The type of service is often classified by specialty. For automobiles this includes engine mechanics and specialists in body and fender work, tires, steering, brakes, and transmissions.

For medical services, providers are divided into physicians, hospitals, pharmacists, laboratories, and so forth. Then each provider group can be classified into specialty types (internal medicine, gynecology, or obstetrics) in a manner analogous to the way that apples can be classified as cooking apples and eating apples. There are also quality classifications of health services. Physicians may be rated on their bedside manner, diagnostic skills, or surgical technique. They are graded into classifications by colleagues, consumers (patients), and third parties. This sorting out based on the type and quality of services is necessary to help close the gap between the supply and demand for medical services.

Assembly. Assembly is the bringing together of homogeneous (sorted out) groups into larger groups. Like sorting out, it is done to facilitate further processing or the marketing activities of storing, handling, and shipping, as well as selling and buying.

For example, a producer cooperative that accumulates apples from many growers can convert low-grade apples to cider and vinegar more efficiently with a large supply and longer production runs than if it has limited quantities and must go through cycles of setting up and shutting down. Handling, storing, and shipping of larger quantities also tend to be more efficient. Conveyer systems and other large handling equipment can be employed, and more economical rail and truckload quantities can be stored and shipped. Selling advantages will accrue when the assembler has larger quantities to sell to such large-scale middlemen as the Great Atlantic and Pacific Tea Company. Efficiencies are likely for both buyers and sellers who do not need to venture into the market as frequently.

Assembly also serves manufacturers. As individual products come off the assembly line and are sorted out, they are assembled in pallet quantities in the immediate area for efficiency in moving to the storage area. They are also assembled in storage to facilitate further handling, storing, and shipping.

Even services are assembled—at least in the latent form of the source. Medical services, for example, that have been sorted out by type and quality are assembled in various local, regional, and national centers. The Menninger Foundation at Topeka, Kansas, is an assembly of high-quality psychiatric services.

Assembly of homogeneous services facilitates the rendering (producing) of medical services and also helps to market the services. A relatively new psychiatrist who joins the staff of the Menninger Foundation, for example, has a full clientele almost immediately. By comparison, the individual psychiatrist who hangs out his shingle in Topeka is a long time getting his own patients.

Throughout the assembly activity, the participants must both provide and acquire marketing information. Consequently, it entails promotion as well as information searching.

Allocation. Allocation, the third function in the equalization process, is the breaking down of a homogeneous (assembly) supply into the smaller quantities that are more appropriate for various users. A wholesaler may buy a carload of apples from a producer cooperative and resell and distribute them to 10 retailers over a period of two weeks. He has both allocated smaller portions from the larger supply and allocated the apples over time and space.

A similar situation would prevail for trail bikes. The manufacturer might sell his entire output (say, 250,000) to 40 wholesalers (allocation) who, in turn, would each resell smaller batches of the bikes to retailers within their territories. Retailers usually sell only one bike at a time. Allocation has occurred over time and space to help equalize the discrepancy of assortments.

Medical and other services are also allocated. When the customer comes to the medical service and receives 10, 20 or more minutes of services from one or more physicians, the type and amount of services needed have been allocated.

Promotion and information searching are also part of the activity of allocation.

Assorting. The final equalization function, assorting, is the bringing together of the proper quantities of the different types and qualities of goods and services that various users want. A retail grocery store, for example, assembles an assortment from which it believes its customers will in turn draw their assortments. Retailers typically assemble their assortments from numerous sources, but their selection of sources is partially dependent on the fit of such assortments to their needs.

Some products and services in an assortment are complementary (gasoline and motor oil) and jointly tend to offer more attraction than if each product appears alone. Others are not compatible within one assortment (live pets and fresh bakery goods) and are less attractive together than separately.

Assorting is concerned with both the breadth and depth of a product and service line. A broad assortment provides a choice among many different types of products and services and will serve many users. Drug, grocery, and hardware stores carry broad assortments and provide customers greater scope for servicing many of their requirements from one outlet. Depth of assortment means that numerous types and/or qualities of *each* product or service are available to the customer. For example, a hardware store may carry over 40 sizes and types of hinges. Within each assortment, customers can get a more precise fit for their particular requirements.

Although the problem of assortment might initially appear easily resolved (simply build a very big assortment of compatible goods), it is not. The larger the assortment, the more different products and brands there are to store, handle, and ship. This means more expense, not only for retailers, but also for wholesalers and manufacturers. Furthermore, too large an assortment makes selling and buying more difficult as communications and search problems increase. At the retail level, relatively large assortments are offered because consumers appear quite willing to engage in more search activities in assortments within a store than among various assortments (stores). These consumers can handle and transport an assortment (a mixture of fruit, meat, and groceries) about as cheaply as they can one type of product (a case of dog food). The same statements *cannot* be made for manufacturers and wholesalers, but even at the retail level, assortments can be too large. This occurs when consumers find the searching and handling activities within an assortment (store) too demanding (of time and space) or when they feel incompatible products are included in the assortment. Convenience stores, for example, often do very well within sight of large supermarkets because customers like the quickness and ease of getting what they want out of a limited assortment.

Assorting of services is as necessary as it is with products. Medical services of various types and qualities, for instance, are frequently clustered within hospitals or clinics. The Mayo Clinic at Rochester, Minnesota, offers a broad, in-depth assortment of high-quality medical services. Sometimes the assortment is merely a group of services located in close proximity, with or without the use of a referral system. But this is also true of product assortments, when a shopping center is viewed as an assortment.

The performance of this activity, like each of the other three equalization activities, requires communication. Sellers engaged in assorting activities, for example, use promotion to inform intermediate, as well as final, prospects about the available product, service, quality, quantity, and price assortments. They use persuasion to attempt to convince prospective customers that their assortments are sufficiently appropriate to warrant their purchase. The various sellers also search for information about the assortments wanted by buyers. And, of course, prospective buyers search among the suppliers to find assortments that best meet their needs. The equalization process, in other words, is *not* just concerned with physical distribution. The search for and the dissemination of information is an integral part.

Markets

The four activities of the equalization process—sorting out, assembly, allocation, and assorting—are illustrated in Figure 2–4. The activities could occur in a different order than in the figure (assembly may take place before sorting out, and assorting before allocation), but the marketing system must perform this equalizing process in *all* types of economies, because all have gaps between the heterogeneity of supply and the heterogeneity of demand.

In the equalization process, a market is not always a necessity. **A market is an agreement between buyers (or lessees) and sellers (or lessors) for transferring use rights to a good or service.** If a society is willing to give up some amount of freedom and individual rights (especially those associated with possession and use of property), then tradition and administrative or political command can be used to perform the equalization process, although perhaps not so efficiently.

Further, a market does not require a *marketplace;* that is, a spatial clustering of buyers or sellers—for example, "the Chicago market." However, a specific place for numerous buyers and sellers to come together is often desirable. Among other things, a public market facilitates publication of the price or *value* the buyers and sellers have

FIGURE 2–4
The equalization process

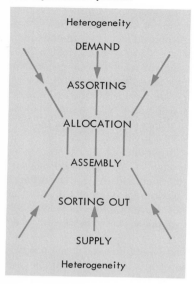

Source: Adapted from J. C. Narver and R. Savitt, *The Marketing Economy: An Analytical Approach* (New York: Holt, Rinehart, & Winston, Inc., 1971).

placed on the goods or services. Numerous buyers and sellers and a public market help ensure that free buyers and free sellers are trading at prices they believe to be a fair measure of value and also provides the pressures on buyers and sellers to reduce remaining discrepancies in assortments. Both the supply side and the demand side of the market must participate in this process, and market price is the single most important bit of information they require for the market mechanism to provide its control of the marketing system.

The equalization process occurs at all levels in the marketing system, sometimes repeatedly at a single level. Institutions constantly seek to discover when it is more efficient to use a market to reduce discrepancies and when administrative mechanisms are more effective. Through *vertical integration* some firms have found it efficient to perform the entire equalization process up to the point of sale to an ultimate consumer. The Great Atlantic and Pacific Tea Company handles the entire process for some of its seafood products, operating a fishing fleet, fish processing and packaging facilities, and wholesale and retail distribution centers. For many other products, no one company can perform the entire process. The gap between supply and demand—product form, time, place, quantity, and value—is so great that specialized activities must be performed by many different firms.

While the equalizing process provides a useful conceptualization of the marketing system, it is too aggregated to give detailed insight into how an overall marketing system operates. Thus it is necessary to disaggregate this process into: (1) marketing functions, (2) institutions which perform them, and (3) the resulting structure of channels of distribution. These comprise the marketing system of a marketing economy. The first two are discussed below, and the third in Chapter 3.

Marketing: Principles and methods

MARKETING FUNCTIONS

The marketing of any product or service focuses on the flow of both the product or service itself and the title to or the right to use that product or service. To obtain these flows, information must also flow, both from suppliers to prospective customers and from prospective customers to suppliers, to facilitate the search for customers or suppliers. Information flows are also necessary to manage marketing systems. Flows of products, services, and rights to use them are facilitated by various financial services, and there must be mechanisms for spreading or transferring the risks that build up in marketing systems.

Marketing functions can be grouped into three categories: (1) those involving the transfer of title or use rights, (2) those providing for the physical supply, and (3) those that facilitate the first two. Within each of these categories are certain more specialized functions.

1. Those involving transfer of title or use rights.
   a) Buying (or leasing for use).
   b) Selling (or leasing for use by others).
2. Those involving physical supply.
   a) Transportation.
   b) Storage.
   c) Standardization and grading.
3. Those facilitating the performance of the above activities.
   a) Financing.
   b) Risk-taking or bearing.
   c) Seeking marketing information.

These eight specialized activities involved in transferring products and services, and the rights to use them, from suppliers to customers are the *marketing functions*. Their performance by various types of organizations or institutions, together with their interrelationships through channels of distribution, comprise marketing systems. These functions are illustrated in Figure 2–5.

FIGURE 2–5
Performance of marketing functions*

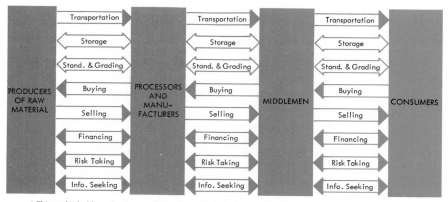

* This method of flow charting was first suggested by R. F. Breyer, who proposed the channel system as an appropriate unit for marketing systems analysis. See his *The Marketing Institution* (New York: McGraw-Hill Book Co., 1937) and *Quantitative Systemic Analysis* (Philadelphia, 1949).

2 / Marketing systems: Functions and institutions

FUNCTIONS THAT TRANSFER USE RIGHTS

Buying or leasing-for-use

The performance of the buying or leasing function in marketing involves a number of distinct but closely related activities whether they are carried out by a manufacturer, a wholesaler, a retailer, or a consumer. These activities include the establishment and implementation of policies and procedures for defining needs; the selection of sources of supply; the "testing" of available products and services; negotiations concerning price, date of shipment, and similar matters; and transfer of title or use rights.

The buying function begins with the buyer's attempt to determine the kinds, quality, and quantity of products and services he needs. Often, of course, it is the demand-stimulating activities of sellers that make the buyer aware of his needs. Once the need has been defined, satisfactory sources of supply must be found. Sometimes the prospective buyer must undertake extensive search, but in other situations the various sellers, through advertising and personal selling, limit this need.

The next step is to determine the suitability of the available products and services. Suitability may be judged by inspection, sample, or description, and the method used in any particular case will depend largely on the characteristics of the products and services. If the goods are highly perishable or ungraded, they are usually bought only after inspection. Where they are uniform as a result of standardized production or grading, purchasing and leasing are often done on the basis of a sample. Description is used either when both buyer and seller are very familiar with the product or service or when one of the parties can provide detailed specifications. After the buyer has determined the products and services that best satisfy his needs and has located satisfactory sources of supply, he must be ready to negotiate the price, terms of sale or lease, delivery dates, and other matters.

This is not to suggest that that is all there is to buying. The buying function receives further attention in Chapters 12 and 13.

Selling or leasing

It is evident that selling and buying complement each other, since both activities are needed to result in the transfer of use rights. Like the buying function, selling involves much more than the act of transferring use rights. It also includes finding buyers, stimulating demand, providing information, and negotiating price, terms of sale, and so forth.

Under the highly competitive conditions of today, personal selling, advertising, and sales promotion are particularly important. These three topics are discussed under the rubric of *promotion, personal selling,* and *advertising* in Chapters 21 and 22. In addition, the selling function receives some attention in Chapter 13.

FUNCTIONS OF PHYSICAL SUPPLY

Few people are aware of the huge costs involved in performing the functions of physical supply. As early as 1966, *Business Week* stated that "moving and storing goods on their way from mine and mill through various subassemblies and assemblies to their final markets costs anywhere from $50 billion to $75 billion a year—$100 billion if paperwork costs are included. This [expense] is now the third highest cost in doing business, trailing only the payout for materials and labor."[9] Even for the individual firm the cost of these functions is great, with one authority writing that for industrial companies "in primary metals, chemicals, and petroleum . . . these costs come to about 25 percent of the sales dollar; in the food manufacturing industry, to 30 percent or more."[10]

Transportation

A change in the use rights of products and services is ordinarily accompanied by a change in their location. A buyer or lessee of a car wants it to be available, usually as soon as possible. A transfer of services requires that either the producer of the services go to the user or vice versa.

As the distance between the producer and the consumer increases, the importance of the transportation function expands, so that its cost makes up a significant part of the whole cost of marketing. This cost is justified by the resulting creation of place utility and by the increased scale of production, specialization of labor, and geographic specialization of production it makes possible. In a later chapter (Chapter 20), detailed consideration is given to the important parts played by the railroad, the truck, the pipeline, and other agencies of transportation in the marketing process. Transportation includes the movement of people to products and services, as well as the opposite.

Storage

The creation of time utility by holding and preserving products and services is necessary throughout the marketing process for a variety of reasons. For agricultural products the typical situation is that of a fairly steady demand and a seasonal production. This is also true for many manufactured products. Furniture manufacturers, for example, often produce various items in their line in batches and may not repeat an item for six months.

With some goods, storage is necessary if regular demand is to be met, not because production is seasonal, but because transportation is seasonal. This situation exists for coal, iron ore, and other products which move by water and may be held up by ice during part of the year.

For some manufactured goods, storage becomes an important function wherever demand is irregular. The demand for skates, snowshoes, and skis for winter sports is of this nature. Since production of these items is most economical if continued throughout the year, storage is used in "off" seasons.

Storage is also necessary as a protection against unavoidable delays in delivery, to meet any reasonable demand, and to permit transportation in economical units. One of the wholesaler's most important functions is to provide a supply of merchandise which is readily available at all times to the retailer, who performs this same function for the consumer. Also, few wholesalers know exactly the size of the orders their salesmen will turn in from day to day, and even if they did, the necessity of

---

[9] "New Strategies to Move Goods," *Business Week,* September 24, 1966, p. 112.

[10] R. P. Neuschel, "Physical Distribution—Forgotten Frontier," *Harvard Business Review,* 45 (March–April 1967), p. 125. Additional support for the accuracy of these cost estimates will be found in J. F. Magee, *Physical-Distribution Systems* (New York: McGraw-Hill Book Co., Inc., 1967), p. 19.

avoiding delays and the cost of transportation in small units would require that they keep some stock.

The storage of services is somewhat different from the storage of products. Services are stored in latent forms, much like a battery stores electricity. To store health services is to have available an unused supply of physicians, hospital facilities, and so forth. With air travel services, storage is in terms of unused capacity available to render the service.

Finally, storage is employed to further public policy, as under our federal agricultural and other commodity-buying programs; as a means of conditioning some products, such as cheese, distilled spirits, and tobacco; and for speculative purposes.

The storage function is performed by a large number of institutions, including manufacturers, wholesalers, retailers, warehouses, cold storage companies, and pipeline operators, as will be considered in later chapters.[11] These organizations, together with those offering transportation services, provide the functions of physical supply.

Standardization and grading

Standardization and grading are closely related activities. The former refers to the actual *setting up* of basic limits or grades into which products or services can be sorted out, while the latter means the actual sorting out of a supply of a given product or service according to established standards.

To illustrate, consider the specifications established by the federal government for wheat. Based on such factors as weight per bushel, percent of damaged kernels, moisture content, and percent of foreign matter, each major kind of wheat is divided into five main classes or grades. Similar detailed standards have been worked out for many other farm products.

Standards are also important in the marketing of services. Various aspects of health services, for example, are classified by type and quality, as was noted above, as are health-care facilities. Hospitals, extended-care facilities, and so forth must meet minimum standards to be approved or accredited.

Several bases are used to define standards, like quality, as in the foregoing wheat illustration; quantity, as exemplified by standards of weights and measures; size or measurement, as in clothing, shoes, and lumber; color, as for paint, oranges, and cotton; service, as with railroad or truck transportation; and price, as illustrated by the "one price" charged to all customers of the same class who purchase similar quantities of goods.

Many methods are employed in the grading or sorting-out process. Eggs may be candled by hand, but a large shipper of oranges or grapefruit will use a machine to grade the fruit according to size. Devices are also available to measure the Btu. content of coal and the butterfat in milk and cream. Electronic machines, X-rays, chemical analysis, and similar aids to grading are used for manufactured goods. Grading is also carried out on a sample basis, as when grain in boxcars is graded by extracting small quantities from various locations in each car. Suppliers of medical and many other services are sorted out through the use of education, training, and qualifying examinations. Quality sorting out is frequently based on the worth of previously rendered services.

Standardization and grading are important to ultimate consumers and industrial

---

[11] See especially Chapter 20. Storage also receives some attention in Chapters 10, 13, and 14.

buyers because they ensure goods and services of uniform quality which can be purchased again and again. The costs of buying and selling are decreased with reduction in the need for continuous inspection. Lower transportation and storage costs result from the fact that only those grades worth transporting or storing are given these services. Once products are graded, comparable products, even though they belong to different owners, may be mixed in the same cars and storage houses, thus economizing on space. Grading also makes financing easier and less expensive. Banks, for example, will loan larger amounts and at lower interest rates on commodities of definitely known grade.

FUNCTIONS THAT FACILITATE

The third major group of marketing functions consists of facilitating or auxiliary services. These functions are facilitating in that they aid in the performance of buying, selling, and physical supply.

Financing

The financing function in marketing includes the provision and management of money and credit necessary to get goods to the ultimate consumer and the industrial user. (Financial transactions required for production are excluded.) The financial function is important because a considerable amount of time must elapse before many goods are processed and placed in the consumers' hands. A manufacturer of trail bikes, for example, ties up many dollars in finished inventory and replacement part orders.

Financing is also important in other phases of marketing. When a retail store sells goods on credit, the store operator is performing a financing service. He may partially shift this function back onto the wholesaler who has extended credit to him; the wholesaler, in turn, may pass part of the burden back to the credit-granting manufacturer. At many points, the assistance of such financial institutions as commercial banks, factors, and commercial installment companies may be sought.

Risk taking

In colonial times, when a seller's market was restricted to his immediate community, marketing risks, it has been observed, were nearly at a minimum. "The seller was acquainted with his market and dealt in small quantities. The seller was also the producer; he would not produce what he was not certain of selling. In fact, early production was mainly on individual order."[12]

Today, however, most production is on a large-scale basis, and producer and buyer are typically geographically separated. In this situation, the marketing of goods and services involves a large number of unavoidable risks and, because few will knowingly assume risks without compensation, the payment for this function is an important marketing cost.

Some examples of marketing risks. Some of the types of risks involved in the marketing process relate to physical deterioration, obsolescence, theft, damage,

---

[12] S. V. Smith, in R. M. Trump (ed.), *Essentials of Marketing Management* (Boston: Houghton Mifflin Co., 1966), p. 2.

waste, extension of credit, and changes in supply or demand, with a resulting impact on price. Products are always subject to such acts of God as fire and flood, and the risk from shoplifting in retail stores is very real. Since movement through marketing channels is frequently time consuming, substantial price changes are possible as a result of both general price level changes and shifts in the demand and supply situation for the specific product. For fashion goods, the demand is subject to such rapid changes that goods which have been in the marketing channel for less than a month can sometimes be sold only at a loss. Fresh fruits, vegetables, and flowers, which are highly perishable, are especially risky. Since so much marketing is carried on by credit, there is also the risk of losses through bad debts. Moreover, there is always the chance that buyers may not like what they have bought, so that merchandise will be returned and repeat sales will not develop. In other words, not only must buyers be sold, but they must remain sold if a business is to be successful. This fact explains many of the after-sale services (such as inspection and repair) that sellers have found it necessary to provide.

Dealing with marketing risks. In some situations, some of the risk may be transferred to others. Losses from fire, flood, and theft can be transferred to insurance companies, and it is possible to insure against loss from price changes in some commodities through the practice known as "hedging."[13] To a degree, some of the risks that cannot be transferred to others may be eliminated or minimized. Thus, the development of cold storage and refrigerated cars has reduced the risks of perishability. The increase in quality and quantity of marketing information is another factor in reducing risk.

The equalization process affects risk in the marketing system. For example, when grey goods (unbleached, unprinted cloth) are converted into prints, they no longer are undifferentiated and salable as a common commodity. They may be worth far less if an undesirable pattern or color set is selected. Consequently, there is risk associated with the change in form, which is reduced by delay in commitment to a specific form. Similarly, there is risk when products and services are moved to a new location, where prices obtainable may not offset the additional costs of transportation.

Consumers and marketing institutions seek ways to reduce risk, such as buying known brands and established styles. It cannot be completely eliminated, however, and some risk remains with the titleholder as the good passes through the channel of distribution. Whether risks are shifted to others, are partly eliminated through new developments and marketing information, or are assumed by titleholders, the element of risk is significant in the total cost of marketing.

Seeking marketing information

As always, marketing decisions can be no better than the facts upon which they are based, and the need for facts and their careful interpretation is growing as markets widen and competition increases. When competition was restricted mainly to the local level, what a similar firm did several hundred miles away was of little importance. But when a clothing manufacturer in Cleveland must compete with competitors located in New York, Chicago, and Los Angeles, he becomes vitally interested in what other firms are producing, how they market their products, the prices they charge, their advertising programs, the reactions of customers to their products, and the attitude of their wholesale and retail outlets to their price policies and their programs

---

[13] See Appendix B.

for mechandising assistance. Likewise, the successful buyer of women's coats for a department store in Milwaukee now needs adequate information on fashion trends throughout the country, since, sooner or later, these trends will influence his customers. And, of course, he cannot buy to best advantage unless he also has detailed facts on the price of available merchandise in the various wholesale markets.

The need for facts in making marketing decisions has led many organizations, particularly the larger firms, to establish groups responsible for information activities. Getting the facts is only part of the story; the information must be interpreted and applied to the situation facing a specific firm. Marketing information and research are discussed in detail in Chapter 17.

SOME OBSERVATIONS CONCERNING MARKETING FUNCTIONS

Other classifications

Some additional observations are pertinent concerning the classification of marketing functions used in this text. There is no unanimity among marketing authorities regarding the number of marketing functions, although many have adopted the groupings we have listed. The list could easily be expanded by subdivision into a much longer one. For instance, in marketing electrical appliances, accounting is performed by various parties to the transaction—by the manufacturer for his marketing activities, by the wholesaler, and by the retailer. Dividing the supply of cotton into smaller units to meet the needs of the individual mill is an activity of the cotton merchant. Packaging bread to ensure sanitation and thus increase salability is an activity of the baker. But these activities are mainly subdivisions of those listed. Because accounting is an adjunct to buying and selling, and dividing and packaging are adjuncts to selling, all of these may be logically excluded. It is believed that the suggested classification of activities or functions is satisfactory for our purposes, provided that the student bears in mind its limitations and recognizes the existence of others.[14]

For various purposes, it is convenient to differentiate certain subdivisions of activities and give them distinguishing names or terms. For example, it has become customary to use the term "product-line planning" (merchandising) to include

the various activities undertaken to adapt to the users' ideas of what is wanted. . . . [More specifically it] includes quality determination as well as measurement, packaging, branding, and display, . . . the selecting of the product to be produced or stocked and the deciding of such details as size, appearance, form, dressing of the product, quantities to be bought or made, time of purchase or production, and lines to be carried.[15]

Thus, product-line planning includes parts of the selling function as well as activities associated with standardization, risk taking, and market information.

Marketing functions essential

Marketing functions are such a necessary part of the marketing task that they must be performed by someone if goods are to be placed in the hands of consumers. Much

---

[14] Readers will find it advisable to refer to other college textbooks on marketing for other types of functional classification. The greatest contrast with our classification will probably be found in books on agricultural marketing. Also see W. P. Dommermuth and C. R. Andersen, "Distribution Systems—Firms, Functions, and Efficiencies," *Business Topics* (Spring 1969), pp. 51–56.

[15] E. D. McGarry, "The Merchandising Function," in R. Cox, W. Alderson, and S. J. Shapiro (eds.), *Theory in Marketing: Second Series* (Homewood, Ill.: Richard D. Irwin, Inc., 1964), pp. 233–34.

criticism of marketing systems is based on the assumption that the cost of marketing would be reduced by the elimination of any particular middleman. There is an old saying in marketing that "you can eliminate the middleman, but you cannot eliminate the functions he performs."

Consequently, omitting a middleman may or may not reduce marketing costs. If that middleman is performing a necessary function efficiently, his removal will mean that someone else must perform that activity, with the result that the marketing cost would not be reduced. In fact, if the new performer is not as efficient as the former one, the cost may even be increased. Consumers can also elect to perform marketing functions and thus reduce the retail price, but such action will not reduce the total cost of marketing. It is, however, sometimes possible to reduce the marketing cost by eliminating those middlemen whose functions may be more economically performed by someone else. In the marketing of food, the chain store system, the voluntary chain, and the cooperative chain operate more economically than the independent wholesaler-retailer channel because it is usually cheaper to perform the wholesale and retail functions when they are substantially integrated. This is not because the wholesaler's functions, such as buying, selling, storage, and risk taking are eliminated; they are not. But the coordination made possible by combining the wholesale and retail activities reduces the extent to which each activity must be performed. This coordination enables the wholesale division of the integrated company to service its stores with a smaller inventory than an independent wholesaler could safely stock, with the result that the cost of the storage function is reduced. At the same time, reordering by store managers through automated devices considerably reduces the buying and selling cost necessary to get goods onto the shelves of the retail store in the integrated organization.

Thus it should be clear that **the main effort to reduce marketing costs should not be on eliminating middlemen but rather on the means of obtaining more efficient performance of the marketing functions.** This increased efficiency can sometimes be obtained by the elimination of middlemen, but in other cases it can come through the introduction of a new middleman specializing in particular marketing tasks.

Pervasiveness of marketing functions

Many of these marketing functions are performed several times in the marketing of a given product. The buying and selling functions are performed each time the title changes hands, perhaps between manufacturer and wholesaler, between wholesaler and retailer, and between retailer and consumer. Storage is performed at the factory, at the wholesale warehouse, and at the store. Grading of fresh fruits and vegetables takes place in both the local market and the central market. Hence, many middlemen are engaged in performing the same function at different stages in the marketing process.

The management of marketing

Finally, although management is not treated as a separate function, it should be emphasized that it is involved in carrying out all of the functions of marketing. It is the responsibility of management to make the various policy decisions necessary for effective buying and selling. It must decide how to finance the business and what risks to take. The various parts of the marketing organization must be coordinated to ensure that policies are followed, and management must constantly evaluate the results of its policies. The skill with which these activities are carried out determines, to a large degree, the effectiveness of a marketing organization. The managerial aspects are discussed in Chapters 17–23.

INSTITUTIONS IN THE MARKETING SYSTEM

The structural components of the marketing system consist of the various individual institutions that perform the entire range of marketing functions, together with the institutional relationships (various firms working together) that comprise the channels of distribution. The institutions can be grouped into three major categories, (1) manufacturers, processors and other producers that perform marketing functions, (2) marketing middlemen, and (3) facilitating marketing agencies. Consumers also perform many marketing functions.

Producers

While many firms are engaged primarily in the production of products and services, their performance of marketing functions is more than incidental. In this group are producers like General Motors, Pillsbury, General Electric, Schlitz, and Procter & Gamble. Some producers do almost all of their own marketing; they use virtually no outside marketing institutions and few if any facilitating agencies. Maytag Dairy Farms, for example, which makes blue cheese, sells its entire output directly to consumers through its own mail-order operation and one sales office outlet. The Fuller Brush Company, Avon Products, Inc.,[16] and other producers of consumer goods market principally through their own direct selling organizations. This practice is even more prevalent among industrial producers such as IBM and Collins Radio Company. In fact, it is more difficult to find producers that perform almost none or only incidental marketing functions than vice versa. Such producers are largely those that produce only resellers' brands or who turn all of their products over to an independent firm for marketing. Some of these arrangements will be described below under the heading of marketing middlemen.

Producers use a variety of structures and structural components to perform marketing functions. Virtually every large marketing producer (as well as many small ones) has a marketing division or group that is under the direction of a marketing vice president. Marketing activities can be oriented and organized in many different ways—by products (product managers or brand managers), activities (director of advertising, sales manager), markets (West Coast manager, Chicago manager). In any event, the emphasis is on marketing planning, selling (both advertising and personal selling), and physical distribution. Some producers make extensive use of manufacturers' sales offices and branches (the General Electric Company and the Maytag Company); that is, they perform wholesaling functions themselves. Some firms operate their own retail stores (Singer Company), and some have their own direct-to-consumer selling forces (Grolier Corporation). These various structural components used by manufacturers in performing marketing functions are examined in later chapters.

---

[16] "Avon to Put More Stress on Costume Jewelry," *Women's Wear Daily,* April 29, 1971, p. 24.

Marketing middlemen

A middleman is an individual or a business concern operating between the producer and the ultimate consumer or industrial user. He specializes in buying and/or selling, but he usually also performs other marketing functions. The local grocery store, whether chain or independent, the large city department store, the mail-order company, and the drug wholesaler are familiar middlemen.

Some middlemen actually take title to the goods in which they deal, as is true of the local grocery store, while others aid in the buying and selling of merchandise without taking title. Those middlemen who take title while performing marketing functions are known as "merchant middlemen," in contrast to the "agent middlemen" (or functional middlemen), who do not take title but merely assist in effecting transfers in ownership or use rights.

Merchant and agent middlemen. Merchant middlemen may be divided into two groups—wholesalers[17] and retailers. Within each group a wide variety of types may be distinguished. The *1967 Census of Business* lists over 80 different kinds of merchant wholesalers, grouped into 21 divisions, such as groceries, dry goods, hardware, machinery, and farm supplies. Similarly, over 90 kinds of retail establishments are recognized, divided into 11 categories, such as food, apparel, drug, furniture, and general merchandise.[18]

The classification into two broad groups of merchant middlemen rests basically upon the markets to which these groups cater. Thus, wholesalers sell mainly to other middlemen (to retailers, for instance), to industrial users (such as public utility companies), or to both; whereas for retailers the ultimate consumer is the main outlet. Notice the word "main"; many wholesalers also sell some goods to ultimate consumers (employees and other friends of the firm), and many retailers sell some goods at wholesale to other retailers. In general, however, there is a fairly clear distinction between their markets. The functions and operations of the various kinds of wholesalers and retailers are discussed at length in Chapters 7–14 of this book.

The most important agent middlemen—those who negotiate concerning buying and/or selling without taking title to goods—are brokers, commission merchants, selling agents, manufacturers' agents, and auction companies.[19] Their major characteristics are indicated by Table 2–1.

Overlapping functions of merchant and agent middlemen. A distinction has been drawn between merchant and agent middlemen, depending on whether they do or do not take title. In practice, however, this clear distinction does not always exist. For example, although brokers do not typically take title to merchandise, agents operating under the name of "broker" sometimes make purchases and sales in their own names. Frequently, some evolution in function takes place without a change in name. As an illustration, years ago southern cotton shippers sold to the New England mills through brokers. Gradually, these brokers began to do more business in their own names by buying from the shippers and selling to the mills. Yet, in spite of their becoming merchant middlemen, the old name of "broker" is still attached to them.

---

[17] Some wholesalers are known as "jobbers." We use the two terms synonymously except in the field of agricultural products, where "wholesalers" and "jobbers" often function quite differently. In the basic materials, semifinished goods, and tool and machinery trades, merchants of this type are commonly known as "dealers," "distributors," and "supply houses."

[18] U.S. Bureau of the Census, *1967 Census of Business, Wholesale Trade: United States Summary* (Washington, D.C.: U.S. Government Printing Office, 1970), pp. 1–11 to 1–14; and *idem, Retail Trade: United States Summary* (Washington, D.C.: U.S. Government Printing Office, 1970), pp. 1–7 and 1–8.

[19] See Chapters 10–14 for more detailed discussion of each type and Table 11–4 for another summary.

TABLE 2–1
Some characteristics of agent middlemen summarized

	Broker	Commission merchant	Selling agent	Manufacturers' agent	Auction company
Products dealt with	Farm products, dry groceries	Livestock and other farm products, dry goods	Industrial goods, piece goods and other textiles, groceries and food specialties	Industrial goods, raw materials, groceries, clothing, dry goods	Fresh fruits and vegetables, leaf tobacco, livestock
Possession of goods	No	Yes, actually handle goods	In some cases	Usually not	Yes
Power over price and terms of sale	Limited by principal	May sell without specific approval of principal, but limits sometimes established	Large degree of authority	Usually strictly limited	Usually free rein, but sometimes principal has right to refuse all bids
Representative of	Either buyer or seller	The seller	The seller	The seller	The seller
Continuity of relations with principal	Not continuous	Usually continuous if services satisfactory	Continuous— sells part of output of principal(s)	Continuous— sells part of output of principal(s)	Not necessarily continuous, but may be if service satisfactory
Services performed*	Provides market information	Receives and prepares goods for market, sells and remits balance; some finance the shipper	Acts as sales department for principal; sometimes finance; aid in advertising and sales promotion; advises on styles and quantity to produce	Similar to those of a salesman; territory restricted	Provides storage and display facilities; sells to highest bidder; sometimes extends credit

*Other than major service of assistance in effecting transfers in ownership.

Consequently, when studying agent middlemen, one must be careful to determine whether or not they are performing the functions of the middleman whose name they bear.

Facilitating marketing institutions

Many institutions which perform, or assist in performing, some marketing functions are not classed as middlemen, since they neither take title to goods nor negotiate purchases and sales. The railroad or trucking company which transports coal from the mine to the local utility performs a valuable marketing function. So does the bank from which the wholesaler or retailer borrows funds to finance his inventories. Yet neither institution takes title or negotiates purchase or sale. Farmers' markets, commodity and livestock exchanges, public warehouses, and advertising agencies are other facilitating marketing organizations. To keep this book within compass, and because some of these institutions are more fully treated in later chapters and in specialized books and courses, we shall not attempt a complete discussion of them here.

SUMMARY

Marketing is found in nations with all types of economic systems because there is a discrepancy of assortments of products and services in all of them. That is, there are gaps in time, place, quantity, and form of products and services between the heterogeneity of supply and the heterogeneity of demand. Marketing systems have evolved to close these gaps through the equalization process, which involves sorting out, assembly, allocation and assorting of goods and services.

These four activities are useful in indicating what marketing is all about, but they do not say much about marketing systems themselves. To get a better overview of the overall marketing system in the United States, the equalization process has been broken down into marketing functions, institutions, and channels of distribution (the subject of the next chapter). In the total marketing system, eight major functions are performed by a variety of merchant and agent institutions and by consumers. These institutions are organized into channels of distribution which close or equalize the discrepancies in assortments.

REVIEW AND DISCUSSION QUESTIONS

1. Explain why it is important to have good measures of performance for our marketing system.
2. Explain the value-added concept of marketing. In what way, if any, does it help measure the performance of our marketing system?
3. Both static efficiency and dynamic efficiency are used when measures of performance are discussed. How are they alike and different?
4. Do you enjoy a higher or lower "quality of life" than your father (grandfather) did at a comparable age? Do you think your son or daughter will experience a higher or lower quality of life than you? Explain in detail.
5. What is meant by discrepancy of assortments? Would this concept apply to Mainland China or to the U.S.S.R.?
6. Was there greater or lesser need for the equalization process before the civil rights and women's liberation movements in the United States?
7. Compare and contrast the concepts of sorting out and assorting.
8. Explain in detail how discrepancy in assortments for automobiles in the United States is resolved through the equalization process.
9. Explain which, if any, of the activities of sorting out, assembly, allocation, and assorting are provided by final consumers.
10. What are the relationships between the activities of the equalization process and the marketing functions?
11. Which one of the marketing functions is most important? Explain why.

12. Name and explain briefly two risks in the marketing process that are physical in nature and two that result from changes in market conditions. Suggest methods for minimizing each.

13. Are such marketing activities as branding, dividing, labeling, pricing, and advertising considered marketing functions? Why, or why not?

14. Distinguish clearly between the terms "standardization" and "grading," giving examples of each practice.

15. List as many facilitating marketing institutions as you can.

SUPPLEMENTARY READINGS

Alderson, W. *Marketing Behavior and Executive Action.* Homewood, Ill.: Richard D. Irwin, Inc., 1957. While he made later elaborations, Chapter 7 of this book may be Alderson's clearest statement of the sorting process.

Cox, R. (in association with **Goodman, C. S., and Fichandler, T. C.**) *Distribution in a High-Level Economy.* Englewood Cliffs, N.J.: Prentice-Hall, Inc., 1965. In a discussion of "The Flows of Marketing," pp. 30–36, the various marketing functions are illustrated.

Cox, R.; Alderson, W.; and Shapiro, S. J. (eds.) *Theory in Marketing: Second Series* Homewood, Ill.: Richard D. Irwin, Inc., 1964. Marketing channels are discussed in Chapter 11 by **R. F. Breyer,** and in Chapter 12 by **F. E. Balderston,** while **E. D. McGarry** analyzes the merchandising function in Chapter 15.

Narver, J. C., and Savitt, R. *The Marketing Economy, An Analytical Approach.* New York: Holt, Rinehart & Winston, Inc., 1971. Solutions to economic problems, the equalization process, and marketing functions and institutions are discussed in Chapters 2, 3, 5 and 6.

Preston, L. E. *Markets and Marketing: An Orientation.* Glenview, Ill.: Scott, Foresman & Co., 1970. Chapters 1 and 2 provide good discussions of markets, marketing and productivity, and efficiency in marketing.

Vaile, R. S., Grether, E. T., and Cox, R. *Marketing in the American Economy.* New York: The Ronald Press Company, 1952. See particularly pp. 113–50, which provide excellent figures and discussions of flows and channels of distribution for various products.

3 The structure of the marketing system

The institutions that are the components of the marketing system have been identified as marketing producers, marketing middlemen, and facilitating agencies. Interrelationships among these various types of institutions as they perform the marketing functions are evidenced in channels of distribution, which taken together form the structure of the marketing system.

CHANNELS OF DISTRIBUTION

A channel of distribution consists of manufacturers, middlemen, and other buyers and sellers involved in the process of moving products and services from producer to consumer. In the marketing of wheat, flour, and bread, for example, the channel shown in Figure 3–1 is common. The wheat is sold by the farmer to the local buyer, who may sell to a commission man, who sells to a miller. The flour made from the wheat may go directly from the miller to the baker, who turns the flour into bread and may reach the ultimate consumer through a channel of distribution from baker to retailer to consumer.

A distribution channel is usually thought of as extending from a producer to a customer who significantly changes the form of the product, regardless of whether he is the ultimate consumer. Thus, the distribution channel for wheat begins with the farmer and ends with the miller; that for the flour begins with the miller and ends with the baker; and that for the bread begins with the baker and ends with the ultimate consumer. Three distinct products and three channels of distribution are involved. The same applies to trade channels for rubber, steel, aluminum, wool, and thousands of other products that pass through numerous middlemen to reach the industrial user

FIGURE 3–1
A channel of distribution: Wheat to bread

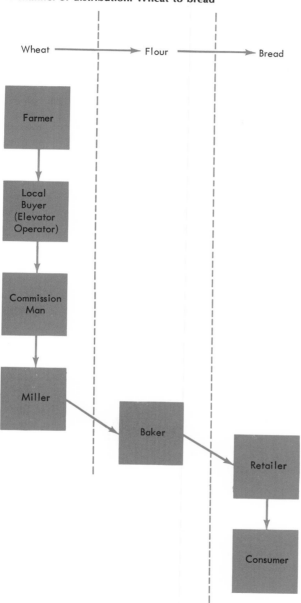

and ultimate consumer in many forms for which the functions vary from product to product.

Major distribution channels

Although there are numerous channels of distribution, those for consumers' goods may be conveniently grouped into the four major types illustrated in Figure 3–2.

1. Producer directly to consumer. This channel of distribution is used for agricultural products, manufactured consumers' products and, especially, services and industrial goods. Farmers may sell their produce to consumers through roadside stands, at municipal markets, and from house to house. The services (insurance) of State Farm Mutual are sold through its own outlets, and brokerage services of firms holding seats on the New York Stock Exchange are often sold through a direct channel. Manufacturers may sell by mail, through their own retail stores (Eastman Kodak Company, Singer Company, Melville Shoe Corporation) or through house-to-house solicitation (Fuller Brush Company, Avon Products, Inc., Electrolux Corporation). Direct sale to users is the most common method of selling industrial goods.

2. Producer to retailer to consumer. Direct sale to large retailers is a common practice among manufacturers of consumers' goods. It is also employed by automobile manufacturers and producers of electrical appliances having a high unit value. Some farmers sell a large part of their output directly to a retailer, and many services are sold through this channel. Income tax services which are originated elsewhere are sold through retail franchises of H. and R. Block and Company, and casualty and

FIGURE 3–2
Major distribution channels for consumers' goods

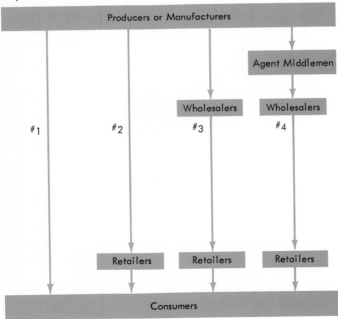

Marketing: Principles and methods

life insurance are sold through independent insurance agents who maintain retail outlets.

3. Producer to wholesaler to retailer to consumer. This channel, often referred to as the "orthodox" or "customary" channel for consumers' goods, is the most widely used of all. Not only are manufactured products moved to consumers in this manner, but large quantities of agricultural commodities follow the same route. As with industrial goods, sometimes another manufacturer substitutes for the wholesaler —as when Hickok Manufacturing Company (men's wear) distributes through the men's toiletries of Lanvin-Charles of the Ritz, Inc. to men's stores and departments or DuPont markets a color film through Bell & Howell.

4. Producer to agent to wholesaler to retailer to consumer. It is not uncommon for some agent middleman to be used between the producer and the wholesaler, or between the producer and the large-scale retailer, to perform important marketing functions. Rather than develop his own sales force, a manufacturer may decide to rely on manufacturers' agents to get his goods to wholesalers. For example, the manufacturer of stuffed toys may use a manufacturers' representative handling a noncompeting line of toys to sell to toy wholesalers. Or the processor of canned goods may have a broker sell 10 thousand cases of canned fruits.

Several channels used for one product. Similar diversity in structure exists in the channels of distribution used to market to industrial users, as described in Chapter 13. Channels of distribution differ, not only among commodities, but even among sellers of the same product. In fact, one manufacturer may employ more than one channel structure in marketing a single product; he may market to wholesalers and also direct to selected retailers. Rather than being static, channel structure slowly but constantly changes in response to shifts in demand and competitive pressures.

Considerable attention is given in this book to promoting understanding of how and why channel structures evolve. Retail channel structure is discussed in Part III, wholesale channel structure in Part IV, and channel structures for industrial goods in Part V. Chapter 19 covers in detail how sellers establish policies for the selection and management of channels. The threefold purpose of this chapter is to provide an overview of the development of channel structures, the major principles for evaluating them, and the conflict for their control.

THE DEVELOPMENT OF CHANNEL STRUCTURES

Transaction efficiency

Man moved away from the completely self-sustaining household as he discovered that specialization in trade and production was a more efficient way to create place, possession, and time utility. This can be called the principle of transaction efficiency, which can be illustrated by considering a primitive community which has learned about specialization of labor in production.[1]

In this community, one family is more skillful than others in making pots, while others excel in making baskets, knives, hoes, or hats. By specializing in the one product for which it has a particular skill, each family can make more of its own

---

[1] This example is the one used by W. Alderson in his original explanation of the development of marketing channels in R. M. Clewett (ed.), *Marketing Channels for Manufactured Products* (Homewood, Ill.: Richard D. Irwin, Inc., 1954), pp. 5–22.

FIGURE 3–3
Exchange without a central market

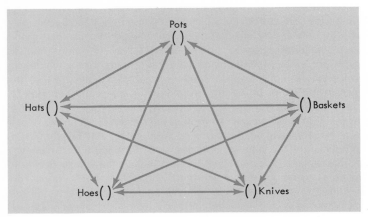

Source: W. Alderson, "Factors Governing the Development of Marketing Channels," in R. M. Clewett (ed.), *Marketing Channels for Manufactured Products* (Homewood, Ill.: Richard D. Irwin, Inc., 1954), p. 7.

product than if each family made all five products. Of course, each then produces a surplus, which it exchanges with the other households for the four needed products they make. To achieve this exchange, 10 fully negotiated transactions are required; 10 trips are made to visit other families and 10 negotiations are made to establish the exchange rate between, for example, hoes and hats. This exchange situation is shown in Figure 3–3.

Now, suppose that the wives in these families discover that they enjoy talking together at these exchange meetings. They might set aside one day each month to meet at the water hole, at which time their husbands could exchange their products. Thus decentralized exchange is replaced by a central market which not only increases exchange efficiency but also provides some pleasant social interaction. The result is illustrated in Figure 3–4.

Only 5 trips (one by each producer) are required instead of 10, and exchange rates are much more quickly negotiated. Place and possession utility are facilitated. The number of fully negotiated transactions has been reduced by half. In general, the savings in number of transactions is $\frac{1}{2} n(n - 3)$, where n is the number of producers, each producing one product. The saving in transactions increases rapidly with the number of products and families. In a farm community of just 100 products and 100 families, for example, the saving from centralized trade would be 4,850 transactions. This number of products is, of course, a fraction of the number required by the modern urban family.

The next step in the evolution of exchange occurs when the pot maker's clever son, who does not like making pots, establishes himself at the water hole as a permanent specialist in trade. Each family can now trade with this dealer rather than with each other. The dealer stocks excess pots, knives, and baskets. A family can acquire time utility as well as place utility because they can trade for any of these items whenever they wish. Based on the number of surplus items he has in stock, the dealer can establish exchange rates so as to equalize supply and demand. For his services,

FIGURE 3–4
Exchange with a central market

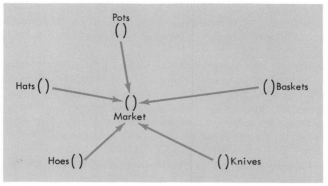

Source: W. Alderson, "Factors Governing the Development of Marketing Channels," in R. M. Clewett (ed.), *Marketing Channels for Manufactured Products* (Homewood, Ill.: Richard D. Irwin, Inc., 1954), p. 7.

he retains one of each product from each producer to take care of his own needs. Even with this payment, the total efficiency and utility in the system is increased because of the trading specialist. Exchange arises out of considerations of efficiency in production. Exchange through middlemen arises out of considerations of efficiency in exchange itself.

Now, if our dealer wanted to exchange with other dealers in other communities—say, exchange acorn meal for fish caught by a tribe near the ocean—the barter system would break down before long. Some dealer would end up with a supply of products which could not be traded as rapidly as he would like. The answer to this problem is resolved by the development of a money system.

Channels of distribution and the equalization process

The efficiency of exchange through middlemen can also be seen by consideration of the equalization process (see Chapter 2). To simplify the discussion, we will consider only the processes of allocation and assorting that occur between manufacturer and consumer. While manufacturer efficiency follows from steady production of a single product, consumer efficiency follows from being able to secure a broad assortment of goods, complementary in use but often unrelated in production, from a single retail source. These differing efficiency considerations of buyers and sellers lead to quantities and types of assortments that are progressively different as a product moves through the channels of distribution. For example, a drug wholesaler has a broader but shallower line than does any one of the drug producers who supply him; the drug retailer has an even broader and much shallower line than any one of his wholesalers; the consumer needs a household assortment much broader and shallower than that carried by any drugstore.

It is the role of the institutions that comprise the channels of distribution to reconcile these quantity and type differences in assortment. When someone discovers a new way to perform the equalization process more efficiently, as did the pot maker's clever son when he discovered he could store a small inventory of each of the five products, this specialist becomes a new institution in the channel structure. Less efficient channel structures are abandoned in due course. If a manufacturer (e.g., Avon Products) finds that it is most efficient to sell his assortment directly to the consumer in her home, a vertically integrated channel (single ownership of various levels) will develop. Of course, some sizable segment of consumers must agree that, from the concept of their personal utility evaluations, this structure is more efficient for them than some other one.

Some channels are efficient with many middlemen involved. Retail grocers usually procure an assortment of fresh meat, fresh produce, frozen foods, dry groceries, and nonfoods. They find that equalizing discrepancies in quantities and assortment is more efficiently done by themselves for some products and by independent wholesalers for others. For instance, they may rely upon one grocery wholesaler to provide their required assortment of dry groceries but on 15 different sources for their fresh meat and fish assortment.

One reason why channel structures become vertically integrated and change slowly (rather than rapidly) is that there are efficiencies that arise from the *routinization* of the transactions. For a transaction to be routinized it must happen according to rules and standarized procedures so that explanations, special communications, and search can be minimized. Even more fundamental is the need for the confidence between buyers and sellers which grows from continued goodwill in the exchange relationships. This principle applies to dealings between retailers and consumers, between middlemen, and between middlemen and manufacturers. Consumer buying, for example, is more efficient when the terms of sale do not have to be discussed with each purchase. (Remember, the channel of distribution has been defined to include the consumer.)

Why then do channel structures change at all? The most obvious reasons are (1) changes in the technology of production, (2) changes in the technology of distribution, and (3) changes in the tastes and life styles of ultimate consumers. But there are other reasons for change which are perhaps more subtle. An important one is the creative innovations of clever competitors within the channel structure. For example, gasoline dealers may add automatic car washes to their assortment, or grocery retailers may add in-store bakeries. In both cases, the importance of the institutions that formerly provided this service or product will be reduced. Another reason is the shifts in costs and efficiencies that occur when any of the above three destabilizing factors occur. In the car wash and bakery illustrations, the new outlets probably will reduce consumer travel costs, reduce the retailers' costs, and increase overall sales volume. When competition is doing its job, more efficient channel structures will slowly force out less efficient channel structures.

Alternative channel structures

The foregoing would seem to suggest that there is only one channel structure for each product and that this channel structure would change only infrequently. In fact many alternative structures are present for each product. Does this mean competition is not working effectively? Some of the answers are suggested in this section, and much of the remainder of this book is designed to help you answer this question.

Some channel structures are long and wide, some are short and narrow, and occasionally some are long and narrow or short and wide. A channel system is said to be *long* when it is composed of many different types of institutions (retailers, wholesalers, facilitating agencies, and manufacturers). It is said to be *wide* when there are many of a given type of institution.

FIGURE 3–5
Marketing channels

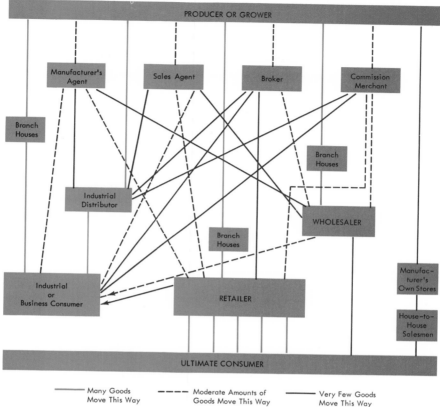

Source: R. S. Alexander, F. M. Surface, and W. Alderson, *Marketing* (3d ed.; Boston: Ginn & Co., 1953).

The long-wide channel is needed, as a rule, to perform the equalization process efficiently when there are many buyers who buy frequently and who are dispersed throughout a large geographical area. Each institution at each level fans out the products and services, with the manufacturer limiting its contact to a manageable number of wholesale relationships (Figure 3–5). The long-wide channel will be used to illustrate three of the reasons why alternative channel structures coexist—geographic differences, producer differences, and market segment differences.

In geographic areas containing many prospective customers, the most efficient marketing approach for a manufacturer with a broad product line may be to perform the wholesaling functions himself through his own branch operations' location. In that same area, a producer with a narrow product line may find it more efficient to use merchant wholesalers than to establish wholesale branches. In low-potential areas of the country, both the broad-line and narrow-line producers, whether large or small, may choose to reach wholesalers through manufacturers' representatives. They simply may find them more efficient than maintaining salesmen in the areas.

Figure 3–5 also suggests that a manufacturer may use different channel structures to reach different market segments. For example, a producer of personal care brushes (hair, tooth, clothes) may (1) sell to wholesalers to reach small retailers, (2) sell directly to large chain retailers, (3) maintain a separate sales force to sell directly to institutional accounts such as hospitals and government, and (4) maintain yet another sales force to sell controlled-brand brushes (resellers' brand) to distributors and even to competing manufacturers.

The largest of these markets—the consumer market sold through retailers—is so large that it is sometimes segmented and sold through different channel structures—such as specialty shops and mass-merchandise discount stores. Some of these channels are high-cost structures because consumers desire the services provided by such channels. "Exception marketing channels," such as selling cosmetics or vacuum cleaners door to door, exist because a profitable market segment desires the utility provided by that method of marketing.

Thus, multiple-channel structures often coexist simply because multiple channels are the most efficient method of marketing to maximize consumer welfare. A useful way to summarize is to visualize the marketing functions performed in the channel and their resultant costs, as in Figure 3–6, which shows three alternative channel structures for the same product made by the same manufacturer and all yielding exactly the same value added in marketing.

First, compare channels A and B. Here we see exactly the same retail and consumer costs. The only difference is that the manufacturer has been able, in channel B, to take over the wholesaling functions himself and earn the same profit for performing these functions as does the wholesaler in channel A. He pays somewhat higher storage, carrying, and promotion costs, but he feels the additional promotion yields better cooperation from his retailers. In channel B, geographic market differences permit a different channel structure with equal efficiency.

Now compare channel B with channel C. In C, the structure through the wholesale functions is exactly the same as B. However, the retailer in C offers more careful buying and more customer service. He also charges a higher retail price. But his customers appreciate his extra services, want them, and can spend less time in shopping. They pay a higher retail price, but the total value added in the *total* channel is the same. Is this channel less efficient? No. The total cost in the channel is exactly the same as the other two. **Several channels can coexist and each yield the same value added by marketing.**

Channel competition. The retailer in channel C provides an example of two forms of competitive rivalry that are not usually discussed in economics. First, the retailers in channels A and B may see that the retailer in C has higher prices. Therefore, they may engage in *horizontal competition* with C by trying to reach over and serve his market segment (gain his customers) through offering a lower price. Their success depends on whether or not they are able to offer the same services as C at a low price or are able to convince consumers in C's market segment that they really do not want the additional service. This reach-over (horizontal) competition can take place between institutions of different types and not just between institutions of the same type. That is, an agent wholesaler can offer horizontal competition to manufacturers' branch offices or merchant wholesalers and vice versa.

To illustrate the second type of competitive rivalry, we need to expand our example. Suppose that C's strategy turns out to be the one that is most popular with consumers—more and more consumers will pay a higher price to receive the additional service. Other *manufacturers,* in competition with the manufacturer in the example, will observe C's success and try to persuade C to carry their product.

FIGURE 3–6

Components of value added by marketing in three alternative channel structures for the same product

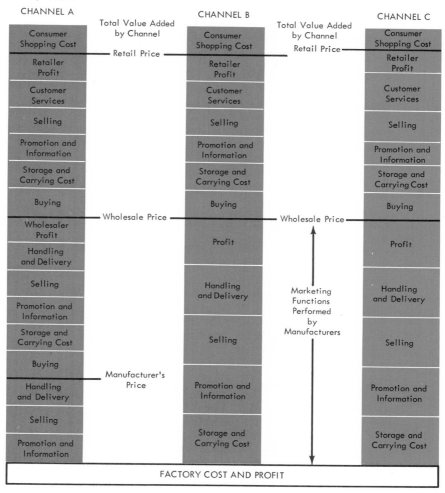

Toward this end, they may offer him special inducements he does not now receive. Thus the manufacturer finds himself in the position of engaging in a form of *vertical competition* for the favor of the most successful retailer serving a particular market segment.

The systems approach to the study of channel structure. This illustration of alternative channel structures is an example of a systems approach. We have looked at the total system and analyzed its environment, functions, institutions, and structure.

We might also describe the existing channels in the market and speculate as to how they developed, as is done in Parts III through V of this book. Or, as in Chapter 19, we could view the system from the vantage point of one institution in the channel and analyze its problems and alternatives. Both of these methods are designed to aid you in understanding why the marketing system functions as it does. It will be useful now to state some specific principles about costs and efficiencies in channels of distribution.

PRINCIPLES FOR SYSTEM COSTS AND EFFICIENCY

Principle of minimum total transactions

The presence of middlemen in the channel of distribution will reduce the total number of transactions involved in marketing a given volume of goods. This is true because the efficiency of trading specialists is greater than that of novices in trade, and a few large exchanges between manufacturer and middlemen are less costly than a very large number of exchanges between consumers and a centralized manufacturer.[2]

This principle makes explicit the concepts illustrated by the primitive community. Specifically, the elements of cost that are reduced by the use of middlemen are as follows:

1. The middleman, through specialization, learns to perform his tasks quickly and with few mistakes.
2. By receiving large shipments in decentralized locations, he reduces the total cost of transit.
3. By reducing the number of transactions and dealing regularly with the same suppliers, he reduces the cost of communication and negotiation between buyer and seller.
4. A decentralized middleman reduces the cost of search incurred by consumers in finding a product at a price they are willing to pay.
5. The middleman becomes a center of information for manufacturer and consumer.

Principle of massed reserves

The existence of middlemen in the channel of distribution will reduce the total amount of goods held throughout the channel to satisfy final demand. This has been called the principle of "pooled uncertainty" because it arises from the uncertainty and the cyclical nature of final demand. If the rate of final demand were known with certainty, retailers would hold exactly the amount of goods demanded by consumers, producers would stabilize their production at this same rate, and no "reserve stock" would be held. But because the rate of final demand is uncertain, retailers carry safety stock.

For example, if 50 retailers sell an average of 10 units per week and require two weeks to get delivery from a manufacturer, they may each carry three weeks' supply, or a total of 1,500 units. This will insure that a sudden jump in demand will not run them out of stock. Now if one wholesaler who provides overnight delivery were to be inserted into this system, the retailers could buy "hand to mouth;" they could stock only enough to last the average week and still be quite sure of never running short. Furthermore, the wholesaler who sells an average of 500 units per week would not need to carry the same three-week supply that the retailers did. Because it is unlikely

---

[2] While this concept can be found in much older literature, it appears in a form similar to that used here in M. Hall, *Distributive Trading* (London: Hutchinson's University Library, 1950), p. 80.

Marketing: Principles and methods

that all retailers would be subject to the same sudden fluctuations in demand in the same direction in the same week, the wholesaler may carry only 1.5 weeks' supply, or 750 units. The total reserves in the system are then 1,250 units (750 plus 500 held by retailers) instead of 1,500 units.

Principle of substitutability

Within the marketing system, it is possible (within limits) to substitute one function for another and still accomplish the same output. If his only function were stocking, the wholesaler in the previous example could be eliminated if the manufacturer could supply one-week delivery by truck rather than two weeks' by train. Then retailers would need to carry only two weeks' supply, or 1,000 units (50 times 20 units). This, of course, is less than the 1,250 units required with the retailer-wholesaler structure. The total cost of the manufacturer-direct-to-retailer structure could be lower than the manufacturer-wholesaler-retailer structure, even with higher truck delivery costs. The shipping function has been substituted for a portion of the stocking function. If the manufacturer discovered that uneven production was less costly than the freight bill for speedy delivery, he might also substitute production for shipping.

The substitutability of inputs into the system gives rise to one of the advantages seen by many manufacturers, wholesalers, and retailers in vertical integration. It is often easier and quicker for a single integrated firm to evolve a more efficient channel structure by making substitutions of freight costs for storage costs or production costs for freight costs than it is for a set of independent businesses to do the same.[3]

However, as will be described in later chapters, there are limits to the advantages of integration. As investment in facilities for quick production, transit, and storage increases, so does the risk of these facilities becoming obsolete. The "lumpiness" of these inputs forces the firm to look constantly for ways to utilize facilities in which it has excess capacity. This task is much more difficult for the integrated firm than it is for a common carrier, a public warehouse, or a merchant wholesaler, all of whom can sell their services to a variety of clients.

Principle of postponement

The risk, and hence cost, of poor allocation of products and services will be minimized if the customization or commitment of a product, service, or assortment to a specific use is delayed to the last possible moment. Postponement can occur in form, time, place, or possession.

An example of form postponement is the practice of not cuffing or hemming men's trousers until they are sold, thereby not commiting them to a specific length beforehand. Time postponement is illustrated by preserving perishable products so they do not become valueless through decay, and consumption can be postponed. Place postponement is illustrated by the book publisher who stores his textbook inventory in a central location and ships to a specific bookstore only when a professor has required the book for a course. Possession postponement is illustrated by the practice of some manufacturers of selling to retailers on consignment. The retailer does not take title to the goods he displays until they are actually sold and, if they are not sold, the manufacturer agrees to take them back.

---

[3] L. P. Bucklin, *A Theory of Distribution Channel Structure* (Berkeley: Institute of Business and Economic Research, University of California, 1966), pp. 83–94.

Thus the principle of postponement is concerned with the shifting of risk within the system. But what is the optimal allocation of each risk within the system? For the manufacturer of pants to shift all risk to the consumer, he would produce grey yard goods only after receipt of an order accompanied by cash and ask the consumer to dye and sew his own trousers. As members of the system, consumers must help to ensure that this risk is allocated in such a way that *consumer utility* and *marketing efficiency* are jointly optimal. In a market economy, competition, working through the marketing system, provides the machinery for allocating risk within the system. Hence, dress trousers are not prehemmed, but work trousers are.

Principle of speculation

A speculative assortment will appear at each point in the distribution channel where its costs are less than the savings to buyer and seller from postponement.[4] Institutions within the channel willingly shift risks to themselves (speculate) by holding goods for a specific use because they believe they have enough knowledge of the system to make more profit by doing so than by shifting the risk to others. A department store provides an excellent example. It carries an extremely broad and deep assortment and offers many customer services in hopes that consumers will purchase their goods at prices that will provide adequate reward for speculation.[5]

Implications for performance measurement

Implications for the measurement of the static efficiency of channel structure include the following points.

Inputs. The buyer is a member of the channel of distribution and can perform some marketing functions. An analysis of channel efficiency that neglects the cost of consumer-performed functions is likely to be faulty.

Outputs. The preceding chapter introduced value added as an aggregate measure of output of a channel. An alternative method of measuring output is to analyze efficiency using more precise measures of *partial* outputs of a system. Three such partial measures are suggested.[6]

1. The average delivery time a consumer must wait, after ordering, before he receives his goods is a measure of the time utility created by the channel of distribution.
2. Market decentralization as measured by the density of retail outlets (or telephones or catalogs) from which the product may be ordered is a partial measure of the search time required of the consumer, the alternative sources available, and the time required to procure the product.
3. The breadth of assortment available to consumers is measured by the quantity of product types, quality levels, and minor variations.

These measures of input and output, even when available, do not completely solve the problem of measurement of performance of the marketing system. How-

---

[4] L. P. Bucklin, "Postponement, Speculation, and the Structure of Distribution Channels," *Journal of Marketing Research*, 2 (February 1965), p. 27.

[5] For a classification of product assortments, see R. F. Breyer, *Quantitative Systemic Analysis and Control* (Philadelphia, 1949), p. 61.

[6] L. P. Bucklin suggests four—the three above plus lot size of final purchase. See his *Vertical Market Systems* (Glenview, Ill.: Scott, Foresman & Co., 1970), pp. 164–74.

ever, if you can remember these principles and their implications, you will be far ahead of many of the participants in, and critics of, the marketing system. You will have an understanding of what the marketing system is attempting to do, why it is doing it, and its degree of efficiency.

CHANNEL MANAGEMENT AND CONTROL

You may have the impression that the channel system is composed of a loose coalition of institutions, each one of which is prompted by the profit motive. You may also think that each institution has little concern for what goes on in the channel except for the levels immediately above and below it. If the assumptions of pure competition (many buyers and sellers, perfect information, "spaceless markets") were applicable to the real world, such a structure would prevail. There would be a quite efficient vertical marketing system controlled exclusively by competitive pressures. But even in the primitive market outlined above, one advantage the trading specialist had was his accumulation of information. Further, although final markets are distributed throughout the globe, large numbers of middlemen are not found everywhere. How, then, do channels operate?

Negotiation and power

Negotiated exchange is the opposite of perfect market exchange in which buyers accept the market price or turn away. In dealings between manufacturers and middlemen, the numbers of buyers and sellers are small enough that negotiation is the rule and not the exception. Negotiation involves power relationships in which the more powerful member usually has the edge and it is unusual for two institutions to have equal power.

In the United States prior to the Civil War, it was the wholesaler who held the greatest power in the channel, for he purchased from foreign sellers or small manufacturers and sold to small, independent retailers. By the second half of the 19th century, a shift in power to the large manufacturer and urban retailer was already underway, although it was the development of the West, not urbanization, that was the dominant force in consumer markets during this period. From 1866 until at least 1921, the manufacturer was gaining power to control channels of distribution, which he was motivated to manage by his discovery that the economies of large-volume production require the development of mass markets.

Following World War I, the automobile, the postwar recession, and large-scale manufacturing led to the growth of concentrated markets in and around urban centers. A new source of power for channel control was the chain retailer, who is vertically integrated and performs his own wholesaling, buys directly from the manufacturer or even engages in manufacturing, and manages the total promotion and selling of the product. Such a retailer also attempts to offer his reputation, rather than that of the manufacturer, as the main source of consumer confidence. The winner of the battle for the consumer's trust will be the institution that will hold the power to control the channel of distribution.

The balance of power today differs among product types. In automobiles, for example, the manufacturer clearly manages the channel of distribution. In food and apparel, the balance of power probably rests with the retailer, while in household appliances, the picture is mixed. The locus of channel power is more likely to be the manufacturer in other countries, although in Japan the wholesaler is still powerful.

The nature of channel conflict

There are conflicts between members of the same channel of distribution which go beyond those thought of as competitive rivalry. A middleman, for example, competes with a manufacturer when he packages, promotes, and sells his own brand along with those of his manufacturer suppliers. The middleman's objective, of course, is to build a "franchise" or credibility reputation for himself rather than for the manufacturer. Even without engaging in this form of direct competitive activity, many areas for conflict exist between manufacturer and middleman and between one middleman and another in the same channel.[7]

Manufacturer direct sale to retailers. Manufacturers, often at the urging of retailers, yield to the temptation to sell directly to the largest and best retail accounts in an area, leaving the least profitable accounts for the wholesaler. Thus the manufacturer is competing with his own wholesalers—an obvious source of conflict.

The discount retailer has provided a good example of this type of conflict. The successful discount operation is too important an outlet for a manufacturer to ignore, but it will demand price concessions that will allow it to sell at prices below that of conventional retailers and below that which will permit wholesalers their normal margins in sales to competing retailers. Some manufacturers have partially solved this problem by producing special models or special brands for direct sale exclusively in discount stores. Although these discount programs have helped to soften the conflict, they have not eliminated it.

Conflict over the storage function. Many of the conflicts between manufacturer and middleman arise over the breadth and depth of inventory which middlemen should carry. No one party is always correct in these disagreements. Some examples of abuses by manufacturers and middlemen may be cited.

1. *Manufacturer loading.* "Loading" is the term applied to the practice of selling far more stock to a wholesaler or retailer than he requires for prudent inventory management. Loading generally stems from poor sales management; salesmen may load their customers in order to meet a quota or win a sales contest, knowing full well that they are losing both the customer's goodwill and an order on the next trip. Sometimes a salesman loads because he feels he can get a middleman to feature a mass display or a special promotion on his product only by getting him in an unsatisfactory inventory position. The usual result is that loading increases cyclical fluctuations in sales and increases conflict.

2. *Complete-line requirements.* A middleman who performs a storage function makes profit on his investment by "turning over" that inventory as many times a year as possible. Thus he prefers to stock only items that are fast sellers. On the other hand, a manufacturer with a broad line in terms of sizes, varieties, prices, models, accessories, and spare parts would like each middleman to carry his complete line. The result is a conflict which arises simply because each institution is attempting to maximize its profit rate. Such suboptimization by channel members may yield a total channel system which does not operate optimally.

Product servicing requirements. Manufacturers of such products as automo-

---

[7] Also see L. J. Rosenberg and L. W. Stern, "Conflict Measurement in the Distribution Channel," *Journal of Marketing Research,* 8 (November 1971), pp. 437–42.

biles, sewing machines, television sets, and white goods (appliances) find that adequate service at and after sale is essential to customer satisfaction. Many manufacturers rely on middlemen to perform repair and installation services or to train servicemen, but some middlemen would prefer not to do so and others perform the service function so badly that manufacturers have had to take it over. In some situations, this has served as a steppingstone to more direct distribution.

Conflict arising from price changes. Middlemen in the United States have not experienced generally declining prices in the past 20 years. However, when selective prices have declined, the protection of the value of stocks held by middlemen has been the source of considerable conflict between institutions in the same channel of distribution. Sellers would like to make sales at previous, higher prices final, and buyers would like sellers to adjust downward the purchase price of products that are unsold at the time of the price decrease.

This conflict commonly occurs at the time of a model change. If middlemen anticipate it, they will be hesitant to order the old model unless the seller provides an incentive. U.S. automobile manufacturers usually handle this problem by allowing their dealers a discount on all units on hand as of a given date. If manufacturers drastically change models without warning, the existing stock may be immediately obsolete, and middlemen expect that they can return, or at least receive rebates on, their existing stock of the old model.

Conflict over aggressive promotion. The promotion and selling strategy of a manufacturer today is expensive and complex. If he advertises directly to end users, he may require complex coordination with the promotional activities of middlemen. If wholesalers are used, for example, it may be necessary for the wholesaler to explain a complex promotional program to each retailer, help him construct a point-of-purchase promotion, and supply all necessary materials and inventory by a specific date that coordinates with national advertising. Many wholesalers with a broad line of products are not equipped to "push" one manufacturer's promotion with any degree of precision. In addition, the wholesaler's salesmen cannot perform such tasks without shorting the attention given other products.

Manufacturers often try to gain extra effort by paying the middlemen (wholesalers and retailers) or their salespeople something extra to handle the promotion. In the long run, such attempts are doomed to failure. The manufacturer will have an expensive promotion and the middleman still has an obligation to give attention to those items he feels will be most attractive to his customers. Wholesalers have a reputation as mere ordertakers; that is, they often will not cooperate with a manufacturer in putting out display materials, "talking up" the products they sell, or aiding the retailer to tie in his advertising with the manufacturer's national advertising programs.

This complaint of the manufacturer undoubtedly is a valid one. The service wholesaler does not and cannot engage in aggressive selling for any particular manufacturer—at least, to any considerable degree. For the average grocery wholesaler with 10,000 to 20,000 items in stock (or for the dry goods wholesaler with up to 250,000 items), to have his salesmen push even a limited number of items would be too time consuming and would result in very high selling costs. Aggressive sales promotion is not one of the functions of the wholesaler; rather, it is the wholesaler's job to provide each retailer with the goods he needs, regardless of the manufacturer. Of course, this should not be taken to mean that wholesalers never push certain items. They do feature special goods from time to time, but they do this for their own advantage and not simply to encourage the sale of the goods of a certain manufacturer. Hence, for the manufacturer who desires to have his products promoted aggressively, some other medium of distribution is needed. Recognition of this fact, coupled with the need for aggressive selling in a highly competitive era, has led many manufacturers to circumvent the wholesaler.

Conflict over other functions.[8] Conflict between channel members is not restricted to the performance of storage, service, risk taking, selling, and promotion functions. Shipping, financing, and information functions are also open to conflict. In seeking their own goals, channel members will continually attempt to shift the performance of all the marketing functions forward or backward, as long as they can do so without losing the margin they receive for performing the function. They will naturally ask for more margin when asked to perform some task out of the ordinary. Such demands are used where the channel member believes a conflict-generating power position will be more profitable than a position of continued cooperation.

For some products, renewed middleman cooperation can be gained through granting an exclusive arrangement to handle a line. There are legal as well as marketing limitations to this approach. For other products, agent middlemen have proved more cooperative than middlemen who carry stock and take title. It should be recognized, however, that this approach does little more than limit the areas for conflict by limiting the functions performed by nonintegrated channel members.

Conclusions regarding channel conflict. The goals of institutions within a single channel system are in conflict with one another, and none are necessarily going to be in accord with the goals of society. In an advanced marketing system like that found in the United States, however, there are reasons why most channel systems perform efficiently. One is that many potentially competitive alternative channel systems exist. A second is that some channel member has found a base of power and a method for playing the role of "channel manager."

Methods of channel management and control

The methods of channel control are: (1) vertical integration through ownership of channel institutions at more than one level; (2) contractual, as in franchising agreements, voluntary chains, and cooperative chains; (3) leadership or consensus.

Vertical integration. The greatest degree of control over a channel system is achieved when one institution simply purchases those above or below it in the channel. This is referred to as vertical integration.[9] When manufacturers own wholesale or retail outlets for their products, they are said to be *vertically integrated forward.* The Singer Company, Sherwin-Williams Paint Company, and the Weyenberg Shoe Company (Nunn-Bush) are examples of vertically integrated marketing organizations whose original source of power was *manufacturing oriented.* All have vertically integrated forward to the retail level.

Retailers who own and operate their wholesale or manufacturing facilities are said to be *vertically integrated backward.* Sears, Roebuck and Company, the Montgomery Ward Division of Marcor Inc., and the large food chains such as the Kroger Company and the Jewel Companies are all examples of vertically integrated marketing organizations whose original source of power was *distribution oriented.* Wholesalers who have integrated forward or backward are less common. Where such firms exist,

---

[8] This section is based on E. H. Lewis, *Marketing Channels: Structure and Strategy* (New York: McGraw-Hill Book Co., 1968), chap. 4.

[9] For a current discussion of this topic see W. R. Davidson, "Changes in Distributive Institutions," *Journal of Marketing,* 34 (January 1970), pp. 7–10.

their power base, too, stems from their expertise in distribution. An example of such a firm is Foremost-McKesson in drugs.

Government also operates integrated channels of distribution in some circumstances. For example, Iowa, Ohio, Pennsylvania, and other states operate integrated retail and wholesale liquor monopolies. The state of California operates as a monopoly "publisher" and distributor of textbooks for all school districts in the state.

Cooperative contracts. Stopping short of combined ownership, channel members often enter into long-term contracts binding themselves to buying and selling arrangements and to facilitating services. Voluntary chains, like Super Value, are individual retailers linked by a sponsoring wholesaler under contractual arrangements.

Retailer cooperative chains, like Certified Grocers, are also linked together through contracts, but here the impetus comes from contractual agreements among retailers who jointly own wholesale operations. Franchise systems also are cooperative contract arrangements.

Exclusive dealership arrangements can be classified as contractual, but such arrangements may be of a less binding nature and depend more on mutual trust than on a legal document.

Leadership. Some channel systems are bonded together and managed solely because channel members accept the leadership and power of one member. The leader may have either a manufacturing orientation or a distribution orientation, but it will most probably have established a "consumer franchise." It has convinced other institutions in the channel that it can be trusted, will be fair in allocating rewards, is an expert marketer, and has an excellent reputation with end users, and that their mutual desire for profit and growth can be achieved through cooperating with it.

Long-term channel structures of the orthodox type—independent manufacturer → independent wholesaler → independent retailer → consumer—illustrate this form of channel management. For such a system to be stable, each channel member must be convinced of the mutual dependence of all members. Each institution acts in cooperation with the others because it realizes that, within the limits of their abilities and environments, cooperation will permit them to survive.

Leadership of such channels is partially based on demonstrated fitness to lead, although this is not sufficient. In addition, a channel leader must have a differential power advantage in order to maintain his position.

Sears, Roebuck and Company, for example, has extensive influence over many of its supplier firms. Sears is in a position to tell many of their suppliers what they want, when and where they want it, the prices they consider appropriate, and even that they doubt if a supplier is big enough to retain both Sears and Wards as customers. These suppliers, of course, can tell the channel leader they are taking no such orders, but if a sizable part of their operation has been devoted to, say, Sears, they may feel constrained to accept orders on procedures to obtain Sears's orders for merchandise.[10]

Bases of power for channel control[11]

The base of power for the distribution-oriented channel leader is different from that of the manufacturing-oriented channel leader.

---

[10] For a discussion of channel management by large retailers, see R. Dickinson, "Channel Management by Large Retailers," in R. L. King (ed.), *Marketing and the New Science of Planning,* 1968 Fall Conference Proceedings (Chicago: American Marketing Association, 1968), pp. 127–30.

[11] This section draws heavily on R. L. Little, "The Marketing Channel: Who Should Lead This Extracorporate Organization?" *Journal of Marketing,* 34 (January 1970), pp. 31–38; and L. W. Stern (ed.), *Distribution Channels: Behavioral Dimensions* (Boston: Houghton Mifflin Co., 1969).

Power base of the distribution-oriented leader. The distribution-oriented firm usually has three advantages it can use to gain consumer confidence and power over the channel. First, it controls access to consumers. Most manufacturers of consumer goods are concerned about getting distribution for a new product. The retailer is the gatekeeper, and he has many demands for his shelf space. His control over retail display is a source of power through which he can set the terms under which he will handle a new product.

Second, he is in direct contact with consumers and fixed in their geographic market area. This direct contact makes it easier for the retailer than for the manufacturer to gain and maintain the confidence of shoppers. The manufacturer is removed in space and does not deal directly with the consumer.

Third, while most distributors are small and small businesses are often inefficient, that charge cannot be made against the large distributor vying for control of the channel of distribution. Large distributors have had a tradition for "lean," low-overhead, efficient operations, which cannot be said for most large manufacturers. This trimness provides another source of power for the distribution-oriented channel leader.

Power base of the manufacturing-oriented leader. The low-overhead distribution organization, however, can work under a disadvantage if manufacturers' staff functions are performed properly. Manufacturers have gained the power to control the channel of distribution through investments in staff activities, such as information management. Manufacturers usually obtain more information and manage it more intelligently than do distributors, thus providing them with a differential advantage and a source of power.

A second staff function that manufacturers perform better than distributors is the recruitment and training of young managerial talent. A steady influx of bright, energetic, hungry people is a source of power for any organization. A third is promotion management. Middlemen tend to accept the leadership of manufacturers who provide complete, multifaceted, well-planned promotions supported by national advertising.

The function that is perhaps the greatest base of power for the manufacturer is research, or more correctly, new product development and introduction. It is innovation, new choices, new products, and new ways of doing things that permit our society to grow; a new product will probably be more valuable to society than a new retail location. Unless he is completely integrated, the distributor can never match this base of channel power for the manufacturer.

Power based on market structure. At this stage in our exploration of marketing, we do not want to go extensively into the economic analysis of market power. However, we will point out the structural characteristics of markets that can provide a base of power to one or another channel member.

1. A high degree of monopsony (one buyer) in distribution in any geographic market. For example, a state liquor distribution department has absolute control over which brands legally reach the public.
2. A manufacturer with a monopoly (one seller). Such a manufacturer has the power to control its channel of distribution if and when it can establish an end user demand for that product.
3. The breadth of a manufacturer's line. Even without vertical integration, companies such as Lever Brothers, General Foods, and Bristol-Myers have a base of power over their channels of distribution because they make a large number of products which go through the same channels and at least a portion of which have met consumer acceptance.

4. The introduction of a new product. This gives a manufacturer a technical and marketing head start on his competition. Old products tend to be standardized and easily produced, and distribution-oriented firms are better able to have them produced and marketed under private labels. As a product matures, the manufacturer's power base disappears.

Implications for performance measurement. As should be evident from the above discussion on the explicit role of power in channel control, the resource-allocation mechanism of pure competition does not provide an adequate model for our advanced marketing economy. Nor does it provide an adequate model which can be investigated to determine whether the marketing channel system is structured in a socially optimal way.

The public policies of this country say virtually nothing about the positive use of power to control a channel to make it perform more efficiently. In fact, there is only one piece of federal legislation which attempts to deal with vertical power relationships in channels of distribution—the Robinson-Patman Act, which is certainly not based on a systems analytic model and has been the subject of severe criticism since its passage in 1936.

We have few notions of what constraints to place on negotiations between channel members. We have few principles on how risk should be diffused through the channel and few ideas on how the locus of power influences innovation. We do not know when vertical integration makes a channel too rigid to change for the public good. Some of these issues will be investigated again in Chapter 25, but you are encouraged to bear them in mind as you read the intervening chapters.

SUMMARY

Chapters 2 and 3 provide an overview of the marketing system. In the previous chapter, the focus was on the processes and functions performed by the marketing system, and the participatory institutions were introduced. This chapter considers the work of these institutions in the evolution, structure, and operations of the channels of distribution within the marketing system.

The need for marketing arises out of the efficiencies that accrue from the division of labor in production. The performance of these functions by marketing specialists arises out of consideration of efficiency in distribution.

Marketing functions can be conducted in a large variety of alternative structures. New technology, changes in consumer wants, and competition cause constant evolution of channel structures within the confines of specified principles of marketing efficiency. The principles developed were those of minimum total transactions, massed reserves, substitutability, postponement, and speculation.

The efficiency with which a channel structure performs its functions is dependent on how well the coalition of institutions in a channel are able to work together. Since the makeup of our society often does not permit the many buyers and sellers required for pure competition, channel members often must reach agreement through negotiation. This creates conflict which arises over the question of which institutions are to perform which functions and how much compensation they are to receive.

The resolution of the conflict is usually in favor of the channel member with the greatest economic power. It may be resolved by vertical integration of the channel, contractual agreement, or extraorganizational leadership.

In Part II the consumer market is discussed. Before moving on, test your understanding of the material in this chapter by working the review and discussion questions.

REVIEW AND DISCUSSION QUESTIONS

1. What is a channel of distribution?

2. What are the major structures of channels for consumer goods? What factors determine the length and breadth of channels of distribution?

3. Explain in your own words the principle of the division of labor as applied to marketing.

4. Show algebraically why the savings in fully negotiated transactions with a central market is $\frac{1}{2} n(n - 3)$.

5. Use the concept of equalization processes to explain why all channels of distribution are not fully vertically integrated.

6. Cite from your own experience some changes in channel structure for particular consumer goods.

7. Explain why a single good is not distributed through a single, most efficient channel structure.

8. Explain why different goods are not marketed through the same channel structure.

9. Is the spread between the manufacturer's price and the retail price of a product a good measure of the cost of marketing? Why?

10. Distinguish between horizontal competition, vertical competition, and vertical channel conflict.

11. Why is the principle of postponement incomplete without the principle of speculation?

12. What was the source of channel power for wholesalers prior to the Civil War? How does this compare to the channel structure you would expect to find today in a developing country?

13. Distinguish in your own words the differences in the sources of power of manufacturing-oriented channel leaders and distribution-oriented channel leaders.

14. How does the cost of national television advertising affect the importance placed on channel leadership by a manufacturer of refrigerators?

15. What information would you want to have in order to compare the performance of the channel structure used by RCA to market television sets (integrated through the wholesale level and service functions) and that used by Motorola (independent wholesale distributors and servicemen)?

SUPPLEMENTARY READINGS

Breyer, R. E. "Some Observations on 'Structural' Formation and the Growth of Marketing Channels." In **R. Cox, W. A. Alderson, and S. J. Shapiro (eds.),** *Theory in Marketing.* Homewood, Ill.: Richard D. Irwin, Inc., 1964. Many insights are to be gained from the excellent writing of this early channel theorist.

Bucklin, L. P. (ed.) *Vertical Marketing Systems.* Glenview, Ill.: Scott, Foresman & Co., 1970. An original collection of advanced works that is suitable for use as a text. There are excellent questions at the end of each chapter.

Clewett, R. M. (ed.) *Marketing Channels for Manufactured Products.* Homewood, Ill.: Richard D. Irwin, Inc., 1954. A classic collection of articles on channels of distribution.

Marketing: Principles and methods

Lewis, E. H. *Marketing Channels: Structure and Strategy.* New York: McGraw-Hill Book Co., 1968. A short but complete volume covering all aspects of channels and channel management.

Moller, W. G., Jr., and Wilemon, D. L. *Marketing Channels: A Systems Viewpoint.* Homewood, Ill.: Richard D. Irwin, Inc., 1971. An excellent new collection of modern writing on channel theory and practice.

Revzan, D. A. *Wholesaling in Marketing Organization.* New York: John Wiley & Sons, Inc., 1961. Covers both systemic and internal points of view and provides a comprehensive view of wholesaling. Chapters 5 and 6 discuss channel structure.

Stern, L. W. (ed.) *Distribution Channels: Behavioral Dimensions.* Boston: Houghton Mifflin Co., 1969. This largely theoretical volume focuses on the conflicts that arise within channels of distribution.

Part II   The environment of the market for consumers' products and services

Parts II through IV are devoted to helping you learn about marketing systems for *consumers'* products and services, as contrasted with industrial products and services. Part II focuses on the environment of consumers' goods marketing, Part III on the retailing system, and Part IV on wholesaling. The environment in which the marketing system exists both influences the system and is influenced by it. In line with the massive attention being given it currently, attention is directed to the major aspects of the environment throughout the three chapters in Part II.

Chapter 4 focuses on consumers and how they make decisions about buying. Scholars of marketing do not believe, as the popular press maintains, that consumers can be influenced and persuaded, although they would like to be able to change attitudes and buying habits. This chapter summarizes what marketers know about individual consumer decision-making processes.

Chapter 5 takes an aggregate or macro view of the many segments of the total market for consumers' products and services. There is an old but robust saying that "markets are composed of people with money and a willingness to buy." Each of these market dimensions are examined.

Chapter 6 points out that as members of the marketing system, consumers have certain responsibilities and rights. They sometimes do not meet their responsibilities, and their rights may be violated. Consumers are being increasingly protected, however, and the types of consumer aids and protection offered by various sources are viewed in some detail. Chapter 6 brings the topic of consumerism into focus.

4 A system of consumer behavior

To be a meaningful venture, marketing must satisfy human needs. The marketing concept helps organizations to achieve their goals and objectives by developing appropriate marketing activities that focus on intended customers.

COMPLEXITY OF CONSUMER BEHAVIOR

Consumer behavior is complex and difficult to observe, and the underlying processes and explanations are obscure. As Bernard Berelson and G. A. Steiner have written: "Human behavior itself is so enormously varied, so delicately complex, so obscurely motivated that many people despair of finding valid generalizations to explain and predict the actions, thoughts, and feelings of human beings—despair, that is, of the very possibility of constructing a science of human behavior."[1] The variety in consumer behavior is apparent. Some buy only Fords, others only Chevrolets. Some buy Cadillacs, Lincolns or Mercedes-Benz. Why? Beer is purchased by only 33 percent of U.S. households; a mere 17 percent buys 88 percent of it. Why? Cake-mix purchase behavior is almost as varied, with only 37 percent of the households purchasing 85 percent and 27 percent of the households not buying any. Why? Human behavior is such that for numerous products a small proportion of all households consumes well over half of all the units sold (Figure 4–1).

A product, a style, or a brand that has sold in large quantities over a considerable period of time may quickly lose favor. Few consumers today use fountain pens, wear

---

[1] B. Berelson and G. A. Steiner, *Human Behavior: An Inventory of Scientific Findings* (New York: Harcourt, Brace & World, Inc., 1964), p. 3.

FIGURE 4-1
Heavy half users

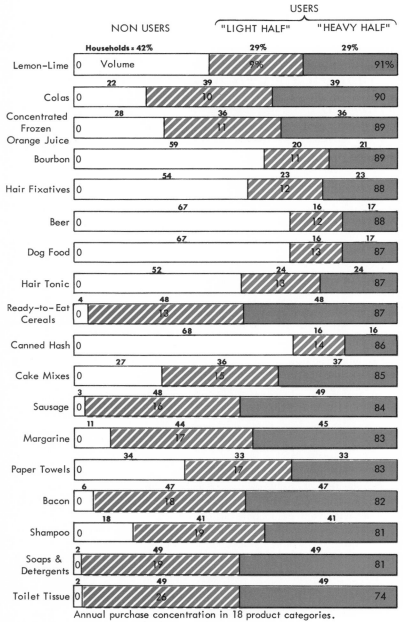

Annual purchase concentration in 18 product categories.

Source: *Chicago Tribune* Consumer Panel data as reproduced in D. W. Twedt, "How Important to Marketing Strategy Is the Heavy User?" *Journal of Marketing,* 28 (January 1964), p. 72.

FIGURE 4–4
Effects of exogenous variables

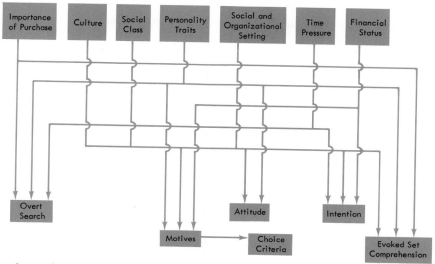

Source: Adapted from J. A. Howard and J. N. Sheth, *The Theory of Buyer Behavior* (New York: John Wiley and Sons, Inc., 1969), p. 92.

the involvement and interest a buyer has in a product or service class, the more attention and search for information he will devote. This also increases awareness of the number of alternatives (brands) and the amount of knowledge he possesses about each.

A prospective apartment renter who is "turned on" by apartments will engage in far more exploratory behavior than one who just needs a place to sleep. The person with the avid interest will know much more about available apartments, and his choice criteria are likely to be more extensive and detailed.

Personality traits. Variables such as need for achievement, self-esteem, self-confidence, anxiety, venturesomeness, and authoritarianism account for a person's enduring disposition in emotion, temperament, and social behavior. Personality theories developed by Freud, Jung, and Murray were viewed as offering complete explanations of behavior. Motivational research in marketing, which grew out of such theories, tried to place sole dependence on traits as explanation of buyer behavior. This simplistic, ad hoc approach has a very poor record, but the use of personality traits as an exogenous variable accounts for some differences in behavior that would otherwise go unexplained.[27]

Personality traits impinge most directly on overt search, motives, attitudes, and evoked-set comprehension. Certainly not all, if even most, of the relationships of personality traits are understood, but researchers have acquired some evidence. For example, the more *anxious* a person, the greater is motivational arousal and the greater are attention and overt search, as well as the magnitude of his evoked set. The more *authoritarian* he is, the narrower his evoked set. The greater *self-esteem* a person possesses, the more likely he is to perceive messages, but the less likely to

---

[27] For a recent review article, see H. H. Kassarjian, "Personality and Consumer Behavior: A Review," *Journal of Marketing Research,* 8 (November 1971), pp. 409–18.

4 / A system of consumer behavior

be influenced. A person with *low self-esteem* is less likely to let communications through his perceptual process, but those that make it through are more likely to influence him.

We would expect an apartment seeker with high *self-esteem* and high *anxiety* to be very active in exploratory behavior (attention and overt search) and a seeker of much information about many apartments (evoked-set comprehension). Also, his perceptual biases would play a heavy role in interpreting the information. Traits should not be examined individually, however, but the dominant set of personality traits of a buyer should be viewed in terms of their influence on his perception and learning.

Time pressure. The amount of time allocated to the act of purchasing compared to the time required determines time pressure. A person may feel he needs four hours a week for six weeks to find a new apartment. On discovery that he must make his decision in the first week with only six hours available (he misread his current lease), he is under time pressure. His behavior will be different than if he had the expected time available.

Time pressure impinges most directly on his search activity (overt search) and on his intention. The more time pressure to which he is subjected, the less search activity he can engage in. This, in turn, will lessen the number of alternatives he can consider and the amount of information he can secure about each apartment (the magnitude of his evoked set).

Time pressure also is an inhibitor—a constraint that the buyer did not recognize as he was forming his attitude and intention. His intention becomes different from attitude as the inhibitor constraint comes to bear.

Financial status. A buyer's financial resources, including income, assets, and borrowing potential, during a specified period of time determine his financial status, which is colored by his perception of it. Financial status influences intentions and motives most directly and acts as a constraint to intention. It causes a buyer to behave contrary to his attitudes because he simply does not have the funds to purchase what he desires. The apartment hunter may prefer the penthouse apartment but intend to rent the first-floor apartment overlooking the parking lot because of his financial status.

Changes in relative financial status have some motivational influence. A person learns to live within his income with a certain standard of living. Even though income rises, he may continue to spend at a level close to the old one. If financial status declines, either absolutely or compared to his expectations, the buyer is likely to become frustrated by the income constraint and become more aroused. At first, he will spend at a rate more like that of his previous *perceived permanent income.* Arousal would likely lead the buyer to perceive more relevant market information—particularly price information. If the buyer becomes exceedingly frustrated, he may shut off virtually all information and become irrational in his purchasing by buying more than he can possibly hope to pay for. For example, he might attempt to rent the penthouse knowing there is no way he can pay for it. Financial status appears to offer an explanation for this type of buying behavior.

Social and organizational setting. Influences from the family, small groups, and reference groups stem from the social and organizational setting. These groups, particularly the family, provide the historical background that makes the buyer what he is in a buying situation.

It is not mere chance that children tend to reflect the behavior and beliefs of their families. The years when they are in the home coincide with the time they are most susceptible to influence. The family interprets the values and life style of its culture to the child, who must learn enough to be tolerated. A child grows to adulthood in the United States eating hamburgers, hot dogs, milk, milk shakes and peanut butter, and he likes football and basketball. The child growing to adulthood in Mexico eats tacos, enchiladas, tostadas, tamales, and refried beans, and he likes bull fighting and soccer. The family and other groups are responsible for differences in attitudes, motives, and other perceptual and learning variables because as the child grows to adulthood he learns from those around him.

Shopping behavior provides a good illustration of the socialization of a child. He begins accompanying family members to the grocery store at a young age. As he grows older he may be permitted to select an item or two, but perhaps he is told that certain items are too expensive or too cheap, too small or too large. Some families sensitize their children to price and others to quality. After a few years the child may be sent to the store alone with a shopping list and buying instructions. He may also be permitted small sums of money in order to learn "to manage money." As he grows older, he accompanies the family on more shopping trips for more items. Clothes are no longer brought home for him; he participates in their purchase. As he is permitted to buy more items, members of the family are close at hand to provide opinions.

Although the family is a major influence, the child and the teen-ager also learn from friends and from the school, church, temple, and other organizations. An individual learns early in life that to be accepted by a group he must conform to it, and the more certain a group is that it is right, the greater conformity it demands from its members. The group, whether the family or the high school cheerleading squad, influences behavior of its members by providing them with support, reinforcement, security, encouragement, protection, and rationale for "proper" behavior. It metes out punishment for deviations in the form of ridicule and shame, lower status, and the threat of expulsion.

The same is true for adult social, political, and work groups. In addition to behavior, such groups also influence values, attitudes, and life styles. We are influenced by groups to which we belong (peer groups) and those to which we aspire. Such groups are called reference groups, the norms of which are adopted by the individual and reflected in his buying behavior.

The apartment seeker of our example is what he is largely because of the environment in which he matured. His immediate family has had a lot of influence, although he does not mirror its attitudes, motives, and behavior. We know, for example, that children are more likely to smoke if both their parents do. An adult who had an alcoholic parent often will not touch liquor. This, however, may represent the agony he sensed. The individual who matured in an environment where a house was merely a place to sleep will have different attitudes and motives about an apartment than one from an environment where a house was a home or a virtual castle. In the latter situation, the apartment seeker is likely to have more fully developed choice criteria, more apartments in his evoked set, and more information about each of them.

Although this chapter is focused principally on the behavior of ultimate consumers, most of what has been said can be generalized to the industrial buyer. Here, however, the additional influence of a small group in the work or formal organization—the design engineer, production manager and his boss, or the purchasing agent—may be paramount, with the other groups being secondary. The industrial buyer will be discussed in more detail in Chapter 12.

Social and organizational settings impinge most directly on the learning variables of motives, attitudes, intention, and evoked-set comprehension. The family and other social groups are also instrumental in interpreting and transmitting to the buyer his social and cultural milieu.

Culture. As the distinctive life style of an aggregate of people, culture represents their adaptation to their environment and their design for living. Culture may emanate from a nationality group (Italian), a religious group (Jewish), a racial group (black), or a regional group (Texas). Culture influences how people relate to other people, the way they perceive things, the products and services they feel they need, and their consumption patterns. It includes knowledge, beliefs, values, art, morals, law, life styles, and customs.

A member of a close-knit culture may find he must conform to his group or be rejected by it. A Mormon, for example, must reject alcoholic and tobacco products; an orthodox Jew abstains from pork and purchases a higher than average quantity of candles. Orientals tend to care for their own elderly members and do not commit them to nursing homes. Blacks, Jews, and Orientals learn through many sources that avenues of success are not as available to them as to nonminority groups, and they therefore pursue certain avenues (sports, education, entertainment) more avidly.

In terms of our consumer behavior model, culture directly affects motives, evoked-set comprehension, attitude, and intention. In turn, these influence overt search and perceptual bias.

The apartment seeker may need an apartment as a goal-object to show his family and friends he is an adult. In some other culture his goal-object might be to contribute to his parent's well-being. The type of apartment a person will consider and the information he wants about apartments (evoked-set comprehension) will reflect his culture. A student from England who is new to Minnesota might not inquire about central heat or a private bathroom, whereas one raised in Chicago would. A student from the culture of Japan would have a different attitude about the size of an apartment that would affect his choice criteria, overt search activities, and perceptual bias. He might not even consider looking at an apartment of more than 500 square feet because of a perceptual bias that such a size would be far too expensive.

Social class. Society is divided into different classes that exhibit distinguishable values and life styles and that are distinct from cultural background. For social class to influence buyer behavior, individuals must feel that they belong to a specific class. Class awareness, values, and life styles are derived from things learned and transferred principally by education and occupation. Family and cultural background can influence the importance placed on class membership, but the mobile individual may change his class through the outside influences he encounters as a young person. The son of a poorly educated farmer may become a college professor; the daughter of a socially prominent family may adopt a hippy life style. Life styles and values assumed may also be independent of the income variable.[28]

A buyer's social class is postulated to directly influence his motives and attitude. In addition, some aspects of social class that are not utilized internally (as the buyer is formulating attitudes) may become constraints and thus affect intention. The buyer's evoked-set comprehension is also affected by his social class.

If the apartment seeker is from the upper middle class, he may place great importance on a prestigious well-appointed apartment. A plush apartment may be a partial goal-object that will help him to know he is succeeding and will encourage his friends to tell him so. His attitude as to what constitutes a satisfactory apartment will be affected by his social class, which will call for a location in a neighborhood

---

[28] For a study that relates social class and income to buyer behavior, see J. H. Myers, R. R. Stanton, and A. F. Haug, "Correlates of Buying Behavior: Social Class vs. Income," *Journal of Marketing,* 35 (October 1971), pp. 8–15.

of his class and a building occupied largely by his social peers. His choice criteria and resulting evoked set will be better explained with the help of social class than without it. Any of these effects he fails to take into account when he is formulating his attitude are likely to become constraints, with the result that his intentions will not be congruent with his attitudes.

Paul Lazarsfeld has indicated that lower social-class individuals prefer sweet chocolate, fabric with a rubbery touch, and strong smelling flowers, while those in the upper class favor more sensory demanding experiences such as bitter-dry tastes, irregular weaves, and less pungent fragrances.[29] William Henry found that greeting cards were purchased less frequently and in fewer numbers by the upper social classes than by the lower classes.[30] Since the consumption patterns and buyer behavior for some goods can be related to social class, this variable, along with culture and income, provides a basis for sellers to segment the markets in which they sell. James M. Carman summarizes the evidence and suggests an approach for identifying social classes.[31]

The seven major exogenous variables discussed above that impinge on the buyer's perception and learning and consequently influence his behavior help explain observed differences in consumer behavior.

The model as a decision-making process

Perception and learning variables can be put together with the set of exogenous variables to form a more comprehensive view of the consumer behavior model as a decision-making process. Figure 4–5 indicates major parts and relationships.

When the consumer is confident he has enough information about the alternatives and their attributes, he will purchase the item that *maximizes his utility per dollar expended*. However, since perfect information is not available and obtaining more information costs time and money, most decisions are made when the consumer is *satisfied* that the utility per dollar expended could not be increased much by further overt search.

The amount of overt search that is necessary before this step in the decision-making process is reached depends on the consumer's *stage of learning*. Three stages describe the range of decision-making behavior: (1) extensive problem solving, (2) limited problem solving, and (3) routinized response behavior.

Extensive problem solving. The buyer is in the extensive problem-solving category when he has very little, if any, applicable prior experience. His attitude box for the product or service class under consideration is virtually empty; he does not know enough about the available alternatives to be able to choose among them. He may not even know the boundaries of the product class that satisfy his goal-object. As a result, the prospective buyer actively seeks a great deal of information about available product characteristics as well as about criteria for evaluating them. His search is likely to lead him to consider many more alternatives than an experienced buyer would. Without direct experience, he will not have in-depth comprehension; his evoked set will be wide but shallow. He will tend to place more reliance on information for evaluation from trusted friends and will use commercial stimuli mainly to identify his range of alternatives and individual product characteristics. Search takes

---

[29] P. F. Lazarsfeld, "Sociological Reflections on Business" in *Social Science Research on Business.*

[30] W. E. Henry, "A Study in the Application of Socio-Psychological Research to the Problems of Business and Industry," *Journal of Social Psychology,* 1948, pp. 33–60.

[31] J. M. Carman, *The Application of Social Class in Market Segmentation* (Berkeley, Calif.: University of California, Institute of Business and Economic Research, 1965).

FIGURE 4–5
Comprehensive view of the buyer model

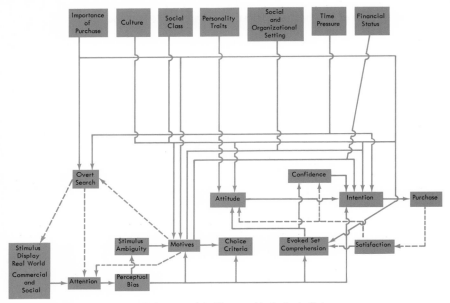

Note: Solid lines represent flows of information; dashed lines stand for feedback effects.

Source: Adapted from J. A. Howard and J. N. Sheth, *The Theory of Buyer Behavior* (New York: John Wiley and Sons, Inc., 1969), pp. 92 and 184.

much time and is not very efficient. Evaluation of choice criteria and product and service characteristics is extensive. The time lapse from start to finish of the decision process will be relatively long.

Limited problem solving. The limited problem-solving category includes buyers with a moderate amount of experience which influences their attitude about the evoked set. Ambiguity among the individual alternatives is present, but not to the extent in the extensive problem-solving category. The buyer may have moderate preference for one alternative over the others, but he is fairly well settled on his choice criteria. He will actively seek information, probably in more depth than before but for fewer alternatives, because his evoked set is smaller. The lapse time from initiation of the decision process to its completion is much smaller.

Routinized response behavior. When the buyer has acquired extensive experience (very firm attitudes) about the alternatives in the evoked set, he is in the routinized response behavior category. There is sufficiently little ambiguity about the alternatives in the evoked set so that he has a strong preference for one or two of them, and he is not likely to actively seek additional information from the environment. Information that does come to his attention will be subjected to extensive perceptual bias to bring it into congruence with his existing attitudes.

For frequently purchased products like toothpaste and gasoline, the buyer, upon sensing his need, will respond almost without conscious thought to buy one of the brands he has been purchasing recently, provided they have maintained or increased

Marketing: Principles and methods

his satisfaction. Through his experience he has learned what he prefers, he has simplified the alternatives to a brand or two, and he proceeds to a purchasing decision virtually without thought.

If there is a long time between purchases, as in buying an automobile or renting an apartment, the buyer is likely to engage in exploratory behavior as each purchase time approaches. However, in routinized response behavior, he is prone to retain his choice criteria pretty much intact and limit his exploration to determination of which alternatives best fit his choice criteria.

Classification of consumer products and services

If discussion of the model of consumer behavior has led you to infer that the buying decision process is influenced by the type of product or service under consideration, you are correct. A buyer in any stage of learning will go through the buying decision process somewhat differently for a cleanser solution for new contact lenses, a first-time rental of an apartment, or an initial purchase of a set of Head brand skis. He will move to another learning stage much sooner for the lens cleanser solution than for the apartment or the skis.

We should recognize that there are different consumer buying patterns not only *among* but also *within* each learning stage. The differences within each stage are due in part to differences in the characteristics of various products and services as they are perceived by the prospective consumers. These characteristics, which lead to differences in shopping behavior, are: (1) the interval of time between purchases or replacement rate; (2) the amount of adjustment, fitting, or service of the good performed by the retailer; (3) the extent of instability in supply assortment, price, quantity, and quality; (4) the degree of homogeneity between brands; and (5) the unit value of the product. Most of these characteristics are also reflected in the margin between the factory and retail price.

To examine this phenomenon we will use a classification that is based *on the way buyers typically go about buying various products and services.*[32] This classification recognizes three major categories: (1) convenience products and services, (2) shopping products and services, and (3) specialty products and services.

Convenience goods. These are products and services the consumer usually desires to purchase with a minimum of effort at the most convenient and accessible location. He behaves this way because these products and services are of relatively small unit value, are frequently purchased, and any one transaction is of relatively minor importance. Compared to the other two types of products and services, convenience goods require relatively little time for the buying decision process. Cigarettes, pay telephones, chewing gum, razor blades, bank checking services, shoe repair, lens cleanser solution, cleaning services, and gasoline are specific illustrations.

Studies make it clear that people actually treat these goods as convenience items. One study of the buying habits of people in Iowa found that

---

[32] M. T. Copeland, *Principles of Merchandising* (Chicago: A. W. Shaw Co., 1924), chap. 5. Significant contributions to Copeland's classification have been made by L. V. Aspinwell, "The Characteristics of Goods," in W. Lazer and E. J. Kelley (eds.), *Managerial Marketing: Perspectives and Viewpoints* (Homewood, Ill.: Richard D. Irwin, Inc., 1962), pp. 633–43; L. P. Bucklin, "Retail Strategy and the Classification of Consumer Goods," *Journal of Marketing,* 27 (January 1963), pp. 50–55; and G. E. Miracle, "Product Characteristics and Marketing Strategy," *Journal of Marketing,* 29 (January 1965), pp. 18–24. Useful empirical research of the theory includes A. K. Kleimenhagen, "Shopping, Specialty, or Convenience Goods?" *Journal of Retailing,* 42 (Winter 1966–67), pp. 32–39; and L. P. Feldman, "Prediction of the Spatial Pattern of Shopping Behavior," *Journal of Retailing,* 43 (Spring 1967), pp. 25–30, 63.

the attraction of a city increased in proportion to its size up to a radius of ten miles, but at that point the trend stopped abruptly in the case of convenience goods such as groceries and drugs. With respect to more occasional purchases, particularly those involving larger amounts of money or factors of style and durability (i.e., shopping goods), the ten-mile limit did not hold. As a matter of fact, the drawing radius for clothes and furniture continued to increase with the size of the city, many consumers traveling fifty to sixty miles to buy in the larger cities.[33]

Another study of women's buying patterns for food revealed a relatively high frequency of purchase, with 26 percent visiting a supermarket at least three times each week, another 26 percent twice each week, and the remaining 48 percent making a weekly visit.[34]

Since customers wish to purchase convenience products and services with a minimum of effort, a seller will usually place them in as many locations as possible; that is, he will attempt to gain maximum exposure to sale.[35] Similarly, convenience store retailers seek locations that are as convenient as possible for consumers.[36] When convenience products and services are sold by stores that deal largely in shopping and specialty goods, the explanation is found in the fact that on occasion it is more convenient for the consumer to buy them in such establishments.

The fact that convenience products and services are placed in numerous locations that are close to the consumer has two important results: The sales of many of these locations are typically small. Therefore, many manufacturers find it too expensive to sell direct to the thousands of individual retailers, and a vast wholesale organization has grown up to handle this type of merchandise.

Shopping goods. Shopping products and services are those that the consumer will usually purchase only after comparing quality, price, and style in a number of stores. Such products and services rarely are standardized. Exactly the same style of dress is seldom found in a number of stores in the same shopping center, nor do two lawyers render the same services. The purchase of shopping products and services often involves a significant expenditure, takes place infrequently as compared with the buying of convenience products and services, is of greater importance and, in general, requires more time for the buying decision process. Furniture, apartments, clothing, legal services, rugs, musical instruments, electrical appliances, and jewelry are in this category.[37] Many other items of lower price, such as those in limited-price variety stores, also fall within this classification.

The marketing of shopping goods is considerably different from that of convenience goods. Because consumers frequently make their comparisons in more than one store before buying, stores handling shopping goods tend to congregate in shopping centers, both in downtown and outlying areas—they thrive best in groups.[38] Depart-

---

[33] W. Alderson, *Marketing Behavior and Executive Action* (Homewood, Ill.: Richard D. Irwin, Inc., 1957), pp. 342–43.

[34] "Frequency of Visits to Supermarket in a Week," *Printers' Ink,* February 11, 1966, p. 39. Also Kleimenhagen, "Shopping, Specialty, or Convenience Goods," especially p. 37.

[35] Consumer buying habits growing out of product characteristics and the manufacturer's marketing channel policy are treated by Miracle, "Product Characteristics and Marketing Strategy," pp. 21–22.

[36] The importance of retail store location in relation to consumer buying habits is discussed by L. Groeneveld, "A New Theory of Consumer Buying Intent," *Journal of Marketing,* 28 (July 1964), p. 24.

[37] A study of consumer shopping habits for electrical appliances is reported in W. P. Dommermuth, "The Shopping Matrix and Marketing Strategy," *Journal of Marketing Research,* 2 (May 1965), pp. 128–32.

[38] A recent study suggests that today's consumer wishes to shop less than did her counterpart of yesterday. For a limited list of shopping-type goods the study disclosed that consumers "visited more than one store in less than one-third of the purchasing situations." The authors of the study conclude that the decrease in the propensity to shop is the result of such factors as widespread advertising which allows the customer to

ment and "five-and-ten" stores furnish good examples. Whereas a very large number of stores handle convenience goods, a much smaller number concentrates on shopping goods. The manufacturer of such goods is frequently less interested in the number of stores that will handle his merchandise than in the quality of the stores that do. If his merchandise is displayed in the better stores, the chances are that the prospective buyer will see it as he shops before making a purchase. Finally, the successful sale of shopping goods demands a large assortment within a store, since the shopper wants to feel he really has a choice.

The smaller number of stores in this field furnishes another point of contrast between the marketing of convenience and shopping goods: A much larger percentage of shopping goods is sold directly from the manufacturer to the retailer without the aid of a separate wholesale organization. The number of stores to call on is not so overwhelming; the size of orders is large enough to make individual shipments economical; and the financial position of these larger merchants makes them better credit risks. Moreover, larger stores prefer to buy direct from manufacturers.

The marketing of shopping services, which is little different from convenience services, is discussed more fully in Chapter 15. Prospective customers will normally compare (shop for) shopping services by talking with prior and current purchasers rather than directly securing such information from the service supplier (loan officers of banks, dentists, lawyers, public accountants, etc.). In town shopping service suppliers do not tend to cluster in shopping patterns.

Specialty goods. Products and services that have a particular attraction for the consumer so that he will go out of his way to purchase them are classified as specialty items. They consist of those products and services that many buyers insist on having and for which they are willing to make a special purchasing effort. Buyers have developed the belief that the products and services of certain suppliers are superior to the general run of possible substitutes and will go to the stores or suppliers handling the ones they want. If the supplier is "out" or the goods are unavailable, substitution may be difficult; the buyers may prefer to wait. The main appeal is not price, it is the qualities thought to lie in the merchandise or service itself. Such products and services tend to be high priced in relation to others of the same type. Examples are certain men's high-grade clothing and shoes, some makes of automobiles and fine watches, fancy groceries, and services of certain trial lawyers, medical specialists, and hair stylists.

Since buyers of specialty products and services are willing to make special efforts to visit suppliers, and since purchases are made rather infrequently and usually involve fairly substantial sums of money, suppliers in this category need neither the widespread distribution required for convenience goods and services nor the major outlets in shopping areas that are necessary for shopping goods. Such sellers may rely on a small number of outlets in each city, and the service supplier may have but one "shop" or office. Consequently, use of the exclusive agency, whereby a dealer is made the sole representative within a certain area, and selective distribution, where a few carefully chosen retailers within a city handle the product, are quite common in the marketing of such merchandise. Since the number of outlets used by any one manufacturer is small, direct sale from manufacturer to retailer is possible, and some manufacturers retail their merchandise through their own stores.

---

preshop, competing alternatives for the use of the customer's time, and greater affluence of many buyers (so that the customer does not feel the need to buy so carefully). See W. P. Dommermuth and E. W. Cundiff, "Shopping Goods, Shopping Centers, and Selling Strategies," *Journal of Marketing,* 31 (October 1967), pp. 32–36.

Overlapping classifications of consumers' goods. Like the overlapping in the classification of goods as consumer or industrial, the three classifications of consumer goods and services also overlap.[39] Products and services fulfilling the same need may be treated as convenience, shopping, or specialty, depending upon the individual consumer's buying habits. For most people staple groceries are convenience goods, but many "shop" for them, and high-priced fancy groceries are typically treated as specialty goods. Medical or legal services may be secured where most convenient in an emergency or for minor needs, but with more ample time and greater need, they can be treated as shopping or even specialty services. Typically, common work shoes are a convenience good and medium-priced women's shoes are a shopping good, but high-priced men's shoes are often purchased by brand—they are treated as a specialty good.

SUMMARY

The behavior of humans is complex and difficult to understand, particularly when it is observed in a casual or nonrigorous manner. Two or more persons with the same set of needs will often respond or behave in very different ways, and two or more persons with different sets of needs will often respond or behave in extremely similar ways.

Man's behavior has intrigued him throughout history. Untold numbers of theories and models of human behavior have been advanced as philosophers, psychologists, psychiatrists, sociologists, economists and, more recently, marketers have struggled to provide meaningful behavioral explanations that will be useful in problem solving and prediction. While our knowledge and understanding of human behavior may be many times greater than that of our forefathers, it still is meager relative to what we would like it to be.

This chapter has formulated a model that will provide as good a framework or perspective of the process of buyer behavior as is currently available. It is based on the assumptions that buying is an exercise in problem solving and that the process is systematic. Specifically, the model relates the manner in which three sets of variables result in consumer decisions: (1) real-world input variables from sellers and the social environment; (2) variables that are internal to the buyer, which are further divided into learning variables (motives, choice criteria, evoked-set comprehension, confidence, attitude, satisfaction, and intention) and perception variables (attention, stimulus ambiguity, overt search, and perceptual bias), and (3) exogenous variables (importance of purchase, personality traits, time pressure, financial status, social and organizational setting, culture, and social class) which influence the external state of the buyer's decision process.

Three stages of learning about a specific product or service will affect the buyer's decision process. When he considers a product or service for the first time, he is in the extensive problem-solving stage. After he has acquired some experience and attitudes about it he will be in the limited problem-solving stage, and after extensive experience has led to firm attitudes about the class of product or services, he will be in the routinized response behavior stage.

Different characteristics of various products and services influence consumer buying processes and behavior patterns. Convenience, shopping, and specialty are the categories into which products and services can be classified.

---

[39] Feldman, "Prediction of the Spatial Pattern of Shopping Behavior," pp. 10–11.

REVIEW AND DISCUSSION QUESTIONS

1. Explain the ways in which economics provides an understanding of consumer behavior that is useful to marketers.

2. How could Freud's concepts of man's id, ego, and superego in his model of human behavior be helpful to a seller of a risqué man's magazine? To a bank loan officer?

3. What are the main reasons for using models of buyer behavior instead of just discussing a large set of influencing variables?

4. What are motives, and how do they help explain the buying decision process?

5. What variables are included in the learning subsystem in the Howard-Sheth model? What are the relationships (influences) of these variables on each other, and how do they jointly influence buying decisions?

6. What are the differences between attitudes and intentions, and which are most likely to reflect actual buyer behavior?

7. Illustrate (explain) the process a consumer goes through learning for the first time to purchase a tennis racket, a cleanser for new contact lenses, or a mobile home.

8. Illustrate that consumers sense only a part of their real environment but, on the other hand, also sense some things that are not really present.

9. What are the major variables within buyers' perceptual subsystems, and how do they relate to each other to provide inputs to learning?

10. Illustrate the perception process of a consumer who is attempting for the first time to make a decision to buy a tennis racket, a cleanser for new contact lenses, or a mobile home.

11. Explain each of the exogenous variables and indicate why they are called "exogenous."

12. Illustrate the influence various exogenous variables have on a consumer who, for the first time, is attempting to make a decision to buy a tennis racket, a cleanser for new contact lenses, or a mobile home.

13. Explain the three stages of learning described in the Howard-Sheth model. Why are there only three stages?

14. Illustrate the buying decision process for a consumer who is about to make a tenth purchase of a tennis racket, a cleanser for contact lenses, or a mobile home.

15. Explain how different types of products and services (convenience, shopping, and specialty) influence the buying decision process and the resulting pattern of buyer behavior.

SUPPLEMENTARY READINGS

Alderson, W.   *Marketing Behavior and Executive Action,* chap. 6, "The Motivation of Consumer Buying." Homewood, Ill.: Richard D. Irwin, Inc., 1957. *Dynamic Marketing Behavior,* chap. 6, "A Theory of Consumer Behavior." Homewood, Ill.: Richard D. Irwin, Inc., 1965. These chapters are excellent sources on some concepts that receive only limited attention in the Howard and Sheth model.

Berelson, B. and Steiner, G. A.   *Human Behavior: An Inventory of Scientific Findings.* New York: Harcourt, Brace & World, Inc., 1964. An introduction to the state of the knowledge of human behavior expressed in 1,045 scientific findings.

Carman, J. M.   *The Application of Social Class in Market Segmentation.* Berkeley, Calif.: Institute of Business and Economic Research, University of California, 1965. Provides a good synopsis of the social class variable and its measurement and applications to marketing.

Engel, J. F., Kollat, D. T., and Blackwell, R. D. *Consumer Behavior.* 2d ed. New York: Holt, Rinehart & Winston, Inc., 1972. A basic book that discusses a broad variety of buyer behavior variables and presents an alternative model of buyer behavior.

Howard, J. A., and Sheth, J. N. *The Theory of Buyer Behavior.* New York: John Wiley & Sons, Inc., 1969. This is the book which presents the Howard and Sheth model in full perspective and detail.

Kassarjian, H. H., and Robertson, T. S. (eds.) *Perspectives in Consumer Behavior.* Glenview, Ill.: Scott, Foresman & Company, 1968. This readings book includes many of the outstanding journal articles on consumer behavior that have appeared in the past 15 years.

Katona, G. *The Mass Consumption Society.* New York: McGraw-Hill Book Co., 1964. The reader will benefit from the background offered by this study of consumer psychology in an affluent society.

Myers, J. H., and Reynolds, W. H. *Consumer Behavior and Marketing Management.* Boston: Houghton Mifflin Co., 1967. Using examples from current marketing situations, the authors relate consumer behavior to buying situations.

Newman, J. W. (ed.) *On Knowing the Consumer.* New York: John Wiley & Sons, Inc., 1966. Part II of this collection of readings is pertinent in connection with this chapter, especially **J. S. Coulson,** "Buying Decisions with the Family and the Consumer-Brand Relationship."

Nicosia, F. N. *Consumer Decision Processes.* Englewood Cliffs, N.J.: Prentice-Hall, Inc., 1966. Presents a review of empirical evidence and theoretical analysis of consumer behavior.

5 The market: People, money, and fashion

It takes three ingredients to create demand for a product or service: people, the ability to buy (money), and the willingness to buy. The big potential U.S. market for consumers' products and services—those produced for personal and household consumption—consists of some 200 million people whose total personal income in 1970 exceeded $800 billion. These people have a large variety of wants and are motivated in their buying activities by a great many influences. If inflation and unemployment continue, will they have the willingness to buy? If so, what will they want to buy? With the birth rate in the United States decreasing and the population getting older, a decline in the demand for toys and baby food and less emphasis on the teen-ager market than on the young family market can be anticipated.

Market segmentation

Success in marketing in the United States today is dependent on a strategy of *market segmentation.* This is a fundamental tenet of modern marketing that has been suggested in previous chapters. Market segmentation is the way in which the marketing system maximizes the alternatives available to consumers. It does so by recognizing that the total market is made up of smaller submarkets (segments) of consumers who have needs that are homogeneous in many demographic, geographic, economic, cultural, and psychological ways. A market segmentation strategy attempts to find such a market and penetrate it to the greatest extent possible by customizing products, services, and marketing efforts to fit its needs. Volkswagen and the Coca-Cola Company, for example, have realized that everybody does not want to buy a "bugmobile" or a cola beverage. Volkswagen has introduced other types of vehicles, and Coca-

Cola also makes Fresca, Hi-C, and a variety of beverages and snack foods. This strategy represents the ultimate extension of the "marketing concept"—giving consumers what they want.

Thus a marketer must look at more than total population and aggregate income. In considering the incomes and other characteristics of the population segments of the potential U.S. market, he must understand that people with money do not automatically constitute a market, except for basic necessities. Most goods and services in the United States are not basic necessities without substitutes. Thus the third ingredient necessary to constitute a market is willingness to buy.

People and money considerations in marketing are fairly easily understood; many of these dimensions and implications will be presented in this chapter. The third ingredient, willingness to buy, is a much more complex dimension that precludes comprehensive discussion in a single chapter. Personal, social, and cultural influences on spending were discussed in the preceding chapter; this one will consider the variations in spending patterns by various social, cultural, and income groups and the influence of fashion on the willingness to buy.

In exploring the three major dimensions of the consumer market, we shall look first at important selected characteristics of the population, placing special emphasis on the changes that are taking place and their impact on marketers. Second, we shall examine patterns of consumer income and significant trends in personal consumption. Finally, attention will be given to fashion and its relevance in the marketplace.

POPULATION TRENDS

Among population changes that are influencing the market for consumer goods are a continuing rise in total population, active changes in status of age groups, changes in the American family, a better educated population, geographic shifts, and the increasing importance of ethnic markets.

Continuing rise in total population

Long-run forecasts of the country's population have proved difficult in the past. Population is a function of the birth rate, the mortality rate, and the immigration rate. The mortality rate is the stable element of the three, while the birth rate has shown significant changes, both upward and downward, during the past 50 years. From 1921 to the end of World War II, immigration was an insignificant factor in population change, but it has grown in importance since that time; in 1970, 17 percent of the population growth was accounted for by immigrants.

Birth rate. The record year for births in the United States was 1957, when 4.3 million children were born. The fertility rate, children born per 1,000 women aged 14 to 44, was lowest (about 70) during the first half of the 1930s. It subsequently increased, took a big jump following World War II, and reached a peak of 123 in the mid-50s. It has now declined to under 90.

The fertility rate is expected to continue to decline, but at a slower rate, in the seventies. However, because the population of women age 20 to 30 will increase sharply (due to effects of the postwar baby boom), the number of births will actually rise. As shown in Figure 5–1, the result will be not only a continued growth in total population, but an increase in the growth rate, which in the late sixties had slowed to 1 percent per year. This may seem like a very low growth rate, but it will double the population in just 70 years!

Marketing: Principles and methods

FIGURE 5–1

Growth of U.S. population, 1930–1970, with projections to 1980

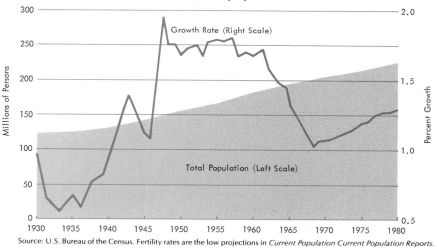

Source: U.S. Bureau of the Census. Fertility rates are the low projections in *Current Population Current Population Reports.*

While the environmental, social, and economic impact of a 1 percent or greater population growth rate may be more important than its impact on marketing, the implications for the marketer can easily be suggested. Each year, over four million mothers need to buy the products required by newly born babies, about three million boys purchase razors (or borrow their fathers') for the first time, some three million girls become potential customers for lipstick, and some 2.5 million young people get married and become purchasers of products necessary for new households. At the other end of the age scale, each period of 12 months finds 1.5 million individuals reaching the age of 65. The majority of these retire, and major changes gradually take place in their buying patterns.

Changes in the age distribution of the population

The under-20 population. The young—those 19 and under—made headlines in the sixties because they were the group with the largest growth. Figure 5–2 makes it clear that during this decade they will likewise make headlines—but for a different reason. The population under 20, about 78 million people, may actually decline during the years to 1980. The trend will not be the same for all age segments of this group. The number of preschool-age children, which has been declining since the mid-60s, will turn upward before the end of the decade. The 6 to 11 age group will actually decline during the decade, and the teen-age group will remain about constant.

Of course, mothers do the buying for preschoolers, so it is the teen-age market segment that will retain dominance in this decade. Marketers have worked hard to understand this segment and have found that when they discover the motivations of teen-age consumers and offer products and services to meet their needs, the rewards are great. The 13 to 19 age group is responsible for purchasing some 16 percent of all the cosmetics sold in this country, 20 percent of the radios, 24 percent of the wrist

FIGURE 5–2
Population change of four age groups, 1960–1970, and projections for 1970–1980

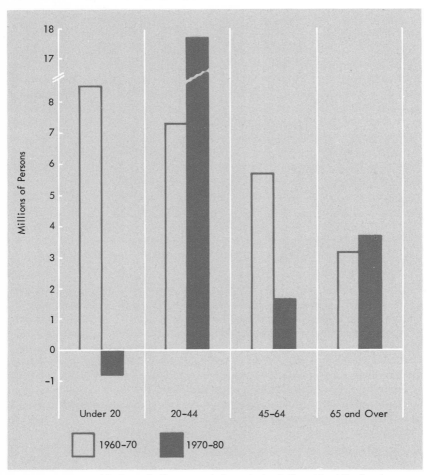

Source: U.S. Bureau of the Census. Fertility rates are the low projections in *Current Population Reports.*

watches, 30 percent of the lower priced cameras, 45 percent of the soft drinks, 81 percent of the records, and "the girls . . . [spend] at least two billion dollars a year" for clothes.[1] Thus it is understandable that manufacturers develop products for this market, which are both packaged and advertised to attract teen-agers, and that retailers often stock certain areas of their stores with merchandise especially for this group.

The young adults. As Figure 5–2 shows, the big news in the seventies is the growth of the young adult market, which is actually more concentrated than that

---

[1] "U.S. Teen-Agers—The Golden, Confusing Years," condensed from *Newsweek* in *Reader's Digest,* August 1966, p. 51.

Marketing: Principles and methods

shown in the graph. Because of the small number of births in the thirties, the number of people 35 to 44 will not start to increase until late in the decade. The greatest growth is concentrated in the 25 to 34 age range, which will increase by 50 percent during this decade. In 1980 there will be more people in the 20 to 24 age group than any other five-year age group.

The impact for economic growth is tremendous. Households in the 25 to 44 age group with earnings of $10,000 to $25,000 will account for 40 percent of all consumer spending by 1980.[2] This group is now entering the labor force and earning money. The increase in young adults is triggering an upsurge of family formations and births, and the number of homes with children still in the nest will increase by nearly 25 percent during the decade.[3] By the last half of the seventies, the rate of formation of new households—which includes families as well as single persons living alone or with friends—is expected to reach 1.3 million per year.

New households and young families make many major purchases such as houses, appliances, and furniture. The result is that young adults consistently spend more than they earn. It should not be surprising, then, that the greatest growth in consumer expenditures in the seventies is forecast for housing, medical care, automobiles, home furnishings, appliances, household operation, personal care, personal business, recreation, and education.[4]

The 65 and over group. The 30 to 40 age group was small during the sixties because of the decline of births in the thirties. This deficit group will move up to the 40 to 50 age bracket in the seventies. Thus the growth in the 45 to 64 group shown in Figure 5–2 is small.

On the other hand, the 65 and over group shows regular and substantial growth of over three million people in each decade. There are 20 million in this age bracket today, and it is estimated that by 2000 the number of those over 65 will exceed 35 million. And life expectancy continues to rise: it was 54.1 years for those born in 1920, 70.5 years for those born in 1967, and it is still higher today.[5]

The trend toward an older population, especially the rising over-65 group, also has significance for marketing. Manufacturers and middlemen selling goods that appeal to these people will have expanding markets, since both the numbers and the incomes of this group are in an upward trend. Marketing to the over-65 group is also influenced by other factors. Among these older people, women are far more numerous than men—seven women for every five men. Most of the women are widows, most of the men are still married. Older Americans carry considerable political heft; comprising over one of every eight people of voting age, they go to the polls in heavier proportions than the rest of the electorate and represent an even larger share of votes actually cast. Nearly one of five is still working or looking for a job. Nearly a third of those over 65 live in just four states: California, New York, Pennsylvania, and Illinois. Florida, Iowa, Nebraska, Arkansas, South Dakota, Missouri, and Arizona also have high proportions of older persons.

Their buying power, now about $60 billion a year, makes older Americans a big and growing market for clothing, health aids, retirement homes, travel, recreation, and a host of other goods and services. Income statistics are somewhat deceptive

[2] F. Linden, *The Consumer of the Seventies* (New York: The Conference Board, Inc., 1969), p. 60.

[3] Ibid., p. 16.

[4] Ibid., p. 64.

[5] U.S. Bureau of the Census, *Statistical Abstract of the United States, 1970* (Washington, D.C.: Government Printing Office, 1970), p. 53.

in this regard. An aged couple with a cash income of $5,500, the median in 1970, would actually be doing as well as a younger couple earning $7,200 a year. Older people benefit from special U.S. income tax allowances, the elimination of Social Security taxes, ownership of a home in many cases, and a differential in medical costs as a result of Medicare.[6]

Changes in the American family

The size of the average family in this country has been on a slow, long-run downward trend, with some short-run interruptions. In 1890, the average family contained 4.9 persons; by 1930, 4.1 persons. The average size today, 3.6 persons, is about the same as it was 20 years ago.[7]

Two marketing implications of this trend are a return to smaller housing units and increased discretionary income. Perhaps the most significant implication is that smaller families facilitate the continuance and return of wives to the work force. As recently as 1947, our labor force consisted of 43 million men and 16.7 million women. By 1970, the men had increased by 10 million to a total of 53 million, but this was overshadowed by a 15 million advance in the number of working women, to a 31.5 million total.[8] In 1970, over one third of all wives comprised 54 percent of the female work force. Figure 5–3 shows that this trend is expected to continue.

Quite apart from sociological implications, the employed wife is catapulting an increasing number of families into the upper earning brackets. In almost half of all husband-wife homes with earnings exceeding $10,000, the wife is employed, and more often than not, her supplementary earnings are necessary to sustain the family in the upper income brackets.[9] This higher income has resulted in the purchase of many additional products and services—homes, appliances, travel, education, and especially clothing. Since many working women believe they need, in effect, three wardrobes—one for the home, one for the job, and one for social activities—it is not surprising that they purchase 50 percent of all women's apparel. With less time for household activities, demand has also been expanded for frozen foods, prepared dinners, and laborsaving devices for the home such as the electronic oven, which promises a golden-brown roast on the table 20 minutes after removal from the freezer and hamburgers in 5 minutes.

Another aspect of American family life which deserves note is the work preferences of the population. Not only have wives returned to work in increasing numbers, but husbands show some reluctance to reduce their work hours. Twenty years ago it was thought that the workweek would decline from the standard 40 hours per week, but the statistics show no sign of this. The average weekly hours worked in manufacturing were the same, 40.6, in 1940 and 1970.[10]

However, this does not tell the whole story. Excluding overtime, average weekly hours may be gradually declining since the mid-60s. More important is the way families desire to spend their leisure time. With some help from Congress, most workers can count on at least nine paid three-day weekends each year. These and

---

[6] From the U.S. Department of Health, Education and Welfare as reported in *U.S. News and World Report,* May 24, 1971, pp. 66–71.

[7] U.S. Bureau of the Census, *Current Population Reports,* Series P-20.

[8] U.S. Bureau of Labor Statistics.

[9] Linden, *The Consumer of the Seventies,* p. 56.

[10] U.S. Bureau of Labor Statistics.

FIGURE 5–3

Number and percent of wives employed, 1945–1970, with projections to 1980

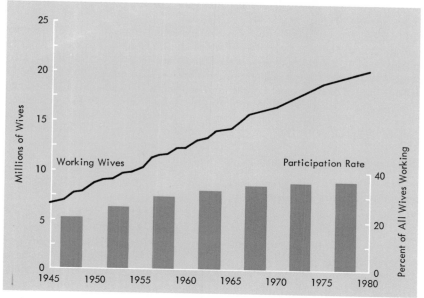

Source: U.S. Bureau of Labor Statistics historical data projected by F. Linden, *The Consumer of the Seventies* (New York: The Conference Board, 1969), pp. 56–57.

experiments with four-day, 10-hour-per-day weeks have proved popular with most workers. Evidently a mobile population can do more with a long weekend than with a shorter work day. Longer paid vacations also are increasing in number. Just two decades ago, 61 percent of union contracts called for a maximum two-week vacation. According to the Bureau of Labor Statistics, in 1967, the maximum was four weeks in 60 percent of the contracts, five weeks in 10 percent, and six weeks in 2 percent of the union contracts.[11] Recreational expenditures are rising with increased leisure time, having jumped from $18.3 billion in 1960 to $30.6 billion in 1967. It is estimated that by 1980 these expenditures will have increased by 8 percent.[12]

Some striking evidence of the impact of these expenditures on both goods and services can be seen. The boom in professional sports is an example in the services area, and recreational vehicles provide an example in the products market. Trail bikes, snowmobiles, campers, and self-propelled homes have all been introduced and become important products in a very few years.

A better educated population

Educational attainments of the U.S. population have steadily improved, and this trend will probably continue into the future. Whereas 29 percent of all people 25 years of age and over in 1940 had attended high school for from one to four years, and

---

[11] As reported in *Business Week*, February 8, 1969, p. 83.
[12] Linden, *The Consumer of the Seventies*, p. 67.

5 / The market: People, money, and fashion

an additional 10 percent had finished high school and gone on to one or more years of college, corresponding figures for 1970 were 51 and 21 percent. By 1980 it is expected that the high school figures will increase to 56 percent and that one in four will have attended college.[13]

This trend toward more education has marketing implications. Since better schooling leads to higher pay, a larger share of consumer spending power flows to the relatively well-educated segments of the community. In 1970, households headed by persons that had college training accounted for less than one fourth of all homes but for one third of total personal income. By 1980, close to 40 percent of all personal income will accrue to homes where the head has at least some college training, and the importance of the high school graduate in the marketplace will rise to about 36 percent of all spending.[14] These families spend above-average amounts for travel services, books, magazines, records, hi-fi, concerts and plays, sports equipment, housing, home furnishings, education, and insurance.

Geographical shifts in population

The striking rise in population has not been shared equally by all parts of the country. Moreover, a high degree of mobility has been demonstrated, with approximately 12 percent of the population changing residence within the same county and 7 percent moving to a new county or state each year.[15] As a result, markets have felt the impact of at least three geographic population trends: (1) toward the southwestern and western states, (2) away from rural areas, and (3) from central cities to the suburbs. The last two trends have resulted in the emergence of population concentrations in a relatively small number of megalopolises—super-cities formed when the suburbs of one urban area join with those of another.

Regional trends. Throughout the history of the United States, there has been a gradual westward shift in population. In 1790, the center of the population was a few miles *east* of Baltimore, Maryland.[16] One hundred years later, it had moved to Indiana; today it is just east of St. Louis, Missouri. The trend continues, with the "Sun Belt" of Florida, Texas, New Mexico, Arizona, California, and Hawaii showing large percentage gains in population.

The westward population shift has forced manufacturers to adjust marketing programs to follow the market. Since the movement has resulted in more people in warmer areas, the demand for such goods as sports clothes, sunglasses, lightweight suits and topcoats, air conditioners, and patio furniture has increased.

An urban nation. It's been "hard to keep 'em down on the farm" since about the end of World War I. Because of rapid increases in agricultural productivity, a large farm population is not required, and migration from farms has been rapid since the end of World War II. Today only 10 million people, 5 percent of the population, live in farm areas. The high point for lived-on land in the nation as a whole was 1920, when about 32 million people, 30.1 percent of the population, lived in farm areas. Rural southern blacks have been moving to northern cities at a steady rate for 30 years,

[13] U.S. Bureau of the Census, *Current Population Reports,* Series P-20.

[14] Linden, *The Consumer of the Seventies,* p. 34.

[15] U.S. Bureau of the Census, *Current Population Reports,* Series P-20.

[16] U.S. Bureau of the Census, *Statistical Abstract of the United States, 1970, op. cit.,* p. 10. The "center of population" is that point upon which the United States would balance if it were a rigid plane without weight and the population were distributed thereon.

but the migration to urban centers is far more general. About one half of the counties in the nation lost population during the decade of the sixties.[17] New immigrants also settle in the cities.

There is another mobility trend at work. Government home loan programs have made it possible for lower middle-income families to own their own homes, largely in the suburbs. The result has been an influx of low-income families into the central cities to replace the flow of middle-income families to the suburbs. On balance, except for growth areas with regional metropolitan boundaries such as Houston, the central cities have experienced a net loss in population. Since the low-income newcomers pay less taxes and require more city services, central cities are in serious environmental, social, and economic trouble. Many of the suburbs may follow a similar pattern of poor management and go through a life cycle ending in deterioration, decay, and death.

In 1970, for the first time, the U.S. Census showed more people living in the suburbs than in central cities. About three quarters of the population could be said to be living in urban or suburban areas. Fully half is huddled along the coasts and the Great Lakes in megalopolises. The largest is the Boston-to-Washington corridor, which runs from New Hampshire to Virginia and includes New York, Philadelphia, and Baltimore. In the Midwest there are three: the Milwaukee-Chicago-northern Indiana area around Lake Michigan, the Detroit-Toledo area around eastern Lake Erie, and the Cleveland-Akron-Pittsburgh area of northeastern Ohio and western Pennsylvania. In the absence of more active population controls, these areas could well grow together to cover an area along the base of the Great Lakes from Green Bay, Wisconsin, to Buffalo, New York.

Next to the East-Coast megalopolis, southern California is the second most important market area in the country, stretching 150 miles from Los Angeles and Orange County south through San Diego. The northern California megalopolis, around San Francisco Bay, includes the cities of San Francisco, Oakland, and San Jose. Texas contains two major urban areas: Houston and Dallas–Fort Worth. It is unlikely that the two California or the two Texas urban clusters will ever merge.

In the South Atlantic area, Florida could become a megalopolis along both coasts and from Tampa on the northwest to Miami on the southeast. The other urban centers of the country which promise to continue to be important regional urban centers are the metropolitan areas of St. Louis, Missouri-Illinois; Minneapolis–St. Paul, Minnesota; Seattle-Everett-Tacoma, Washington; Atlanta; and Kansas City–St. Joseph, Missouri-Kansas.

With half the population in the suburbs, it is not surprising that this group does not constitute a single homogeneous market segment. Suburbanites represent the plurality of America—high income/low income; growing/stagnant; Catholic/Protestant/Jewish; Republican/Democratic. A suburbanite has mobility and easy access to a big central city, but he is not necessarily a commuter to that city. Industry, retailing, entertainment, and even culture have moved to join him.

The successful national marketer has found how to serve the single-family-house suburbanite by researching his needs, moods, social patterns, attitudes, values, and life styles. Poor rural and urban consumers are not so well served by the marketing system simply because they do not represent significant profitable market segments and it appears that they will continue to decline in importance in the seventies.

---

[17] U.S. Bureau of the Census, *1970 Census of Population,* Preliminary Reports.

Ethnic changes in the population

Market segments have often been profitably defined on the basis of ethnic culture—race, religion, or national origin. From its base of mainly English settlers, the United States opened its arms to foreign immigrants from many parts of the globe after the War of 1812. Before 1880, they came in large numbers from Germany and Ireland; after that time, from Poland, Italy, and China. First- and second-generation immigrants maintained much of their foreign culture, and marketers who understood the special needs of these groups were able to serve them well.

While World War II brought peoples of many lands, from 1921 to 1950 the only growing ethnic markets were the Jewish and Puerto Rican populations of New York. By 1970, immigration was up again to 375,000 people per year, with Mexico and the Philippines accounting for 20.3 percent. The next greatest number was Italians, with 6.7 percent. Native American Indians numbered only 800,000 in 1970—less than half the number of foreign-born Italians in the country. These Italians, Latin Americans, and Mexicans comprise ethnic market segments that have attracted the attention of marketers.

The most important ethnic market segment is the native American Negro. The blacks are catching up in American society; they now number 23 million, over 11 percent of the population. And, in central cities, the percentage of the total U.S. Negro population is greater than that for whites. While the median income of a black family in 1969 was about $3,600 below that of a white family, there has been improvement, as shown in the income distributions in Figure 5–4. Futher, the median school years completed in 1969 for Negroes over 25 years of age, 9.6 years, was up 1.4 years over 1960. The increase for whites was 1.3 years. The total annual spending of Negroes is estimated to be about $30 billion.[18]

FIGURE 5–4

Percentage distribution of families by annual before-tax income groups (constant 1968 dollars)

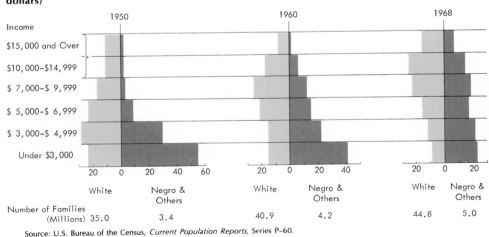

Source: U.S. Bureau of the Census, *Current Population Reports*, Series P–60.

[18] *Statistical Abstract of the United States, 1970*, p. 109; and "Why the Negro Market Counts," *Business Week*, September 2, 1967, p. 64.

Marketing: Principles and methods

By no means is there unanimity on how to sell to the Negro market. Although blacks are, in the main, native Americans, they have formed a unique subculture. To develop a market segmentation strategy for blacks requires, by definition, "customizing the product, services and all marketing efforts to fit the needs of this submarket." Negroes have said that much promotion directed to them has an "Oreo" character (like the Oreo cookie—black on the outside and white on the inside).[19] While blacks are entering the mainstream of American life, preference for their own culture must be recognized by the marketer.

CONSUMER INCOME AND EXPENDITURES

Besides knowing the number and characteristics of the population that constitutes his market, the marketer must also know something about consumer incomes and expenditures. Three basic facts concerning current income and expenditure patterns of consumers in the United States will be examined:

1. Average income, while rising and providing the highest standard of living in the world, is still low in relation to the wants of consumers. Moreover, although income is distributed more evenly among its recipients than ever before, many families continue to have very low incomes.
2. The expenditure pattern varies according to the income group of the consumer, although the variations are less today than formerly. It also varies with the passing years.
3. Total retail sales, as well as sales in specific fields, are closely related to disposable consumer income.

Rising income and its significance to the marketer

Changing consumer income. Since the Great Depression of the 1930s, personal income in the United States has literally leaped forward. Even allowing for inflation (1958 dollars), per capita disposable personal income more than doubled from $893 per year in 1933 to $1,795 in 1955. By 1970 it had risen to $2,580.[20]

While these averages are an indication of increasing prosperity, an area of concern is how these incomes are distributed among the families of America. It would not be desirable if incomes had risen sharply for highly paid executives and members of powerful unions while the number of Americans living in poverty actually increased. The change in this distribution of income can be seen in the changing shape of the "income pyramid" in Figure 5–4 above. The figure shows considerable progress toward inversion of the pyramid. Even by 1950, the poor did not comprise the modal tier, and by 1960 it had moved up to $7,000–$10,000 range. By 1968, the inversion of the pyramid was not quite complete, but it is forecast that it will be by 1980. Nonwhite families enjoyed an even greater redistribution of income during the period.

Using a family income of $3,000 in 1968 prices as a rough measure of the poverty line, you can see that the number of families below that line was cut in half—from 10 million to 5 million—between 1950 and 1968. These figures show a tremendous expansion in the potential market for consumer goods, but it would be well to realize

---

[19] "Marketing to Blacks Still Mystifies Whites, Speakers Advise Conference," *Advertising Age,* June 2, 1969, p. 19.

[20] *Economic Report of the President* (Washington D.C.: Government Printing Office, 1971), p. 215.

that average figures do not tell the whole story. In 1969, four states—Mississippi, Arkansas, Alabama, and South Carolina—had an average per capita personal income under $2,600 per year. On the basis of money income per family (as in the figure), this amount is equivalent to $7,200 per year.[21]

Income and marketing opportunities. While the social significance of disappearing poverty is great, you should also appreciate the significance for marketing of this shift in income distribution. As family income rises above the poverty level, choices can be made in the marketplace for other things besides the necessary food, clothing, and shelter. This additional buying power is called *discretionary income*. It is up to the marketer to find ways to help consumers achieve the most from these dollars.

The decade of the seventies will continue to experience a dramatic expansion in the number of families with incomes exceeding $10,000. The number will more than double to almost 35 million, about half of all families. Thus, if inflation can be controlled, the nature of the market in this decade could shift "from mass to class."[22]

Consumer wealth. As families save and invest from their incomes, they will accumulate a stock of wealth. It has been argued that as this wealth gets bigger, its marginal utility decreases, so that, as income rises, the *proportion* spent on current consumption also rises. Although there is little empirical validity for this argument, there is some truth in the maxim that "money burns a hole in one's pocket." Liquid assets—funds in checking and savings accounts and savings bonds—provide the means for instant consumption. The median liquid assets held by families have increased steadily in the past decade, up 40 percent in five years to $730 per family in 1969. In that year, 18 percent of the families in the population were holding $5,000 or more in liquid form.[23]

Consumer debt. Another source of funds for consumer expenditures is through the expansion of consumer debt. Nonmortgage consumer debt took a jump in 1955 as a result of unusual demand for durables, and monetary authorities have kept a close watch to make sure that it does not create some form of economic imbalance. A number of relevant statistics are given in Table 5–1.

TABLE 5–1
Some statistics on consumer debt

| Year | Total nonmortgage consumer debt | | Percent of GNP | Total debt as a percent of GNP | Installment credit repayments as a percent of disposable personal income |
	Outstanding (billions of dollars)	Percent of disposable personal income			
1929......	7.1	8.5	6.9	186.0	n.a.
1949......	17.4	9.2	6.8	174.0	8.2
1959......	51.5	15.3	10.7	172.0	12.6
1969......	122.5	19.4	13.2	182.0	15.0

Source: *Economic Report of the President* (Washington, D.C.: Government Printing Office, 1971), p. 270.

[21] *Statistical Abstract of the United States, 1970*, pp. 320 and 325.

[22] Linden, *The Consumer of the Seventies*, p. 52.

[23] Institute of Social Research, *1969 Survey of Consumer Finances* (Ann Arbor, Mich.: University of Michigan, 1970).

The table shows that the consumer is shouldering an increasing proportion of the total debt in the economy, while the ratio of total debt to total annual output has remained quite stable over a period of time. The question, then, is whether it is appropriate for consumers, rather than business or government, to increase their share of this debt. Experts believe that it is, as long as delinquencies and loan defaults do not start to increase rapidly. When this happens, the cost of borrowing becomes so high that consumers will not want to pay the price. In addition, overextended families, which are often low-income families, will find it increasingly difficult to be participants in American affluence.

To ensure that consumers know what they are paying to borrow money, market-ers and lenders have supported consumer credit counseling services, and Congress has passed the "Truth-In-Lending" Act, which requires complete disclosure of the cost of borrowing. As long as borrowers and lenders are prudent and borrowers are well informed on the price they pay to consume now rather than later, growing consumer debt can be a help rather than a hindrance to marketing and to continued prosperity.

The implications of continued inflation. The American economy experienced short periods of generally rising prices following World War I, World War II, and the Korean conflict. The cause was the classic situation of buyers bidding up prices because demand exceeded supply. From 1921 to 1945, the price level did not increase at all. From 1952 to 1964, the average annual increase exceeded 1.5 percent in only four years.

Since 1965, however, inflation has been persistent and increasing, as illustrated by the trend in the Consumer Price Index shown in Figure 5–5. The cause is

FIGURE 5–5
Consumer Price Index, 1952–1970 (1967 = 100)

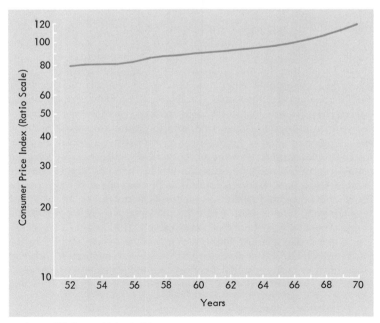

Source: U.S. Bureau of Labor Statistics.

a combination of the impact on the economy of the Southeast Asian problem, private and public efforts to keep the marginally employable working, pockets of excess demand, and price increases that followed wage increases in excess of productivity increases in major industries which must bargain with powerful labor unions.

The impact of this inflation on the consumer market is substantial. The increase in prices shown in Figure 5–5 means that a dollar in 1951 was worth only 65 cents in 1971. A recent study concluded that inflation "is the most disruptive force in the economy today, and is responsible for many of the problems now facing society."[24] In addition to widespread labor interruptions, it hits most at the incomes of the poorest citizens; retired people on fixed incomes; young, newly married couples who cannot afford a home and consumer durables; and homeowners.

If consumers believe the rate of inflation will continue upward, they may increase their purchasing and borrowing in anticipation of higher prices. If they believe prices are going to go down, or if price increases cause all their spending to go for necessities, discretionary spending could decline substantially. If this were to happen it is not clear, given the present economic structure, that prices would decline. Finally, selective, excessive wage increases, which lead to general price increases, typically reduce most of the real incomes of those lower income consumers who are just achieving some small amount of discretionary income. Such a result frustrates the inversion of the income distribution pyramid shown in Figure 5–4.

Expenditure patterns

Variations by income groups: Engel's laws. It is to be expected that expenditure patterns will vary at different income levels and according to the composition and life-cycle stage of the family. Some of these variations are suggested by Table 5–2, which shows how income was spent in 1960 and 1961 by families of different income groups.

In the middle of the 19th century, a German statistician, Ernest Engel, concluded, on the basis of a study of the family budgets of working-class families that the proportion of family income spent for food decreases as income increases. The data of Table 5–2 make it clear that this particular law is still true, and logically so. Since food is essential, even a low-income family must purchase it in substantial quantities. Although, as family income rises, the family can increase somewhat the quantity it consumes and the quality can rise appreciably, it soon discovers that other purchases are more attractive than more and better food, and the proportion spent for food begins to drop.

Another of Engel's laws stated that the proportion of family income going for housing, household operation, and household furnishings remains about the same regardless of income. The situation today is somewhat more complex. The percentage spent for housing and household operation (necessities) decreases until income reaches $15,000 per year, where it turns up. The percentage spent for household furnishings and equipment increases until incomes reach $7;500 and then levels off. The explanation is that today a house is more than just necessary shelter. In the income range where discretionary income permits, we spend a larger percentage of our income to make our domiciles beautiful, comfortable, and prestigious possessions.

The same appears to be true for clothing. Where Engel said this percentage would

---

[24] "What Inflation Is Costing Americans," *U.S. News and World Report,* May 17, 1971, pp. 23–25.

Marketing: Principles and methods

TABLE 5–2

Consumer expenditures by family income groups, 1960–1961 (percentage of total consumption expenditures)

		Family income before taxes					
Item	All families	Under $3,000	$3,000– $4,999	$5,000– $7,499	$7,500– $9,999	$10,000– $14,999	$15,000 and over
Food, beverages, and tobacco	27.8	32.4	29.9	28.4	27.4	25.9	23.1
Housing and household operation	24.0	30.4	25.1	23.8	22.8	21.8	23.6
Household furnishings and equipment...................	5.2	4.1	4.8	5.3	5.5	5.5	5.4
Clothing and accessories...............	10.2	7.1	9.0	9.9	10.6	11.5	12.2
Transportation..........	15.2	8.6	14.5	16.0	16.1	16.7	14.9
Medical care	6.6	8.5	7.0	6.6	6.3	6.2	6.1
Personal care...........	2.9	3.0	3.1	2.9	2.9	2.8	2.5
Recreation and equipment	4.0	2.2	3.4	3.8	4.3	4.8	4.7
Reading and education	1.9	1.3	1.4	1.7	1.9	2.5	3.5
Other goods and services	2.2	2.3	1.8	1.8	2.2	2.3	4.0
Total expenditures	100.0	100.0	100.0	100.2	100.0	100.0	100.0

Source: Based on F. Linden, *Expenditure Patterns of the American Family* (New York: National Industrial Conference Board, 1965), p. 18.

remain the same, as income increases we place a greater value on being fashionable and spend an increasing proportion of our income on clothing.

Ernest Engel could not foresee the automobile and hence did not consider transportation expenditures in his analysis. The pattern in this category is the reverse of that for housing. In 1960, families in the middle-income ranges increased the percentage of their income spent for transportation (purchase and operation) as income increased. In upper income brackets, however, the percentage leveled off. Would the same trend be true today?

Finally, Engel concluded that expenditures for such items as recreation and education, as well as savings, rise more rapidly than income. Logic would seem to be on his side: Once a family has met its needs for food, housing, and essential clothing, additional income might well be used to meet those seemingly never-fulfilled desires for more expensive clothing and more recreation, education, and savings —items for which the very lowest incomes provide little. And the data of Table 5–2 support Engel, with relative expenditures for both recreation and education advancing with the income level. Other studies also substantiate Engel in his conclusion on savings.[25]

Significance to marketing. If the income redistribution pattern in Figure 5–4

---

[25] General support for Engel's laws, as modified by the discussion in the text, is also found in studies made in other countries. See P. R. Cateora and J. M. Hess, *International Marketing* rev. ed. (Homewood, Ill.: Richard D. Irwin, Inc., 1971), pp. 340–41

continues, and if we can bring the disenfranchised into the mainstream of affluent American society, then increasing similarity in spending patterns might be anticipated. But our modified versions of Engel's laws also suggest how expenditures will change as family incomes rise generally. For example, one might expect the market for clothing (especially more expensive items), recreation, and education to expand far more than that for food. Moreover, we can anticipate a considerable amount of "trading up," that is, desire for and purchase of better quality merchandise. This is partially due to a desire for individualism or distinctiveness; we do not want to look and act like everyone else, and higher incomes provide an opportunity to express individuality.

These expenditure patterns also shed light on the economist's assumption that human wants are unlimited. For generations, that assumption has seldom been questioned, but of late several students have expressed the opinion—to quote Reavis Cox—that "capacity to consume may be more drastically limited than we sometimes think." Professor D. F. Blankertz adds that "even in a materialistic economy, an end to, or a palling of, acquisition could occur," and Arnold Toynbee has stated bluntly that "there is a limit to human wants in terms of consumer goods, even when these wants are artificially stimulated by a high-powered advertising industry."[26] However, the facts still seem to justify the economist's assumption that individuals shifting into higher income brackets still find wants to satisfy. To quote a study by the McGraw-Hill Economics Department: "The U.S. consumer has not lost his appetite for more and better goods."[27] And a report of the National Planning Association states: "The 'economy of abundance' in which all desired objectives become possible is unlikely to figure as the economic environment in which our goals will be implemented over the next decade."[28]

True, wants may take a different form. They are already shifting from a desire to accumulate *things* to a desire for a more beautiful and peaceful environment. We will continue to strive to make our lives better and the world a better place to live, and these efforts require economic activity and marketing. Human wants are indeed insatiable.

In addition to recognizing both differences and similarities of expenditure patterns for various income groups, the marketer needs to be aware of how these patterns change from year to year and from decade to decade. He will find that keeping up with the changing tastes of consumers can be a mighty trying ordeal.

The disposable income of the consumer is that part of his income which he can choose to spend or save. Thus it includes all the money he receives, even for welfare, social security, and the like, but it excludes such elements as payroll and direct personal taxes. The famous British economist, John Maynard Keynes, was correct in his statement that consumer expenditures can usefully be expressed as a stable percentage of disposable personal income. There is a close positive relationship between retail sales and disposable income. Since 1948 total consumer spending for products and services has stayed within a range of 90 to 94 percent of disposable personal income.

---

[26] D. F. Blankertz, "A Marketing Analysis of Suburban and Urban Expenditure Patterns," in R. Cox, W. Alderson, and S. J. Shapiro (eds.), *Theory in Marketing* (Homewood, Ill.: Richard D. Irwin, Inc., 1964), p. 309; and Toynbee, "A July 4 Question for the U.S.: Where Will the Coming Social Revolution Stop?" *London Globe and Mail,* July 4, 1961, p. 7. Also E. B. Weiss, "Will We Flee from Possessions?" *Advertising Age,* October 18, 1965, pp. 122 and 124.

[27] "Soaring—and Then Some," *Business Week,* July 16, 1966, p. 25.

[28] L. A. Lecht, *The Dollar Cost of Our National Goals* (Washington, D.C.: National Planning Association, 1965), p. 50.

Marketing: Principles and methods

Several developments may weaken the close relationship between retail sales and disposable income. Three of these are the importance of durable goods in today's standard of living, since such purchases can be postponed for considerable periods; the growth of consumer credit, which makes it possible to buy in advance of income or to decrease purchases more rapidly than income falls; and the backlog of liquid assets upon which the consumer can draw to make purchases or into which funds can be placed if purchases are deferred. To date, however, these factors have not upset the long-standing sales-income relationship.

Because of the close relationship of retail sales to disposable income, manufacturers' and wholesalers' sales also show a close correlation with the same factor. Moreover, there is a high degree of correlation between disposable income and retail sales in a number of specific fields of business. This relationship should make it clear to manufacturers and middlemen of consumer goods that their prosperity is linked with that of the country. Although it is possible for the sales of an individual manufacturer or middleman to move against the trend, sales as a whole will rise as disposable income gains and fall as it decreases. Consequently, close attention to those factors that bear on the trend of income is important.

FASHION AND THE DIFFUSION OF INNOVATION

With the differences that exist between the various demographic, social, cultural, and economic segments of the consumer market, the process through which new ideas, life styles, and goods and services are diffused through the society is vital to the marketer. The process of diffusion of fashion goods is more fascinating than that of all other consumer products.

Style and fashion defined

A *style* is a "characteristic or distinctive mode or method of expression, presentation, or conception in the field of some art."[29] There are styles of furniture, of dresses, and of houses—for example, the Duncan Phyfe chair, the miniskirt, and the Cape Cod house. A *fashion* is a style which happens to be popular at a given time. If we should find increasing numbers of women wearing the hoop skirt, we would say that it is coming back into fashion. Although styles do not change, fashions do—a Cape Cod house always has the same characteristics, but it may not always be in fashion.

Historic origins of fashion

Fashion is as old as civilization. The adornment of the body is the center of fashion attention, and the way one wears one's hair, for example, has been controversial since the beginning of society. In the mid-19th century, Englishmen refused to send their sons to schools where headmasters and teachers had long hair. The advent of bobbed hair in the 1920s resulted in repercussions as loud as those of the present-day long-hair controversy.

Before 1750, fashions changed quite slowly and their influence was confined largely to limited kinds of merchandise owned by the rich. Indeed, in the Puritan era, those who devoted much attention to fashion were somewhat suspect, as is suggested by legislation proposed in England in the 1700s:

---

[29] P. H. Nystrom, *Economics of Fashion* (New York: Ronald Press Co., 1928), p. 3.

All women of whatever age, rank, profession, or degree, whether virgin, maid or widow, that shall impose upon, seduce and betray into matrimony any of His Majesty's subjects, by scents, paints, cosmetic washes, artificial teeth, false hair, Spanish wool, iron stays, hoops, high-heeled shoes or bolstered hips shall incur the penalty of the law now in force against witchcraft and the like misdemeanors and that marriage, upon conviction, shall stand null and void.[30]

Clothing fashions began to play an important role in the stream of cultural change after 1750, often taking their cues from world developments. Fashion monthlies in Paris and London in 1850 were as elegant as *Vogue* at its best. Marie Antoinette is believed by some to be the last member of royalty to be a fashion leader, but Nystrom reports that the popular but unfashionable Lafayette set American fashions for women and men back five years as a result of a visit in 1823, a Hungarian patriot established a new fashion in men's hats as the result of a visit in 1851, and Prince Albert started a new fashion with his long frock coat in 1860.[31] In our day, the impact on American fashion of Jacqueline Kennedy during the sixties cannot be denied.

From 1750 to 1935, fashion evidenced stable cyclical patterns which have been the subject of empirical investigation.[32] Since 1935, however, the diffusion of fashion through society has been a more complex process which requires a more detailed analysis for understanding.

The diffusion of fashion

The diffusion process has been defined as the spreading of (a) a new idea or innovation (b) through specific channels of communication from one individual to another (c) within a social system (d) over time.[33] While the concepts and theory of the diffusion of innovation through the social system can apply to new ideas, new products, or new life styles, the innovation we are concerned with here is a new fashion. "New," therefore, is not measured by the time since discovery, but since the introduction of the fashion in the commercial market.

The communication channels through which fashion is diffused are both commercial and noncommercial and both personal and impersonal. Thus, study of the diffusion of fashion must be concerned with mass-media communication, communication within the channels of distribution, promotion by manufacturers and retailers, and the social network through which one individual communicates an idea or influences the ideas of another. Because personal sources of influence are more important than impersonal ones, an understanding of the fashion diffusion process requires an understanding of the social system.

All products and services are subject to life cycles, but they can decline and die because of technological obsolescence, as well as fashion obsolescence. Although fashion goods are only concerned with the latter, the length of cycles varies. A fashion with a very rapid cycle is called a *fad*. The stages of the fashion cycle, as shown in Figure 5–6, are *introduction, trial, popular adoption, maturity,* and *decline.*

Fashions are introduced by designers at fashion shows scheduled at particular times of the year. At these shows, the press, other designers, a few wealthy consumers, and some manufacturers are *made aware* of the fashion, *evaluate* it, and may *try* it. If key *opinion leaders* in various social and commercial groups are *early*

---

[30] *House & Garden,* quoted in *Reader's Digest,* September 1965, p. 145.

[31] Nystrom, *Economics of Fashion,* pp. 84–85.

[32] J. M. Carman, "The Fate of Fashion Cycles in Our Modern Society," *Proceedings of the Fall Conference of the American Marketing Association* (Chicago, 1966), pp. 722–37.

[33] E. M. Rogers, *Diffusion of Innovations* (Glencoe, Ill.: The Free Press, 1962), p. 16.

FIGURE 5–6
The fashion cycle

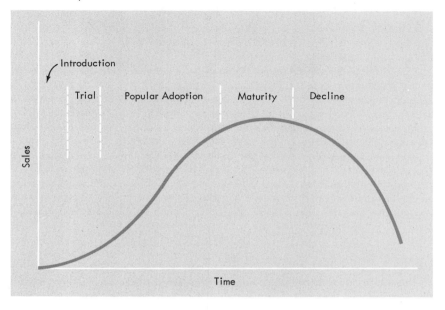

adopters of the fashion (i.e., like it and are willing to buy), large manufacturers will adapt it for mass production and sale at lower prices, putting the stage of popular adoption underway. This process creates an S-shaped sales curve which after a period of time reaches a plateau, the maturity stage. For some products, maturity and decline may be slow, but for fashion goods, the decline is much more steep than growth.

Opinion leadership and interpersonal communication. Diffusion, then, must begin with the adoption process, since for the new fashion to spread it first must be communicated by individuals within the social system to other individuals. The communicators in the system must play two roles: early adoption and opinion leadership. T. S. Robertson, in summarizing empirical studies of the diffusion process, has concluded that early adopters have characteristics in common: they are younger, read more, are not risk avoiders, and are heavy users of the product category in which they innovate.[34]

Early adopters also have high social participation. Their interest in both formal and informal social organizations and groups may mean that opinion leaders have a propensity to be early adopters. Information about new fashions is believed to flow from mass media to opinion leaders and then through a series of other opinion leaders whose influence depends on the number of social contacts they make and the extent to which their opinions are respected. The most often cited research on this point studied the diffusion of a new drug among physicians. Socially integrated doctors adopted the new drug sooner than social isolates.[35]

---

[34] T. S. Robertson, *Innovation and the Consumer* (New York: Holt, Rinehart & Winston, Inc., 1971).

[35] J. S. Coleman, E. Katz, and H. Menzel, *Medical Innovation: A Diffusion Study* (Indianapolis, Ind.: Bobbs-Merrill Co., Inc., 1966.)

"Trickle-down" theory of fashion diffusion. Historically, the adoption and diffusion process has been based on a "trickle-down" model of fashion adoption which places emphasis on the vertical flow of adoption from higher to lower socioeconomic classes. Nystrom describes geographic and vertical flow processes—geographically from Paris to New York to Chicago to St. Louis to Des Moines, etc., and vertically from upper class to lower class.[36]

Paris is the traditional center for introduction of women's clothing fashions. The creative art of *haute couture,* in which designers sign their dresses like painters or sculptors, began around 1860. In 1928, Nystrom reports, the 80,000 dressmaking establishments in Paris derived most of their volume from individual customers in Paris or other parts of France. English women came next in dollar volume of sales, and professional buyers from the United States probably ranked third.[37] However, professional buyers were only permitted to the third showing of a season's new designs—the first was for the press and the second for individual buyers. By 1957, the number of firms had dropped to about 200, and 30 percent of the Paris volume was accounted for by professional buyers. Paris is no longer the only center for new designs, however. Italy, England, and the United States all exert influence on the clothing fashions of today.

Fashion diffusion in the current environment

The trickle-down theory of fashion is incomplete because in concentrating on vertical diffusion it ignores horizontal diffusion within classes. Other reasons why regular fashion cycles fail to exist today can be ascribed to advances in production and communication technology, changes in life styles, and changes in the social system.

Horizontal diffusion. With increasing education and income, the relative size of cultural classes within our society has changed, and mobility from class to class has increased. A very large middle class and blurred class boundaries have magnified the importance of diffusion within a class. The preferences of the opinion leaders and early adopters within a social group are as important to diffusion as those of leaders and adopters in another segment of society.[38]

Production technology. Mass-produced clothing and large-scale retailing are now the rule, not the exception. If low-income consumers desire low-priced copies of the newest high fashions, the production and marketing system can now fill this need, although it would not have been able to do so 50 years ago. Because well-known American or French designers, with a few exceptions, do not offer medium-priced fashions, suppliers of popularly priced fashionable clothing market their products in a way designed to the needs of this market segment.

Paris now has two major shows a year—the last weeks of January and July. High-priced, exact copies of the July showing appear in American stores in mid-September, just six weeks after introduction. American manufacturers work on a four-season basis, but with a six- to eight-week lag between order and delivery.

Communication technology. All communications media, particularly television, have speeded up fashion cycles. Cycles in dress, which previously had a fre-

---

[36] Nystrom, *Economics of Fashion.*

[37] Ibid.

[38] C. King, "Fashion Adaptation: A Rebuttal of the Trickle Down Theory," *Proceedings of the Winter Conference of the American Marketing Association* (Chicago, 1963), pp. 108–25.

quency of a generation, now are complete in as few as six years. Messages spread by these media not only speed up the diffusion process but contribute to increased fashion consciousness.

Changes in life styles. In earlier times when life was simpler, people had work clothes and dress-up clothes. Today they need many different outfits to fit the occasion. Diversity has even replaced singularity of fashion for a single point in time or a particular function. At a formal affair today, one may see women in full-length dresses, knee-length cocktail dresses, and pants—all in fashion.

Social changes. Current attitudes toward fashion stems from many changes in society. Four that are important in explaining the fashion explosion that began in the sixties are education, affluence, increased leisure time, and youth.

Education fosters an appreciation of beauty, but it can also contribute to a desire for individuality. The craving for individuality that was at its height in the 1960s promoted diversity in fashion.

The impact on marketing of affluence is demonstrated in the fashion world. Fashion interest has revived in every period of rising general prosperity. With the increase in discretionary income unmatched in history, is it any wonder that interest in fashion is likewise unmatched?

Increased leisure time also has the effect of increasing interest in fashion. Those who work long hours have little opportunity to think of fashion, to shop for fashionable things, or to wear their fashionable clothing, all of which are conducive to rapid fashion diffusion.

But it is the youth of the country who have provided the unique ingredient in today's fashion world. In the 1960s the 16–24-year group increased by about a third. Members of this group spent 40 percent more on clothing than the average American.[39] More important, they became fashion leaders, creating a climate that made fashion a new force in the market and drove apparel expenditures higher and higher. Perhaps it was their numbers, perhaps it was their education, perhaps it was their money, perhaps it was their way of life—perhaps it was all of these. In any case, it was the young who conditioned the market for long hair, it was the young who made mod-style clothing popular with men, and it was the young who forced Mary Quant's miniskirts out of London to worldwide distribution.

There are other instances of fashions that have been inspired by other than the designers for the very rich, but the pervasiveness of youth as the fashion setter is unparalleled. Society is more inclined to accent youthfulness in their total life styles. Will this mood continue to 1980 or, like the young people who set this mood, will it mature into young adulthood?

Can fashion be controlled? Since fashion trends are so important to the business community, business groups have tried to exercise control over them. One example is the chemise in women's clothing, introduced in 1957. In sharp contrast with previous styles, the chemise was a loose-fitting dress worn without a belt. It was heavily promoted by both manufacturers and retailers but, after a few months, it disappeared from view. Stanley Marcus, president of Nieman-Marcus, the famous Texas fashion stores, explained this failure in fashion control by saying that the industry tried to move the style too rapidly and did not give enough weight to the natural fashion cycle, and the validity of his statement is underlined by the fact that something similar to the chemise later reappeared in the shift or loose-fitting dress. In practice, it is difficult to predict consumer reactions to different styles and even to rationalize

---

[39] E. Carruth, "The Great Fashion Explosion," *Fortune*, October 1967, p. 164.

5 / The market: People, money, and fashion

unsuccessful promotions, as any apparel manufacturer or buyer will witness. Many variables, ranging from consumer behavior to product design, are involved.

A recent example was the attempt to kill the miniskirt in favor of the midiskirt for the spring and fall 1970 seasons. The man and woman on the street rebelled; stores were left with many of the unwanted fashions, and some conducted formal funerals for the midiskirt. The jump from mini to midi was simply too drastic. There has never been a time when a shift of that magnitude took place in a single year. What the drastic shift did accomplish was a gradual lengthening of skirts and increased diversity of fashion—for example, hot pants.

Many occurrences similar to the foregoing have convinced some observers that even a large business group can neither check a fashion trend nor create one. Admitting this conclusion, other students of the fashion industry believe that the active promotion of a fashion trend already under way may shorten its cycle by encouraging people to accept the fashion at a faster rate than they otherwise would. Still others look toward the day when the cycle will be better understood and controlled.

Marketing implications

Consumer goods marketing may have been permanently influenced by the fashion explosion of the sixties. The extension of this trend brings the promise of major rewards but carries demands for newer, more efficient forms of marketing. An end is nowhere in sight to the consumer's passion for fashion in all kinds of merchandise. Manufacturers of electric refrigerators, home furnishings, cameras, watches, men's clothing, and cosmetics, as well as women's dresses, must emphasize fashion in the goods they produce. People for the most part do not purchase these items as basic necessities. Their willingness to buy is explained, at least partially, by fashion. The universality of fashion, awakened style consciousness, greater acceptance of design innovation, and an upsurge of the arts have put every consumer goods marketer squarely in the fashion business.

Retailing's response has been the spawning of off-beat shops catering to special wants, the evolution of the boutique, the creation of new retailing services, refinements in merchandise control systems, and new thinking in store design that lays out departments to cater to the way people prefer to shop. Even retailers who succeeded for many years without giving too much attention to fashion currently find it essential to comb the fashion centers of the United States and Europe for ideas. The J. C. Penney Company for example, has specialists in buying offices in California and Europe to keep up with the new young fashion makers.

Retail buyers can get abundant information on coming trends from textile producers, manufacturers, trade papers, and buying offices and agents, who offer assistance to retailers at a fee. But buyers must also watch the local street scene, competitors' windows, sales records, and the shoppers in their own stores. They must be flexible enough to acknowledge mistakes and clear out slow-selling merchandise and should be on the lookout for suppliers who will make rapid deliveries on reorders of fast movers.

Manufacturers and middlemen have also found that the increasing importance of fashion has added to the risks and costs of doing business. Automobile manufacturers spend more than $1 billion annually to retool for new lines, largely for styling reasons. The promotion of fashions also involves large expenditures; a women's apparel manufacturer's fashion show for the trade and press alone may cost from $10,000 to $50,000 or even more. With a change in fashion, large markdowns may be necessary to clear out existing stock. To avoid such large markdowns, retailers may try "hand-to-mouth" buying, with more frequent purchases in smaller lots, which increases the cost of the buying function and places more risk on the manufacturer. Thus fashion is a major factor in marketing strategy for many kinds of goods.

The individual manufacturer or middleman finds it especially difficult to attempt to control fashion trends. Probably the most he can do is to accept fashion trends as given facts and try to conduct his business advantageously within their limits. He does have the responsibility of trying to discover trends so that the merchandise he markets meets the demands of his customers. He should also follow the fashion cycle closely, so that he will be practically out of stock of a particular style before the cycle turns downward and will, at the same time, be accumulating stock of another style on the rising part of the curve. To rush into full production or to place large orders early in the fashion cycle may prove as disastrous as to have large stocks of goods on hand when the cycle turns downward.

Successful fashion marketing requires flexibility, up-to-date information, and detailed analysis. The market is so volatile that many fashion manufacturers have merged in order to spread the risks of commitment to a single fashion. Consumers can be fickle and unpredictable. For example, Bobbie Brooks forged to the front in women's apparel manufacturing by concentrating on the stability of sportswear, but in 1966 young women suddenly stopped buying sportswear classics, and the firm experienced very large losses in that year and the next.[40]

The manufacturer of fashion goods and the middlemen who handle them not only should define their markets carefully but should also decide upon the phase of the fashion cycle in which they desire to operate. Very few can successfully cater to several income groups of the population at the same time or operate profitably in more than one or two stages of the fashion cycle.

SUMMARY

Discussion about markets for consumer products and services in this chapter has been in aggregate terms rather than dealing with the behavior of individual consumers. Markets have been examined as being composed of people who have money and are willing to spend it.

Relatively good measures of population and its various characteristics and distribution are available for the United States. They show, for example, that while the birth rate is currently declining, the absolute number of births is still increasing because there are so many couples of child-producing age. The 65-and-over group is also showing regular and substantial growth.

Not only are current population statistics readily available, but demographers are able to prepare relatively good forecasts for the future. This is true because the death rate remains relatively stable, the birth rate has followed a fairly predictable pattern, and most of the population is already present and merely aging at the rate of one year per year. The changes from rural to urban, region to region, and central city to suburban areas are also relatively free of surprises.

Reliable measures and forecasts of population change facilitate careful attention to resulting marketing implications. The larger group of older people, for example, leads to the purchase of more health aids, retirement home services, and certain travel

---

[40] *Women's Wear Daily,* August 23, 1968, p. 14.

and recreation facilities. As the size of the average family decreases, smaller package sizes and home sizes should result.

Another major dimension of a market, in addition to population, is money. Economic factors are not as well measured, nor are they quite so easy to forecast. Yet the marketer generally has adequate measures and forecasts about money to enable him to plan his marketing activities.

The third ingredient in composition of a market is willingness to buy. Markets for all but necessities are composed of people not only with money but with a willingness to buy, which is a very complex and pervasive dimension. It involves an analysis of social, cultural, and economic influences on values, tastes, attitudes, life styles and behavior. Insights into these factors were provided in this chapter through an analysis of the diffusion of fashion in society.

In our analysis of marketing, memorization of specific facts of market dimensions are not called for. The various facts are merely used to point out what has been the situation, the changes that are occurring, and the marketing implications of these changes. It is not necessary that you continually keep current on the changing dimensions of markets. Facts themselves are quite meaningless; it is what you can *learn* from facts that is important. It is of more value to retain a framework of the dimensions of the total market which can be used to define, analyze, and market to individual segments. The dimensions to be considered, as suggested in this chapter, are demographic, geographic, economic, cultural, and psychological.

The review and discussion questions that follow are designed to help you learn about the market for consumers' products and services.

REVIEW AND DISCUSSION QUESTIONS

1. From library reading, explain the major changes in the population growth rate portrayed in Figure 5–1.

2. What would be the impact on marketing of zero population growth?

3. If the U.S. population were to grow at the rate of 2 percent per year, in what year would our population be double what it is today?

4. Suggest the impact on the retailer of the trend toward suburbia.

5. Summarize the immediate past and prospective population changes by age groups as reflected in Figure 5–2 and point out their significance to marketers.

6. Evaluate the case for treating Negroes as forming a segmented market.

7. Summarize the content of each of the most recent issues of U.S. Census Bureau, *Current Population Reports,* Series P-20, P-25, P-60.

8. How does (or does not) a strategy of market segmentation increase the efficiency of marketing?

9. List the implications for marketing of a population in which half of all adults are high school graduates and an additional 25 percent are college graduates.

10. Define each of the following terms, carefully distinguishing one from another: personal income, money income, disposable personal income, discretionary income.

11. Using the information in Chapter 4, state and defend how you believe the percentage of income spent for transportation varies with income today.

12. "In our affluent society, the idea that human wants are unlimited is no longer valid." Appraise this statement.

Marketing: Principles and methods

13. Discuss the relationship between fashion and the cost of marketing. Would society be "better off" if "fashion were abolished"?

14. What is the significance of diffusion of innovation for the marketer of a new breakfast beverage?

15. Distinguish between vertical and horizontal diffusion.

SUPPLEMENTARY READINGS

Bowen, W. "The U.S. Economy Enters a New Era," *Fortune,* March 1967, pp. 111–15, 246. "The great boom has come to an end, and the performance is not likely to be matched in the next few years," is the author's conclusion.

Brooks, J. *The Great Leap.* New York: Harper & Row, 1966. Changes in the United States since 1939 are detailed and, to some degree, appraised.

Carruth, E. "The Great Fashion Explosion," *Fortune,* October 1967, pp. 162–65, 210–17. With fashion "a more potent market force than ever," the writer concludes that "the fashion industries competing for consumer dollars . . . have to run harder than ever." The article emphasizes fashion trends for both men and women.

Coleman, J. S., Katz, E., and Menzel, H. *Medical Innovation: A Diffusion Study.* Indianapolis, Ind.: Bobbs-Merrill Co., Inc., 1966. This work provides the detail of a drug innovation diffusion study.

The Conference Board, Inc. *A Guide to Consumer Markets, 1970.* New York, 1970. An up-to-date analysis of consumer spending patterns.

Contini, M. *Fashion.* New York: Odyssey Press, 1965. The more than 500 illustrations of *haute couture* from the days of the Pharaohs to the present suggest that today's fashion has ancient ancestry.

Houthakker, H. S., and Taylor, L. D. *Consumer Demand in the United States, 1929–1970.* Cambridge, Mass.: Harvard University Press, 1966. Making extensive use of a dynamic model of demand, the authors view consumers' expenditures for over 80 commodities from 1929 to 1961 and project the demand for each through 1970.

Jarnow, J. A., and Judelle, B. (eds.) *Inside the Fashion Business.* New York: John Wiley & Sons, Inc., 1965. The authors' survey of literature on fashion has produced a comprehensive book on the subject.

Linden, F. *Market Profiles of Consumer Products.* New York: National Industrial Conference Board, 1967. Contains tables of consumer spending patterns from the Bureau of Labor Statistics 1960–61 Survey of Consumer Expenditures.

Robertson, T. S. *Innovation and the Consumer.* New York: Holt, Rinehart & Winston, 1971. A new and comprehensive treatment of the diffusion of innovation.

Rogers, E. M. *Diffusion of Innovations.* Glencoe, Ill.: The Free Press, 1962. A complete review of empirical studies of diffusion processes.

U.S. Bureau of the Census *1970 Census of Population.* Washington, D.C.: Government Printing Office, 1971. The basic volumes from the newest population census contains far more detail than could be provided in this chapter.

6 The consumer in the marketing system

. . . his customers are to be his idols; so far as he may worship idols by allowance, his is to bow down to them, and worship them. . . .
Daniel Defoe, Complete English Tradesman, 1776

The primary objective of any marketing system is to allocate scarce resources efficiently and in such a way as to satisfy to the greatest extent possible the needs of man.
page 3 above

. . . The marketing concept means that an enterprise views its products and services as the adaptation of their resources, processes, and marketing activities to the characteristics and wants of prospective buyers.
page 7 above

There's an explanation why consumer issues have become good politics. In the very broadest sense, consumerism can be defined as the bankruptcy of what the business schools have been calling the marketing concept.
Business Week, September 9, 1969, p. 95

If the realization that the "consumer is king" is such an old and enduring idea, how is it that the phenomenon popularly known as consumerism has become such a salient issue in our society in the past decade? In considering this question it is useful to bear in mind that the consumer is a member of the marketing system and to recall that in Chapter 2 we defined a market as an agreement between a buyer (consumer) and a seller, and in Chapter 3 the consumer as a member of a channel of distribution.

The consumer movement is no more than an organized effort to improve the effectiveness with which the consumer fulfills his role as a member of the system. There is a general recognition that the individual consumer may be operating under a severe handicap in performing the buyer's role by himself—some sellers have more market power than individual consumers. Thus, government has often found it necessary to help the consumer as he performs his functions in the system. President Kennedy, in a special message on protecting the consumer interest, March 15, 1962, set forth certain rights of consumers, including:

1. The right to safety, to be protected against the marketing of goods that are hazardous to health or life.
2. The right to be informed, to be protected against fraudulent, deceitful, or grossly misleading information, advertising, labeling, or other practices, and to be given the facts he needs to make an informed choice.

3. The right to choose, to be assured, wherever possible, of access to a variety of products and services at competitive prices and, in those industries in which competition is not workable and government regulation is substituted, to be assured of satisfactory quality and service at fair prices.

4. The right to be heard, to be assured that consumer interests will receive full and sympathetic consideration in the formulation of government policy and fair and expeditious treatment in its administrative tribunals.

These consumer problems and rights are the subject of this chapter, which is divided into two major sections. The first concerns the problems of the consumer as a buyer, including those concerned with the safety of products; availability of adequate information to make value comparisons; deceptive practices; and the role of advertising in consumer choice. The second section describes the assistance the consumer receives from private organizations, business, and government.

THE PROBLEMS OF THE CONSUMER AS A BUYER

Health and safety

The most obvious and generally accepted of President Kennedy's consumer rights is the right to expect that products purchased will be safe when used in their intended manner and purpose. The implied warranty of a seller to this effect has its roots in common law, as codified and reaffirmed by judicial precedent. The need for more protection than that provided by an implied warranty was recognized early in U.S. history. It does little good to put the processor of a poisoned food product out of business after someone has been killed, nor is an implied warranty effective in preventing the adulteration of food and cosmetics that may hasten death although they do not kill instantly.

The first major federal legislation designed to protect the consumer in this area was the Pure Food and Drug Act of 1906, which established the Food and Drug Administration, now a part of the U.S. Department of Health, Education, and Welfare. It took over 20 years of consumer and government arguing, plus considerable muckraking, to get this bill through the Congress. A major revision to the act was passed in 1938, again only after considerable consumer agitation. Laws governing the labeling of contents and of safety and health hazards began with the 1906 Act.

After over 50 years of experience, one might think that these fundamental procedures for protection of consumer safety would have been well established. However, they were not. The matter of product safety became an issue again in the 1960s, when the spotlight shifted from food, drugs, and cosmetics to automobiles, tires, television sets, electrical appliances, and toys. This time it was consumer activists such as Ralph Nader who led the fight for passage of the Federal Traffic Safety Act in 1967, a new meat inspection act, and the Flammable Fabrics Act. Later, the FDA's Bureau of Product Safety began the testing and regulation of toys. Subsequent crises over the safety of such items as specific foods, new drugs, the automobile, and Christmas ornaments suggest the need for assurance of the continuing vigilance of government as a protector of consumers.

Consumer information

Consumers need to perform buying functions in the marketing system well enough to ensure efficient allocation of resources in their own interest. They must have the information and exercise the judgment necessary to select those products and services that will give maximum satisfaction in relation to cost. This section will consider the kinds of information buyers should have available to them and problems consumers have in finding and using this information.

Quantity. The quantity declaration on packaged products may not always be obvious, as became evident in hearings that led to the passage in 1966 of the Fair Packaging and Labeling Act. Prior to implementation of this act, the declaration of contents on the package was often difficult to find. Now it has to be in plain sight on all packages; packages with slack fill or false bottoms have been eliminated; meaningless qualifying words like "jumbo quart" have been eliminated; and the number of different package sizes has been reduced. The declaration of quantity on packaged products may prove to be a useful device in consumer education for conversion to the metric system.

On the other hand, legislation cannot solve technical problems in stating quantities, the most important of which is a difference in density. For example, a can of vacuum-packed corn will contain more corn than a can of the same weight packed in water. How is the consumer to know when such distinctions exist or are important unless he is a regular purchaser of the product and is willing to experiment?

Quality. In many instances the consumer's lack of quality information is apparent. Take the case of a used automobile, offered for sale as one of good quality. "It has been used by a schoolteacher who drove it carefully, and it has gone but 31,000 miles," says the salesman. Actually, it is a former taxicab with 150,000 miles of service behind it, but with a new coat of paint to cover up these facts. Or consider a pair of men's shoes retailing for $29.95. Next to it is a pair at $21.95. Can the average consumer judge the relative qualities of these two pairs of shoes? As for carpeting, one authority on retail pricing states that "It is difficult for the occasional carpet buyer to distinguish between $6.95 and $9.95 carpet." He reports that one manufacturer has 39 different qualities in his line, and adds that ". . . the consumer is befuddled by the various carpeting materials and probably has to rely on the salesman for advice."[1] Many customers are unaware that practically all brands of aspirin are identical, irrespective of wide price differences. Few can detect functional differences between cake mixes, TV sets, or brands of gasoline (even with octane declarations).

Much attention has been given to this problem over the years. The attempted solutions fall into five categories: standardization, testing and grading, certification, informative labeling, and branding.[2]

Standardization. Standardization of contents and identification of packages help the consumer to measure quality. For example, he can be sure that products such as mayonnaise or peanut butter will always contain the same ingredients in relatively fixed proportions. The U.S. Department of Agriculture establishes standards for some foods, the Food and Drug Administration for other foods and drugs. The U.S. Bureau of Standards and the Federal Trade Commission also have authority to regulate standards for some products. A problem with standardization is that the standards usually are established near minimum quality levels and allow little room for quality improvement without addition of the word "imitation" to the name. Standardization is discussed in more detail in later chapters.

Testing and grading. Testing and grading are conducted by both government

---

[1] A. F. Jung, "A Different Retail Price Pattern: The Case of Carpeting," *Journal of Business,* 38 (April 1965), pp. 184–85.

[2] See H. B. Thorelli, "Testing, Labelling, Certifying: A Perspective on Consumer Information," *British Journal of Marketing,* 4 (Autumn 1970), pp. 126–32.

and private organizations. The standards used in comparative testing may be based either on product characteristics or on performance. Grading on composition and characteristics is conducted extensively on agricultural products by federal and state departments of agriculture. Characteristics considered for a typical fruit or vegetable, for example, may be percent water, firmness, color, and absence of defects. The best known private organization doing comparative performance testing is Consumers Union, which tests a full range of consumer products, from whiskey to automobiles, rating products as "best buy," "acceptable," or "not acceptable." Some problems of grading are: standard tests and measures are often not available; the selection of characteristics tested is subjective; and grading must be done by assigning weights to test results based on individual tastes which differ greatly among consumers.

Quality certification.   Seals from private or government organizations are sometimes used on labels to indicate that a product meets the specification of quality established by the issuing institution. The concept here is that quality is such a complex technical matter that the consumer needs to know only that a recognized authority certifies something about it. The "DOT" (Department of Transportation) imprint on tires is an example of a fairly new government quality seal program. The ambiguity of this system is a disadvantage, but like a brand name, symbolic information is a useful technique in consumer communications.

Informative labeling.   The alternative to quality seals on a product is to include a label or tag which provides detailed information. Color fastness, percentage of key ingredients, nutritional information about foods, and technical specifications of hi-fi equipment or appliances have all been labeled. In order to be effective, some institution other than the seller must police the labels and ensure that the information is factual and clearly presented. Perhaps the greatest disadvantage of informative labeling for consumers is that the information provided is often so complex that they will not attempt to read and understand it.

Branding.   Branding is simply a form of quality certification for which the certifying institution is the seller. Insofar as sellers want to build and protect their goodwill with consumers, this form of quality certification has much value. It is an efficient technique for communication, but unfortunately, sellers often puff their products, and many brands convey little about quality level. In addition, the extensive use of multiple branding by sellers permits them to lower quality of one brand without damaging the image of leading brands.

Price as an indicator of quality.   In the absence of other indicators of quality, consumers often use obvious but unrealistic cues such as fragrance, color, finish, and packaging as indicators of quality. The most bothersome of these proxy quality cues is price.[3] When used as an indicator of quality, price enters into both the numerator and denominator of the expression that defines value:

$$\text{Value/Unit quantity} = \frac{\text{Satisfaction/Unit quantity}}{\text{Price/Unit quantity}}$$

$$= \frac{f(\text{Price})/\text{Unit quantity}}{\text{Price/Unit quantity}}$$

---

[3] The evidence of this relationship is strong. See J. D. McConnell, "The Price-Quality Relationship in an Experimental Setting," *Journal of Marketing Research,* 5 (August 1968), pp. 331–34; J. E. Stafford and B. M. Enis, "The Price-Quality Relationship: An Extension," *Journal of Marketing Research,* 6 (November 1969), pp. 456–58; and A. G. Bedeian, "Consumer Perception of Price as an Indicator of Product Quality," *MSU Business Topics,* 19 (Summer 1971), pp. 59–65.

The result is that when quality comparisons are difficult to make, for example in the purchase of a fine imported wine, high-priced products may actually be preferred to low-priced ones, and the demand curve could actually slope upward! Quality falsification by some sellers and social waste due to a failure to allocate resources in a way that maximizes value for all are further disadvantages. Thus it is important for society and for the marketing system that consumers are quality conscious and have available real measures of quality.

Price. When the consumer is ignorant of price itself, it can be obtained only by the lengthy procedure of "shopping around." Failure to possess accurate price information is easy to understand in view of the great number of items bought, the frequency of price changes, and the widespread usage of price promotions. It is possible for two supermarkets in the same block to sell many items at price differences of from 5 to 10 percent. Investigation has shown that the consumer may pay as much or even more for an item advertised as a bargain than was asked for it in everyday business, which is encouraged by retailers and manufacturers who use inflated "suggested list price" tags. The Federal Trade Commission has taken action against this practice.

An interesting illustration of the problems of price comparisons may be found in the experiments in supermarket *unit pricing,* which began in some areas in 1969.[4] Unit pricing is the display of the price per pound or per quart of products on grocery store shelves; the net price of the item is shown as usual on each container. The unit price is provided so that the shopper can compare prices between packages containing different quantities without solving two division problems. Of those shoppers who have noticed this additional information, about 60 percent claim they use it in making choices.[5] However, for frequently purchased products where preference patterns have been established, the price-per-unit labels appear to lead to little brand switching. There are two disadvantages: the inability to make quality comparisons, particularly among products with different densities, can lead to consumer confusion, and unit pricing programs are costly to operate and maintain, particularly for smaller stores, which are at a competitive disadvantage with chain stores.

The Truth-in-Lending Act passed in 1968 is an example of legislation intended to help consumers determine price—in this case, the price of credit. Because the calculation of interest is simple in theory but complex in practice, it is not surprising that most consumers still do not understand these calculations. However, the presence of the information has called consumer attention to a pricing problem where previously no accurate information existed. This law has brought to light a number of inconsistencies in the calculation of interest charges. Almost all lenders calculate daily interest using a 360-day year rather than a 365-day year, and most retail stores calculate monthly interest on the *previous* month's balance without deducting returns or payments. An obvious alternative, used by J. C. Penney and the bank credit-card plans, is adjusting the balance for payments and credits. Suits brought as a result of the attention generated by the new law may cause many stores to shift to computing interest on the average daily balance outstanding during the month.

Nonuse of product information. A substantial part of all purchasing is of the "unplanned" or "impulse" variety, which is not associated with careful use of product knowledge, even when it is available. Richard H. Holton calls this the problem of the

---

[4] Unit pricing, of course, has been common for years in the selling of products offered in random quantities, such as meat and cheese.

[5] J. M. Carman, "A Review of Unit Pricing in Supermarkets," *Journal of Retailing,* 48 (Winter 1972).

"quality of demand" and argues that competition cannot do an adequate job of resource allocation in those markets where consumers cannot or will not use adequate information to make them competent as household purchasing agents.[6] The ideal conditions for consumer performance would be: (1) the item is frequently purchased by the specific individual, (2) the quality and performance characteristics of the product are known to the buyer before purchase or immediately after use, (3) the rate of technological change in the product is slow relative to the frequency of purchase, and (4) the offers of competing sellers are known, readily comparable, and stable over time. These conditions are frequently not present, and it is not necessarily desirable that they should be. In all other market situations, the consumer must work to obtain the information required to perform buying functions effectively.

It is becoming increasingly difficult to be an intelligent buyer. In part, this trend results from the shift of the production of many consumer products from the home to the factory. Further, the number of products to select from has expanded, both in kinds and in models or varieties; a large majority of the consumer goods volume of many firms comes from items that did not exist a decade ago. Moreover, many of today's products are more complex than their counterparts of yesterday—the electric refrigerator versus the icebox, the automatic clothes washer versus the washboard and tub—and "science and technology have constructed a body of technical information about materials and products so vast that even the well-informed consumer can know relatively little of it."[7]

While the unavailability or high cost of obtaining the necessary information represents a serious lack to consumers, the nonuse of the knowledge that is available at low cost also constitutes a major problem. As a problem of consumer motivation, it is apart from business and government responsibilities to protect consumers from unsafe products, fraud, deception, confusion, and concentration of monopoly power.

Protection from unfair or deceptive practices

If consumers have problems in finding and using honest information about products and services, they will often be prey to sellers who are willing to use deceptive and confusing practices in order to gain sales. The ingenuity of unscrupulous sellers has often been noted by social philosophers. A list of fraudulent selling practices would be very long and would require frequent additions. In addition to deceptive advertising, which is discussed in the next section, other unfair practices can be considered under three headings: fraudulent selling practices, confusing selling practices, and special problems of the disenfranchised consumer.

Fraudulent selling practices. The most common types of fraudulent selling practices are briefly noted below. There are others, and many of these practices are often used in combination.

1. *Misrepresentation.* The number of cases of misrepresentation runs into the thousands and keeps enforcement staffs in the Food and Drug Administration, Federal Trade Commission, Postal Service, and state attorney general offices busy constantly. The misrepresentation often concerns the material, performance, quality, or origin of the product. Special legislation has been passed to cover the labeling of wool, fur,

---

[6] R. H. Holton, "Business and Government," *Daedalus* (Winter 1969), pp. 47–48.

[7] R. Cox, in association with C. S. Goodman and T. C. Fichander, *Distribution in a High-Level Economy* (Englewood Cliffs, N.J.: Prentice-Hall, Inc., 1965), p. 182.

and synthetic fibers because of abuses in this area. Land sales, such as retirement lots sold sight unseen, constitute another common area for fraudulent misrepresentation.

2. *Weights and measures.* The supervision of the weights and measures used in trade has been the responsibility of the states since the time that bulk products were weighed by retailers and there were still retail butchers to weigh their thumbs along with the meat. Efficiency in trade at all levels requires fair and honest weights and measures, even in the age of prepackaging, which is subject to vigilant governmental policing.

3. *Deceptive practices in direct selling.* Door-to-door personal selling is a proven successful method of marketing. In recent years it has grown in popularity because of the added convenience it provides. The basic key to the success of direct selling is that it prevents consumer search for information by attempting to close the sale in the home before he can shop. This entrapment provides the opportunity for many forms of deceptive practices, often upon the poor and poorly educated, which have long brought shame to the marketing system generally and direct selling specifically.

One effective method of reducing these frauds is a law which is currently being passed by or introduced into the legislatures of most states to establish a three-day cooling off period on any home solicitation contract. Any time during this period the buyer can back out of such an agreement.

Most direct sales frauds involve selling a product, usually on a time contract, at a very high price under the deception that a "special low price" is being offered only to this buyer, under the guise that it is the salesman's first sale, this sale is the first in the neighborhood, or the buyer has won a prize that entitles him to a big discount.

4. *Bait and switch.* Perhaps the most common of all deceptive selling practices, this fraud involves offering an item of unmistakable good value at an extremely low price. The object is to get the prospective buyer into a sales demonstration where he is switched away from the advertised item (which the swindler has no intention of selling) to another one selling at a much higher price. When used with automobile repair service, this swindle is called "lo-balling," and the low repair price is intended to get the customer's car into the shop so that the garage can find "other needed work" on which very high prices are charged.

5. *Combination offers.* This fraud involves selling a product at a very low price along with an agreement to buy a service connected with the product over a long period of time. Any low price on the product is more than compensated for by charging very high prices for the service, which is usually of low quality. This scheme has been used extensively in the selling of food freezers and subscriptions to food-freezer plans and in selling encyclopedias with annual supplements.

6. *Fear appeals.* This fraud is a homeowners version of protection extortion in organized crime. It has been practiced by "furnace inspectors" who tear down a furnace and then refuse to reassemble it because it is unsafe, "termite inspectors" who bring their own termites, "roofing inspectors" who tear off shingles, and "chimney inspectors" who clog chimneys.

Confusing selling practices. The six practices discussed above are blatant frauds. Incidence of such frauds among companies with national reputations is lower than that among regional companies with less investment in goodwill. However, sellers of all sizes sometimes engage in promotional practices which, while not obviously fraudulent, are designed to confuse rather than inform the consumer. Five examples will illustrate this type of unfair promotional practice.

1. *Price points during inflation.* One object of the Fair Packaging and Labeling Act was to facilitate price comparisons between similar items by standardizing package sizes. A seller who has been selling a 12-ounce size for 29 cents has a problem in an inflationary period when his labor and material costs go up. Often he prefers to reduce the pack size to 10¾ ounces rather than increase his price. His competitor, seeing this move, may choose to increase his price even more by selling 11¾ ounces for 32 cents. (Can you calculate these prices per ounce in your head?) These are attempts to mask a price rise—to confuse rather than inform.

2. *"Free" goods.* The Federal Trade Commission has long had trouble with regulation of the word "free" when used in combination offers. It attempts to prohibit use of the wording "buy one quart, get one free," when the intent is "our price on a half-gallon is half that of some leading brands."

3. *Negative-option sales plans.* These plans are commonly used by book-of-the-month and record clubs. A book or record offering will be mailed and must be purchased unless the buyer exercises his option of notifying the seller that he does *not* want to purchase. The charge is that such plans confuse the buyer into thinking he must purchase the items offered.

4. *Promotional games.* Supermarkets, gasoline marketers, and manufacturers use "sweepstakes," contests, and other games of chance as promotions fairly regularly. Most complaints about such promotions are that they confuse the consumer into believing his chances of winning are much greater than they in fact are, for the purpose of gaining a sale. Complaints of this nature have been filed against such reputable firms as Reader's Digest Association, Inc., McDonald's Corporation, and Coca-Cola Company.[8]

5. *Confusing packaging.* The shape and label on packaged goods is a potential source of consumer confusion when the buyer is not able to see the product itself. A rectangular package with a square bottom is an efficient shape for shipping and storing. In self-service stores, however, the area of the package facing the customer is important, and sellers often make wide, tall, "skinny" packages in order to increase shelf facing area. Some sellers go even further by adopting odd-shaped containers that are even wider, adding false bottoms, and practicing slack fill (filling a container so that nonfunctional air space remains above the product). Generally, retailers have been ineffective in stopping these packaging practices. Thus competitive pressures drive manufacturers away from the shapes desired by both consumers and retailers. The Fair Packaging and Labeling Act of 1966 has generally been successful in bringing about more socially desirable package shapes and clear and accurate descriptions of the quantity of contents.

Illustrations of package contents on labels are another area of concern. Some products simply do not look good in pictures, and to improve the situation they may be shown in use. Consumers often charge that such pictures are deceptive, such as cherry pies pictured with far more cherries than the pie actually contains. Toys are another target for complaints of this type. The problem of making vignettes pleasing but not deceptive is difficult and hard to regulate.

Special problems of the disenfranchised consumer. A unique set of buying problems is faced by the poor or disenfranchised consumer. If the marketing system

---

[8] Citations and summaries of these actions may be found in "Legal Developments in Marketing," *Journal of Marketing,* 35 (January 1971), pp. 83–84; (July 1971), p. 84; (October 1971), p. 77; and (January 1972), p. 83.

used by the mainstream of American society is also to serve those disenfranchised from it, it must arrive at creative solutions to these special problems. The central argument is that marketing and consumption are so much a part of our society that it is not possible to bring the poor back into the mainstream without first making them participants in the marketing system. Thus it is important to help the poor learn to spend money wisely as well as to help them earn a living.

If the reader doubts the existence of a disenfranchised market segment, a look back at Figure 5–4 will show how income distributions differ among races. Even when the races are combined, there is a bulge in the distribution under $5,000 per year and another in the $7,000 to $15,000 categories. A marketing system designed to efficiently serve an affluent society creates a trap for the poor.

1. *Affluent society assumption.* American society functions under an assumption of affluence. As the demand for public transportation declines, an automobile becomes a necessity. It is assumed that everyone has a telephone for private communication and a television set for mass communication. Rural and urban poor cannot help their children escape the poverty trap unless they can be educated to cope with modern urban life.

2. *Aspiration for ownership.* Mass-media messages increase consumer aspirations and the "need" for the fine products displayed there. If the disenfranchised do not have the income to obtain at least some of these products and services, the result may be frustration, mental illness, or antisocial behavior. In addition, the poor are often reluctant or unable to travel beyond their own small world and remain locked into a ghetto neighborhood, although they are strongly motivated to obtain the goods and services they see in the affluent society around them. At the same time, they have little ability or opportunity to earn their way.

3. *Retailing services.* The retailer who serves the poor is not the efficient merchant who is a participant in the marketing system we discuss in this book. There is little economic incentive for him to serve this community, for the residents have little money to spend. The result is that the poor are denied all four of President Kennedy's consumer rights.

One type of retailer who does want to serve such neighborhoods is the merchant who is a member of the community. Regardless of his good motives, however, he is almost always small, inefficient, unprofitable, and unable to bring to the community the fruits of an efficient marketing system.

Unscrupulous merchants may come to the community because they believe they can make more profit by cheating the poor than by selling honestly to the affluent. They often survive by selling poor quality merchandise at exorbitant prices, usually on credit.

Installment lending to the disenfranchised is a system virtually unknown elsewhere. Those who make a profit lending to the poor must charge interest rates or build charges into the price of their products that will cover high collection costs and high default rates.[9] Finance charges in excess of the value of the product purchased are not unusual. The disenfranchised cannot engage in comparative shopping for credit, are not knowledgable about price or terms, and will not be given credit by "mainstream" lending institutions.

4. *Legal rights.* Finally, the disenfranchised buyer is not aware of his legal rights

---

[9] For a more detailed description of these problems see D. A. Aaker and G. S. Day, *Consumerism: Search for the Consumer Interest* (New York: The Free Press, 1971), Part 5.

Marketing: Principles and methods

of redress in a conflict with a seller and can often become a party to a sales contract which the seller can enforce under the law.

The problem of the marketing system in serving the poor is perhaps the only one facing the system that cannot be solved by minor changes in structure and increased efficiency on the part of all system members in the performance of their functions. Providing equal opportunities to the disadvantaged requires equality in opportunity for education, employment, and housing, as well as for consumption. Changes in no single subsystem of our social system are alone sufficient to solve the problem.

The role of advertising

The primary objective of advertising is to sell the product or service being advertised. It is a message paid for by a seller for the purpose of influencing sales. Its tasks are to: (1) attract the attention of the prospective receiver of the message; (2) provide information about the product, what it does, where to get it, and how to use it; (3) build a liking for the product; and (4) instill a desire to own it.

Thus the advertising message is a vehicle for attitude change which can increase the consumer's knowledge and enable him to reach a decision as to what to buy. Advertising also creates a number of problems, such as deceptive practices, undesirable secondary social effects, and the influence of large advertising expenditures on market performance. A discussion of the last of these problem areas is delayed until Part VIII of this book.

Deceptive advertising. Most charges of misrepresentation in advertising concern false testimonials and claims for performance. The rule governing the regulation of such claims, which has been developed by judicial interpretation over the years, is that it is not necessary to prove intent or actual deception, but only a tendency to mislead or deceive. Nor need the person who could be misled be an "average" consumer; the public includes the ignorant, the unthinking, the gullible, and even children. Current interpretation of what constitutes deceptive advertising can be illustrated by examples of practices that have been curtailed, juxtaposed with examples of "acceptable" practices.

Mickey Mantle endorsed both Camel cigarettes and Bantron, an antismoking pill; when he endorsed a brand of milk he did not consume, the Federal Trade Commission suggested he desist.[10] Yet a dramatization of Jane who "almost never had dates" suddenly swept into the arms of a handsome man after switching to brand X deodorant soap is accepted as innocent puffing which is not misleading.

Lite Diet, Hollywood, and Profile breads were all found to be making deceptive claims that their products would help in weight loss, when they in fact contain the same number of calories per pound as other breads, but they use thinner slices. Yet commercials can show men admiring their slim wives who claim to stay that way by drinking diet cola because it contains far fewer calories than regular colas.

The Campbell Soup Company was charged with using false advertising when it placed marbles in the bottom of a bowl of noodle soup in order to cause the heavy noodles and chicken to break the surface of the soup during television photography. Yet a breath-freshening toothpaste can visibly cause Jane's kisses to fly across the television screen to land on the cheek of the man she has been pursuing.

---

[10] *Time,* August 18, 1961, p. 68.

These examples demonstrate that the line between healthy competitive puffery and deception—that is, between desirable and undesirable persuasive messages—is a difficult one for the layman, the lawyer, or the government regulator to draw.

Social effects. Advertising is often criticized not because it misrepresents products, but because of the undesirable secondary social effects it is alleged to cause. Since it is a major institution of social influence (persuasion) in American life, such allegations are understandable. Such an institution, not unlike the executive branch of government, is going to receive criticism whether or not it is deserved. In fact, it is surprising that attitudes about advertising are not more strongly held than they are. In a national survey in 1964, 15 percent of the population said advertising needed immediate attention and change, ranking it fifth in a list of 10 items.[11] In 1970 another national survey using a different question format asked people to rate the importance of 98 social issues of the day. "Dishonest advertising" ranked below the top 10, with 24 percent of respondents considering it a most important problem.[12]

So many social critics and journalists, as opposed to social scientists, have criticized advertising that the task of separating real problems from popular thinking is difficult. The following six influences of advertising in America encompass social criticisms which may have merit.

1. *Influence of advertising on aspirations.* It is desirable for those in a free society to aspire to increase their real income (broadly defined for differences in taste and not restricted to dollar income). Those in some societies have higher aspirations than those in others and work harder to accomplish this goal. Advertising and the life style depicted in the media increase this aspiration for income. But does it also contribute to aggregate real income so that people are able to close the gap between level of income and aspiration? Could it be that advertising reduces the incentive for productivity so that we are becoming more consumption oriented and less production oriented? If this were true, the gap would be widening, "bliss" would be farther away, and frustration and decay could set in. This could indeed be the case for those for whom opportunity is blocked. The situation for society in general is not clear and is widely debated by social philosophers.[13]

2. *Influence of advertising on values.* Advertising may also alter values toward work, thereby making us more hedonistic than we would otherwise be, and may alter other values in ways that we *personally* feel are not desirable. There is no consensus or regulation as to what values we should hold, but it is important that we think about, discuss, and formulate our own ideas about desirable and undesirable values. Does advertising make us too materialistic? Does it emphasize and make rigid our sexual roles? Does it make us too hedonistic or dull our senses and capacity for creativity? Does puffery in advertising lead us to believe that a little deceit is all right? These are important questions, particularly with regard to young children, and it is difficult to collect empirical evidence on them. No one answer applies to all.

3. *Influence of advertising on morals.* The impact of advertising on morals has been viewed inconsistently over the years. Probably for historical reasons, few broadcast media accept liquor advertising, while print media do. The codes of the National

---

[11] R. A. Bauer and S. A. Greyser, *Advertising in America: The Consumer View* (Boston: Harvard University Graduate School of Business Administration, 1968), p. 87.

[12] J. S. Coulson, "New Consumerists' Breed Will Fade Away," *The Marketing News,* Mid-June, 1971, pp. 5–8.

[13] A detailed analysis of these ideas has been developed by R. S. Weckstein, "Welfare Criteria and Changing Tastes," *American Economic Review,* March 1962, pp. 133–53.

Marketing: Principles and methods

Association of Broadcasters and all publishers list products and services for which they will not accept advertising. Yet beer and wine, pornographic movies, and war toys are advertised, and sex has been used to help sell many consumer and industrial products. It has been alleged that the drug culture has been encouraged by advertising of pain relievers that depicts the taking of a pill as bringing both relief of pain and a sense of euphoria and pleasure. How does a society decide on acceptable moral standards? Is advertising the correct aspect of the issue on which to focus?

The effect of misleading advertising on our basic honesty and trust in our fellow man is one moral question on which we might attempt to collect evidence and establish public policy. Perhaps we should expect a higher level of honesty in advertising than we expect from society generally, but should the same apply to all promotional practices? Should a seller not be allowed to say that he has a better product and provides more service than his competitors?

4. *Influence of advertising on life styles.* There has been considerable feeling lately that advertising leads to life styles that are homogeneous, mediocre, in poor taste (not defined), and "thing" oriented rather than "idea" oriented. Since such feelings are clearly matters of personal taste, any analysis of these charges is far beyond the scope or competence of the authors. However, these are charges which we should not dismiss lightly as individual buyers or sellers. Were it not for private advertising, would you spend more money and time on parks, natural beauty, and the arts? And if you would, would this be a better life style?[14]

5. *Influence of advertising on program content.* It is argued that since advertising media rates depend on the number of viewers or readers, the media must present programs that attract large audiences. The largest audiences watch bland, escape-type entertainment shows. The media are at the mercy of their advertisers to present material that sells, and what sells is a "wasteland." Much of the motivation for this argument seems to come from creative people who have shows to be sponsored. Their usual suggestion is more media subsidized by tax funds.

Although this criticism is not without merit, the case is not so obvious. Successful print media today are those that find highly specialized audience segments and provide them with in-depth materials on narrow topics, perhaps because of the absence of such materials on the broadcast media. Cable or recorded television may relieve the shortage of in-depth TV programming. Media regulated by the FCC might also be required to sell all time at average rates rather than at rates that vary by time slot.

As in any market, media must seek to offer the mix of service that brings the greatest amount of utility to the greatest number of consumers. For most things in this country, market mechanisms do a good job directing suppliers to provide the outputs that achieve this goal, but the market mechanism for the purchase of broadcast entertainment is not a normal one. Under the current system, consumers pay for the broadcast through the price they pay for advertised products. The advertiser is left with the decision of which programs to buy, and he buys time on programs with large consumer acceptance.

With subsidized media, consumers pay for the broadcast through taxes. Freedom to influence programming would be reduced to some even less direct, political process. Subsidization does not appear to be a way to increase consumer control and reduce advertising control over program content.

---

[14] For a development of this thesis, see J. K. Galbraith, *The Affluent Society* (Boston: Houghton Mifflin Co., 1958), chap. 18, and "Economics as a System of Belief," *American Economic Review,* 60 (May 1970).

6. *Influence of advertising on product improvement.* Social critics claim that advertising makes it cheaper for a seller to differentiate his product on psychological factors than on functional product advantages. Actually, few examples of *successful* new product introductions in which the product did not have real and important differences can be found. What can be observed are products that had real advantages when they were introduced and have been able to retain a strong competitive position through advertising (e.g., Camel cigarettes and Log Cabin syrup), and product groups where "real" technological improvements are difficult, but advertising is used in an attempt to introduce "phony" new products (e.g., cigarette brands). Most of these latter campaigns fail to do as well as ones for products with observable advantages for buyers.

The consumer's position as a buyer today

What conclusion is reasonable concerning the consumer's present position as a buyer? Does he have the ability (and does he use it) to guide the economy to the production and marketing of those products that best meet his wants? Some observers believe that the answer to this question is negative. Professor E. S. Mason of Harvard states: "In an economy whose supreme talent is devoted not only to the creation of the new product but to making the customer like it, this sovereignty [of the consumer] turns out to be limited indeed."[15] Others, even after considerable study of the question, claim

we simply do not know enough about this aspect of marketing . . . to draw very firm conclusions. . . . We have reason to believe that they [consumers] are neither so well served as the partisans of marketing maintain nor so badly abused as its more vociferous critics assert. Beyond that it is not very safe to go.[16]

Because the majority of business firms realize that their goodwill and future profitability are at stake, they attempt to avoid practices that will be widely considered as undesirable. There probably has been considerable improvement in the honesty of advertising claims simply because the education and standards demanded by the public have gone up. Many advertisers have discovered that although "consumers may be willing to be flattered, cajoled, or entertained," they do "not really wish to be deceived."[17]

In the final analysis, however, the consumers' best defense is to avoid apathy in buying, to seek and use information, to seek vehicles for voicing objections, and be skeptical that General Motors, AT&T, or any other seller is looking out for their best interests. While government has some responsibilities for consumer protection, just as sellers look out for their own well-being, consumers have responsibilities to be efficient and knowledgable buyers and to be vocal in their opposition to monopoly power, abuses, and inefficiencies in sellers. To achieve these ends, consumers engage in many activities sponsored by private organizations, business interests of various types, and the government.

---

[15] E. S. Mason, "The Apologetics of 'Managerialism'," *Journal of Business,* 31 (January 1958), p. 9.

[16] Cox, Goodman, and Fichandler, *Distribution in a High-Level Economy,* p. 241.

[17] W. Alderson, *Marketing Behavior and Executive Action* (Homewood, Ill.: Richard D. Irwin, Inc., 1957), p. 184.

Marketing: Principles and methods

ASSISTANCE TO THE CONSUMER AS A BUYER

Private organizations

The consumer movement in the United States has had three periods of active and rapid growth.[18] The first began in about 1891 and lasted about 15 years. The second, beginning in about 1927 after a lapse of two decades, also lasted 15 years. The third began two decades later in 1962 and is still in progress. Each period produced private organizations of consumers that had neither business or government support and provided some form of consumer pressure group.

The Consumers' League of New York City, founded in 1891, grew by 1903 to a national federation with 64 branches in 20 states. This group was concerned with the labor movement, particularly minimum hours and wages and sanitary working conditions. In the second period, in 1929, F. J. Schlink founded Consumers' Research, Inc., to do product testing. It did not involve itself in labor issues, but in 1935 its refusal to bargain collectively with a union led to labor troubles of its own. The dispute led to the foundation by subscribers and strikers of a new organization, Consumers' Union of the U.S., Inc. (CU), which within three years was larger than Consumers' Research. The circulation of CU's magazine, *Consumer Reports,* fell to about 50,000 during World War II but recovered to 800,000 by 1963. During the third period of the consumer movement it has grown rapidly to a circulation of over 2 million.

The current period has been marked by the introduction of a number of independent consumer organizations, the most notable being the Consumer Federation of America (CFA) and Ralph Nader's volunteer agencies. CFA is a federation of local organizations, headquartered in Washington, D.C., which comes closer to being a consumer lobbying organization than any of its predecessors. Its financial base is deeply rooted in organized labor. Ralph Nader is truly an independent consumer advocate. Few leaders of the consumer movement since its beginning have been so successful. Nader has founded a number of institutions in order to provide administrative organizations for his work: The Center for Study of Responsive Law, Center for Auto Safety, Public Interest Research Group, and Project on Corporate Responsibility.

Other consumer organizations active today are the Cooperative League of the USA, professional societies such as the American Council on Consumer Interests and the American Home Economics Association, some women's organizations, and state and local consumers' leagues, councils, and associations.

The natural appeal of independent consumer organizations is that they represent buyers performing their own marketing functions without reliance on government bureaucrats. Their disadvantage is that, since we are all consumers, they do not form homogeneous or close-knit special-interest groups which can effectively do battle. Only Consumers' Union has a really broad-based constituency, and this following stems from the services their magazine provides rather than their political efforts. CU meets a market test—it successfully sells a product in the open market. The voluntary organizations, business aids to consumers, or government cannot make that statement.

---

[18] For an excellent history of the consumer movement see R. O. Hermann, *The Consumer Movement in Historical Perspective* (University Park, Pa.: Department of Agricultural Economics and Rural Sociology, The Pennsylvania State University, 1970).

Business aids to consumers

A number of businesses and business groups find it in their enlightened self-interest to provide consumers with some help in buying. These include magazine institutes, individual firms, trade associations, and Better Business Bureaus.

Magazine institutes. A few private magazines, notably *Good Housekeeping,* have extended aid to the consumer by financing tests of the products advertised in them. Like Consumers' Union, the Good Housekeeping Institute has its own testing laboratory (some magazines use outside commercial laboratories) to which all its advertisers must submit their products. But unlike *Consumer Reports,* which accepts no advertising, at *Good Housekeeping* there is a close tie between the activities of the Institute and those of the advertising department. When the magazine is convinced that the product is satisfactory and that its proposed advertisement is valid, the product is allowed to bear the *Good Housekeeping* seal of approval, and advertisements are accepted. In addition, the magazine gives all its readers a guarantee that it will either replace or refund the purchase price of any product carrying its seal that is defective or does not perform as advertised.[19]

However, these institutes do not (1) publish lists of nonapproved items, (2) give any idea of the relation of quality and price among items which might be used for the same purpose, or (3) tell the basis of their ratings. In addition the Federal Trade Commission has disclosed that the seal of *Parents' Magazine* has been awarded in some instances on the basis of reports and tests submitted by the applicant or the recommendations of nontechnical employees of the magazine and without independent or magazine-financed tests.[20]

Individual firms. The major way in which an individual business helps the consumer is a direct result of its attempt to attract and retain patronage. Although a clever advertisement or an attractive store may entice a customer into his first purchase, continuous patronage rests mainly on the broad basis of consumer goodwill. Hence, it is essential that the company follow policies that will lead to satisfied customers. Most manufacturers and middlemen realize that the sale of suitable products and services will do this. Almost all will replace a new product a customer finds unsatisfactory. Moreover, both manufacturers and middlemen spend great sums for research to improve present products and develop new ones, thus fulfilling a major social responsibility.

Among the middlemen that give consumer protection through their own merchandise testing laboratories are Sears, Roebuck and Company, Montgomery Ward and Company, the Great Atlantic and Pacific Tea Company, R. H. Macy & Company, and J. C. Penney Company.[21] Products are tested in their laboratories *before* they are placed on sale. Those that are misrepresented by attached tickets or labels are discovered and eliminated, or they are advertised as being of the quality revealed by the tests. Some department stores have experimented with placing labels on their products that give specific data in understandable terms concerning the serviceability of the merchandise. A few of the food chains, such as the Great Atlantic and Pacific

---

[19] "Guaranty Seal: The Offer Still Stands," *Business Week,* March 19, 1966, p. 192.

[20] *Re Parents' Magazine Enterprises, Inc.,* F.T.C. Dkt. C–1133, CCH 17,751, November 1966.

[21] For details, see "Sears' Appliances Lead New Products," *Printers' Ink,* January 27, 1967, pp. 51–52; "New Test Laboratories," Montgomery Ward *Annual Report,* year ended February 1, 1967, p. 9; "Product Testing and Development," J. C. Penney *Annual Report,* year ended January 28, 1967, p. 11; and "Penney's Testing Moving into Era of Expansion," *Women's Wear Daily,* March 11, 1970, p. 41.

Tea Company and Safeway Stores, Inc., use government standards for the basis of labels on some of their private-brand goods.

Trade associations. In attempts to look after the interests of their members, trade associations often provide aid to consumers and the public. Some formulate codes of ethics and play a leading role in stopping deceptive selling practices. The National Canners' Association has set up an inspection system to be sure that food is placed in cans by member manufacturers under sanitary conditions. The Major Appliance Consumer Action Panel (MACAP) was founded in 1970 by three trade associations to resolve disputes between consumers and sellers of household appliances.

Some trade associations have also taken the lead in establishing standards: package size standards (food processing associations), quality grades (coal, hardwoods, and even brooms), safety standards (American Gas Association, among others), and even performance standards. Standardization may be handled by a trade association directly, but the American National Standards Institute has been established by many business organizations expressly for this purpose. Businesses also support independent consumer research organizations such as Committee for Economic Development, Consumer Research Institute, Inc., and Marketing Science Institute.

When consumer interest is in conflict with members' interests, however, the trade association is most likely to look after its own short-run interest. Consumers should not expect business trade associations to look after consumer welfare except when it is clearly to the association's advantage.

Better business bureaus. In 1911, at a meeting of the Associated Advertising Clubs of the World, a discussion of "What Is the Matter with Advertising?" led to the conclusion that the trouble was a lack of confidence in advertising on the part of the public. To improve the situation, a central organization (now known as the National Better Business Bureau, with 2,300 members from business firms or organizations operating nationally or regionally) was established "to build and conserve public confidence in advertising and business generally." When it was found that the bureaus did not work well enough to protect consumers and the free enterprise system (in 1970, about 40 percent of telephone calls to bureaus were blocked by busy signals),[22] a new national organization (Council of Better Business Bureaus, Inc.) of local bureaus and the national bureau was formed in 1970 to increase efficiency. Working with member bureaus, the council is designed to: develop programs for self-regulation, provide information and education to consumers, improve methods to protect consumers from fraudulent business practices, participate in public affairs affecting business and consumers, and monitor advertising, selling practices, credit, warranties, performance, and safety of products and services.[23]

In regard to deceptive advertising and selling practices, the procedure of the various bureaus is worthy of commendation. In addition to investigation of consumer complaints about unfair advertising, they check local newspaper advertisements and other forms of sales promotion. When an advertisement looks suspicious, an employee of the bureau makes an investigation, which often involves the purchase of the advertised merchandise to see whether it fulfills the seller's claims. If an inaccuracy is disclosed, a representative of the bureau calls on the guilty advertiser and suggests,

---

[22] H. Bruce Palmer, "Consumerism: The Business of Business," *Michigan Business Review,* 23 (July 1971), pp. 12–17.

[23] Ibid.

on the theory that cooperation is better than coercion, that a correction be printed or that he desist from that type of advertising in the future. Usually this step is sufficient. Where it is not, the case is reported to local newspapers and other advertising media, the great majority of which will not permit the use of their advertising facilities by a persistent offender. If further steps are needed, and if a state fair-advertising statute exists, action may be brought against the offender. These steps may be supplemented by announcements in the various publications of the bureau itself, in which the inaccuracy of certain advertisements are made public. The National Better Business Bureau uses comparable methods in the national field.

Better business bureaus have a good track record. They do work. However, consumers should not expect CBBB, trade associations, or any other business group to *protect* them. Business is on the other side in a game in which both buyer and seller are trying to get the better of a trade. The various business groups basically attempt to maintain the kind of environment in which they want to operate. This may not be the ideal consumer environment.

Governmental efforts to protect the consumer

Government aid to protect the consumer is not new. In the 18th century, the English Parliament sought to protect the male consumer against the effects of some products used by women to "seduce and betray" him into matrimony.[24] Today, government protection for the consumer may be less slanted toward the male, but it exists at all levels—local, state, and federal.

Local and state government measures. Except for schools, the consumer-aid activities of cities are quite limited. A few of the larger cities (New York, Chicago, Miami) have active consumer affairs offices. Most cities have ordinances regulating the activities of itinerant merchants, in most cases because local businessmen did not want such competition, but they also provide some consumer protection.

Many consumer problems are more appropriately handled at the state level. Most consumer frauds are localized and are attacked most effectively by county or state agencies. Prior to the past decade, state activities were confined typically to such matters as the establishment of sanitary standards for processing and distributing goods, including restaurants; weights and measures regulations; small loan and install-ment credit measures; false advertising; and, in a few instances, required grading or marking of such agricultural consumer goods as eggs, potatoes, and apples.

In contrast to these earlier efforts, since 1959 about a dozen states have estab-lished some form of consumer representation in the executive branch of the state government. All 50 states provide protection against consumer frauds in goods and services through the state attorney general's office. About half the states have "little FTC acts" or "deceptive practices acts" which are considered adequate by present-day standards of consumer protection. Insurance, banking, and investment protection are usually the responsibility of separate state departments.[25] The states also coordi-nate or are responsible for weights and measures departments, some of which have been expanded to handle more general consumer problems. There is a general feeling that government should organize so that there is a single visible and accessible agency

---

[24] See pp. 115–16 above.

[25] Many of these departments fall under the influence of the industry they are designed to regulate and become poor protectors of consumers.

that consumers can contact by letter, telephone, or in person when they have a problem.

For efficiency in trade, states have attempted to establish similar legislation in some areas of consumer protection. The Uniform Commercial Code is the most important of such laws (see Chapter 25). The *Printers' Ink* model advertising code to govern deceptive advertising was thought to be very progressive in 1911 when it was written but is "too business oriented" to satisfy consumer activists today. In recent years, consumer law experts have been trying to develop a comprehensive model consumer protection code for state use. Some states have passed sections of this model code. For example, in 1971 California passed a new "class-action" bill so that consumer groups can sue a seller in the name of a class of all buyers who may have been similarly defrauded, abolished the protection formerly available to lenders who buy consumer installment debt paper so that they now have responsibility for valid consumer complaints, and established a three-day cooling-off period on home-solicitation contracts. All three of these statutes are parts of the model consumer protection code.

Local and state governments are also contributing an increasing amount of aid to consumers through courses in consumer education in public school systems. Illinois and Massachusetts have been particularly active in this effort in recent years. However, such courses face two serious barriers: teen-agers are less receptive to the materials because they have not yet experienced many real consumer problems, and business and consumer groups fail to agree on the "fairness" of course materials, which inherently contain value judgments rather than facts and principles. The solution to this problem may lie in teaching more economic principles at the secondary level and less "how to shop" materials.

Federal government aids. It is at the federal level that consumer aid has flowered. It is difficult to find a department or agency which does not help the consumer in some way: the Postal Service in prohibiting the use of the mails in selling fraudulent goods; the Public Health Service in checking the spread of dangerous diseases and inspecting food on interstate railroads; the Bureau of Home Economics of the Department of Agriculture by its publication of consumer buying guides and its studies of quality standards. The Department of Agriculture also is conducting research on consumer products, establishing grades on agricultural products, certifying the quality of many products, and inspecting or establishing inspection standards for all meat and poultry. The Federal Reserve Board administers the Truth-in-Lending law and helps to protect bank deposits; the Security and Exchange Commission protects investors; the Interstate Commerce Commission has improved its protection of consumers in moving household goods. The Civil Aeronautics Board protects the rights of airline passengers, and the Department of Transportation has established a National Highway Traffic Safety Administration. The National Bureau of Standards has established standards of measurement and encouraged simplification. Especially noteworthy are the activities of the Federal Trade Commission, the Food and Drug Administration, and the President's Office of Consumer Affairs.

1. *Federal Trade Commission.* The authority of the FTC to protect consumers stems primarily but not exclusively from the 1938 Wheeler-Lea Amendment to the Federal Trade Commission Act and the labeling acts—wool (1939), fur (1951), textile fibers (1958), flammable fabrics (1953 and 1967)—so consumers could know what materials they were buying. Wheeler-Lea extended Section 5 of the 1914 Act to forbid unfair or deceptive acts or practices in commerce and added four new sections, 12 to 15, which supplemented the 1938 Food, Drug, and Cosmetic Act to authorize the

FTC to move broadly against deceptive or misleading advertising. Prior to that time, Section 5 would apply only if injury to a competitor could be proved.

Currently, consumer protection activities are centralized in the Bureau of Consumer Protection and make up about two thirds of the Commission's work. The Commission also maintains 11 field offices. The authority of Section 5 is very broad. Most criticism of past FTC lethargy has been caused by lack of action or budget, not lack of authority to protect consumers. The FTC can attack any deceptive selling or advertising practice in interstate commerce or in the District of Columbia.

The actual consumer-protecting work of the Commission takes various forms. Many cases of alleged deceptive practices are filed with it by business competitors. These situations are investigated, and complaints are issued where necessary. It takes action against false advertising uncovered by its own staff of investigators, who review the advertisements appearing in a large number of magazines and newspapers and scripts covering radio and television advertising. Better industry practices are also encouraged by the issuance of industry guides to such things as deceptive pricing, guarantees, tire advertising, labeling of shoe materials, promotional allowances, and "cents-off" labels (under additional authority in the Fair Packaging and Labeling Act).

The 1960s were not good years for the Commission. After 50 years of life it appeared to have "hardening of the arteries." Many authorities in 1970 called for it to be disbanded, maintaining that consumers and competition would be better off without it than with it doing so little. Instead President Nixon brought in new leadership and gave it new life, and it shows signs of becoming an aggressive guardian of consumer rights. For example, it now makes available to the public the *FTC Consumer Alert,* which reports FTC consumer-related activities.

2. *Food and Drug Administration.* Originally in the Department of Agriculture, the Food and Drug Administration (FDA) is now a part of the Department of Health, Education, and Welfare. Unlike the FTC, which is an independent regulatory agency, FDA belongs to the executive branch of the federal government. Its powers are based mainly on the Food, Drug, and Cosmetic Acts of 1906, 1938, and 1962.

The FDA has certain responsibilities for foods, drugs, cosmetics, and therapeutic devices, including those assigned to it by the Fair Packaging and Labeling Act of 1966. In general, the law forbids the shipment in interstate commerce of such goods if they are injurious, adulterated, or falsely labeled, although certain exceptions are made as regards injurious items if they are labeled properly. Most foods using artificial coloring, artificial flavoring, or chemical preservatives must be so labeled, and drug labels must warn of habit-forming products. New drugs cannot be offered for sale and chemicals cannot be added to food products until the manufacturer has satisfied the FDA that it is safe for use under the conditions set forth on its labels. Enforcement is secured by FDA inspection at least every two years of every plant producing drugs; through orders that certain products be withdrawn from the market; and by collecting samples on interstate shipments, seizing goods being shipped in violation of the law, and prosecuting the shippers of such goods. The agency also has some responsibility for approval of advertising and labeling of drugs.

The FDA has taken many steps to carry out the law, such as: (1) revising advertising and labeling standards for vitamins and mineral preparations; (2) setting minimum amounts of key ingredients for cake mixes, canned foods, and other prepared products; (3) restudying a long list of drugs and food additives on the market to be sure they meet conditions in the act as amended in 1962 and additional consumer probing in 1971; (4) taking vigorous enforcement steps, including court action, against leading drug companies to eliminate what the FDA considers as advertising which fails to disclose unpleasant side effects and contraindications; (5) establishing regulations of certain promotions specified in the Fair Packaging and Labeling Act; (6) testing the safety of toys and baby equipment such as car seats;[26] (7) designing and improving the nutritional information on food labels; (8) testing drugs for efficacy as well as safety; and (9) the approval of all new food, drug, and cosmetic products.

To carry out its activities, the Food and Drug Administration has 17 regional offices, over four thousand employees and an annual budget of just under $110 million. The FDA has always had a difficult time in obtaining a budget adequate to meet its responsibilities. As late as 1954, the staff was cut to less than 800 employees. Both presidents and Congress have been embarrassed from time to time by the activities of the FDA, which often moves against large, highly respected corporations that have considerable political lobbying power.

There has been considerable animosity between the FDA and the firms subject to its jurisdiction. They charge the agency sometimes moves too rapidly, as in the matter of banning cyclamate artificial sweeteners, and at other times too slowly, as in approval of new drug products. On balance, the FDA has a record which is perhaps the finest of all consumer protection agencies. Its responsibilities for both scientific and marketing activities require a large, diversified, and expert staff. The question is not whether its services are necessary but how it can meet, with a limited budget, all its responsibilities objectively, efficiently, and free of political pressure.

3. *Office of Consumer Affairs.* In 1964 President Kennedy named a Special Assistant to the President for Consumer Affairs and established in the executive branch a Consumer Advisory Council, for which the consumer affairs assistant serves as executive secretary. The concept of having a strong consumer voice close to the president was accepted, and the function has become more permanent with each administration. The position is now known as Director, Office of Consumer Affairs (OCA), Executive Office of the President. Each of the three directors to date has been an intelligent, attractive, articulate woman. The Consumer Advisory Council, with 12 members, continues to operate, and the staff of the office has grown increasingly effective. In 1971 it began publication of *Consumer News,* which reports all current activities of government in protecting consumers. Consumer complaints sent to OCA tend to receive attention—either from the seller or appropriate government agency.

As early as 1966, there was serious discussion as to the merits of a reorganization that would establish a Department of Consumers at the cabinet level. The department would absorb all of the consumer activities of other government departments and independent regulatory agencies. While such a reorganization is still possible, the continued success of the Office of Consumer Affairs probably argues against it. A visible, persuasive voice close to the president which can prod and coordinate both consumer groups and government agencies may well be a better place for a consumer advocate than a cabinet secretary, who could easily lose power to influence other special-interest group secretaries such as labor, agriculture, and commerce.

THE FUTURE IN THE CONSUMER MOVEMENT

The consumer movement, along with other fundamentally right activities such as the pursuit of peace, motherhood, and religion, seems subject to fashion cycles. Society is capable of concentrating on only a few issues at one time. If a 15-year cycle

---

[26] Responsibility for safety of products other than foods, drugs, cosmetics, toxic substances, and automobiles was transferred in 1973 to the Consumer Product Safety Commission, a new agency.

in consumer activity continues, we should enjoy lively consumer debate until about the end of 1976 before the nation tires of these issues. By then, we will see additional legislative protection for poor consumers, some changes in redress procedures for both individual small claims and class actions, more powers and more money for the FTC and FDA, and perhaps some reorganization of consumer protection activities.

Is that all the additional protection consumers need? It is difficult to say, for the consumer movement represents an excellent example of the marketing system in action. When sellers get hit by consumer complaints, they usually make some change in their methods of operation. When the sellers do not change, legislation often follows. Before long, all obvious abuses around which consumer groups can organize are gone. Journalists, feeling the public is tired of the topic, write on other things. The public finds other interests to support, hopefully continuing to be alert buyers.

This is not a sad ending. The current period of consumer activism, like previous periods, has breathed new life into old protectors of the consumer interest and added new safeguards. The marketing system will survive and operate more effectively as a result of an alert and vocal movement—and even a little muckraking.

SUMMARY

Consumers, from time to time in history, have found that they have rights and that if those rights are unguarded, they will be violated. They have the right to safety in the products and services they buy. They have the right to be truthfully informed so they can make knowledgeable decisions. They have the right to choose from a variety of product and service alternatives, and finally, they have the right to be heard in the formulation of government policy.

Many consumers either do not know about these rights or do not care enough about them to safeguard them. Under such conditions neither business firms nor government will continually go out of their way to maintain these rights. Injurious products, false and/or misleading advertising, deceptive packaging, false weights, and other consumer abuses multiply until finally the tolerance level of the more sensitive consumers is exceeded. They react by forming consumer groups, alerting less aware consumers, and supporting consumer spokesmen. Slowly consumer rights grow more prestigious, and it becomes good business to pay more attention to consumer rights. When business moves too slowly or not at all, consumers seek redress through government. Legislation is passed which, if the consumer is vigilant, protects him and not the businessman.

This scene was not enacted for the first time in the late 1960s and early 1970s, nor will it be the last time it appears. Each time it is reenacted new areas of consumer protection come under the jurisdiction of government—truth in lending, truth in packaging and so forth. However, it is doubtful if relatively more of the consumer's world is protected, because his decisions and activities apparently expand faster than his protection.

This chapter focused first on the problems of the consumer as a buyer: problems of safety of products; of obtaining adequate information about quantity, quality, and price; of deceptive practices, and of advertising. As consumers, you are already somewhat familiar with many if not most of these problems. Now that you have a framework for viewing consumer problems, we hope you will stay alerted to them.

The second focus of this chapter was on the assistance consumers receive from private organizations, from business, and from government. Each consumer movement has generated private organizations to help organize and perpetrate its activities.

Consumers' Union, for example, is an outgrowth of an earlier movement. Consumer Federation of America and Ralph Nader and his institutions represent private organizations that have arisen from the current movement.

Business assistance to consumers normally arises from enlightened self-interest. Magazine seals of approval may help consumers, but they are likely to be of even more help in selling advertising space. Better business bureaus are basically operated to aid businessmen to police the activities of their competitors. Trade associations primarily help member firms. In each of these situations, however, some benefits are likely to flow to consumers. Consumers should not place complete trust in business to guard their rights. Business rights come first and consumer rights come second, and they are not always compatible.

Local, state, and federal government has long been a protector of various consumer rights. Not that all or even most legislation is designed to protect consumers (as will be seen in Chapter 25), but there is meaningful government protection. The Federal Trade Commission, the Department of Agriculture, the Federal Reserve Board, the Securities and Exchange Commission, the Interstate Commerce Commission, the Federal Communications Commission, the Food and Drug Administration, and many other government groups help provide some consumer protection.

In the final analysis, private organizations, business, and government can assist consumers in securing their rights. However, the consumer's well-being is influenced more by his own interest, desire, and action as an informed and intelligent consumer than by anything else.

REVIEW AND DISCUSSION QUESTIONS

1. Give an actual example of a violation of each of President Kennedy's consumer rights and an example of government protection of each.

2. Give two examples of products for which you feel the quality of demand is high and two for which it is low. Relate your reasoning to the material in Chapter 5.

3. Is it becoming easier or more difficult for the consumer to be an intelligent buyer? Why, or why not?

4. Give examples of products for which quality information is given by: (a) standardization, (b) consumer grading, (c) quality seals, and (d) informative labeling.

5. "There is nothing wrong with advertising as such; the fault, if any, lies with the advertiser. We should not confuse the tool and its user." Discuss.

6. Give an example of an actual purchase made by you or your family for which you used price as an indicator of quality. Discuss.

7. Formulate several currently useful generalizations which in your judgment best describe the present position of the consumer as a buyer.

8. Find five advertisements you feel are socially undesirable. Using the framework presented in this chapter, state the reasons for your belief in each case.

9. Evaluate the aid received by consumers from Consumers' Union of the U.S., Inc.

10. Support or contest the statement that "it is in the competitive struggle for the consumers' purchases, supplemented by the growing sense of social responsibility among members of the business community, that the consumer finds his greatest protection."

11. Based on your visit to a local better business bureau, prepare a brief report covering its recent activities, how it is financed, and how it processes a complaint received from a

citizen. Interview some local businessmen to get their opinions of the value of the better business bureau.

12. Outline and appraise the effectiveness of the efforts by state governments during the past decade to aid the consumer as a buyer.

13. Find the wording of Section 5 of the Federal Trade Commission Act of 1914 and the new wording provided by the Wheeler-Lea Amendment of 1938. Explain the significance of this change.

14. What are the main provisions of the Pure Food and Drug Act of 1906? What were the important changes made by the acts of 1938 and 1962?

15. Prepare a short report on the materials reported in *Consumer News* and the procedure for obtaining this publication.

SUPPLEMENTARY READINGS

Aaker, D. A. and Day, G. S. (eds.)   *Consumerism: Search for the Consumer Interest.* New York: The Free Press, 1971. A collection of 30 readings on the current consumer movement.

Alexander, G. J.   *Honesty and Competition: False-Advertising Law and Policy under FTC Administration.* Syracuse, N.Y.: Syracuse University Press, 1967. This complete book on the interdiction by the Federal Trade Commission of deception in advertising particularly explores the conflict between the Commission's two roles: protecting consumers and enhancing competition.

Bauer, R. A. and Greyser, S. A.   *Advertising in America: The Consumer View.* Boston: Harvard University Graduate School of Business Administration, 1968. A comprehensive study of what Americans think of advertising.

Bell, C. S.   *Consumer Choice in the American Economy.* New York: Random House, Inc., 1967. Among many other subjects Professor Bell deals with the problem of consumer protection: "Keeping markets actively competitive . . . is undoubtedly the most efficient and powerful technique for protecting consumers."

Gordon, L. J. and Lee, S. M.   *Economics for Consumers.* 5th ed. Cincinnati, Ohio: American Book Co., 1967. Although written for an elementary course in economic principles from the consumer point of view, this will be helpful for the student who has not given much thought to the consumer.

Grether, E. T.   *Marketing and Public Policy.* Englewood Cliffs, N.J.: Prentice-Hall, Inc., 1966. Covers the entire range of problems concerning marketing and public policy.

Howard, M.   *Legal Aspects of Marketing.* New York: McGraw-Hill Book Co., 1964. An excellent short volume summarizing the legislation that affects marketing.

Kohlmeier, L. M., Jr.   *The Regulators.* New York: Harper and Row, 1969. An excellent and up-to-date review of the record of the independent regulatory agencies, such as the FTC, in protecting the public interest.

Lavidge, R. J. and Holloway, R. J. (eds.)   *Marketing and Society: The Challenge.* Homewood, Ill.: Richard D. Irwin, Inc., 1969. An excellent collection of current readings on the social problems of marketing.

Preston, L. E. (ed.)   *Social Issues in Marketing.* Glenview, Ill.: Scott, Foresman and Co., 1968. The readings in this volume focus on four issues: the social point of view, marketing efficiency and costs, fair competition, and consumer welfare.

U.S. National Commission on Food Marketing   *Food from Farmer to Consumer.* Washington, D.C.: Government Printing Office, 1966. The majority and minority recommendations on such subjects as a department of the consumer, grade labeling of food, packaging and labels, and the buying problems of the consumer will be found on pp. 101, 109, 130–31, and 150–51. Unfortunately, too many of the majority recommendations are based on subjective judgment and not on the basis of evidence.

Part III *The retailing system*

Retailing institutions are the final link of the marketing system for consumer products and services. A great variety of institutions perform the numerous marketing functions that make up the retailing system or, more accurately, subsystem.

Discussion of the retailing system is divided into three chapters. Chapter 7 is concerned principally with the development of the retailing system in the United States. This longitudinal analysis not only indicates where the system has been and now stands, but it also should give some insight into where it is going.

Chapter 8 concentrates on small-scale, group, and direct systems of retailing. A large portion of the retailing structure fits into these categories. While you may think you, as a consumer, already know a lot about retailing, you may find a number of surprises in this chapter.

The final chapter in Part III focuses on large-scale retailing systems. Corporate food, department, and discount stores, and a number of other retail giants, are discussed.

When you have completed Part III you should have a good idea about how the component institutions and activities of the retailing system fit into the total marketing system and into the overall concepts of this book. From Part I you should have gained a composite framework or overview of the marketing system, as well as a view of the major component systems. Each of the other parts should help you fill out this framework. In Part II, for example, you were exposed to the consumer system. Part III logically moves to a discussion of the retailing system, which provides much of the input into the consumer system. Part IV, as you might anticipate, features the wholesaling system for consumer goods, a major input into the retailing system.

147

7 Development of the retailing system

The industrial development of the United States has been marked by a gradual transfer of the production of goods desired by the consumer from the household to the factory. Goods made in the home were the basis of the pioneer's economic existence. He raised his grain and milled it in his own (or his neighbor's) mill, and his wife made the bread. His woolen jacket was produced by the labors of his immediate family. The tallow candles which lighted his cabin were homemade. The few things that he needed and could not produce were obtained at the trading post, which he visited perhaps no more than three or four times a year.

Mass production has meant the end of consumer self-sufficiency. As factories have produced a greater share of goods, distribution has become a new problem calling for massive transportation, communication, and financial systems. The trading post has given way to a complex system of middlemen and direct retailing.

This and the following two chapters focus on the retailing system—particularly the institutions related directly to the sale or rental of products and services to the ultimate consumer for personal nonbusiness use. Most of the retailing system operates through retail stores and retailers. However, nonretailers—those whose primary activities are not selling to ultimate consumers—such as farmers, manufacturers, and wholesalers, also engage in the retailing system. We use the term "retailing system" throughout these chapters, recognizing that it is in reality a subsystem of the marketing system.

The primary objective of the retailing system is to make products and services available to ultimate consumers. The retailing system is one of the major components in the marketing system that performs the equalization process to remove the discrepancy of assortments. It engages in all four of the equalization process activities—sorting out, assembling, allocating, and assorting. Its primary activities, however, are allocating and assorting, i.e., breaking down homogeneous supplies into the quantities and assortments or mixes that ultimate consumers want. In performing these activities, the retailing system engages in the transfer of title or use rights, physical distribution, and facilitating functions.

The composition of the retailing system is continually evolving in response to an ever-changing environment, new technology, and the pressure of competition. This chapter examines this evolution in the United States and concludes with an overview of the current situation and trends looking toward the future. The major institutional components of the retailing system are reserved for Chapters 8 and 9.

The relative position of the retailing system in the overall marketing system is shown in Figure 7–1. As can be seen, it is positioned between the ultimate consumer and the various supply systems.

FIGURE 7–1
The retailing system in the total marketing system

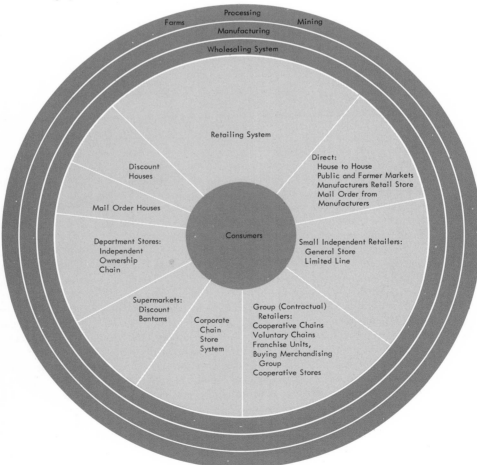

Marketing: Principles and methods

EVOLUTION OF RETAILING

The trading post

Retail institutions—those marketing institutions engaged primarily in selling consumer products and services to ultimate consumers—have gradually evolved in response to changing conditions. Trading posts, founded very early in the history of the United States, were our first retail institutions. At these posts, products from Europe were exchanged for animal furs and other goods brought in mainly by the Indians, although to some extent also by the few white settlers. As the settlers increased in number, a change took place in the character of the trading post: It was gradually turned into a general store to serve the settler rather than to trade with the Indian. This evolution was taking place in the eastern parts of the country during the late 17th and early 18th centuries, although in the Middle West the trading post as such was still important at the end of the 18th century.[1]

The Yankee peddler

Another retailer from whom the early settler could buy some of the things he desired was the Yankee peddler from New England, where he apparently first appeared in the 17th century.[2] Gradually, he expanded his territory to cover the country as far west as the Mississippi River and as far south as Louisiana.

The wares of the Yankee peddler consisted mainly of "Yankee notions"—articles such as scissors, tinware, and pins and needles, although he also carried groceries, patent medicines, and dry goods. Some of the peddlers made the goods they distributed; they usually specialized in a limited line of wares. Others bought a variety of merchandise for resale and were "walking W. T. Grants." Originally, most peddlers traveled on foot, carrying their packs on their backs, but as success came their way—and it often did—they took to horseback. As roads improved and profits increased, they began to use wagons. Some even engaged rooms in country hotels as display quarters, rather than calling directly on customers. Because their lives were very hard, most peddlers were relatively young men. The scarcity of currency led them to accept goods in payment for their wares, so that, like the general store, they served in the double capacity of bringing goods into a section and taking products out of it to be disposed of in another. The acceptance of beaver skins, of rags to be resold for the making of paper, and of knitting and crocheting to be resold in town was common.

The peddler was apparently shrewd, and often his love of a good bargain led him to sharp practices, so that he has been described as "notoriously dishonest" and as a "person whose ingenuity in deception is confessedly very great."[3] Because of the nature of his wares, his dealings were largely with the women of the family, on whom he practiced a good deal of applied psychology. He has been called the original baby praiser; he encouraged Mrs. Smith to buy by telling her that Mrs. Jones had made a similar purchase; he often left a luxury article in the house of a prospective purchaser

---

[1] P. H. Nystrom, *Economics of Retailing,* Vol. I (New York: Ronald Press Co., 1930), p. 76.

[2] R. E. Gould's *Yankee Storekeeper* (New York: McGraw-Hill Book Co., 1946) gives a good description of early peddling and storekeeping in New England, and Harry Golden's *Forgotten Pioneer* (New York: World Publishing Co., 1963) relates the trials and tribulations of the peddler in both North and South.

[3] F. Presbrey, *History and Development of Advertising* (New York: Doubleday, Doran & Co., 1929), p. 167.

for a few days so that the women of the family would use it and then find that to part with it would be too difficult; and he offered the famous "guarantee" which applied to all articles "if well used." When dealing with the man of the family, he never forgot the farmer's pride in his oncoming crops. Although his methods were not always those of the highest character, the peddler was an important retailer in the late 17th and early 18th centuries. He served to introduce new goods to the sparsely settled districts and to open up inland trade for the growing manufacturers, functions quite different from those performed by his present-day counterpart, the house-to-house salesman.

The general store

Despite the importance of the peddler at the beginning of the 18th century, the general store—a nondepartmentized store carrying merchandise in a number of lines, such as groceries, hardware, dry goods, and drugs—was the typical retail institution at that time.[4] Of course, stores handling larger assortments in limited lines did exist, but they were in cities having a population of five thousand or over, and there were only about 12 of these.[5] Not only did the general store sell manufactured goods to nearby settlers, but it bought or bartered for many local products, such as woolen and linen check, tallow candles, butter, homewrought nails, flax, and furs. Thus the general store also served as a transfer agency between the villagers and the neighboring farmers. Long-term credit, usually of a year's duration, was customary. The store served as the village post office and as the center of social life for the male members of the community. In contrast with the itinerant peddler, "the storekeeper was to be found all the year round in every town, village, and hamlet in New England. He ministered to the needs of male and female alike. He made contacts that were permanent. He served the wants of the whole community rather than of isolated families. . . ."[6]

One student of retail history has written that there were certain conditions which, at the time,

virtually made the general store type of establishment the only one capable of surviving. Various pioneer conditions limited the sales volume in any given line, and consequently the merchant endeavored to increase his trade by adding dissimilar lines of goods, hence his establishment was a general store. The sales volume was restricted by such things as the high degree of self-sufficiency of the early settler, the predominance of agriculture as the main occupation, the prevalence of production for use rather than for sale, the meagerness of transportation facilities, the high cost of transportation, and the scarcity of specie or purchasing power.[7]

As the towns in the eastern part of the United States grew into cities, the general store found it impossible to meet all the demands made on it. Its stock of goods consisted of so many classes that its selection in each was limited. As early as 1800

---

[4] For a description of the New England store of 1840, see *Annual Report of the Massachusetts Bureau of Statistics of Labor* (1899), pp. 58–64.

[5] F. M. Jones, "Retail Stores in the United States, 1800–1860," *Journal of Marketing,* 1 (October 1936), p. 134.

[6] H. A. Wooster, "A Forgotten Factor in Industrial History," *American Economic Review,* 16 (March 1926), p. 18.

[7] E. J. Sheppard, "A History of the Wholesaling of Groceries and Other Food in Central Ohio, with Particular Reference to the City of Columbus, 1797–1936," in *Abstract of Doctoral Dissertations,* No. 31 (Columbus: The Ohio State University Press, 1940), p. 308.

the limited-line store began to push it out of the East, although as late as 1860 it was important in other parts of the country. Although the general store may still do as much as 0.5 percent of our total retail business, its sales are confined mainly to certain agricultural sections and some suburban areas. Even here, its percentage of total retail sales is declining, and this trend will probably continue.

The limited-line store[8]

The limited-line store, a nondepartmentized store having the bulk of its sales in a certain broad line of merchandise, such as food or dry goods, is not a new development. As early as 1789 the *Boston Directory* indicated that limited-line stores could be found in fields such as bakery goods, books and stationery, boots and shoes, china and glassware, drugs, dry goods, groceries, hardware, jewelry, lumber, millinery, ship chandlery, and tobacco. With the development of industries to provide merchandise formerly made in the home, and with the growth of cities in which they could operate profitably, there was an increase in both the number and the kinds of limited-line stores. Beginning about 1835, the wholesale manufacture of men's clothing began; and by the late forties, men's clothing stores were fairly common. The village shoemaker gave way to the factory; and by the late fifties, retail shoe stores appeared in the larger cities. For 1860 a list of 56 kinds of specialized retail stores has been compiled;[9] and when the first complete Census of Distribution was taken in 1929, well over 100 kinds of the limited-line store were listed. This institution is the typical kind of store in present-day retailing.

During the first half of the 19th century, when the limited-line store was developing in one field after another, it usually specialized in a narrow range of goods. In 1853 a writer in the *United States Economist* noted that "we have a dealer in hosiery, a dealer in lace, a dealer in perfumery, a dealer in pocket handkerchiefs, a dealer in shawls, and a house is just starting to keep nothing but suspenders!"[10] Following the Civil War, however, this movement reversed itself, and several closely related lines of merchandise were combined to give the limited-line stores of today.

Certainly, the stores of 1850 were anything but attractive when contrasted with modern ones. One student of business history has described the "typical retail stores of 1850" as having "small quarters, with selling largely confined to the street floor; goods piled on shelves with no attempt at attractive display; cheap and ugly fixtures; no heat in cold weather, except in the proprietor's office, and stifling temperatures in the summer; very little window dressing, if any; a dingy interior during the day and gas or oil-lamp light at night."[11] And he adds: "Misrepresentations of quality, short measure, and other sharp practices[12] were frequently encountered, and selling prices almost everywhere depended upon the customer's ability to bargain with the salesman."

Like other retail institutions, most of the early limited-line stores were indepen-

---

[8] This section owes much to Jones, "Retail Stores in the United States," pp. 134–42.

[9] Ibid., p. 136.

[10] May 28, 1853, p. 92. Quoted by R. M. Hower, "Urban Retailing 100 Years Ago," *Bulletin of the Business Historical Society,* 12 (1939), p. 92. For a picture of retailing in the 1850s, see also Hower, "Captain Macy," *Harvard Business Review,* 18 (Summer 1940), pp. 479–81.

[11] Hower, "Urban Retailing 100 Years Ago," p. 93.

[12] One of the jokes of the period tells of the groceryman who calls to his son in the cellar: "Sand the sugar, water the vinegar, and get up stairs for evening prayer." Presbrey, *History and Development of Advertising,* pp. 297–98.

dent establishments. Since they were generally quite small, they found it most convenient to purchase their goods from a nearby wholesaler, who, in turn, bought from the manufacturer. These retailers often extended credit to customers and offered delivery service, but their small size made it impossible for them to give their customers the many services offered by present-day large department stores. Although most limited-line stores are still independent and small and offer a limited number of services, it should be noted that the majority of the chain store systems of this country are made up of limited-line stores. Thus, we find chain store organizations operating food stores, drugstores, millinery shops, candy stores, and others. This development is discussed below.

Large-scale retailers

Types. The *department store*—a retail store which handles a wide variety of lines of merchandise such as women's ready-to-wear and accessories, men's and boys' wear, piece goods, small wares, and home furnishings, and which is organized into separate departments for purposes of promotion, service, accounting, and control —is largely a product of the post–Civil War period. Its development did not take place until large cities and mass production made it a suitable and needed retail establishment. Beginning in the late 1860s, however, and especially in the years immediately following the depression of 1873, the department store grew rapidly until about 1920. Since then, few new large department stores have been established, except as suburban free-standing units or in outlying shopping centers, although sales have increased significantly as a result of these *branch stores.* Along with the growth of the department store has come the development of the large *departmentized specialty store,* which is especially important in the retailing of men's and women's clothing and accessories on a departmental plan of organization. It renders many services similar to those of the department store.[13]

Modern *mail-order retailing* was an even later development than the department store. As early as 1870, E. C. Allen was selling washing powder, engravings, and novelties by mail from Augusta, Maine; but Montgomery Ward & Company did not come into existence until 1872, and Sears, Roebuck and Company dates from a watch and jewelry mail-order business begun in Minneapolis in 1886. Following these early beginnings, other successful mail-order firms were founded; and soon after the turn of the century they had become important enough to throw a real scare into the small country merchants. In a number of communities, these retailers organized "trade at home" clubs and made it a practice to obtain and burn mail-order catalogs. Later, independent merchants also fought the expansion of chain stores in their communities.

Although the original *chain store* company can be traced back to the year 1859, when a Mr. Gilman opened a tea store in New York City, actually the growth of the chain store is even more recent than that of the department store or the mail-order business. Its main growth dates from the second decade of the present century. Partly in response to this development, formerly independent retailers, especially those operating limited-line stores, have joined together—sometimes with wholesalers—to conduct group buying and other activities. The resulting organizations, known as *cooperative* and *voluntary chains,* have continued to expand to the present time.

---

[13] Specific examples of this type of store are Lord & Taylor, New York City; I. Magnin & Company, San Francisco; and Maurice L. Rothschild & Co., Chicago.

Marketing: Principles and methods

During and since the thirties, *supermarkets* have been established, first by independents and later by chain operators. Basically, most of these stores are in the food field, but some are in drugs and women's apparel—and even the so-called "food supermarkets" usually handle many nonfood lines of merchandise. Finally, the past 20 years have seen the rapid spread of *discount houses* (i.e., mass merchandisers). While they were originally devoted mainly to the sale of appliances, furniture, and other consumer durable goods at below-normal prices, "soft goods" and foods now account for an important share of their volume. Like the supermarkets, some discount houses are operated as independent stores and others as units of chains.[14] As to location, some are free standing while others are in shopping centers and in central business districts.

Mass production and mass retailing. The emergence of these forms of large-scale retailing parallels that of large-scale production in industry. The production of vast quantities of goods required a mass system of distribution, and large-scale retailers meet this demand.

Shifts in marketing power. Large-scale retailing, as noted in Chapter 3, has brought about shifts in marketing power. In the early days of small manufacturers and small retailers, it was comparatively easy for the wholesaler to dominate the marketing scene. The manufacturer was too busy with production problems to spend time in developing a market. He left that to the wholesaler, who was in a position to drive hard bargains with the manufacturer, since his threat to buy from another producer was enough to "bring him into line."

Gradually, the power shifted from the wholesaler to the manufacturer. The latter, having enlarged his plant and put in order his production organization, was able to devote time to marketing. He showed his dissatisfaction with the wholesalers' domination by placing his own brand name on his product to build goodwill for himself; he utilized widespread advertising to sell his merchandise; he began to bypass the wholesaler and sell directly to the retailer; and in a smaller number of cases, he even avoided the merchant-retailer and went directly to the ultimate consumer. The result was a period during which the manufacturer dominated both the wholesaler and the retailer.

The development of large-scale retailing gave rise to a further struggle for control, with the retailer attempting to replace the manufacturer as the dominant figure. Large retail concerns able to bargain for all or a substantial part of the output of a producer are in a far different position than the small retailer. Many of them have developed their own private brands and have obtained widespread consumer acceptance for them.[15] Moreover, they can threaten the manufacturer with setting up their own factories if prices are not satisfactory. Thus, the General Foods Corporation, a merger of a number of noncompetitive manufacturers, was formed partly to permit its constituent manufacturers to cope better with the bargaining power of the chain stores. Although in many fields the manufacturer is retaining the dominance he had won from the wholesaler and in some cases is even strengthening it, one can safely say that the power of the retailer has been greatly increased by the development of large-scale retail organizations.

---

[14] Some of the discount house chains are owned by long-established chains—for example, the Woolco stores of the F. W. Woolworth Company and the K-Mart stores of the S. S. Kresge Company.

[15] Private brands account for 20 percent of all sales by the Great Atlantic & Pacific Tea Company, 50 percent of W. T. Grant sales, and over 90 percent at Sears, Roebuck and Company and Montgomery Ward & Company. For additional discussion, see D. J. Duncan, C. F. Phillips, and S. C. Hollander, *Modern Retailing Management* (Homewood, Ill.: Richard D. Irwin, Inc., 1972), pp. 393–94.

Automatic vending machines

U.S. retailers have traditionally relied on salespeople to sell merchandise to ultimate consumers. Among the exceptions to this practice are mail-order houses and firms operating self-service stores, which are discussed in Chapter 9. Another exception is the retailer who sells through automatic or coin-operated vending machines.

Current status. The use of vending machines as a method of retailing has grown slowly but steadily since the late twenties. Although census data show sales through vending machines of $2.04 billion, or about 0.67 percent of all retail sales, these figures considerably understate the importance of this method of retailing. Many vending machines are located in stores, and their sales are reported in the figures for these establishments. Vending machines probably actually dispense merchandise valued at more than $6 billion annually, and the total may well reach over the $7 billion level in the next few years.[16] The industry is also expanding in Europe.

For many years, automatic vending was limited chiefly to the sale of such items as cigarettes, pay telephone services, and candy, and these items are still significant. As shown in Table 7–1, cigarettes represent the largest dollar volume for any one

TABLE 7–1
Vending machine sales by major type of item, 1970

Item	Sales
Packaged confections	$ 671,314,000
Bulk confections	304,416,000
Cigarettes	2,116,506,000
Cigars	18,208,000
Soft drinks (cups)	379,623,000
Soft drinks (bottles, cans)	1,117,255,000
Hot drinks	471,795,000
Ice cream	50,513,000
Milk	152,567,000
Hot canned foods	70,678,000
Prepared foods	223,923,000
All others	582,531,000
Total	$6,159,329,000

Source: G. R. Schreiber, "1971 Census of the [Vending] Industry," *Vend,* May 1971, p. 37.

product sold by this method. But milk, fruit and vegetable juices, shoeshines, ice cream, postage stamps, soft drinks, restroom facilities, insurance policies, hosiery, jewelry, men's shorts and handkerchiefs, novelties, railroad tickets, car-parking spaces, and car-washing services are also obtainable today through these machines. Technological advancements in quick freezing of foods, dehumidification, and electric cooking have enabled operators to enter the frozen-food business, to serve hot sandwiches and beverages, and to dispense complete meals, with the result that machines are widely used for in-plant feeding. In some areas, vending machines are being

---

[16] U.S. Bureau of the Census, *1963 Census of Business, Retail Trade: United States Summary,* BC 63–RAI (Washington, D.C.: Government Printing Office, 1965), pp. 1–7 and 1–8; and G. R. Schreiber, "1971 Census of the [Vending] Industry," *Vend,* 25 (May 1971), pp. 33–64.

Marketing: Principles and methods

placed in supermarket and shopping center parking lots where they will be available for round-the-clock selling.

The future of vending. The fact that vending machines are in wide use almost everywhere people tend to congregate is evidence of their practicality and acceptance by consumers. They are of special value in the retailing of relatively low-priced and highly standardized convenience goods and in providing a source of supply when stores are not open or are not located nearby. Sales through coin-operated machines should continue to gain as the machines are improved and adapted to additional items, as coin-change devices become more widespread, and as vending companies attain a higher level of efficiency, in part through mergers and internal expansion.

Yet there is little likelihood that the automatic vending machine will revolutionize the retail distribution of many kinds of goods.[17] Relatively few products have all the characteristics necessary for sale through machines, and consumers dislike the fact that they can neither examine products prior to the purchase nor return them to the machine. Vending also involves a relatively high expense-to-sales ratio—the machines themselves are costly, and both maintenance and servicing are expensive.

Changing retail institutions: A summary

The history of retailing depicts changing institutions in an effort to fit retail establishments to the needs of the changing marketing and economic systems. The trading post gave way to the general store and to the "tin" peddler. The peddler gave way to the general store; but as the limited-line store began to develop, it gradually pushed the general store out of well-populated districts until it exists now largely as a small-town retail institution. Since the Civil War, large-scale retailing has come to play an increasing part in distribution, which has put the retailer in a much stronger position than he held earlier. Finally, there has occurred a limited growth of retailing through the automatic vending machine.

Current methods of retailing. Retailing in the United States is currently carried on by at least four distinct methods. The first and most important of these is through the retail store, to which the customer comes to make selections or from which he orders by telephone or by mail. About 97 percent of all retail sales is made in this manner. The second method is retailing by mail, in which orders are solicited by catalogs, advertising in publications, and correspondence, with shipments by mail, express, or freight. This method, illustrated by the mail-order house, accounts for about 1 percent of all retail sales. House-to-house selling, the third method, is responsible for nearly another 1 percent of total retail sales. Finally, 0.67 percent of all retail volume is handled by automatic vending machines, but this figure might somewhat exceed 1 percent if sales through vending machines located in retail stores were included.

The retail institution cycle. The evolution of retailing tends to support the thesis that there is a "wheel" or cycle in retailing institutions. Periodically, an innovator comes along with some new retailing ideas. Although at the outset he is

ridiculed, scorned, condemned as "illegitimate" . . . he attracts the public on the basis of the price appeal made possible by the low operating costs inherent in his innovation. As he goes along he trades up, improves the quality of his merchandise, improves the appearance and

---

[17] M. L. Morris, "Growth Parameters for Automatic Vending," *Journal of Retailing,* 44 (Fall 1968), pp. 31–45.

standing of his store, attains greater respectability. Then, if he is successful, comes the period of growth, the period when he is taking business away from the established distribution channels that have clung to the old methods. Repeatedly something like this has happened in American distribution. The department stores took [business] away from the smaller merchants in the cities in the late 19th and early 20th century; the original grocery chains took it away from the old wholesaler–small-retailer combination; the supermarkets then began taking it away from the original grocery chains to the extent that the latter had to climb on the supermarket bandwagon. And today the discount houses and the supermarkets are taking it away from the department stores and variety chains.

During this process of growth the institution rapidly becomes respectable in the eyes of both consumers and investors, but at the same time its capital investment increases and its operating costs tend to rise. Then the institution enters the stage of maturity. It has a larger physical plant, more elaborate store fixtures and displays, and it undertakes greater promotional efforts. At this stage the institution finds itself competing primarily with other similar institutions rather than with old-line competitors. The maturity phase soon tends to be followed by topheaviness, too great conservatism, a decline in the rate of return on investment, and eventual vulnerability. Vulnerability to what? Vulnerability to the next revolution of the wheel, to the next fellow who has a bright idea and who starts his business on a low-cost basis, slipping in under the umbrella that the oldline institutions have hoisted.

Sometimes the wheel turns slowly and at other times it turns faster. In the department store field the revolution has been very slow, but in the food distribution field the wheel has been turning rapidly. The point is that sooner or later marketing institutions seem to arrive at the point of vulnerability, and then they face the dilemma that they must either innovate and evolve or be content with fighting a rearguard action and dropping into positions of secondary importance. For instance, the strictly service type of retail grocery store, with emphasis on credit, telephone, and delivery service, has all but vanished from the scene. Likewise the old-time service wholesale grocer who failed to innovate in the direction of supermarket or voluntary chain operation is today almost extinct.[18]

RETAILERS IN THE UNITED STATES TODAY

Retail establishments and sales

During 1967 over 1.76 million establishments carried on retailing by one or more of the four main methods, and their total sales were some $310 billion.[19] To provide perspective, Table 7–2 gives fairly comparable information on the number of stores and retail sales for selected years beginning with 1929. In examining these figures, bear in mind the substantial decline in the price level between 1929 and 1933 and the increase following the latter year, especially since 1939. By no means has the physical volume of goods sold at retail fluctuated as much as the dollar sales. It is evident that the past quarter of a century has seen a striking increase in both dollar and physical retail sales. Since the gain in total number of stores has been relatively small, the average sales per store has shown a rapid rise.

What kinds of goods are sold by these retailers? What percentage of retail sales is by independent stores and by chain or multiunit stores? How large are retail establishments? It is to these questions that we now turn our attention.

---

[18] M. P. McNair, "Significant Trends and Developments in the Postwar Period," in A. B. Smith (ed.), *Competitive Distribution in a Free-Level Economy and Its Implications for the University* (Pittsburgh: University of Pittsburgh Press, 1958), pp. 17–18.

[19] Throughout this volume the *Census of Business* is relied upon for the number of retail establishments. The student should be aware, however, that there is some evidence the census "seriously understates the number of retail establishments, both in total and in most lines of trade." See W. E. Cox, Jr., "The 'Census' of Business. Some Contrary Evidence," *Journal of Marketing*, 31 (July 1967), pp. 47–51.

TABLE 7–2
Stores and sales, selected years, 1929–1970

Year	Number of stores (000 omitted)	Total sales (000,000 omitted)	Average sales per store
1929	1,476	$ 48,330	$ 33,000
1933	1,526	25,037	16,000
1935	1,588	32,791	21,000
1939	1,770	42,042	24,000
1948	1,770	130,521	74,000
1954	1,722	169,968	99,000
1958	1,788	199,646	112,000
1963	1,708	244,202	143,000
1967	1,763	310,214	175,000
1970	n.a.	364,571	n.a.

Source: *Census of Business.* Not included in the 1963 sales figures are the $1.8 billion made by commissaries, exchanges, and eating places operated for military personnel by the Department of Defense. Sales in Alaska and Hawaii are included for 1963 and later years. The 1970 figure is from U.S. Department of Commerce, *Survey of Current Business,* June 1971, p. S–5.

Sales by kind of retail business

Table 7–3 shows retail sales classified by the main kind of business in which each establishment is engaged. The importance of food retailing is immediately apparent when the dollar sales given are seen as percentages of total sales. Food stores in 1967 accounted for over 22 percent of all sales, or just over 30 percent when eating and drinking places are included. Automotive retailers were responsible for over 18 percent, with filling stations handling 7 percent more. Department stores—which some students erroneously think of as the "typical" retailer—transact less than 11 percent of retail volume.

TABLE 7–3
Retail sales by kind of business, selected years, 1948–1970 (billions of dollars)

Kind of business	1948	1954	1958	1963	1967	1970
Food	$ 29.2	$ 39.8	$ 49.3	$ 57.1	$ 70.3	$ 81.5
Automotive group	20.1	29.9	31.9	45.4	55.6	62.8
Filling stations	6.5	10.7	14.2	17.8	22.7	26.5
Eating and drinking places	10.6	13.1	15.3	18.4	23.8	27.9
Apparel and accessory stores	9.7	11.1	12.6	14.0	16.7	20.4
Department stores	9.4	10.6	13.4	20.5	32.3	38.5
Lumber-building materials group	11.1	13.1	14.3	14.6	17.2	14.5
Furniture and appliance stores	6.6	9.0	10.1	10.9	14.5	16.8
Variety stores (limited prices)	2.5	3.1	3.6	4.5	5.4	7.0
General and general merchandise stores	3.9	4.2	4.9	4.9	5.8	(n.a.)
Drug and proprietary stores	4.0	5.3	6.8	8.5	10.9	12.8
All others	15.2	20.1	24.0	27.6	35.0	55.8
Totals	$128.8	$170.0	$200.4	$244.2	$310.2	$364.5

Source: Same as Table 7–2, except that the figures have been adjusted to the more recent census definitions for each type of outlet.

Table 7–3 classifies by "kind of business" the 97 percent of retail sales accounted for by retail stores. The 3 percent transacted by nonstore retailers (door-to-door distributors, operators of merchandise vending machines, and mail-order houses) is not classified but reported in the "all others" category.

Sales by independent and chain stores

A large majority of retail stores are independently owned, but chain stores account for a disproportionately large percentage of all retail sales. More precise figures are presented in Table 7–4. Since it has taken the chains over 30 years to increase

TABLE 7–4
Sales by independent and chain stores

	Percent of all stores	Percent of all sales
One-store retailers	88	60
Two-or-more–store retailers	12	40
Totals.......................	100	100

their share of total sales from 30 to 40 percent, it does not seem that the field of retailing will soon become dominated by a few giant organizations.

Size of retail establishments

The typical retail establishment in the United States is very small. Measured by number of employees, the 1967 Census of Business revealed that 78 percent of all establishments in operation on March 12, 1967, had five or fewer paid employees, and an additional 9.2 percent employed fewer than nine workers. At the other extreme, about 1.3 percent of the establishments had 50 or more employees.[20] When annual sales are used as the measure of size, nearly 49 percent of all stores in 1967 had sales of less than $50,000 for the year, and they transacted about 5.7 percent of all retail business. At the opposite end of the scale, about 6 percent of the stores transacted 57.2 percent of retail business, with each of these units having annual sales of $500,000 or over.[21] Thus it is clear that the retail structure is made up of a large number of very small establishments, a moderate number of medium-sized ones, and a small number of very large stores.

Small-store operating difficulties. The difficulties of operating a very small store so as to make a profit are not easily overcome, even in periods of full employment and high income. For example, consider the hypothetical case of a store with sales of $100 per day (6 day week) or $31,200 annually.

---

[20] U.S. Bureau of the Census, *1967 Census of Business, Vol. I, Retail Trade: Subject Reports* (Washington, D.C.: Government Printing Office, 1971), p. 3–1

[21] Ibid., pp. xvii, 2–2.

Marketing: Principles and methods

```
Sales .............................................................    $31,200
Less cost of merchandise ..........................................     23,400
                                                                      ─────────
    Gross margin .................................................    $ 7,800
Less expenses, before payroll:
  Insurance, taxes, repairs, upkeep, light,
    heat, advertising ............................... $2,000
  Rent (4 percent of sales)......................... 1,248    $ 3,248
                                                      ──────    ─────────
    Balance ......................................             $ 4,552
```

In this store, $4,552 is left for payroll and profit. Even if the proprietor operates the store without outside help, it will provide less than $100 per week for salary and profit.

Why do such stores continue in business? Some are operated by individuals otherwise incapable of employment, whose living expenses are met from sources other than store earnings. Others exist to sell the products of the farm, dairy, or manufacturing business in which the proprietor is primarily engaged. Still others take only the spare time of the proprietor or members of his family, who are primarily occupied otherwise or are employed in highly seasonal occupations. Many of them are largely personal-service businesses in which merchandise sales are incidental, such as automobile paint shops or repair shops. Or, like restaurants, they are in fields where a substantial part of the gross margin goes for preparation of merchandise within the establishment. In such instances a much greater gross margin may be obtained than is indicated in the foregoing hypothetical case.

GEOGRAPHIC DISTRIBUTION OF RETAIL SALES

The shifts in population discussed in Chapter 5—from one section of the country to another, from farms to cities, and from central cities to suburban areas—have had noticeable impact on retailing. Relatively few people are willing to travel any appreciable distance to make retail purchases. There has been a fairly close correlation between the percentage of population and the percentage of retail sales in each of the census geographic areas. New England, for example, has 5.7 percent of the total population and 6.1 percent of the retail trade; Middle Atlantic, 18.5 and 18.7; West South-Central, 9.9 and 8.8; and Pacific, 12.8 and 14.1. By the same reasoning, 64.5 percent of the U.S. population is now concentrated in 233 Standard Metropolitan Statistical Areas (SMSAs) accounting for just over 70 percent of retail sales.[22]

The suburban movement has been especially important in bringing about a relative loss of retail sales of stores located in central business districts (CBDs). Well aware of the consequences, some stores have abandoned their downtown stores to concentrate on suburban locations. Others have supplemented their downtown locations with outlying units and have sought to protect their downtown stores through supplying ample parking space, undertaking joint promotions, providing free transportation, and adopting similar measures. In some cities, business and the national government have cooperated to institute long-range, expensive, and extensive rebuilding of CBDs.

─────────

[22] In essence, a Standard Metropolitan Statistical Area is a county or group of contiguous counties with a total population of at least 100,000 and a central city with a minimum population of 50,000. These figures are based upon the *1967 Census of Business* and comparable figures as given in the U.S. Bureau of Census, *Statistical Abstract of the United States, 1970* (91st ed.; Washington, D.C.: Government Printing Office, 1970), pp. xiii, 16, 839, 854, and 883.

Retail structure of the metropolitan area

While there are significant differences in the retail structures of the 233 SMSAs in the United States, it is possible to present a structure analysis that is applicable in a general way to all of them. Each area seems to contain an older central business district (CBD), one or more older secondary shopping districts, and a variety of planned shopping centers, as well as free-standing stores and clusters of neighborhood businesses.

The central business district. The old heart of the retail structure of the city, which is an integral part of each SMSA, is the central business district. Most means of intracity public transportation and major road arteries converge on the CBD. In most cities it is composed of two areas—the core and the frame. The main mode of movement in the core is pedestrian, because the core is quite compact, usually not exceeding a square mile, and it has grown vertically rather than horizontally.[23] In the core are concentrated many of the area's leading shopping and specialty-goods stores —department stores, departmentized specialty stores, and limited-line independent and chain stores engaged in selling such merchandise as apparel, furniture, shoes, and jewelry. These stores are typically much larger in both floor space and sales than the average store in the city, and they draw a far greater part of their total business from nonresidents than do other city retailers. In addition, there are a number of convenience-goods retailers—drugstores, cigar stores, and grocery stores.

Although the area covered by the CBD core is small, it draws customers from the entire SMSA, so that its total sales form an appreciable although declining part of the total sales of the SMSA. The CBD frame area is less intensively utilized and less compact. Retail stores needing larger display or immediately adjacent storage space—automotive dealers, home furnishing outlets, lumber and building material suppliers, wholesale outlets—may locate in the frame area instead of in outlying areas.

The older secondary shopping districts. The older secondary shopping districts of the SMSA came into existence mainly as the city increased in population and spread over a broader area. Gradually it became more convenient for some of the people to buy at least part of their shopping and specialty goods outside the older CBD. Consequently, stores located on neighborhood business streets expanded to supply more of the wants of the people living in the vicinity. Several centers which have developed in this manner may be found in most large cities, located on the old main traffic arteries leading from residential districts to the CBD. Others of these secondary shopping districts developed within the smaller towns that have gradually been absorbed by the SMSA. Regardless of their origin, to a considerable degree the kinds of goods sold are similar to those sold in the main shopping district, but the stores are smaller, selection may be more limited, people are not attracted from such wide areas, and the sale of convenience goods is relatively more important.

Shopping centers. A major response to the suburban growth of cities and the principal reason for the relative decline of retail sales in CBDs has been the rapid growth of outlying planned shopping centers. These centers usually consist of one or more anchor or generator stores, such as department stores, which generate traffic, with a cluster of smaller stores and extensive parking facilities in readily accessible locations. Unlike the older CBDs and secondary shopping districts, these centers are carefully planned, developed, and controlled by one organization. There are basically

---

[23] R. F. Murphy and J. C. Vance, Jr., "A Comparative Study of Nine Central Business Districts," *Economic Geography, 30* (October 1954), pp. 302–30.

two kinds of center sponsors: (1) real estate organizations, such as Taubman Company, Rouse Company, Irvine Company, and Ogden Development Corporation, which expect to make a profit on their centers by leasing all the units to others, and (2) large retailers, alone and jointly through subsidiary corporations, such as May Realty and Investment Company (May Department Stores) and Alstore Realty Corporation (Allied Stores Corporation), who are generators in their own centers but lease out the other space.

In 1971 there were an estimated 12,000 shopping centers in the United States. They had sales of $117 billion or approximately one third of all retail sales.[24]

Shopping centers have been classified into three major types: neighborhood, community, and regional. This classification is based largely on the breadth and depth of the assortment of products and services they sell and on the size of the market from which they draw their customers.

1. *Neighborhood shopping centers.* These are the most numerous but the smallest of the three types of centers, usually occupying under 100,000 square feet of retail space and containing from 5 to 15 stores. They specialize in convenience goods and services and draw most of their customers from the immediate neighborhood (within five minutes' traveling time) around the center. A grocery supermarket typically serves as the generator or anchor store. Strung out from it is likely to be some combination of drugstore, variety store, florist, barber and beauty shop, laundry, dry cleaner, bakery, snack bar, or appliance repair shop, and a free-standing gas station. While initially planned, the neighborhood shopping center frequently falls into a loose coalition of stores. On occasion, a shopping goods retailer (a shoe store or a dress shop) may be found in such a center, but his likelihood of survival is low because he is not grouped with retailers of similar products. He is outside consumers' regular shopping patterns for shoes or dresses.

2. *Community shopping centers.* These are the intermediate-size centers containing from 100,000 to around 300,000 square feet of leasable area and typically housing 15 to 25 retail stores. They usually are anchored by a department store branch or a full-stock variety store such as W. T. Grant, F. W. Woolworth, or J. J. Newberry. The other outlets are likely to include the types of stores found in the neighborhood center plus a shoe store or two, several clothing stores (for men, women, and children), a jewelry store, a restaurant, and perhaps a movie theater. It offers a mixture of shopping and convenience goods and services.

The community shopping center draws most of its customers from a radius of one and a half to two miles, with very few customers regularly traveling more than three to four miles. The two most common configurations for community centers are the L or an I with the generator at the origin of the L or near the center of the I. Figure 7–2 depicts these arrangements.

3. *Regional shopping centers.* These are the largest planned centers. The largest one, Woodfield, in Schaumburg, Illinois, contains 2 million square feet and 215 shops, including the largest stores Sears, Roebuck and Company and J. C. Penney Company have ever built and the largest Marshall Field and Company suburban store. According to its developer, it was designed to compete for shoppers with downtown Chicago. There are now a number of centers with over 1 million square feet of retail space and over 100 shops. More commonly though, regional centers contain from 400,000 to 1 million square feet of leasable space and contain from 40 to 100 stores.

---

[24] "Shopping Centers Grow into Shopping Cities," *Business Week*, September 4, 1971, p. 34.

FIGURE 7–2
Two community shopping center arrangements

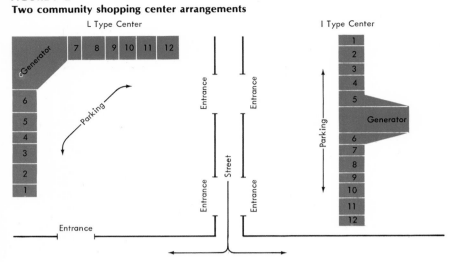

Regional centers are further distinguished from the other two types in that their primary emphasis is on shopping goods and services, and they attract customers from relatively large market areas. Most of their customers come from within a 30-minute driving radius, but the larger regional centers draw from a considerably greater distance. Regional centers are further distinguished from community centers in that they usually have two or more generators (anchors), with some regional centers containing four or five. Two regional center configurations illustrating multiple generators are shown in Figure 7–3.

It has become more common in recent years for regional center developers to include high-rise office buildings, apartment complexes, and hotels or motels in close proximity to their retail structures. For some time it has also been common practice to include medical arts centers, professional buildings, and financial centers in the regional centers.

Some of the newer regional centers that readers might have the opportunity to examine, besides Woodfield, are North Park in Dallas; Newport Center south of Los Angeles; South Hills Village in Pittsburgh; Franklin Park Mall in Toledo, Ohio; Highland Mall in Austin, Texas; Perimeter Mall in Atlanta, Georgia; The Mall in Columbia, Maryland; Eastridge in the San Jose area; and two downtown centers—Broadway Plaza in Los Angeles and one in Worcester, Massachusetts.[25]

Large free-standing stores.   Another type of retail location is the large free-standing store. Normally located in the suburban parts of the metropolitan areas, this type of store is usually a discount or mass-merchandise store, a department store, or a departmentized specialty store. It is typically a unit of a chain or a branch of a downtown store.

1. *The free-standing discount or mass-merchandise house.*   The fact that discount houses are not always welcomed into the newer shopping centers has forced

---

[25] For a study of seven major Cleveland shopping centers see W. E. Cox, Jr., and E. F. Cooke, "Other Dimensions Involved in Shopping Center Preference," *Journal of Marketing, 34* (October 1970), pp. 12–17.

FIGURE 7–3
Regional shopping center configurations with two and four generator stores

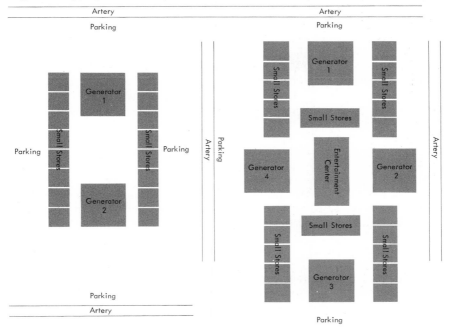

some discount retailers to turn to the free-standing store as an alternative. For many others, however, this decision is a matter of choice; the real estate vice president of S. S. Kresge Company states that for K-Marts "we favor free-standing units."[26] Back of this policy is the belief of many discount retailers that the free-standing store gives them a lower rental, complete freedom of choice on merchandise lines (in centers, merchandise restrictions are typically included in leases), better parking facilities (usually around a greater part of the store building), and a larger flow of traffic for the types and quality of merchandise they offer for sale. By "ringing a city" with units (for example, E. J. Korvette, Inc., has used the "cluster" approach around New York, St. Louis, Chicago, and Baltimore), a substantial promotional program is possible at a relatively low cost per store.

2. *The department store and the departmentized specialty store.* During the late 1920s and the 1930s, as Sears, Roebuck and Company began to develop its chain of department stores, the firm's management correctly interpreted the trend to the suburbs and began to open free-standing units in such areas. At the same time, a few downtown department and departmentized specialty stores started to serve these areas through branches, that is, stores usually smaller than (and dominated by) the parent stores.

---

[26] "Nailing Down Locations Is the Key to Kresge's Expansion," *Chain Store Age* (Supermarket Executives Edition), December 1965, p. E15. In contrast, practically all of the Woolco units of the F. W. Woolworth Company are in shopping centers.

Today most department stores prefer to locate their branch stores in shopping centers rather than free-standing locations. However, grocery supermarkets, home furnishing retailers, and some other departmentized specialty stores will use free-standing store locations.

Neighborhood business streets and plazas. Far more numerous than any of the foregoing types of locations in the metropolitan area are neighborhood business streets, made up mainly of convenience-goods stores located one next to the other or with only reasonably small distances between them. Here are many grocery stores, superettes, meat markets, small bakery shops, fruit and vegetable stores, small variety stores, and drugstores, although a few of the smaller shopping- and specialty-goods stores are located on these streets. In the majority of cases these streets follow the main arteries of traffic throughout both the city and its satellite towns and villages. The stores are relatively small and attract business from the immediately surrounding area.

In recent years a development somewhat comparable to the controlled shopping center has taken place in regard to neighborhood business streets. Instead of developing gradually as in the past, in some areas a large building—sometimes known as a "shopping plaza"—has been constructed and its various sections rented out to several retailers. Ample parking space is usually provided.

In spite of competition from stores in other parts of the metropolitan area, those located on neighborhood business streets have demonstrated a remarkable vitality. One student of retailing trends attributed their continued success to the fact that people "don't always select the best buys at the lowest prices. They don't anticipate their needs, and consequently are always patronizing some neighborhood store to fill in what they forgot on an orderly shopping trip."[27]

The future of the central business district. The decentralization of shopping areas has proceeded so rapidly that it gives rise to the question: Does it eventually mean the end of the CBD? Victor Gruen, head of the well-known firm of architects, engineers, and planners, believes that the city will end up "like a doughnut—all the dough on the outside, and a hole in the middle" unless downtown is adapted "to new business sources and forces, and (is set free) from strangulation by (the) automobile. . . ."[28] Both retailers and customers agree that today's downtown presents great problems for them: Customer access difficulties, limited parking, high land cost, substantial property taxes, high building cost, difficulties in moving merchandise into the store and in delivering it to the customer, split ownership of land and buildings, old retail structures. No wonder Montgomery Ward & Company's corporate manager of real estate as early as 1964 said: ". . . Time is running out for most downtowns that do not have realistic plans in process."[29] The late Frank Lloyd Wright even proclaimed that the CBD would disappear.

We believe that the CBD, while relatively less important than in past decades, will remain of great significance to the retailer. Some observers are of the opinion that, as urban renewal programs are completed and downtown high-rise residential buildings are constructed, middle-income families who have moved to the suburbs

---

[27] P. D. Martineau, "Customers' Shopping Center Habits Change Retailing," *Editor & Publisher* (October 26, 1964), pp. 16, 56.

[28] Quoted by Walter Guzzardi, Jr., "An Architect of Environments," *Fortune* (January 1962), p. 136.

[29] Quoted by S. O. Kaylin, "Research and Development Program: Key to Ward's Dynamic Leap," *Chain Store Age* (Supermarket Executives Edition) (December 1964), p. E16.

may return to the cities.[30] In addition, low-cost housing subsidized by the government may induce many families to remain in the cities.

In the larger cities the great congregation of stores in the downtown area offers a breadth of merchandise assortment not matched by the largest of the planned shopping centers. The desire to "make a day" of a shopping trip will continue to bring many from the outlying areas to the central shopping area, while the thousands who work in that area or who come to the city as out-of-town visitors will continue to find it convenient to buy there.

Moreover, in many cities the downtown merchants, in cooperation with transit authorities and city-federal governments, are making efforts to increase the attractiveness of downtown shopping. Somewhat typical is little Keokuk, Iowa (pop. 14,459), where an urban renewal grant was utilized to clear the entire south end of the CBD and build an enclosed mall-type community shopping center in its place. In a similar redevelopment in Worcester, Massachusetts, a regional shopping center opened its first doors in the CBD in 1971. In downtown Los Angeles, the Broadway Plaza is a single-block complex of about 40 stores, an office building, and a hotel.[31] Express highways leading directly to the heart of the city are being built, and public transportation systems are being modernized and unified to give better schedules. More downtown parking facilities are becoming available, through additional parking lots, underground developments, and ramps or mechanical devices to provide above-the-ground parking. A combination of fringe parking lots plus public transportation (in a few instances, without charge) to the CBD is being used in some cities. Downtown retailers are modernizing their stores, establishing shopping malls, adopting night hours, and joining together on promotional programs similar to those of shopping centers. In the light of such developments, there is far greater optimism among many merchants about the future of downtown areas than has prevailed for many years.

EXPENSES OF RETAILERS

Although recent reports of the Bureau of the Census have not included an average retail expense figure, over three decades ago expenses were reported as 23.9 percent of total sales.[32] This figure covered all wages (including an imputed wage for the proprietor), rent, interest on borrowed money, taxes, insurance, administration, office expenses, and other expenses exclusive of payments for merchandise. Interest on capital invested, except for borrowed money, was not considered; and since it obviously should be, its inclusion at 5 percent would add about 1 percent to the total expense figure. In general, then, we may say that the cost of retailing in 1935 was about 25 percent. With the inflationary trend that has existed since the date of this figure, we may reasonably assume that it is somewhat larger today. Operating expenses in chain food stores, for example, advanced from 16.77 percent of sales in 1955 to 20.97 percent in 1967–1968.[33] The validity of the assumption is also suggested by Table 7–5.

---

[30] Professor W. L. C. Wheaton, quoted by Mitchell Gordon, "Shape of the Future," *Wall Street Journal,* January 30, 1967, p. 1.

[31] "Shopping Centers Grow into Shopping Cities," *Business Week* (September 4, 1971), pp. 34–38.

[32] U.S. Bureau of the Census, *1935 Census of Business,* Vol. I, *Retail Distribution: Summary Statistics* (Washington, D.C.: Government Printing Office, 1937), pp. 1–16.

[33] "Food Chain Performance and Trends," *Progressive Grocer* (April 1968), p. 69.

TABLE 7–5
Operating expenses of selected retail businesses

Kind of business	Total expenses (percentage of net sales)
Appliance, radio, and television dealers	25.5
Bakeries	39.5
Bookstores	35.1
Confectionery stores	26.1
Dry goods and general merchandise stores*	26.9
Furniture stores†	38.3
Grocery stores‡	11.5
Hardware stores	29.3
Jewelry stores	47.8
Men's wear stores§	32.0
Paint and wallpaper dealers†	30.6
Shoe stores (family)	31.9
Variety stores	26.7

* Annual sales $100,000 to $200,000.
† Annual sales less than $250,000.
‡ Annual sales less than $200,000.
§ Handling men's wear only.
Source: National Cash Register Company, *Expenses in Retail Businesses* (Dayton, Ohio, n.d.).

As noted in Table 7–5, there are wide variations in the expenses of various kinds of retail business. Among other factors responsible for these variations are the sales volume of the store, the population of the place in which the store is located, and the kind of goods sold.

Influence of sales volume

Careful analysis of expense ratios of stores selling similar types of merchandise and in cities of comparable populations supports the following conclusions:[34]

1. The ratio of expenses to sales tends to fall as one goes from the very small, to the medium-sized, to the larger stores. To cite a single example, in larger cities, hardware stores with annual sales under $20,000 in one year had an expense ratio of 32.1 percent, which fell to 30.4 percent for the $20,000–$50,000-volume stores and to 24.7 percent for still larger stores.

2. The point of lowest average cost, however, is reached rather quickly in some fields. In fact, in certain cases the very largest stores operate at expense ratios considerably above those of medium-sized stores, in part because they assume more functions. They tend to buy in larger amounts and therefore to take over part of the wholesale function, and they usually render many more services than do the small stores. In contrast, the smaller store depends upon the wholesaler to undertake the cost of buying from manufacturers, storing merchandise, and extending credit. Moreover, the larger stores must advertise extensively to attract customers from a wide

---

[34] Supporting data for these conclusions are available from a variety of sources. For department and specialty stores, for example, see the annual reports of the National Retail Merchants Association, New York City; for hardware stores, those of the National Retail Hardware Association, Indianapolis, Indiana; and for furniture stores, those of the National Retail Furniture Association, Chicago.

Marketing: Principles and methods

area; they have to deliver to these widely scattered buyers; and in many cases, they offer liberal return-goods privileges and other services. All these activities increase their costs considerably.

It should be emphasized that the higher operating expense ratio for the larger stores does not necessarily result in higher prices. By partially bypassing the wholesaler and buying direct from the manufacturer, larger stores can buy more cheaply, so that even with a higher markup than small stores take, their prices may in fact be lower. Moreover, because of the greater volume of business, the large store may take a smaller margin of profit, and this also tends to keep its prices down. Many large stores, however, do sell at higher prices than their small competitors and make no attempt to conceal that fact. They maintain that their offerings of superior assortments, attractive surroundings, and a large number of customer services justify higher prices. Their sales and profit experiences seem to support this position.

Influence of population

Readily available data also make it clear that, with some exceptions, operating expenses tend to be higher in the larger than in the smaller cities. Thus the larger furniture stores in cities of less than 20,000 population operate at 31.4 percent, whereas comparable stores in somewhat larger communities operate at 36.2 percent, and in still larger cities at 38 percent.

The reasons for this trend are quite clear. In cities, competition seems to be keener, with the result that stores are forced to spend a larger percentage of their sales in advertising. Competition may also force stores to add services for which no separate charge is made against the consumer, such as additional help to give faster service and more liberal exchange privileges. Delivery service is more expensive in larger towns, since customers are scattered over a greater area and more time is lost due to heavier traffic. City stores also have to pay higher salaries, and the increase in salaries is greater proportionately than the increase in sales. Finally, rental cost also advances faster than sales.

Once again, it cannot be assumed that the higher expenses of the large city stores necessarily mean higher prices. They may or may not, depending on the circumstances; the larger volume of business in city stores may enable them to buy their merchandise for less, and they may be satisfied with a smaller profit margin.

Influence of kind of merchandise

As noted in Table 7–5, the expenses of retailing vary widely from field to field, from an average of 11.5 percent for grocery stores to 47.8 percent for jewelry stores. A study of the stores in this table, together with observation of others in various fields, indicates that among the major factors resulting in high expense ratios are the following: (1) large investment in an inventory with limited sales, as in many jewelry stores; (2) substantial amount of conversion or processing, such as is required in restaurant operation; (3) considerable individual attention to the customer; (4) high degree of technical knowledge necessary in selling; (5) cost of delivery and other "free" services; (6) large installation cost, such as that involved in electric garbage disposals; (7) special attention needed for some merchandise, such as that involved in uncrating, refinishing, and polishing furniture; and (8) operations conducted in high-rental areas. The converse of these factors results in low retail costs.

A quick glance back at Table 7–2 will establish the point that the past three decades have seen little change in the total number of stores. But this apparent stability conceals the fact that during these years, several hundred thousand retail concerns (some of which operated more than one store) went out of business and were replaced by about the same number of retail enterprises. Many of the firms going out of business do so because they fail to make a profit; in other words, the enterprise is a failure. Dun and Bradstreet reports that 10,748 businesses of all kinds failed in the year ended December 31, 1970, and 4,650 of these failures were in the retail field, almost 20 percent of them in the automotive area.[35]

Among businesses as a whole, most failures are attributable to managerial short-comings resulting from inexperience or incompetence. Such shortcomings operate so quickly that typically over half the failures occur during the first five years of operation. Retail failures follow the same pattern, with 9 out of 10 casualties accounted for by inexperience or ineptitude on the retailer's part (Table 7–6), and from 30 to 40 percent

TABLE 7–6
Why retail businesses fail, year ended December 31, 1970

Apparent cause	Percentage of firms
Neglect	2.3
Fraud	1.1
Inexperience, incompetence	89.6
Inadequate sales	45.2
Heavy operating expenses	6.5
Receivables difficulties	3.8
Inventory difficulties	6.2
Excessive fixed assets	2.7
Poor location	6.4
Competitive weakness	24.1
Other	1.5
Disaster	1.3
Reason unknown	5.7
Total number of failures	4,650

Source: *Dun's Review,* March 1971, p. 114. Since some failures are attributed to a combination of causes, percentages do not add up to 100 percent.

of the failures occurring within the first five years. Many retail stores fail because retailing is easy to enter. There are no required schools, examinations, qualifying licenses, nor union membership. Further, only limited capital is often required. Consequently, many poorly qualified, underfinanced people open retail establishments.

Failures are not pleasant, but the great ease of entry into retailing encourages competition and provides added alternatives to consumers. Retailers find it very difficult to gain and maintain anything approaching a monopolistic position.

---

[35] "Business Failures," *Dun's Review,* March 1971, p. 114, and L. R. Blau, "Measuring Business Mortality," *The Conference Board Record,* February 1971, pp. 28–32.

SOME CURRENT TRENDS IN THE RETAILING SYSTEM

Several years ago a leading authority on retailing stated that "at no time in this twentieth century has the dynamic and changing character of retail distribution been more in evidence than is the case today."[36] Developments have continued to emphasize the changes taking place, so that the retailing system exists in a state of ferment.

Change in the retailing system

Evidence has been presented indicating the basis of turmoil in the retailing system—the striking gain in retail sales; the suburban movement; the development of shopping centers; the deterioration of downtown areas and efforts to check and, if possible, to reverse this trend; the rise of metropolitan areas and megalopolises; present and future possibilities of retailing through automatic vending machines; the growing significance of fashion; and shifts in purchases as the age distribution changes in the population.

Other aspects of the present ferment in the retailing system will be made clear in the next two chapters. We shall especially note current trends for various types of retail institutions and focus attention on the newer forms of stores—bantam or convenience-type stores, branch stores, and discount houses. The growing role of self-service in the retailing system will be examined, and the increasingly competitive situation faced by the retailer will be discussed.

But there are other factors in the current revolution in the retailing system that need to be brought to the reader's attention. Representative of these factors are the following:

1. The greatest retail building and modernization program in history.
2. An increase in the floor space of the retail establishment, as evidenced in the replacement of the old-line grocery store with the modern supermarket and the ever-increasing size of the discount or mass-merchandise house.
3. Supplier competition for shelf space in retail stores, particularly in supermarkets, discount houses, and other self-service stores.
4. A trend toward Sunday and night shopping hours, which is part cause and part result of another factor—family shopping.
5. Greater emphasis on sales promotion as a means of meeting competition.
6. "Scrambled merchandising," the tendency for the retailer to broaden his lines— the food store adds nonfood items, the milkman also delivers orange juice, and the drugstore sells "everything."[37] Even the gasoline service station is adding to the variety of its products and services, many of which are not even remotely associated with automobiles—garden tools, washers and dryers, and restaurant service.[38]
7. The growth of franchising or licensing—Kentucky Fried Chicken, Baskin-Robbins, Holiday Inn, Aamco Automatic Transmissions—which has provided the

---

[36] McNair, "Significant Trends and Developments in the Postwar Period," p. 1.

[37] Some authorities suggest that there is a retail cycle or accordion during which retailers swing from narrow lines to broad lines and back again. See S. C. Hollander, "Notes on the Retail Accordion," *Journal of Retailing*, 42 (Summer 1966), pp. 29–40, 54.

[38] An excellent illustration is afforded by the F. W. Woolworth Company, which is increasing the number of its stores, establishing the Woolco discount chain, expanding its advertising, and placing greater emphasis on wearing apparel.

independent businessman with a new strength as well as a new set of head-aches.[39]

8. The rapid development of rentals. Customers are being attracted by the "rental" store or department by the continuing popularity of "do it yourself" techniques, to avoid the necessity of capital outlays, and to realize savings. Numerous types of equipment are available under rental arrangements, and automobiles are rented on a wide scale.

9. The long-run possibilities of automation in the retailing system as new technological developments make its adoption both practical and less costly. Besides automatic vending machines, it is evident in (1) current experiments with the fully automated store, (2) mechanical devices to move merchandise from receiving points to stockrooms and onto the sales floor, and (3) electronic data processing (EDP), which is already yielding benefits in such areas as accounting, merchandise control, buying, and credit operations. Some authors even see the replacement of many retail stores by a highly automated central distribution facility, with the customer engaging in push-button purchasing from the home.[40]

10. The widespread practice of leasing departments, particularly in department stores and discount houses.

11. The many mergers and acquisitions that involve retail organizations, and government activities to check those that unduly restrict competition.

12. The ever-increasing reliance on credit as a means of stimulating retail sales, with $119.7 billion consumer credit outstanding in 1970 as compared with $39 billion in 1955.[41]

SUMMARY

A good understanding of the past history of the retailing system in the United States should provide some suggestions as to future evolution. Past changes in the system have tended to be in response to changes in buyers' needs and in the marketing and economic systems. The trading post gave way to the traveling peddler who gave way to the general store, as population concentrations increased, increased supplies of goods became available, and travel conditions eased. The general store was slowly squeezed out as population was concentrated more thickly and as more goods became available. To gain larger market shares and profits, retailers carried deeper assortments and differentiated their offerings in their attempts to be unique from the increasing number of other stores.

Comparable changes are ongoing within the retailing system of today, at an ever faster pace. These changes reflect the competitive efforts of merchants to take advantage of unserved consumer needs that result from changes in the environment of the retailing system. Such efforts often cause retailing institutions to follow an evolutionary cycle called the "wheel of retailing."

Retailing fits in the overall marketing system between the consumer level and the wholesale middlemen. The principal objective of the retailing system is to make

---

[39] For a penetrating look at franchising, see G. G. Burch, "Franchising's Troubled Dream World," *Fortune* (March 1970), pp. 116 ff.

[40] A. F. Doody and W. R. Davidson, "Next Revolution in Retailing," *Harvard Business Review,* 45 (May–June 1967), pp. 4–20 ff.

[41] *Statistical Abstract of the United States,* 1970, p. 450. For some additional trends, see W. Gross, "Retailing in the Seventies: A Projection of Current Trends," *Baylor Business Studies* (February, March, April 1969), pp. 19–31.

goods and service available to ultimate consumers. It engages in the four equalization process activities—sorting out, assembling, allocating, and assorting—as described in Chapter 2.

This chapter should have given you a better perspective of those parts of the retailing system that you have experienced as a consumer and helped you organize your thoughts about various facets of retailing into more meaningful explanations. For example, you could explore the retail structure in cities with which you are familiar to see if they have a CBD, older secondary shopping districts, free-standing stores, neighborhood business streets, and plazas and shopping centers. Can you discern what types of shopping centers are present and distinguish between neighborhood, community, and regional shopping centers?

A persistent question in retailing is whether CBDs are worth saving. They grew large when mass transportation funneled consumers from large areas into the downtown area. With the disfavor of mass transit and the popularity of the automobile, is there any need for such concentrations of retail goods and services in a single location? Perhaps old CBDs are better locations for parks, zoos, and other city services.

The point to such questions is that retailing never stands still. It is constantly in a state of ferment. To be successful as a retailer or in understanding the retailing system, you must learn what is occurring so you can analyze why it is occurring. Some facts and statistics are presented here not because we expect you to remember them for long but because they will help you draw conclusions and help you understand the dynamic processes within the retailing system.

The next two chapters will help you continue to learn about the retailing system as they focus on specific types of retail institutions. You should ask about each type: what role does it play in the retailing system (i.e., why is it present), how did it evolve to its present condition, what changes are ongoing at this time, and why are they occurring?

REVIEW AND DISCUSSION QUESTIONS

1. What marketing functions are performed by the retail store? Does the number of functions performed vary among stores in different fields? Between large and small stores? Between independent and chain stores? Explain.

2. In your own words, define "retailing," a "retailer," and a "retail sale." Discuss the three concepts in relation to the following situations:
    a) A farmer selling his own home-grown fresh vegetables at his own roadside stand.
    b) A college bookstore selling books and supplies to students.
    c) A Fuller Brush salesman selling brushes from door to door.
    d) A supermarket selling groceries to the ultimate consumer.
    e) A farm equipment store selling a tractor and fertilizer to a farmer.
    f) A department store selling a refrigerator to a housewife.
    g) A clothing store selling baseball uniforms to the local professional team.

3. Trace briefly the evolution of retailing in the United States up to the time of the larger organizations, indicating the conditions responsible for the development of the various retail institutions.

4. Prepare an essay not to exceed 1,000 words in length on the topic "Factors Responsible for the Emergence of Large-Scale Retailing Organizations in the United States."

5. Discuss the present status and probable future of retailing through automatic vending machines.

6. What is the "retail institution cycle"? Can you think of any exceptions to this cycle?

7. Describe and indicate the current importance of each of the four major methods by which retailing is carried on in the United States today. Which method holds the promise of the most rapid future growth? Why?

8. In 1967 retail sales in dollars were over seven times what they were in 1939, yet the number of retail establishments in those two years was about the same. What are the implications and the significance of these facts?

9. Define an SMSA. What is its implication for marketing?

10. What are the elements making up the retail structure of the typical SMSA? Briefly describe each element.

11. Discuss the effects on the CBDs of the continued growth of planned shopping centers. Be sure to give particular attention to the measures adopted by downtown businessmen to improve their position. In your judgment, are CBDs doomed? Support fully your answer.

12. What general conclusions can be drawn regarding retail expenses by kind of store, by sales volume of store, and by size of city?

13. What are the major causes of failure of retail stores? In your judgment, what methods would be most effective in reducing retail failures? Why?

14. State and support your conclusion as to the future of the fully automated store.

15. Explain briefly five major developments in the current retail revolution—other than automatic vending machines and the automated store—and their significance.

SUPPLEMENTARY READINGS

Dolan, J. R.   *The Yankee Peddlers of Early America.* New York: Clarkson N. Potter, 1963. The functions of the early peddler, with many details as to what and how he sold, are highlighted.

Duncan, D. J., Phillips, C. F., and Hollander, S.C.   *Modern Retailing Management.* Homewood, Ill.: Richard D. Irwin, Inc., 1972. A new version of a standard text in the retail field which treats all major aspects of retailing.

Goeldner, C. R. (ed.)   *Automatic Merchandising.* Chicago: American Marketing Association, 1965. In this excellent listing, the literature available on automatic merchandising in books, reports, bulletins, articles, dissertations, directories, and other sources is summarized.

Mahoney, T., and Sloane, L.   *The Great Merchants.* Rev. ed. New York: Harper & Row, 1966. The evolution of retailing, as seen through the lives of outstanding retailers and the organizations they created, is set forth.

Nystrom, P. H.   *Economics of Retailing,* Vol. I. New York: Ronald Press Co., 1930. An excellent discussion of the historical development of retailing.

B. Earl Puckett Fund for Retailing Education, Inc.   *A Bibliography for Students of Retailing.* New York, 1966. Consists of 259 basic titles plus a supplementary list of about 2,500 titles.

Reilly, P. J.   *Old Masters of Retailing.* New York: Fairchild Publications, 1966. This fascinating and revealing account of the innovations and contributions of 35 retailers was written by the late, long-active head of the Associated Merchandising Corp.

8 Retailing: Small-scale, group, and direct systems

Since the days of Ben Franklin, it has been generally held that the small businessman is the backbone of our country and the salvation for its future. In the dream of many Americans to work for themselves, the independent store offers one of the most promising avenues. Many young people today are successful originators of boutiques, health food stores, leather shops, candle and novelty shops and a variety of other small stores. Others who have worked the 40-hour week for somebody else for too long see possibilities in the promise of the franchise operation—"If you have $10,000 to invest, we'll train you and set you up in a profitable business." Groups of individuals with causes in common have seen the cooperative store as a promise for lower priced books or foods, for securing hard-to-locate health foods, or as an outlet for their arts and crafts.

Small, group, and direct retailing systems in the United States will be examined in this chapter. The evolution and current importance as well as the future of each of these types of retailing will be considered, and reasons for success as well as failure will be suggested. While the initial focus is on small retailing, many who started out as small retailers are no longer small, and this facet is also discussed.

SMALL-SCALE RETAILERS

Little agreement exists among businessmen, trade associations, governmental agencies, congressional committees, or marketing writers as to the precise definition of "small business" as distinguished from "medium-sized" or "large" business. For our purposes, a useful dividing line between small-scale and other retailing is annual sales of $100,000. We will use this figure, however, as a rough criterion only, and much of the discussion is applicable to somewhat larger retailers. As a general rule, these "small" retailers operate what are best described as "independent stores."

Characteristics and importance of the independent retailer

The typical independent store is a small, nonintegrated establishment lacking any appreciable degree of specialization in management or employees. It is owned and operated as an individual unit. The owner of the store usually acts as manager, and, if it is very small, he may perform all the essential functions himself. This is true of about 37 percent of all independent stores, and nearly 14 percent more give employment to only one additional person.[1] In other independent stores the division of labor is more fully developed, and the owner-manager is assisted by a number of full-time and part-time employees.

Most independent stores are under the proprietorship form of business organization, but some are partnerships and corporations. According to the latest complete census data, over 74 percent of all retail establishments are proprietorships or partnerships, and their average annual sales are about $77,000, compared to over $463,000 for corporations.[2]

The independent store accounts for about 87.5 percent of all retail units and about 60 percent of retail sales. In absolute terms, census data show 1,543,193 one establishment retailers, with total annual sales of over $186.7 billion.[3]

That the majority of these independent stores fall in a small-scale classification is also evident from census figures. Of the 1,458,783 independent stores that *operated throughout the entire year* of 1967, 1,067,093, or over 73 percent, had sales of less than $100,000. A further breakdown of sales is shown in Table 8–1, which shows that one half of all stores have an annual volume of less than $50,000 but comprise a small fraction of total retail sales.

The fact that it is possible to operate a small retail store successfully is of consider-

TABLE 8–1
Number and sales volume of one-establishment retailers with sales of less than $100,000 in 1967 (including only stores operating entire year)

Sales volume group	Number of stores	Annual sales (in billions)
$50,000–$99,999	283,869	$20.0
$30,000–$49,999	211,650	8.2
$20,000–$29,999	154,849	3.8
$10,000–$19,999	195,448	2.8
$ 5,000–$ 9,999	128,418	.9
Less than $5,000	88,011	.3
Total	1,062,245	$36.0

Source: U.S. Bureau of the Census, *1967 Census of Business*, Vol. I, *Retail Trade: Subject Reports* (Washington, D.C.: Government Printing Office, 1971), pp. 4–256.

[1] U.S. Bureau of the Census, *1967 Census of Business*, Vol. I, *Retail Trade: Subject Reports* (Washington, D.C.: Government Printing Office, 1971), p. 3–1.

[2] U.S. Bureau of the Census, *1967 Census of Business*, Vol. I, *Retail Trade: Miscellaneous Subjects* (Washington, D.C.: Government Printing Office, 1971), p. 5–103.

[3] U.S. Bureau of the Census, *1967 Census of Business*, Vol. I, *Retail Trade: Subject Reports*, p. 4–1.

able social significance in an economy of free private enterprise. Such an economic system relies on the entry of individuals and firms into a field and the exit of those individuals and firms that find the field unprofitable. The Susan Ives Stores, Inc., now a sportswear chain of over 20 units, grew from a single store opened in 1953 by a 24-year old retailer with an investment of a few hundred dollars.[4] Practically all of today's large retail establishments and organizations, including such giants as R. H. Macy and Company and the Great Atlantic and Pacific Tea Company, came from humble beginnings.

The two most prominent types of small independent stores in the retailing system are the general store and the limited-line store.

The independent general store

The general store handles a number of lines of merchandise without any significant degree of departmental organization. To broaden its merchandise lines, it may also offer a catalog from which selections can be made. These stores typically are located in smaller rural communities, especially in the dominantly agricultural states of the South Atlantic, West North-Central, and East and West South-Central regions, and their lines of merchandise are broad enough to take care of many, if not most, of the community's needs. Groceries and related commodities constitute at least half the sales volume of general stores, with such items as dry goods and notions, apparel and shoes, hardware, home furnishings, farm implements and supplies, and gasoline and oil contributing to the balance.

The total number of such stores decreased from 104,089 in 1929 to 9,474 in 1958, and the classification was dropped in the 1963 census. Some of these stores went out of business, while others so shifted their merchandise lines that they fell in other census classifications; the remaining stores were absorbed in the "grocery store" and the "general merchandise store" groupings. Although the general store will continue to serve the needs of certain areas, no factors are now foreseeable to reverse its downward trend.

The small, independent limited-line store

The limited-line store is a nondepartmental retail establishment handling one major line of merchandise, such as groceries, shoes, or men's clothing. Many—probably most—of these stores handle some merchandise outside the major line. Women's shoe stores typically handle handbags, hosiery, and gloves; tobacco stores sell candy, and many drugstores sell small electrical appliances, toys, books, radios, and other items. This tendency toward scrambled merchandising has gone so far that in many cases the designation of limited-line store should no longer be applied.

A larger number of limited-line stores is not now independent; the typical chain store organization consists of a number of limited-line stores. Our attention is confined to the limited-line independent store, however, which is the most important type of small-scale retailer in the retailing system.

The main competitors of the small, independent limited-line shopping or specialty goods store are the department store, the departmentized specialty store, and the

---

[4] "How to Succeed in Retailing When You Really Try Hard," *Women's Wear Daily,* March 22, 1967, p. 40.

chain store. For the limited-line convenience goods store, however, the chain store and the group-activities independent provide the major competition.

The small store has the advantages of personal contact of owner with customers and of owner with employees, freedom of action, and the profit incentive. It often will carry a more complete line *in its chosen field* than is carried by its larger competitors. Its goods tend to be located on or near the ground level, so that they are more accessible. Better salesmanship through better knowledge of merchandise and customers is possible. In addition, the smaller store may cater to a particular segment of the population, such as the student buyer. In the important matter of operating cost, data are not available for an adequate comparison between the large department or departmentalized specialty store and smaller limited-line stores.

The small limited-line store also has disadvantages. It is often so small that it lacks buying power, specialization by functions is less possible, and poor management is common. It does not obtain as many sales from "impulse buying" as does the store with broader assortments of merchandise. And the small store also finds it less possible to offer as many "free" services as does the larger department store.

The development of outlying shopping centers has dealt more harshly with the small downtown store than with the large department or departmentized specialty store. Both of the latter retailers usually have sufficient prestige to be invited into controlled shopping center projects and can generate sufficient sales to pay the higher rent. Consequently, the impact on their downtown sales is typically more than offset by the attraction of new customers in the centers. But the small limited-line independents may not achieve a similar solution. While many of them have made the transition to shopping center locations, many more have remained downtown, where they compete for a decreasing volume of business. In such a location, they should be avid supporters of downtown renewal projects; yet they often lack the funds or the foresight necessary to finance their business during the period required for carrying out the renewal project.

Is the independent on the way out of the retailing system?

Among students of marketing, the future of the small independent retailer has been a favorite subject ever since the rapid growth of chain stores during the 1920s. Since World War II the continued increase in size of the larger retail organizations such as Sears, Roebuck and Company and Safeway Stores, Inc., and the further development of mass merchandisers and shopping centers have focused attention on the question of whether or not the small independent is on the way out.

Two students of this subject have found that "despite many prevailing prophecies of doom, there is underway growing strength in small retailing. . . . This strength could reverse, or at least hold in check, the gradual trend toward consolidation in the retailing system."[5] Specifically they point to (1) the small retailer's current ability to practice quasi integration through franchise and group activities, (2) the limitations of large-scale retailing (such as burdensome union contracts and difficulties in providing meaningful incentives),[6] and (3) the developing diversity of consumer markets

---

[5] A. F. Doody and W. R. Davidson, "Growing Strength in Small Retailing," *Harvard Business Review.* Vol. 42, No. 4 (July–August 1964), p. 69.

[6] Supporting this point is an analysis of Internal Revenue data developed from income tax returns which suggests that the economies of size in retailing are limited, with the most efficient size frequently being far smaller than the largest firms in the field. E. Douglas, "Size of the Firm and the Structure of Costs in Retailing," *Journal of Business,* 35 (April, 1962), pp. 158–90.

which calls for flexibility of independent operations (special services, the boutique offerings, health food stores). And they conclude:

The extent to which the small retailer will once again become a major competitive force will depend on the vigor and aggressiveness with which he accepts the challenge and develops programs appropriate to his given line of business. This will require a philosophy of innovation rather than of imitation and the full cooperation of all organizations that stand to gain from this development. Obviously, not all small retailers will participate in this opportunity, but for those who do, a bright future lies ahead.[7]

That the independent does have strengths which can make him a formidable competitor is attested to by the former president of a leading food chain.

. . . the independent operator, with one, two and three stores, employing his family and friends, being on the ground floor, doing his ordering, writing his own advertising, handling his own personnel, greeting his own customers, is the toughest kind of competition we are facing today. Give me any corporate chain next door, any time, in preference to a good, smart, aggressive independent operator who is not afraid to work. We know how to fight the corporate chain—our problems are his problems and vice versa. But it is tough to fight an individual, or 100 individuals all shooting at you from 100 different directions.[8]

We believe the small independent retailer will continue to play a significant part in the retailing system. To thousands of small merchants, retailing is a way of life as well as a way to make a living. They will not abandon it. In addition, there are thousands of innovative Americans, young and old, who are not satisfied with present retail stores and their offerings and who feel they can successfully do the "thing" that they and many consumers want. Retailing remains as an endeavor that is relatively easy to enter—it takes hard work, ideas, and financial backing (in that order) to open a small store. There will continue to be many new small stores opening in response to the market's needs.

GROUP ACTIVITIES OF RETAILERS

The increasing competition independent merchants have experienced has necessitated stronger efforts to improve efficiency and to attract more customers. They have bought from cash-and-carry wholesalers (the customer pays cash and transports his purchase) to reduce the cost of their merchandise, copied chain store policies and methods, and converted credit and delivery food businesses to cash-and-carry stores in order to lower prices. Stores have been rearranged and modernized, with many of them placed on a self-service or self-selection basis, and operating methods and costs have been carefully scrutinized. Independent merchants have opened supermarkets and discount houses and secured locations in shopping centers, as well as seeking aid from manufacturers, wholesalers, trade associations, and the federal government. Attempts have been made to attract customers by broadening merchandise lines, adding special services, and upgrading personnel.

Forms or types of group activities

Many independent retailers have joined together to carry out certain group activities for their mutual benefit, such as pooled buying direct from the manufacturer. As groups have discovered that buying power is only one factor (and not the main

---

[7] Doody and Davidson, "Growing Strength in Small Retailing," p. 79.

[8] H. V. McNamara, former president, National Tea Company, in "Common Ground," *Super Market Merchandising,* August 1960, p. 112.

one) in the success of the chain store, they have copied other chain store practices, such as joint advertising, featuring the same items as "leaders" in each store, painting stores a similar color to simulate a chain, adopting uniform fixtures, and establishing warehouses. Some independents have been united by a wholesaler, who becomes their major source of supply and plans many of their joint activities. Others have been franchised by manufacturers or other franchisers. Thus there are four major kinds of organizations for group activities by formerly independent retailers: (1) retailer buying and merchandising groups, (2) retailer cooperatives, (3) voluntary chains sponsored by wholesalers, and (4) franchise organizations. The last three are often referred to as contractual systems because the retail units are integrated voluntarily with suppliers through contracts.

Two points should be emphasized. First, this trend toward group activities is of major significance and deserves careful study. It has been estimated that these contractual systems account for 35 to 40 percent of all retail trade in the United States.[9] Without them, far more independents would have succumbed to chain store competition than has been the case. Second, it is impractical to limit the discussion of group activities to stores with annual sales of $100,000 or less. Many of the former independent supermarkets that are supplied by cooperative or voluntary wholesalers have sales substantially above this level, for example, and the discussion must be broad enough to include them.

Buying and merchandising groups. The simplest type of retailer cooperation is the buying and merchandising group. Many of these organizations are informal, frequently operate without a place of business, and do not appear in the statistics of the number of merchants engaging in group activities.

These groups usually limit their activities to the pooling of orders in an attempt to get lower prices from wholesalers and manufacturers. A number of grocers (or hardware dealers) in a certain city may meet informally from time to time and appoint one of the group to act as buyer for certain items. This member may make all purchases in his own name and have the items delivered to his store, where the others agree to call for their parts of the order. In some groups a different member acts as buyer each week; in others, each member specializes in goods of a particular type.

In such informal buying groups the price advantages may be offset by a number of operating disadvantages. In some lines, various members of the group may be handling different brands, so that group buying is limited to a small number of identical items carried by all members. Dissatisfaction with the "deals" made may be a source of irritation, as may be the slowness of some members in picking up their purchases from a common delivery point. Finally, if the group is merely shopping among the wholesalers, it may not obtain prices as low as it might if it could perform the wholesale functions and buy direct from manufacturers.

A number of these buying groups use group advertising to the extent that they jointly select and advertise "leaders." A common group name often is adopted to identify all the stores. If these group-buying and advertising activities prove successful, the group tends to evolve into a cooperative chain by opening its own warehouse, or into a voluntary chain by organizing around one wholesaler as the major source of supply.

Cooperative chains.[10] In marked contrast with the more or less loosely organ-

---

[9] W. R. Davidson, "Changes in Distributive Institutions," *Journal of Marketing,* 34 (January 1970), pp. 7–10.

[10] For the story of a successful cooperative chain see "Twin County Grocers," *Super Market Merchandising,* June 1966, pp. 22–24.

ized buying and merchandising groups are the cooperative chains. To form one of these organizations, the retailers become the stockholders of a wholesale company established to serve themselves. As stockholders, the retailers elect the board of directors, typically from among the retailer-members. Voting is usually based on the number of shares of stock held by each member, although often each member has one vote regardless of the number of shares he holds. Two of the largest cooperative chains in the food field are Associated Grocers and Certified Grocers.

The main connecting link between the wholesale company and the retailer member is stock ownership. The sale of stock to members (most cooperative chains require a certain minimum holding for membership) is the chief source of working capital for the wholesale company. Additional funds may be obtained from initiation fees, which range from $10 to $50 a member, and from members' cash deposits in those cooperative chains that require a deposit as a guarantee that all bills will be met promptly. Many of the cooperative wholesale companies are operated on a nonprofit basis; that is, they add to the cost of their merchandise a markup which is not in excess of their cost of operation. Other cooperative wholesalers pay dividends on their common stock as a means of distributing their earnings to the retailers, or the "dividends" are divided on a patronage basis.

A second connecting link between the wholesale company and its retailer members is the formal contract used by many of them. These contracts may bind the wholesale organization to perform certain services for the member, such as the preparation of advertising, aid in store remodeling and relocation, store supervision, and providing private brands. In return, the retailer may agree to pay certain dues or fees, to follow store-remodeling requirements, to concentrate a certain percentage of his buying with the wholesale firm, to pay his bills according to the rules of the organization, and to cooperate in group promotions. It should be emphasized, however, that in the retailer cooperatives the contract is a secondary means of keeping contact between the member and the wholesale house. Stock ownership is the main link. This situation is in contrast to the voluntary chain organization, where the contract, although less important than formerly, still has primary importance.

Voluntary chains.[11] Most voluntary chains have been formed by wholesalers who have felt the impact of chain store development, although some of the most successful ones have been organized by chains themselves, and a few manufacturers have established somewhat similar relationships with the retailers of their products. Two large voluntary chains in the food field are Super Valu and the Independent Grocers Alliance of America (I.G.A.). Realizing that their success depends on that of the independent retailer, wholesalers have adopted programs to aid him. They have even gone so far as to rent buildings, place fixtures and stock in them, open them for business, and then sell them to a retailer who will sign a contract for the wholesaler's services.

Typically, the agreement between the wholesaler and each retailer member of the voluntary chain is set forth in a written contract. The wholesaler agrees to provide a variety of services: to furnish sales "leaders," to develop a sales promotion program, to plan advertising for the group and to carry out some of it, to furnish material as an aid in window trimming or in setting up floor displays, to provide supervisors who visit member stores and offer assistance and advice on merchandising and manage-

---

[11] For case histories of two of these organizations see Seymour Freedgood, "Uncle to 1,700 Grocers (Super Valu)," *Fortune,* (March 1965), pp. 130–33; and "Wetterau Foods, Inc.," *Progressive Grocer,* April 1966, pp. 302–9.

ment, to set up an accounting system, to aid in store remodeling, to help in selecting new store sites and even in the financing of a new store and its equipment, to assist in the training of store personnel, to provide uniform store signs, and to furnish a rather complete line of private-brand merchandise. As an indication of the financial aid extended to retailer-members, one survey of 56 major voluntary chain wholesalers reports that 25 of them "frequently" and 21 "occasionally" take leases on stores and then sublet to their retailers; comparable figures for financing retailers' fixtures are 23 and 25.[12] Some wholesalers even establish "schools" to which independents and their employees can go for more intensive training.

In return for the wholesaler's services, the agreement typically provides that the retailer will act upon the advice of the wholesaler, concentrate a certain percentage of his purchases with him, remodel his store along the lines suggested, display the sign of the group, feature the "leaders" in his advertising, "push" the voluntary chain private brands, and keep his accounts according to a suggested system. In addition, the retailer usually contracts to pay certain fees to compensate the wholesaler in part for his services.

The cost of these services has proved so great that voluntary group wholesalers have an operating cost ratio which, while substantially below that of the traditional general-line grocery wholesaler, is above that of the cooperative wholesale houses. Some have reduced these services in an effort to cut costs; for example, some of the wholesalers operating within the I.G.A. will accept only one order a week from the retailers they serve, consolidate orders for retailers in the same locality or territory, and collect cash on delivery, thus eliminating a billing cost.

Franchise systems. Many independent retailers are franchisees. The franchise arrangement is an agreement whereby a franchiser—often a manufacturer—who has developed a pattern or format for a particular business extends to franchisees the right to operate such a business, provided they follow the established pattern.

Two basic types of retail franchise arrangements predominate in the United States.[13] The more traditional one is for manufacturers to franchise retailers of finished products. This is used extensively by producers of passenger cars and trucks, farm equipment, petroleum products, shoes, and paint. The second arrangement has been the area of major growth during the 1960s and 1970s, the service-sponsor–retailer agreement, which is built around a service-product package where the product or service must be processed or performed by the retailer (franchisee).[14] This is the type of franchise arrangement used by Howard Johnson's, Dairy Queen, McDonald's, Holiday Inn, Avis, Hertz, Manpower, Kelly Girl, H & R Block, and many others. It is often known as trademark licensing because the retailer buys the right to apply the trademark to his output.[15]

---

[12] W. F. Whittier, "The Financing of Voluntary Group Affiliated Retailers in the United States," address at Sixth International Food Conference, Copenhagen, Denmark, June 1966 (privately printed), pp. 8 and 10.

[13] Franchise arrangements are not limited to the retailing system. At the wholesale level Coca-Cola, Pepsi Cola and other manufacturers of soft-drink syrups franchise wholesalers. At the manufacturing level, Sealy bedding provides an illustration.

[14] W. P. Hall, "Franchising—New Scope for an Old Technique," *Harvard Business Review,* 42 (January–February 1964), pp. 60–72.

[15] Not all of the units in a franchise system are owned by independent retailers. Holiday Inn, H & R Block, and other franchisers own and operate some of their own units. In the fast-food systems, an estimated 10 to 12 percent of all the units were owned by the franchisors in 1970. U. B. Ozanne and S. D. Hunt, *The Economic Effects of Franchising* (Madison, Wis.: Graduate School of Business, University of Wisconsin, 1971), p. 3–11. Some franchisors, e.g., Sambos' and Dunkin' Donuts, go 50–50 ownership with each of their franchisees. "More Mouths to Feed," *Barron's,* April 26, 1971, p. 5.

Marketing: Principles and methods

The franchisee normally pays for his franchise in several ways:

1. A straight fee (the average among fast-food franchisors in 1970 was $7,500).
2. A royalty as a percent of sales (the median fast-food franchise royalty in 1970 was 4 percent, but the extremes ranged from 1 percent to 18 percent).
3. Purchase of various services, materials and products from the franchisor.

Franchise arrangements vary from those that are highly permissive toward the franchisee to those that rigidly limit his prerogatives. Franchise contracts typically include clauses on location; merchandise and service lines to be sold; product, material, and service purchases; sales volumes; store appearance; promotional efforts; prices to be charged; and records to be maintained. Location, in fact, is such a prime consideration that in fast foods and other convenience goods and services, franchisors more often than not select the sites before selecting the franchisees.

1. *Franchising's contribution to small business.* The franchise arrangement has provided many opportunities and encouragement to individuals to enter the retail field. There are franchisors in fast foods, groceries, regular foods, laundry, dry cleaning, campgrounds, motels, automotive repair, rental products, and many other products and services, and within these categories there are numerous franchise systems.[16] For example, just in the fast-foods area there were estimated to be 300 to 400 franchisors with around 750 franchise systems operating approximately 35,000 units in 1969. There were over 103 hamburger (major product) systems with over 5,000 outlets; 75 chicken systems with a total of almost 3,000 units, and 48 ice cream systems with almost 9,000 outlets. In 1970, the McDonald system contained 1,600 units and had sales of $675 million, Kentucky Fried Chicken, with 3,500 units, recorded sales of $700 million, and International Dairy Queen, with 4,000 units, had total sales of $450 million.[17]

A study by U. B. Ozanne and S. D. Hunt indicated that about 68 percent of the fast-food franchisees were not self-employed in their immediate prior employment, and 36 percent said they would not have been self-employed except for the franchise alternative. The study estimated that fast-food franchising provided between 13,700 and 26,000 small businesses that otherwise would not have been possible.[18]

2. *Franchising as an aid to helping minorities into retailing.* Franchise systems, however, have not provided much expanded opportunity for minority member ownership. The fast-food study indicated that only about 1.5 percent of all franchisees appeared to be members of minority groups, as shown in Table 8–2. And only a few minority-owned franchise systems—All-Pro Chicken, Inc.; Jet Foods Corporation, and Rib-Cage International, Inc.—probably accounted for a large share of the black-owned units. The major explanations appear to be that few interested minority families have the necessary funds, or can secure needed additional funds from other sources, including franchisors. Further, few have the necessary business and managerial experience or appear interested in franchise businesses.[19]

3. *Franchised businesses: Are they small and are they successful?* The Ozanne and Hunt study pointed out that fast-food, dry cleaning, and convenience grocery

---

[16] A franchisor may have several franchise systems. International Industries (a franchisor), for example, operates several franchise systems, including International House of Pancakes, Orange Julius, and Copper Penny.

[17] Ozanne and Hunt, *Economic Effects of Franchising,* chap. 3; and "No Burned Fingers," *Barron's,* April 12, 1971, p. 3.

[18] Ibid., p. 2–8.

[19] Ibid., pp. 2–23 and 2–24.

TABLE 8–2
Minority member ownership of fast-food franchises

Ethnic Group	Percent of total U.S. fast-food franchises
American Indian................................	0.1%
Mexican American.............................	0.7
Negro	0.6
Puerto Rican....................................less than	0.1
Other minority	0.1
	1.5%

Source: U. B. Ozanne and S. D. Hunt, *The Economic Effects of Franchising* (Madison, Wis.: Graduate School of Business, University of Wisconsin, 1971), p. 6–17.

franchises are small businesses with average annual unit sales in 1969 respectively of $140,000, $53,000 and $180,000.[20] It seems reasonable to conclude that most, but certainly not all, franchised retail operations should be classified as small. As to success and failure rates, a 1968 study concluded that the average failure rate among the franchisees of 70 franchisors was only 1.6 percent per year.[21] However, the Ozanne and Hunt study estimated failures between 1.3 percent and 6.7 percent during 1969.[22]

Success, however, should be defined more broadly than simply staying in business or dropping out. Table 8–3 reports the income (owner's salary plus other payments to his household plus profits) of 800 fast-food franchisees for 1969. Over 25 percent of the franchisees received *under $10,000* from their franchise, while less than 25 percent of the franchisees had over $25,000 income.

TABLE 8–3
Franchisee income in fast foods, 1969 (includes salaries, wages, and other payments to franchisee)

Income	Percent
Less than $5,000..	10.4
$ 5,000–$ 9,999...	15.4
10,000– 12,499...	10.7
12,500– 14,999...	7.0
15,000– 17,499...	14.0
17,500– 19,999...	7.5
20,000– 22,499...	7.1
22,500– 24,999...	5.1
25,000– 29,999...	4.8
30,000 and over...	18.1
	100.1 (rounding error)

Source: U. B. Ozanne and S. H. Hunt, *The Economic Effects of Franchising* (Madison, Wis.: Graduate School of Business, University of Wisconsin, 1971), p. 5–2.

---

[20] Ibid., pp. 3–20, 9–5, 9–10.

[21] J. F. Atkinson, *Franchising: The Odds-On Favorite* (Chicago: International Franchise Association, 1968).

[22] Ozanne and Hunt, *Economic Effects of Franchising,* p. 3–27.

Group activities in the grocery and supermarket fields

All four types of group activity discussed above can be found today in the grocery or supermarket fields. Although group activities did not significantly develop until the middle 1920s, their origin can be traced back at least to 1887, when a group of retailers formed the Baltimore Wholesale Grocery Company. The following year another group of grocery retailers, this time in Philadelphia, formed the Frankford Grocery Company. In contrast with the early formation of a few retailer cooperatives, voluntary chains seem to date from the General Purchasing and Distributing Company of San Francisco, formed in 1916. By this date, some 15 retailer organizations had been formed. That the sales of both voluntary and cooperative chains have gained steadily since 1939 is indicated by Table 8–4.

In 1968 the voluntary and cooperative chain groups claimed the membership of 80,500 food stores with annual sales of $37.8 billion.[23] It should be emphasized,

TABLE 8–4
Number of warehouses and sales of groceries and related products by voluntary chain and cooperative chain warehouses, 1939, 1954, 1963, 1967, and 1968

Year	Voluntary chain warehouses		Cooperative chain warehouses	
	Number of warehouses	Sales (in billions)	Number of warehouses	Sales (in billions)
1939	638	$ 0.7	136	$0.2
1954	574	2.5	193	1.3
1963	708	5.4	161	2.9
1967	734	7.4	173	4.1
1968	749	11.0	277	6.9

Source: 1939, 1954, 1963, and 1967 figures are from U.S. Bureau of the Census, *1939 Census of Business,* Vol. II, *Wholesale Trade: Summary Statistics* (Washington, D.C.: Government Printing Office, 1942), pp. 156–57; *1954 Census of Business,* Vol. III: *Wholesale Trade: Summary Statistics* (1957), pp. 1–4; *1963 Census of Business, Wholesale Trade: United States Summary,* BC63–WA1 (1965), pp. 1–11; *1967 Census of Business,* Vol. 3, *Wholesale Trade: Subject Reports* (1971), pp. 1–9. 1968 figures are from "36th Annual Report of the Grocery Industry," *Progressive Grocer,* April 1969, p. 80.

however, that a rapidly rising number of the retailers affiliated with these groups are chain store operators (two-or-more–store retailers) rather than true independents (one-store retailers). To illustrate the point, of all the supermarket chains in the United States belonging to the Super Market Institute, 24 percent are supplied through voluntary chain wholesalers and 39 percent through cooperative wholesalers.[24] While most of the chains served by the groups fall in the 2- to-10–store size, some are appreciably larger. For instance, Food Fair's 45-store Pacific Coast division is served by a cooperative chain, Certified Grocers of California, Ltd., because the president of this division does not believe it is economical to operate "your own warehouse until you are doing at least $200 million in annual volume."[25] Consequently, when it is stated that the groups' percentage of total food business has advanced from 35 percent in 1947 to

---

[23] "36th Annual Report of the Grocery Industry," *Progressive Grocer,* April 1969, p. 63.

[24] *The Supermarket Industry Speaks, 1969* (Chicago: Super Market Institute, 1969), p. 24.

[25] Arthur Rosenburg, quoted in "Catalyst of 'Warehouse-Less' Supermarket Growth," *Chain Store Age* (Supermarket Executives Edition), December 1966, p. 44.

over 44 percent today,[26] it must be realized that much of this gain is by chain stores using groups for their wholesale activities. Although data are not available for an exact figure, we estimate that over half of the retail sales reported by the group retailers take place in chain units (organizations with two or more stores) rather than in independent stores.

Some of the present-day groups are very large. The I.G.A., a voluntary chain which was founded in 1926, now has over 4,000 member stores in the United States and parts of Canada, with annual sales in excess of $3 billion.[27] Certified Grocers of California, Ltd., a cooperative chain dating from a buying group established in 1922, serves over 1,827 stores with annual sales of more than $471 million.[28] Other large groups include the Red & White Food Stores of Buffalo; Royal Blue Stores and Cardinal Food Stores of Chicago; and Super Valu Stores of Minneapolis. Buying and merchandising groups, however, seem to be on the decline. Some of them are going out of business, being taken over by wholesalers, or establishing their own warehouses and thus becoming cooperative chains.

Group activities in other fields of retailing

The development of group activities among independent retailers in other fields has not gone so far as in foods, but in both the drug and the hardware trades there are probably more stores in these organizations than in regular chains. Group activities among druggists are not new; a drug retailer buying pool was formed as early as 1887 in New York City and in 1888 in Philadelphia. As early as 1929 the Federal Trade Commission estimated that 30 of these organizations in the drug field had a total membership of 7,550 retail stores.[29] Most of these were of the cooperative type, with few buying groups and voluntary chains. Although recent census data are not available, one study concluded that a decade ago at least 3 out of every 10 drugstores in the country were tied in with a manufacturer, a wholesaler, or other retailers in one of the three main forms of group activities.[30] The Walgreen Company, a chain store firm, has long engaged in voluntary chain operations.

Group activities have also developed in the automobile accessory, furniture, dry goods, television and electrical appliances, variety, restaurant, and lumber fields. Gamble-Skogmo, Inc., which operates a combination wholesale, chain store, and mail-order business, has over 3,100 authorized dealers.[31] These dealers "are independent retailers whose stores carry the 'Gamble' name, who procure their merchandise from the company's wholesale facilities, carry a substantial volume of its private brand goods, and have available to them the services and counsel of the Gamble-Skogmo central service and regional organizations."[32] Most of the growth

---

[26] National Commission on Food Marketing, *Organization and Competition in Food Retailing* (Washington, D.C.: Government Printing Office, 1966), p. 33. Another source reports that the groups did 29 percent of the 1947 food business and 51 percent in 1966. "34th Annual Report of the Grocery Industry," *Progressive Grocer,* April 1967, p. 74.

[27] *Printers' Ink,* March 24, 1967, p. 3.

[28] "36th Annual Report of the Grocery Industry," p. 85.

[29] Federal Trade Commission, *Chain Stores: Cooperative Drug and Hardware Chains* (Washington, D.C.: Government Printing Office, 1932), p. 3.

[30] W. T. Kelley, "The Franchise-Wholesale System in Co-operative Drug Stores," *Journal of Retailing,* 33 (Winter 1957–58), pp. 184–91.

[31] Gamble-Skogmo, Inc., *Annual Report,* year ended January 31, 1967, p. 10.

[32] Gamble-Skogmo, Inc., *Facts About Gamble-Skogmo, Inc.* (Minneapolis, Minn., n.d.), p. 13.

in the restaurant business in recent years has been due to the extensive expansion of franchise systems ranging from the many fast-food systems like McDonald's to the regular food systems like Nino's Steak House. Of course, the franchise food service business is not all new. Most of the restaurants (and motels) operated under the Howard Johnson name are independent units under franchise arrangements.

Manufacturers who distribute through franchise organizations are quite common. Men's clothing produced by the manufacturing division of Bond Stores, Inc., is sold through a group of associated stores located in the smaller towns and cities. Bond provides merchandise and merchandising assistance in return for purchase of clothing by the independent retailer. Major shoe, automobile, paint, and tire manufacturers have similar arrangements.

Outlook for the future

Despite limiting factors, many who have studied the development of group activities are enthusiastic about their future possibilities within the retailing system. Although this type of organization has probably not yet significantly lowered the total operating cost for group wholesalers and retailers, it has increased the merchandising ability of the affiliated retailer and enabled him to meet his local competition more effectively. It is reasonable to conclude that certain economies will be effected by the mergers that have taken place and that the competitive power of the groups will be strengthened. The continued evolution of such groups is anticipated.

DIRECT RETAILING

Two additional forms of retailing are sales made directly to consumers without the use of middlemen—a practice commonly referred to as "direct retailing"—and retailing by consumers' cooperatives. Direct retailing will be discussed first.

Methods of selling direct to consumers

The sale of consumer goods direct to the ultimate consumer without intervening middlemen is the simplest form of retailing. The point of sale serves to classify the various operations: sale at production point, sale at consumption point, and sale between the production and consumption point.

Sale at production point. The farmer who builds a roadside stand on his farm to sell his products to the public is engaged in direct retailing. The same is true of the men's clothing manufacturer who opens a retail shop on the ground floor of his factory. In both these cases the merchandise passes directly from producer to consumer at production point, and middlemen are not required for the performance of the necessary marketing functions.

Sale at consumption point. In cases of direct sale by producers or manufacturers to consumers at the point of consumption, the seller takes the initiative. There are three methods: (1) house-to-house selling, or "huckstering," as it is often called when agricultural products are sold, (2) selling by mail, and (3) selling by telephone.

1. *House-to-house selling.* This method of direct sale is used for a wide variety of items, including vacuum sweepers, radios, television sets, furniture, brushes, cooking utensils, hosiery, cosmetics, household chemicals, vitamins, books, stationery,

magazines, and many food products, such as dry groceries, baked goods, fruits and vegetables, milk, and other dairy products.[33] The Bureau of the Census reported 77,632 direct-selling establishments—the sales offices or headquarters from which crews of canvassers operated to sell from house to house—in 1967 with sales of $2.5 billion. These sales represented an increase of almost $122 million as compared with 1963. In view of generally increased prices, however, it appears that house-to-house selling is decreasing in relative importance. In 1963 it accounted for about 1.0 percent of all retail sales, and in 1967 it was only 0.8 percent. It is also likely that sales by many users of this method were not included in the census figures.[34]

Three main influences related directly to competition have encouraged some manufacturers in recent years to turn to door-to-door selling. First, the rise in competition in many consumer goods markets has necessitated different approaches to the consumer, including such a "hard sell" technique as house-to-house selling. Second, inability to match the tremendous advertising expenditures of major competitors has led some firms to turn to direct selling at the consumer's door. Finally, the fact that some firms have done very well using direct-selling organizations has encouraged others.[35]

The problems of house-to-house sale from the manufacturers' point of view are largely (1) recruiting large numbers of salespeople, (2) high turnover rate among sales personnel, (3) high sales costs, (4) control of a sales force made up of "nonemployees" and many part-time salespeople, (5) local ordinances preventing or harassing door-to-door selling, (6) need for highly aggressive sales management and promotion, and (7) damage to the company reputation through misrepresentation by sales personnel.

Of these limitations, the high cost of selling, with resulting relatively high prices, is especially serious. Not only are the commissions paid to salesmen necessarily large, but the direct-selling organization faces a substantial cost in recruiting, training, and supervising salesmen—a cost made especially high by the employment of many part-time salesmen and the rapid turnover of both part-time and full-time sales personnel. In many cases a firm must hire three people in the course of a year to keep one on the job. Even the better known organizations have difficulty in this connection, especially during the periods of full employment.

The influence of heavy consumer advertising on television and in other media in changing consumer attitudes toward house-to-house salesmen should not be underestimated. Avon Products, Inc., for example, advertises in women's magazines regularly, in addition to television spot announcements.

Among the better known companies selling products from house to house are Electrolux Corp., for vacuum cleaners; Avon Products, Inc., for cosmetics; the Fuller Brush Company, International Housewares, Inc., and Stanley House Products, Inc., in the brush and home products field; and *Reader's Digest* and Grolier encyclopedias in the publishing area. There are many other less well-known firms.

Several years ago the founder of the Fuller Brush Company described the typical Fuller Brush Man as a salesman who "travels eight hundred miles a month by car,

---

[33] Abroad, manufacturers also employ house-to-house selling for a wide variety of products, and several manufacturers from the United States have developed important house-to-house selling organizations in foreign markets—Avon Products, Inc., Wear-Ever Aluminum Co. of America, Fuller Brush Co., and Tupperware.

[34] U.S. Bureau of the Census, *1967 Census of Business, Retail Trade: Subject Reports,* p. 1–8.

[35] Avon Products, Inc., with sales in excess of $408 million annually, had a better than 13 percent return on sales in 1965 and 37 percent on stockholders' equity. "The Fortune Directory of the 500 Largest U.S. Industrial Corporations," *Fortune,* June 15, 1967, p. 203.

walks six miles a day during which he rings one hundred twenty-five doorbells, and takes twenty-five orders which average three dollars."[36] Salesmen's commissions in various house-to-house firms vary from 20 to 40 percent of sales, and gross margins of 40–50 percent of sales are common. Most of the salesmen are really independent dealers, since they buy their merchandise from the manufacturer at wholesale prices and sell to the consumer at retail—thereby relieving the company of such tax obligations as social security, unemployment compensation, and workmen's compensation.[37] As to organization, the Avon structure is quite typical: the sales representative, who covers from 200 to 300 households, reports to a resident manager. Each resident manager is responsible for from 100 to 200 sales representatives and, in turn, reports to a district manager.[38]

Although the majority of house-to-house salesmen take orders and then call back to make delivery or rely on mail service, some of them have their merchandise with them. The "home shopping service" department of the Jewel Companies, which is basically a middleman rather than a manufacturer, represents this type of house-to-house selling. In early 1967, it had 2,109 routes which served 500,000 customers each week in some 44 states with about 300 food and related items and more than 2,600 general merchandise items.[39] Under the firm's cooperative franchise plan, each route operator is rewarded on the profitability of his operation rather than only on sales, thus giving him a goal identical with that of the company.

Some of the firms selling from house to house make use of the "party" technique. Under this plan the salesman's first job is to locate a housewife who will serve as hostess. She invites a group of friends or neighbors to her home for a party—for breakfast, mid-morning coffee, luncheon, mid-afternoon cake, or in the evening—and the salesman then demonstrates his wares. For acting as hostess, the housewife receives a gift or cash, the value of which frequently varies with the sales made during the party. The Tupperware division of the Rexall Drug and Chemical Company affords a good illustration of a firm using this technique; its plastic housewares are sold exclusively by home-party selling in some 30 countries throughout the world.[40] Women's wearing apparel valued at more than $50 million annually is sold through the party plan by Beeline Fashions of Bensenville, Illinois, and the Jewel Companies have established a subsidiary, Joya Fashions, to sell both women's and men's clothing by this technique.[41]

2. *Mail-order and telephone selling.* Sale at the point of consumption through mail-order and telephone solicitation is used by both manufacturers and farmers. A number of dress manufacturers, especially those located in California, sell by mail, and specialty merchandise, such as hand-woven ties and some makes of shoes, as well as books and candy, are sold both by mail and telephone. Firms producing flower and vegetable seeds and some orchardists use these same methods. The Maytag Dairy Farms, which operates seven farms in Iowa, sells thousands of pounds of blue cheese each year by mail. They maintain a mailing list of over 140,000 persons and contact

[36] A. C. Fuller, *A Foot in the Door* (New York: McGraw-Hill Book Co., 1960), p. 183.

[37] There are exceptions to this arrangement: the salesmen representing Electrolux Corp. are employees, so the firm "deducts Social Security payments from commission checks and provides health insurance and a pension plan." Editors of Wall Street Journal, *How They Sell* (New York: Dow Jones & Co., 1965), p. 187.

[38] For a description of how Grolier, Inc. sells encyclopedias, see "Smart Earnings Advance in the Works at Grolier," *Barron's*, March 8, 1971, p. 30.

[39] The Jewel Companies, *Annual Report*, year ended January 28, 1967, p. 4.

[40] Rexall Drug and Chemical Company, *Annual Report*, 1966, p. 10.

[41] "Apparel Salesmen Take Samples to the Party," *Business Week*, July 15, 1967, pp. 148 and 152.

each one from one to three times a year, depending on their prior purchases. Manufacturers supplement direct-mail advertising with advertisements in magazines, newspapers, radio, and television.

Sale between production and consumption points. Two other methods of direct sale to consumers involve taking initiative by both the consumer and the producer, since the sale is made in between the production and the consumption points. One of these methods is sale through the retail public market; the other is sale through the manufacturer's retail store.

1. *Retail public and farmers' markets.* Although the retail public market has declined in importance in this country, it still offers a significant outlet for many farmers. Most of these markets are, as the name implies, publicly owned; the municipality constructs the building and leases space to various sellers. A few of them, even though called "public" markets, are actually owned by private interests. In either case the method of operation, i.e., through the leasing of space to sellers, is the same. The items sold in such markets are comparable to those sold at roadside markets: fruits and vegetables, eggs, poultry, butter, and honey and maple products. Fresh fish and meats are sold at some. Farmers' wives sometimes use them to sell homemade bakery products or nonfood items, such as hooked rugs. Satisfactory data on the amount of goods sold through retail public markets are not available.

Found mainly in suburban and rural areas, "farmers' markets" were originally simply privately owned markets to which growers could bring their produce for direct sale to consumers. Gradually, retailers of other merchandise lines were attracted to the location, so that today many so-called "farmers' markets" actually are shopping centers dominated by middlemen who sell a wide variety of merchandise at relatively low prices. Unlike the regular shopping centers, however, the facilities are frequently very simple (open sheds, quonset huts, and unpaved parking lots are not uncommon), they may be used largely on weekends, and the auction method of sale is used for some merchandise. Large-scale promotions supported by all the retailers in the market create a carnival or circus atmosphere and attract large crowds. A few years ago it was estimated that there were about 1,000 farmers' markets with annual sales in excess of $1 billion, but it seems likely that their current number is considerably less, as some have "traded up" to become regular shopping centers, others have been converted to discount houses, and some have gone out of business.

2. *Manufacturers' retail stores.* Among the manufacturers who operate retail stores, under either their own or other names, are such well-known firms as the Eastman Kodak Company, selling photographic supplies; Bond Stores, Inc. and Hart, Schaffner & Marx, selling men's and women's apparel; Florsheim Shoes; Fanny Farmer Candy Shops; and the Sherwin-Williams Company, selling paint and related products. Manufacturers of baked goods, ice cream, hats, automobiles, and women's hosiery also operate their own retail outlets. In some cases the integration of manufacturing and retail stores began from the retail level, as it did with the Melville Shoe Corporation, operators of Thom McAn and other shoe stores. In these cases, after a successful retail store operation, control was established over manufacturing facilities.

Frequently, manufacturers operating their own stores also sell many products purchased from other manufacturers. For instance, although Bond Stores, Inc. manufactures all of its men's suits, topcoats, and overcoats, it purchases such other items as shoes, ties, hats, and women's apparel. Likewise, the bookstores operated by Doubleday & Company, Inc. sell books produced by many other publishers.

Use of direct sale to consumers by middlemen

Most of the methods used by manufacturers or farmers to sell directly to consumers are also used by middlemen. Some roadside markets are operated by merchants who purchase merchandise from farmers and resell it to the public, and house-to-house selling is employed by such middlemen as the Jewel Companies. Some department stores sell the larger household appliances on a house-to-house basis. Even mail-order selling in this country is used predominantly by nonmanufacturers. Telephone orders are accepted by many retailers operating through stores, and many merchants operate in the retail public markets and the farmers' markets. Most of the discussion of this chapter, therefore, is applicable to middlemen as well as to those manufacturers and farmers who use these methods of sale.

Reasons for direct retailing

Some manufacturers and farmers who engage in direct sale expect to increase their profit by receiving retail rather than wholesale prices for their products. Thus, those farmers who sell through their own roadside markets are usually able to get a higher price than if they sold to dealers; and, in some instances, by selling superior merchandise, they obtain higher than average retail prices. Likewise, manufacturers selling through their own retail stores are able to secure the full retail price. It should be noted, however, that the higher prices obtained by manufacturers and farmers selling direct to consumers will increase their total profits only if they can perform the retail functions for less than the gross margin of middlemen. To illustrate: An item of merchandise for which a manufacturer can receive $1.00 at wholesale sells at retail for $1.50, thereby providing a gross margin of 50 cents to cover the retailing functions. Only if the manufacturer can perform these retailing functions for less than 50 cents will direct sale add to his total profits.

Another reason for direct retailing is to obtain more aggressive selling. Manufacturers of electrical household appliances often require the aggressive selling characteristic of this method of sale as well as the opportunity to demonstrate their products. In the home the customer's attention can be concentrated on the item or items being offered by the salesman. Other manufacturers open their own stores to be sure that their merchandise is well displayed and demonstrated, that the store carries a full line of their items, and that salesmen are well trained in selling methods. Still other manufacturers sell direct because they wish their products to reach the consumer in a satisfactory condition—for instance, candymakers whose products are perishable and require special handling. Manufacturers also engage in some direct selling so that they can better serve the middlemen who handle the bulk of their output. They believe that through some experience in retailing, they can adapt their product better to the consumer's wants and gain knowledge they can pass on to their dealers. Their stores are operated as laboratories.

Direct sale to consumers also may be the result of inability to obtain satisfactory outlets. A farmer with a large crop of strawberries may find that all the local retailers have an ample supply, and sale at a roadside stand or even from house to house may be his only opportunity to achieve a satisfactory price, or the only way he can sell at practically any price. Direct retailing also has been used to convince a middleman that he should stock an item. A manufacturer may have found the more orthodox channels of distribution closed to him, so he resorts to direct sale as a method of introducing his product to the market. In still other cases the seller has turned to direct retailing so that he can control his product all the way to the ultimate consumer, thereby assuring himself of an outlet, making it possible to control retail prices, and allowing him to offer more satisfactory repair and other services after the product has been sold.

Direct retailing in the future

Major trends in the marketing and economic systems of the United States are working both against and in favor of direct sale to household consumers. On the one hand, as the production unit has grown larger, the producer and consumer have become more widely separated, which makes direct retailing much more difficult. On the other hand, the growing intensity of competition under large-scale production in some fields has encouraged the producer to seek ways of controlling his product all the way to the consumer. Some producers seek this control through advertising, others through direct retailing. Although serious obstacles lie in the path, it seems likely that direct selling by manufacturers, especially through their own retail stores and house-to-house salesmen, has not yet reached the peak of its development.

CONSUMERS' COOPERATIVE ASSOCIATIONS

Nature and purposes of consumer cooperation

A consumers' cooperative is a voluntary association of ultimate consumers, organized to fulfill some of their needs for products and services. Cooperatives have been organized to provide medical care, housing, credit, electricity generation and distribution, rural telephone service, insurance, recreation, meals, lodging, supplies and books for college students, frozen-food lockers, and other services.

The following discussion will be confined to still another phase of the cooperative movement, retail store cooperative associations.[42] A retail store cooperative is a store owned and managed by a group of ultimate consumers who use the store as a source of supply for merchandise.[43] Instead of buying groceries, for example, at an independent or chain food store, they set up their own store. They provide the capital, usually through the purchase of stock. A board of directors is elected, which in turn hires a manager for the store. A store site is selected, and the necessary equipment and stock are purchased. If a number of such stores come into existence in a limited area, they may find it advisable to form their own wholesale house, which will buy for them from farmers and manufacturers. Merchandise may even be packed under the cooperative's private brand. And a final possible development is for the wholesale society to engage in the manufacture of some of the products it sells to its affiliated cooperative stores.

In the main, the economic aim of a cooperative retail store is lower net prices for members, although some members of cooperative associations look upon their organization as a means of abolishing capitalism as an economic system. In this discussion, however, we shall treat consumers' cooperative as a part of our marketing organization rather than concern ourselves with its effect on the capitalistic order.

---

[42] Another type of cooperative, the farmers' purchasing association, also handles many consumers' goods. However, it deals dominantly in industrial goods. For discussion, see Chapter 14.

[43] Most cooperative stores also sell to nonmembers, but usually without benefit of the patronage dividend.

Marketing: Principles and methods

Basic principles: The Rochdale plan

Cooperative societies operating retail stores were attempted in European countries long before 1844, the date at which the modern cooperative movement places its origin. These earlier cooperatives, however, were not successful, and they gradually went out of business. It remained for a group of flannel weavers in Rochdale, England, who organized as the Rochdale Society of Equitable Pioneers, to develop certain basic principles which, when applied to the earlier ideas of Robert Owen and others, led to the success of cooperatives. These principles, collectively known as the "Rochdale plan," are six in number: (1) open membership, (2) democratic control, (3) sales at prevailing prices and with patronage dividends, (4) limited interest on capital, (5) sales for cash, and (6) educational activities.

Open membership. The Rochdale plan places no limitation on membership. Whether or not a person joins a cooperative society is a voluntary matter; but if he desires to join, the possibility is open to him regardless of his political and religious views. To become a member, all he has to do is to subscribe to one or more shares of the society's stock.

Democratic control. The Rochdale pioneers opposed the domination of a society by a few individuals, and maintaining open membership was one way of avoiding clique control. A more direct way of achieving this same end was found in limiting the number of votes per member. In the modern corporation, voting is based on the number of shares held by the voter, but in a cooperative society, only one vote per member is allowed, regardless of the number of shares held. Although any member may be elected to the board of directors, an additional safeguard against clique control is provided, in some societies, by preventing reelection of a member to the board until after a certain period has elapsed. Other societies, however, have found that in the interest of efficiency, it is wise to allow certain directors to be reelected indefinitely. This decision illustrates one of the many points where cooperative principles and efficiency in operation come into conflict.

Sales at prevailing prices and patronage dividends. Some of the cooperative societies that failed in the years before the development of the Rochdale principles attempted to pass savings on to their members by selling at prices below those charged by other merchants. This procedure had the obvious advantage of making clear to members the savings they were realizing, but because it did not allow for the accumulation of adequate reserves, it often led to failure. In addition, it gave nonmembers the same price advantage as members and, by antagonizing competing storekeepers, led to price wars.

The Rochdale plan calls for sale at going market prices so as to allow the society to make a profit[44] out of which reserves may be accumulated. All earnings in excess of those needed in the business are returned to members, thus resulting in a lower net cost of merchandise for the members. These dividends to members are paid according to patronage, on the theory that they should go to those who make them possible by using the cooperative.

Limited interest on capital. In contrast with the owners of common stock of modern corporations, members owning stock issued by cooperative societies receive a definitely limited rate of dividends—commonly 4 to 6 percent—because the cooperatives prefer to return the bulk of their savings to members on a patronage basis. Although limiting the return on capital invested in a cooperative makes it more difficult

---

[44] Those in the cooperative movement commonly refer to their profit as a "saving" or a "surplus."

to raise funds, a number of other ways to obtain money are open. Weekly fees or annual dues may be collected; members may make loans to the society; profits or "savings" may be retained. Once a society is successfully established, borrowing in the name of the cooperative is possible just as it is to a private firm.

Sales for cash. Although many cooperative societies in the United States transact part of their business on a credit basis, the original Rochdale plan called for all sales for cash. By eliminating the costs of credit extension, the cooperative was in a better position to sell at prevailing prices and return a larger patronage dividend to its members.

Educational activities. From the beginning, the cooperatives have realized the necessity of educational activities to foster the cooperative spirit, urge loyalty to the movement, and encourage its development. Many present-day cooperatives make some effort in this direction by using part of each year's profits for financing lectures, distributing literature, and sponsoring classes in cooperation.[45]

Importance of consumers' cooperatives in the retailing system

In the United States. Consumer cooperation is far from a new idea in the United States, a buying club having been formed in Boston in the same year that the Rochdale pioneers formulated their plan in England. Yet the growth of the cooperative movement has been slow, and many societies have failed. It has been estimated that

TABLE 8–5
Growth of U.S. consumers' cooperatives, 1929–63

Year	Number of cooperative retail stores	Total annual sales (in millions)	Percentage of total retail business
1929	2,463	$ 180	0.37
1939	3,698	224	0.50
1948	4,398	1,066	0.80
1954	6,135	1,704	1.00
1958	5,964	1,306	0.66
1963	6,480	2,097	0.86

Source: See U.S. Bureau of the Census, *1963 Census of Business: Legal Forms of Organization*, BC63–R55 (Washington, D.C.: Government Printing Office, 1965), and earlier comparable census publications.

for 1903, there were only 200 cooperative stores in existence, and a study covering 1906 discovered only 343 local associations.[46] Census figures showing more recent developments are given in Table 8–5. However, these figures, small as they are, vastly overstate the cooperative's share of consumer goods sales. Some 57 percent of the current cooperative establishments accounting for 71 percent of cooperative sales are hay, grain, feed, farm supply, and farm equipment stores organized mainly to provide farmers with supplies (industrial products) rather than to sell consumer products. Less

---

[45] As early as 1846, the Rochdale pioneers placed one half of their yearly earnings in an educational fund to provide for the establishment of a library and classes for children.

[46] F. E. Parker, "Consumers' Co-operation in the United States," *Annals of the American Academy of Political and Social Science*, May 1937, p. 92.

Marketing: Principles and methods

than 20 percent of cooperative sales are of consumer products, with the bulk accounted for by gasoline service stations and food stores.[47]

In other countries. Outside the United States retail and wholesale cooperatives are more important components in the retailing systems. The societies handle 6.2 percent of the retail business of Western Europe,[48] and in several countries their sales ratio is substantially above this figure. About one fourth of all British families are now believed to hold membership in retail cooperatives; and, despite considerable dissatisfaction with what many Britishers believe to be outdated policies and practices,[49] the societies account for over 9 percent of total retail sales.[50] In Sweden one family in three does some buying through a cooperative, giving the societies about 17 percent of that nation's retail business.[51] The two major associations in Switzerland handle nearly 10 percent of all sales at retail.[52] Moreover, in these countries the stores are well served by large wholesale societies, which also engage heavily in manufacturing.

How does it happen that a form of retailing and wholesaling that is so important abroad is not more important in the United States? The answer is made clear by an analysis of the cooperative's possible economic advantages and limitations within our retailing system.

Outlook for consumers' cooperatives

The main economic aim of the cooperative movement is to supply members with quality merchandise at competitive prices and still pay a patronage dividend. Cooperatives hope to achieve their goal of quality merchandise by the careful selection and labeling of the merchandise they sell. They seek competitive prices and patronage dividends by making a tax saving, by eliminating the retailer's profit, having lower operating costs, and reducing their cost of merchandise below that of private businesses.

Possible tax saving. Private retail firms operating as corporations pay income taxes on their profits, which results in a direct reduction in the net profits of the private business. On the grounds that "surpluses" returned as patronage dividends belong to members and not to the association, cooperatives are not required to pay taxes on their earnings (profits, savings, or surplus) distributed as patronage dividends.[53] Consider the case of a private firm and a cooperative, each with a profit before taxes

[47] U.S. Bureau of the Census, *1963 Census of Business, Retail Trade: Legal Forms of Organization,* BC63–RS5 (Washington, D.C.: Government Printing Office, 1965), pp. 5–1 to 5–14. This series has been discontinued as of the *1967 Census of Business.*

[48] D. Carson, "Marketing in Italy Today," *Journal of Marketing,* 30 (January 1966), p. 14. The countries included by Professor Carson in arriving at the 6.2 percent average are Austria, Belgium, Denmark, Finland, France, Germany, Iceland, Ireland, Italy, Netherlands, Norway, Sweden, Switzerland, and United Kingdom.

[49] Reports one observer of British retailing: "To the majority of shoppers . . . the general impression of co-operative trading is that of an old-fashioned, cumbersome giant which is out of touch with the consumer of the 1960's." And, again: ". . . co-operative societies have lagged sadly behind in adapting their methods to current distribution requirements." C. Fulop, *Competition for Consumers* (London: Institute of Economic Affairs, 1964), p. 118.

[50] W. G. McClelland, "Some Management Problems Now Facing British Retailers," *Journal of Retailing,* 41 (Spring 1965), p. 8.

[51] C. M. Wieting, "Sweden's Co-operatives Move Ahead," *News for Farmer Cooperatives,* December 1965, p. 5.

[52] J. M. Hess and P. R. Cateora, *International Marketing* (Homewood, Ill.: Richard D. Irwin, Inc., 1966), p. 472.

[53] *United Co-operatives, Inc.* v. *Commissioner of Internal Revenue,* decided by United States Tax Court, September 29, 1944.

of $1 million. Each organization wishes to retain $500,000 of this sum in the business and to return the balance to stockholders or patrons. The private company would pay an income tax (most of it at the 48 percent maximum rate) computed on the *entire* $1 million; the cooperative would pay a tax just on the $500,000 retained in the business. Moreover, the cooperative could escape tax even on the $500,000 retained in the business by giving patrons shares of stock or promissory notes with long maturities, although in this case the cooperative member would be required to declare on his tax returns the value of the stock or promissory note. Such tax savings represent a decided advantage to the cooperative.

Ability to undersell private stores.   Since cooperatives have little or no advantage in the way of lower operating cost and lower buying prices, whatever lower prices they offer must come largely from the elimination of profits and a reduction in taxes. In most fields where active competition persists, the profit margin is fairly small. Moreover, even this source of saving may be eliminated unless cooperative management is fairly efficient. As far as taxes are concerned, expressed as a percentage of sales, the cooperative's saving is not great—even though it is large enough to be considered by many private businessmen as a discrimination against them. Thus, under the retailing system in the United States, the cooperative form of retailing generally fails to offer lower prices to its members. In the late 1960s, for example, numerous consumer cooperatives were undertaken as a means to mobilize efforts for self-improvement in ghetto communities. Virtually all failed because they lacked professional managers and the profit incentive and a profit measure to help them gauge their efficiency. Student cooperatives, when not subsidized by universities (free or reduced rental rates, management, bookkeeping systems), usually meet similar fates.

Other problems.   The mobility of our population is not conducive to the development of cooperatives. Unless a family expects to remain in a place for some time, so the argument runs, it may not find it worthwhile to join a society because the possible savings for a short period would be so small. Even if a society does attract persons who will not remain for long in one place, the problems that a constantly changing membership entails may be significant.

The cosmopolitan nature of our population and the absence of a community of interest among large segments of our people have also retarded the growth of consumer cooperation. Associative efforts in this country have been most successful in those regions where one nationality predominates and, even there, mainly in the rural areas and smaller towns and cities.

It does not seem that consumers' cooperatives will experience any appreciable growth in the United States.[54] Left to stand upon their own feet and forced to meet the competition of private retailers in the marketplace, the cooperatives face serious problems. Managerial know-how and efficient operation are just as essential in the cooperative establishment as they are in the private store. The future of both types of retailers lies in the competence they demonstrate in achieving that know-how and operating efficiency.

---

[54] A study of British retailing concludes that cooperatives are also losing ground in that country. They did 11.2 percent of all retailing in 1957, 10.2 percent in 1961, and were estimated to have handled 9.2 percent in 1966. McClelland, "Some Management Problems," p. 8. And in Italy, where the cooperative stores are "small and not at all up-to-date, . . . the total number of cooperative stores has been almost stationary" for many years. Giancarlo Ravaggi, "Retailing in a Developing Economy—Italy," *Journal of Retailing,* 43 (Spring 1967), p. 43.

SUMMARY

Owners of small-scale, group, and direct retailing systems—small businessmen— have for years been touted as the economic backbone of the United States. There can be no doubt that they will continue to be important components in the retailing and marketing systems.

Most small-scale retailers manage a single independent store that lacks any appreciable degree of specialization in employees or management. Over half of the independent stores have fewer than two employees, including the owner-manager. However, independent stores hold an important place in the retailing system, accounting for almost 88 percent of all the retail units and almost 60 percent of all retail sales.

At one time in the history of the United States, the independent general store was the most common type of retail outlet. Today the independent limited-line store— grocery, shoe, clothing, tobacco, drug—far outnumbers any other type of retail outlet. Many arguments have been advanced, however, that the independent limited-line store will fade from the scene. They are frequently located in deteriorating CBDs, they have little opportunity to relocate or establish in new shopping centers, they cannot afford the relatively high rent of shopping centers because of their limited volume, they lack sufficient funds for mass merchandising, and so forth. Our collective judgment, however, is that independent limited-line stores will be a major component in the retailing system for a long time.

One of the chief reasons for the continued survival and success of the independent retailer is his ability to take part in group activities. Four of these basic types of activities in the United States are buying and merchandising groups, retailer cooperatives, voluntary chains, and franchise organizations. Buying and merchandising groups are, for the most part, informal groups of merchants who engage in joint buying and promotional activities. They operate without the advantages of a wholesale house or a salaried manager and simply cooperate with one another through their existing facilities. Cooperative chains are distinguished by joint ownership by retailers of a wholesale house. Voluntary chains, on the other hand, are formed by wholesalers, with participating retailers agreeing to concentrate their purchases and to buy certain other services from the sponsoring wholesaler.

The most dramatic group effort in recent years has been the franchise system. The finished-goods franchised retailer (Ford dealers, Nunn-Bush Shoes, and Magnavox dealers) has been present, popular, and generally profitable for many years. The service-sponsor franchised retailer (H & R Block, Hertz, and Dairy Queen) has provided the rapid and sometimes controversial recent growth. These franchisees buy the right to use a trademark and may buy ingredients needed to produce and sell a set of products and services. Of course, they are not all new; such retail fast-food franchise systems as A & W root beer and MadeRite have been present for over 30 years.

Direct retailing and consumers' cooperatives are two other types of retailing considered in this chapter. Direct retailing systems of manufacturers sell directly to consumers without the use of middlemen, as in door-to-door or mail-order selling. Some wholesalers also sell directly to consumers. Sizable numbers of consumers seem to prefer the direct channel, although expenses of these sellers and, in turn, the prices of directly sold products tend to be higher than for wholesaler-retailer distribution. Because consumers normally do not engage in as much search or travel for products that are sold and delivered to their door, however, direct sellers' prices may be more in line than they appear to be at first glance.

Consumers' cooperatives are receiving renewed attention in the United States. Most university towns and most large cities have at least one consumers' cooperative which may deal in groceries, health foods, housing, books, day schools or any of a large number of commodities and services. Their number, while growing, is still not substantial in the total retailing system. Because the federal government last counted consumers' cooperatives in 1963, we cannot be very definite about just what has occurred in cooperative marketing.

The facts we have presented in this chapter on small-scale, group, and direct retailing systems are most useful as a basis for seeking explanations. On that note, we encourage you to review the statistics in this chapter after you have read the next chapter on large-scale retailing systems.

REVIEW AND DISCUSSION QUESTIONS

1. Explain fully the social significance of the small retail store in the United States.

2. What is a variety store? What chance does the small independent variety store have against the competition from large variety chains of the Woolworth, Kress, or Kresge type? Why?

3. Discuss the possibilities of continued existence in this country of the small grocery store, the dry goods store, and the commissary store.

4. Appraise the future of the small independent retailer in the United States.

5. Explain briefly the chief differences between a "regular" chain organization, such as A & P, Safeway, or Woolworth, and a "voluntary chain" organization, such as I.G.A., Red & White, or the Ben Franklin Stores.

6. List the main similarities and differences of the cooperative chain and the voluntary chain.

7. "The challenge of the future lies in the willingness of group-activity retailers to cooperate and to delegate supervisory authority to a central agency so as to make the best use of specialists and division of labor." Do you agree? Justify your answer.

8. Do franchise systems appear to strengthen or weaken the position of small independent retailers in the United States? Explain.

9. What are the salient differences between franchise systems and each of the other cooperative arrangements?

10. You have been employed by a small manufacturer of cosmetics to plan his marketing program. Evaluate house-to-house selling for his products.

11. Discuss the value of mail-order selling for a manufacturer of cosmetics.

12. Comment on the following statement: "Direct sale to the consumer is the lowest cost method of retailing primarily because it eliminates all the expenses and profits of the wholesaler and retailer."

13. What developments are likely to occur in direct retailing in the foreseeable future? State your reasons.

14. As national policy, should an effort be made to encourage the expansion of consumers' cooperatives in the United States? Give reasons for your conclusion.

15. Compare and contrast a retail store cooperative and the more usual type of retail institution on the basis of organization, ownership, operations, and overall social and economic philosophies.

SUPPLEMENTARY READINGS

Bunzel, J. H. *The American Small Businessman.* New York: Alfred A. Knopf, Inc., 1962. So difficult is the life of the small retailer (and the small manufacturer and wholesaler) that the author concludes: "Small businessmen claim to be the cornerstone of American Democracy, but it is doubtful if they can be counted upon to furnish imaginative and constructive leadership."

Cahill, J. *Can a Smaller Store Succeed?* New York: Fairchild Publications, Inc., 1966. The author, well versed in small-store problems and experiences, reviews the problems of the smaller specialty store in this country.

Clark, T. D. *Pills, Petticoats, and Plows.* Indianapolis, Ind.: Bobbs-Merrill Co., Inc., 1948. This history of the country store in the South from 1865 to 1915 discusses not only operating methods but social influence. It should be read for an understanding of the important part played by this marketing institution in the lives of the people of the South.

Duncan, D. J., Phillips, C. F. and Hollander, S. C. *Modern Retailing Management: Basic Concepts and Practices.* 8th ed. Homewood, Ill.: Richard D. Irwin, Inc., 1972. A new edition of a standard text in the retail field which treats all major aspects of retailing.

Gould, R. E. *Yankee Storekeeper.* New York: McGraw-Hill Book Co., Inc., 1946. The field of small-town retailing is made more vivid as this Maine Yankee tells his life story as a storekeeper.

Kelley, P. C. and Lawyer, K. E. *How to Organize and Operate a Small Business.* 3d ed. Englewood Cliffs, N.J.: Prentice-Hall, Inc., 1961. *Manual of Small Business Operation.* 4th ed. Englewood Cliffs, N.J.: Prentice-Hall, Inc., 1962. These volumes cover the essential factors involved in establishing a small business. The latter provides checklists helpful to those considering their own small stores.

Ozanne, H. B. and Hunt, S. D. *The Economic Effects of Franchising.* Madison, Wis.: Graduate School of Business, University of Wisconsin, 1971. A detailed report on an empirical study of franchisors and franchisees, with special emphasis on fast foods, laundry–dry cleaning and convenience grocery franchising. Includes an excellent bibliography.

Preston, L. E. (ed.) *Managing the Independent Business.* Englewood Cliffs, N.J.: Prentice-Hall, Inc., 1962. The editor has assembled and condensed considerable "material [which] originated as a series of lectures presented by members of the faculty of the School of Business Administration of the University of California (Berkeley) on television." The small retailer will find this source of information of much value.

9 Retailing: Large-scale systems

While small-scale retail establishments constitute by far the largest segment of retailing systems in the United States, the growth of large-scale institutions has been rapid, especially since 1900. Their number is constantly augmented by the most successful of the small-scale retailers, who gradually expand their operations to bring them into this classification. Today, over 45 percent (and perhaps as much as 50 percent or even more)[1] of our total retail business is accounted for by the five types of large-scale retailers to be discussed in this chapter: the chain store organization, the supermarket, the department store, the discount house, and the mail-order house.

As a general rule, these large-scale retailers have developed because there are advantages of size in retailing just as in other economic activities. The large-store or chain operator, as compared with the small-scale retailer, can integrate retailing activities with those of wholesaling and manufacturing, spread his risks, practice a greater division of labor, afford to experiment and carry on research activities, extend merchandising ideas developed by one store to other stores or departments, achieve greater financial strength, employ exceptionally able managers, purchase in larger quantities, use equipment which is too expensive for the small firm, and acquire the prestige which goes with size. But these gains of size may be offset, at least in part, by certain disadvantages: the "red tape" of large organizations, the problem of finding able managers, difficulties in maintaining good relationships with employees and the public, slowness in getting decisions, lack of personal incentive by employees, machinery necessary to maintain control of the organization, legal restrictions on pricing freedom, and higher tax rates. The applicability of these generally favorable and unfavorable factors to the five kinds of large-scale retailers will be considered below.

---

[1] Census data do not make it possible to be very precise on this matter. Although Chapter 7 gives 60 percent as the 1967 share of sales by independent stores, this classification includes many large-scale retailers such as independent supermarkets, independent discount houses, and independent department stores.

THE CHAIN STORE SYSTEM

A chain store organization is composed of two or more stores of similar type which are centrally owned and managed. An individual chain store is simply one unit or link in the chain store organization.

Major characteristics

A chain store system has four main characteristics: (1) central ownership, (2) central management, (3) similarity of stores, and (4) two or more units.

Central ownership implies that all the stores of the system are owned by a corporation, a partnership, or (as in some of the smaller chains) a single individual. *Central management* means that the individual stores in the chain do not have autonomy of operation. Instead, the buying, selling, and other operating policies are formulated at the chain's central, regional, or divisional headquarters. These policies are then enforced throughout the chain (or throughout one division, if the firm practices decentralization of management), although, in practice, exceptions may be made and the policies may differ for various groups of stores within the chain or division because of different operating conditions.

In general, the phrase *similarity of stores* refers to reasonable similarity in the line of goods carried, in the appeals made to the buying public, and often in store appearance. For instance, all units of the Great Atlantic & Pacific Tea Company tend to handle the same basic products; they make their main buying appeal on price; and many of the stores are similar in appearance and layout. These factors make possible a higher degree of standardization, which lies at the root of the success of the chain form of organization.

The *number of stores* necessary for a group to be called a chain is a minor matter. The foregoing three requirements—central ownership, central management, and similarity of stores—are fundamental. In early editions of this book a minimum of four stores was required, since the Bureau of the Census used a similar definition. Now that it is possible to make use of census data with a two-store definition, it seems advisable to use this more natural division between an independent and a chain store.[2]

Growth

Chain store growth was so rapid during the 1920s that its earlier development may be overlooked. This is unfortunate because many present-day chain store systems (or their predecessors) had their origins in the 19th century, and it was during this time that some of the existing policies and practices were first applied and tested. The close of World War I marked such an important change in the rate of chain store expansion, however, that it is a convenient dividing line.

Development to 1918. The origin of the first modern chain store is usually given as 1859, when the first unit of the Great American Tea Company, which was to become the Great Atlantic & Pacific Tea Company, was established in New York City. Although known as a "tea" store, it also carried coffee, spices, and a limited number of other food products. By 1869, there were six such stores. As additional

---

[2] The U.S. Bureau of the Census uses the term "multiunit firm" to include all those operating two or more establishments in the same general kind of business. In contrast, the *Progressive Grocer*, in its annual reports on the grocery industry, lists as "independent stores" those with 1 to 10 units and as "chain stores" those with 11 or more units.

stores were opened the line of merchandise was broadened, so that by 1910 the company's 370 stores were full-fledged grocery stores.

These early stores were distinctly different from those now operated by A & P. They encouraged the sale of merchandise by the use of premiums; they were large in size for those days and were located only in important cities; and they used house-to-house selling, by means of a salesman traveling by horse and wagon, to get additional business. It was not until 1912 or 1913 that the company made an abrupt· shift in its retailing methods by opening its "economy" stores. These units were typically so small that they could be staffed by just one man. Their inventory consisted of a fairly complete line of grocery products sold on a cash-and-carry basis under a low-price policy. With the change to this type of store, rapid expansion began. Early in 1915, the company reported 938 stores, 554 of which were of the economy type and had been opened within a two-year period.

After the founding of the present A & P, there was a gap of 13 years before the first unit of a second important chain was established, as shown in Table 9-1. This firm was also a "tea" company; it was not until 1879 that the first unit of an important chain outside the grocery field was established.[3] In that year, F. W. Woolworth opened his first store in Utica, New York. In 1882, J. G. McCrory began what was to become the second variety chain in Scottdale, Pennsylvania.

Federal Trade Commission data on 1,718 chain systems indicate that 58 of them were in existence by 1900, and by 1918 this number had increased to 645 systems operating 29,200 retail units.[4] A few chains were even then of considerable size: Kroger was operating 550 grocery stores and annual sales were approaching $26 million; the A & P had 3,799 stores and sales of $152 million; and Woolworth's 1,039 stores had annual sales of $107 million. Chains were also developing in a greater number of fields, but the chain store in 1918 was not important enough to give the independent merchant cause for worry, except in a few areas.

1918 to 1929: The chain store era. From the point of view of retailing, the years from 1918 through 1929 may well be referred to as the "chain store era." A few figures will show the magnitude of the development that took place. In contrast with its 1918 estimate of 29,200 chain store units in 26 retail fields, by 1929 the Federal Trade Commission reported 87,800 units in these fields. For all retail fields the first business census count, taken for 1929, reported over 216,000 chain units.

The growth of chain systems is emphasized also by the increasing percentage of total retail sales transacted in chain units. Starting slowly with about 4 percent in 1919 and 6 percent in 1923,[5] by 1929 they were doing almost 30 percent of retail business.

By that time the chains had invaded field after field which had earlier been considered quite unsuitable for their methods of retailing. In the early twenties, it was freely predicted that chain store methods were unsuited for items of large unit price,

---

[3] Prior to this time, of course, retailers in various fields had experimented with branch stores. For example, in 1872, John Wanamaker had branch clothing stores in Pittsburgh, Baltimore, Richmond, Memphis, St. Louis, and Louisville. See J. H. Appel, "Reminiscences in Retailing," *Bulletin of the Business Historical Society,* 12 (December 1938), p. 83. F. W. Woolworth, however, was the first to develop an important chain in the nonfood field.

[4] Federal Trade Commission, *Chain Stores: Growth and Development of Chain Stores* (Washington, D.C.: Government Printing Office, 1932), p. 63.

[5] J. P. Nichols, *Chain Store Manual* (New York: Institute of Distribution, 1936), p. 11; P. H. Nystrom, *Chain Stores* (Washington, D.C.: Chamber of Commerce of the United States, 1928); also see Nystrom's *Economics of Retailing,* Vol. I (New York: Ronald Press Co., 1930), p. 376.

Marketing: Principles and methods

TABLE 9–1

Some chain store systems established before 1900

Date of first unit	Company	Field of operation
1859	Great American Tea Company[a]	Groceries
1872	Jones Brothers Tea Company[b]	Groceries
1879	F. W. Woolworth Company	Varieties
1880	Owl Drug Company[c]	Drugs
1882	Kroger Grocery & Baking Company[d]	Groceries
	James Butler	Groceries
	J. G. McCrory[e]	Varieties
1883	D. A. Schulte, Inc.	Cigars
	Childs Grocery Company[f]	Groceries
1886	J. W. Crook Stores Company[g]	Groceries
	H. C. Bohack	Groceries
1887	Acme Tea Company[f]	Groceries
1888	George N. Dunlap Company[f]	Groceries
1889	Childs Company	Restaurant
1892	John R. Thompson	Restaurant
1894	Melville Shoe Corporation	Shoes
	G. R. Kinney Corporation[h]	Shoes
1895	Ginter Company[i]	Groceries
1896	S. H. Kress[j]	Varieties
1897	S. S. Kresge	Varieties
	O'Keeffe's, Incorporated[i]	Groceries
1898	Frank Shattuck Company	Restaurant
1899	National Tea Company[k]	Groceries
	John T. Connor Company[i]	Groceries
	Jewel Tea Company[l]	Groceries

[a] Now Great Atlantic & Pacific Tea Company of America.
[b] Now Grand Union Company.
[c] Now owned by Rexall Drug and Chemical Company.
[d] Now Kroger Company.
[e] Now part of Rapid-American complex.
[f] Now Acme Markets, Inc.
[g] Absorbed by Kroger Company.
[h] Controlled by F. W. Woolworth Company.
[i] Now First National Stores, Inc.
[j] Controlled by Genesco, Inc.
[k] Controlled by George Weston, Ltd.
[l] Now a division of Jewel Companies, Inc.
Sources: *Moody's Industrials;* annual reports; and interviews with executives of companies.

because such items demanded a quality of salesmanship chain stores could not obtain. Yet in 1929, there were 1,460 chain units in the furniture and home furnishing business and 1,290 units of motor vehicle dealers' chains.[6] It had also been argued that chain development would be quite impossible where personal service was important. But, although chain store growth was slower in such fields, in 1929 the beauty parlor chains had sales in excess of $15 million; undertaker chains had $2 million; and optical goods chains had nearly $7 million. It was argued further that chains could not flourish in fashion goods fields. Yet in 1929, there were 3,062 millinery chain units and 2,240 women's apparel shops. However, it was true in 1929 (as it is today) that

[6] The data in this paragraph are from U.S. Bureau of the Census, *Fifteenth Census of the United States, 1930, Distribution,* Vol I: *Retail Distribution* (Washington, D.C.: Government Printing Office, 1933), Part I, p. 30.

the chains experienced their greatest expansion in trades where highly standardized operations were possible.

1929 to 1948. During the 1930s and the days of World War II the development of the chain store was very different from what it was in the 1920s. As Table 9–2 shows, by 1948 the number of chain units was substantially below that of nearly 20 years earlier. The percentage of total retail business accounted for by chain systems had changed little, however, and their dollar sales were nearly triple those of 1929. It is clear from these facts what the chains were doing in the thirties and forties. After greatly increasing the number of units between 1919 and 1929, during the next two decades the chains weeded out the poorer stores and replaced smaller stores with fewer but larger ones, thus strengthening and consolidating their position. These trends were especially evident in the food field.

TABLE 9–2
Chain store units and percentage of total retail sales, 1929, 1939, 1948, 1954, 1958, 1963, and 1967

Year	Number of chain store units	Percentage of total retail sales
1929	216,524	29.6
1939	201,040	30.6
1948	162,655	29.6
1954	167,027	30.1
1958	182,735	33.7
1963	219,783	36.6
1967	220,131	39.8

Source: U.S. Bureau of the Census, *1963 Census of Business, Retail Trade* and *1967 Census of Business, Retail Trade* (Washington, D.C.: Government Printing Office, 1965 and 1971).

Developments since 1948. After 1948, the chains resumed their expansion in terms of both number of units and percentage of total retail sales. Today the total number of retail units is not much larger than it was in 1929, but their share of retail sales has increased by one third and is growing faster than the growth in number of stores.

1. *Expansion in shopping centers.* This growth relates particularly to the shopping center development. Promoters of these centers have diligently wooed chain stores as tenants, and the chains have eagerly sought the sales possibilities these centers offer. This is not to imply that chains have ceased all downtown expansion; rather, their emphasis has been placed on shopping centers. To cite just three examples: During one year, Rose's Stores, Inc., a variety store organization, opened six new units, of which five were in shopping centers; 12 of the 13 new units opened by Lerner Stores Corporation, a women's apparel chain, were similarly located;[7] and the junior department store chain of W. T. Grant Company added 51 new stores, all of them in shopping centers or free standing.[8]

2. *Larger stores, broader merchandise lines.* Another trend of the last decade

---

[7] Rose's Stores, Inc., *Annual Report,* 1966, p. 10; and *Women's Wear Daily,* April 4, 1967, p. 26.

[8] W. T. Grant Company, *Annual Report,* fiscal year ended January 31, 1967, p. 3.

Marketing: Principles and methods

has been a further move toward still larger units. Food chains, which opened units of 5,000 square feet in the mid-1940s, now require 15,000 to 25,000 square feet or more. Variety store chains, drug chains, and others show a similar development.[9] J. C. Penney Company opened a 280,000-square-foot store at Roosevelt Field, Long Island in 1969 and its largest store, in Woodfield Center in Schaumburg, Illinois, in 1971. It has several other stores in excess of 150,000 square feet, in contrast to its typical store of 15,000 to 20,000 square feet a few years ago.

The trend toward larger chain units is a reflection, in large part, of another trend—the broadening of merchandise lines. In today's chain drugstore unit, drug items frequently account for a small percentage of total sales. General merchandise or nonfood departments occupy 6 percent of the selling area of supermarkets. The large Grant City units operated by the W. T. Grant Company contain garden shops, automotive service centers, radio and television departments, restaurants, furniture, and rug areas, as well as the firm's more traditional merchandise. Stanley C. Hollander has found such merchandise scrambling to be "one of the most prominent characteristics of contemporary distribution,"[10] and it will likely persist into the next decade of chain store development.

3. *More stores, increased sales.* The number of stores and sales of chain store companies, at least in the food field, continue to increase. As indicated by Table 9–3,

TABLE 9–3
Sales and number of stores in food store chains, 1963 and 1967

Units in chain	Number of stores		Sales (000)	
	1963	1967	1963	1967
2 or 3 stores	9,008	6,599	$ 2,929,924	$ 3,483,825
4 or 5 stores	2,134	1,997	1,076,560	1,223,920
6 to 10 stores	2,361	2,472	1,615,680	2,038,786
11 to 25 stores	3,225	3,452	2,327,665	3,494,087
26 to 50 stores	2,249	3,250	1,742,747	2,778,595
51 to 100 stores	2,701	2,740	2,839,552	4,003,697
101 or more stores	19,391	23,434	18,350,027	23,741,088
Totals	41,069	43,944	$30,882,155	$40,763,998

Source: U.S. Bureau of the Census, *1967 Census of Business, Retail Trade: Subject Reports* (Washington, D.C.: Government Printing Office, 1971), p. 4–2, and *1963 Census of Business, Retail Trade: Subject Reports,* pp. 4–4, 4–5.

the total number of stores in food chains from 1963 to 1967 increased from 41,069 to 43,944 (7 percent) while sales increased from about $31 billion to almost $41 billion (32 percent). Chains with five or fewer units have actually decreased in number. Many new chain firms have also come into existence in the rapidly growing discount house field. At the same time, such long-established chain systems as Sears, Roebuck and Company, J. C. Penney Company, W. T. Grant Company and others have demonstrated their continued ability to grow.

4. *Foreign operations.* Although Woolworth and a few other chains have long operated stores in other countries, this practice has become increasingly common

---

[9] "32nd Annual Forecast of Construction, Modernization and Equipment," *Chain Store Age,* January 1971, p. 3.

[10] S. C. Hollander, "Notes on the Retail Accordion," *Journal of Retailing,* 42 (Summer 1966), p. 30.

during the past two decades. Among the many U.S.–based chains also operating in Canada are Safeway Stores, Inc., with over 250 units; S. S. Kresge Company, with over 100 units; and W. T. Grant Company, with its controlling interest in the units of Zeller's Limited. Safeway also has over 50 stores in West Germany, the United Kingdom, and Australia; and directly or through joint ventures the Jewel Companies have supermarkets in Italy, Belgium, and the first of a proposed chain of discount houses in Spain.[11] The Walgreen Company, through an affiliate known as Sanborns, operates a group of stores in Mexico. Sears, Roebuck and Company has more than 60 units in Mexico and South America; at least one unit in Spain; and about 30 stores operated under Simpson-Sears, Limited, in Canada. In addition to over 2,000 domestic stores, Woolworth-controlled units may be found in Canada, West Germany, Mexico, the United Kingdom, and Spain. In view of the opportunities in foreign markets, it is likely that the next decade will witness even more expansion in other countries on the part of U.S.–based chain store systems.[12]

Position today. Referring again to Table 9–2, it can be seen that in 1967 the chain accounted for about 40 percent of all sales made by the retailing system. This ratio varies widely by kind of business. Chains are responsible for nearly 84 percent of all variety store sales but not quite 17 percent of sporting goods sales. Chains transact almost 61 percent of shoe store sales, 58 percent of food sales, 39 percent of drugstore business, and about 14 percent of hardware sales.[13]

Table 9–4 summarizes 1970 earnings and employees for the 25 largest chain organizations. By any of the measures shown in the table, Sears, Roebuck is a giant even among the large chain store companies.

The firms listed in Table 9–4 are gigantic retailing machines, with hundreds of stores and thousands of employees serving millions of people. Their tremendous sales volume, reflecting wide public acceptance, has been attained through alert merchandising efforts and continuous innovations. To cite but one example: The J. C. Penney Company in recent years has, among other innovations, granted credit, added private-brand kitchen and laundry appliances produced by the Hotpoint Division of the General Electric Company, increased its emphasis on fashion merchandise, opened larger stores, entered the mail-order business, and established catalog sales departments in some of its stores.[14] Such adjustments and continued attention to efficiency of operation have been responsible for the contributions of chain stores to the rising standard of living in the United States.

Success in the chain store business, despite the growth of many organizations, is by no means automatic. In recent years, for example, competition has forced the former limited-price variety chains to add higher priced lines and diversify their offerings. Some, like Woolworth and S. S. Kresge, have established discount chains (Woolco department stores and K-Mart); others, like J. J. Newberry, Neisner Brothers, and S. H. Kress Company, have reduced or omitted their dividends because of lower earnings and/or the desire to conserve capital needed for expansion; and still others

---

[11] U.S., Mexican, and Spanish Companies Plan Spain's First Discount Stores," *Business Week,* July 15, 1967, p. 84.

[12] Some of these opportunities, as well as the problems involved, are set forth in M. Y. Yoshino, "International Opportunities for American Retailers," *Journal of Retailing,* 42 (Fall 1966), pp. 1–10, 76.

[13] U.S. Bureau of the Census, *1967 Census of Business, Retail Trade: Subject Reports* (Washington, D.C.: Government Printing Office, 1971), pp. 4–8, 4–37.

[14] The recent evolution of the J. C. Penney Company is detailed in John McDonald, "How They Minted the New Penney," *Fortune* July, 1967, pp. 110–13, 160–65.

TABLE 9–4

Sales, earnings, and employees of the largest chain store companies, 1970

Rank 1970	Company	Sales ($000)	Assets ($000)	Rank	Net income $000	Rank	Net income as percent of sales	Employees	Rank
1	Sears, Roebuck (Chicago)	9,262,162	7,623,096	1	464,201	1	5.0	359,000	1
2	*Great Atlantic & Pacific Tea (New York)	5,650,000	957,073	6	53,000	8	0.9	120,000	5
3	*Safeway Stores (Oakland)	4,860,167	875,705	10	68,892	5	1.4	96,760	6
4	J. C. Penney (New York)	4,150,886	1,627,055	3	114,096	2	2.7	145,000	3
5	*Kroger (Cincinnati)	3,735,774	767,777	13	39,732	9	1.1	83,813	7
6	Marcor (Chicago) (Montgomery Ward)	2,804,856	2,459,730	2	59,637	7	2.1	127,100	4
7	S.S. Kresge (Detroit)	2,595,155	926,227	7	66,994	6	2.6	80,500	8
8	F. W. Woolworth (New York)	2,527,965	1,436,297	4	76,624	4	3.0	225,275	2
9	Federated Department Stores (Cincinnati)	2,096,935	1,165,770	5	82,169	3	3.9	75,700	9
10	*Food Fair Stores (Philadelphia)	1,762,005	363,472	22	10,636	30	0.6	30,000	21
11	*Acme Markets (Philadelphia)	1,650,249	336,448	23	12,530	28	0.8	35,283	17
12	*Jewel Companies (Melrose Park, Ill.)	1,628,496	486,059	19	23,962	15	1.5	48,314	13
13	*National Tea (Chicago)	1,512,282	265,993	30	9,868	31	0.7	31,000	20
14	*Lucky Stores (San Leandro, Calif.)	1,488,715	275,234	29	23,475	16	1.6	26,000	26
15	*Winn-Dixie Stores (Jacksonville)	1,418,916	201,337	36	27,615	13	1.9	27,700	23
16	Gamble-Skogmo (Minneapolis)	1,296,704	771,896	12	15,066	24	1.2	24,275	30
17	W.T. Grant (New York)	1,259,116	807,628	11	39,577	10	3.1	65,000	10
18	Allied Stores (New York)	1,225,070	921,506	9	14,801	25	1.2	50,000	12
19	City Products (Des Plaines, Ill.)	1,207,127	519,414	17	24,772	14	2.1	33,600	19
20	*Grand Union (East Paterson, N.J.)	1,200,831	236,731	33	15,741	23	1.3	25,000	28
21	May Department Stores (St. Louis)	1,170,383	925,380	8	31,873	11	2.7	56,000	11
22	Dayton Hudson (Minneapolis)	969,287	691,357	14	18,970	20	2.0	27,000	24
23	*Allied Supermarkets (Detroit)	952,142	228,459	34	(4,852)	50	–	17,000	39
24	Southland (Dallas)	950,721	289,189	25	14,430	26	1.5	18,900	37
25	R.H. Macy (New York)	907,029	579,264	16	20,660	19	2.3	37,500	16

*Food chains.

Source: "The Fifty Largest Retailing Companies," *Fortune*, May 1971, pp. 196–97.

are subjecting their entire operations to close scrutiny in an effort to minimize their costs. In today's markets, only the more efficient chain organizations are able to prosper.

Factors in chain store development

Among the social and economic factors that have influenced the growth of chain stores are the following:

1. The movement of population toward the urban areas which made possible the location of chain units close together and facilitated the solution of warehousing, transportation, advertising, and supervision problems.
2. The increased use of automobiles and the building of good roads, which made shopping easier for customers and deliveries to and from warehouses and stores easier.
3. The sharp rise in prices, particularly on food items, which turned many consumers into "bargain hunters" and enabled chain stores to capitalize on consumers' moods.[15]
4. The growth of installment buying, which caused many people to economize on certain necessities and to turn to the chain stores to effect savings on their purchases.
5. The shopping center development, and the desire of landlords to secure the well-financed chains as tenants.
6. The overall inefficiency of the retailing and marketing systems, which provided a fertile field for chain store growth because, especially in the early days of this development, the greater efficiency of the chain system in both retailing and wholesaling gave it a distinct advantage over other middlemen.

Chain store policies and practices. The policies and practices of the chains themselves, together with the inherent advantages of this type of operation, also contributed importantly to their success. These policies and practices may be classi-fied under two major headings: the low-price appeal of the chain store and improved retailing practices.

1. *Price appeal.* Almost from its origin, the chain store has emphasized price as a means of gaining patronage. In 1867 the A & P (then the Great American Tea Company) proclaimed its low-price policy. Today, most major chains continue the traditional policy of low prices and low margins; in fact, price appeal still plays the greatest part in chain store advertising, despite a tendency to give more attention to assortments, quality of merchandise, and store services. The appeal is also supported by facts. Study after study shows that the chains have undersold their competitors. Even though their advantage has declined relatively during the past 25 years as their

---

[15] In his *Only Yesterday* (New York: Harper & Bros., 1931), p. 5, the late Frederick Allen describes what "Mr. and Mrs. Smith" were discussing in May 1919: "Mr. and Mrs. Smith discussed a burning subject, the High Cost of Living. Mr. Smith is hoping for an increase in salary, but meanwhile the family income seems to be dwindling as prices rise. Everything is going up—food, rent, clothing, and taxes. . . . Mrs. Smith, confronted with an appeal from Mr. Smith for economy, reminds him that milk has jumped since 1914 from 9 cents to 15 cents, sirloin steak from 27 cents to 42 cents a pound, butter from 32 cents to 62 cents a pound, and fresh eggs from 34 cents to 62 cents a dozen."

As early as 1916, it was recognized by some that rising prices would aid the chains. For example, T. H. Price wrote in November of that year that "the economy that the present high price of food will compel seems likely to increase the appeal of the chain store for . . . [the] public. . . ." See his article on "The Chain Grocery Store," *Outlook,* November 22, 1916, p. 690.

Marketing: Principles and methods

competitors have gained in efficiency and new types of stores have emerged, it is still significant, especially when the chain's private brands are taken into account. One study, for example, shows food chains still underselling independent retailers by 8 percent and group or affiliated retailers by 2.5 percent.[16] For this price advantage, three factors are responsible: the chain's low operating cost, its buying advantage, and its low profit margin.

a) Operating cost. Chain store organizations are able to perform the wholesale and retail functions more economically for at least the following reasons:

1. They frequently limit the free services they offer, such as credit, returns and adjustments, and deliveries.
2. In the grocery, variety, drug, and some other fields, they operate increasingly on the self-service plan.
3. They turn over their stocks more rapidly than many independent stores and reduce expenses through savings on interest charges, storage space, and insurance.
4. Through standardization of fixtures, equipment, store arrangement, order forms, and similar programs and methods, they effect savings in purchasing and in the number of employees required.
5. They reduce the advertising cost per store because one advertisement covers all stores within a particular trading area.
6. They make possible (particularly in the larger organizations) a division of labor through assignment of people with varying abilities to the jobs they can do best, thus reducing the total wage bill.
7. Chain store systems operating warehouses and providing their own transportation find it possible to salvage boxes, barrels, sacks, and wastepaper through developing a "cost consciousness" on the part of the store managers.
8. They achieve greater sales per square foot of floor space and per employee, as compared with independent stores.
9. They place the locating, designing, and equipping of new stores in the hands of experts, thus achieving efficiency in operation and minimizing the number of units which fail to operate at a profit.
10. Through integration of wholesale and retail activities, some reductions in costs are effected, such as the elimination of the wholesaler's salesmen. This integration is being made more effective as wholesale and retail inventories are coordinated through electronic data processing systems.
11. The chains' superior access to capital through the national securities market both reduces their capital costs relative to that of smaller merchants and aids them in financing cost-saving technological innovations.
12. Chains are able to train personnel through all levels of management more systematically than their independent competitors.

b) Buying advantage. The buying advantage of the chain is made up fairly equally of buying power, or the ability to command lower prices, and buying skill, or the ability to buy wisely.

---

[16] P. E. Nelson and L. E. Preston, *Price Merchandising in Food Retailing: A Case Study* (Berkeley, Calif.: University of California, Institute of Business and Economic Research, 1966), table 7, p. 27. Also see the price comparisons reported in one of the technical studies made in connection with the work of the National Commission on Food Marketing, *Organization and Competition in Food Retailing* (Washington, D.C.: Government Printing Office, 1966), chap. 16, "Comparative Performance of Chain, Affiliated, and Unaffiliated Independent Food Retailers."

c) Low profit margin.   The third major reason why chains undersell their competitors is that most chains operate on the basis that a small profit per dollar of sales will lead to a larger turnover and greater aggregate net profits. Insofar as chain profit margins are below those of their competitors, this element aids the chains to undersell other retailers.

2. *Effective retailing practices.*   There have been other factors in the success of the chains besides their ability to undersell competitors. Briefly, the chain has attempted to provide prompt and courteous store service; clean, modern, attractive, and well-located stores; and good-quality merchandise in relation to price.

Some limitations to chain store growth

It is evident that chain stores have assumed an important place in the distribution system. Four major groups of influences, however, have limited their development: (1) certain inherent disadvantages, (2) resentment against some of their methods, (3) antitrust policy, and (4) competition from other retailers.

Inherent disadvantages.   Some disadvantages to chain store operations include the following factors.

1. *Limited interest of personnel.*   The chain store, in common with all large-scale business, finds it difficult to maintain the same personal interest of its employees in the success of the organization as that found in independent stores. As the chain grows and the store manager, the supervisor, and perhaps a district manager stand between the salesperson and the general manager, the feeling of direct responsibility decreases.

2. *Standardization difficulties.*   The high degree of standardization in chain stores gives rise to certain disadvantages. So that turnover may be rapid, the stock carried in each store may be so standardized that the customer has a limited selection from which to choose. Prices may be set at headquarters, and the manager may have limited authority to meet local conditions. The selling of fashion goods and high-priced goods is difficult to standardize, so some chains dislike to stock such items. "Free" services like credit and delivery demand considerable local autonomy and make difficult the standardized control desired by top executives. The standardized and impersonal store operated by many chain organizations, therefore, does not appeal to all customers.

3. *Relative inefficiency.*   Finally, the mere size of the chain company gives rise to certain problems. In most cases, perhaps, a vast amount of "red tape" and paperwork are involved. Decisions may be made quickly, but it may take a long time to put them into operation. Moreover, those making decisions have to rely on information furnished by others, and their lack of firsthand knowledge of a problem may result in poor decisions. For these reasons, a certain degree of inefficiency may creep into a chain organization; and, unless quickly corrected, these inefficiencies can cause the demise of a business.[17]

Resentment against methods and policies.   The chain store is not the only form of large-scale retailing which has stirred up resentment against some of its policies and methods, but it has probably suffered most from the resulting criticism. During the 1930s, when the "antichain movement" was at a peak, it was argued that:

---

[17] For an illustration where they almost did, see L. A. Mayer, "How Confusion Caught up with Korvette," *Fortune*, February 1966, pp. 153–54 ff.

1. The chains are monopolistic.
2. They use unfair practices, especially "loss leaders," to remove independent competitors.
3. They are a detriment to community life because—
   a) Absentee ownership removes their interest in the community.
   b) Money is drained from the community.
   c) They do not pay their proportion of taxes.
   d) They are unfair to local bankers.
4. They are unfair to their employees, since they—
   a) Force long hours.
   b) Pay low wages.
   c) Encourage dishonesty (such as underweighting).
   d) Offer little chance of advancement.

In general, most of these charges were in the nature of half-truths—just valid enough to be readily acceptable by many people. The chains gradually changed their policies, however, so as to minimize those parts of the charges which were valid, with the result that this limitation to their future growth has been minimized. Yet public resentment against them remained strong enough during the 1930s and 1940s to support a considerable amount of antichain legislation.

Antitrust policy. While our federal antitrust policy has not limited the *internal* expansion of chain store systems (that is, through the opening of additional stores), the Federal Trade Commission has sought to curtail their *external* growth by restricting their acquisition of other firms and forcing them to dispose of some of the stores already acquired.

For example, the Commission reached an agreement with the Federated Department Stores in August 1965 "by which the chain agreed to table its merger thinking for five years." In another somewhat typical case, the Grand Union Company agreed to sell 10 supermarkets in New York State that it acquired in 1958 and to obtain prior approval on sizable supermarket acquisitions in localized areas where it already had stores.

Of even greater significance than Commission action, however, was a decision of the U.S. Supreme Court in May 1966 *un*merging Von's Grocery Company and Shopping Bag Food Stores, both of Los Angeles. The merger took place in 1960, and the combined sales of the two firms constituted just 7.5 percent of the area's retail grocery sales. Breaking new ground, the Court in effect ruled that "mergers of substantial, healthy competitors must be blocked in a market that is still highly competitive but tending toward an oligopoly—where a few giants operate."[18]

Early in 1967 the Federal Trade Commission issued formal merger guidelines for food distributors. The statement indicated that all acquisitions and mergers resulting in combined annual retail sales of more than $500 million will receive the Commission's "attention and consideration." The guidelines require large firms to notify the Commission at least 60 days prior to any such merger or acquisition.[19]

Competition from other retailers. While inefficiency is still present in independent operations, in recent years they have provided much keener competition,

---

[18] See "High Court Bars Merger of Rivals," *Business Week,* June 4, 1966, p. 36. For the actual decision see *United States* v. *Von's Grocery Company,* et al. (S. Ct., May 1966). Also see the analysis of this case by C. F. Phillips, Jr., "Legal Developments in Marketing," *Journal of Marketing,* 30 (October 1966), pp. 68–69.

[19] "FTC Announces Formal Merger Guidelines for Cement, Food-Distribution Industries," *Wall Street Journal,* January 18, 1967, p. 3.

so that the earlier competitive advantages the chain derived from reduced marketing costs have been decreased. Wholesalers have taken steps to cut operating costs and to give better service to independent retailers. Voluntary and cooperative chains have strengthened the competitive position of their affiliated retailers. Many independents have profited from studying chain store methods of location, store arrangement, display, pricing, and advertising; and some of them have opened large supermarkets, giant discount houses, home and garden shops, and other types of modern retail establishments. Interchain competition has also become intense, especially in the large cities and in shopping centers. While the chain store systems remain an efficient method of distributing merchandise, under today's competitive conditions there is little reason to believe that they will greatly increase their present percentage of total retail sales in the foreseeable future.

THE SUPERMARKET

One of the large-scale retail institutions which has developed in the retailing system in this country is the supermarket. Since 1930 it has grown rapidly, and today both independent and chain supermarkets are found in all sections of the United States. Currently the supermarket is also gaining acceptance in other countries, including, among others, England, Switzerland, West Germany, Italy, and Belgium.

A supermarket defined

It is difficult to formulate a satisfactory definition of a supermarket that is comprehensive enough to cover all types of stores operating under this name. However, the following broad definition will serve: A supermarket is a departmentized retail store having annual sales of $1 million or more in a variety of merchandise, and in which the sale of food, much of which is on a self-service basis, plays the major role.[20]

Although the early supermarkets were established by independent retailers as a means of combating the chain, by 1968 over 52 percent of supermarkets and over 53 percent of their sales were controlled by chains. Of the nonchain supermarkets, practically all (82 percent) are affiliated with cooperative or voluntary chains. Since earlier sections of this chapter have been devoted to the chain store as such, in the discussion which follows we shall concentrate attention on features of the supermarket that apply regardless of whether the store is operated by a chain, an independent, or a retailer affiliated with a voluntary or cooperative chain.

Development and current importance

Stores with many of the supermarket's characteristics have existed for some time, but the type as we know it developed on the West Coast during the late twenties and in the East during the depression of the early thirties. Seldom have customers been as sales-conscious, seldom has as much "distress" merchandise been available, and seldom have as many large buildings suitable for supermarkets been vacant as in late 1932, when the first eastern supermarket was opened in Elizabeth, New Jersey. Its

---

[20] This definition is similar to that of the Super Market Institute, which describes a supermarket as "a complete, departmentalized food store with a minimum sales volume of one million dollars a year and at least the grocery department fully self-service." See Super Market Institute, *The Super Market Industry Speaks: 1967* (Chicago, 1967), p. 3.

Marketing: Principles and methods

immediate success led others to copy its operating methods. As the independent supermarkets began to undersell chain food stores and cut into their sales, the chains also turned to this type of operation.

Statistics on the early period of supermarket growth indicate the general trend. As early as 1938, supermarkets had annual sales of $1 billion; and by 1948, this had increased to $7.8 billion.[21] Table 9–5 provides figures showing that the striking growth of supermarkets has continued in recent years to the point that there are now over 36,000 such stores in this country doing over $55 billion in annual sales, or 74 percent of total grocery sales.

TABLE 9–5
Statistics on supermarket growth, selected years, 1957–1968

Year	Number of supermarkets	Sales (in billions)	Percentage of grocery sales
1957	18,843	25.2	60
1959	22,523	32.4	70
1962	28,102	39.1	75
1965	31,309	44.8	76
1968	35,900	54.5	74

Source: "The True Look of the Super Market Industry, 1965," *Super Market Merchandising*, April 1966, p. 39; and "36th Annual Report of the Grocery Industry," *Progressive Grocer*, April 1969, p. 61.

Factors contributing to supermarket growth in the retailing system

Price appeal. Without doubt, price appeal is a major reason for the growth of supermarkets. With relatively high merchandise turnover, a small profit per dollar of sales, and a large sales volume, they have undersold many of their competitors. To continue such underselling, in recent years so-called discount supermarkets have been opened, that is, stores with less expensive equipment and fixtures, often operating without trading stamps and carry-out personnel, and sometimes with merchandise displayed in cartons. These discount supermarkets may undersell the more conventional store by 1 or 2 percent although it is not yet firmly established that, as other units of the discount type move into an area, they can continue to be profitable with such a price differential.[22] A low-price appeal is also characteristic of the supermarkets within the discount department stores that have become a significant factor in the retailing system during the past two decades.

Increased services. Price appeal, although important, is not the only factor in the supermarket's growth. Buyers are attracted by the supermarket's "one-stop shopping," where, under one roof, they can buy all their food as well as many other kinds of merchandise. The parking facilities offered are another inducement. The fact that supermarkets have taken the lead in remaining open during the evenings and on Sundays (with an increasing number of them open 24 hours a day on a seven-days-a-week basis) when many customers find it most convenient to buy, has added to their

---

[21] "The True Look of the Super Market Industry, 1958," *Super Market Merchandising*, April 1959, p. 82.

[22] C. Day, "Discounting Drops Its Hemline," *Supermarketing*, April, 1970, pp. 17–24.

appeal. Customers have also been attracted by the facilities they offer, such as check cashing service, "music while you shop," and restrooms. The desire of shopping center promoters to include supermarkets in their developments is another element in explaining the growth of this retail institution.

The bantam store. Recent experience suggests that there is a place for a "bantam" or convenience type of supermarket within the retailing system.[23] These stores handle a more limited variety of brand-name products than their larger namesake and prices are somewhat higher, but they usually compensate for these limitations by convenient locations and typically long hours—frequently, 24 hours a day or at least 7 A.M. to 11 P.M.—on a seven-days-a-week basis. Sunday is their busiest day. Operating with a minimum of personnel, these "vest-pocket" supermarkets cater to customers who desire fast and convenient service. Although the typical sale is under $3, their careful inventory control and low labor costs often enable them to earn more per dollar of sales than the conventional supermarkets.[24]

Most of these convenience stores are chain operated by organizations such as the 7-Eleven of Dallas, Texas, with more than 2,300 stores; Li'l General Stores, Inc., with about 400 stores in the South; Utotem, Inc., with 300 stores in the Southwest; and the Lawson Milk Company, operating more than 550 stores in the Midwest. That stores of this type are fulfilling a need is shown by the fact that their number increased from an estimated 5,000 in 1964 to 7,800 in 1967, and their annual sales exceed $1 billion.[25]

Bantam stores are providing tough competition in numerous markets and are leading some supermarkets to change their operations. Some supermarkets are remodeling their stores so when the main store is closed evenings and Sundays the bantam department can remain open.[26]

Future of the supermarket

The supermarket has won a place for itself in the retailing system. Although it may not add to its percentage of total grocery sales, a growing population and the development of new shopping centers in suburbia provide the background for a further rise in the number of supermarkets and in their total sales. The majority of supermarkets will remain mainly food stores, but some operators may add many nonfoods; and still others will continue the current trend toward diversification by opening limited-line stores restricted to such merchandise as drugs, liquor, or home and garden supplies.[27] We may also expect many new supermarkets to be located within discount houses. And, of course, if automation eventually reduces substantially the cost of operating the supermarket, its percentage of total food sales may begin to advance again.

---

[23] Typically, this store has an annual sales volume of about $165,000, so that it is not, strictly speaking, a supermarket as that term is defined in this chapter.

[24] For extensive data on bantam-type store operations, see *The Journal of Convenience Stores* (New York: United Publishing Company).

[25] R. D. Hershey, Jr., "Convenience Stores Filling Their Role," *New York Times,* January 23, 1966, pp. F1, 12; "Full-Fledged Boom for Convenience Stores," *Progressive Grocer,* April 1967, p. 60; "How Bantams Are Blanketing the U.S.," *Chain Store Age* (Supermarket Executives Edition), May 1967, pp. 34–35, 42; and "Marsh Joins Bantam Boom," *Non-Food Business,* July, 1967, p. 42.

[26] "Bantam, Super Now Under Same Roof," *Chain Store Age* (Supermarket Executives Edition), September 1969, pp. E–71, E–72.

[27] "The Grocery Business," *Forbes,* November 1969, pp. 34–49.

THE DEPARTMENT STORE

A department store is a retail organization which sells a wide variety of merchandise, including piece goods, home furnishings, and furniture; is organized by departments; has large sales; sells mainly to women; is located typically in the downtown shopping district or in a shopping center; and usually offers a large amount of "free" service.[28] Two of these characteristics deserve brief comment.

Typically, the large department store has four or five major divisions devoted to merchandising, advertising and sales promotion, operating activities, personnel, and control, each under a vice president or another major executive. As far as merchandise is concerned, it is segregated into departments to facilitate its purchase and sale—such as piece goods, floor coverings and women's wear departments.

The latest census figures show that the 5,792 U.S. department stores had annual sales of $32.3 billion. They accounted for 10.4 percent of all sales in the retailing system and the average unit had annual sales of $5.6 million, as contrasted with $179,000 for the all-store average.[29] The department store is a large retail organization, relative to retail stores in general.

Classifications of department stores

Two useful ways department stores can be classified are (1) ownership and (2) the income class to which they appeal.

Ownership. Classified on the basis of ownership, department stores may be described as (1) independents, (2) ownership-group stores, and (3) chain stores. If we define *independent* as single-unit firms, there were 609 such department stores in 1967 which transacted about 6 percent of all department store business.[30] If the definition is expanded to include those former single-unit firms which have opened nearby branches, from 15 to 20 percent of all department store sales would be included. Many of these stores are closely owned by their founders or by descendants of founders and closely resemble the single-unit firms.

Ownership groups were originally composed of stores that have been in existence for a long period of time and have been brought together under central ownership. Many of these groups have also opened new units. Actions by the Federal Trade Commission have so limited the possibility of growth by further acquisitions, however, that these firms have now turned mainly to internal growth. While in most of these groups the central ownership has been accompanied by some degree of common management and central control, in some groups the stores have been allowed to carry on much as before. They have their own buyers, plan their own advertising, and, in general, maintain their own individuality. In most cases, they even retain their original names, although in some groups most of the names have been changed to that of the holding company. Federated Department Stores, Inc. is a good example of an ownership group.[31]

---

[28] Because departmentized specialty stores have most of the characteristics mentioned, it has become customary to distinguish the two types by the fact that the department store carries piece goods, house furnishings, and furniture, whereas the departmentized specialty store does not. This distinction, of course, is rather arbitrary, since in assortments carried (in other lines), services rendered, departmental organization, and other matters, the stores are very similar.

[29] *1967 Census of Business, Retail Trade: Subject Reports,* pp. x, 1–4.

[30] Ibid., p. 4–1.

[31] In England many department store amalgamations have also taken place. C. Fulop, *Competition for Consumers* (London, England: Institute of Economic Affairs, 1964), p. 48.

The *chains* are the fastest growing element in the department store field. Like ownership groups, they have central ownership, but they also have the other characteristics of chain systems—central management, similar type of store, and two or more stores in each group. The difference between the two classes lies to an important degree in the amount of central control exercised over the stores. Probably the best examples of department store chains are the complete department stores operated by Sears, Roebuck and Company and Montgomery Ward & Company (now a division of Marcor).

Table 9–6 provides current sales and earnings for some of the leading ownership groups and department store chains.

Income group. An axiom in the department store field is that each store must define its market and its place in the fashion cycle. Certainly, no one store can appeal successfully to all income groups and all social classes. To illustrate the point: ". . . higher income groups are more demanding of services from stores than are the lower groups; similarly, the lower income classes are less critical of self-service."[32]

TABLE 9–6
Department store sales and income, 1970 (ownership groups except where noted)

Company	Net sales, 1970 ($000)	Net income ($000)	Net income as percent of sales
Sears, Roebuck (chain)	$9,262,162	$464,201	5.0
Montgomery Ward (Marcor) (chain)	2,804,856	59,637	2.1
Federated	2,096,935	82,169	3.9
Allied Stores Corp.	1,225,070	14,801	1.2
City Products	907,029	20,660	2.1
May Department Stores	1,170,385	31,873	2.7
Dayton Hudson	969,287	18,970	2.0
R. H. Macy (chain)	907,029	20,660	2.3

Source: "The Fifty Largest Retailing Companies," *Fortune*, May 1971, pp. 196–97.

A store attempts through its merchandise offerings, customer services, and design of store and layout to develop a personality that is reflected in the desired image in the minds of its customers and prospective customers.[33] That is, it defines its market and then caters to this market. Such stores as Saks–Fifth Avenue of New York City, Marshall Field & Company of Chicago, and Bullock's, Inc., of Los Angeles are examples of firms appealing to the middle high-income group. They handle high-quality merchandise, sell at relatively high prices, and offer much "free" service. The stores in this group are few in number but enjoy great prestige in their communities. In contrast, most independent and ownership-group department stores, plus a few of the chain department stores, appeal to the middle income group. Less exclusive merchandise is handled, prices are more moderate, and services are both fewer in number and less elaborate in nature. Many of these stores emphasize price, or value

---

[32] D. J. Rachman and M. Levine, "Blue Collar Workers Shape Suburban Markets," *Journal of Retailing*, 42 (Winter 1966–67), p. 12.

[33] For some empirical evidence, see W. Lazet and R. G. Wyckham, "Perceptual Segmentation of Department Store Markets," *Journal of Retailing*, 45 (Summer 1969), pp. 3–14.

in relation to price, as a major sales appeal, as do the majority of the chain department stores, which handle merchandise that can be sold at low prices and appeal mainly to the lower income groups.

No department store, however, sells *all* its merchandise to people in a specific income group; some stores may find all classes represented among their customers. Moreover, some department stores, especially those making their main appeal to the upper or middle income groups, operate "budget floors," bargain basements, or even self-service departments in an attempt to attract buyers from the lower income groups.[34] Through cut-price sales to "clean out" merchandise, a store may also appeal to a lower income group than that usually sought. These exceptions, however, do not invalidate the rule followed by the majority of department stores to the effect that a certain income group dominates the actions of the store.

Leased departments

The leasing of departments has been characteristic of the department store for some time, as it is of the discount house and—to a lesser degree—of the supermarket. A leased department is a section of a store that is operated by an interest that is independent of that controlling the store. For many years department stores have used leased departments for millinery, optical goods, jewelry, furs, books, groceries, shoes, candy, soda fountains, restaurants, beauty salons, and barber shops. Leasing arrangements are prevalent among both merchandise and service departments, with perhaps 1 of every 12 merchandise departments and one of every 2½ service departments being leased. Discount stores have utilized even more leased departments. A recent study indicated that over 60 percent of the food, millinery, snack bar and shoe departments in discount stores are leased and, on the average, about 25 percent of all departments are leased.[35] The leased department uses the credit and delivery system of the stores; its advertisements may appear under the store's name; and, as a rule, no separate name appears in the section it occupies in the store. Few customers are ever aware that certain departments are leased.

Branch stores

Originally, branch stores differed from local chain stores in that they were dominated by a parent department store, with the management of each branch usually subordinate to that of the main unit. Stock for the branch frequently came through the parent store. Generally, the branch store made no pretense of carrying as complete a stock as did the main store; and in many cases, it was in fact a departmentized specialty store. Other branch stores sold a relatively small number of items from their own stock but took orders to be filled directly from the parent store or warehouse. While many branches still operate according to these earlier methods, increasingly the branch has become a larger unit and has achieved a greater degree of independence from the parent store. Today, some of them are really separate stores, making

---

[34] Bargain basements originated as a means of selling odds and ends to a lower income group than that normally sought by the store. Today, however, so that the bargain basement will not "cheapen" the entire store, most bargain basements purchase their merchandise through their own buyers, use separate advertising space, and sometimes have independent entrances.

[35] W. R. Davidson, A. F. Doody, and J. R. Loury, "Leased Departments as a Major Force in the Growth of Discount Store Retailing," *Journal of Marketing,* 34 (January 1970), pp. 39–46.

purchases directly from manufacturers and adapting both merchandise and operating policies to the particular needs of the community and the competition existing therein.[36] Other branches are organized according to chain store principles, with major management functions including buying at a single headquarters.

The future of the department store

Prior to the last decade, department stores experienced a long period during which their percentage of total sales in the retailing system steadily declined. In contrast with their more than 9 percent share in 1933, they dropped to 7.3 percent in 1948 and to 6.2 percent in 1954.[37] During these two decades the independent department stores were especially vulnerable. They lost members to the ownership groups and felt the impact of competition from such chains as Sears, Ward, Penney, and Grant.

Despite the growth of the discount house, the past 10 years or so have witnessed a revival of the department store. Instead of the 2,761 stores of 1954 doing 6.2 percent of all retail business, the 1967 census reported 5,792 department stores accounting for 10.4 percent of all sales in the retailing system. Even though these figures overstate the case, since an indeterminant number of discount houses was included by the census in the department store category, they do indicate substantial real growth. Moreover, there is a new aggressiveness evident at the management level of department store organizations. While we may expect more independent stores to be absorbed by the ownership groups, those remaining independent can have a good future if they are well managed and willing to open branch units and expand into shopping centers. Most ownership groups and chain department stores have substantial plans for modernization and expansion.

THE DISCOUNT HOUSE

One of the most significant developments in the "marketing revolution" in the United States is the so-called "discount" house or mass-merchandise store. Although existing in a rather primitive form for more than three decades, this institution has emerged as a growing, highly competitive member of the retailing system only since 1950. Emphasizing the sale of merchandise at less than "list" or suggested prices, it is found in all sections of the country—particularly in the larger cities and their suburbs. Although not all discount houses qualify as large-scale retailers, most of them do.

Types and importance

Characteristics of full-line discount houses.[38] A discount house, as we see it here, is a retail establishment which has all or most of the following features:

1. A broad merchandise assortment, including both "hard" and "soft" goods and frequently food as well, which in scope (but not in price class) resembles the department store.

---

[36] "Merchandising Policies for Branch Stores," *Stores,* August 1969, pp. 55–57.

[37] Census data. For each year mentioned see *Retail Trade: Subject Reports.*

[38] For a detailed narrative of K-Mart and Target stores, see W. H. Teninga and D. J. Dayton, "A Tale of Two Discounters," *Stores,* July 1969, pp. 51–55.

2. Price as the main sales appeal. While few careful price studies are available, the consensus is that discount nonfood prices range from 2 to 15 percent lower than those of full-service competing stores, with the advantage in food at the lower end of this range.[39] As a further step to create a price image, and despite the trading-up policy of some discount houses, price lines are aimed at low- and middle-income families.
3. A relatively low operating cost ratio for the types of merchandise carried. Operating costs average about 28 percent, while those for department stores average closer to 32 percent.
4. Relatively inexpensive buildings, equipment, and fixtures. In contrast to a construction cost of $15–$25 per square foot for a shell for a department store, the discount house building may cost from $10 to $18.
5. Low-rent locations, although more discount houses are going into shopping centers and paying higher rents.
6. An emphasis on self-service operation with a minimum of salespeople where self-service is not applicable. Whereas payroll in a department store may equal 18 to 22 percent of sales, in the discount house this cost may be between 6 and 10 percent.
7. Limited customer services such as credit and delivery, or offering these services at a special charge to the customer.
8. Emphasis on rapid turnover of merchandise. Through relatively low prices and a rigid limitation of merchandise to the fast-moving items, the typical discount house turns its inventory about six times a year. However, such firms as King's Department Stores and Zayre's achieve from 12 to 15 stock turns annually.
9. Less use of merchandise and accounting controls than in the typical chain or department store, but organized on a department basis.
10. Low profit as a percentage of sales (1 to 2 percent is quite common). However, the return on investment is very satisfactory (10 to 20 percent is not unusual).
11. Long hours, frequently from 10:00 A.M. to 10:00 P.M. and often including Sunday.
12. Large stores, with 50,000 to 100,000 square feet on one floor being common and 200,000 square feet or more not being too exceptional.[40]
13. Large parking area.
14. A carnival atmosphere based on extensive sales promotional activities, including advertising, in-store display and promotions, and major special events.
15. Frequent use of leased departments. The most significant growth of leased departments in recent years has been among discount houses. Even the Woolco stores of the F. W. Woolworth Company and the K-Mart units of the S. S. Kresge Company lease some of their departments, and many discount houses rely upon leasing for a substantial part of their sales.[41]

---

[39] A study of prices in four conventional supermarkets and three discount supermarkets in Rhode Island disclosed the latter undersold the former by an average of 5.8 percent. "How Much Lower Are Discount Prices?" *Super Market Merchandising,* April 1966, pp. 32–33. A study of three discount stores and four department stores in Syracuse, N.Y., indicated soft goods, when considered as a group, were priced lower in the discount stores. R. Dardis and L. Skow, "Price Variations for Soft Goods in Discount and Department Stores," *Journal of Marketing,* 33 (April 1969), pp. 45–50; E. W. Cundiff and R. C. Andersen, "Competitive Food Pricing of Discounters," *Journal of Retailing,* 39 (Spring 1963), p. 16; and A. F. Jung, "Retail Pricing Policies on Small Appliances," *Journal of Retailing,* 41 (Spring 1965), p. 18.

[40] 150,–200,000 Sq. Ft. Stores Increase 24%" (Discount Census 71/72 Facts and Figures), *Discount Store News,* August 23, 1971, p. A23.

[41] "Takeover of Top Departments Up Slightly," *Discount Store News,* August 23, 1971, p. A21.

Importance of the full-line discount house. The full-line discount house has had a spectacular rate of growth during the past 15 years. It is estimated that as of June of 1971 there were 4,344 discount stores, of which about 333 were opened in the year ending June 1971. Their sales in 1971 were estimated at $25.6 billion, including connecting supermarkets, up from $22.5 billion the previous year and less than $3 billion in 1960.[42]

Other low-margin retailers. There are many other retailers with some of the features of the full-line discount house, and some of these add the word "discount" to their name. The food supermarket which has added a limited number of nonfood lines sometimes tries to capitalize on the current popularity of the discount house. Other food supermarkets have adopted the designation "discount food stores" for some of their units after giving up trading stamps, limiting their stocks to the more rapidly moving items, eliminating their carry-out service, and reducing their markups. Some apparel retailers have placed their dresses on pipe racks, adopted self-service selling, and entered upon an aggressive promotional program under the designation of discount house. Appliance retailers and hardware stores are among others who have switched to the new name. Older bargain-type stores that operate without a basic inventory, depending heavily on out-of-season, closed-out, and discontinued items, are also sometimes termed discount houses. In this text all these retailers are excluded from the discount house classification.[43]

What about the future?

It is evident that discount houses have assumed a role of importance in the retailing system. In a relatively few years they have achieved annual sales of more than $25 billion, a volume which far exceeds the combined sales of all mail-order houses, vending machines, and house-to-house distributors. While one might think that in an affluent society the appeal of this type of retailer to potential customers would decline, such has not been the case. Despite some failures (characteristic of all retailing) well-managed discount firms have manifested an awareness of the changing status of their customers and potential customers by "trading up" their stores, their merchandise, their services, and their public relations. If such alertness is demonstrated in the years ahead, the sales of this institution may reach $35–$40 billion by 1980. And even if these sales levels are not attained, there is no doubt but that the discount house has many years of growth ahead of it.

The discount house and channels of distribution

The growth of discount houses has forced many manufacturers and middlemen to reexamine their marketing policies, especially those related to price and distribution channels. In this process, manufacturers have maintained close watch over the measures adopted by their competitors, reviewed the nature and extent of widespread price cutting, and studied the probable reaction of their distributive outlets to contemplated changes in policies. They have attempted to judge the future of fair-trade laws

---

[42] Annual census of discount stores in *Discount Store News,* August 23, 1971, pp. A1 and A15.

[43] *Discount Merchandiser* suggests a sixfold classification of discount operations: "closed-door" or membership discount department stores, "open-door" discount houses, supermarket discount centers, specialty-type discount stores, soft-goods supermarkets, and department stores operating discount departments. *A Prospectus for the Discount Merchandiser* (New York: Super Market Publishing Co., n.d.), p. 4.

Marketing: Principles and methods

and appraised the effects of off-list selling on the future status of the wholesale distributor. Alternative courses of action designed to solve their problems are carefully considered.

In some instances, manufacturers have decided to maintain resale prices and to make every effort to keep their merchandise out of the stores of discounters. As sales through these retailers have increased, however, most manufacturers have actively sought them as members of their channel of distribution. In an effort to minimize the price advantage of the discount house and retain distribution through other retailers as well, some manufacturers (the General Electric Company, for example) have reduced the wholesale and retail margins on some products. Other manufacturers have relied upon heavy promotions to keep their products on the shelves of both discounters and nondiscounters.

The success of the discount house has also forced many of the more conventional retailers to adopt some of the discounters' policies and methods to guard against the loss of additional sales volume. Such department stores as Macy's in New York and Abraham & Straus of Brooklyn have reduced prices to meet all competition. Others have attempted to "trade up" their merchandise and service to attract a different clientele or have turned to self-service basement stores, longer store hours with more night openings, more extensive promotions, reduced customer services, and emphasis on private brands. Without examining these steps in detail, it seems safe to conclude that discount house competition can best be met by adopting policies regarding prices and customer services that are based on knowledge of customer wants and preferences.

THE RETAIL MAIL-ORDER HOUSE

A retail mail-order house is an establishment that receives its orders by mail and makes its sales (deliveries) by mail, parcel post, express, truck, or freight. The number of such houses has increased steadily since 1929, the first year for which complete data are available, rising from 271 in 1929 to 5,948 in 1967. Throughout this period, however, their total sales in the retailing system did not exceed 1.3 percent. In 1967, their total sales of $3.1 billion accounted for about 1 percent of all retail sales.[44]

Actually, retail sales by mail in the United States somewhat exceed the 1 percent figure, but we do not know by what amount.[45] Some store retailers have sales by mail which are excluded from the foregoing statistics because they are not predominantly mail-order retailers. Department stores probably receive more orders by mail than any other single type of store. Although some of these firms issue catalogs, the bulk of their mail-order business is acquired from people who are attracted by newspaper advertisements. Some manufacturers also sell direct to ultimate consumers by mail. We will not consider these other types of mail-order selling but will concentrate on the retail mail-order house, which is a distinctive type of retailing institution.

Main types

Retail mail-order houses are of three chief types: the department store merchandise house, the other general merchandise firm, and the specialty house. The *department store merchandise house,* as the name indicates, offers a wide, varied assort-

---

[44] *1967 Census of Business: Retail Trade: Subject Reports,* p. 1–7.

[45] In England, mail-order firms do 3 percent of the retail business, but the English firms operate quite differently from those in the United States. The catalogs go "to agents who visit customers to collect orders and later deliver the goods." Fulop, *Competition for Consumers,* p. 122.

ment of merchandise such as might be sold by a large department store, including convenience, shopping, and specialty goods. It is best exemplified by Alden's, Inc., a division of Gamble-Skogmo, Inc.; Montgomery Ward & Company (Marcor); Sears, Roebuck and Company; and Spiegel, Inc., a division of Beneficial Finance Company. The 1967 census reported (Table 9–7) that 2,833 department store merchandise houses had sales of nearly $2.1 billion, an average of $735,500 per establishment. This figure is somewhat deceiving, however, because of the census practice of including more than 1,000 catalog order stores (but not catalog desks) operated by Sears, Ward, and other large chains as separate establishments.

The *other general merchandise houses* carry lines which, while covering several departments, are far less broad than those in a department store. In 1967 their sales per establishment were about $2 million and the 115 mail-order houses of this type had sales of $231 million.

The *specialty mail-order house* sells a relatively limited line of goods. Census data for 1967 show 1,482 specialty mail-order houses with total sales of over $700 million, or close to $500,000 per establishment. Food and books are the most important lines in the specialty group.

TABLE 9–7
Number and sales of retail mail-order houses by kinds of business, 1967

Kind of business	Number of establishments	Sales (000 omitted)
Department store merchandise	2,833	$2,083,801
Other general merchandise	115	231,037
Specialty Mail-Order		
Furniture, home furnishings	79	153,712
Books and stationery	133	81,847
Food	188	62,071
Women's ready-to-wear	43	51,653*
Automotive merchandise	24	26,180*
Other apparel	51	63,003
Other	964	265,729
Totals	4,430	$2,911,200

*Authors estimate based on 1963 *Census of Business* report.
Source: U.S. Bureau of the Census, *1967 Census of Business, Retail Trade: Subject Reports* (Washington, D.C.: Government Printing Office, 1971), p. 1–7. Note: Includes only establishments with payroll.

Development

The sale of goods by mail is not new either in this country or abroad. It was not until the early 1870s, however, that companies operating exclusively on the mail-order plan were formed in this country. The present Montgomery Ward & Company (Marcor) was established in 1872; Sears, Roebuck and Company, the largest of the retail mail-order houses, dates from 1888, when Richard W. Sears and his associate, Alvah C. Roebuck—a watchmaker—issued their first catalog, devoted solely to watches.

The conditions of the times—isolated farm life, inadequacies of rural retailing, growth in farm income, increasing literacy, and postal developments—undoubtedly created a situation in which mail-order selling could develop. But it was the operating policies followed by the mail-order firms—wide assortment of goods, relatively low prices, customer service, and good management—which encouraged the rural and small-town consumer, as well as many others in larger cities, to buy by mail.

Operating costs

Mail-order selling has certain cost advantages as compared with retailing through a store. These benefits include the following: (1) low rental costs because of "off Main Street" locations; (2) inexpensive fixtures and equipment; (3) relatively low-priced labor, although this advantage is rapidly disappearing; (4) a greater opportunity to apply automation to its operations; (5) no newspaper advertising; (6) limited customer services of the traditional store type; and (7) payment of delivery (transportation cost) by the customer, so that this item does not appear as a cost of doing business for the company.

At the same time, there are elements which serve to increase the operating costs of the mail-order house. These cost disadvantages are: (1) the high production and distribution cost of catalogs—estimated at more than $2 per catalog; (2) returns of merchandise, encouraged if the customer is not completely satisfied, which involve considerable handling expense; (3) maintenance of full assortments of merchandise for a long period of time—beyond the six-month "life" of the semiannual catalog—to ensure filling of all orders received; (4) return of money for orders that cannot be filled during abnormal conditions of supply; and (5) the packing and handling charges involved, made higher because of the large number of small orders received.

When a balance is struck between these two sets of factors, one may conclude that the mail-order house has a net cost advantage over many of its store competitors in the retailing system, although this advantage may not be great. For this conclusion, however, we must rely mainly on the statements of retail executives rather than upon actual cost data. The fact that executives of both Ward and Sears have long maintained they could afford to sell for about 4 percent less by mail than through their own retail stores is quite convincing evidence.[46]

Conclusions on mail-order retailing

Mail-order retailing in the traditional sense seems to have passed its relative peak of development in the United States. This conclusion does not mean that individual companies will cease to grow, nor should we be surprised at the establishment of new companies selling by mail. It does seem, however, that this type of retailing probably will not increase its share of the total retail business. This has been the dominant factor leading a number of mail-order firms into chain store retailing.

At the same time, mail-order selling possesses certain advantages which will enable it to retain its significance in the American retailing system. Despite changing social and economic conditions, there are still rural areas which are poorly served by local stores, especially in the matter of adequate assortments of merchandise; and there are many cases of farmer isolation where mail-order buying is convenient. Besides, many customers in areas adequately served by retail stores are attracted by the convenience of telephone[47] or mail ordering of the wide variety of fully guaranteed goods sold at relatively low prices and on convenient credit terms by the mail-

---

[46] "Retailing: Where It's Always Spring," *Time,* January 21, 1966, p. 69B.

[47] As early as 1966, Sears reported it received more orders by phone than by direct mail; statement of Board Chairman Austin Cushman in *Discount Store News,* December 12, 1966, p. 2.

order houses.[48] Years of satisfactory relationships with customers have built a large amount of goodwill, which aids in holding old and attracting new business. Under these circumstances, mail-order houses will continue to meet the needs of many consumers, and the well-managed organizations will continue to grow, even though their proportion of the total retail business will remain small.

SUMMARY

Large-scale retailing systems are so important in the United States that as much as 50 percent of all retail sales is made by chain stores, supermarkets, department stores, discount houses, and mail-order houses. Advantages of size in retailing have given rise to these retailers. While all of the advantages are not on the side of large size, enough are that most of the five types of large retailers have experienced considerable growth since their beginning.

The granddaddy of chain stores in the United States is the Great Atlantic and Pacific Tea Co. started by its predecessor in 1859. Over 20 of the current large chain store organizations got their start before 1900. Currently, chain store organizations account for almost 40 percent of total retail sales. In one product line—variety store—they dominate sales, and in shoes and foods they account for over half of the sales. They are relatively unimportant in sporting goods stores, florist shops, and other types of operations where size does not convey efficiencies. Sales by chain stores relative to the retailing system as a whole have had a slow but steady growth over the past 25 years which appears likely to continue. The retailing environment continues to be favorable toward multistore operations, as resentment against them has virtually disappeared.

Supermarkets, which may be operated by a corporate chain, group, or independent merchant, are relatively new institutions in the retailing system, having had their growth in the 1930s. Today they dominate grocery merchandizing in the United States, with almost 75 percent of all sales. They have been the leading exponents of low price and mass display appeals. Discount supermarkets, which attempt to reduce expenses and prices by several percentage points compared to more conventional supermarkets, have been quite popular in recent years. Because their special features (less service, lower prices, higher volume operation) are not unique advantages, they have been widely copied. The discount supermarket provides a good illustration of the point made in Chapters 1 and 3 that a dynamic marketing system will continue to offer consumers new assortments of services and prices. An example is the development of the bantam store, which offers more convenient locations and quick service on a relatively short line of products at somewhat higher prices.

Department stores, like chain stores, have been present in the United States for a long time. They currently account for over 10 percent of all retail sales and appear to be growing. Most department stores are independent (single ownership), members of an ownership group, or units in a chain store organization. As community and regional shopping centers have increased, department stores have grown in numbers and sales. Most community and regional centers anchor around one or more department stores.

The discount house is the newest of the five large-scale retail institutions examined in this chapter. While some forms began over 30 years ago, the 1950s marked the emergence of the modern discount store. The growth of K-Mart and Woolco

---

[48] P. L. Gillett, "A Profile of Urban In-home Shoppers," *Journal of Marketing,* 34 (July 1970), pp. 40–45.

stores in the late 1960s and early 1970s provides a good illustration of the popularity of this type of store, as masses of consumers have been attracted to these lower price, mass merchandising, minimum service-rendering institutions. Discount houses have upset many traditional distribution channels. They normally buy direct from manufacturers, and many of them buy manufacturers' brands and sell them at prices lower than those offered by more conventional retailers. Many a full-service retailer (and wholesaler) has discontinued Zenith or RCA or some other formerly favorite brand when they found discounters regularly promoted these brands at prices at which they could not operate.

The final large-scale retail institution discussed in this chapter is the retail mail-order house. Sears, Roebuck and Company and Montgomery Ward (Marcor) mail-order divisions represent two of the oldest giants in this field. This type of institution is relatively minor in the U.S. retailing system, accounting for about 1 percent of sales. Most consumers apparently prefer to travel to a retail store, examine the merchandise, make a purchase, and take the items home with them. It seems likely, however, that mail-order sales will maintain a stable share of total retail sales in the United States.

REVIEW AND DISCUSSION QUESTIONS

1. "As a general rule, large-scale retailers have developed because there are advantages of size in retailing as in other economic activities." Do you agree or disagree? Support your position with evidence.

2. Define "chain store system" in your own words. Some authors require that an organization possess at least 4 stores (or perhaps as many as 11) before it is considered to be a chain store system. Argue the merits of this position.

3. In view of the current trend toward decentralization, how do you justify the statement that central management is "one of the most distinctive characteristics of chain organization"?

4. Define "buying advantage" as it applies to the chain store and suggest its significance to the growth of chains in the United States.

5. Explain the main factors that will probably limit supermarket growth in the future.

6. Discuss the significant developments among supermarkets in recent years and the factors responsible for them.

7. In your judgment, what is likely to be the place of the supermarket in the distribution structure in the future? Discuss this question with a supermarket operator in your community, report his opinions, and appraise their validity.

8. Explain why bantam (convenience) food stores have expanded rapidly in total number and sales in the past 10 to 15 years.

9. Distinguish among independent, ownership-group, and chain department stores, giving two examples of each type.

10. Briefly discuss the advantages and disadvantages of the present-day independent department store as compared with the chain department store.

11. Indicate the current importance of, and the reasons for, the leasing of departments in department stores.

12. Comment concisely on the probable future of the department store as a marketing institution.

13. What are the characteristics of the full-line discount house? Explain how each contributes to the success of this retail institution.

14. Discuss the impact of the discount house on the marketing policies of manufacturers producing the kinds of merchandise sold by these establishments.

15. Summarize the chief characteristics of the retail mail-order house and indicate its present importance in the marketing system.

SUPPLEMENTARY READINGS

"Annual Discount Store Census" *Discount Store News,* August 23, 1971. Statistics covering over 4,000 discount houses in the United States, their distribution among states and selected areas, and the expansion plans of discount chains are considered in this annual study.

Cassady, R., Jr. *Competition and Price Making in Food Retailing.* New York: Ronald Press Co., 1962. The subtitle of this book is "The Anatomy of Supermarket Operations." Among other subjects, it discusses the dynamics of retail food store competition.

Federal Trade Commission *Concentration in the Retail Food Business.* Washington, D.C.: Government Printing Office, 1962. Perhaps the major contribution of this study is the emphasis on chain store growth during the period 1948–58.

Gist, R. R. (ed.) *Management Perspectives in Retailing.* New York: John Wiley & Sons, Inc., 1967. A readings book which contains many of the better articles on retailing that appeared in the 1960s.

Gist, R. R. *Retailing: Concepts and Decisions.* New York: John Wiley & Sons, Inc., 1968. A basic book in retailing that discusses many retailing topics in some detail.

Kane, B. J. *A Systematic Guide to Supermarket Location Analysis.* New York: Fairchild Publications, Inc., 1966. Techniques and sources of information concerning location analysis.

Lebhar, G. M. *Chain Stores in America, 1859–1962.* 3d ed. New York: Chain Store Publishing Corp., 1963. Divided into three main parts—development, struggle against opposition, and present maturity—this comprehensive review of the chain store business is "must" reading for the student of marketing.

Markin, R. J. *The Supermarket.* Rev. ed. Pullman, Wash.: Washington State University Press, 1968. A comprehensive developmental study, plus a forward-looking examination of supermarket activities.

McNair, M. P. and May, E. G. *The American Department Store, 1920–1960.* Bulletin No. 166. Boston: Bureau of Business Research, Graduate School of Business Administration, Harvard University, 1963. This analysis of performance, based on Harvard reports, develops "a . . . better perspective on the behavior of significant ratios . . . over a long-run period."

Nelson, P. E. and Preston, L. E. *Price Merchandising in Food Retailing: A Case Study.* Berkeley, Calif.: University of California, Institute of Business and Economic Research, 1966. This study of retail prices for food disclose (1) wide differences from store to store, (2) chains underselling group retailers who, in turn, undersell independents, (3) the absence of price leadership, and (4) variable-price merchandising, that is, "the frequent upward and downward manipulation of prices on selected items . . ."

Part IV The wholesaling system for consumer products and services

The focus in Part IV remains on consumer products and services, but in the wholesaling system. As a component of the host marketing system, the wholesaling system is positioned between processers and manufacturers and between manufacturers and retailers.

A large variety of functions is performed by numerous types of wholesale institutions. These wholesalers, the functions they perform, and the environment within which they operate are examined in two chapters. Chapter 10 is concerned with the wholesaling environment and the structure of wholesaling, and Chapter 11 features wholesale institutions and functions.

Study of Part IV should give you an understanding of how the wholesaling system is evolving and will continue to evolve. The fit of the wholesaling system into the total marketing system should also be made apparent.

10 Wholesaling: Environment and structure

In study of the evolution of trade, the most efficient channel system for performing marketing functions is often found to include specialized middlemen between manufacturers and consumers. Retailers and retailing have been viewed; our focus now turns to wholesalers and wholesaling. Like retailing, wholesaling is undergoing numerous changes as middlemen make adjustments to allow them to operate profitably in their changing environments. An understanding of the marketing channel system requires an understanding of these changes.

Analysis in this area is handicapped by the lack of separate data for consumer products and industrial products. Since we wish to make full use of census data, we shall include wholesalers of both kinds of products in this chapter. However, the balance of Part IV will consider the wholesaling of consumer products only, and industrial products will be covered in Part V.

WHOLESALING DEFINED AND ILLUSTRATED

Individuals or business firms engage in wholesaling when they primarily sell to or negotiate sales with those who buy for purposes of resale or industrial use.[1]

---

[1] Wholesale trade, as defined in the *1967 Standard Industrial Classification Manual* and as covered in the *1967 Census of Business,* includes establishments primarily engaged (1) in selling merchandise to retailers; to industrial, commercial, institutional, and professional users; or to other wholesalers; or (2) in negotiating as agents in buying merchandise for or selling merchandise to such persons or companies. Importers selling merchandise at wholesale in the U.S. market and exporters are included in wholesale trade. The Definitions Committee of the American Marketing Association defines a wholesaler as "a business unit which buys and resells merchandise to retailers and other merchants and/or to industrial, institutional, and commercial users but which does not sell in significant amounts to ultimate consumers." See R. S. Alexander, *Key Marketing Words—What They Mean,* Management Aids No. 127 (Washington, D.C.: Small Business Administration, 1961). Also see D. A. Revzan, *Wholesaling in Marketing Organization* (New York: John Wiley & Sons, Inc., 1961), pp. 2–4.

Illustrations of wholesalers dealing with firms who buy for resale would be a sales branch of a manufacturer such as General Foods Corporation which sells coffee to a grocery retailer; a Texaco bulk station which sells gasoline to a local filling station; a sugar broker who negotiates sales between a refinery and a food chain; or an apple buyer who assembles products from a number of orchards and sells them to Safeway Stores. Examples of wholesalers dealing with industrial or business users are the merchant who buys office equipment from A. B. Dick Company for resale to other manufacturers for use in their own offices, a Reliance Electric sales branch selling electrical controls for use in a shoe plant, a Texaco bulk station selling lubricants to the Parker Pen Company, or a cotton broker negotiating the sale of cotton to a textile mill.

The wholesaler may be visualized as any middleman who serves between an extractive, manufacturing, construction, transportation, communication, service, or utility industry and another of these industries. He also serves between retailers, government agencies, and other middlemen. He performs important functions relating to the time interval between production and consumption, the product types and assortments involved, the location of consuming areas and, to a lesser degree, the points of manufacture. In this position, he may be considered "the eyes and ears of the marketplace" in some channel systems.

Wholesalers and retailers differentiated

While some retailers buy directly from manufacturers and thus perform wholesale functions, retailers are excluded from our concept of wholesaling because they sell primarily to ultimate consumers. Moreover, wholesalers frequently offer for sale a wider variety of products than do retailers, cover a larger area or territory, sell at lower prices, usually buy and sell in larger quantities, and have different operating methods.

Large wholesalers may buy many items in carload lots and resell to retailers in dozen-item lots or even less. Even the smaller wholesalers buy in quantities far in excess of those in which they resell. This buying in large quantities and breaking down into smaller lots is one of the main services that wholesalers perform for both manufacturers and retailers. Yet it should be realized that many wholesalers actually buy in smaller lots than do some retailers; consider the large-scale buying done by such integrated retailers as the mail-order companies and department stores. The tendency for the wholesaler to buy on a "hand-to-mouth" basis, to avoid storing goods and for other reasons, and the growth of large-scale retailing have made this characteristic of wholesaling less distinct.

As to operating methods,[2] wholesalers usually operate warehouses which serve mainly as storage facilities rather than as sales quarters. Except for some wholesalers, produce markets, and other central markets such as the Merchandise Mart (Chicago), wholesale establishments are generally not frequented by the customer. Instead, purchasing is usually done in the retailers' stores, over the telephone or from salesmen sent out by the wholesaler. As a result, warehouses are usually located in less accessi-

---

[2] It is beyond the scope of this volume to discuss the operating methods and problems of wholesalers, although brief reference to them will be made in subsequent chapters. For details concerning all phases of management, see Revzan, *Wholesaling in Marketing Organization,* pp. 107–518; T. N. Beckman, N. H. Engle, and R. D. Buzzell, *Wholesaling: Principles and Practice* (3d ed.; New York: Ronald Press Co., 1959), pp. 219–634; and R. M. Hill, *Wholesaling Management: Text and Cases* (Homewood, Ill.: Richard D. Irwin, Inc., 1963), pp. 85–678.

ble and less attractive quarters, where rents are lower but railroad and trucking facilities are available. In recent years, however, many wholesalers have moved into better locations and have built modernistic structures designed to permit automation of some functions, particularly those related to the physical handling of merchandise. Hibbard, Spencer, Bartlett & Company, a hardware wholesaler who moved from an old building on the north bank of the Chicago River east of Michigan Avenue in Chicago to new, improved facilities in Evanston, Illinois, is a case in point. But most wholesalers have been far behind retailers in modernization programs because of their belief that expensive showplaces are not necessary to attract patronage.

Wholesalers and producers compared

Many manufacturers and producers of raw materials perform wholesaling functions in selling direct to retailers or to industrial users. Census data on wholesaling, however, exclude such individuals or firms on the ground that they are primarily producers. Consequently, except where they operate sales branches devoted to wholesaling, they will be excluded from the statistics given in this chapter.[3]

DEVELOPMENT OF WHOLESALING IN THE UNITED STATES[4]

The development of wholesaling in the United States may be conveniently divided into three periods: (1) that preceding 1800, (2) that between 1800 and 1929, and (3) that since 1929. It is for this last period only that detailed statistics on wholesaling are available from the Bureau of the Census.

Prior to 1800

Wholesaling activities during the colonial period of the United States were related to import and export trade. As interior towns developed, domestic wholesale activities became necessary. Frequently, these were carried out by the general store operator, who exchanged the imported wares he secured at seaport cities for the agricultural products of his customers.

Despite the passing of many years,

up to the nineteenth century the internal [wholesale] trade of the United States had undergone very little change from colonial days. The country was still a frontier community with two-thirds of its population on the Atlantic seaboard. Even as late as 1802, according to a description by the French traveler, Michaux, goods, consisting largely of firearms, small metal articles, dry goods, and other valuable commodities, were transported from Philadelphia to Pittsburgh in large covered wagons, drawn by four horses, two abreast.[5] There appears to have been relatively little competition in internal wholesale trade, possibly because none of the powerful wholesaling concerns which were to make their appearance later had yet been established.

---

[3] The division drawn by the census between a manufacturer and a wholesaler is rather flexible. A manufacturing establishment is classified under wholesaling if its "manufacturing is secondary" to its sale of goods produced by others.

[4] For a more complete history of wholesaling, one on which these paragraphs are largely based, see Beckman, Engle, and Buzzell, *Wholesaling: Principles and Practice,* pp. 61–86.

[5] E. L. Bogart, *Economic History of the American People* (New York: Longmans, Green & Co., Inc., 1930), p. 350.

Most of the wholesaling of the period was divided between the frontier trading posts and the country general stores on the one hand, which continued as in colonial days to assemble the raw produce of the land, and, on the other hand, importers who also dealt in the more profitable goods of domestic manufacture.[6]

Even up to 1800 the bulk of our wholesale business was closely related to our foreign trade.

Growth, 1800–1929

After 1800, however, and especially after the Civil War, wholesaling grew at a more rapid pace. For example, in 1808 a wholesale house for domestic merchandise, as distinct from an importing house, was established. Moreover, although most wholesalers also engaged in retailing, after the War of 1812 wholesale and retail functions were gradually separated, although the separation of wholesaling from neither importing nor retailing was marked until after the Civil War. Even today, many wholesalers continue to purchase goods from foreign manufacturers, and some of them get such quantities from this source that they are known in the trade as importers rather than as wholesalers.

Previous to the Civil War, most wholesalers handled general merchandise because their main customer was the general store operator who wished to purchase a broad list of wares from a single source. After the Civil War, however, when the limited-line store gradually replaced the general store, wholesalers began to specialize in such single lines as groceries, hardware, and drugs. Thus, in the second half of the 19th century, as large-scale production increased the distance between the manufacturer and the consumer and as transportation facilities made this separation possible, the "wholesaler" gradually changed (1) from an importer to a middleman dealing mainly in domestic merchandise, (2) from a combined wholesaler-retailer to a wholesaler, and (3) from a general-merchandise wholesaler to a more specialized middleman. The development of domestic, large-scale production required a large wholesaling sector to perform the important marketing processes of allocating and assorting to a consumer market still expanding across the continent. To a large degree, these three transitions were completed by the end of the century.

During the latter part of the 19th century, wholesalers of various types also came into prominence, even though merchant wholesalers continued to play the dominant role. Brokers and commission houses were widely used; some manufacturers began to open sales branches and offices; and assemblers developed to handle the flow of farm products to major markets.

Wholesaling since 1929[7]

The year 1929 is a significant one in marketing history, since it marks the date when the first extensive Census of Distribution was taken in the United States. At that time, as the data in Table 10–1 reveal, there were 163,830 wholesaling establishments in this country, with sales of $65.4 billion. Although wholesalers, like other businessmen, experienced serious problems during the depression of the 1930s and were

---

[6] Beckman, Engle, and Buzzell, *Wholesaling: Principles and Practice,* p. 80.

[7] For a somewhat old but excellent summary of some significant developments in one segment of wholesaling, see P. D. Converse, "Twenty-five Years of Wholesaling: A Revolution in Food Wholesaling," *Journal of Marketing, 20* (July 1957), pp. 40–52. For later information see "38th Annual Report of the Grocery Industry," *Progressive Grocer,* (April 1971).

faced with demands that they "be eliminated to save the middleman's profit," they demonstrated a surprising tenacity and endurance. Their sales decreased to less than $54 billion in 1939, but the number of establishments grew to 190,379. Comparable figures in 1948 were over $180.6 billion and 216,099 establishments, and such increases have continued. By 1967 establishments, including Alaska and Hawaii, numbered 311,464, with sales of about $459 billion.[8] This tremendous growth furnishes convincing evidence of the essentiality of the wholesaler in the distribution system.

TABLE 10–1
Wholesale establishments, sales, inventories, and paid employees

Business census year	Establish- ments (number)	Sales (in thousands)	Inventories end of year (at cost; in thousands)	Paid em- ployees
1967	311,464	$459,475,967	$28,117	3,518,969
1963	308,177	358,385,749	20,149	3,088,706
1958*	287,043	285,726,904	15,009	2,807,661
1954	250,322	233,976,052	13,046	2,554,700
1948	216,099	180,576,659	9,965	2,305,403
1939	190,379	53,766,426	3,822	1,553,062
1929	163,830	65,378,051	5,195	1,549,910

*Alaska and Hawaii included as of 1958. Alaska had 254 wholesale establishments and Hawaii had 793 in 1958.
Source: U.S. Bureau of the Census, *1963 Census of Business,* Vol. IV, *Wholesale Trade: Summary Statistics* (Washington, D.C.: Government Printing Office, 1966), Table 2, pp. 1–9.

Some factors explaining the growth of wholesaling

Why has wholesaling become so important to the economy? What conditions led to its growth, as outlined in preceding paragraphs, and what forces are responsible for its current status? As one student of the subject suggests: "Wholesaling developed in structure as attempts were made by producers and other business firms . . . to solve the problem of marketing . . . and to bridge the growing marketing gap between the various types and levels of producers at one end, and . . . of users at the other."[9] This gap grew out of the following forces:

1. The development of diversified, large-scale mass production in factories located at a distance from the areas of principal use of the output thus produced.
2. An increase in the volume and proportion of such production made prior to, rather than for, the specified order of users.
3. A corresponding increase in the number of levels of intermediate-user consumption between the production of basic raw materials at the beginning of the channel and the areas of final use at the end of the channel.
4. The increasing need for adaptations of products to the needs of intermediate and final users in terms of quantities, shapes, packages, and other elements of assortments, as well as in pricing arrangements.

---

[8] Wide variations occurred, however, in the growth pattern of different kinds of wholesalers and in different areas. For evidence, see the *1967 Census of Business,* Vol. IV, *Wholesale Trade: Area Statistics* (Washington, D.C.: Government Printing Office, 1970), and "Wholesalers in Manhattan Drop to Three," *American Druggist,* October 10, 1966, p. 29.

[9] Revzan, *Wholesaling in Marketing Organization,* pp. 10–11.

5. Continuing increases in both the quantities and the varieties of goods and services in relation to the foregoing.
6. The necessity of establishing primary and intermediate markets (organized and unorganized) in which the various stages of wholesale exchange and the establishment of wholesale price levels (systematic and unsystematic) would take place.[10]

Thus constant changes in the technology and products of manufacturers, in the desires of end users, and in retail structure have increased the need for middlemen specialists to perform marketing functions at the wholesale level.

THE STRUCTURE OF WHOLESALING

In turning to an analysis of the wholesaling structure, we shall consider the types of institutions through which wholesaling is conducted, the size of establishments in the wholesale field, the kinds of goods these middlemen sell, the geographical or spatial pattern of wholesaling, and the customers served by wholesalers.

Wholesaling institutions

The growth of wholesaling institutions is even more impressive when broken down by type of institution. Data for the five major types of wholesale institutions in the United States from 1929 to 1967 are given in Table 10–2. Two of these, merchant wholesalers and manufacturers' sales branches and offices, have grown during the period since 1958 at a rate equal to the economy overall. Growth of the other institutions has been somewhat slower.

Merchant wholesalers. The *1967 Census of Business* classifies merchant wholesalers into five categories, as follows: (1) Wholesale merchants and distributors primarily engaged in buying and selling merchandise in the domestic market and performing the principal wholesale functions, such as buying, stocking, and selling; (2) importers buying and selling goods on their own account principally from foreign sources; (3) exporters primarily engaged in purchasing goods in the United States and selling them to foreign customers; (4) terminal grain elevators with sizable storage space which buy and sell grain received mainly by rail or barge rather than directly from farmers by truck.

Merchant wholesalers as a group have consistently constituted the most important type of operation, measured both by number of establishments and by sales. As to number, they increased from 77,079 in 1929 to 212,993 in 1967. This represents the number of "establishments"; number of firms in that year was 232,783—94 percent had only one establishment, 3 percent had two, 2 percent had three to five, and only 1 percent had six or more.[11]

Manufacturers' sales branches and offices. Owned and operated by manufacturers and mining companies apart from their "plants," manufacturers' sales branches and offices are the second most important type of wholesale establishment as measured by sales. The sales offices exist primarily as points out of which manufacturers' salesmen may work or to which customers may come to place orders. Sales branches serve these same purposes; in addition, they house stocks from which deliveries can be made. Manufacturers' sales branches and offices have been the fastest growing

---

[10] Ibid.

[11] U.S. Bureau of the Census, *1967 Census of Business,* Vol. III, *Wholesale Trade: Subject Reports* (Washington, D.C.: Government Printing Office, 1971), Table 11.

Marketing: Principles and methods

TABLE 10–2

Wholesale establishments and sales by type of operation

	Merchant wholesalers	Manufacturers' sales branches and offices	Petroleum bulk stations and terminals	Merchandise agents and brokers	Assemblers of farm products	Total all types
1967						
Number of establishments.........	212,993	30,679	30,229	26,462	11,101	311,464
Sales (millions of dollars).........	206,055	157,097	24,822	61,347	10,156	459,476*
1963						
Number of establishments.........	208,997	28,884	30,873	25,313	14,110	308,177
Sales (millions of dollars).........	157,392	116,443	21,485	53,245	9,820	358,386*
1958						
Number of establishments.........	190,492	25,240	30,520	26,666	14,125	287,043
Sales (millions of dollars).........	122,060	87,820	20,252	46,589	9,005	285,727*
1948						
Number of establishments.........	129,117	23,706	28,351	18,138	16,787	216,099
Sales (millions of dollars).........	76,533	50,800	10,483	32,840	9,920	180,576
1939						
Number of establishments.........	98,037	17,926	30,825	21,083	22,508	190,379
Sales (millions of dollars).........	21,811	14,254	3,808	11,779	2,114	53,766
1929						
Number of establishments.........	77,079	16,863	19,611	18,467	31,810	163,830
Sales (millions of dollars).........	28,212	16,175	2,390	14,517	4,084	65,378

* Figures rounded.

Note: Data for Alaska and Hawaii included beginning with 1958.

Source: U.S. Bureau of Census, *1967 Census of Business*, Vol. IV, *Wholesale Trade: Area Statistics* (Washington, D.C.: Government Printing Office, 1970), Table 2.

segment of the wholesaling structure since 1929. In that year they contributed 24.7 percent of total wholesale sales; in 1939, 26.5 percent; in 1958, 30.7 percent; and by 1967, they had reached 34.2 percent.

Petroleum bulk stations and terminals. Petroleum bulk stations, terminals, and liquefied petroleum gas facilities are distinguished from other wholesale establishments primarily by their physical characteristics. They operate bulk storage and distributing facilities (on railroad or other transportation lines) for gases, gasoline, oil, and other petroleum products. Their number has not increased in 15 years (it was 30,229 in 1967), and their sales—made largely to retailers, commercial and industrial users, and farmers—accounted for 5.4 percent of total wholesale sales in 1967.

Merchandise agents and brokers. Merchandise agents and brokers numbered 26,462 in 1967 and accounted for almost 15 percent of wholesale sales. As noted, they are described as "functional middlemen"; they negotiate purchases and/or sales but do not, as a rule, take title to goods.[12] As the census points out, in addition to

TABLE 10–3
Number of wholesale establishments, sales, and operating expenses by type of operation, 1967

Type of operation	Number of establishments	Sales (in millions)	Operating expenses (percentage of sales)*
Merchant wholesalers, total	212,993	$206,055	13.5
Wholesale merchants, distributors	204,783	181,776	14.4
Importers	5,171	10,354	10.3
Exporters	2,272	9,508	4.1
Terminal grain elevators	767	4,418	4.5
Manufacturers' sales branches, sales offices, total	30,679	157,096	7.2
Manufacturer's sales branches—with stock	16,709	67,175	11.3
Manufacturers' sales offices—without stock	13,970	89,922	4.1
Petroleum bulk stations, terminals, total	30,229	24,822	(NA)
Refiner-marketer bulk stations, terminals	16,611	17,224	(NA)
Other bulk stations, terminals	13,618	7,597	(NA)
Merchandise agents, brokers, total	26,462	61,347	4.0
Auction companies	1,594	4,792	2.9
Merchandise brokers for buyers or sellers	4,373	14,030	3.2
Commission merchants	5,425	14,068	3.4
Import agents	270	1,790	2.2
Export agents	548	3,372	1.9
Manufacturers' agents	12,106	15,257	6.4
Selling agents	1,891	6,889	4.2
Purchasing agents, resident buyers	255	1,146	3.6
Assemblers of farm products, total	11,101	10,155	8.6
Country grain elevators	6,477	5,590	7.1
Other assemblers of farm products	4,624	4,565	10.4
U.S. total	311,464	$459,476	—

*Entries for merchandise agents and brokers represent brokerage or commission received.
Source: U.S. Bureau of the Census, *1967 Census of Business*, Vol. IV, *Wholesale Trade: Area Statistics* (Washington, D.C.: Government Printing Office, 1970), Table 2.

---

[12] The *Census of Business* sales figures for merchandise agents and brokers represent the value of the goods in the transaction; their "operating expenses" reported are the commissions received from these sales, not actual expenses.

negotiating purchases or sales, they furnish valuable marketing information to their clients. Paid on a fee or commission basis, they may represent either buyers or sellers. Some serve only one client; others, a group of clients. Many specialize according to kinds of goods; for example, there are sugar brokers, fruit and vegetable auctioneers, and livestock commission men.

Assemblers. Assemblers are wholesalers who deal mainly in farm products, although some handle fish and seafood. Basically, their function is (as their name implies), to assemble and market such products at local producing points or in the cities of producing regions. By purchasing from a number of small farmers (or fishermen) or other local market dealers, they assemble sufficient quantities for economical handling and shipping. In contrast to many wholesale establishments which buy in large quantities and break them up into smaller lots to meet the needs of their customers (such as the small retailer), assemblers buy in relatively small lots and consolidate them into larger lots to meet the desires of commission men or carlot wholesalers in central markets, or of industrial users. Assemblers are engaged in assembly and sorting, whereas most other wholesalers are engaged in allocating and assorting. As will be described in Chapter 14, these institutions have undergone considerable change since 1948.

Wholesalers further detailed. Table 10–3 is presented in order to serve as a point of reference for later discussion and to give the student an overall picture of the wholesaling structure and the operating expenses involved. This table shows a further breakdown of the types of wholesalers given in Table 10–2.

Size of wholesale establishments

To understand wholesaling institutions better, it is necessary to examine their size. Size may be measured in several ways: by annual sales volume—giving full recognition to the advancing level of wholesale prices; by number of employees—recognizing both paid and nonpaid employees; and by single-unit versus multiple-unit firms. The discussion here is limited almost entirely to size as determined by sales volume.[13]

Some statistics on the average number of proprietors and paid employees per establishment may be helpful in gaining an understanding of the nature of the various types of wholesale institutions. More detailed statistics are available in the *Census of Business*. In 1967, manufacturers' sales offices and branches had the largest average number per establishment with 22; next came merchant wholesalers with 12. Agents, brokers, and assemblers averaged about eight employees and proprietors per establishment, while petroleum bulk stations were the smallest, with just over five persons.[14]

In the discussion of retail establishments, it was indicated that an overwhelming number are of very small size. The average annual sales per store in 1967 was only $175,000.[15] As would be expected, the typical wholesale establishment is much larger, with the 1967 average of sales per establishment being nearly $1.48 million, and for merchant wholesalers alone, $968,000.[16]

The great range in the sales of wholesale establishments is demonstrated by the data in Table 10–4, which shows that sales are concentrated in the upper sales-size

---

[13] For details concerning the other bases, see Beckman, Engle, and Buzell, op. cit., pp. 99–108.

[14] Calculated from U.S. Bureau of the Census, *1967 Census of Business*, Vol. IV, op. cit., Table 2.

[15] See Table 7–2.

[16] See Table 10–2.

TABLE 10–4

Size of sales of wholesale establishments in 1967

	Establishments		Sales	
Sales volume (annual)	Number	Percent of total	Amount (in millions)	Percent of total
U.S. Total*	311,464	100.0	$459,476	100.0
$20 million or more	2,663	.8	138,612	30.4
$15.0–$19.9 million	1,268	.4	21,755	4.8
$10.0–$14.9 million	2,665	.9	32,371	7.1
$5.0–$9.9 million	8,564	2.7	58,843	12.9
$2.0–$4.9 million	25,153	8.1	76,714	16.8
$1.0–$1.9 million	34,824	11.2	48,714	10.7
$500,000–$999,999	49,611	15.9	35,189	7.7
$200,000–$499,999	73,643	23.6	23,944	5.2
Less than $200,000	105,200	33.8	10,170	2.2

* Includes only those establishments operating entire year; 2.6 percent of all establishments with 2.2 percent of sales did not operate for entire year.

Source: U.S. Bureau of the Census, *1967 Census of Business,* Vol. III, *Wholesale Trade: Subject Reports* (Washington, D.C.: Government Printing Office, 1970), Table 2–1.

groups and the greatest number of establishments is in the lower ones. This shape is a common one for distributions of firms by sales, but the distribution for wholesaling is more extreme than most. The largest 13 percent of the firms do 72 percent of the business, while the smallest 73 percent of the firms do 15 percent of the business. It will be recalled that a large number of small establishments and a small number of large ones are also characteristic of the retail field.

Kinds of goods sold by merchant wholesalers

Another major factor in understanding the structure of wholesaling is the kinds of goods sold by wholesalers. A general picture is provided in Table 10–5 for a selected number of merchant wholesalers. These data also reveal sales trends between 1963 and 1967. Wholesale businesses that enjoyed rapid growth during the period were distributors of automobiles, metals, electrical appliances, paper products, and groceries.

To explain the differences in growth rates shown in the table, keep in mind that the distinction between a wholesale and a retail transaction is the purpose for which the product is purchased. For example, a car sold to a retailer for use either in his business or for resale is considered a wholesale transaction. If the same car were purchased by a final consumer for use by his family, it would be a retail transaction.

Geographical structure of wholesaling

The geographical structure or spatial pattern of wholesaling in the United States has been influenced by a large number of factors, including the location (and changes in location) of manufacturing plants and other processing units; points of consumption or use; availability of transportation facilities and the charges related thereto; proximity of financial institutions that can provide needed funds; cost of establishing suitable facilities, including local and state taxes; and governmental rules and regulations

Marketing: Principles and methods

TABLE 10–5
Sales and growth rates of selected kinds of merchant wholesalers

	1967 sales (in millions)	Compounded annual growth rate, 1963–67
Consumer goods		
Grocery, general line	$ 15,548	7.2
Piece goods, notions, and dry goods	4,578	6.0
Beer, wine, and distilled spirits	10,444	6.5
Drugs, drug proprietaries, and sundries	4,748	7.0
Tobacco and tobacco products	5,315	3.2
Electrical appliances, TV and radio sets	5,718	8.2
Hardware	3,197	5.7
Industrial goods		
Industrial and commercial machinery, equipment and supplies	13,231	3.6
Metals and coal	11,863	10.6
Automobiles and other motor vehicles	5,345	10.6
Paper and paper products, excluding wallpaper	6,422	8.0
All merchant wholesalers	$206,055	7.0

Source: U.S. Bureau of the Census, *1967 Census of Business*, Vol. IV, *Wholesale Trade: Area Statistics* (Washington, D.C.: Government Printing Office, 1970), pp. 1–9 to 1–10.

regarding shipments. The important variations that exist among the many manufactured and agricultural commodities are too numerous to be considered here.

To gain some understanding of the spatial structure of wholesaling, it is necessary to know more than just where wholesalers are located. It is also of interest to know how they happened to get there. The nonstocking wholesaler obviously wants to be near his customers, but the merchant wholesaler or manufacturer's sales branch must also consider the location of his sources of supply and the transportation facilities available.

The breadth of line and quality of service provided also influence location. Since few retailers visit wholesalers, the need to locate close to customers involves considerations different from those in retailing. The wholesaler may trade off product and service assortments with delivery time. He seeks to provide either immediate delivery of an unspecialized array of goods or forward delivery of specialized goods. As competition in wholesaling increases, the product-service-delivery time assortment will be adjusted to meet the unique needs of customers. These assortments will not all be the same as wholesalers adjust their assortments to the needs of important customers or segments of customers.

To specialize more, the wholesaler will have to broaden his geographic coverage; to narrow his geographic field, he must broaden his product and service assortment. If the total demand increases so that it attracts competitive entry in his area, the wholesaler can and must increase service in order to retain his competitive position.[17]

With these considerations as central to the location decision, wholesaling has developed with a *regional* rather than a *national* or *central-city* orientation. Service and specialization requirements prevent the development of many national wholesal-

---

[17] This proposition is made by J. E. Vance, Jr., *The Merchant's World: The Geography of Wholesaling* (Englewood Cliffs, N.J.: Prentice-Hall, Inc., 1970), p. 78.

ers. Thus analysis of spatial markets and the historic and economic factors that led to the development of particular regional market structures is necessary for an understanding of the geography of wholesaling.

Since the time when most wholesalers were import agents, competitive pressures have forced wholesalers to base their location decisions on the needs of customers in their market areas. As trade practices matured, communications and transportation facilities improved, and the population became more urban, wholesalers found it less important to be near suppliers and more important to be near the growing regional clusters they served. Wholesaling centers develop first near market centers at the end of transportation "fingers" which extend from the manufacturing and import centers to regional population clusters. Today's centers have their roots in the water and rail transportation centers of yesterday.

In terms of national importance, the Middle Atlantic states of New York, Pennsylvania, and New Jersey rank high, with over one quarter of all wholesale business. The

TABLE 10–6
Wholesale sales of the most important wholesale centers, 1967

Metropolitan area	Sales (in millions)
New York, N.Y.–Northeast New Jersey Consolidated Area	$82,102
Chicago–Northwestern Indiana Consolidated Area	33,269
Los Angeles–Long Beach–Anaheim–Santa Anna–Garden Grove–San Diego Consolidated Area	23,968
Cleveland–Akron-Canton-Youngstown-Warren, Ohio-Pittsburgh, Pa. Consolidated Area	17,050
Detroit–Toledo, Ohio Consolidated Area	14,677
San Francisco–Oakland-San Jose Consolidated Area	13,936
Philadelphia, Pa.–New Jersey	13,216
Boston	10,436
Dallas–Ft. Worth Consolidated Area	8,880
Washington–Baltimore Consolidated Area	8,837
Atlanta	8,498
Minneapolis–St. Paul	8,470
St. Louis, Mo.–Illinois	8,409

Source: U.S. Bureau of the Census, *1967 Census of Business*, Vol. IV, *Wholesale Trade: Area Statistics* (Washington: U.S. Government Printing Office, 1970), pp. 1–41 to 1–50.

New York–Northeast New Jersey Consolidated Area alone did 18 percent of the country's wholesale business in 1967, and the Philadelphia Standard Metropolitan Statistical Area (SMSA) did 3 percent. Many sales are made to customers in other areas. The second most important of the nine geographic divisions of the country is the East North-Central. The fastest growing divisions, the Pacific and South Atlantic, rank third and fourth, respectively.

A more useful way to analyze the geography of wholesaling is to study the regional centers by SMSAs rather than geographic divisions. The 13 most important are shown in Table 10–6, with the largest reflecting the location of retail and industrial buyers. The magnitude of these differences may be surprising.

Another helpful measure of wholesaling importance is the ratio of wholesale sales to the population of the metropolitan area. A regional wholesaling center would be identified by areas where this ratio is above average. On this basis, Kansas City; Charlotte, North Carolina; Memphis; and Portland, Oregon are important wholesale centers, in addition to the 13 shown in the table.

Wholesale sales by class of customer

The distribution of sales by merchant wholesalers among their various kinds of customers for selected years from 1939 to 1967—as well as for merchant wholesalers of automotive equipment, meat, and electric supplies for 1939 and 1967—is shown in Table 10–7. Particularly noteworthy among merchant wholesalers in general is the sharp increase in the proportion of sales made to industrial and other commercial

TABLE 10–7
Merchant wholesalers—percentage distribution of sales by class of customer, 1939–67

Type of operation and year	Amount (in millions)	Percentage distribution				
		To industrial and commercial users	To consumers and farmers	To retailers	To wholesale organizations	Export
Merchant wholesalers, total						
1967	$206,055	37.0	1.6	39.4	14.5	5.9
1963	139,305	37.6	1.2	40.8	14.5	5.9
1958	94,779	31.7	1.6	45.9	15.3	5.5
1948	75,838	31.8	1.6	46.9	13.7	6.0
1939	21,973	23.6	1.9	58.9	11.6	4.0
Automotive equipment						
1967	7,389	13.2	4.6	45.9	32.6	2.4
1939	488	10.6	4.3	69.9	14.0	1.2
Meat and meat products						
1967	7,395	33.9	1.2	40.3	21.8	0.7
1939	501	14.4	2.7	72.7	9.9	0.3
Electric supplies, apparatus and equipment						
1967	5,695	75.0	1.3	15.8	4.0	0.9
1939	430	49.7	1.3	42.7	4.9	1.4

Source: U.S. Bureau of the Census, *1967 Census of Business*, Vol. III, *Wholesale Trade: Area Statistics* (Washington, D.C.: Government Printing Office, 1970), Table 2.

users (from 23.6 percent in 1939 to 37 percent in 1967) and the decline in the proportion sold to retailers (58.9 percent to 39 percent). Among wholesalers of meat (72.7 percent versus 40 percent) and of electric supplies and apparatus (42.7 percent versus 16 percent), the decline in sales to retailers is even more pronounced. These declines are the result of manufacturers integrating forward and large retailers integrating backward into wholesaling. Wholesaling functions are still performed, but to a lesser extent by the independent merchant wholesaler.

WHOLESALING COSTS AND PROFITS

Expenses of wholesaling

As used by the Bureau of the Census, "operating expenses include payroll as well as other overhead expenses of the establishments and prorata share of any general office expense, but does not include the cost of merchandise for sale nor income or excise taxes. Any withdrawals by owners or part owners of unincorporated businesses are not included."[18]

Because the functions performed by different types of wholesalers are so different, an average expense figure for all of wholesaling would have little meaning. For merchant wholesalers alone, it was 13.5 percent of sales in 1967, unchanged from 1963. Tables 10–3 (above) and 10–8 (below) show operating expense ratios for other types of wholesale operations and merchant wholesalers in different lines of business. These ratios indicate that wholesaling functions are much less expensive to perform than are retailing functions.[19]

No major functional classification of wholesaling expenses has been published by the federal government since 1948. The most helpful studies of expenses compare similar-type firms operating in comparable locations and doing substantially the same volume of business. Such studies should be made over a series of years, so that trends can be noted. In virtually every line of business there are trade associations and trade journals that publish operating statistics for wholesaling firms. Such comparisons are of value to the wholesaler in evaluating his own operating results and detecting points of strength and weakness.

The *Census of Business* does provide statistics on operating expenses by size of establishment as well as by type of operation and field of business. Average operating expenses (figured as a percentage of sales) decrease as sales increase, in the fashion predicted by economic theory. The very large merchant wholesalers have significantly lower average cost ratios. However, when analyzed by field of business, there are cases in which average costs increase for the very largest firms.

Operating ratios by type of operation. Data on operating expenses by types of operation for 1967 are presented in Table 10–3. These expenses varied from 4.0 percent of sales for agents and brokers to 14.4 percent for merchant wholesalers. Those for manufacturers' sales branches were 11.3 percent; for sales offices, 4.1 percent; and for assemblers, 8.6 percent. Comparable data for petroleum bulk plants and terminals are not available.

Although other factors, such as location of establishment and kind of business, also have a bearing on the relative operating expenses of different wholesalers, it should be noted that they line up in a logical fashion, based on functions performed and services rendered. As we have seen, agents and brokers provide largely a specialized service in the negotiating of sales or purchases. They carry little stock and extend a relatively small amount of credit. In contrast, cost-increasing functions, particularly carrying inventory, are performed by manufacturers' sales branches and many merchant wholesalers. Note that the largest operating expense ratios (11.3 percent and 14.4 percent, respectively) are for these two types of operation.

---

[18] U.S. Bureau of the Census, *1967 Census of Business,* Vol. IV, *Wholesale Trade,* p. 55–3.

[19] For a statement of retailers' expenses, see Chapter 7.

TABLE 10–8
Operating ratios for selected merchant wholesalers

	Mean 1967 operating expenses (percent of sales)	1969 median net profit		1969 median net sales to tangible net worth (times)	1969 median net sales to inventory (times)
		As percent of sales	As percent of tangible net worth		
Automotive equipment	23.2	2.13	8.11	3.80	4.9
Women's and children's clothing, furnishings, and accessories	16.3	1.39	8.90	5.69	8.8
Drugs and drug sundries	14.3	1.34	7.38	5.97	6.3
Electrical appliances, TV and radio sets	13.8	1.29	7.98	6.15	6.0
Electrical apparatus and equipment	12.9	1.63	8.17	5.64	7.3
Electronic parts and equipment	20.6	2.35	8.72	4.90	4.2
Groceries, general line	6.4	.58	6.81	10.72	11.2
Hardware	19.7	1.48	4.85	3.72	4.5
Industrial machinery and equipment	17.9	1.51	7.05	4.67	7.4
Lumber and millwork	13.0	1.80	8.42	5.42	7.6
Metal service centers	14.5	2.09	7.94	4.02	5.2
Piece goods	12.4	1.34	5.71	5.04	6.1
Plumbing and heating equipment and supplies	17.7	1.74	6.91	3.99	5.8
Tobacco and its products	5.9	.46	6.25	12.72	17.7

Source: 1967 operating expenses from 1967 Census of Business, Vol. IV, Wholesale Trade (Washington, D.C.: Government Printing Office, 1970), Table 2; all others from "The Ratios of the Wholesalers," Dun's Review (October 1970), pp. 72–73.

Operating ratios by kind of business

Operating ratios for merchant wholesalers in a number of different kinds of business are shown in Table 10–8. The profitability (as a percent of tangible net worth) for these businesses ranges from 4.85 percent for hardware to 8.90 percent for women's clothing and accessories. Only two types of business earned below 6.25 percent on net worth. This fairly narrow range of profit performance is below that for manufacturers in comparable kinds of businesses.

More meaningfully, the table also shows the different ways in which this profit is earned. Grocery and tobacco wholesalers take a very low margin of profit on sales (less than 0.6 percent) but turn their inventory over very rapidly (more than 11 times each year). Automotive and electronic equipment distributors are in fields in which the number of items they must carry in stock is increasing rapidly. Thus their inventory turns over more slowly, but each item sold carries a greater margin on profit. All four types end up with profit rates on assets in the middle of the range. For the hardware wholesaler, his inventory turnover and his margin on sales are low. The result is a poor profit performance.

The variation in average operating expenses can also be seen in the table. In 1967 these expenses ranged from 5.9 percent of sales for those handling tobacco and tobacco products to 23.2 percent for those dealing in automotive equipment. Again, hardware operating expenses are higher than other consumer nondurables such as groceries. These differences are explained by variations in the character of the merchandise sold, the marketing functions performed, and the services rendered.

WHOLESALING SUCCESS FACTORS

Failures in wholesaling, like failures in retailing, are caused by competition, insufficient financial resources, and poor management. In 1970, Dun and Bradstreet reported that 984 wholesale businesses failed,[20] somewhat more than in 1969 but considerably below the number in 1965. Nevertheless, the fight for profitability is particularly tough for the wholesaler. While performance in 1968 and 1969 was better than that for most of the post–World War II period, the total dollar profits of merchant wholesalers actually declined during that period.

Wholesalers who are expanding are doing so by: (1) knowing their local customers, (2) understanding customer problems and providing additional services when the opportunity arises, (3) giving constant attention to the handling and management of inventory, (4) developing industrial, institutional, and commercial customers as well as retailers, (5) integrating vertically into retailing, (6) upgrading performance in selling and promotion functions, and (7) modernizing paper flow and data processing.

The independent wholesaler is not likely to ever gain enough power to become the channel leader for very many products. However, he is likely to remain profitable by performing certain marketing functions more efficiently than can any one else in the channels he serves.

SUMMARY

Because the purpose of this chapter has been to examine the environment and structure of wholesaling in the marketing system in the United States, it has been descriptive by design. The distinction between a wholesaler and a retailer is that the

---

[20] "Business Failures," *Dun's Review,* February 1971, p. 91.

latter makes a majority of his sales to consumers for final use, while the former makes over half of his sales to other institutions for resale or for use in processing or selling activities. A wholesale transaction is made with other wholesalers, manufacturers, processors, or retailers; a retail transaction is made with an ultimate consumer and is intended for his own use. Many wholesalers do some retailing and many retailers do some wholesaling, but the key to the classification is whether the establishment is primarily engaged in wholesaling or retailing.

Five major types of wholesale institutions have been distinguished in the United States through the collection of census data. They are merchant wholesalers, manufacturers' sales branches and offices, petroleum bulk stations and terminals, merchandise agents and brokers, and assemblers of farm products.

Merchant wholesalers take title to the merchandise in which they deal; hence, they are *merchants*. Manufacturers' sales branches and offices, in a sense, are not wholesalers at all but manufacturers' operations engaged in wholesaling activities. Petroleum bulk stations and terminals and assemblers of farm products are classified by type of products handled. Merchandise agents and brokers, on the other hand, are *agents;* they do not take title to the merchandise they "handle." These distinctions are investigated in Chapter 11.

Large wholesalers account for the greatest share of wholesale sales, although small wholesalers are the most numerous. This is similar to the pattern in retailing. Wholesaling is not evenly distributed among the population as is retailing. A useful measure of the importance of a wholesaling center is to divide wholesale sales by the area's population. The larger the ratio, the more important is the wholesaling activity. Transportation centers or hubs persist as wholesale centers.

While wholesale operating expenses vary widely among different types of wholesalers, they are generally lower than retail operating expenses. Wholesaling has had some poor periods in its history and has been the target for vertical integration in many fields, but the independent wholesaler is not declining in importance. However, to have survived since World War II, an independent wholesaler has had to be efficient, aggressive, and flexible.

The next chapter and those in Part V will investigate some of the ways the wholesaler performs his particular marketing functions. You should be able to integrate this description of the independent wholesaler's role into the total vertical channel system described in Chapter 3.

REVIEW AND DISCUSSION QUESTIONS

1. In your own words, differentiate between the terms "middleman" and "wholesaler," and between a "wholesale sale" and a "retail sale." Give examples in each case.

2. Compare and contrast the operations of a distributor and a manufacturers' agent selling electronic equipment.

3. Summarize the most significant developments in wholesaling in the United States before World War II.

4. Based on a study of current business periodicals, prepare a paper not exceeding 1,500 words in length on the topic "The Changing Importance of Wholesalers since World War II."

5. Explain why wide variations occur in the growth patterns of different kinds of wholesalers and in different areas of the country.

6. Define a merchant wholesaler and indicate the chief classifications into which such wholesalers may be grouped.

7. Since retailers far outnumber wholesalers and also sell at higher prices, how do you explain the fact that the total volume of wholesale sales is greater than that for retailing?

8. What useful information may be summarized from a detailed, careful analysis of the number and sales of wholesalers classified by sales volume (Table 10–4)?

9. Of what value to the marketer are census data on wholesaling related to regions, divisions, standard metropolitan statistical areas, and states? Be specific.

10. How do you explain the fact that about half of the U.S. wholesaling business ($217 billion of $459 billion) is done in only two of the nine census divisions, the Middle Atlantic and East North-Central?

11. Through study of the section of Volume IV of the *1967 Census of Business, Wholesale Trade* devoted to Standard Metropolitan Statistical Areas, develop significant generalizations concerning the concentration and dispersion of wholesale sales in such areas.

12. Explain briefly the important recent trends in the sales of merchant wholesalers to their different classes of customers.

13. Study the operating costs of some regular type of wholesaler, i.e., drugs, groceries, hardware, for a recent five-year period. Discuss the significant changes that have taken place. If none has occurred, explain why.

14. Explain the major factors responsible for the cost differences among merchant wholesalers shown in Table 10–8.

15. Assume you have been asked to speak before a group of wholesalers on the subject "Opportunities for Cost Reduction and Profit Improvement." What information would you present?

SUPPLEMENTARY READINGS

Bartels, R. (ed.) *Comparative Marketing: Wholesaling in Fifteen Countries.* Homewood, Ill.: Richard D. Irwin, Inc., 1963. Sponsored by the American Marketing Association, this collection of articles describes and interprets wholesaling activities in a variety of cultural settings.

Beckman, T. N. and Doody, A. F. *Wholesaling.* Small Business Bulletin No. 55. Rev. ed. Washington, D.C.: Small Business Administration, 1965. A bibliography of governmental and nongovernmental publications on all phases of wholesaling and a valuable guide to supplementary reading for the student.

Beckman, T. N.; Engle, N. H.; and Buzzell, R. D. *Wholesaling: Principles and Practice.* 3d ed. New York: Ronald Press Co., 1959. This volume has been a "standard" in the wholesaling field for many years.

Converse, P. D. "Twenty-five Years of Wholesaling: A Revolution in Food Wholesaling," *Journal of Marketing,* 22 (July 1957), pp. 40–52. This analysis by a careful student of marketing provides valuable information on the development of various concepts and the contributions of early authors.

Davis, R. T. *A Marketing Professor Looks at Wholesaling: Challenge and Opportunity.* Washington, D.C.: National Association of Wholesalers, 1966. In this 9-page pamphlet, the author presents an excellent summary of the contributions of wholesaling, recent trends, and existing opportunities.

Hill, R. M. *Wholesaling Management: Test and Cases.* Homewood, Ill.: Richard D. Irwin, Inc., 1963. This well-rounded treatment of the management problems facing wholesalers also examines the nature and significance of wholesaling. Also see the author's *Techniques of Measuring Market Potential for Wholesalers,* Bulletin No. 820. Urbana: Bureau of Business Management, University of Illinois, 1962.

Kelley, E. J. and Lazer, W. (eds.) *Managerial Marketing: Perspectives and Viewpoints.* 3d ed. Homewood, Ill.: Richard D. Irwin, Inc., 1967. See especially **E. H. Lewis,** "Trends in Wholesaling," pp. 516–21; and **T. N. Beckman,** "Summary Statement from 'Changes in Wholesaling Structure and Performance,'" pp. 522–25.

Lopata, R. S. "Faster Pace in Wholesaling," *Harvard Business Review,* 47 (July–August 1969), pp. 130–42. An excellent description of the current status of the merchant wholesaler.

Moller, W. G., Jr. and Wilemon, D. L. *Marketing Channels: A Systems Viewpoint.* Homewood, Ill.: Richard D. Irwin, Inc., 1971. Readings 5, 11, 15, 16, 27, 28, and 31 are an excellent supplement to this chapter.

Revzan, D. A. *Wholesaling in Marketing Organization.* New York: John Wiley & Sons, Inc., 1961. This volume, covering both the external and the internal points of view, represents a clear and comprehensive analysis of wholesaling.

Revzan, D. A. *The Marketing Significance of Geographical Variations in Wholesale/-Retail Sales Ratios: Parts I and II.* Berkeley: University of California, Institute of Business and Economic Research, 1966 and 1967. These two publications develop significant ratios in wholesale-retail sales based on 1963 data from the Census of Business.

Revzan, D. A. *A Marketing View of Spatial Competition.* Berkeley, 1971. Chapters 4 and 5 develop the concepts of spatial competition and then apply them to an analysis of wholesale trade.

Vance, J. E., Jr. *The Merchant's World: The Geography of Wholesaling.* Englewood Cliffs, N.J.: Prentice-Hall, Inc., 1970. A short and fascinating volume which examines the principles applying to the distribution and organization of U.S. wholesaling activities.

11 Wholesaling: Institutions and functions

A bewildering array of wholesaling institutions and functions is present in the marketing system in the United States. Each of the thousands of institutions is somewhat different from the others. To help untangle this complexity, organizations engaged principally in wholesaling activities have been classified on the basis of several characteristics which are important to the other institutions in the channel system. This system is strongly dependent on the classification used by the Bureau of the Census because this is the one for which statistics are available. It is not necessarily the most useful classification for today's marketing system.[1]

First, middlemen who take title to the merchandise in which they deal are known as *merchant* middlemen; those who do not take title are known as *agent* middlemen. Second, merchant wholesalers are further classified as to the assortment of their product line—*general line, specialty,* or *general merchandise*. Third, merchant wholesalers are also classified on the completeness of the services and functions they provide. Merchant wholesalers who perform all wholesaling functions are called *full-service wholesalers,* and the other merchant wholesalers are called *limited-service wholesalers*. Fourth, agent wholesalers, as well as merchant wholesalers, are classified on the basis of the market size they serve: *local, regional,* or *national*. Fifth, the main bases for the agent wholesaler classification are the functions provided (selling, buying, etc.) and for whom the functions are provided (the buyer or the seller).

Finally, wholesaling activities managed by manufacturers are designated as

---

[1] For a more complete discussion of this point, see D. A. Revzan, *Wholesaling in Marketing Organization* (New York: John Wiley & Sons, Inc., 1961), chap. 2.

manufacturers' branches or sales offices—not as wholesalers; and certain activities (public warehousing, trade shows, and central markets) are classified as *facilitating institutions*—not wholesaling organizations.

The first part of this chapter is designed to acquaint you with the major types of wholesaling organizations that are available and are used in channel systems. The second part focuses on the major functions performed by wholesaling organizations in the marketing system and provides insight as to why they are used.

CLASSIFICATION OF WHOLESALERS

The geography of wholesaling was discussed in the previous chapter. Because the number of national wholesalers is small, classification by geographic coverage will be omitted here. The other classifications are discussed in the following order:

1. Merchant wholesalers by function
   a) Full-function wholesalers by product assortment
      (1) General-line wholesalers
      (2) Specialty wholesalers
      (3) General merchandise wholesalers
   b) Limited-function wholesalers
      (1) Rack jobbers or service merchandisers
      (2) Cash-and-carry wholesalers
      (3) Drop shippers
      (4) Mail-order wholesalers
      (5) Truck jobbers
2. Agent middlemen
   a) Brokers
   b) Commission merchants
   c) Selling agents
   d) Export and import agents
   e) Auction companies
   f) Purchasing agents and resident buyers
3. Manufacturers' sales branches and offices
4. Facilitating institutions
   a) Public warehouses
   b) Central market facilities
   c) Trade shows and exhibits

Full-function merchant wholesalers

Based on the degree of product specialization, three types of full-function (or full-service) merchant wholesalers can be distinguished: general-line, specialty, and general merchandise wholesalers.

General-line wholesalers. As measured by annual sales volume, general-line wholesalers are the most important service wholesalers. Catering to large numbers of limited-line stores, this type of service wholesaler attempts to meet their needs by carrying a fairly complete line of merchandise in a particular category such as groceries, hardware, or drugs. In 1967, census data revealed there were 2,543 general-line grocery wholesalers, 591 in the hardware field, and 374 handling drugs.

A study of dry goods wholesalers some years ago concluded that the chief advantages of general-line firms over specialty houses are as follows:

(1) They can more completely fill the needs of their retail customers [and] this tends to lessen competition as it enables the retailers to get their merchandise from fewer sources, thereby decreasing the sales pressure; (2) retailers are more dependent on them, especially during times of scarcity, and are thereby more loyal and better customers; and (3) the volume per customer and per salesman is larger, resulting in greater volume from fewer customers and smaller areas.[2]

Specialty wholesalers. These wholesalers differ from the general-line wholesalers in that they carry a limited number of items within one field. Thus we find that the specialty wholesaler in the grocery field may specialize in just frozen foods; in the dry goods field, in hosiery and lingerie; and in the drug field, in toilet articles or proprietary medicines. Although they represent an even more recent development than general-line wholesalers, the specialty wholesalers are already more important in many fields, from the point of view of numbers. In the hardware field in 1967, there were 2,922 specialty wholesalers, as against 591 general-line wholesalers.[3] Sales in this field also exceeded those of the general-line wholesalers.

To the retailer, the specialty wholesaler offers the advantages that come from a high degree of specialization. Although his stock may be limited in scope, it is complete in the items carried. Because turnover is fairly rapid, the merchandise may be fresher; or if fashion is involved, it may be more up to date. Further, the salesmen of such wholesalers may be experts in the few items they sell and able to offer worthwhile advice to the retailer. On the other hand, the limited stock carried makes it too expensive to call on smaller retailers who cannot buy in quantities, and the time that the retailer must spend interviewing salesmen is increased.

To the wholesaler, operation on a specialty basis has attractions. The more limited stock simplifies the management problem because less unsalable merchandise may be accumulated and stock turnover may be increased. In addition, less capital is needed to begin business, and less knowledge is required. But these advantages are gained through the acceptance of a higher cost of doing business. Apparently, the higher overhead per item when fewer items are handled is not offset by lower interest cost resulting from a faster turnover, less obsolete merchandise, and greater sales within the limited line carried. Of the fields covered in Table 11–1, none of the specialty wholesalers has a lower cost ratio than the general-line wholesaler.

General merchandise wholesalers. General merchandise wholesalers, rather than carrying reasonably complete stocks in a particular line or specializing in the handling of a limited number of items in a given field, maintain inventories of a number of unrelated lines such as groceries, hardware, dry goods, furniture, and electrical supplies. These wholesalers find their main outlet through general stores, just as they did in the 19th century, although many of them also sell to limited-line country stores, such as drug, hardware, and electrical appliance stores. They are found mostly in the southern, midwestern, and western parts of the country. In 1967 the *Census of*

[2] J. R. Bromell, *Dry Goods Wholesalers' Operations* (Washington, D.C.: Government Printing Office, 1949) p. 13.

[3] U.S. Bureau of the Census, *1967 Census of Business,* Vol. IV: *Wholesale Trade: Area Statistics* (Washington, D.C.: Government Printing Office 1970), p. 1–10. Census data do not allow separation of information on service wholesalers from that on wholesale merchants in general. Nor do they make possible a complete separation by kinds of business between service and limited-function wholesalers. Consequently, these statistics include both service and limited-function wholesalers.

TABLE 11–1
Operating expenses of selected general-line and specialty wholesalers, 1967 (net sales = 100 percent)

Field	General line	Specialty line
Drugs 12.0		16.3
Merchandise 10.1		—
Groceries 6.4		11.6 (dairy products)
Hardware 18.3		22.6

Source: U.S. Bureau of the Census, *1967 Census of Business,* Vol. IV, *Wholesale Trade: Area Statistics* (Washington, D.C.: Government Printing Office, 1970), Table 2.

Business reported 387 general merchandise wholesalers with sales of $1.5 billion.[4] The number of establishments is less than half that of a decade earlier.

Limited-function wholesalers

The present importance of limited-function wholesalers such as cash-and-carry wholesalers and drop shippers has sometimes been grossly exaggerated. The *Census of Business* has not reported separate data on these middlemen since 1958. In that year only 10,232 of the 287,000 wholesalers were limited-function wholesalers, including both consumer and industrial goods.

Although data are not available, it is probable that the greatest part of limited-function wholesaling is now carried on through limited-function departments of regular wholesalers. Thus while independent limited-service wholesalers are of marginal importance per se, their operating methods and the conditions responsible for their development are of interest because they have also caused many full-function wholesalers to provide limited-function services. The five types of limited-function wholesalers outlined above will be considered here.

Rack jobbers or service merchandisers. The rack jobber or service merchandiser has grown rapidly since 1952, primarily in response to the increasing sale of nonfood items in supermarkets. The rack jobber typically sets up merchandise racks, keeps them stocked with merchandise, and charges the retail establishment only for the merchandise that is gone from the rack (or display) when he restocks. His racks usually contain merchandise that is somewhat foreign to the host store; grocery stores, for example, have used rack jobbers for hardware, cosmetics, and hosiery. One source reports that sales of the major categories of such items—health and beauty aids (about 67 percent of sales), hosiery, housewares, soft goods, magazines, toys, stationery, and phonograph records—in supermarkets grew from $0.28 billion and 1.5 percent of total sales in 1954 to $5.12 billion and 5.8 percent of total sales in 1970.[5]

Nonfoods have become so important that some chains now perform the wholesale functions for some product lines (notably health and beauty aids) or buy direct from manufacturers. Still, half of all nonfood items in grocery stores are supplied by this growing type of wholesale middleman.

Sales opportunities for rack jobbers are not restricted to supermarkets, however.

---

[4] U.S. Bureau of the Census, *1967 Census of Business,* Vol. IV, *Wholesale Trade;* p. 1–11.

[5] "Nonfoods: New Surge Anticipated," *Progressive Grocer,* 50 (April 1971), p. 97.

Perhaps as much as 20 percent of their $2 billion sales in 1970 went to department, drug, hardware, and discount stores. The industry is composed of about 500 firms, the largest of which service over 5,000 retail stores each.[6]

To call the rack jobber a limited-function wholesaler is almost a misnomer, for he offers sophisticated service on a narrow line of items that are big profit items for retailers. He provides complete inventory management, furnishes the retailer with display fixtures, preprices the products, carries all risks by guaranteeing sale and allowing return of damaged, unsold, or slow-moving merchandise, delivers the merchandise, and writes the order. Perhaps most important, he relieves the retailer of all responsibility for advertising and point-of-purchase promotion. He performs these functions for 12 to 16 percent of sales, about the same as a full-service drug wholesaler.

Cash-and-carry wholesalers. Cash-and-carry wholesalers may be distinguished from service or regular wholesalers by the following factors: (1) their customers call at their places of business to obtain the merchandise; (2) cash is usually required at the time of purchase or soon thereafter; (3) they generally carry a very limited line of the fast-moving items in their field; and (4) salesmen are not widely used to call on customers. It is not at all certain that cash-and-carry wholesalers reduce the *total* cost of marketing, because it is more expensive for the retailer to visit the cash-and-carry wholesaler's establishment to get his merchandise than to buy from a service wholesaler. However, this limited-function wholesaler does provide an excellent source for fill-in or emergency needs. Further, for small resellers, he provides a means of buying in less than case lots.

Drop shippers. The drop shipper has a relatively low cost of operation. In 1948, the latest year for which data are available, his costs were 4.4 percent of sales, as contrasted with 12.5 percent for all merchant wholesalers. To a large degree, this lower cost is a result of eliminating the wholesale warehouse function. He does this by placing his orders with the manufacturers and having them ship direct to the retailer. This does not necessarily mean a lower total cost of distribution; in fact, it may result in a higher distribution cost because he forces storage back onto the manufacturer, who may not be able to provide this function as economically as the specialized wholesaler can. In addition, the cost of transportation may be considerably increased because of the smaller sized shipments the manufacturer must make to the retailer.

Drop shippers are found in fields such as construction materials where merchandise is bulky (so that substantial savings can be achieved by the elimination of handling at the wholesale level), when retailers frequently purchase in carload lots, and where two or more buyers live in the same area. Carload shipment to the area coupled with local delivery to the buyers can result in lower transportation costs and speedier delivery.

Mail-order wholesalers. Mail order as a distinctive kind of wholesaling is probably passing from the field. In 1929, there were only 41 wholesalers doing over 50 percent of their business by this method, and their total sales were about $46 million. By 1935 their number had increased to 189 but their total sales were only $14 million. Since that time, they have not been classified separately by the Bureau of the Census.

Before the development of good roads and automobiles, the mail-order whole-

---

[6] "Racking up Profits," *Financial World,* 133 (February 4, 1970), pp. 20–22.

saler was important in reaching rural retailers. At the present time, however, the ease with which these retailers can be visited by the salesmen of the service wholesaler or by the manufacturers' salesmen has changed the picture. Since the goods bought from a mail-order wholesaler often have to come from some distance, there are resulting delays in delivery and increases in cost.

Truck jobbers.[7] Merchant middlemen who combine the functions of salesmen and of delivery men are known as truck jobbers. Typically, they sell for cash from a stock limited to nationally advertised specialties and fast-moving items of a perishable or semiperishable nature. Most of these wholesalers are concentrated in the grocery, tobacco, and sundries fields, where they usually carry a few specialties—such as potato chips, salted nuts, and candy—on their trucks. They make some 30 to 35 calls a day on retailers and deliver stock as orders are received.

The truck jobber is far from being a new development. His predecessor, the "wagon distributor," can be traced back to colonial days. Yet the 1930s saw a rather rapid expansion in the number of this type of wholesaler. In 1929 the Census of Distribution reported only 817 establishments, whereas in 1939 there were 2,398. By 1958 they had grown to 7,351 establishments with sales of $1.5 billion, but they suffered a sharp decline by 1963.

Although truck jobbers offer manufacturers a means of obtaining aggressive selling—because they carry few items—and aid the retailer in obtaining a more rapid turnover of merchandise by keeping shelves organized and well stocked, they suffer the disadvantage of operating at a high cost. Operating delivery trucks during daylight hours in urban areas today is costly and in some areas virtually impossible. In addition, they provide much service for a small order. In 1963, their costs were 13 percent of sales.

Agent middlemen

Agent middlemen—those negotiating the buying and/or selling of goods without generally taking title to them—also compete with the service wholesaler, but this competition is less extensive than it appears from total sales data. In 1967, for example, only 17.6 percent of their sales, $10,797 million, were to retailers, while 39.4 percent of merchant wholesalers' sales, or $81,186 million, were to retailers.[8] Statistics on agent middlemen in selected consumer goods fields are shown in Table 11–2. Note how much more important agent middlemen are in groceries than in other fields.

Brokers. A broker is an independent agent middleman whose principal function is to bring the buyer and the seller together. In consumer products, merchandise brokers, the most important agent middlemen, actually function as manufacturers' representatives; that is, they represent sellers. In 1967, they helped market $14 billion worth of consumer and industrial products.

Grocery and food specialties constitute the most important consumer product handled by brokers. Table 11–3, which presents the main product fields in which food brokers operate, shows that they are faring quite well in today's competitive market. Note the amount of dispersion among brokerage fees between products. The size of

---

[7] The Bureau of the Census lists these as "wagon and truck jobbers." The term "wagon distributor" developed historically because sales were originally made from wagons. Since this operation today is typically carried on from trucks, many years ago the authors adopted the more modern term "truck jobbers."

[8] U.S. Bureau of the Census, *1967 Census of Business,* Vol. III, *Wholesale Trade: Subject Reports,* Table 4–1.

TABLE 11–2

Number of establishments, sales, and operating expenses of agent middlemen in selected fields, 1967

Type, by kind of business	Number of establishments	Sales (in millions)	Commissions received (percent)
Automotive equipment.................................	688	$1,105	5.5
Drugs, proprieteries, and sundries...	220	504	5.6
Piece goods, woven fabrics............................	411	1,682	3.3
Women's and children's clothing	762	1,462	5.6
Frozen foods..	365	1,546	3.8
Groceries and related products 2,174		9,123	3.1
Electrical appliances, TV and radio sets	252	490	5.7
Hardware...	436	462	6.1
Home furnishings and floor coverings..............	531	665	5.9

Source: U.S. Bureau of the Census, *1967 Census of Business*, Vol. IV, *Wholesale Trade: Area Statistics* (Washington, D.C.: Government Printing Office, 1970), Table 2.

TABLE 11–3

Relative importance of food brokers by type of product, 1967 and 1958

Type	Number of establishments		Sales (in millions)		Brokerage fee (percent)	
	1967	1958	1967	1958	1967	1958
Frozen foods..................	365	257	$1,546	$ 574	3.8	3.7
Dairy products	233	252	1,141	771	3.9	3.4
Confectionary	288	210	448	266	5.3	4.7
Poultry, seafood, and meat	351	307	1,222	997	2.4	2.4
Fresh fruits and vegetables 1,029		986	2,467	1,877	4.7	4.5
Other grocery and related products...........2,174		2,447	9,123	6,377	3.1	2.3

Source: U.S. Bureau of the Census, *1967 Census of Business*, Vol. IV, *Wholesale Trade: Area Statistics* (Washington, D.C.: Government Printing Office, 1970), Table 2; *1963 Census of Business*, Vol. IV, *Wholesale Trade: Summary Statistics* (Washington, D.C.: Government Printing Office, 1966), p. 1–23.

the average firm is growing; each may represent as many as 20 noncompeting manufacturers. The number of manufacturers using food brokers is near an all-time high. To obtain national distribution with food brokers may require arrangements with as many as 50 organizations, since brokerage organizations offer only regional coverage.[9]

The success of the food broker is due to his ability to do detailed promotion and effective selling at costs below those of a manufacturer selling a narrow or seasonal

---

[9] "Food Brokers: A Comprehensive Study of Their Growing Role in Marketing," *Grocery Manufacturer* (December 1969).

Marketing: Principles and methods

product line direct. Sunsweet Growers, Inc., for example, uses brokers to sell prunes. By selling this product along with others, the brokers can give strong selling effort at a cost below that of a national Sunsweet sales organization. In addition, the brokerage fee is only paid when sales are made. Thus, through the broker, even the small producer can quickly establish contact with potential buyers over a wide area; and because the small manufacturer pays on the same commission basis as does his larger competitor, he is not at a cost disadvantage. On his part, the broker is able to make his knowledge of the market available to the manufacturer on a relatively low fee basis, since he is free to work for a number of sellers.

Commission merchants. In practice, commission merchants are difficult to distinguish from brokers, although in theory they differ in that they always represent sellers, have the right to accept offers of buyers without first getting the principal's approval, and actually have possession of the goods they sell.[10] In 1967 the Bureau of the Census reports that 5,425 *commission merchants* had sales of $14.1 billion. [11] Relatively small amounts of manufactured consumer goods were included in these sales, and they were largely in the dry goods (mainly piece goods) field. In this field, the commission merchants receive merchandise from their principals on consignment, provide storage, find buyers, negotiate prices, make deliveries, extend credit, make collections, and deduct their commissions before remitting the balance to their principals.

The importance of commission merchants is not increasing, primarily because of the lack of control their principals can exert, particularly with respect to selling prices. Once goods are turned over to them, commission merchants may sell them at any price they consider satisfactory without seeking further advice from their principals. This pricing freedom may be necessary to move perishable products in glutted markets, but few manufacturers are willing to yield so much control when other middlemen are available.

Selling agents. Selling agents engage in wholesaling a considerable amount of manufactured consumer goods in the dry goods field, with lesser amounts in clothing and furnishings, groceries and foods, and furniture and house furnishings. In 1967 they numbered 1,891 and had sales of $6.9 billion, including both consumer and industrial goods, and their commissions were 4.2 percent of sales.[12] For 1958 the figures were: number 2069, sales $7 billion, and expenses 3.6 percent.

The decline in the number of selling agents during the past decade probably results more from horizontal mergers among smaller manufacturers and vertical integration by retailers who buy directly from manufacturers than from inefficiency on the part of these operators.

The basic differences between the selling agent and the manufacturers' agent arise out of the fact that the former takes over all the selling activities of a company, whereas the latter is really a salesman on an independent basis who sells in a restricted area. Specifically, selling agents differ from manufacturers' agents in the following respects: (1) they sell all or a major part of the output of one or more products of the clients they serve; (2) they are less limited in sales territory; (3) they have considerable latitude with regard to prices and terms of sale, whereas the authority of the manufacturers' agent is limited; and (4) they frequently finance their clients and offer

---

[10] The term "merchant" used here is unfortunate since this term is also used to connote a middleman who takes title. The commission merchant does not take title; he is an agent.

[11] U.S. Bureau of the Census, *1967 Census of Business*, Vol. IV, *Wholesale Trade*, Table 2.

[12] Ibid.

assistance in connection with advertising and other sales promotion activities. The use of manufacturers' agents in marketing industrial goods is discussed in some detail in Chapter 13.

In the textile and canned goods fields the selling agent usually takes over the selling activities for a number of companies. Thus by handling the outputs of several small mills or canning factories, he is able to reduce the selling cost for each firm. He may engage in advertising, operate sales offices, and place salesmen on the road. In addition, in fields where style and fashion are important elements (as in textiles), he may offer advice to the mill as to what should be produced. In many instances, financial aid is also extended to those for whom he sells, and he may go so far as to handle all credit and collection problems for the manufacturer. Consequently, the selling agent may afford an advantageous means of distribution for the small-scale manufacturer who desires to market his product over a fairly wide area and who needs continuous representation in that area.

Frequently the selling agent has been criticized by manufacturers for having what is described as a stranglehold on those for whom he sells, the argument being that the agent, through his control of markets and of his client's finances, may exert pressure on the client to sell at unreasonably low prices, thereby making it easier for the agent to sell and collect his fee. There are illustrations of this situation, but there are also examples of long-established relations between manufacturers and selling agents which have been to the advantage of both parties. A selling agent can provide an ideal method of sale for many manufacturers.

Export and import agents. These agents may be any one of the four kinds already discussed, except that they specialize in the buying and selling of goods in foreign trade. In 1967, 270 import agents had sales of $1.8 billion. Export agents numbered 548 in 1967 and enjoyed sales of $3.4 billion.

Exporters did better than importers during the first seven years of the 1960s. Since then the reverse has been true. While the U.S. trade balance has worsened in recent years, the total volume of international trade has increased. Agents in this trade are likely to experience the competitive pressures of vertical integration that are common for all middlemen but, as long as world trade expands, the opportunity for their continued growth should remain. More will be said about global marketing in Chapter 16.

Auction companies. Auction companies, which primarily engage in selling merchandise on an agency basis through the auction method, are not important in the sale of manufactured consumer products, although some clothing, furniture and home furnishings, automobiles, and general merchandise are sold through them. Data are unavailable to indicate the volume of manufactured products sold at auction, but overall figures indicate that 1,594 such firms had total sales of $4.79 billion in 1967. Both statistics show absolute declines since 1963.

Purchasing agents and resident buyers. These agent middlemen engage in buying merchandise for a limited number of customers on a continuing basis. In 1967, when they numbered 255, they negotiated sales of $1.1 billion at a commission of 3.6 percent. Only the last statistic has changed to any extent since 1958 (up from 2.7 percent). They are the least important agent middlemen in the distribution structure. An example of their use may be found in department stores who employ resident buyers in key markets such as New York and Paris. They assist the buyers with market information and make buys that are necessary when the store's buyer cannot travel to the market.

Manufacturers' sales branches and sales offices

A manufacturer cannot proceed very far in planning for a direct-selling sales staff before he faces two questions: First, shall all salesmen work out of the factory headquarters, or shall sales offices be established with a manager in charge of all salesmen within a specific geographic area? Second, shall stocks be established at such offices, thereby turning them into branches?

As consumer markets have become larger and more concentrated in urban areas and competition has become more intense, more manufacturers have decided that the increased financial and managerial problems connected with performing their own wholesaling functions are worth the effort. In recent years there has been a trend toward distribution through branches by manufacturers of consumer goods. In the appliance field, for example, many manufacturers, facing an uncertain and highly competitive market, have reluctantly reached the conclusion that the number of good distributors is not sufficient to meet the needs of the appliance manufacturers. Branches are located mainly in the large cities (or prime markets); in other areas, independent distributors are commonly used. The increase in vertical integration has progressed; in 1967 over one third of all wholesale sales were made by manufacturers' branches (see Table 10–2). Accounting methods and census procedures probably result in an actual understatement of the amount of wholesaling functions performed by manufacturers.

However, modern transportation and communications methods make it possible for a manufacturer to contact many customers without establishing any branch offices at all. For selling and information purposes, he can use traveling shows and displays, closed-circuit television, and leased telephone lines to contact customers. Nor need the traveling salesman of today spend weeks on the road. With modern highways, air travel, and geographically concentrated markets, he can often work out of a home office at a cost lower than that required to establish a branch office. The mails also are a medium for selling and information exchange. Many small manufacturers find direct-mail promotion and catalog sheets to be efficient selling tools, although the catalog is mostly used by manufacturers of consumer goods to obtain orders for fill-in merchandise. Improved transportation and other facilitating institutions also encourage manufacturers to sell direct to retailers.

Facilitating institutions

Manufacturers and retailers who want to avoid dealing with merchant wholesalers may turn selling functions over to agent middlemen and perform other of the wholesaling functions themselves. Alternatively, they can sell direct and use other institutions to facilitate direct sale. Three such institutions are discussed here: public warehouses, central markets, and trade shows.

Public warehouses. Public warehouses are storage facilities owned by individuals or companies who hope to make a profit on the renting of space to others. In 1967 there were 9,433 of these establishments in the United States, with a floorspace of 392.9 million square feet.[13]

---

[13] U.S. Bureau of the Census, *1967 Census of Business,* Vol. III, *Wholesale Trade,* Table 1.

Such warehouse firms usually specialize in some particular line with warehousing facilities built for the handling of that line. As a rule, they offer a number of services in addition to storage; they will receive merchandise in carload or smaller lots, remove it from the cars, place it in storage, and—upon the receipt of orders for such merchandise (the orders, of course, must be approved by the one placing the goods in storage)—they will pack it in smaller lots, ship it, and issue invoices.

The public warehouse is an ideal development from the point of view of the manufacturer who wishes to sell direct to the retailer. It relieves him of the necessity of financing a number of private warehouses located at strategic geographical points. If the inventory is collateral for a loan, the public warehouse gives the lender the security he requires. The manufacturer also need not divide his energies to be sure that his private warehouses are well managed. Although the manufacturer who has a large and steady volume of business at a particular point may find a private warehouse cheaper to operate, many manufacturers are not in this position. The small manufacturer, the large manufacturer having small volumes in particular markets, and the manufacturer of seasonal goods will probably find the public warehouse cheaper than the private one. Public warehouses provide a means of securing wide distribution of spot stocks and financing such stocks at a reasonable cost.

Central market facilities.   Some 15 central markets have been developed in North America to encourage the manufacturer to sell direct to the retailer. Instead of the manufacturers of related lines of merchandise being scattered all over the central market city, large buildings are available in which a number of them can rent suitable space. Probably the two best illustrations are found in Chicago—the Merchandise Mart and the American Furniture Mart—but similar facilities are now available in apparel and other lines such as the Dallas (Texas) Apparel Mart, the California Mart (Los Angeles), Western Merchandise Mart (San Francisco), High Point (North Carolina) Furniture Mart, Miami International Merchandise Mart, and the Atlanta Mart. Seattle, Denver, St. Louis, and New Orleans also have marts with floor space of over one million square feet. New York has no specific merchandise mart but has office buildings that serve this purpose: women's wear on Broadway; toys, gifts, and housewares on Fifth Avenue.[14] Merchandise marts have actually increased in importance since the 1950s when jet travel made it easier for smaller retailers to get to shows. The Dallas Mart opened in 1955, Atlanta's new building was occupied in 1961, and Miami's opened in 1968.

1. *The Merchandise Mart.*   The Merchandise Mart can be described as a store for storekeepers. Eighteen of its twenty-one floors are packed with clothes, curtains, rugs, chairs, tables, silverware, notions, toys, dishes, jewelry—all the merchandise commonly found in U.S. department stores, but here the merchant is the customer and the manufacturer is the man behind the counter.

The number of buyers and lines displayed in the Merchandise Mart has continued to increase since its opening in 1932. Today, more than a million separate items are displayed by several thousand manufacturers. At the annual International Home Furnishings Show, the 700 sample rooms on 10 floors of the Mart building are specially decorated to attract purchasers.

2. *The American Furniture Mart.*   This Mart is housed in the largest building in the world devoted to a single industry—furniture and related items. It contains permanent exhibits of some 1,250 leading manufacturers of furniture and major

---

14 "Trade Marts Take Over the Selling," *Business Week,* November 9, 1968, pp. 78–82.

household appliances, hard and soft floor coverings, and numerous related items. It is the center of semiannual "markets" of about one week's duration. These markets attract retailers from all parts of the country who visit the exhibits of various manufacturers, learn about current developments in the various lines, and place many orders for delivery during the following six months. In addition, numerous buyers visit the Mart weekly to order needed merchandise. Both the American Furniture Mart and the Merchandise Mart arrange definite programs and showings during the market periods.

Trade shows and exhibits. Though old, the trade show is a growing institution through which sellers, usually manufacturers, can display their wares for buyers, usually retailers or industrial users. New York City has an annual home furnishings show and a toy fair; Chicago, a national shoe fair and the millinery exhibition; and Hollywood, a semiannual fashion show. None of these are permanent exhibits such as those housed in the American Furniture Mart and the Merchandise Mart; rather, they are temporary gathering places for sellers and buyers of specific kinds of merchandise.

A large showing of consumer products, although not especially conducive to careful buying by the retailer, does offer him certain advantages. He can actually see the merchandise rather than depend on a catalog or description. Moreover, with products of competing manufacturers located close together, he can make direct comparisons in a minimum of time. He can also note the purchases of those retailers who are recognized as astute buyers.

The number of such shows in industrial marketing has grown from approximately 400 in the late 1930s to perhaps 4,000 today. In Europe, the name "trade fair" is more common; "exhibition" is the name usually applied to a group of displays assembled in conjunction with a convention or a trade association or professional society. European trade fairs date from the 12th century and have grown in popularity as an institution to facilitate international trade. American manufacturers display at such shows as the International Furniture Fair in Cologne, Germany.

From the manufacturer's point of view, the trade show is useful for introducing new products or fashions, maintaining a company image, identifying potential customers, demonstrating nonportable equipment, obtaining new ideas and market feedback from customers and competitors, and even hiring personnel. However, few orders are written at most shows; a follow-up direct sales call is usually required to close a sale. The disadvantage of trade shows for manufacturers is that they are a costly medium of promotion for which it is difficult to evaluate effectiveness.[15]

FUNCTIONS PERFORMED BY INDEPENDENT WHOLESALE MIDDLEMEN

The previous sections may have suggested that the importance of the independent wholesale middleman is declining. In fact, during the past decade, industrial products middlemen grew a bit faster than the economy generally and consumer products wholesalers grew a bit slower than aggregate growth. Even here, however, some types of wholesalers who were under intensive competitive pressure, such as furniture and appliance wholesalers, did better than average.

The predicted demise of the independent wholesaler is not a new phenomenon.

---

[15] J. M. Carman, "Evaluation of Trade Show Exhibits," *California Management Review,* 11 (Winter 1968), pp. 35–44.

Even in the late years of the 19th century, when the modern wholesaler was just emerging, the feeling prevailed that he was a useless middleman and doomed to pass out of the distribution picture in the near future. The following quotation is from a letter written in 1897 to a young man recently employed in a wholesale hardware firm:

It is very unwise for you to start your business life in the wholesale jobbing trade, because any time you spend upon it will be wasted. The wholesale merchant has no place in these progressive times. You may take my word for it that within ten years there will be no more wholesale establishments in the United States.[16]

The wholesaler has retained his importance in the marketing structure for two main reasons. First, he has adjusted his operations to changing conditions through innovations of various kinds which have brought growth in the face of much adversity and numerous forecasts that "his days are numbered." One careful student gives the following reasons for the resurgence of the regular wholesaler:

1. His role as the "eyes and ears" of the marketplace, including his many services both to manufacturers and to customers.
2. Recent internal managerial changes designed to meet his competition more effectively, including more efficient warehousing, adoption of aggressive sales promotional methods, addition of new lines and dropping of unprofitable ones, and increasing use of multiple-type operations.
3. Manifestation of operational flexibility in terms of geographical adaptability, sales-size and multiunit characteristics, and kind of business. The regular wholesaler is found in more kinds of business than any other type of wholesale middlemen; there are no important kinds of business classifications in which there are no regular wholesalers.
4. Beneficial effects of protective legislation for independent middlemen, such as the Robinson-Patman Act.[17]

The second reason why the wholesaler continues to be important is that he has evaluated and strengthened the essential services he offers to the retailer on the one hand and to the manufacturer on the other. A more detailed discussion of the functions he performs will aid in understanding the wholesaler's continued health. It is useful to remember that most retail establishments are small and not part of large chain organizations. Furthermore, as more of the population has become urban, the area of sparse consumer markets has actually enlarged.

Buying activities

A rather apt description of the service wholesaler is contained in the phrase "the retailers' buying agent." The magnitude of this task is evident in the experience of a midwestern dry goods wholesaler some years ago. Analysis of his records revealed that on a certain day he received, either by direct mail from retailers or through his salesmen, a total of 88 orders which called for 1,849 items produced by 1,121

[16] J. R. Sprague, The Middleman (New York: William Morrow & Co., 1929), p. 2.

[17] Revzan, op. cit., pp. 596–98. For another close observer's list of nine "specific wholesaler values" that have contributed to the resurgence of this middleman, see R. T. Davis, A Marketing Professor Looks at Wholesaling: Challenge and Opportunity (Washington, D.C.: National Association of Wholesalers, 1966), pp. 5–6.

Marketing: Principles and methods

manufacturers. His average order was for 21 items from 13 manufacturers. To serve as the retailers' buying agent meant that he had to have contact with all these sources of supply in order to have the products on hand when they were demanded.

Of all the services the wholesaler performs for retailers, the "buying agent" function is the most important. It begins with some attempt on his part to anticipate retailers' demands; and, since these are dependent on consumer needs, study of probable trends in consumer demand is also required. Some wholesalers attempt to forecast retailer demands by sending buyers into the main market centers to see what is forthcoming. Others keep in close touch with leading manufacturers to get information on new merchandise.

Once the wholesaler has anticipated the demands of his retailer customers, he contacts qualified suppliers. Selecting the best suppliers is not an easy task, in part because of the large number of producers. For the average retailer merely to approach one tenth of the manufacturers who make the products he sells would keep him so busy that he would have no time to run his store. The wholesaler makes these contacts for him. The average grocery wholesaler stocks from 10,000 to 20,000 items; the drug wholesaler, from 20,000 to 60,000; the electrical goods wholesaler, from 4,500 to 30,000; the hardware wholesaler, from 20,000 to 60,000; and the dry goods wholesaler, up to 250,000.[18] For the average small retailer the wholesaler is indispensable; and for the large retailer, he is a valuable resource for maintaining proper assortments of merchandise and as a supplier of "fill-ins," i.e., goods bought in small quantities to last until the retailer's shipment arrives from the manufacturer.

Many wholesalers are not satisfied with waiting for manufacturers' salesmen or sending their buyers on occasional trips to the central markets. They also rely on resident buyers or establish their own central market buying offices.

Selling assistance

Whereas the term "buying agent" describes the wholesaler from the retailer's point of view, the term "selling agent" best describes him from the manufacturer's point of view—since the wholesaler acts as a medium through which the merchandise produced by the manufacturer is put into the hands of the retailer. Many manufacturers operate on a small scale and produce only a few products or a number of items of relatively low unit value, so that in most cases he relies on the wholesaler to perform a large part of the job of selling to retailers.

The selling function includes: (1) finding a buyer, (2) promoting the product to him, (3) negotiating the terms of sale, and (4) transferring title. It is in the performance of the second of these functions that the independent wholesaler is most likely to prove unsatisfactory to the manufacturer. The importance of the selling service performed by the wholesaler for the manufacturer is clearer in light of the number of retailers each manufacturer would otherwise have to contact, many of whom are located in small towns or are scattered through sparsely populated areas. Then too, the majority of retailers, including many of those located in the larger cities, are so small that for a large number of manufacturers to send salesmen to call on them would be prohibitive. The wholesaler, by consolidating a number of small orders into one

---

[18] These statistics are from T. N. Beckman, N. H. Engle, and R. Q. Buzzell *Wholesaling: Principles and Practice* (3rd ed, New York: Ronald Press Co., 1959), p. 132. Other related information may also be found in this book.

bill of goods, may find this business profitable, whereas it would not be so if each item or small group of items had to be sent direct from the manufacturer.

Even though the wholesaler acts as the manufacturer's selling agent, the manufacturer continues to have selling responsibilities. While agent middlemen usually are more successful in promotion than merchant wholesalers, few wholesalers give a manufacturer's product the promotional "push" he feels it deserves. Consumer products manufacturers who spend millions of dollars to promote their products cannot afford to let selling and distribution break down in the middle of the channel. As a consequence, many manufacturers end up selling to wholesalers, selling to retailers, and selling to ultimate consumers, too.

Transportation assistance

The wholesaler offers at least two important services in connection with transportation. First, he decreases the cost of this function by purchasing in larger lots than the average retailer; consequently, merchandise is brought to the wholesaler's warehouse at a lower unit transportation cost. This lower cost plus the cost of delivery from the warehouse to the retailer may be less than the cost on small shipments direct from the manufacturer to the retailer. If quantities purchased are sufficient to obtain carload rates, an even greater saving in transportation cost is realized.

Second, because the wholesaler assembles merchandise from a large number of scattered manufacturers and makes it accessible to the retailer, quicker delivery results. Thus, the retailer is able to carry less stock and still be reasonably sure of getting any item he needs on short notice. The net result is that less money is tied up in stock, less storage space is necessary, and fresher merchandise is made available. The wholesaler's service thus makes possible the present-day practice of many retailers—"hand-to-mouth" buying.

Storage facilities

Closely related to delivery is the storage function performed by the wholesaler. Next to buying, this is probably the wholesaler's most important function. Storage facilities for many items must be specially built and require a considerable investment, as when cold storage is necessary. For many goods the storage facilities are not expensive (most dry groceries, for example, may be stored in practically any place where they are protected from the weather), but the large investment in merchandise that storage entails prevents the retailer from assuming this function.

Many wholesalers have attempted to reduce their role in the storage function by shifting it back onto the manufacturer and, to a lesser extent, forward to the retailer. Whether they realize it or not, such action means they are relinquishing one of their most important reasons for existence.

By buying ahead for storage, wholesalers permit manufacturers to smooth out their production and thus to reduce production cost, as well as to buy raw materials in advance and in larger quantities. Although buying ahead has decreased in recent years, enough of it is still done by wholesalers in many fields to give the manufacturer some saving in production cost. Moreover, if storage were performed to a greater extent by the manufacturer, he would find it necessary to keep spot stocks scattered all over the area in which he wished to sell, to provide the quick delivery desired by retailers. Such a plan would be more expensive than having the stocks of many manufacturers concentrated among a few wholesalers.

Financial aid

The merchant wholesaler aids the retailer and the manufacturer in financing, both directly and indirectly. For the retailer, he extends credit directly on purchased goods. Indirectly, he reduces the need of financing by offering prompt delivery service, thus permitting the retailer to maintain smaller stocks. For the manufacturer, the merchant wholesaler finances inventories when he buys merchandise ahead, receives a shipment, and pays for it. Not only would the manufacturer have more inventory to carry without him, but the *total inventory in the system* would be greater.

Without the wholesaler, also, the manufacturer would have to extend credit to the retailer, thus increasing and complicating his credit problems. Moreover, since the credit standing of the wholesaler is often better than that of the retailer, credit risk is reduced for the manufacturer. Wholesalers also tend to pay their bills more promptly than retailers. Retailers usually buy from wholesalers or manufacturers on "open account," with discounts given for payment within a few days. Except for the loss of this cash discount, however, it is exceptional for any penalty to be attached to delayed payments, and many retailers obtain open account terms for the length of a selling season. Over the years, retailers have been able to place an increasing share of the financing function on wholesalers and manufacturers; manufacturers are often happy to have a merchant wholesaler with whom to share this burden.

Assuming risk

The wholesaler reduces the risks of the manufacturer in several ways by purchasing ahead before buyers are known; by storing merchandise, thus lessening losses from price changes, fashion shifts, and physical deterioration; and by extending credit to retailers. The merchant wholesaler also assumes risk for the retailer by guaranteeing the merchandise he sells and making adjustments quickly. Since the manufacturer stands back of his merchandise, no additional protection from the wholesaler may seem needed. Sales to a particular retailer, however, might be so small that, rather than make an adjustment, the manufacturer would risk incurring the retailer's ill will. But when the retailer buys from a wholesaler, regardless of who made the particular product under question, the *total* business of the retailer may be important enough to the wholesaler that a prompt adjustment will be made.

Providing information

Because he is closer to the ultimate consumer than is the manufacturer, the wholesaler is often in a position to evaluate and provide the producer with information on consumer buying trends. Some manufacturers believe such data to be so valuable that they conduct periodic surveys among wholesalers. However, many manufacturers prefer to go directly to the consumer for this information.

Most wholesalers offer a greater information service to their retailers by providing them with market information and general advice. Yet some wholesalers are very backward in offering this service, probably because they fail to recognize the close connection between their own success and that of their customers. If ever the small retailer should disappear, the need for the wholesaler as he now exists would greatly diminish, if not vanish. Progressive wholesalers recognize this and have gone to considerable expense to assist the retailer to meet competitive inroads upon his business. Wholesalers are particularly helpful in furnishing independent retailers with information concerning general market conditions, shifts in consumer demand, new products, price trends, and fashion developments, and in assisting him to adjust to these changes.

Providing managerial assistance to the small retailer

Some wholesalers have reduced their cost of doing business by limiting the inventory they stock, asking retailers to pick up merchandise, requiring payment in cash, and selling by mail or telephone rather than through a salesman. The number of these limited-function wholesalers has not grown in recent years, in contrast with full-function wholesalers. The wholesaler has found that the way to succeed is not to reduce the marketing functions performed but to expand the services offered to retailers.

The service wholesaler, in particular, is closely concerned with the survival of small independent retailers, which is dependent on their ability to be aggressive merchants. Many wholesalers have offered them managerial aid. As early as 1925, the Southern Wholesale Dry Goods Association undertook a cooperative educational program to aid the small retailer and to check the inroads of the chain store. A few years later, Butler Brothers set up a chain of stores in the hope that its customers (retailer merchants) "will visit the Scott Store nearest him as a medical student visits a clinic."[19] It was expected that the independent retailer would learn principles of display and stock control from these model stores and would get general advice from the store manager. The company believed that the operation of its stores would also enable it to sense what the public wanted and thus put it in a position to be of greater service to the retailer.

In more recent years, other wholesalers have undertaken to train their salesmen so that they can give advice to retailers. They have developed forms of dealer assistance which may include some or all of the following activities:

1. Counsel with dealers regarding the acceptability of products.
2. Provide the dealer with merchandise specials for promotional use.
3. Distribute information bulletins with merchandising ideas and trade news.
4. Encourage and help dealers to organize sales-building programs.
5. Give the retailer advice and help in promotions, including (a) selling and promotional ideas, (b) setting up promotions and adapting them to the store, and (c) supplying promotional materials such as circulars, newspaper advertisements, catalogs, posters, banners, and pennants, and showing him how to use them.
6. Help retailers modernize stores.
7. Provide training for store owners and sales personnel.
8. Establish model stock programs.
9. Establish accounting systems.
10. Provide modern data processing services for accounts receivable, cost accounting, and inventory control.

Although many retailers do not require such assistance, some of them, particularly the smaller ones, do. In fact, they often expect and depend upon it.[20]

---

[19] *Chain Store Age* (General Merchandising Edition), January 1929, p. 28.

[20] The extent to which a wholesaler may go in providing assistance to his retailer customers is illustrated by the case of the drug wholesaler who performed the following services for his account *while the retailer was in Europe:* (a) evaluated the location for the new store; (b) compiled a forecast of its probable sales; (c)

Formation of voluntary chains

From the retailer's point of view, a voluntary chain is an agency through which the wholesaler may offer (1) a location service, by means of which the retailer is given expert advice on the selection of a better location; (2) a stock control service, by which his stock may be kept more up to date and yet be reduced in dollar value; (3) a window-trimming and display service, through which suggestions for well-trimmed windows and easily constructed but effective displays are furnished; and (4) the service of a number of retail-trained supervisors who visit the retailer to aid him in solving his current problems. Insofar as these services strengthen the wholesaler's customers, they make the wholesaler's position more secure. In addition, the voluntary chain offers certain direct advantages to the service wholesaler.

Improving sales and profits. The voluntary chain contract between wholesaler and retailer provides a bond which encourages (or requires) the retailer to concentrate his buying with the chain wholesaler. To the extent that this concentration takes place, it may increase the total business and profit of the wholesaler. In fact, unless increased business does result from his voluntary chain operation, the service wholesaler cannot perform the added services called for without a substantial increase in his operating expenses. It is this concentration of business which tends to cut down on his selling cost, since the salesman may sell a larger order on a single call.

Promoting private brands. Through the formation of a voluntary chain the wholesaler is able to get retailers to "push" his private brands.

Reducing merchandise cost. Lower cost of merchandise for the wholesaler may come about in two ways: large-volume buying that results in quantity discounts and is made possible through increased sales, and advertising and merchandising discounts. By gathering a number of independent retailers together in a voluntary chain, a wholesaler improves his chances to sell an advertising and special promotion service to the manufacturer. In return for an advertising allowance, the wholesaler may agree to feature the manufacturer's product in his promotional efforts and have members of his group call the item to the attention of their customers.

INTEGRATION WITHIN WHOLESALING

Vertical integration

Years ago a few wholesalers believed that the best way to meet the competition of chain store organizations was to join them, and they attempted to form chains of their own. Generally speaking, however, these attempts were not successful. The wholesaler's expertise is in the area of dealing with the independent retailer, not buying him out.

Horizontal integration

While some local wholesalers have purchased other local wholesalers to form stronger regional organizations, there appear to be few economies from operation of

---

drew up a rough budget for the store; (d) estimated its personnel needs; (e) prepared the opening order; (f) marked each case at the warehouse for location in the store according to the layout based on traffic flow analysis; (g) hired and trained clerks for the store; (h) handled advertisng, public relations, and merchandising; and (i) furnished a work force to help with the opening sale. See "A Marketing Concept for Hardware Wholesalers," *Hardware Retailer,* May 1959, p. 69.

national wholesale organizations. More common is group buying by noncompeting wholesalers. Sometimes the members of the group are bound together in a common voluntary chain organization or by joint ownership of a private brand name. In a few instances, service wholesalers have joined together to form a wholesale chain. Whatever the form of organization, large-scale buying by wholesalers is a step toward the improvement of their power in the channel of distribution.

Perhaps the most important move on the part of the wholesaler in his attempt to meet changing conditions has been to improve his own efficiency. Warehouses have been modernized and mechanized to reduce handling cost, better accounting and inventory control systems have been installed, data processing systems have been automated, selective selling has been used to a greater degree, time and cost studies have been inaugurated to improve sales control and reduce operating costs, efforts have been concentrated on fewer lines and grades of merchandise, faster delivery has been offered, the indiscriminate granting of credit has been reduced, and wholesalers' salesmen have been more carefully selected and trained to increase their selling efficiency. All these activities are part of the attempt to cut the cost of wholesaling and thus reduce the price of goods going through the channel of distribution between independent wholesaler and independent retailer.

SUMMARY: PRESENT OUTLOOK FOR THE SERVICE WHOLESALER

The field of wholesaling is in a period of rapid change as manufacturers, retailers, and other wholesalers engage in a continuing battle to find ways to perform marketing functions more efficiently than can the full-service merchant wholesaler. Some manufacturers eliminate him from their channels of distribution through direct sale to the ultimate consumer by such methods as house-to-house selling and the establishment of their own retail stores. Other manufacturers who become dissatisfied with the service wholesaler assume his functions and distribute direct to the retailer—a practice which is encouraged by many retailers who prefer to buy directly from the manufacturer. Some independent retailers compete with the wholesaler through group activities—buying clubs, cooperative chains, and voluntary chains; other retailers, such as the chain store, the mail-order house, the department store, and the discount house, are so large that they purchase the bulk of their merchandise directly from the manufacturer. Wholesalers themselves try to increase their profit by limiting their product lines or the marketing functions they perform.

Table 11–4 provides a summary of the type of functions that wholesale middlemen perform. The number of limited-function combinations is so great that the service wholesaler must be aware of the necessity of adopting progressive methods of conducting his business and strengthening the essential services he performs in the scheme of distribution. It seems to be true that

as long as great distances separate manufacturers and retailers, as long as many manufacturers are relatively small-scale operators and produce a limited line of merchandise, as long as many retailers are located in small communities and in otherwise inaccessible places, and as long as large numbers of retailers operate on a small scale and buy in small quantities, so long will wholesalers be an indispensable medium for translating concentrated production into widely diffused retail distribution.[21]

---

[21] Beckman, Engle, and Buzzell, op. cit., p. 145.

Marketing: Principles and methods

TABLE 11–4
Functions performed by wholesalers

	Buy for customers	Sell	Ship	Stock	Take title	Grade	Finance customers	Provide information to buyers and sellers
Full-service merchant wholesalers	Yes	Yes	Yes	Yes	Yes	Sometimes	Yes	Yes
Limited-function merchant wholesalers	Yes	Yes	Sometimes	Yes	Yes	Sometimes	Sometimes	Yes
Manufacturers' sales branches	No	Yes	Yes	Yes	Yes	No	Yes	Yes
Manufacturers' sales offices	No	Yes	No	No	Yes	No	Yes	Yes
Petroleum bulk stations	Sometimes	Yes	Sometimes	Yes	No	Sometimes	Sometimes	Sometimes
Auction companies	No	Yes	No	No	No	Sometimes	Sometimes	Sometimes
Merchandise brokers	Sometimes	Yes	No	No	No	Sometimes	No	Yes
Commission merchants	No	Yes	Yes	Sometimes	Sometimes	Sometimes	Sometimes	Yes
Import agents	Sometimes	Yes	Yes	Sometimes	Sometimes	Sometimes	Sometimes	Yes
Export agents	Sometimes	Yes	Yes	No	Sometimes	No	No	Yes
Manufacturers' agents	No	Yes	Sometimes	Sometimes	No	No	No	Yes
Selling agents	No	Yes	No	No	No	Sometimes	Sometimes	Yes
Resident buyers	Yes	No	Yes	No	Yes	Yes	Sometimes	Yes
Assemblers of farm products	Yes	Yes	Yes	Yes	Sometimes	Yes	No	Yes

Given these conditions, the elimination of the service wholesaler will not remove the need for his services but will simply transfer their performance to someone else. To a considerable degree, the future of the wholesaler comes down to the question of whether or not there is anyone else who can perform his functions more economically and as well.

Although the service wholesaler may continue to lose some relative ground as manufacturers and retailers take over more of the wholesale functions, the future of the progressive wholesaler is brighter today than it has been for some time, perhaps since the days prior to the rapid growth of chain stores. The fact that the number of regular wholesalers actually has increased in each census year since 1929, reaching an all-time high of 213,000 in 1967, is significant. There can be little doubt that since 1945, the service wholesaler has demonstrated remarkable ability to make the adjustments and innovations necessary to function effectively in our economy; present indications are that he will continue to do so.

REVIEW AND DISCUSSION QUESTIONS

1. "To analyze the basic causes of the conflict of interest between manufacturers and service wholesalers, you have to trace a bit of economic history starting in the 1800s and coming up to now. You must understand (a) why the wholesaler before 1900 was traditionally in a position of importance, (b) how he operated during those times, and (c) what attitudes he developed toward changing conditions. Part of the conflict stemmed from basic changes in the manufacturing side of the economy. Finally, the emergence of large-scale activity in retailing completed the 'squeeze' on the wholesaler." Analyze and explain these evolutionary patterns.

2. One of the important factors contributing to the growth of local wholesalers is the cost advantage they enjoy. How may this cost advantage be explained?

3. What, in your opinion, are the chief reasons for the resurgence of the service wholesaler in recent years? Explain.

4. Visit a service wholesaler in your city, or in a nearby one, and obtain the manager's reasons for the recent growth in the importance of wholesaling. Check his ideas against your own and those given in the textbook. Ask him to comment on the charges that wholesalers often (a) do not sell aggressively or cultivate the market intensively, (b) neglect the storage function, and (c) are indifferent to the promotional helps furnished by the manufacturer.

5. Summarize the major causes of dissatisfaction on the part of the manufacturer with the services of the wholesaler. Suggest concrete ways by which these may be overcome.

6. "The future of the service wholesaler depends upon the future of the small-scale retailer. By the same token, the future of the small-scale retailer depends on the increased efficiency of the wholesaler and the aids he can furnish to the small retailer." Do these two statements merely take the reader around a circle? Explain.

7. Some retailers have considered eliminating the wholesaler in favor of buying direct from the manufacturer. If the wholesaler were eliminated, what would happen to the total cost of distribution? Discuss. In bypassing the wholesaler, which of his functions and services could the retailer take over most easily, and which would be most difficult for the retailer to perform? Discuss.

8. Explain the meaning and significance of the following statement: "The wholesaler may be eliminated from the marketing channel but the functions he performs cannot."

9. Among the services performed by the wholesaler for the retailer, which, in your judgment, have become increasingly important in recent years? Why?

10. "Because his role is frequently misunderstood, the wholesaler is the target of much manu-

facturer criticism." What is the nature of this criticism? Suggest methods by which it may be overcome.

11. Define "rack jobber" in your own words. What are the major characteristics of products best suited to distribution through this middleman?

12. Discuss the statement: "The rack jobber's future is tied closely with the growth of nonfood items in supermarkets; his opportunities for service in other retail stores are severely limited."

13. How do you explain the fact that "more manufacturers are now using food brokers than ever before in our history"? Do you expect this growth to continue? Why?

14. Differentiate between the "selling agent" and the "manufacturers' agent." How may the existence of each be economically justified?

15. Which type of agent middlemen, if any, is most apt to be used in each of the following cases? Defend your choice in each instance.
    a) A salmon canner on the Pacific Coast who packs an unlabeled product available for private branding.
    b) A cereal manufacturer with his own sales force and national distribution decides to market a new unrelated product, namely, a line of small appliances.
    c) A small manufacturer of fishing tackle.
    d) A canner of corn who packs under his own national brand. He has no other product in his line.
    e) An Alabama cotton textile mill manufacturing gray goods.
    f) A manufacturer of luggage and some other leather goods who has his own sales force to cover his presently developed market east of the Mississippi River. He wants to expand his market to include the Rocky Mountain and Southwest regions, plus the metropolitan areas of the Pacific Coast.

SUPPLEMENTARY READINGS

All of the readings listed at the end of Chapter 10 also are applicable here.

Boyd, H. W., Jr. and Clewett, R. M. (eds.) *Contemporary American Marketing: Readings on the Changing Market Structure.* Homewood, Ill.: Richard D. Irwin, Inc., 1962. An older collection that is still of value today.

Bucklin, L. P. (ed.) *Vertical Marketing Systems.* Glenview, Ill.: Scott, Foresman & Co., 1970. A collection of the latest thinking of the experts in the field.

Cox, R. (in association with **Goodman, C. S. and Fichandler, T. C.**) *Distribution in a High-Level Economy.* Englewood Cliffs, N.J.: Prentice-Hall, Inc., 1965. "Wholesale Agencies of Distribution" and "Recent Developments in Wholesaling" are covered on pp. 50–58.

McNair, M. P. and Berman, Mira (eds.) *Marketing through Retailers.* New York: American Management Association, 1967. In this compilation of 26 articles presented at an association forum, the critical importance of manufacturer-retailer cooperation in maximizing results is emphasized. All main aspects of the problem are reviewed.

National Association of Wholesalers Washington, D.C. This federation of 39 national commodity line associations is a fertile source of information on all aspects of wholesaling. Operating and merchandising results of affiliated associations are available only from each commodity line association. For example, **National Wholesale Druggists Association,** *NWDA 1966 Operating Survey.* New York, 1967.

U.S. Small Business Administration *Management Research Summaries.* Washington, D.C.: Government Printing Office, 1952. No. 100, *Inventory Control for Small Wholesalers;* No. 104, *Wholesalers' Services to Food Retailers;* and No. 133, *Analyzing Food Brokers' Costs and Margins* are of special interest in connection with this chapter.

U.S. Small Business Administration *Wholesaling.* Small Business Bibliography No. 55. Washington, D.C.: Government Printing Office, 1965.

Part V The marketing system for industrial products and services

The focus in Part V is on the marketing systems for industrial products and services, in comparison with the emphasis in Parts II through IV on consumer products and services. While industrial products are usually classified into six groups, in this book they are discussed in four chapters—three in this part of the book and one in the next. Business services are discussed in Chapter 15 as part of the topic of Part VI, marketing in special fields.

Chapter 12 is concerned with providing an overview of the system for marketing industrial products and services, with special emphasis on buyer behavior of industrial purchasers and on other environmental influences on this marketing system. As you study the chapter, try to list the major differences and similarities between the environment for the consumer and industrial products marketing systems.

The marketing systems for manufactured products provides the central focus in Chapter 13. We suggest again, as a learning device, that you compare and contrast these systems with marketing systems for consumer products and try to determine why things are as they are.

Chapter 14, the last chapter in Part V, should not mislead you by its title, "Marketing Agricultural Products." Agriculture is merely the topic chosen to illustrate how a total marketing system operates. It is designed to help you see how a system is integrated in all its aspects. Agricultural products provide a useful illustration of a marketing system for both industrial and consumer products.

12 Marketing industrial products and services: The environment

Two major types of products and services have been distinguished: consumer and industrial. For the past several chapters, attention has been centered on consumer products and services—the market for them and the retailing and wholesaling structure involved in their distribution. Industrial products and services are submitted to a similar analysis in this chapter and the two that follow.

In studying the way the marketing system performs the equalization process between producers and industrial users it is important to keep in mind two important characteristics of the industrial market which make it different from the consumer market: the number of customers is much fewer, and users are commercial institutions, not households.

INDUSTRIAL PRODUCTS AND SERVICES DEFINED AND CLASSIFIED

Industrial products and services are those consumed by: (1) organizations in producing and distributing consumer or other industrial products and services, (2) other business firms, and (3) government. Using the words of the Definitions Committee of the American Marketing Association: "The distinguishing characteristic of these goods is the purpose for which they are primarily destined to be used, in carrying on business or industrial activities rather than for consumption by individual ultimate consumers or resale to them."[1]

---

[1] R. S. Alexander et al., *Marketing Definitions* (Chicago: American Marketing Association, 1960), p. 14.

One authority notes the relative neglect of attention to industrial marketing and the reasons for it as follows:

Any careful survey of marketing literature will disclose that a relatively small amount of it is devoted to the problems and techniques of marketing industrial goods. . . . [In part, this lack of emphasis] may be . . . that, particularly before the Second World War, marketing as a management function was not so highly developed in companies making and selling industrial goods as it had been in the consumer goods field. . . . [In addition,] the marketing function tended in many cases to be shared by, and possibly overshadowed by, managers of other functions [the engineers in the organization, for example]. . . . Finally, industrial products are very often highly technical products, and perhaps those who would study and write about the problems involved in marketing industrial products have been deterred to some extent because of their technical character.[2]

Whatever the reasons for this neglect, it is not because industrial products are unimportant. From the input-output tables for the United States in 1963, it can be estimated that almost 35 percent of the value of all business transactions was attributed to sales of inputs to industrial users.

Classification of industrial products and services

Industrial products and services may be classified into six distinctive groups: (1) raw materials, (2) component parts and materials, (3) major capital equipment, (4) operating supplies, (5) accessory equipment, and (6) business services. Consumer products and services are classified as convenience, shopping, or specialty on the basis of the buying habits of purchasers, partially determined by purchase frequency and usage rate. In contrast, industrial products are classified according to the uses to which they are put, also partially determined by purchase frequency and usage rate.

The marketing of business services, discussed in Chapter 15, includes engineering, accounting, legal, and banking services; purchased maintenance such as gardening, painting, equipment repair and window washing; and purchased employee services such as food and medical services. The other classes of industrial products are discussed below.

Raw materials.   Raw materials are defined by the Definitions Committee of the American Marketing Association as "those industrial goods which in part or in whole become a portion of the physical product but which have undergone no more processing than is required for convenience, protection, or economy in storage, transportation, or handling." They may be classed conveniently into two groups with different marketing methods and problems. First, many farm products are used as raw materials—for example, wheat, tobacco, and cotton (see Chapter 14). Second, natural products such as petroleum, iron ore, and lumber also serve as raw materials. Natural raw materials may be classified into six divisions:[3]

1.   Animals—wild animals, fish.
2.   Land—space, agricultural soil, grasslands.
3.   Forests—for lumber, paper, watershed, wildlife.

---

[2] E. R. Corey, *Industrial Marketing: Cases and Concepts* (Englewood Cliffs, N.J.: Prentice-Hall, Inc., 1962), p. v.

[3] Some products classified as natural products are really borderline cases between this class and farm products. Lumber and fish are examples. Although they are referred to as "natural products," they can be regenerated or even raised on farms and harvested. Some raw materials, such as metals, can also be recycled and reprocessed from scrap.

4. Minerals—iron, nonferrous metals, petroleum, coal, fertilizers, building materials, other nonmetals.
5. Water—for consumption, production, power, heat exchange, navigation.
6. Atmosphere—to live, to produce gasses.

Three environmental characteristics have significant influence on the marketing systems for raw materials: the limited supply, the small number of producers, and the importance of transportation.

Limited nonreproducible supply. Whereas the supply of farm products is to a large degree controllable by man, the supplies of extracted raw materials are produced by nature at a very slow rate, as in the case of crude oil, or not produced at all, as in the case of elements. Because the supplies of most natural products are scarce in relation to the demand for them, there is a continual search for undiscovered sources and for synthetic products to serve as substitutes.[4] From the point of view of marketing, the limited supply of natural raw materials has been a factor encouraging users to integrate their manufacturing with the limited sources of supply. Thus we find that large companies engaged in the refining of oil also engage in exploration and drilling for a part of their crude oil. Many refiners also own their own pipelines, tank cars, and tankers. The large steel companies have integrated as far back as the ore mines and coal mines, besides controlling some of the agencies engaged in transporting these natural products. Large copper-smelting companies own copper mines, and large paper manufacturers own enormous tracts of forests.

This integration between the supplies of the natural products and the companies engaged in using them as raw materials considerably simplifies the marketing of the products of this class. To a large degree, it reduces the need for independent middlemen. Yet middlemen are still important in this field, especially as a source of supply for nonintegrated manufacturers.

Relatively few producers. Although not true for all natural products (such as bituminous coal), a further factor in reducing the need for independent middlemen in this field is the limited number of companies engaged in obtaining natural products. For example, in 1969, 23 copper mines owned by 10 firms produced over 90 percent of the copper in the United States; and a similar, but less concentrated, situation prevailed among iron ore mines.[5]

Transportation of particular importance. Transportation's vital role in the marketing of natural products is a result of two factors: these products are bulky in relation to their value, and they are often found at considerable distances from markets. The first factor is illustrated by such products as iron ore, petroleum, sand and gravel, and building stone. Examples of the second factor are aluminum mines in Canada; crude oil wells in northern Alaska, the Near East, and Indonesia; and copper mines in the western states. Processing and even some refining for these products takes place close to markets on our east and west coasts. Under such conditions the cost of transportation constitutes a significant part of the total marketing cost.

It should be emphasized that not all natural products serve solely as raw materials

---

[4] For the long-run statistics on prices, output, and consumption of raw materials, see Neal Potter and F. T. Christy, Jr., *Resources for the Future, Inc.* (Baltimore, Md.: Johns Hopkins Press, 1962); H. H. Landsberg, L. L. Fischman, and J. L. Fisher, *Resources of America's Future: Patterns of Requirements and Availabilities, 1960–2000* (Baltimore, Md.: Johns Hopkins Press, 1963); and *U.S. Energy Policies: An Agenda for Research* (Baltimore, Md.: Resources for the Future, Inc., 1968).

[5] U.S. Department of the Interior, *Minerals Yearbook, 1969,* Vol. I (Washington, D.C.: Government Printing Office, 1970), pp. 464 and 572–76.

for the industrial market. Coal, for instance, is used both as an industrial and a consumer good; and even when consumed in the industrial market, it falls into the category of "operating supplies" rather than that of "raw material." A further example is afforded by fish. Although large quantities of these are industrial goods in that they serve as the main raw material for certain manufacturers engaged in processing them for future use (drying, fish meal, canning), large quantities are sold in the natural state to ultimate consumers and must be considered consumer goods.

Component parts and materials. Component parts and fabricating materials also enter into the physical product being produced. Unlike raw materials, however, they have already undergone some processing in addition to that necessary for convenience in marketing. Natural and synthetic fabrics, electric or gasoline motors (such as those on power lawn mowers), and automobile steering wheels are examples.

In purchasing, most companies draw a distinction between standardized components which can be ordered from a variety of suppliers and specialized components produced to the buyer's specifications. Because components become a part of the product, very large volumes of business may be involved. In such situations, general management and engineering will work closely with the purchasing department in the selection of suppliers. If the component is a branded unit which will be recognized by the user of the product, the marketing manager may also participate in choosing a source of supply that he feels will help in selling the product.

An assured source of supply is an important consideration in vendor selection. The importance of lasting vendor relationships results from the need for uniform production and uniform quality. A constant level of quality is helpful in maintaining smooth production. Thus, purchases are often made on contracts which usually call for delivery at stated intervals during the contract period. A price protection clause, through which the seller agrees to credit the buyer for any price reductions made to others during the contract's life, is common. Contracts involving large sums of money usually need the approval of the buying company's chief executives and are typically negotiated between the executives of the buying and the selling companies.

Even when contracts are used, the buyer often has a second or even third source of supply that may be given as much as a third of the business. If the main supplier fails to perform, the other sources are prepared to take over a major share of the business.

When volumes are large, long-term contracts common, and direct negotiation important, there is a strong tendency for the user and the supplier to deal directly in the marketing of components. However, agents may be found in situations where materials are standardized or where users are in isolated locations. In such situations, the seller is glad to be relieved of the problem of building a selling organization. Selling agents, for instance, are used by a number of the smaller manufacturers who wish to minimize their own selling activities—the agent taking over the whole selling problem. Other small companies, and even large companies in those areas where sales are small, make use of the manufacturers' agent. The general trend, however, is to use direct sale where it is economically practical.

Some manufacturers of fabricating materials and parts have tried to increase their sales by branding their products and advertising them on a wide scale to the ultimate consumer. Rubber-heel manufacturers urge the ultimate consumer to purchase shoes made by manufacturers using their heels, and makers of automobile batteries attempt to build consumer preference for cars that install their products.

The motivation for these activities is twofold. First, sellers of component parts and materials will have a selling advantage if they can tell potential customers that consumers recognize and prefer their heels, motors, or batteries on the products they buy; a power lawn mower manufacturer may recognize that it will be easier to sell machines powered by Briggs and Straton engines, for example. Second, a large and profitable replacement market may develop with the customer or the customer's customers. This is particularly true if the component has a life which is less than that of the entire assembly. In some of these situations (e.g., automobile tires) it is common for suppliers to sell in the original-equipment market at little or no profit in order to sell replacements to consumers at high profit margins.

Major capital equipment. Major capital equipment includes installations of plant, machinery, and equipment used to produce the product or service. They do not become a part of the physical product and are used up slowly by wear or obsolescence. Examples include chemical process equipment, steel-making furnaces, computer systems, and metalworking machinery.

The purchase of capital installations or equipment is influenced by executives in several business functions. Marketing management may be involved, since the equipment may determine the quality and quantity of product they have to sell. Production management is consulted, since their unit costs will be affected. Engineering is involved because it is responsible for the design and specification of the equipment. Finally, the treasurer will be involved because he must find the funds to pay for it. For this reason most firms have appropriations committees or "capital budgeting" committees which make decisions on capital expenditures only after careful calculation of the expected value of the future stream of profits the equipment is expected to produce. If the equipment is to replace existing equipment that is not worn out, the calculation will be of future "savings in use" of the new equipment over the old.

The flow of funds into the firm for large capital purchases is not great enough for even the largest firms to make decisions without careful planning, rationing, and fund allocation. Companies that have sufficiently long records of profitable operation can usually secure needed funds by borrowing from financial institutions or by public offerings of securities. With continued high corporate tax rates and increasing interest rates, many firms prefer to lease equipment or buy it on an installment plan.

Spending for capital equipment is also subject to wide swings over the business cycle. Production capacity must be expanded when demand for products is greatest, and this is also likely to be the time when money is in shortest supply and interest rates are highest. Figure 12–1 shows the relation of new plant and equipment expenditures to gross national product. Capital equipment represents one of the most volatile elements in national expenditures; the figure shows wide fluctuations since 1949.

Purchasers of equipment installations typically prefer to buy directly from manufacturers. Direct sale is common because of the relatively small number of potential users, the concentration of the market, the large unit of sale, and the need of technical sales service. Since this equipment requires installation by on-site engineers of the manufacturer even if sales are consummated through middlemen, the manufacturer may consider it advisable to do the whole job. Manufacturers who sell basic equipment over a wide territory often find it advantageous to establish sales offices or branches in the leading industrial centers. These serve as storage points for the company's products, although they are more often used to store repair parts.

Though the bulk of installations is sold direct, such middlemen as manufacturers' agents, industrial machinery and equipment distributors, mill supply houses, and, to a lesser degree, selling agents and brokers, are important in the marketing of these

FIGURE 12-1
Business expenditures for new plant and equipment as a percentage of gross national product

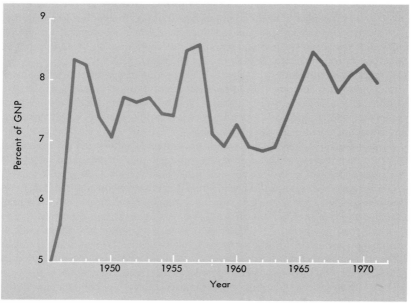

Sources: U.S. Office of Business Economics and Securities Exchange Commission.

products. Indirect sale may be used in one or both of two situations: the equipment is relatively low in price and fairly well standardized, or the potential buyers are relatively small and widely scattered.

Accessory equipment. The accessory equipment group resembles the capital equipment group in that such goods do not enter the final product and are exhausted only after repeated usage. However, their life is shorter than that of installations; and, whereas installations determine the product to be produced and set the scale of operations, accessory equipment merely facilitates the operation of the plant. Examples are trucks, conveyors, typewriters, and time clocks.

The buying of accessory or facilitating equipment usually rests with junior executives of a company rather than senior executives, as is the case in the purchase of installations. Purchases of accessory equipment are more frequent than those of installations, the products are more standardized, and the sums involved are smaller. Consequently, the purchasing officer relies mainly on his experience with previous suppliers, catalogs, and the advice of foremen and department heads.

1. *Direct sale.* Selling methods used by manufacturers of accessory equipment vary widely and are both direct and indirect. Although middlemen are much more important than in the marketing of installations, many manufacturers of accessory equipment that is of rather high unit value, is of low unit value but sold in large orders, or is sold to a large number of different types of users (e.g., Xerox duplicating machines) find that direct sale is economical and preferable. This preference is explained largely by the closer contact of the manufacturer with his customers and the oppor-

tunity provided his salesmen to demonstrate the suitability of equipment to the buyer's requirements. Moreover, the cost of training salesmen for accessory equipment is considerably less than that necessary for installations because the technical features of such equipment are not so great. Sales offices and sales branches with stocks are sometimes maintained to strengthen direct-selling efforts.

2. *Indirect sale.* Other manufacturers find that their products (e.g., small power tools) are salable to industrial users in a number of fields, that their unit sales are small, and that the potential buyers are widely scattered. To have their salesmen cover such a market would be very expensive; the additional sales such contacts might produce would not compensate for the added sales expense. Hence the middleman may perform a useful function in serving a number of manufacturers whose products have similar markets, thus spreading the overhead cost.[6] In addition, the storage function is more important on standardized equipment, and a middleman may be well equipped to give this service. Finally, the credit position of the smaller buyers is often rather precarious, and the manufacturer may not want to tie up funds in such accounts. Investigation of and collection from a large number of small and widely scattered accounts is expensive. Under any or all of the above circumstances, a manufacturer of accessory equipment may well decide to sell through industrial distributors and agent middlemen, maintaining just the small sales force needed to contact these middlemen.

The use of middlemen by accessory equipment manufacturers is more satisfactory than it is for manufacturers of installations, since they can sell standardized items better than they can those that demand a considerable degree of technical knowledge and require a long period for negotiating sales. Middlemen are often used in markets where buyers are widely scattered, and the company's own salesmen are confined to areas where many buyers are concentrated.

3. *Missionary salesmen.* Missionary salesmen are employees of manufacturers who work with distributors' salesmen to help them carry out the manufacturers' marketing program. They are sometimes employed by manufacturers of accessory equipment who distribute their products through middlemen, mainly to overcome some of the difficulties encountered when middlemen are used. These salesmen may be very valuable, for example, to a manufacturer of equipment of a technical nature requiring knowledge that the middlemen's salesmen do not possess. A few missionary salesmen may travel for a short period with each distributor salesman to train him to sell the product, particularly to close sales. Since salesmen handling a large number of items are unable to "push" any particular product, a missionary salesman may also be employed by the manufacturer to travel with each salesman and introduce new products to the possible buyers. Orders obtained by this method are *turned over* to the distributor for filling, and repeat orders are placed through the distributor's regular salesmen.

The use of missionary salesmen also creates certain problems. They add to the selling cost of the manufacturer, and this cost increases the longer they are employed. Distributors' salesmen may come to depend upon them so much that when they are withdrawn, sales fall off rapidly. Or it may be that the task of educating the distributors' salesmen is an endless one because of the high rate of turnover among such salesmen. Thus what was expected to be a temporary program may become quite permanent.

---

[6] Although far larger than the average, one Chicago mill supply house is said to list 23,000 items, many of which are competitive.

Under such circumstances, the manufacturer might well wonder why he did not adopt a direct-selling plan in the first place.

Operating supplies. Supplies that do not become part of the finished product but are consumed in facilitating the operation of an enterprise are known as operating supplies. They are of short life and are often subdivided into three types: maintenance, repair, and operating (MRO) supplies. Examples are office supplies, fuels, lubricants, janitorial supplies, and power transmission belts.

While some frequently used supplies may be purchased on contract, most are purchased as needed from a variety of single sources. If the factors of standardization of product and relatively low unit value are added to the need for frequent purchasing, it can easily be understood why such buying tends to become quite routine in nature. Usually, in the first instance of buying the purchasing agent and his associates may consider the products of several companies. If the kind selected proves satisfactory, subsequent buying tends to become largely routine. Requisitions from various departments will be acted upon almost automatically by the purchasing department.

In the purchasing of such supplies as office stationery, brushes, and electric bulbs, the decision of the buyer as to the source of supply is influenced to a large degree by price, although the nearness of the supplier and his dependability are also considered. Since such items are quite standardized and various manufacturers handle similar goods, it is understandable why price differences among companies become of first-rank importance. Where quality varies, price is not such a dominant consideration.

From a marketing point of view, operating supplies have many characteristics that are similar to those of convenience products in the consumer products field. Both have broad geographic markets: As the market for coffee is nationwide, so firms in all sections of the country make use of office and janitorial supplies, lubricants, and other operating necessities. Both types of products tend to be bought in relatively small quantities. Because the unit of value is low and standardization has proceeded far enough to make satisfactory substitutes available, buyers will not go to any considerable trouble in making purchases. Manufacturers, therefore, arrange to have adequate supplies located near all possible customers. Finally, if the supplies are sold on credit, the small size of each purchase and the distance between the manufacturer and the buyer work against credit extension by the manufacturer.

These characteristics of operating supplies tend to encourage the use of indirect selling. For some supplies, however, direct selling is important. Lubricants are largely sold direct because the manufacturers sell a technical service along with the product; they offer to study each manufacturer's machinery and suggest the most efficient lubricants. Even here, however, direct sale is used in selling only to fairly large users. As a general rule, the marketing of operating supplies is carried on through industrial distributors, although some manufacturers also make use of the manufacturers' agent.

Classification of markets for industrial products and services

The market for industrial products and services comprises all the users and potential users of such regardless of their location or class purchased. While this market is a broad one compared to the consumer market, there are relatively few buyers. There are only 11 million industrial users, as compared with 62 million consumer households. In fact, there are far fewer than 11 million "live prospects," for this number includes many sole proprietorships. Only 3.5 million businesses have employees and pay employer social security taxes, and the number of corporations is only slightly over 1.5 million.[7] These are broken down by industry in Table 12–1. The 197,000 manufacturing concerns in this group operate just over 311,000 establishments.

For a particular industrial product, the number of users is far smaller. For example, General Electric motors are sold to more than 205,000 customers, but over 90 percent of the firm's business is concentrated among about 5,000 large purchasers. Even for producers of operating supplies, which are usable in practically the whole field, the number of possible customers is much less than for consumer goods. The producer of an operating-supply item used by manufacturing establishments can cover perhaps 20 percent of the market by calling on the 544 largest establishments (0.2 percent) and more than double that portion by visiting 4,861 plants (1.6 percent).[8] Makers of a product which might be used by all the manufacturing plants in the United States can probably reach 75 percent of the market by calling on 10 percent of the plants—those with 100 or more employees.

In addition to being limited in number, the industrial market is concentrated geographically. Consequently, two useful classifications are by type of user and geography.

TABLE 12–1
Number of selected active corporations by type, 1967

Type of industrial user	Number (in thousands)
All industries	1,502
Mining	14
Construction	123
Manufacturing	197
Transportation, communication, electricity, and gas	66
Wholesale trade	143
Retail trade	316
Finance, insurance, and real estate	399
Service industries	221

Source: U.S. Bureau of the Census, *Statistical Abstract of the United States, 1970* (Washington, D.C.: Government Printing Office, 1970), p. 468.

Types of industrial users. One of the most useful classifications of the industrial market is that of the Standard Industrial Classification (SIC) system, which is used by all federal agencies. Major SIC classifications are shown in Table 12–2. The structure of the classification makes it possible to classify establishments by industry on a two-, three-, or four-digit basis according to the degree of detail in information that may be needed. Most industry statistics are available in four-digit SIC classifications. The Bureau of the Census has expanded the scheme to include five-digit product classes and, in some cases, even seven-digit product codes. For example, SIC product 2844511 (suntan lotions) is a part of 28445 (other cosmetics and toilet preparations),

---

[7] U.S. Bureau of the Census, *Statistical Abstract of the United States, 1970* (Washington, D.C.: Government Printing Office, 1970), pp. 460–80.

[8] U.S. Bureau of the Census, *Census of Manufactures, 1963,* Vol. I, *Summary and Subject Statistics* (Washington, D.C.: U.S. Government Printing Office, 1966), pp. 2–8, 2–9.

TABLE 12–2
Standard Industrial Classifications of the United States

Division A.	Agriculture, forestry, and fisheries:	
	Major Group 01.	Agricultural production
	Major Group 07.	Agricultural services and hunting and trapping
	Major Group 08.	Forestry
	Major Group 09.	Fisheries
Division B.	Mining:	
	Major Group 10.	Metal mining
	Major Group 11.	Anthracite mining
	Major Group 12.	Bituminous coal and lignite mining
	Major Group 13.	Crude petroleum and natural gas
	Major Group 14.	Mining and quarrying of nonmetallic minerals, except fuels
Division C.	Contract construction:	
	Major Group 15.	Building construction—general contractors
	Major Group 16.	Construction other than building construction—general contractors
	Major Group 17.	Construction—special trade contractors
Division D.	Manufacturing:	
	Major Group 19.	Ordnance and accessories
	Major Group 20.	Food and kindred products
	Major Group 21.	Tobacco manufactures
	Major Group 22.	Textile mill products
	Major Group 23.	Apparel and other finished products made from fabrics and similar materials
	Major Group 24.	Lumber and wood products, except furniture
	Major Group 25.	Furniture and fixtures
	Major Group 26.	Paper and allied products
	Major Group 27.	Printing, publishing, and allied industries
	Major Group 28.	Chemicals and allied products
	Major Group 29.	Petroleum refining and related industries
	Major Group 30.	Rubber and miscellaneous plastics products
	Major Group 31.	Leather and leather products
	Major Group 32.	Stone, clay, glass, and concrete products
	Major Group 33.	Primary metal industries
	Major Group 34.	Fabricated metal products, except ordnance, machinery, and transportation equipment
	Major Group 35.	Machinery, except electrical
	Major Group 36.	Electrical machinery, equipment, and supplies
	Major Group 37.	Transportation equipment
	Major Group 38.	Professional, scientific, and controlling instruments; photographic and optical goods; watches and clocks
	Major Group 39.	Miscellaneous manufacturing industries
Division E.	Transportation, communication, electric, gas, and sanitary services:	
	Major Group 40.	Railroad transportation
	Major Group 41.	Local and suburban transit and interurban passenger transportation
	Major Group 42.	Motor freight transportation and warehousing
	Major Group 44.	Water transportation

which is part of industry 2844 (toilet preparations), which is part of major group 28 (chemicals and allied products), as shown in Table 12–2.

Geographic classification. The industrial goods market is characterized by geographic concentration as well as concentration in terms of number of firms. Based on the value added in manufacturing, a seller of industrial goods or services will find over 26 percent of his market in just five Standard Metropolitan Statistical Areas

TABLE 12–2 (*continued*)

Division E. (*continued*)
        Major Group 45.   Transportation by air
        Major Group 46.   Pipeline transportation
        Major Group 47.   Transportation services
        Major Group 48.   Communication
        Major Group 49.   Electric, gas, and sanitary services
Division F.   Wholesale and retail trade:
        Major Group 50.   Wholesale trade
        Major Group 52.   Building materials, hardware, and farm equipment dealers
        Major Group 53.   Retail trade—general merchandise
        Major Group 54.   Food stores
        Major Group 55.   Automotive dealers and gasoline service stations
        Major Group 56.   Apparel and accessory stores
        Major Group 57.   Furniture, home furnishings, and equipment stores
        Major Group 58.   Eating and drinking places
        Major Group 59.   Miscellaneous retail stores
Division G. Finance, insurance, and real estate:
        Major Group 60.   Banking
        Major Group 61.   Credit agencies other than banks
        Major Group 62.   Security and commodity brokers, dealers, exchanges, and services
        Major Group 63.   Insurance carriers
        Major Group 64.   Insurance agents, brokers, and services
        Major Group 65.   Real estate
        Major Group 66.   Combinations of real estate, insurance, loans, laws offices
        Major Group 67.   Holding and other investment companies
Division H. Services:
        Major Group 70.   Hotels, rooming houses, camps, and other lodging places
        Major Group 72.   Personal services
        Major Group 73.   Miscellaneous business services
        Major Group 75.   Automobile repair, automobile services, and garages
        Major Group 76.   Miscellaneous repair services
        Major Group 78.   Motion pictures
        Major Group 79.   Amusement and recreation services, except motion pictures
        Major Group 80.   Medical and other health services
        Major Group 81.   Legal services
        Major Group 82.   Educational services
        Major Group 84.   Museums, art galleries, botanical and zoological gardens
        Major Group 86.   Nonprofit membership organizations
        Major Group 88.   Private households
        Major Group 89.   Miscellaneous services
Division I.   Government:
        Major Group 91.   Federal government
        Major Group 92.   State government
        Major Group 93.   Local government
        Major Group 94.   International government
        Major Group 99.   Nonclassified establishments

(SMSA). In addition, federal government purchasing activity is centered in Washington, D.C.

Construction activity, trade, finance, and services cluster near population centers that are also the areas of high manufacturing activity. The main markets are in just six states: New York, California, Ohio, Illinois, Pennsylvania, and Michigan. These states, plus New Jersey, contribute more to the value added by manufacture than all of the other states together.[9] The extent of this concentration is shown vividly in the industrial map of the United States, Figure 12–2.

While the big industrial states have remained the same for some decades, industrial markets have moved with the people—south and west. The greatest percentage growth since 1947 has occurred in the Pacific, west south-central, and south Atlantic geographic areas.[10] By industry, the concentration is still more extreme: furniture in North Carolina, southern California, and Michigan; steel in Pittsburgh and Chicago; automobiles in Detroit; rubber in Akron; electronics in New England and California.

FIGURE 12–2
Industrial map of the United States

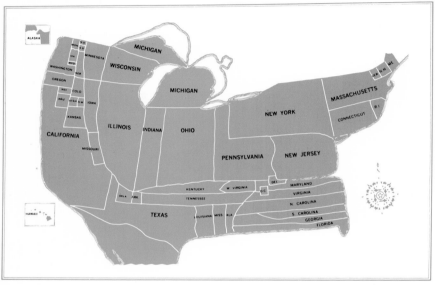

Map reproduced through the courtesy of Russell T. Gray, Inc.

The area of each state is shown in exact ratio to the other states, based on the value added to products by manufacture, according to the *Census of Manufacturers, 1967.*

BUYING BEHAVIOR OF INDUSTRIAL PURCHASERS

As ultimate consumers are motivated in their purchase behavior by a complex of considerations (see the model of consumer buyer behavior in Chapter 4), so is the behavior of industrial buyers influenced by many factors. Perhaps the greatest difference between the consumer behavior model and the industrial buyer behavior model is the influence of the work organization on decisions in the purchasing process. In many other respects there is considerable similarity between the two processes.

The model to describe industrial buying behavior (Figure 12–3), therefore, is quite similar to that presented for consumer behavior. There is an analogous subsys-

---

[9] U.S. Bureau of the Census, *1967 Census of Manufactures* (Washington, D.C.: Government Printing Office). Note that these statistics include only manufacturing activity.

[10] Ibid. The west south-central area contains Arkansas, Louisiana, Oklahoma, and Texas; the south Atlantic area includes West Virginia and all the states on the Atlantic Ocean from Delaware south to Florida.

Marketing: Principles and methods

tem for each subsystem in the consumer behavior model. In addition the organization learning variables are added. The individual buyer learning subsystem has been simplified into one "box" because the variables and relationships are the same as those shown in Figure 4–2.

Stage of learning[11]

The industrial purchasing process, as the consumer process, can be divided into three stages based on the extent to which the buyer has learned how to make a particular buy and the extent to which sources of supply have been established: (1) new task, (2) modified rebuy, and (3) straight rebuy.

FIGURE 12–3

A model of industrial buyer behavior

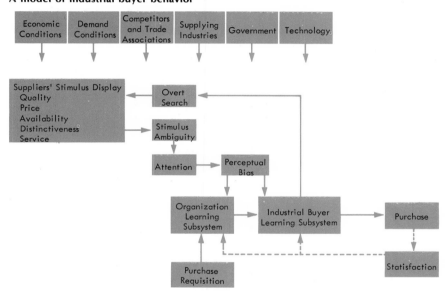

New task. The new-task stage corresponds to extensive problem solving in that the buyer has no experience with purchasing this item. His knowledge of alternatives and attitudes toward vendors (suppliers) is not well established and he must develop rather complete information. The search process, therefore, will be most elaborate at this stage, and new-task buying will be described most completely below.

Modified rebuy. The stage of learning called modified rebuy exists when the purchase requirement is not new but some event has occurred to alter the alternative sources of supply or the buyer's evaluation of them. The change may have occurred in the marketplace, such as a technological innovation (e.g., a new material), a new vendor aggressively seeking the business, or a rapidly changing competitive situation.

[11] See P. J. Robinson, C. W. Faris, and Y. Wind, *Industrial Buying and Creative Marketing* (Boston: Allyn & Bacon, Inc., 1967), pp. 22–38.

It may also have been generated within the buying organization, by changes in the quantity required in production, quality specifications, the service need, or buying policy.

In this stage the buyer has existing attitudes about various suppliers. However, he will actively search, will be receptive to offerings of new suppliers, and will reevaluate his alternatives.

Straight rebuy. The straight rebuy stage is the industrial counterpart to routinized response behavior in the consumer behavior model of Chapter 4. The requirement is a continuing one with which the buyer is familiar. He will check the price and availability of the item from a list of alternative suppliers about whom he has well-formed attitudes, and the purchase decision will be made from a supplier on this list. The majority of industrial purchases are of this type.

Organization learning subsystem[12]

The detail of the organization learning subsystem for a new task is shown in diagram form in Figure 12–4.[13] Note that like the buyer learning subsystem, the organization has goals (motives), holds attitudes, has an evoked set, and holds specific attitudes toward risk (the reciprocal of confidence). Empirical evidence suggests that

FIGURE 12–4

The organization learning subsystem

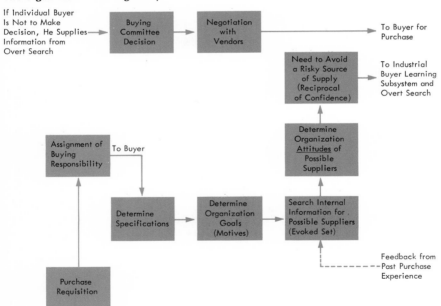

---

[12] The objective here is to study industrial buyer behavior in order to understand the marketing of industrial goods.

[13] See F. E. Webster, Jr., "Modeling the Industrial Buying Process," *Journal of Marketing Research,* 2 (November 1965), pp. 370–76.

organization variables are the most important factors in determining source of supply.[14]

The buying decision process is usually triggered from outside the purchasing department by the issuance of a purchase requisition by some other department. The requisition outlines (usually in insufficient detail) the item or service to be purchased. The purchasing department then assigns the buying responsibility to a particular buyer—often a specialist in purchasing that particular class of product or service.

Multiple purchasing influence. Even after assignment of the requisition, the buyer will not conduct his search or make his decision without consultation with a number of other persons in the organization. Types of organizational influence will vary among types of organizations. For example, influences on government or university purchasing will differ from those on a buyer at a branch manufacturing plant of Westinghouse Electric Company. Several people are involved in the buying decision, with the exception of smaller purchases of operating supplies and routine reordering of raw materials and fabricating parts and materials. This is especially true in the purchase of installations, where not only the engineers of the company participate but often the top executives as well. Such purchases are so important to the welfare of the company that no single man is authorized to make the final decision.

As one writer notes, "the inescapable fact [is] that the *chain of influences in most industrial buying situations is long, involved, and even mysterious.*"[15] To illustrate this "long and mysterious involvement," the results of a broad study of industrial purchasing practices may be cited:

the number of persons who function in the purchase of plant equipment and supplies ranged from one to nineteen; the average of all transactions studied was nearly five. In less than 1 percent of the transactions were all the buying functions performed by one individual; in only 9 percent of the transactions were two individuals involved, and in the largest number of instances, from 3 to 5 participated. The general superintendent appeared in 53 percent of the transactions, the plant engineer in 40 percent, the department head in 37 percent, the president in 34 percent, the general manager in 21 percent, [and] the finance committee in 16 percent. . . . The purchasing officer appeared in 92 percent of all the transactions.[16]

One generalization that can be made is that as the technical complexity of the item increases, the influence of the involved technical personnel on the purchase decision increases and the influence of the purchasing agent decreases.

Even for some routine purchases, the buyer cannot make the purchase until he clarifies some of the information on the requisition with the originating department. For a new task, the job of determining specifications (through physical properties, chemical composition, performance standards, samples, or blueprints) for even a reasonably simple part or material will involve much interaction between the buyer and other members of the organization.

Organization goals. Goals are the organization's motives. They are not quite the same as the basic drives of the individual, but survival remains as the primary goal. This goal will show itself in operating policies that may vary through time. For example, at some times organizations may place more pressure on the purchasing depart-

---

[14] For some recent evidence see Yoram Wind, "Industrial Source Loyalty," *Journal of Marketing Research,* 7 (November 1970), pp. 450–57.

[15] C. E. Walsh, "Reaching Those 'Hidden' Buying Influences," *Industrial Marketing,* October 1961, p. 165. Italics in original.

[16] W. B. England, *Procurement: Principles and Cases* (4th ed.; Homewood, Ill.: Richard D. Irwin, Inc., 1962), pp. 677–78.

ment to conserve cash or to buy at lower prices than at other times. Some firms also have policies that give preference to nearby suppliers.

Reciprocity is also a factor in buying. Today the "we will buy from you if you will buy from us" idea is often referred to as "trade relations." This subject is discussed at some length in Chapter 24.

Internal information sources. Most organizations keep files on possible sources of supply and evaluations of vendors with whom they have dealt in the past. The value of this information will vary with the organization and sophistication of the purchasing department. It could be elaborate enough to provide the entire *evoked set* of alternative suppliers the buyer will use in reaching his recommendation.

A well-organized purchasing department will rate suppliers on their past performance, store these evaluations in computerized files, and make them available to the buyer. While the buyer may hold personal attitudes as to the dependability of a supplier, such ratings indicate the organization's attitude toward him.

Risk avoidance. Organizations, like people, vary in their tolerance for risk and ambiguity, but most are motivated by a desire to reduce risk. A high need to avoid risk in the new-task purchase stage may lead to one of two extremes. It could cause the buyer to narrow his search to a few known suppliers that have received high performance ratings in the past. In this case, high need for risk avoidance would lead to increased loyalty to known sources. Alternatively, a high need for risk avoidance could lead to very extensive search. In this case the buyer will do everything possible to locate new sources of supply.

Marketing implications. The result of these organization factors is to constrain and direct the buyer in his own search behavior to particular suppliers and to particular sources of information. The seller is often confused by buyer behavior he cannot understand. Often the answer can be found by talking to other people in the organization, but it is difficult to know which ones.

The titles carried by a firm's employees frequently give little indication of purchasing influence. Whereas in one company the plant engineer may have as much influence as the purchasing agent, in another he may have no influence, and the vice president (or the design engineer, the treasurer, or the general manager) is the important individual. Thus many industrial calls by salesmen are on the "wrong" man. It is in view of these problems of reaching the "right" men that advertising takes on special significance in the marketing of industrial products and services. Through the placing of advertisements in carefully selected media, many of the key men in a specific situation may be influenced even though they are not contacted by a salesman.

Evaluation of alternatives. If the buyer is not given the authority to make the purchase decision, he will make his report on alternative vendors to the organization (often to a buying committee). This report will be tempered by the perceptual bias of his own internal search and overt search. Buying committees are most common in retailing organizations where marketing, not production, considerations are paramount.

The buying committee is of particular interest to the seller for two reasons. First, it may provide him an opportunity to make a presentation to the entire committee that is not filtered through the buyer's perceptual bias. Second, the buying committee can bring to play a variety of personal and political forces at work within the organization which would not be present if a single buyer had the authority to make the purchase. For example, one influential committee member's negative attitude toward a particular vendor could become very important in the decision process. The seller

Marketing: Principles and methods

can use these forces to his advantage if he discovers them in time, or they can work against him.

The organization also can be important in the evaluation of alternatives and the eventual decision if the buyer desires to negotiate with the seller over the terms of the purchase. Such negotiations are common in the purchase of capital installations and raw materials. Negotiations for the purchase of expensive and complex items routinely can extend for periods of many months.

Individual buyer learning subsystem

It is important for the seller to try to understand the impact of the organization on the individual buyer. Within this organizational context is a complex individual who is going through the same learning processes and coping with the same structure of personal motives, job-oriented motives, personality, roles, selective perception and retention, choice criteria, evoked set, attitudes and confidence that was studied in Chapter 4. The buyer will try to minimize conflict within the organization, avoid uncertainty through overt search, and improve the information available to both himself and his organization.[17] Appeals directly to the personal motives of the buyer certainly play a role in industrial marketing. For example, 60 percent of the buyers interviewed by one of the authors reported they were motivated by a need for recognition of accomplishment through advancement. Recognition by top management and salary increases were also mentioned.[18] Social ties, favors, and ego enhancement can also help the salesman get an order—particularly if the product offerings of competing sellers are nearly the same.

Overt search and the perceptual subsystem

The industrial buyer gains recognition and advancement by performance on his job, largely measured by how carefully he seeks out and deals with vendors. Because the buyer of industrial products and services must keep the profit motive of his firm always in mind, increasing attention in recent years has been devoted to "value analysis." This concept involves careful study of all relevant factors in the purchasing decision in an effort to obtain the maximum value in terms of quality, service, and price. As a rule, therefore, industrial buyers know what they require in products and services from their sources of supply in order to attain the desired profit objective. Consequently, the appeals that sellers make to them are primarily on the basis of quality, price, availability, distinctiveness, and service.

Specific appeals. The buyer may be attracted to a certain product because it is superior to competing products in giving a *lower cost of production.* Such economy may arise from the fact that the machine is more reliable, with the result that production holdups are less frequent, it can be operated with fewer men, it has a longer life and thus involves smaller yearly depreciation charges, or it will increase the output of the plant. Even the purchase of items to ensure additional comfort for employees (for example, air-conditioning equipment) may be for the purpose of lowering production cost by increasing employee efficiency. Or the buyer may find that the use of a certain machine will result in a high *uniformity of output*—a feature especially

---

[17] Robinson, Faris, and Wind, *Industrial Buying,* pp. 101–9.

[18] D. J. Duncan, *Some Basic Determinants of Behavior in Industrial Purchasing* (Berkeley: University of California, Institute of Business and Economic Research, 1965), p. 5.

attractive to a manufacturer producing a branded product where standardization is important.

Again, the buying motive may lie in the fact that a certain piece of equipment is *flexible;* that is, it can be used in producing products of various sizes or qualities or in various kinds of work. Often purchases are made because the buyer feels that the *salability* of his product will be increased. In the purchase of fabricating parts, for example, the deciding factor may be that the parts offered by one company are branded and well known so that their presence in the finished product will provide a good "talking point." And, finally, many industrial products and services are purchased because they will give *protection* to their user. Fire sprinkler systems are also sold by this appeal.

Need for technical advice. A knowledge of the technical qualities of many products, especially in basic equipment, is another factor in overt search. To sell today's complex electronic systems and other sophisticated machinery, the salesman must have full knowledge of their operations and applications, and the continuous improvements being made in them, in order to advise users of their capabilities. Even for such products as lubricating oils and greases, industrial buyers require competent technical assistance; there are several hundred types and grades of lubricants, each tailor-made for specific purposes.

Therefore, if the salesman is going to help the customer to purchase products best suited to his needs, and if appropriate standards of service are to be maintained, proper training both in technical knowledge and in selling techniques is essential.

Good salesmen required. Since industrial products are purchased mainly on an economic basis by well-informed purchasers, a salesman of industrial products should be trained to meet the buyer's needs. He should be prepared to (1) make an intelligent presentation of his product; (2) furnish prices promptly and accurately on request; (3) provide information on new developments—new uses, improvements in manufacturing methods, latest engineering and research data; (4) help the buyer to avoid overstocking; and (5) give prompt attention to errors and omissions on shipments, invoices, and credits.

A dependable supply required. An adequate supply of raw materials must be available at all times; shutdowns are expensive. Modern industry operates with a large overhead cost, and important elements of the total cost of production continue even when a plant is not in production. A forced shutdown may cause the transference of orders from the affected manufacturer to another with sufficient raw materials. Moreover, if the shutdown continues for some time, skilled labor may be lost.

Uniform quality essential. The emphasis on quality and dependability of raw materials, operating supplies, and fabricating materials and parts in industrial buying grows out of the very nature of manufacturing industries. In the first place, efficient manufacturing rests largely upon the effective use of automatic machinery, and such machinery requires dependable materials, parts, and supplies. When a weaver is operating one or two looms, for instance, the breakage of a thread in warp or woof is of relatively little importance; but when he operates dozens of high-speed automatic looms, frequent breaking of the yarn overcomes the very purpose for which automatic machines were perfected. Second, high-priced labor makes materials of the right quality imperative, since production delays caused by unsuitable supplies interfere with the operation of the machine and greatly increase labor costs. Third, to permit quantity production of standardized products requires an assured supply of materials of uniform quality. Finally, considerable consumer demand exists for high-quality finished products which cannot be met without a complementary demand for high-quality materials and parts.

Exogenous variables

As in consumer behavior or any other system, the industrial buying system is influenced by the economic, technical, and social systems in which it resides. These environmental forces are the exogenous variables in the industrial buying model; seven of the most important (shown in Figure 12–3) are discussed below. Similarities between these and the exogenous variables in the consumer behavior model can be readily seen.

Technology. The rate of technological change in the industry will have a significant influence on purchasing. When change in products, manufacturing processes, or raw materials is occurring rapidly, the purchasing department has little chance to establish regular sources of supply or to learn much about market conditions. Thus a greater percentage of the purchases are "new tasks" and the influence of technical groups is greater than if technology were more stable. Sometimes, as in the case of the computer and air freight, technological changes have a direct effect on the buying procedure within the firm.

Government antitrust enforcement. The United States has laws which make it illegal to sell like goods to competitors at different prices. These laws regulate the behavior of both buyers and sellers. The extent to which government is enforcing regulations against illegal price discrimination will influence buying and industrial marketing procedures. In markets under government scrutiny, sellers must be very careful not to agree in negotiations to offer a price that could be held to be illegal. This subject will be discussed in more detail in Chapter 25.

Government environmental control activities. Regional, state, and federal regulations designed to improve the quality of the environment in which we live also have an influence on purchasing. Regulations concerning water use and pollution, air pollution, thermal pollution, noise pollution, and solid waste disposal have a tremendous impact on manufacturing practices and the machinery, suppliers, and materials used in manufacturing. Since pollution control usually increases the cost of production, the industrial buyer must be sure that the items he buys meet pollution-control standards and that their cost does not put his company at a competitive disadvantage to companies subject to a different set of standards.

The supplying industry. The competitive structure and performance of firms supplying an item also influence buying procedures. If the item is a commodity and suppliers are few and large (for example, in sheet steel), the purchasing company may be at a disadvantage in securing the prices and services desired. The seller will attempt to make the buyer dependent on him as a source of supply. The buyer will attempt to stockpile, purchase on contract, and secure alternative sources of supply. When there is a greater number of sources of supply, the buyer may keep a number of vendors competing for the business to ensure that competitive pressures on price, quality, and service work to his advantage. If the item is a component purchased in large quantities to the buyer's unique specifications, the buyer may offer one or two suppliers very large orders to make them more dependent on this business, thus exerting pressure for lower prices.

Competitors and trade associations. Since the Great Depression of the 1930s it has been possible for competitors in most industries to solve common supply problems through trade association activities. These may take the form of a simple exchange of information about suppliers at meetings and conventions or extensive selling by suppliers through convention exhibits and entertainment. Trade associations also provide the vehicle for competitors to bargain collectively with suppliers with whom they are having trouble. This practice is most common in dealing with regulated suppliers such as railroads. The trade association can bring pressure on the regulating agency while the companies negotiate with the carriers.

Demand conditions.   The buying organization's marketing efforts have an impact on its purchasing activities. If demand for products declines, pressure is put on the purchasing department to reduce costs and inventories. If demand jumps, pressure is put on purchasing to increase inventories to meet increased production. Thus, changes in tastes and styles in the buyer's market exert exogenous pressures on the industrial buying process.

Economic conditions.   The impact of fluctuations in general business conditions has such a significant impact on industrial marketing and buying that the marketer should have a more detailed understanding of the nature of demand for industrial goods. The remainder of this chapter is devoted to this topic.

CHARACTERISTICS OF DEMAND FOR INDUSTRIAL PRODUCTS AND SERVICES

Economics teaches that the most important determinant of personal consumption expenditures is income—when consumers' incomes increase, they buy more. It is not possible to make a similar simple statement about the demand for industrial products and services, chiefly because it is derived from the demand for the products and services they help to produce. For example, a general falling off in the demand for automobiles and appliances means that the manufacturers of these products will reduce their demand for raw materials, operating supplies, and parts. During such periods, manufacturers of steel find it impossible to induce manufacturers of automobiles to make purchases. When the demand for automobiles again begins to increase, the demand for steel likewise grows.

The fluctuations in the demand for industrial products and services will be greater than the fluctuations in final consumer demand. It is important to understand why this is so. In the case of raw materials and component parts and materials that go into the product, there are two reasons for such fluctuations: inventory and anticipation of price changes. In order to ensure smooth production, a manufacturer will carry substantial stocks of raw materials, perhaps four times the current rate of weekly production. If a decline in final demand causes a reduction in that production rate of 25 percent, the materials inventory will be sufficient for more than five weeks. Thus the producer stops buying materials until he can bring his stocks into line. Fluctuations in materials needs are even greater because the manufacturer also has finished inventories in his channels of distribution. He and his distributors will reduce their purchases by more than 25 percent in order to bring their stocks into line. If the manufacturer feels that his refusal to buy will cause raw material prices to fall, he may cut his purchases still more in anticipation of a price reduction.

When final demand increases, the reverse amplification of demand fluctuations takes place. When distributors rush to increase their inventories to cover the jump in demand, the manufacturer increases his production rate by a percentage greater than the increase in final demand. He then may increase his raw materials safety stock by a greater percentage than production and may buy an additional increment if he expects material prices to increase. Copper provides an excellent illustration of demand fluctuation in raw materials. Even after recovery from the wild fluctuations of the Great Depression and World War II, fluctuations in demand in excess of 25 percent over a two-year period have been the rule, not the exception.

In the case of facilitating supplies and services, which do not become a part of the product, demand is still derived, but fluctuations will be about equal to production changes because safety stocks are zero or small.

Derived demand for capital equipment

Fluctuations in the demand for major capital equipment and accessory equipment are also greater than fluctuations in the final demand from which it is derived. In addition to the rate of production and anticipation of price changes, there are six other major factors which affect the fluctuations in the demand for capital equipment. All six have to do with the desire of the businessman to change his production capacity.

Anticipation of changes in business conditions. The business firm is required to anticipate changes in general business conditions. In periods of prosperity, businessmen tend to be optimistic; they often enlarge their plants and install heavy equipment to take care of anticipated future business. Although this means that the downswing of the business cycle finds many firms in an overexpanded condition, during the upswing of the cycle it results in large sales of "heavy" business goods. If the anticipated demand not only fails to materialize but sales actually begin to fall off, all desire to buy heavy equipment vanishes. Products already installed are more than adequate to meet the demand.

The durable nature of capital equipment. Further, the life of such equipment under light usage is vastly increased; and, during periods of recession, businessmen continue to use machinery long after it otherwise would have been replaced. Thus the stage is set for a rapid increase in the demand for basic equipment when the business cycle turns upward.

The amount of excess capacity. If a firm forecasts that their demand will increase 10 percent per year for the next three years in an industry which is operating at 80 percent of capacity, the firm is likely to be eager to increase its own capacity now so that it can meet the anticipated increase in demand. However, if the industry has had chronic overcapacity and is now operating at an average of 50 percent, the firm may be reluctant to increase its capacity even if it is operating above the industry average.

The rate of innovation. An industry such as aerospace or electronics that has enjoyed a rapid rate of technological development both in products and production processes will have more of a need (independent of business conditions) to buy capital equipment than will firms in a mature industry with a slow rate of innovation.

The availability of funds and government monetary policy. The firm generates funds internally roughly equal to its profits plus depreciation charges. It generates funds externally from banks and by issuing securities. Government monetary policy is aimed at keeping the sum of these two sources on a steady plane. When business conditions are bad and profits low, government makes money available at low interest rates to encourage investment in capital equipment. When profits are high and business activity is at a boil, the Federal Reserve System tries to reduce the supply of money banks have to lend.

Many economists question the extent to which this policy has been successful in reducing fluctuations in capital investment. One problem is that firms with excess capacity have little motivation to invest in plant and equipment no matter how low interest rates are. Another problem is that the government's central bankers have had only mixed success in knowing when to increase and when to decrease the supply of money.

Depreciation and government tax policy. Depreciation on capital equipment is a tax-deductible expense. As long as tax rates remain unchanged, charging more depreciation during the early years in the life of a plant or piece of machinery will delay (but not remove) the need to pay taxes on the income the depreciation charge offsets. To postpone the payment of income taxes is like borrowing money from the government at no interest. For large industrial concerns, accelerated depreciation is an important source of funds. Therefore, government has, on a few occasions, attempted to stimulate investment in plant and equipment by offering rapid depreciation charges against taxes. During 1971, such a proposal was a major issue of fiscal policy. There is little doubt that such a policy would stimulate investment, but it is questionable as to whether it would dampen the fluctuations in the demand for capital equipment.

There is an abundance of statistical evidence on the wide fluctuations in the demand for capital equipment. One example was shown in Figure 12–1, where capital expenditures were shown as a percentage of gross national product.

Marketing implications

What are the implications for marketing of these environmental characteristics of derived demand for industrial goods and services? We will discuss just two: pricing and promotion.

Pricing implications. One implication of derived demand is that it is price inelastic. If all producers of an industrial product reduce their price, demand will not increase by enough to recover the revenue lost by the price reduction. This follows from the fact that, as a rule, any particular type of industrial good accounts for such a small part of the price of the item whose production it aids that the price of the completed product is not materially affected. Even a 20 percent cut in the price of such an important material as the steel used in making typewriters would have little impact on the price at which typewriters are sold, because so much of their cost is accounted for by wages, other materials and parts, general overhead, and cost of distribution.

It is true, of course, that a particular producer may increase the demand for his product by a price cut even if the demand for the ultimate good is not increased. This result may be a consequence of the buyers transferring some orders to the price cutter instead of giving them to his competitors. Competition is so keen, however, that a price cut by one firm is usually met by similar action on the part of competitors, and a significant shift in patronage does not usually result. Because of this reaction to a price cut, such action may result in a smaller profit margin for all in the field rather than an increase in demand for the output of any one producer. In fact, the action may set off a price war which would be disastrous to all producers for perhaps an extended period of time.

Consumer promotion. When a component part is identifiable to the consumer, when a replacement market exists, or when a material is in competition with others, sellers of industrial goods have sometimes undertaken promotional activities directly to consumers. For example, the Du Pont Company has frequently undertaken consumer advertising of its synthetic resins and fibers. The seller must be very careful that such expenditures are going to increase his profit in the long run, for consumer advertising is a very expensive form of promotion by industrial marketing standards.

The rationale for these activities when a replacement market exists is self-evident. Consumer advertising of identifiable components is a good way to gain and hold customers if the advertising is successful. For example, a General Electric motor in a power tool marketed by a small manufacturer helps sell the power tool and helps General Electric hold a customer.

Of these three situations, the competition between materials is perhaps the most interesting. Most materials compete with substitute materials, and gaining preference by the ultimate consumer is one way to hold off this competition. The market for beverage cans, for example, is a very important one for both steel and aluminum producers. Therefore, both groups tell consumers about their ecological attributes. They believe ecology has an appeal which is salient, i.e., important, to consumers. Steel will rust and hence go back to nature; aluminum won't. Aluminum scrap is valuable enough for producers to pay consumers to return their empty cans; steel scrap is not. At the same time, both sides must constantly guard against inroads by returnable glass bottles or new polyvinyl chloride bottles.

Producers of new synthetic materials have additional reasons to promote them to consumers. One is that they often have patent protection and thus have much to gain from successful advertising. Perhaps more important, consumers must be helped to overcome their fear that new synthetic materials are just "cheap substitutes."

SUMMARY

In contrasting the marketing of industrial products and services with consumer products and services, it has been noted that the industrial market differs in two major dimensions. First, the number of prospective customers is relatively limited. There are about 11 million industrial users, only 3.5 million of whom have employees, compared with about 62 million consumer households. Secondly, the customers are commercial institutions—manufacturers, hospitals, schools and so forth—and not households.

A useful definition is that industrial products and services are those consumed by organizations in producing consumer or other industrial products and services or in conducting an enterprise. The definition is based on the purpose for which the products and services are intended for use by the immediate purchaser.

Industrial products and services have been classified into six groups: raw materials, component parts and materials, major capital equipment, operating supplies, accessory equipment, and business services. With the exception of services, this classification is based on the uses to which the products are normally put. It also reflects some differences in purchasing and marketing behavior.

The industrial market in the United States can be broken down into market segments according to the types of products industrial users produce. This is facilitated by the federal identification of each firm with an SIC code number. In each category, a wealth of information is collected that is useful in assessing the market potential of various firms.

Compared to the consumer market, the industrial market is geographically concentrated. Over one fourth of the customers are located in only five SMSAs. Seven states—New York, California, Ohio, Illinois, Pennsylvania, Michigan and New Jersey—combined account for more value added by manufacturing than all of the other 43 states together. Further, numerous industries—furniture, steel, rubber, automobiles, and electronics—are concentrated geographically.

Because the buying process for industrial buyers is not much different from that for consumers, the buyer behavior model in Chapter 4 can provide the basis for the industrial buyer model in this chapter. The major differences arise because: the goals of the firm are more economic and less hedonistic than those of a household, and the organization of which the industrial buyer is a member is larger and therefore has more influence on purchase decisions than would be true for a household. Another difference between the two models is in the exogenous variables that influence the decision process. Those affecting the industrial buyer in particular are: technology, government antitrust enforcement, government environmental control activities, the supplying industry, competitors and trade associations, demand conditions, and general business conditions. A final difference is that the gain from search for the industrial buyer is likely to be greater than that for the consumer because the size of the purchase is often large. The implications for marketing are that the seller is well advised to give more emphasis to individually supplying each buyer with specific information about his product than would be prudent in consumer goods marketing.

In summarizing this chapter, we remind you that the demand for industrial products and services is, for the most part, a derived demand from consumer demand as influenced by government economic stabilization policy. That is, the demand for these products and services is derived from the demand for the products and services they help to produce. Because of derived demand, sales to the industrial market fluctuate much more than sales to the consumer market, which has meaningful marketing implications. Marketing in the industrial market is decidedly different from marketing to the consumer market. To make sure that you understand these differences and similarities, we recommend consideration of the review and discussion questions.

REVIEW AND DISCUSSION QUESTIONS

1. Into what major groups may industrial products and services be classified? What useful purposes, from a marketing point of view, are served by such a classification?

2. How do you think the marketing activities of a manufacturer of a plastic molding resin material will differ from those of the molder who sells plastic custom-molded component parts?

3. Find some examples of branded and promoted component parts. What are the reasons the manufacturers engage in these activities?

4. Calculate personal consumption expenditures as a percentage of gross national product for the years 1947 to the present and compare your percentages to those in Figure 12–1. Comment on the differences.

5. What is the marketing significance of the fact that fluctuations in demand for industrial products and services are wider than those for consumer products and services?

6. For any three-digit SIC manufacturing industry, prepare an analysis of the number, size,

Marketing: Principles and methods

and location of each of the four-digit groups within the industry, using the latest *Census of Manufactures* as your source of information.

7. From the *Census of Manufactures,* make a list of the 15 SMSAs that add the most value by manufacturing. Also record the number of establishments in each of these SMSAs. Now go to the *Census of Business* and find the number of merchant wholesalers and manufacturers' agents selling electrical apparatus, equipment and supplies, industrial machinery and equipment, and industrial supplies. What are the maketing implications of this analysis for a manufacturer of industrial machinery?

8. Based on the discussion in the text, describe the industrial buying behavior for a modified rebuy; for a straight rebuy.

9. Based on the discussion in Chapter 4, compare and contrast the factors that come to play in the industrial buyer learning subsystem.

10. Discuss the marketing implications involved in the multiple purchasing influence at work in the buying of industrial products and services.

11. Do you think more purchasing agents than housewives read direct-mail advertising?

12. Should companies absolutely forbid their buyers to be entertained or receive gifts from salesmen? Defend your answer.

13. Why will the bargaining power of a General Motors purchasing agent differ from that of a small machine tool company?

14. Trace the impact on demand for ripsaws used in lumber mills that would result from a 15 percent reduction in residential construction.

15. An extruder is the machine used to produce automobile tire treads. What is the competitive significance of a price cut of 25 percent by a manufacturer of extruders?

SUPPLEMENTARY READINGS

You should also consult the readings listed at the end of Chapter 13.

Alexander, R. S.; Cross, J. S.; and Hill, R. M. *Industrial Marketing.* 3d ed. Homewood, Ill.: Richard D. Irwin, Inc., 1967. A valuable treatment of all aspects of the industrial market will be found in this volume. It provides detailed information in an area where data have been quite limited.

Corey, E. R. *Industrial Marketing: Cases and Concepts.* Englewood Cliffs, N.J.: Prentice-Hall, Inc., 1962. In this excellent casebook, sections 1 and 2 offer illustrative material for the subjects covered in this chapter.

Dickinson, R. A. *Buyer Decision Making.* Berkeley: University of California, Institute of Business and Economic Research, 1967. Analyzes buyer behavior in selecting vendors by department stores.

Duncan, D. J. *Some Basic Determinants of Behavior in Industrial Purchasing.* Berkeley: University of California, Institute of Business and Economic Research, Marketing Research Program, 1965. Analyzes the intracompany and external forces influencing the behavior of the purchasing officer.

Levitt, T. *Industrial Purchasing Behavior: A Study of Communication Effects.* Boston: Harvard University, Graduate School of Business Administration, Division of Research, 1965. Emphasizing the importance of integrating three factors in all buying situations—the source of the buying message, the message itself and its presentation, and the audience or prospective buyers—the author contributes to our understanding of industrial purchasing. Also see his "Communications and Industrial Selling," *Journal of Marketing,* 31 (April 1967), pp. 15–21.

Mill & Factory *Industrial Market Analysis '64–'66.* New York, 1967. This 59-page booklet details the characteristics of the industrial market, with comparisons for 1939, 1951, and 1966.

Revzan, D. A. *A Comprehensive Classified Marketing Bibliography.* Supplements No. 1 and No. 2 to Part I. Berkeley, Institute of Business and Economic Research, University of California, 1963. In supplements to a similar compilation in 1951, publications relating to industrial marketing are listed. Supplement No. 1 covers books published between 1950 and 1962, and Supplement No. 2 lists government publications, research monographs, and articles from professional journals for the same period.

Robinson, P. J., Faris, C. W. and Wind, Y. *Industrial Buying and Creative Marketing.* Boston: Allyn & Bacon, Inc., 1967. An easy-to-read, comprehensive treatment with an excellent bibliography.

Webster, F. E., Jr. and Wind, Y. *Organizational Buying Behavior.* Englewood Cliffs, N.J.: Prentice-Hall, Inc., 1971. This is the most complete treatment of this subject.

Westing, J. H., Fine, I. V. and Zenz, G. J. *Purchasing Management, Materials in Motion.* New York: John Wiley & Sons, Inc., 1969. This leading text in industrial procurements also contains case materials.

13 *Marketing manufactured industrial products: System functions, structure, and institutions*

The functions, structural characteristics, and institutions in the marketing system for industrial products which make it a unique and dynamic part of the total marketing system comprise the subject of this chapter. The focus is narrowed to encompass only *manufactured* industrial products, including major capital equipment, accessory equipment, operating supplies, and component parts and materials.

The first section discusses three unique functional characteristics: (1) product servicing, (2) financing by leasing, and (3) the use of catalogs and trade shows to communicate with potential buyers. The structure of the channels of distribution used to market manufactured industrial products is examined in the second section, and the third describes two important middlemen, the industrial distributor and the manufacturers' representative. The unique characteristics of marketing to government are considered in the final section of this chapter.

UNIQUE FUNCTIONS IN INDUSTRIAL MARKETING

Product servicing

Buyers of industrial goods have long recognized the need for and dependence on satisfactory servicing of the products they purchase.[1] This places great responsibility upon the manufacturer either to render the service himself or to have it performed

---

[1] For an excellent discussion of the types, objectives, and measurement of technical product services, see L. S. Simon, "Measuring the Market Impact of Technical Services," *Journal of Marketing Research* (February 1965), pp. 32–39. Also see Jack Wertis, "How Good Are Your Product Profits?" *Industrial Distribution,* 57 (February 1967), pp. 41–45.

effectively by other agencies. For convenience of discussion, these services are divided into two groups: (1) those performed before the sale is made and (2) those carried on after the sale is consummated.

Presale services. Offering presale services is a convincing sales argument, especially when the buyer's needs are highly individualized as well as technical in nature. They are also of great value to a company marketing, for example, a new type of equipment, the benefits of which are difficult to judge except by those well acquainted with its operation.

Examples of technical sales services are numerous. The marketer of electronic equipment designed to control production in a plant must present the potential buyer with a complete analysis of how such equipment can improve his operations. A company interested in selling packaging machinery to a candy manufacturer may make a detailed investigation of the candymaker's market which may lead to the conclusion that an important part of his potential market is being overlooked. A number of package designs appropriate for use in developing this market may be submitted, with estimates as to the cost of developing machinery to produce the suggested packages. Or again, a company selling lubricants may offer to send experts to the plant of a potential customer to give recommendations as to the correct lubrication for each machine. Some firms use workshops and product demonstration centers to acquaint prospective customers with their products and to demonstrate how customers' problems can be solved through use of the manufacturers' equipment.

Postsale services. Services are also frequently rendered after purchase, especially for equipment. These services have become more necessary as more sophisticated machines have been developed in recent years; a seller may train the operators of a complex machine after it is installed. Even more important, perhaps, is the need of maintaining a staff of men to serve as troubleshooters. Because production trouble with basic equipment can close down a section or even an entire plant, a machinery manufacturer must stand ready to give repair service at any time. Computer manufacturers, for instance, maintain personnel and facilities for servicing their products within a few hours of a failure at many points throughout the United States. Sellers of such equipment may also provide periodic inspection service designed to minimize delays in production that are caused by breakdowns of machinery. Thus manufacturers of major equipment for industrial uses find it necessary to sell service as well as products.

Leasing of industrial equipment

The leasing of industrial equipment, another important characteristic of the industrial market, has been practiced for years by firms such as the United Shoe Machinery Corporation and International Business Machines. These earlier leasing arrangements were limited chiefly to expensive major equipment or installations. Today, companies can lease machine tools, trucks, cars, office equipment, operating supplies, and hundreds of other items. In fact, the practice has expanded so rapidly in recent years that many companies have been organized to do nothing but facilitate leasing. In the data processing field alone more than 100 computer leasing companies have been established under such names as Leasco Computer Inc., ITEL Computer Leasing Corporation, Data Automation Co., and Diebold Computer Leasing Inc. By purchasing data processing equipment from manufacturers and leasing it to their customers at rates lower than those charged by the manufacturers, these companies render a real service and realize a profit in the process. Other leasing firms include United States Leasing

Corporation (San Francisco), which purchases capital goods and leases them to factories and offices, and the National Equipment Leasing Corporation (Pittsburgh), through which the General Electric Company leases its diesel locomotives. In addition, firms which have traditionally offered credit services, such as the Commercial Credit Company, have become important factors in the leasing of industrial goods; and, currently, commercial banks are attempting to add this service.

A specific leasing plan. The leasing plan offered by one machine tool manufacturer, Warner & Swasey, provides that the industrial user:

1. Deposits 10% of the purchase price. . . .
2. Chooses one of three payment plans, which can run as long as 16 years:

	Under plan A	Under plan B	Under plan C
Percent of purchase price paid each year as rent............	36	24	18
For a period of	2 years	3 years	4 years
At which time he may return the machine, having paid (percent)	72	72	72

If he keeps the machine, he pays a lower rental until seven years are up, when he has paid a total of 114%. He then may extend the contract for nine years at 6% rent per year or send the machine back to Warner & Swasey.

3. Can include an option to buy the machine if he wishes. The terms: 105% of the purchase price plus 5% for each year he has had it. Rent payments already made apply against the price.[2]

Reasons for leasing. It is not difficult to see why some manufacturers have turned to leasing to supplement outright sale or as the sole method of placing their products on the market.[3] Some equipment is so expensive that potential users hesitate to make purchases. This factor is especially important if (1) the equipment offered represents a new development, (2) the equipment depreciates or becomes obsolete rapidly (e.g., automobiles and computers), (3) the equipment requires frequent specialized maintenance, (4) the need for the installation is uncertain or sporadic, or (5) the firm lacks adequate finances or wishes to conserve its working capital for other corporate purposes. To smaller companies the payment of a monthly rental or of a royalty per unit produced may not be an undue burden. If the machine is new or the need for it uncertain, the buyer will feel more like trying it out, since he can return it if it proves unsatisfactory or unnecessary. In addition, the use of a lease may enable the seller to obtain more for his machines.

Although the desire to conserve working capital and enjoy the freedom of allocating it to other particular needs is the major reason why industrial users prefer leasing, there may also be tax advantages. Since rental payments are fully deductible as a business expense (so long as there is no option to purchase), and since they typically exceed the normal depreciation rate allowed by the Internal Revenue Service, the final net cash cost may not be much more than under outright purchase. Even though

---

[2] Material provided by the company.

[3] For another analysis of the advantages and disadvantages of leasing, see *Leasing versus Buying,* a booklet prepared by a committee of the National Association of Purchasing Agents (New York, 1963).

the surcharges on leased equipment run to 4 to 6 percent per year of the original cost of the equipment, so that the total dollar amount paid is greater, these additional dollars may be charged against operating income. Thus the net number of the dollars *after* taxes is far less than the gross extra cost of leasing.[4] Moreover, keen competition among leasing firms has resulted in relatively low down payments, long credit periods, and modest surcharges.

Information and promotion in industrial marketing

A major task of promotion in industrial marketing is to inform potential buyers about a supplier firm and its products. Periodicals directed toward specifiers and buyers usually contain information sections on new products along with a postal card the buyer can use to request additional information about any product featured or advertised. The magazine publisher forwards these requests for additional information to the appropriate manufacturer. Some business publications have also experimented with a telephone inquiry service for readers.

While industrial advertising must attract the attention of the customer, the copy of the advertisement usually discusses the quality, delivery, distinctiveness, cost savings, and service provided by the firm. Figure 13–1 shows an industrial advertisement used by the Century-Fox Company. (Note that the advertisement mentions the reader service card at the bottom.) User benefits are emphasized, and case histories frequently are used to document claims.

The salesman's job is made easier because the buyer is made aware of the company and its products. A McGraw-Hill Publications Company study in 1970 showed that advertising boosted the average sales per call for commodity products by $129.[5]

Use of catalogs. The standardized nature of many industrial products enables buyers to rely upon catalogs in placing orders. One study of 512 purchases in which 1,383 different products were given consideration disclosed that 471 were purchased or discarded entirely on the basis of printed information; for 360 additional products the decision to see the manufacturer's salesman was based on a catalog or other printed material.[6] The catalog is especially useful in providing information to buyers on fabricated parts, operating supplies, and repair parts for major equipment. Two pages of a typical catalog from Flex-Weld, Inc., are illustrated in Figure 13–2.

The catalog of an individual manufacturer may be a modest six-page brochure or an elaborate publication of hundreds of pages. The International Harvester Company spends more than $1 million in preparing its products catalog.[7] Depending upon the trade channels used by the specific manufacturer, the catalog may be sent to middlemen, users of the products, or both. Many manufacturers also use catalogs in

---

[4] The "present value" technique of comparing the cost of owning or leasing is advocated and illustrated in R. F. Vancil, *Leasing of Industrial Equipment* (New York: McGraw-Hill Book Co., Inc., 1963). Also see R. H. Butz, "Leasing or Buying: Which Is the Best Bargain?" *Air Conditioning, Heating, and Ventilating News* (November 28, 1966), pp. 18–19.

[5] *Business Week* (November 14, 1970), p. 103.

[6] Sweet's Catalog Service, *The Need for Printed Product Information in Industrial Buying* (New York: F. W. Dodge Corp., n.d.), pp. 3, 6, and 8.

[7] Kathryn Sederberg, "At Harvester Catalogs Do Real Sales Job," *Industrial Marketing,* 49 (October 1964), p. 104.

Marketing: Principles and methods

FIGURE 13-1
Typical industrial advertisement

**New 10-Ton
Floor Press**
Features rugged 10,000
PSI hand pump at con-
venient working height
(½ HP motor pump
optional), and single
or double-acting ram
with adjustable plate.
Work platform adjusts
easily from 6½" to 44".
Width 22½", height 60".

Only $262

Who besides Century-Fox offers hydraulic tools at such low cost?

NOBODY! Because Century-Fox specializes in
building high-quality, low-cost products for industry. Other C-F hydraulic tools include: 2"
pipe and conduit bending set in a handy metal
carrying chest, plus heavy duty one-shot bend-
ers up to 6 inches. Remote-control pumps,
solid rams, and hollow rams with complete
attachments. Jacks from 1½ to 100 tons capacity. 1000 and 2000 lb. shop cranes. All
designed and built to give your customers long
service life. Write for details.

**Only
$115**

44-102 R1

New Mini-Power Kit
Four tons of concentrated hydraulic power in a
convenient 30 lb. package. Includes pump, ram,
metal chest, and all attachments needed to lift, push,
bend, straighten, spread or clamp.

CENTURY-FOX CO.
1005 PERKINS AVENUE, WAUKESHA, WISCONSIN 53186
AREA CODE 414-542-2235
Division of Hein-Werner Corp.

146   CIRCLE 146 ON READER SERVICE CARD

Source: *Industrial Distribution,* 61 (May 1971), p. 146.

FIGURE 13–2
Two pages from a typical industrial catalog

FLEX-WELD
ANNULAR CORRUGATED
DIESEL EXHAUST HOSE

STAINLESS STEEL FWSS-DE

Nominal Hose I.D. Inches	Nominal Hose O.D. Inches	Approx. Weight Per Ft. Lbs.	Min. Static Inside Bend Radius	Min. Inside Bend Radius Intermittent Flexing	Max. Lateral Offset Per Ft.	Max. Axial Movement Per Ft.	Unbraided Max. @ 70°F Operating Pressure	Max. Operating Temp.
1½	2.19	1.27	2.7	28	1.25	.14	50	1500°F
2	2.75	1.35	3.5	36	.96	.14	45	1500°F
2½	3.17	1.50	4.0	46	.82	.21	30	1500°F
3	3.74	2.13	4.7	55	.74	.21	30	1500°F
3½	4.29	2.13	5.5	60	.65	.21	25	1500°F
4	4.82	2.64	6.1	65	.60	.21	20	1500°F
5	6.00	3.62	7.5	89	.47	.21	20	1500°F
6	6.94	4.00	8.5	103	.42	.21	18	1500°F
8	9.00	4.82	11.0	155	.30	.21	16	1500°F
10	11.00	5.70	13.6	163	.20	.21	10	1500°F
12	13.00	6.3	16.5	187	.17	.21	5	1500°F
14	14.50	7.0	19.0	230	.15	.21	5	1500°F
16	16.50	8.5	22.0	268	.13	.21	5	1500°F

CARBON STEEL FWCS-DE

Nominal Hose I.D. Inches	Nominal Hose O.D. Inches	Approx. Weight Per Ft. Lbs.	Min. Static Inside Bend Radius	Min. Inside Bend Radius Intermittent Flexing	Max. Lateral Offset Per Ft.	Max. Axial Movement Per Ft.	Unbraided Max. @ 70°F Operating Pressure	Max. Operating Temp.
1½	2.19	1.36	2.7	33	1.2	.14	50	800°F
2	2.75	1.87	3.5	40	.90	.14	45	800°F
2½	3.22	1.95	4.0	50	.72	.21	30	800°F
3	3.73	2.72	4.7	58	.65	.21	30	800°F
3½	4.30	2.85	5.5	66	.55	.21	25	800°F
4	4.81	2.97	6.1	70	.50	.21	20	800°F
5	6.00	3.40	7.5	100	.36	.21	20	800°F
6	6.90	4.25	8.5	110	.33	.21	18	800°F
8	9.00	7.85	12	160	.20	.21	15	800°F
10	11.00	9.28	13.7	180	.19	.21	12	800°F
12	13.00	10.26	17.0	210	.17	.21	10	800°F

FLEX-WELD
BUTT-WELDED
ANNULAR
CORRUGATED
HOSE

BRONZE

FWB-30 — Unbraided
FWB-31 — Single Braided

Nominal Hose I.D. Inches	Product Number	Approx. Weight Per Ft. Lbs.	Nominal Hose O.D. Inches	Min. C/L Bend Radius for Intermittent Flexing	Min. C/L Bend Radius for Static Bend	Maximum Working Pressure @ 70° P.S.I.G.	Maximum Test Pressure @ 70° P.S.I.G.	Rated Burst Pressure @ 70° P.S.I.G.
¼	FWB-30	.18	.49	6	1	125	175	4200
	FWB-31	.26	.55	6	1	1050	1575	
⅜	FWB-30	.30	.69	7	1⅛	100	150	3000
	FWB-31	.42	.75	7	1⅛	750	1125	
½	FWB-30	.40	.84	8	1½	60	90	2000
	FWB-31	.54	.90	8	1½	500	750	
¾	FWB-30	.70	1.23	10	2⅛	45	67	1700
	FWB-31	.92	1.29	10	2⅛	425	640	
1	FWB-30	1.00	1.51	12	3	40	60	1500
	FWB-31	1.26	1.57	12	3	375	560	
1¼	FWB-30	1.25	1.87	16	4	25	50	1200
	FWB-31	1.57	1.93	16	4	300	450	
1½	FWB-30	1.75	2.20	18	5	20	30	1200
	FWB-31	2.15	2.27	18	5	300	450	
2	FWB-30	2.30	2.75	20	7	15	25	750
	FWB-31	3.02	2.83	20	7	190	285	
2½	FWB-30	2.60	3.23	22	8	10	20	700
	FWB-31	3.32	3.31	22	8	175	265	
3	FWB-30	3.50	3.72	24	12	10	20	650
	FWB-31	4.38	3.80	24	12	165	250	
3½	FWB-30	3.80	4.29	27	14	10	20	625
	FWB-31	4.68	4.37	27	14	155	230	
4	FWB-30	4.20	4.82	32	16	10	20	475
	FWB-31	5.50	4.90	32	16	120	180	
5	FWB-30	6.00	5.96	40	18	10	20	450
	FWB-31	7.93	6.10	40	18	115	175	
6	FWB-30	7.00	7.20	50	20	8	16	325
	FWB-31	8.93	7.36	50	20	80	120	

Refer to page 4 for explanation of pressure ratings. For higher pressure requirements, contact FLEX-WELD, INC.

NOTE: Refer to page 12 for elevated temperature correction factors and live length required for offset or lateral motion. For pulsating or shock pressure applications, consult FLEX-WELD engineers. Larger sizes available on application.

Source: Catalog No. 100A, Flex-Weld, Inc., Bartlett, Illinois.

which their products are indexed and advertised together with those of their competitors. The use of such common catalogs (which are often referred to as trade directories, to distinguish them from publications of sellers) is the result of buyer preference. Space in these volumes is sold to manufacturers much as advertising space is sold. In some instances the printed material in the catalog is supplemented by additional information on microfilm.[8]

Some of the common catalogs limit the products listed to those used in a certain trade or industry. Illustrations of this type are afforded by Reinhold Publishing Corporation's *Chemical Engineering Catalog* and its *Chemical Materials Catalog;*[9] Gulf Publishing Company's *Pipe Line Catalog* and its *Composite Catalog* for the gas and oil drilling-production operator;[10] Pitman Publishing Company's *Food Processing & Marketing;*[11] McGraw-Hill's *Modern Packaging Encyclopedia;* and the specialized catalogs issued by Sweet's Catalog Service, a division of the F. W. Dodge Corporation, such as *Product Design Catalog File, Plant Engineering Catalog File,* and *Industrial Construction Catalog File.*

In contrast with the more specialized catalogs are those which list products and services used by buyers in many trades. Three of these annual trade directories are especially well known. *Sweet's Architectural Catalog File* consists of several bound volumes, the exact number varying from year to year, published by Sweet's Catalog Service. The *Thomas Register of American Manufacturers* is made up of six volumes which contain comprehensive lists of manufacturers arranged alphabetically under 75,000 product classifications and is "consulted 120,000 times a day" by prospective buyers.[12] *MacRae's Blue Book* is a single volume containing a comprehensive list of sources of supply for various types of industrial products.

Since catalogs serve the purpose of representing a company when the salesman is not present, and since they are used frequently as reference guides to desirable sources of supply, their importance in the sale of industrial goods should be evident. No manufacturer should overlook the possibility of using them in formulating his marketing program.[13]

Trade shows. As described in Chapter 11, the trade show or industrial exhibit, perhaps the oldest form of business promotion, is still important today. Sponsored by a single manufacturer, several producers of complementary products, competing manufacturers in a given field, a trade association, or an industrial distributor, the trade show provides buyers an opportunity to become acquainted with and purchase available industrial goods and to obtain technical advice about them. From the point of view of the exhibitor, the industrial show offers a way to discover potential buyers, make sales, uncover new uses for existing products, introduce new products and lines, demonstrate equipment, introduce sales personnel to customers, and even to locate needed personnel.

---

[8] "Industry Starts a Run on Microfilm Banks," *Business Week* (June 17, 1967), pp. 66 ff.

[9] For details, see *Industrial Marketing,* 50 (September 1965), p. 43.

[10] *Industrial Marketing,* 52 (May 1967), p. 137.

[11] *Industrial Marketing,* 51 (November 1966), p. 115.

[12] *Industrial Marketing,* 52 (June 1967), p. 96.

[13] A study by the Industrial Advertising Research Institute covering 300 purchasing agents and engineers of 67 manufacturers and designed "to establish concrete guidelines for creating catalogs that measure up to buyers' needs" revealed that "a well-made catalog is a very persuasive salesman." Other results indicated that the degree of satisfaction for the user depended on the quality of the indexing and format coupled with the completeness of the information. Generic names, prices, and pictorial treatments were only of secondary importance. See "New Critique of Catalogs," *Industrial Marketing,* 52 (March 1967), pp. 70–71.

Figure 13–3 shows the important channel structures for manufactured industrial goods. These can be contrasted with the five major structures for channels of distribution for consumer goods shown in Figure 3–1.

The term "agent middlemen" includes brokers, selling agents, and manufacturers' representatives. Direct sale, Channel No. 1, includes sales made through manufacturers' branch offices. The smallest sales volume occurs through the fourth channel, which is also the least direct, although a substantial number of small manufacturers of light general-purpose equipment do market through this channel. As a general rule, trade channels for industrial products are shorter than channels for consumer products, so that fewer middlemen are involved and direct sale is relatively more impor-

FIGURE 13–3

Major distribution channels for manufactured industrial products and services

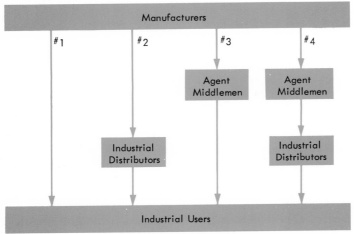

tant. We estimate that over three quarters of all manufactured industrial products move direct from manufacturer to user, or from manufacturer to user through an agent middleman. Less than one quarter of these products is handled by an industrial distributor.

The relative importance of industrial distributors compared to manufacturers' agents is difficult to measure, however, because the distributor adds value by performing the functions of transportation, storage, financing, and some physical production, while agents do not. There is evidence that in the past two decades industrial distributors have increased their importance, particularly in electronics and metals. The percentage increase in sales by these two types of middlemen in selected product lines is shown in Table 13–1.

In metals, the increased importance of imports and specialty steels, continued inflation, labor stoppages in the steel industry, increased fabrication by distributors, and the high cost of money have all contributed to the increased sales of service centers. In electronics, the intense competition and the rapid rate of technological

Marketing: Principles and methods

TABLE 13–1
Percentage increase in sales of industrial middlemen to industrial, commercial, and federal government users, 1962 to 1966

Increase in sales	Industrial distributors	Manufacturers' agents
Sales of all industrial distributors and manufacturers' agents	34.1%	8.9%
SIC 5063 Electrical Apparatus, Equipment, and Supplies	33.4	34.4
SIC 5065 Electronic Parts and Equipment	57.6	28.9
SIC 5084 Industrial Machinery and Equipment	53.5	55.5
SIC 5085 Industrial Supplies	42.6	48.0
SIC 5091 Metals	63.5	36.1

Source: Calculated from *1967 Census of Business,* "Wholesale Trade Sales by Class of Customer."

growth have resulted in rapid change in the channels of distribution employed by manufacturers. Many companies have shifted from indirect to direct channels, while others have shifted from agents to inventory-carrying distributors. The result has been a big increase in sales for distributors of new space-age electronic equipment without a similar increase being enjoyed by distributors of more traditional electrical equipment such as large motors and controls.

Table 13–2 provides current information on the importance of industrial distributors for selected tools, equipment, and supplies. But, despite a trend toward indirect sale for some industrial products, direct sale still predominates in this field. Can you explain why the percentage of precision measuring instruments sold through distributors is so small?

Direct sale

As pointed out in the previous chapter, direct sale to users is an important distribution channel for all kinds of manufactured industrial goods. This method of sale is used especially for heavy machinery and equipment and for products purchased in large quantities such as sheet steel and newsprint; but it is also used by such organizations as the Monsanto Company, a manufacturer of chemicals and related products, which operates agricultural centers in the Midwest to sell its fertilizer, herbicides, and pesticides directly to farmers.

Problems encountered in direct sale. No manufacturer, of course, should undertake a direct-selling program without giving careful consideration to the problems and risks it involves. One of these is finance. Direct sale may involve the establishment of sales branches, organizing and training a larger sales staff than would be necessary otherwise, and extending credit to a large number of buyers. Some small firms that might like to sell direct may find the financial obligations too large and too risky for them to assume. Marketing expense with direct distribution is almost entirely fixed for any time period and does not vary much as sales go up or down. The marketing expense of distributors or agents, in contrast, is only paid, either through the distributors' discount or agents' commission, if the product is sold.

TABLE 13–2
Proportion of selected products purchased from industrial distributors 1965

Product	Percent of buyers purchasing products from distributors in amounts of		
	100%	95–50%	49–1%
Cutting tools and abrasives			
Grinding wheels and coated abrasives	84.8%	6.5%	2.9%
Twist drills, taps, dies, reamers	93.6	2.8	2.1
Carbide, diamond or ceramic tipped tools	88.8	6.6	4.3
Saws (hack, band, circular)	87.1	4.3	1.5
Wire brush wheels, buffers	91.7	0.8	—
Mechanics tools			
Hand tools, vises, files, pipe tools	97.3	1.4	—
Hand precision tools (micrometers, calipers)	87.2	5.6	1.6
Precision measuring, testing equipment, counters	59.7	7.3	8.0
Powered equipment and supplies			
Light production machines (drill presses, bench grinders, etc.)	80.2	5.0	4.1
Portable electric tools	88.5	3.6	4.3
Pneumatic tools	75.5	3.7	6.6
Pipe, tubing, valves and fittings			
Pipe, tubing and fittings—metal	85.5	4.4	5.8
Pipe, tubing, valves, fittings—plastic	89.8	—	—
Valves—metal	86.8	2.4	4.7
Packing and gaskets	65.0	—	—
Steam traps, regulators, separators	81.1	3.7	2.7
Pneumatic, hydraulic equipment and supplies			
Pumps and compressors	51.9	10.4	5.1
Power cylinders, controls, accessories	59.0	8.0	7.0
Power transmission equipment			
Chain and sprockets	70.6	17.4	6.4
Clutches, brakes, coupling, speed reducers	66.1	16.9	2.4
Flat belts and drives, pulleys	80.0	10.0	5.8
Stock gears and gear drives	66.7	12.5	7.5
V-belts and drives, sheaves	82.8	10.0	2.1
Bearings			
Anti-friction (ball, roller, needle)	81.2	6.0	5.3
Plain bearings, bearing metals and plastics	81.3	3.2	6.2
Pillow blocks and flange units	84.0	5.9	5.0
Retaining rings and seals	80.8	5.6	2.4

Even if the financial problem can be met, selling direct involves more managerial problems than can be successfully handled by many companies. Managers of some firms are better producers than marketers; they can produce first-rate goods, but they lack the ability to formulate and carry out an effective direct-selling program. They are unwilling to devote the time and attention required to solve the problems of training a large sales staff or choosing effective sales promotional methods and of providing adequate service facilities. Although some manufacturers attempt to minimize these managerial problems through the purchase of established distributors, others prefer to rely on sale through independent distributors.

The decision as to whether or not to establish sales branches is frequently a most difficult one for the direct-selling manufacturer. For the company with extensive sales

TABLE 13–2 (continued)

Product	Percent of buyers purchasing products from distributors in amounts of		
	100%	95–50%	49–1%
Materials handling equipment			
Hoists (electric, air, hand)..77.9		6.2	4.5
Floor and hand trucks, casters and wheels................76.5		4.8	5.3
Slings, wire rope and chain....................................77.0		3.6	4.5
Jacks, benders and movers (air, hydraulic, and hand)..91.2		1.1	2.2
Industrial rubber products			
Rubber hose, couplings, assemblies 86.4		5.8	2.8
Conveyor belting 71.3		11.7	6.4
Mats and molded rubber products 65.3		7.0	5.0
Metals			
Metals—ferrous (bars, rods, sheets, shapes)...............68.4		9.0	12.8
Metal—nonferrous (bars, rods, sheets, shapes)...........67.0		9.1	6.7
Flat ground stock, tool steel..................................84.2		5.6	3.8
Fasteners			
Bolts, nuts, screws, washers, rivets.........................79.0		9.1	7.7
Cap and socket screws...83.4		8.0	4.3
Electrical and electronic equipment			
Motors..51.1		13.4	12.8
Lamps (incandescent and fluorescent)......................83.8		2.1	4.0
Motor starters and controls...................................65.0		12.4	6.5
Safety equipment			
Fire extinguishers..93.0		2.8	0.7
Safety clothing, gloves, goggles.............................82.7		4.9	4.2
Protective coatings and paint			
Paints, coatings and epoxies..................................42.2		10.7	10.7
Painting equipment (sprays, brushes)......................80.7		4.3	4.3
Maintenance and production equipment and supplies			
Lubricating equipment and devices.........................73.4		6.7	3.6
Lubricants, oils, greases, coolants 41.8		6.2	6.9
Unit heaters, fans, ventilators, dust collectors............64.7		9.1	7.6
Industrial tapes and adhesives................................83.5		4.4	4.3
Welding equipment and supplies............................82.9		9.3	2.1
Steel shop equipment (shelving, bins, benches, slotted angle) 85.3		4.6	1.6

Source: "How Much Do Buyers Buy from Distributors?" *Industrial Distribution,* 56 (May 1966), p. 44.

operations, branches offer a means of decentralizing the supervision of the sales staff as well as many other functions. More specifically, the manufacturer may expect his sales branches to aid his direct-selling staff in such ways as (1) providing a field headquarters, (2) allowing quicker delivery of merchandise than is possible from the factory, and (3) serving as points from which quick repair and maintenance service may be rendered. These advantages, however, will not be realized without a significant financial outlay for buildings, equipment, and investment in inventory, and the managerial problem is increased. Such branches often are not necessary, especially for industrial products with a relatively low weight in relation to their value, because rapid delivery by air makes it possible to serve the entire country from a single shipping point. One-day delivery is possible, often with a net saving compared with the cost of running the older field-warehouse system.

The manufacturer should also consider the cost of direct sale as compared with indirect channels of distribution. The costs of performing selling, transportation, storage, financing, risk-taking, and promotion functions will differ among alternative channel structures. For selling alone, the cost of maintaining a field sales force has increased rapidly in recent decades—at a rate of 10 percent per year since the mid-fifties. Today, the average cost of an industrial sales call is over $55.[14] Because most direct selling expense is fixed, sales per salesman must be high to absorb these costs. When they are not, independent middlemen offer definite advantages.

Finally, even if satisfactory solutions to these problems can be found, there remains the task of maintaining favorable relationships with those distributors the company plans to retain.

Agent middlemen

Many manufacturers, particularly smaller ones whose finances are limited and whose customers are scattered, seek the assistance of various types of agent middlemen in the marketing of their products. These agent middlemen assist the manufacturer by locating buyers, negotiating sales, and furnishing marketing information. Their compensation usually is in the form of fees or commissions based upon either the dollar amount of the transaction or the number of units sold. While *brokers* and *selling agents* are used to market industrial goods, the most important agent middleman is the *manufacturers' representative,* which is discussed in detail below.

Brokers are commonly used in the sale of used plants, machinery, and equipment. Selling agents are often used by small producers of standardized products such as small coal mining companies, lumber mills, and chemical companies. They have filled a continuously important role in the textile field.

Using more than one channel

Although direct sale is the dominant channel in the marketing of manufactured industrial goods, many producers find it advisable to use a combination of channels. They sell direct to large industrial users when such action seems desirable from the point of view of the costs involved and customers' preferences. They use agent middlemen and industrial distributors advantageously in areas where potential customers are scattered and the cost of reaching them through salesmen from the main office or from sales offices or branches is prohibitive. The manufacturer's problem, therefore, becomes one of determining the conditions and circumstances under which he will sell direct, use industrial distributors, use agent middlemen, or use some combination of these methods.

Selling to industrial users and ultimate consumers. Many manufacturers of industrial goods find that their products are also in demand as consumer goods. A manufacturer of pumps may produce one model for large industrial companies and smaller models for household use. An electrical manufacturer may produce everything from electric bulbs to turbogenerating plants. Flour is sold to both bakers and

---

[14] D. M. Phelps and J. H. Westing, *Marketing Management* (Homewood, Ill.: Richard D. Irwin, Inc., 1968), p. 824, and H. H. Hoffman, "U.S. Steel Takes Another Look at Harnischfeger," *Industrial Marketing,* 54 (July 1969), p. 49.

Marketing: Principles and methods

household users; automobile batteries and tires to both automobile manufacturers and owners. Grocery manufacturers find an industrial, institutional, restaurant, and government market, as well as the home. And in recent years the diversification programs of various companies involving both industrial and consumer goods have created new marketing problems for them, as is illustrated by the experience of the Norton Company.[15] A long-time producer of industrial goods, Norton acquired the National Research Corporation to gain new products—and then found it necessary to organize a separate division to market its first creation, the NRC Space Blanket, a protective covering for outdoorsmen. It had never made a consumers product before. Under

FIGURE 13–4
Marketing channels of paper manufacturer selling to industrial and household consumers

Industrial channels of distribution

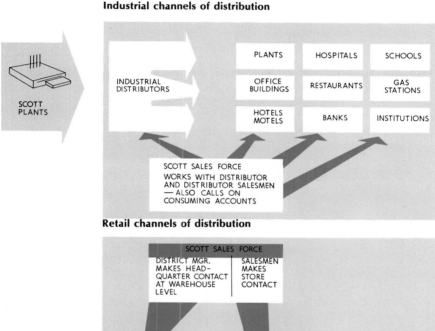

Retail channels of distribution

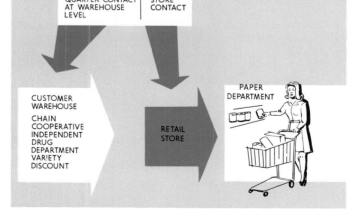

Source: *A Marketing Career with the Scott Paper Company* (Philadelphia, n.d.), pp. 22–23, 30–31.

---

[15] See "Norton Gives Itself a Selling Lesson," *Business Week,* January 8, 1966, p. 70.

the foregoing and similar circumstances, the manufacturer faces the problem of organizing his marketing system to reach both markets with a minimum degree of conflict.

Where the products are quite distinct, are sold in different markets, and call for different sales appeals or for different advertising methods, it is desirable to segregate the sales department into an industrial goods division and a consumer goods division. The need for technical knowledge and for an understanding of actual operating problems in selling to the industrial market requires salesmen of a different type than for consumer goods. Segregation of the sales force is more effective as well as less costly because it permits the better trained and higher paid men to be used in the particular segments of the market they are best qualified to serve.

The channels of distribution used by the Scott Paper Company to reach both household consumers and industrial users are shown in Figure 13–4. Separate directors for retail marketing and industrial marketing report to the marketing vice president. Figure 13–5 portrays the channels used by a large electrical manufacturer in cultivating these two markets.

FIGURE 13–5
Marketing channels of electrical manufacturer selling to industrial and consumer products markets

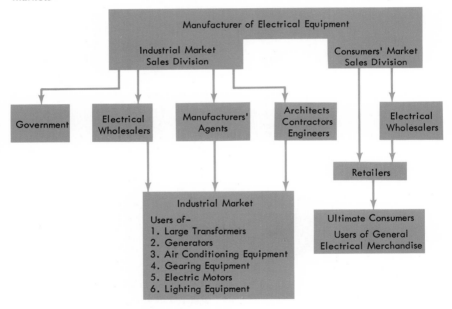

IMPORTANT MIDDLEMEN IN THE MARKETING OF INDUSTRIAL PRODUCTS

The industrial distributor[16]

Despite the importance of direct sale in the marketing of industrial goods, certain middlemen—particularly the industrial distributor are of considerable significance in

[16] For a comprehensive discussion of the industrial distributor, see T. N. Beckman, N. H. Engle, and R. D. Buzzell, *Wholesaling: Principles and Practice* (3d ed.; New York: Ronald Press Co., 1959), pp. 151–64.

Marketing: Principles and methods

this field. The term "industrial distributor" is commonly used to cover all merchant wholesalers selling to industrial and commercial users and performing all marketing functions, particularly stocking. Examples are mill supply houses, cutting tool distributors, machine tool distributors, oil well supply houses, and steel service centers. These merchants purchase goods outright from manufacturers, store them until needed by their customers, and sell to industrial users. Their counterpart in the consumer goods field is the regular service wholesaler; but whereas the latter sells to retailers for distribution to consumers, the former sells directly to users, who generally purchase in rather large quantities.

To serve their customers most effectively, industrial distributors are located mainly in geographical areas having a high concentration of industrial establishments such as California, Illinois, New York, Ohio, and Texas. Thus 53 percent of the chemical supply houses, selling 55 percent of the total volume, are located in five states; and 56 percent of the firms selling construction machinery and handling 65 percent of total volume are in seven states.[17] In other fields the situation is similar.

Basic types of distributor operations. Many industrial distributors have established their businesses since World War II, and both old and new firms have adapted their lines and services to the changing needs of customers. A comprehensive survey of these middlemen by *Industrial Distribution* magazine revealed that more than 60 percent of them started business after 1945 and that about 20 percent have been in business a decade or less. Three basic types of distributor operations were identified: general-line distributors, comprising 18 percent of the total; specialists, 61 percent; and combination houses, 19 percent. As the name indicates, the general-line distributor carries a broad assortment of items in a number of related lines. The specialist handles a limited number of related products such as power transmission or electronic items, whereas the combination house deals in a broader line (electrical or hardware, for example) or carries on a retail business as well.

The "average" distributor. It is difficult to describe an "average" industrial distributor since they vary in type, sales size, number of employees, and geographic coverage. However, a 1968 survey of industrial distributors found that the median firm employs four outside salesmen and does about 23 percent of its business through inside telephone salesmen. The average invoice carries a value of $72, and stock turns over four times per year. Each outside salesman makes an average of seven calls per day servicing 125 accounts and generating $300,000 in business annually.[18]

While the average distributor is a business of moderate size, as in most of the businesses we have studied the bulk of the business is concentrated among the larger firms. For instance, although there are just 91 distributors of electrical supplies and apparatus (27 percent of all) with annual sales in excess of $2 million, these firms do 72 percent of all the business.[19]

Table 13–3 gives an aggregate picture of the major types of industrial distributors. The product lines most frequently carried by the industrial suppliers in the table are maintenance and repair items, cutting tools and abrasives, bearings, rubber and plastic products, and fasteners.

---

[17] R. S. Alexander, J. S. Cross, and R. M. Hill, *Industrial Marketing* (3d ed.; Homewood, Ill.: Richard D. Irwin, Inc., 1967), p. 221.

[18] Industrial Distribution, *The 1968 Census of Industrial Distribution* (New York: McGraw-Hill Book Co., Inc., 1968). A follow-up survey by *Industrial Distribution* in 1969 indicated that the number of salesmen, volume per salesman, and stock turn have increased since the 1968 study.

[19] Alexander, Cross, and Hill, *Industrial Marketing,* pp. 223–24.

TABLE 13–3
Statistics of important types of industrial distributors

SIC number and type of distributor	Number of establishments	Sales (in millions)	Inventory, end of year, at cost (in millions)	Operating expenses (percent of sales)	Percentage distribution of sales		
					To industrial and commercial users	To federal government	For export
5063. Electrical apparatus, equipment and supplies	4,961	$5,695	$ 652	13.8	75.0	2.9	.9
5065. Electronic parts and equipment	4,116	3,209	341	20.6	48.1	4.6	9.6
5081. Commercial machinery and equipment	5,931	1,929	241	25.6	65.9	3.0	1.6
5082. Construction, mining machinery and equipment	3,022	3,652	937	18.7	87.9	1.4	2.5
5084. Industrial machinery and equipment							
Food processing	440	257	24	18.7	55.8	1.0	5.6
General-purpose industrial	1,682	1,046	152	91.8	60.3	2.5	4.8
Metalworking	1,173	1,107	121	16.2	86.3	2.9	1.4
Materials handling	1,061	709	88	22.9	78.0	2.4	.7
Oil well, oil refining, pipeline	1,746	1,477	177	11.8	79.8	.3	9.3
Other industrial	2,693	1,507	210	21.0	74.7	1.1	6.5
5085. Industrial supplies	7,658	5,198	679	20.2	76.7	2.0	1.9
5086. Professional equipment and supplies ...	4,633	2,893	388	22.7	72.9	3.0	1.8
Part 5091. Metals service centers	2,659	7,875	1,296	14.5	71.6	1.1	3.3

Source: 1967 Census of Business, Vol. IV, Wholesale Trade: Area Statistics (Washington, D.C.: Government Printing Office, 1970).

Services of the industrial distributor. The industrial distributor provides services to the manufacturer as well as to the buyer.

1. *To the manufacturer.* The industrial distributor generally performs the same functions for the manufacturer of industrial products that the regular wholesaler does for the producer of consumer products; he is the "service wholesaler" of industrial products. It should be kept in mind that the distributor is most successful in selling to the small plant, where buying volume is too low to be attractive to the direct-selling manufacturer, and that, as plant size goes up, the distributor's advantages go down.

Because he handles fewer lines and items than does the service wholesaler of consumer products, and because industrial products are usually purchased with greater deliberation than are consumer products, the industrial distributor becomes more familiar with each product and gives it greater attention. He provides the manufacturer with a staff of salesmen who cover their territories at frequent intervals and are in close touch with the needs of their customers and prospects. Since the distributor is a "local" institution, he may have knowledge as to those individuals in the buyers' plants who exert the greatest influence on purchases. Moreover, he is able to gather suggestions for improving products and pass them on to the manufacturer.

Distributors perform a useful service to manufacturers by storing products at strategic locations and making them available on short notice to customers. In recent years, with technology contributing to the number and variety of products as well as to better facilities for handling them, this warehousing function has increased in importance.[20] Distributors also cover the markets in which customers and prospects are scattered and, because they represent a number of lines, they can do so at a cost often much lower than if the manufacturer sold direct. In addition, they may render financial assistance to the manufacturer by paying for products in advance of resale, reduce his credit losses (because his accounts are fewer and of better quality), handle his adjustments and complaints, and contribute local prestige to the products they handle. Finally, they serve as "service stations" for the manufacturer's product, since they maintain a stock of repair parts and are usually staffed to supervise installations, especially minor ones.

2. *To the buyer.* Some buyers of industrial products prefer to buy through middlemen who handle the products of many manufacturers because of the assortment they offer and the service they provide. This preference has been indicated by the figures given in this chapter concerning their share of purchases from industrial distributors (Table 13–2). Buyers prefer the services of industrial distributors because:

1. Being able to buy many kinds of items on one order or by interviewing one salesman improves communication between buyer and seller, reduces the number of purchase orders and invoices written, and saves the buyer's time.
2. They provide an economical source of supply for small buyers, since the distributor buys in relatively large quantities and achieves transportation economies, as compared with the small buyer who purchases directly from a distant manufacturer.
3. They secure quicker delivery, especially important in emergency, and store-door service.
4. They make possible small-quantity buying, thus reducing the buyer's need of

---

[20] A special report by *Industrial Distribution* entitled "Warehousing with the Experts" explains the essential factors involved in the planning of suitable storage facilities and presents three case histories as illustrations. See the issue of April 1967, pp. 37–74.

storage space and avoiding tying up funds. This probably accounts for much of the growth of industrial distributors since the mid-1960s.

5. Repair parts can be obtained speedily so as to avoid shutdowns.
6. Nearby technical services and product information are available.
7. Complaints are settled more easily because buyer and seller are located close enough together that personal contact is possible.
8. There is a double guarantee of products, by the manufacturer and by the distributor.
9. Easier and quicker credit approval is possible, since buyer and seller know each other.
10. They provide a good source of market information.

Some limitations of the industrial distributor. Not all buyers of industrial goods agree as to the importance of the industrial distributor. Probably the chief drawback to selling through distributors is the preference of many users for buying directly from the producer. Most large industrial users refuse to buy in any other way. Because of their financial strength, ample storage facilities, and bargaining power, they can insist upon the lower prices that direct quantity buying usually affords. Since buyers of major installations of equipment, for example, arrive at decisions to purchase only after long negotiations, distributors are usually not prepared to make the detailed investigations and recommendations which precede the decision to purchase. Furthermore, some manufacturers are dissatisfied with the type and number of services they receive from distributors and therefore sell directly, even though their costs are higher. Conversely, many distributors are not pleased with the services they obtain from the manufacturer. Effective results from both points of view, of course, can be secured only when there is a clear understanding and fulfillment of the responsibilities and obligations on the part of each. Certainly, the manufacturer cannot expect satisfactory results from industrial distributors unless they are selected carefully, given assistance through advertising and a sales personnel training program, and offered an adequate financial incentive to "push" the manufacturer's product.

Manufacturers' representatives

The prime function of the manufacturers' representative is to sell the noncompetitive products of several manufacturers in the allotted territory and under the conditions prescribed. Some of them also store goods from which deliveries are made. They are usually paid on a commission basis, normally from 10 to 15 percent of sales, although there are instances in which as little as 5 percent or as much as 25 percent is paid.

In 1967 there were approximately 10,000 manufacturers' agents in the United States selling industrial goods, and their sales totaled over $12 billion.[21] Although exact data are not available, some years ago it was estimated that they sold two or three times as much industrial goods as consumer goods.[22] Table 13–4 shows the importance of manufacturers' representatives in marketing specific classes of industrial products. In total, over half of the manufacturers selling to industrial users employ agents to some extent.

---

[21] U.S. Bureau of the Census, *1967 Census of Business, Vol. IV, Wholesale Trade: Summary Statistics* (Washington, D.C.: Government Printing Office, 1970).

[22] T. H. Staudt, *The Manufacturers' Agent as a Marketing Institution* (Washington, D.C.: Bureau of the Census, 1952), p. 34.

TABLE 13–4
Number and sales of manufacturers' agents and brokers selling industrial products

SIC number and type of business	Number of establishments	Sales (in millions)
5029. Chemicals and allied products.................................	470	$ 757
5063. Electrical apparatus, equipment and supplies...............1,030		1,242
5065. Electronic parts and equipment................................1,315		1,977
5081. Commercial machinery and equipment......................	610	288
5082. Construction and mining machinery and equipment......	170	192
5083. Farm machinery and equipment	106	114
5084. Industrial machinery and equipment.........................2,193		2,482
5085. Industrial supplies...1,122		1,037
5086. Professional equipment and supplies.........................	283	223
5087. Service establishment equipment and supplies.............	327	362
5088. Transportation equipment, excluding motor vehicles ..... Part	281	462
5091. Metal sales..	746	1,995
5092. Petroleum and petroleum products........................... Part	282	482
5096. Industrial and personal service paper........................	285	434
Totals	9,220	$12,047

Source: *1967 Census of Business*, Vol. IV, *Wholesale Trade: Area Statistics* (Washington, D.C.: Government Printing Office, 1970).

Why manufacturers' representatives are used. One manufacturer who relies entirely on manufacturers' representatives justifies this policy in these words:

Our main reason for using reps is simply that they have demonstrated their superior ability to sell. A salesman on a company payroll with a salary, or salary and commission arrangement, is not as "hungry" as is a straight commission man. Where the company salesman will tend to coast, the rep will push harder, no matter how many units he has already sold. Our reps work strictly on commission, and either they sell or they don't eat. This is not just a hardnose attitude. It is good business, and furthermore, it helps us select the right persons to represent us in today's highly competitive markets. The man who wants to make the most money actually prefers to sell on commission because this places no limit on his income. He is not complacent enough to want a salary.[23]

The major services manufacturers' representatives can supply for the producers of industrial products are as follows:

1) They usually have a thorough knowledge of the territories in which they operate and of the users and potential users of the manufacturers' products located therein. They often know personally the executives who influence the purchase of goods in the firms upon whom they call, which ensures a fair, and perhaps preferred, presentation for the manufacturer.

2) They are generally, through the technical knowledge they possess, equipped to provide adequate demonstrations of the products they sell. They are also prepared to render sales engineering services of various kinds which are necessary for the choice of the product best adapted to the purchasers' needs.

---

[23] Statement of R. B. Bunn, general manager of B. H. Bunn Co., Chicago, which distributes its package-tying machines in the United States and many foreign markets through 75 manufacturers' agents. See "Why We Like Reps," *Industrial Marketing,* 47 (February 1962), pp. 85–86.

13 / Marketing manufactured industrial products

3) Since they handle far fewer products than do salesmen of industrial distributors, they are in a position to "push" the lines they do handle. Thus the manufacturers' agent may sell a dozen or so lines, whereas the large industrial distributor may have several hundred made up of 10,000 to 60,000 specific items.

4) They provide a highly flexible method of selling, since they may be used to contact industrial consumers, to supplement a direct-selling organization, or to work with mill supply houses and other types of distributors.

5) They enable the manufacturer to effect savings in his selling expense, especially in areas where his markets are "thin." Since they usually solicit orders for a number of noncompeting manufacturers, they spread their costs over several products, thus reducing the expense per unit sold. Furthermore, because they are commonly paid on a commission basis, the manufacturers incur selling expense only when sales are made.

6) They provide a way for a manufacturer to enter a market that is new to him.

7) They are capable of providing manufacturers with an excellent source of market information.

Some limitations of manufacturers' representatives. As compared with building his own sales organization, the manufacturer using agents gives up direct control of the sales personnel selling his products. In practice, less promotional work and developmental selling may be carried on. If the buyer purchases in small amounts, the cost of delivery from the factory may be relatively high. In some instances the manufacturers' agent may even represent competing producers. For these and other reasons, the manufacturer frequently decides to utilize manufacturers' representatives in those areas where consideration of cost; difficulty of control; selecting, training, compensating salesmen; and similar factors make it inadvisable to sell direct, even though elsewhere he uses his own sales branches. Where the problems involved in the maintenance of his own sales organization result in costs and difficulties out of proportion to the results likely to be obtained, the manufacturer may use manufacturers' representatives.

Part of the difficulty some manufacturers have experienced with manufacturers' representatives may be attributed to their own unwillingness to recognize the changing status of this middleman. One observer notes, for instance, that "unfortunately, today's company sales managers do not fully understand the operation of a manufacturers' representative organization. Their concept is outdated."[24] He recommends personal attention to the individual salesmen of the agent's organization as a method of motivating them to greater efforts on behalf of the particular manufacturer's products.

If a manufacturers' representative is very successful, he can work himself out of a job. When a market becomes a big one, the manufacturer usually finds he can give better service and achieve better communications at a lower cost by selling direct.

A few manufacturers have gone even further to strengthen their own sales organizations. After using agents originally to build distribution for their products, they have sought more control over selling activities by absorbing the former representatives into their own organization. An illustration of a firm taking this step is afforded by the Hewlett-Packard Company, producers of precision electronic instruments. After 23 years of selling its products through manufacturers' representatives, they entered upon a program of acquiring these agents—and results have justified the move.

---

[24] Vito Dipalo, "Putting the Mfg's Rep on the Company Team," *Industrial Marketing,* 52 (March 1967), p. 72. Also see W. F. Baker, "How to Get a Good Sales Rep . . . and Keep Him," *Industrial Marketing,* 52 (August 1967), pp. 68–70.

SELLING TO GOVERNMENT

Taken as a group, government buyers represent by far the largest customer for the industrial market. The performance of marketing functions in selling to government has a number of characteristics which make it unique.

Market segments

While one might expect the purchases of different cities and states to show considerable differences, the needs of government units at the same level and function are quite similar. Many of these purchases are also influenced by programs supported at the federal level.

Organizationally, too, buying procedures show similarities across jurisdictions. Rigid procedures and extensive clerical activity are more important than short-run efficiency in purchasing because of statutory requirements aimed at achieving other public policy objectives and protecting the public's funds. Procedures are also complicated because purchasing functions often report to multiple elected authorities such as city councils.

The relative importance of various government market segments to the producer of manufactured industrial goods is shown in Table 13–5. The dominance of the U.S. Department of Defense is striking. It is so important and so unique that many of the points made here apply only to defense procurement, but this should not be interpreted as meaning that other government buying is simple or not important.

TABLE 13–5
Relative importance of selected agencies in government purchases of goods and outside services, 1967 (percent)

Federal government, including purchases made through prime contractors:	
Department of Defense	45
NASA	3
Atomic Energy Commission	2
HEW, Development of Health Resources	2
Postal Service	1
General Services Administration	1
State and local government, including purchases made from federal grants:	
Education	18
Highways	6
Mass Transit	2
Housing and Community Development	2
All other	18
	100

Source: Authors' estimates from U.S. Executive Office of the President: *The Budget of the United States Government, Fiscal Year 1972* and *Economic Report of the President* (Washington, D.C.: Government Printing Office, 1971).

General-purpose needs for the federal government are purchased by the Federal Supply Service of the General Services Administration (GSA). Unique needs are purchased by the purchasing offices of departments and independent agencies. In either case, almost all purchase decisions are made on the basis of open competitive bidding. With expensive formal procedures and competitive bidding, the government requires considerably more lead time than industry to make a purchase decision. The result is that government must carry higher safety stocks.

A seller can obtain information on purchasing procedures from GSA or the agency concerned. A useful place to begin is with the *U.S. Government Organization Manual,* which is revised annually.

Within the Department of Defense, the Defense Supply Agency is responsible for direct purchases. It also coordinates the purchase activities of the three services. The organization of the actual contracting function differs by branch of service. The Army uses a decentralized system; the Air Force, on the other hand, centralizes its procurement in the Air Materiel Command at Dayton, Ohio.

Geographic concentration

A federal agency located outside of Washington, D.C., can often procure a standard item from a local dealer under a contract previously negotiated by the GSA in Washington. Thus even when procurement is local, the purchase decision is often made in Washington. The same is true with defense spending, in which government contracts produce income for all the states based on decisions made in Washington. California, for example, receives the largest share of defense business; the economic impact of defense spending on California is more than double that reported for New York, the second leading state. In California the greater importance is in subcontracts rather than prime contracts, reflecting the tendency for suppliers to cluster around major industrial buyers.

One buyer and few sellers

While the standard operating supplies purchased by the General Services Administration do not differ in any major way from the supplies purchased by private commercial organizations, the needs of the Defense Department are unique. There is only one buyer, and the technology required for production has developed as the specialty of just a few sellers. Such technological specialization often provides the seller with a virtual monopoly. The market structure for this situation (one buyer and one seller) is called "bilateral monopoly," in which competition is replaced by bargaining between the two parties. The classical economic guarantee provided by the price mechanism of a free, competitive market structure is often totally lacking. Nonetheless, the government has established policies that cause it to rely on private industry to provide these defense requirements. It must then bargain to try to achieve a "fair" price for the products it buys.

Emphasis on research and development

A major portion of such defense procurement is in items where the arms race forces the government to buy at the forefront of technological advance. In addition, there is a public policy of government support for important basic research that appears to be in the public interest but cannot be justified by its private market potential. For example, the National Science Foundation has dedicated its efforts almost entirely to basic research which is in the long-run public interest. In 1969, government paid 45 percent of industry's research and development bill. This figure

---

[25] "R & D Spending Shoots for a 7% Gain," *Business Week,* May 23, 1970, p. 102.

is expected to drop to 37 percent in a few years.[25] From the supplier's point of view, this advanced technology greatly increases the risk that can result from a fixed-price contract bid.[26] The government has been trying unsuccessfully since World War II to find a procurement procedure which will solve the problems for both buyer and seller that have resulted from the situation.

Importance of subcontracting

One way for a seller to avoid at least a part of the problems of selling to the government is to seek subcontract work wherein the prime contractors are the defense specialists. This practice spreads some of the risk and avoids some of the government red tape because the subcontractor is dealing most directly with another firm and has responsibility for only a part of the total system being purchased by the government. Often a subcontractor can actually gain considerable profit advantage over his prime contractor. Because of the very large size of some government systems procurements, subcontracting is a common practice.

Government authority to audit and renegotiate

Because of the absence of market forces and the presence of high-risk technology, the government has the authority to audit, through the General Accounting Office, the books of contractors for some fixed-price and all cost-type contracts. When unauthorized costs have been charged to the contract by the supplier, the government has the authority to void or renegotiate the contract. The 1951 Renegotiation Act applies to contracts and subcontracts with the Department of Defense, the Armed Services, NASA, GSA, and the Maritime Commission. The government can, and regularly does, recover "excess profits" from contracts covered by the act.

Advertised versus negotiated contracts

Government purchases are made on one of two procedures: advertised bidding or negotiation. Formal advertising is used to purchase most standardized goods and services but is not popular in defense contracting. The 1947 Armed Services Procurement Act requires that advertised bidding be used and that "award be made to that responsible bidder whose bid, conforming to the invitation for bids, is most advantageous to the government, price and other factors considered." Examples of "other considerations" are directing some purchases to small business or distressed labor areas. All price information on advertised bids is public information and is useful to competitors in planning their bidding strategy for the next invitation to bid.

The law states 17 reasons for exemptions from competitive bidding, but negotiation is usually permitted in just three circumstances: (1) specialized supplies and investment or extended periods of preparation are required; (2) experimental, developmental, or research work is called for, or (3) there is an insufficient number of suppliers to respond to a request for advertised bids. Purchases of major weapon systems, like the Antiballistic Missile System, usually qualify for negotiated contracts for more than one of these reasons. Selection in such cases is more likely to be made on the basis of technical and managerial competence than price.

---

[26] For an insightful analysis of this problem, see H. D. Drake, "Major DOD Procurements at War with Reality," *Harvard Business Review* 48 (January–February 1970), pp. 119–40.

Marketing implications

Under advertised procurement or negotiated contracts the government buyer clearly does not have the same degree of freedom in selecting suppliers as does his industrial counterpart. In advertised bids, the freedom of information and constraints of other government policies restrict the buyers' freedom. In negotiated contracts, the shortage of suppliers is often the limiting feature. These and other unique features have caused companies interested in this business to set up specialized departments or even subsidiary companies to market to government.

The largest contractors to the Department of Defense clearly specialize in government business (see Table 13–6), but these companies are the exception, not the rule. Many companies sell to government. Because of the special nature of the customer, most of these sales are direct. Of the 100 largest Department of Defense contractors, all but 9 appear on the list of *Fortune's* 500 largest companies. The share of business from government for the 100 largest is about one third of their total volume.[27] As

TABLE 13–6
Large defense contractors, 1967

Company	Rank in DOD contracts*	Rank in Fortune's 500	DOD contracting, percentage of total sales*
McDonnell Douglas	1	16	72
General Dynamics	2	32	82
Lockheed Aircraft	3	30	77
General Electric	4	4	17
United Aircraft	5	33	50
Boeing	6	19	32
North American Rockwell	7	28	28

*Does not include NASA or other government agencies.
Source: A. E. Lieberman, "Updating Impressions of the Military-Industrial Complex," *California Management Review,* 11 (Summer 1969), p. 61.

the 1971 experience of Lockheed Aircraft Company suggests, the return on investment in the 100 largest firms with a balanced customer mix is greater than the return on investment of those with a very high percentage of government business. This lower return on investment occurs despite the fact that government contractors often receive capital equipment from the government and have government support for their research and development expenditures.[28]

The marketing department of a major government contractor will differ significantly from that of other firms selling in the industrial market. For one thing, selling is given another name, such as "program management" or "applications engineering." The chief tasks of such departments are to keep communications open with government influentials and to prepare proposals and presentations for their consideration. Another difference is the importance of the contract administration group,

[27] A. E. Lieberman, "Updating Impressions of the Military-Industrial Complex," *California Management Review,* 11 (Summer 1969), pp. 51–62.

[28] For a detailed discussion, see R. J. Levine, "Defense Jobs Tied to Capital Outlays," *The Wall Street Journal,* January 10, 1972.

which is a marketing liaison function between the government and engineering and production.

One final difference is that, since advertising is not an allowable contract expense, the advertising and promotion done by government contractors is treated as public or employee relations. This diffusion of marketing has presented many problems for government-oriented companies. They seem not to have the ability to organize a marketing effort which is effective in competing in normal industrial or consumer markets. Whether such firms can survive in periods of declining defense budgets is an interesting question.

SUMMARY

In reviewing the marketing system for industrial products, particularly those that are manufactured, it is useful to contrast its features with the system used by manufacturers to sell consumer products.

There are three functions in the marketing of manufactured industrial products that are unique: product servicing, financing by leasing, and information and promotion.

Short, direct channels of distribution are the most important in industrial marketing. Some manufacturers, however, elect to be represented by independent agents rather than to establish their own sales force. In this way they reduce the risk of high fixed costs, since agents' commissions are only paid if a sale is made.

Selling through industrial distributors has the same effect, but the chief reason for using this important type of middleman institution is because the allocating and assorting processes and many marketing functions that industrial users desire can be performed more efficiently by the distributor than by the manufacturer. A manufacturer must sometimes use more than one type of channel structure to serve all his markets in the most efficient manner.

The final section of this chapter described the structure and institutions in the marketing system serving the government market.

REVIEW AND DISCUSSION QUESTIONS

1. What are the main channels of distribution for manufactured industrial products?

2. Account for the widespread use of direct sale in the marketing of industrial products.

3. "No manufacturer should undertake a direct-selling program without giving careful consideration to the problems and risks it involves." What are some of these problems and risks, and how can they best be handled by the manufacturer?

4. Define the term "industrial distributor" in your own words. Visit an industrial distributor in your area (provided one is located nearby) and ask him to describe his activities. Upon the basis of this interview, what changes, if any, would you make in your definition?

5. Summarize the major services the industrial distributor performs (a) for the manufacturer and (b) for his customers.

6. Table 13–1 shows that the sales of manufacturers' representatives to industrial users from 1962 to 1966 increased only 8.9 percent. From data in the *1967 Census of Business,* determine the percentage increase in sales of manufacturers' agents to wholesalers.

7. How do you explain the growing reliance placed on catalogs by industrial buyers?

8. Prepare a paper of some 1,500 words on the topic "Current Developments in the Leasing

of Electronic Data Processing Equipment." (With the approval of the instructor, some other type of equipment may be chosen.)

9. Discuss the merits and limitations of using manufacturers' agents (or representatives) from the point of view of the manufacturer.

10. Prepare a short paper (800–1,000 words) on the topic: "The Manufacturers' Representative: His Present and Probable Future in the Marketing of Manufactured Industrial Goods."

11. Under what conditions is it advisable for the manufacturer of industrial goods to use more than one, or a combination of, trade channels? Illustrate with specific examples obtained from outside reading.

12. Assume that you are a manufacturer of diesel engines for trucks. Point out the possible channels of distribution you might use, and discuss the relative merits of each.

13. Explain briefly the advantages a manufacturer of a product in demand both by industrial users and ultimate consumers might gain from the segregation of his sales force according to the market.

14. List the ways in which the government market differs from other industrial goods markets.

15. For each marketing function, write a brief paragraph describing how and where each is performed in the channels of distribution for Defense Department contracts.

SUPPLEMENTARY READINGS

The reader should also consult the readings listed at the end of Chapters 12 and 19.

Beckman, T. N.; Engle, N. H.; and Buzzell, R. D. *Wholesaling: Principles and Practice,* chap. 9, "The Industrial Distributor." 3d ed. New York: Ronald Press Co., 1959. The chapter cited from this basic book on wholesaling will be of special interest.

Diamond, W. T. *Distribution Channels for Industrial Goods.* Columbus: The Ohio State University, Bureau of Business Research, 1964. The author reports on his questionnaire investigation of the channels used and the margins allowed distributors by manufacturers.

Dodge, H. R. *Industrial Marketing.* New York: McGraw-Hill Book Co., 1970. This is the newest text on the subject. Chapter 17 is on defense marketing.

Drake, H. D. "Major DOD Procurements at War with Reality." *Harvard Business Review,* 48 (January–February 1970), pp. 119–40. An excellent analysis of current procurement problems.

England, W. B. *Procurement Management: Principles and Cases.* 5th ed. Homewood, Ill.: Richard D. Irwin, Inc., 1970. In an outstanding text and casebook in this field, the author covers all aspects of industrial procurement.

Industrial Distribution *The 1968 Census of Industrial Distribution.* New York: McGraw-Hill Book Co., Inc., 1968. The most complete statistics on industrial distributors broken down into meaningful product lines.

Lee, Lemar, Jr. and Dobler, D. W. *Purchasing and Materials Management.* New York: McGraw-Hill Book Co., 1971. Chapter 25 is on government purchasing.

Machinery and Allied Products Institute *Leasing of Industrial Equipment.* Washington, D.C., 1965. Major aspects of the leasing problem are covered in this compilation of essays.

"Machines without Owners" *Fortune* (August 1962), pp. 112–14. The development of the practice of leasing equipment is traced in this article.

Manufacturers' Agent Publishing Company *Verified Directory of Manufacturers' Representatives, 1969.* 9th ed. New York, 1969. This biennial directory lists over 15,000 representatives grouped alphabetically by state and city and shows products carried and area covered.

Neace, M. B. *Manufacturers' Agent: Bibliography.* Washington, D.C.: Small Business Administration, 1962. This 12-page bibliography provides a valuable reading list.

Vancil, R. F. *Leasing of Industrial Equipment.* New York: McGraw-Hill Book Co., 1962. Both equipment leasing techniques and how to compare the cost of leasing versus owning are considered in this volume.

14 Marketing agricultural products

The diverse ways in which the marketing system performs the equalization process—sorting out, assembling, allocating, and assorting—are easiest to observe in the marketing of agricultural products. Therefore this product category will be used to illustrate the operations of the complex marketing system in the United States.

Many farm products, such as fluid milk, eggs, and fresh fruits and vegetables, are practically ready for the ultimate consumer when they leave the farm. A portion is processed or preserved through drying, canning, or freezing. Other products are processed as raw materials and sold to industrial users (e.g., grain for industrial alcohol) or to consumers (e.g., grain for whiskey). Figure 14–1 shows the flow of agricultural products through a multitude of different marketing institutions and channels of distribution. While this chart does not indicate the role of all the facilitating institutions, it does show the relative importance of each flow.

Farm products are classified as: (1) fruits and vegetables, (2) grains, (3) feed grain and hay, (4) fibers, (5) miscellaneous crops (e.g., tobacco), (6) livestock, (7) poultry, and (8) animal products (wool, milk, and eggs). The industries associated with the production, processing, and marketing of these products comprise the largest sector of economic activity in the United States and in the world.

The organization of the chapter follows the systems approach. Environment, constraints, and marketing functions are discussed, followed by sections on agricultural marketing institutions in assembling and assorting processes, marketing by grocery manufacturers, marketing institutions in allocating and assorting processes, and cooperative marketing. The final section is on the important role of government in controlling agricultural marketing.

325

FIGURE 14–1
Flow of food from sources to destinations, 1963* (in billion dollars)

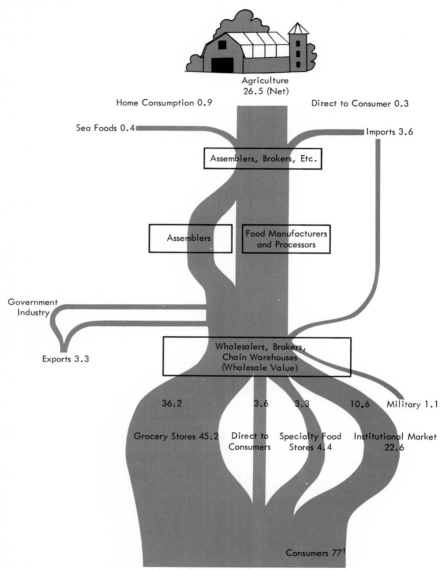

Agriculture
26.5 (Net)

Home Consumption 0.9   Direct to Consumer 0.3

Sea Foods 0.4   Imports 3.6

Assemblers, Brokers, Etc.

Assemblers   Food Manufacturers and Processors

Government
Industry

Wholesalers, Brokers, Chain Warehouses (Wholesale Value)

Exports 3.3

36.2   3.6   3.3   10.6   Military 1.1

Grocery Stores 45.2   Direct to Consumers   Specialty Food Stores 4.4   Institutional Market 22.6

Consumers 77†

* Contributions of industries supplying transportation, equipment, containers, energy, etc., not shown separately.
† Includes farm consumption and direct farm sales
Source: Courtesy of Economic Research Service, U.S. Department of Agriculture.

The marketing system for agricultural products, like the marketing system for manufactured products, is influenced greatly by the characteristics of the product, production, and consumption. In this case, product and producer characteristics lead to extensive use of middlemen in marketing agricultural products to either retailers or industrial users.

Small scale of farming

In 1971, the government estimated there were 2.9 million farms in this country, averaging 389 acres each. In states with large commercial agricultural production, like California, the average size was about 200 acres above the national average. These figures represent a decrease of 40 percent in number and an increase in average size of 138 acres since 1954.[1] Since 1935, there has been a continuous decrease in the number of farms and a steady increase in average size, but farms under 50 acres still numbered 637,000 in 1964. Not only is the average annual income per farm relatively small, but it is obtained from a number of different products—a fact which further complicates the marketing problem of the farmer, since it means that he has a relatively small amount of each product to sell. Moreover, it is too expensive for the farmer to develop the marketing organization necessary to sell direct to consumers or even to retailers.

Partly because the farmer operates on a comparatively small scale, his special problems include the following factors.

Limited information and finances. Most farmers lack the knowledge of market conditions necessary for successful marketing. Consequently, they are glad to turn over their marketing problems to middlemen, who devote all or a considerable part of their time to such problems. Moreover, many farmers need funds as soon as the crops are ready for marketing, if not sooner—funds which middlemen frequently provide.

Slow adjustment of supply to decline in price. In most markets, the output of producers responds quite readily to price changes. Although there is a tendency for this same relationship to hold for farm products, it takes a much longer period for it to show itself—especially in the case of price declines. For example, since 1967 the price of wheat has fallen as a result of oversupply. While wheat farmers in the United States and Canada did cut back production (about 10 percent), there is no other cash crop they can quickly plant to replace the wheat. The result has been that the supply has continued to exceed demand and prices have continued to decline. This sluggishness of market response in supply increases the need for middlemen to perform storage, financing, and risk-taking functions.

Importance of assembly. Despite widespread production, processors of agricultural raw materials prefer to buy in large quantities in central markets in order to ensure them of adequate inputs for their large-scale processing plants. Because of this, middlemen are required to perform the necessary sorting and assembly activities.

---

[1] U.S. Bureau of the Census, *Statistical Abstract of the United States, 1970* (Washington, D.C.: Government Printing Office, 1970).

Product characteristics

Factors which are especially characteristic of agricultural products include (1) specialized production areas, (2) seasonal production, (3) variation in quality and quantity of production, and (4) bulkiness and perishability.

Specialized production areas. The production of most commercial agricultural crops has become localized in specialized areas. Even crops that are produced in many parts of the country must be shipped to the population centers on both coasts. New York City absorbs the bulk of the surplus eggs produced in New York, New Jersey, and Pennsylvania, but these three states supply little more than 10 percent of that city's demand, and large quantities are shipped in from more distant states. Seventy-five percent of all fruit coming to market is produced in Florida and California. Thus middlemen are required to market products over vast geographic areas.

Seasonal production. Seasonal production and fairly steady demand throughout the year, coupled with government price support programs that encourage overproduction, create important storage problems for many farm materials. For example, off-farm commercial wheat storage capacity is equal to about one year's production, and stocks of 900 million bushels have not been unusual in recent decades. For cotton, the movement of the crop to market begins in August, and by the end of December considerably over four fifths of the total has left the growers' hands. Consumption by domestic mills, on the other hand, is spread fairly uniformly throughout the year. Under these conditions, which are typical of many farm products, the importance of the storage function by middlemen is obvious.

There are two general types of normal storage in addition to government stocks. One is that which equalizes seasonal production; the other is the storage in the channels of distribution that is required to maintain the flow of goods through the system. This second type stores about three weeks' supply of food in wholesale and retail marketing channels. About 90 percent has been preserved by canning, bottling, drying, or freezing. The remainder is fresh or in cold storage.

Processors are also an important part of the storage structure either by holding substantial amounts of either raw materials or finished products. For example, cereal manufacturers hold large amounts of grain but try to minimize finished inventories. On the other hand, tomato processors and canners must can the entire year's crop at harvest time and carry the inventory in the form of canned product. They then often offer wholesalers special price inducements to buy and store large quantities of this pack.[2]

The technology of preserving perishable foods and the total cost of storage to the marketing system go hand in hand. Technological change has been rapid. Advances have even been made in older forms of preserving, such as the curing of meat and cheese. Milk, vegetables, and fresh fruits can now be held for relatively long periods of time simply by very careful control of temperature, humidity, and ventilation.

The greatest advances, though, have been made in drying and freezing technology. Quick-freeze techniques now exist which do not cause loss of flavor or harm the appearance of meat. Marketing is often required to introduce such innovations to the public. Low consumer acceptance of frozen poultry formerly caused turkey processors to have considerable excess capacity for over half the year. In the past decade, however, careful freezing, quality control, and marketing have permitted

---

[2] R. L. Kohls, *Marketing of Agricultural Products* (New York: Macmillan Co., 1967), p. 321.

Marketing: Principles and methods

leading turkey producers to sell branded frozen birds at a premium price. The resulting smoothing of production has thus accomplished an overall increase in the efficiency of marketing turkeys.

To meet these varied needs for storage, a wide variety of private and public warehouse facilities have been developed. In 1967 over 500 million cubic feet of public refrigerated storage space and a like amount of private refrigerated space was available for food products.[3] Public bulk freezer storage space now amounts to about 325 million cubic feet. About 10 percent of bulk freezer storage space is in Kansas City.[4] There, caves left by limestone mining in the bluffs around the city form inexpensive, dry, cool storage areas large enough for trains and trucks to enter for loading. Virtually every big food chain in the nation utilizes this storage service for frozen foods, with individual truckloads being called out to company warehouses as needed. Manufacturers of baked goods, TV dinners, pizza pies, turkeys, and Christmas candy also smooth production by storing finished inventory in these caves.

Public warehouses may be operated under supervision of the U.S. Department of Agriculture or the states. A third party verifies the quantity, condition, quality, and insurance on inventory in storage, and warehouse receipts for stored products may be accepted by banks as collateral for loans. Thus the public warehouse plays a role in the financing function as well as the storage function. The negotiable nature of the warehouse receipts also greatly facilitates the transfer of title, as well as reducing the amount of physical handling.[5]

Variation in quality and quantity of production. While increased use of capital coupled with new technology has had a dramatic impact on increasing productivity and yield per acre, agriculture still uses nature's soil, sun, and rain as inputs to the production process. The result is variation in quantity and quality produced each year. This variation places special demands on the standardization and grading, storage, and risk-taking functions. Middlemen specializing in these functions have proven to be the most efficient institutions for performing them.

Bulkiness and perishability. Transportation is also an important specialized business for marketing agricultural products. The bulk of products in relation to their value, the distance they must move to market, and sometimes the factor of perishability all figure in the transportation function. Even the shipment of cattle from feedlot to slaughterhouse is a job performed by a specialist in order to reduce weight loss and injury. These elements go far to explain the relatively high cost of transporting farm food products in this country, which amounted to $5.1 billion in 1964. This amount is 11.1 percent of the total marketing cost of domestic farm food.[6]

The major change in transportation during the last few decades has been the increasing use of the motor truck. In 1929, truck transportation accounted for only 24 percent of the total, but it has now risen to 80 percent.[7] Water transportation is of lesser importance in terms of dollars but is significant in the shipment of grain.

---

[3] There is a sizable discrepancy in this statistic between the *1967 Census of Business,* Vol. IV, and *Agricultural Statistic, 1967.*

[4] "Kansas City Is Capital for All Frozen Storage," *The New York Times,* August 11, 1968, p. F–15.

[5] Kohls, *Marketing of Agricultural Products,* p. 323.

[6] U.S. National Commission on Food Marketing, *Food, From Farmer to Consumer* (Washington, D.C.: Government Printing Office, 1966), p. 11. This percentage is somewhat higher than that reported by the quarterly publication of the U.S. Economic Research Service of the Department of Agriculture, *Marketing and Transportation Situation.*

[7] U.S. Bureau of the Census, *Census of Transportation,* 1967. On a ton-mile basis, the share to trucks is slightly lower.

Freight rates have always been a matter of concern to agricultural producers. Rural agitation was a main force leading to the creation of the Interstate Commerce Commission in 1887. Freight tariffs are very complex and can offer substantial advantages to shippers of some agricultural commodities. For example, the transit privilege permits a shipper to stop a shipment en route for processing (or storage) and then reship it to the original destination at the original through rate. Wheat can thus be shipped from a western point to the East with a stop for cleaning, grading, and milling, and the flour can then continue at the original through rate from the initiating point to its eastern destination.

For truckers, the "agricultural commodities exemption" clause of the Interstate Commerce Act provides that motor carriers which transport agricultural commodities do not fall under federal regulation. For these exempt commodities, rates are usually established by direct negotiation between truck owners and marketers.

In recent years, food distributors have made significant advances in reducing transportation costs. Computers are used extensively to plan shipments in carload lots over the most direct routings, special packaging materials have been used in innovative ways to reduce breakage, package and pallet sizes have been standardized, and handling costs are undergoing constant improvement.

Other marketing functions

In addition to the factors of size and product characteristics, agricultural marketing provides some unique problems for the performance of other marketing functions.

Market information. An efficient marketing system depends on all buyers and sellers having adequate, accurate, and timely information. When either group is composed of large numbers of generalists, as in the case of farmers and consumers, the provision of adequate information for efficient operation of market mechanisms can be a problem. To overcome this problem in the marketing of agricultural goods, government has been active in supplying information to all members of the marketing system.

Much of this work is the product of the Agricultural Marketing Service of the U.S. Department of Agriculture. The Federal Market News collects and distributes information on prices, supplies, and demand conditions for cotton, dairy products, poultry, fruits, vegetables, grain, livestock, and tobacco. Working in cooperation with the various states, market news reporters are stationed at the important markets of the country. The various offices are tied together by leased wire and telephone. News media and middlemen can pick up Market News releases by subscribing to a wire service. Daily, weekly, and monthly summaries are then distributed free of charge.

For information other than price, mail questionnaires are used by the Statistical Reporting Service to estimate crop size, acreage planted, herd size and condition, processor production, crop conditions, and so forth.

Finally, the Economic Research Service interprets and appraises current market information and makes predictions concerning future trends. Their reports are issued in a large number of serial publications called "situation reports."

Standardization and grading.[8] Because they are products of nature, agricul-

---

[8] Agricultural Marketing Service, U.S. Department of Agriculture, *Checklist of U.S. Standards for Farm Products,* Series 210 (Washington, D.C.: Government Printing Office, 1961), and U.S. Department of Agriculture, *Grade Names Used in U.S. Standards for Farm Products,* Agricultural Handbook No. 157 (rev. ed.; Washington, D.C.; Government Printing Office, 1965) provide two excellent sources of information on this subject.

tural products vary widely according to the area in which they are grown, the care taken of them both in the production and in the marketing process, and other factors. At the same time, many consumers demand fairly uniform products. With a high degree of nonuniformity at the producing end and a demand for uniformity at the consuming end, the importance of standardization and grading is self-evident. But the significance of this function does not end here. Standardization of agricultural products permits selling goods while they are in transit, by means of the telephone and telegraph. It reduces transportation and storage costs, facilitates financing, and gives meaning to market news. In addition, it speeds up the settlement of claims between shippers and the transportation agency, because, with the grade known, the market value can quickly be ascertained. And paying on the basis of grade encourages the producer to improve the quality of his crop.[9]

Standards and grades used in the marketing of agricultural products are of four types: (1) quantity standards, (2) minimum quality standards and standards of identity, (3) quality grades for producers, processors, and middlemen, and (4) consumer quality grades.

1. *Quantity standards.* Quantity standards have their roots in the Middle Ages, the U.S. Constitution, and turn-of-the-century agricultural legislation. Their continued need is demonstrated by the Fair Packaging and Labeling Act of 1966. Trade and commerce would be difficult if quantities could not be measured in well-known, standardized units.

2. *Standards of identity.* Standards of identity are statements of minimum ingredients required for products with common names generally recognized by consumers. The Food and Drug Administration has established standards for most common food mixtures, e.g., jam, margarine, juice, nectar, fruit ade, fruit drink, mayonnaise, and peanut butter. The Department of Agriculture establishes standards of identity for "natural" foods such as cheddar and "swiss" cheese. Identity standards for food are minimum standards; products whose main ingredients fall below them must be labeled "imitation." The question of whether the Food and Drug Administration now has authority to extend these programs to cover minimum nutritional standards has not been settled.

3. *Quality grades for producers, processors, and middlemen.* Quality grades yield most of the benefits due to standardization and grading. The Agricultural Marketing Act of 1946 gave broad power to the Secretary of Agriculture to establish such standards for most agricultural products, including grain, meat, poultry, dairy products, and fruits and vegetables. Earlier legislation in this area dates from 1907. Today over 300 farm products are covered by standard grades, which, because they are intended to be used by specialists, can be technical and complex.

4. *Consumer quality grades.* Consumer quality grades have been much slower in development. While standards of identity are used constantly by consumers (often without their knowledge), grade designations are found on few consumer products. In foods, only natural commodities such as meat (e.g., prime, choice, good, and commercial beef), poultry, and dairy products reach the consumer with grades.

There are three main reasons. First, all consumer preferences are not the same. Some consumers prefer heavy sugar sirup with fruit, others prefer a light sirup. Second,

---

[9] For a discussion of the importance of grading from the points of view of operational efficiency and pricing efficiency, see G. S. Shepherd and G. A. Futrell, *Marketing Farm Products,* 5th ed. (Ames, Iowa: Iowa State University Press,1969), pp. 197–99.

quality is a multidimensional concept which cannot be measured on a simple, unidimensional scale.

Third, it has not been demonstrated that standardization is healthy for competition at the retail level. Sellers compete by differentiating their products and identifying these differences with brands, and standardization could stifle innovation. The same is not true for raw agricultural commodities. In markets for these products, standards put small sellers on an even footing with large ones, intensify price competition, and facilitate efficiencies in distribution. Thus, while standardization increases competition and efficiency in markets for raw materials, a similar case for retail markets can be built only after careful consideration of other characteristics of competitive rivalry. More will be said on this subject in Chapter 24.

Protection of health. Because most agricultural products are for human consumption, the Food and Drug Administration, the Department of Agriculture, states, and cities have taken steps to assure that food is produced, packaged, and marketed under sanitary conditions. The Meat Inspection Act of 1907 authorizes inspection of animals, meats, and packing establishments to assure that products will be fit for human consumption. More recent legislation extended inspection to poultry products and processing plants and has brought state inspection requirements up to federal standards. State and local governments have set up required health standards for milk, milk processing, food stores and restaurants, and similar activities not in interstate commerce.

MARKETING INSTITUTIONS IN ASSEMBLING AND SORTING PROCESSES

Historically, the structure of the distribution channels for agricultural products, while composed of different types of middlemen, had a characteristic pattern of flow from producer to "local" markets to "central" markets. Post-processing channels were similarly characterized by two distinct steps. This pattern is shown in Figure 14–2.

In some cases, "secondary central markets" could be found. Processors built plants around these central markets, which were usually population centers. Country buyers, cream stations, country grain elevators, and commission buyers at the local level purchased products for sale to central-market buyers. The assembly and sorting processes were distinct and terminated in well-defined central markets. The institutions at each level in the channels were made up substantially of independent firms. Local market institutions, as R. L. Kohls has observed, "were independent businesses buying from farmers and selling, sometimes through commission agents, to the processors and wholesalers in the cities. Processors were largely engaged only in processing activities. Wholesalers were entities separate from retailers."[10]

While vestiges of the centralized channel structure with well-defined levels remain, central markets have declined in importance. Vertical integration also makes it more difficult to identify unique institutions performing marketing functions at each level of the channel, as pointed out by Kohls.

---

[10] Kohls, *Marketing of Agricultural Products,* p. 241. Much of this introduction is based on Kohls's discussion in Chapter 15.

Marketing: Principles and methods

FIGURE 14–2
Traditional assembling, processing, and allocating channels for agricultural products

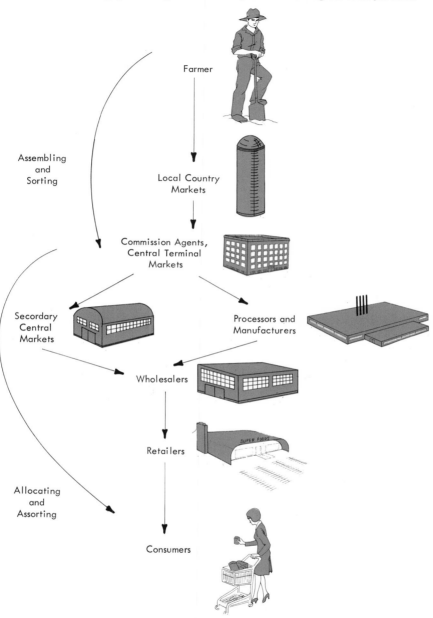

Farmer

Assembling
and
Sorting

Local Country
Markets

Commission Agents,
Central Terminal
Markets

Secondary
Central
Markets

Processors and
Manufacturers

Wholesalers

Retailers

Allocating
and
Assorting

Consumers

Decentralization means that farm products move from farms and into the hands of processors and wholesalers without utilizing the services of the older, established terminal facilities. Buying agents of the processors, wholesalers, and the giant retail firms contact producers and take title to the products in the production area. . . . These firms themselves have often moved out of the cities into the production area to build their slaughterhouses and canning plants, enabling producers to deliver their products directly to the plant door.[11]

As is the case with other marketing institutions and channel structures, the move to decentralized markets has been caused by changes in technological, environmental, and demand factors. Reasons for the growth of decentralized markets include:

1. Development of the truck and highway system, which has vastly increased the flexibility of the assembling and allocating processes.
2. Continued improvement in the speed and flexibility of communications and the quality and quantity of market information.
3. Improved techniques of preserving and storing.
4. Improvement in grading, which has permitted the transfer of products by sample or simple description.
5. Growth of the number of large, specialized production units (farms), which has made assembly on the farm sufficient for purchase by wholesalers.
6. Development of large-scale chain retailers performing their own wholesaling functions.
7. Backward and forward integration by processors creating new economies of scale in assembling, processing, and allocating.

Vertical integration has been practiced mainly by retailers and processors. Meat packers now own and operate both country buying points for livestock and wholesaling facilities for meat. Retail chains may operate their own wholesaling facilities, canning plants, produce-buying agencies, and even cattle herds. Integration results in the centralization of resource allocation decision making and distribution within the firm rather than in the market. Marketing functions are performed within integrated firms rather than by specialized marketing institutions.

The first five reasons for the growth of decentralization given above are also factors that have made vertical integration possible. The two go hand in hand.

Middlemen in local markets

The first step in assembling products from farmers is carried out in the local market. This may be merely an open-air meeting place, either at a crossroad point or in a small town, where farmers with products to sell may contact one or more buyers interested in buying for resale, or it may be the offices of potential buyers located fairly close together in a small town. In other cases the market may be established where special facilities exist for handling the product; for instance, a local market for apples may grow up around a large cold storage warehouse. Regardless of their facilities, such markets are necessarily located near the farmers, and consequently there are many of them.

Sales at local markets usually result from direct negotiation between buyer and seller, although in a few cases the auction method is used. Such auctions are usually referred to as "shipping-point auctions," to distinguish them from those located in the central markets.

---

[11] Ibid., p. 243.

Middlemen of many kinds operate in the local market. Salaried local buyers for meat packers are common in livestock markets, and there may also be some independent buyers who take title to the products they buy. Some of the buyers in the local market are commission agents for central-market buyers or processors. Another buyer for many farm products is the local cooperative association, discussed later in this chapter. Processors with local plants may supply them from local markets or contract to purchase output before it is harvested. All local markets offer the farmer cash for his output at a minimum of inconvenience and delay.

In wheat assembly, the country elevator remains dominant in the local market. Country grain elevators account for about half of the sales of all types of assemblers of farm products.[12] These local elevators are of three main types: independent, line, and cooperative. Independent elevators are single elevators operated as private business enterprises. Line elevators are controlled by private companies that operate two or more elevators. Cooperative elevators, organized singly or in statewide groups, are controlled by the farmers themselves, the profits being divided among them. The importance of a particular type varies in different areas.

Middlemen in central markets

From local markets or directly from large growers, agricultural consumer products are frequently concentrated further by moving them into a smaller number of central or terminal markets. These markets are located in important transportation centers and, in contrast with many local markets which lack special handling facilities, are well equipped to perform all the handling functions, including storage for the wide variety of products that enters them by truck, rail, or ship. Here also are found facilities such as auctions and financial institutions which expedite the performance of the essential sorting and allocating activities involved in the marketing of the various commodities. Major processors and exporters locate close to the terminal markets for immediate commodity processing. In some terminal markets, organized trading takes place on the floor of a commodity exchange; in all of them, well-recognized methods of trading have developed.[13]

For wheat, terminal markets are located at points where the elements of transportation facilities and rates, nearness to producing areas, and size of demand for wheat from millers, manufacturers, and exporters are in the most favorable combination. Twelve of outstanding importance are Chicago, Duluth, Milwaukee, Toledo (these four being lake ports), Indianapolis, Kansas City, Minneapolis, Omaha, Peoria, Sioux City, Wichita, and St. Louis.

Independent country elevators usually sell by consignment to a terminal-market operator, on a "to arrive" basis, or "on track." The consignment method of sale consists of sale through commission men, often termed "cash grain commission merchants," located in the terminal markets. These men receive the grain and take samples to the floor of the commodity exchange, where they offer it to the highest bidder. Following the sale, they make the collection, deduct commission and handling expenses, and return the balance to the country elevator. Many commission houses employ solicitors to canvass country elevators to encourage them to consign to their houses.

---

[12] U.S. Bureau of the Census, *1967 Census of Business,* Vol. IV, *Wholesale Trade: Area Statistics* (Washington, D.C.: Government Printing Office, 1970), p. 1–9.

[13] See "The Commodity Exchange as a Facilitating Marketing Institution," Appendix B below.

The consignment method of sale exposes the country elevator operator to the dangers of price fluctuation between the time he buys from the farmer and the time he sells in the terminal market. Since price fluctuations are often of considerable magnitude, there is a real danger in this method. To lessen the risk, some country elevator operators hedge the grain as they buy it and close the hedge as they sell in the terminal market.

Sales made "to arrive" also remove the evil of price fluctuations as far as the country elevator is concerned. Such sales take their name from the fact that although a definite price has been offered the country elevator by buyers from the terminal market, the elevator is responsible for the grain in all other regards until it arrives at its destination.

A relatively small amount of wheat is sold to terminal buyers "on track" at the country shipping point. By this method, not only does the country elevator operator eliminate the risk of price fluctuations during the period of transportation, but he also avoids arranging for the actual transfer of the grain to the point of destination.

Cooperative and line elevators may employ the same selling methods but also have their own representatives in the terminal markets and sell directly to millers.

The main buyers in the terminal markets are the large elevator companies, millers, cereal manufacturers, and exporters. Brokers are also active. Of these, the terminal elevator companies, those which own or lease large storage facilities, are most important.

Terminal elevators do more than merely provide storage. Much of the wheat they receive must be cleaned and conditioned, since it may be warm or wet. These terminal elevator companies, which are classified as merchant wholesalers, sell largely to millers, cereal manufacturers, and exporters.

Millers, cereal manufacturers, and exporters that buy in terminal markets commonly purchase through their own representatives, although some of the smaller ones use brokers. Where commodity exchanges are in existence, purchase of membership is often less costly than paying commissions. They also buy direct from the terminal elevator firms rather than on the exchange, as noted above.

The independent grain merchant and the elevator operator represent the only independent wholesale institutions to take title in accumulating agricultural products that have not declined in importance since 1963 as a result of vertical integration (see Table 14–1).

In the cotton trade, several of the larger textile mills maintain buying offices in central markets rather than using the services provided by independent middlemen. This is a clear example of vertical integration in the cotton industry. These firms buy from local-market middlemen, have their own salaried or commissioned buyers in the local market, and also buy direct from the larger growers. On the selling side, they deal with spinners in the United States and with foreign spinners or importers.

Many local-market buyers prefer to sell through commission firms in the central markets. In the case of livestock, these firms receive the animals and see that they are properly unloaded into the yards. After a sale, they deduct their commission and remit the balance to their principals. Other central-market middlemen include brokers, cooperative associations, and factors.

Table 14–2 shows the most important sellers and buyers in both country and terminal grain markets. Note, however, that the terminal-market elevators often resell the grain they have purchased in the same markets, after having performed the storage and conditioning functions.

TABLE 14–1
Number and sales of wholesale establishments taking title engaged in the accumulation process for agricultural products

Type of operation	1967			1963	
	Number of establishments	Sales (thousands of dollars)	Percent of sales in commodity line	Number of establishments	Sales (thousands of dollars)
Terminal grain elevators	767	4,417,609		633	2,999,800
Assemblers of farm products, total	11,101	10,155,511	100.0	14,110	9,820,245
Country grain elevators	6,477	5,590,708	55.0	7,653	5,059,224
Other grain elevators	343	n.a.			
Livestock	1,246	1,586,904	15.6		
Fresh fruits and vegetables	1,169	1,005,925	9.9		
Eggs (shell)	750	347,312	3.4		
Feeds	3,473	332,344	3.3		
Cotton (raw)	179	260,793	2.6		
Milk and cream (fluid)	264	241,186	2.4		
Peanuts (unroasted)	73	136,428	1.3		

Source: U.S. Bureau of the Census, *1967 Census of Business*, Vol. IV, *Wholesale Trade: Area Statistics* (Washington, D.C.: Government Printing Office, 1970). pp. 1–9 and BC 67–WS 7, p. 359.

TABLE 14–2
Sellers and buyers in country and terminal wheat markets

Country markets		Terminal markets	
Sellers	Buyers	Sellers	Buyers
Farmers	Elevator operators	Commission men	Terminal elevators
Farm buyers	Track buyers	Brokers	Millers
	Representatives of terminal-market buyers	Representatives of country-market buyers	Cereal manufacturers
	Local millers	Merchants	Exporters
	Local cereal manufacturers	Terminal elevator firms	Brokers
	Exporters		

MARKETING ACTIVITIES OF GROCERY MANUFACTURERS

As noted above, vertical integration results in the performance of more marketing functions within a single firm and in resource allocation decisions that previously were made by a market mechanism being made within the firm. A grocery manufacturing firm may integrate marketing functions not only to make a profit on the performance of those functions but also to gain control over the purchase of raw materials and the sale of finished goods. Thus it performs all marketing functions in order to try to gain control of the marketing channels to ensure a profit on the performance of its manufacturing operations.

Few processors assume a passive role in marketing. Producers are often small and disorganized. The same is usually true of consumers. But the processing firms and food chains are usually not small and seldom disorganized. Thus the struggle to be the most powerful force in the channel of distribution is between processing firms and food chains. The winner of this struggle is probably determined by which group is most favored and respected by the consumer.

This "consumer franchise" is, to a large extent, determined by the amount of processing required (i.e., form utility added) and the extent of technological and product innovation a product group enjoys. These factors dictate the amount of capital equipment and skilled human technology that must be employed. And it is these fixed investments which strongly influence the importance placed on channel control by individual firms and hence their attitudes toward other institutions in the marketing channel.

Value added in farm-produced food

The value added by manufacturers differs among agricultural products. Analysis of these differences is complicated because the statistical data available do not differentiate between *marketing value added* and *manufacturing value added*. Because of the statistical problems that stem from vertical integration, many overlook the importance of the marketing activities of manufacturers.

The share of value added going to the major types of marketing institutions for a variety of agricultural food products is shown in Figure 14–3. While the figure does not separate marketing value added from manufacturing value added for processors and distributors, it is useful in demonstrating the differences between products.

FIGURE 14-3

Percentage distribution of consumer's dollar according to institution, selected farm food products, 1964

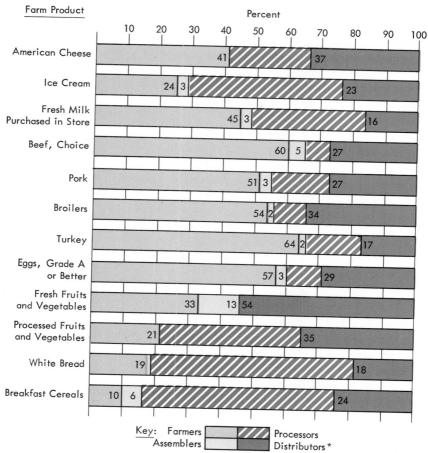

* Except for ice cream, milk, and bread, includes all distribution costs, even those performed by processors.

Source: Adapted from U.S. National Commission on Food Marketing, *Food from Farmer to Consumer* (Washington, D.C.: Government Printing Office, 1966), pp. 14–15.

The farm share for meat and poultry products is high because the raw nutrients are "processed" by the animal before sale by the farmer. Thus less value must be added by the manufacturer. Notice that the value added to beef by the meat packer is one of the lowest. Because of the additional processing required for sausage and other pork products, the value added for pork is greatest of the meat products. Fresh fruits and vegetables are unique because of their perishability and absence of processing. The processor's share is greatest where the value added in manufacturing is greatest: ice cream, milk, processed fruits and vegetables, bread, and cereal.

For all farm-produced foods, 60 percent of the consumer's food dollar goes to marketing and manufacturing, even after excluding food consumed in restaurants. The trend in this percentage has been upward since 1945, chiefly because consumers have demanded more value added in convenience preserving, semiprepared foods, convenience packaging, attractive stores, large parking lots, and greater variety. While a portion of this shift can be called a change in consumer tastes, it provides another example of the effect of specialization of labor. Consumers find it more desirable to have factories process their food than to do so at home and prefer to shop in one supermarket with large variety of brands and products than in several small specialty shops.

Processors have responded with many innovations in preserving, preparation, and packaging. When innovations are adopted, consumers and distributors must be told about the new product. Thus processors must engage in advising distributors, elaborate personal selling to and cooperative promotion with retailers, and extensive consumer advertising in order to provide to consumers the benefits of new technology and new products. Unfortunately, the data are not sufficient to segregate the dollar value of these marketing costs. However, we can describe in more detail some of the marketing activities of manufacturers by looking at both their buying and selling activities.

Buying functions[14]

Any manufacturer must assure himself of an adequate amount of raw materials of the quality he desires at the lowest possible cost. The grocery manufacturer may do this by taking over the assembling and sorting processes himself for his own competitive safety and to make his buying power more effective as a price-setting force.

Food processors procure raw materials in a variety of ways. Varying degrees of vertical integration are represented by the three types of contracts most often made with producers.

Market-specification contracts. Contracts which simply specify some of the product characteristics that will be acceptable to the manufacturer are known as market-specification contracts. They usually also establish some basis of payment for the crop. Such contracts attempt to integrate standardization and market information but not financing and risk taking.

Resource-providing contracts. The kind of production resources to be used is specified in resource-providing contracts. The manufacturer provides the producer with financing ranging from operational to fixed investment financing and a degree of managerial help and supervision. Product prices are usually based on the open market. In this situation, the only marketing function not integrated by the buyer is risk taking. For example, one corn-products manufacturer who has developed a special variety of corn that best satisfies his needs contracts directly with farmers for its production.[15] Milk processors buy on contract and operate their own truck routes to pick up milk at the farms.

Management and income guaranteeing contracts. Processors are taking an increasingly active part in urging farmers to produce the desired quantity and quality of product. Many processors use field men to work closely with producers. Contracts

---

[14] This section is based on Kohls, *Marketing of Agricultural Products,* chaps. 5 and 15.

[15] Ibid., p. 90.

Marketing: Principles and methods

in these cases also provide for assumption of the risk-taking function by the manufacturer, usually by establishing price, quantity, and quality in advance of production. For example, canners often contract with the farmer for product in advance of planting. In return for a guaranteed price, the farmer gives up a substantial part of his normal managerial responsibility. Producers may specify wages, seed, and cultivation of the crop. The manufacturer comes close to having all responsibility short of ownership.

Selling functions

It is in the vertical integration of selling functions that the marketing activities of food processors are most evident. The manufacturers of frequently purchased consumer packaged goods, including food, are among the largest advertisers in the country. (Examples include Procter & Gamble, General Foods, General Mills, and Kellogg. More specific information on advertising expenditures will be found in Chapter 22.) This advertising is devoted to branded goods such as cereals, coffee, partially prepared baked goods, and canned foods. The strategy of manufacturers in performing these selling and information functions directly to consumers is to counter the power of the large retailers in consumer markets by directly building a consumer franchise. Less obvious is the fact that manufacturers also perform many transportation, storage, standardization and grading, and risk-taking functions for middlemen. They hold inventory and pay transportation charges to large chains and wholesalers. When chains or wholesalers hold inventory, the manufacturers often protect it against price decreases.

Manufacturers with a relatively full line of products often maintain large field sales forces which not only service chain headquarters and large wholesalers but also make "detail" calls on retail stores. If the manufacturer's line of products is limited, these selling functions will often be performed by a food broker. Here again, it is not possible to generalize across all product lines. Standardized products that carry government grades and sell as commodities are processed for distributors to their own specifications and carry distributor labels. For product groups in which innovation is more common (e.g., cake mixes and breakfast foods), the manufacturer tries to maintain control over marketing down to the consumer level. Many manufacturers try to do both. Canners sell a prestige line, e.g., Green Giant, Del Monte, which they brand and advertise to consumers and at the same time process canned goods for distributors' labels.

The meat-packing industry has largely become its own wholesaler. It is handling a perishable commodity that has wide fluctuations in volume over a short period. In order to keep such a product moving effectively, many packers consider it imperative to have control of the distributive channel through to the retailer, and they operate their own wholesaling establishments.[16] In the census classifications, these are referred to as "manufacturer sales branches with stocks."

Manufacturers, either through their own sales force or through brokers, also sell directly to other manufacturers, e.g., bakers, restaurant chains, institutions, and government.

---

[16] Ibid., p. 91.

We shall not attempt at this point to describe and analyze the marketing activities of wholesalers and retailers for agricultural products. The activities of food retailers were described in Chapters 8 and 9 and of wholesalers in Chapters 10, and 11, above. It should be emphasized, however, that "backward integration" by these institutions has taken them into processing and even production of agricultural products.

Distributors of fresh fruits and vegetables and seafoods also can be classified as assemblers of food products. Distributors purchase directly from farmers or from middlemen in local markets and accumulate sufficient quantities for economical handling and shipping to retail stores. In addition, they frequently grade, pack, and store the commodities handled. As G. S. Shepherd and G. A. Futrell have noted,

Today there are few food processing industries into which some chain has not integrated. Some leading examples are meat packing, cheese, condensed milk, ice cream, fluid milk, bakery products, coffee roasting, soft drinks, soaps and bleaches, salad dressing, and canned fish. It is easier to cite the exceptions—certainly tobacco products and most cereals are the outstanding holdouts. But even these holdouts may go.

In addition to vertical integration through ownership, many food retailers have become tied—through contracts or informal agreements—with their suppliers. The familiar result here is the so-called "captive supplier."

Vertical integration by food retailers into food processing is possible because they have developed their own brands which are acceptable to consumers. Consequently, chains can easily overcome what is perhaps the main barrier to successful entry into food processing, the difficulty of developing acceptable brands. Moreover, because they have access to substantial financial resources, capital outlays are not serious barriers to entry in many fields. Finally, they can quite easily overcome the other main barriers to entry, technical and business know-how, by buying out going concerns. . . .

Vertical integration reduces the number of bargaining transactions and ownership transfers necessary to move goods from producer to consumer. The importance of this is commonly overlooked. A considerable part of the total cost of distributing food products is incurred for the purpose of bringing about ownership transfers at various stages in the marketing process. Brokers' fees, wholesalers' commissions, salesmen's salaries, advertising expenditures—all are partially chargeable to the efforts of sellers and manufacturers to find retail outlets for their goods. Obviously the greater the number of such buyers and sellers and the more functionally specialized they are, the greater the number of ownership transfers necessary to move the commodity forward toward the consumer.[17]

In summary, many observers believe that large retailers have been more successful at backward integration than food processors have been at forward integration.

AGRICULTURAL COOPERATIVE MARKETING

When the consumer's cooperative was examined in Chapter 8, its major objective was found to be lower prices (taking into account patronage refunds) which would enable household consumers to stretch their dollars over additional want-satisfying products. In cooperative marketing by farmers, the chief purpose is to obtain a higher income for producers. Regardless of the specific purpose, cooperation among both consumers and producers is the result of the conviction that benefits may be obtained through joint or associative effort that cannot be secured through individual effort

---

[17] Reprinted by permission from *Marketing Farm Products,* Geoffrey S. Shepherd and Gene A. Futrell, 5th ed., © 1969, Iowa State University Press, Ames, Iowa, pp. 282–83.

alone.[18] Organizations established by groups of farmers to market their products and to purchase needed supplies and other products are known variously as "agricultural marketing cooperatives," "marketing cooperatives" or "cooperative marketing associations."

Cooperatives versus typical business corporations

Differences. The agricultural marketing cooperative, although typically incorporated, differs in several significant respects from the ordinary business corporation. These differences center around the three "hard-core" principles of (1) democratic control by member patrons, (2) limited returns on equity capital, and (3) services at cost to member patrons. Although the board of directors is elected by the stockholders, each stockholder typically has only one vote, regardless of the number of shares of stock he owns.[19] Thus, whereas in a regular corporation a man may obtain control through ownership of 51 percent of the stock (or less if the stock is widely held), this result is impossible in a cooperative, in which democratic control is the aim.

Some cooperatives will receive products for sale from both members and nonmembers, but most of them restrict their business to members. Occasionally, nonmembers permitted to use the cooperative facilities are automatically made members by withholding their patronage dividends until a sufficient sum is accumulated to buy the qualifying share of stock.

Most cooperatives have a dividend policy different from that of the ordinary corporation. Instead of returning the profits of the business to the stockholders in relation to the number of shares held, cooperatives pay the stockholders a set rate of interest on their shares and distribute the remainder as a patronage dividend. That is, the patronage dividend is paid in proportion to the sales or purchases members have made through the cooperative. Such a distribution is based on the theory that earnings should go to those who make them possible by giving business to the association.

Similarities. As in the ordinary business corporation, the day-by-day management of a cooperative marketing association usually rests with a hired executive. Where the business is small, management may be a part-time job. The manager is appointed by and reports to the board of directors; the board, in turn, is responsible to the members.

Development of cooperative marketing

While the first attempts at collective farm marketing date from 1810, the prominence of agricultural cooperatives stems from periods of rural depression beginning in 1873, when the Grange (Patrons of Husbandry), founded in 1867 as a fraternal order, began to undertake collective activities. Growth of cooperatives continued at a fairly steady rate, until in 1920 there were 1,800 associations.

Beginning in 1920, a new flurry of cooperative activity was set off by the postwar slump in agricultural prices. This led to the passage in 1922 of the Capper-Volstead Act, which recognized the legal right of farmers to act together cooperatively, and

---

[18] An early rallying cry among cooperative members was: "United We Stick, Divided We're Stuck—Let's Get Together."

[19] Although this is a cooperative principle, in practice it is often modified, with voting placed on a patronage basis.

14 / Marketing agricultural products

FIGURE 14–4

The number and annual volume of farmer cooperatives by state, June 30, 1969

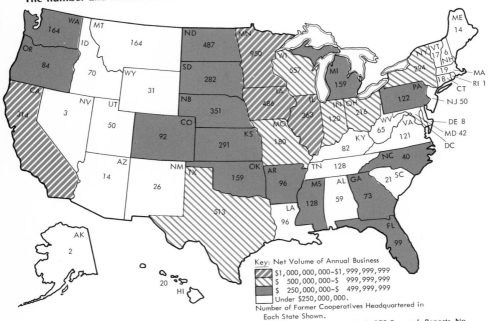

Source: U.S. Farmer Cooperative Service, "Statistics of Farmer Cooperatives, 1968–1969," *FCS Research Reports,* No. 16 (Washington, D.C.: U.S. Department of Agriculture, 1970), Table 9.

the Cooperative Marketing Act of 1926, which "gave the Department of Agriculture its first clear instructions from Congress to encourage the development and growth of cooperatives."[20] The total membership of marketing cooperatives changed but little between 1926 and 1940—rising slowly to a peak of 2.7 million in 1935–36 and falling gradually to 2.3 million in 1939–40. Then it expanded sharply to an all-time high of 4.3 million in 1955–56, falling back to 3.2 million at the present time.[21]

Sales of present cooperative marketing associations are concentrated in dairy products, grains (including soybeans and soybean meal and oil), livestock and livestock products, and fruits and vegetables. These fields account for about 77 percent of all cooperative sales. It is estimated that cooperatives market about 25 percent of all farm products at some stage in the marketing process, their share of the market having gradually increased since 1926.[22] This share varies widely from commodity

---

[20] D. G. Angevine, "Where Do We Go from Here?" *News for Farmer Cooperatives,* January 1967, p. 6.

[21] U.S. Bureau of the Census, *Statistical Abstract of the United States, 1970* (Washington, D.C.: Government Printing Office, 1970), p. 589. There is some double counting in these figures, since a farmer may belong to more than one cooperative.

[22] J. K. Samuels, "In Marketing—Reaching Potential and Improving Capacities," *News for Farmer Cooperatives,* January 1967, p. 7.

Marketing: Principles and methods

to commodity: cooperatives market 10 percent of the eggs, 13 percent of the livestock, 40 percent of the grain, and 65 percent of the milk.[23]

Geographic distribution and size. The geographic distribution of farm cooperative activity is shown in Figure 14–4. Minnesota and Wisconsin have the largest number of cooperatives, while California, Minnesota, Iowa, and Illinois are most important, in that order, when measured by volume of business. In California, cooperatives do 11 percent of all their business. They are responsible for the marketing of about 80 percent of the state's citrus fruits, 60 percent of the walnuts, 65 percent of the state's lima beans, and 33 1/3 percent of its raisins, prunes, and apricots.[24] In contrast, cooperatives do less than one half of 1 percent of their business in Connecticut.

Income-raising methods of cooperative marketing associations

Cooperatives employ several methods of achieving their goal of increasing the incomes of their members. The cooperative has attempted: (1) to raise the selling price of the commodities marketed; (2) to absorb some of the profit from the middlemen's functions and pass this back to the farmer; (3) to find ways to reduce the cost of performing the middlemen's functions so as to absorb not only their profit but something in addition, and (4) to lower the farmer's cost of production, which, other things remaining the same, will increase his income.

Attempts to increase prices for products sold. Cooperative price bargaining with processors in the area and withholding supply so that prices do not fall drastically in periods when crops are abundant are two attempts to raise prices. Others are improving quality through standardization and grading, supporting new product development, and cooperative promotion.

Absorbing the middleman's profit. Cooperative marketing organizations, with a few exceptions, serve to replace other middlemen in the channel of distribution. Local cooperative elevators, for example, replace the local independent and line operators. If the cooperative elevator can be run as efficiently as the private elevator, the profits which would be earned by the latter will accrue to the former. When these profits are paid as patronage dividends to the farmers, their incomes are increased.

Reducing the cost of marketing. Among farmers' cooperatives, vertical integration is probably the most significant development in recent years. Good illustrations of this trend are afforded by the local livestock shipping association that establishes a local processing plant to produce cured hams and bacons, specialty sausages, and other meat products; the grain cooperative that sets up feed mills, soybean-processing plants, and a fertilizer plant; and the cotton cooperative that constructs a plant to make insecticides for use in cotton production. Integration is also extensive among milk cooperatives, where the nature of milk products—butter, cheese, dry and evaporated milk, and ice cream—is conducive to such an arrangement.

A specific instance of integration is afforded by California Canners and Growers, Inc., and Tri-Valley Growers Inc. Between 1957 and 1963, Cal Can purchased six private canning companies with successful operations. The association grew to a membership of over 1,000 growers. By 1964 it was integrated into a single organization for production, canning, and brand marketing of fruits and vegetables. This step was undertaken for the usual reasons for vertical integration—better control over

---

[23] Ibid.

[24] Information supplied by the Berkeley (California) Bank for Co-operatives.

sources of supply, strengthening of bargaining ability and of market position, and improvement in profits.

Lowering the cost of production.   In addition to their main function of performing essential marketing activities in the sale of their members' products, many cooperative associations effect substantial savings in the cost of supplies, equipment, and machinery to their members through purchasing them cooperatively.

Factors limiting growth

Cooperatives represent a type of vertical integration—in this case, by the small independent farmer. As such, they belong to the wave of the future. However, the small family farm may not be a part of this wave. Centralized associations are likely to be healthier in the future than local cooperatives. We are in an age when the large-scale production unit is the only one which is economically viable. The limiting factors to growth of cooperatives are all associated with small size: inefficient business methods, lack of cooperation between members, efficiency below that of private business, lack of adequate leadership, and lack of resources to engage in large-scale technical development.

Types of cooperative marketing associations

The six major types of cooperative marketing associations are listed below.

Local associations.   The most numerous type, local cooperatives operate exclusively at the local market level.

Federated associations.   In federations of a number of local associations, the local associations usually assemble, grade, and pack while the federated association establishes grades, advertises, locates markets, arranges transportation, and solves marketing problems of a regional and national nature. Land O'Lakes Creameries, Inc., is an example of this type of federation. It markets dairy and poultry products for some 400 local cooperatives in Minnesota, Wisconsin, North Dakota, and South Dakota.

Centralized associations.   Unlike the federated type, a centralized cooperative is a large regional cooperative in which all decision making is centralized. The individual grower is a member of the central co-op, not of a local association. The centralized association concerns itself with assembling, grading, packing, standardizing, financing, and promotion. Examples are Sunmaid Raisin Growers' Association, the California Almond Growers Exchange, and Agway, Inc.

Terminal sales associations.   Terminal sales associations—also known as terminal commission associations—are located in central markets, where they function as commission men. Although a large part of the products they handle and sell are sent to them by the local cooperative associations, large private shippers and growers also consign products to them. Since terminal sales associations operate on cooperative principles, prevailing commission rates are charged, and patronage rebates are made to keep the organizations on a cost basis. Such associations are of special importance in the marketing of livestock.

Collective bargaining associations.   Collective bargaining associations are most numerous in the marketing of fluid milk.[25] In many ways, these associations resemble trade unions. They do not usually handle the products of their members,

---

[25] They also exist in the marketing channels for such products as sugar beets and fruits and vegetables.

but each member signs a contract by which he agrees to deliver his milk only to private distributors approved by the association and at prices it has accepted. This contract gives the association a large amount of bargaining power when dealing with the distributors, since their supply of milk may be checked if a price agreement cannot be reached.

Although there are many bargaining associations in existence, there is a decided tendency for them to evolve into some type of central cooperative marketing organization by taking over at least part of the physical activities involved in handling fluid milk and its products. Even when they do not actually handle milk, they may assume such functions as advertising, laboratory analysis designed to improve quality of product, and purchasing of feed and supplies for members. The movement toward state price fixing of fluid milk has been important in hastening this trend, for this automatically takes price bargaining outside the direct influence of the association.

National sales and service associations. At various times in the history of cooperative marketing, some of the local, federated, and centralized associations handling a particular commodity have joined together as members of a national sales and service association. Such an organization exists or has existed for grain, fruits and vegetables, pecans, wool, cotton, and other commodities. Some of these national associations are really gigantic marketing organizations; others serve merely to coordinate the activities of their members and to provide pertinent information.

GOVERNMENT AND THE CONTROL OF AGRICULTURAL MARKETING

The role of government in providing market information, standardization and grading, and protection of health is designed to facilitate the operation of markets as the control system in the marketing of agricultural products. Government is also concerned with regulating markets in order to achieve socially desirable goals which, it is believed, would not be achieved with free market control.

The socially desirable goal in this case is the maintenance of the family farm. While the size of the individual production unit will continue to increase, it continues to be the public policy to keep farming a small-scale industry relative to food processors and food distributors.

Because agricultural prices are so unstable, the prices received by farmers are far more subject to decline than are the prices they pay. Through merger and vertical integration, processors and distributors have grown to be large and powerful. Faced with these two factors, the farmer has been concerned with how to stabilize, and hopefully increase, his income through increased market power, bargaining power, and government power. Professor John Kenneth Galbraith, who calls this the "countervailing power" of those subject to the power of processors and distributors,[26] states that government should foster the development of countervailing power when necessary to hold other oligopolistic power in check. We have seen an example of this process in the enabling legislation and the activities of farmer cooperatives. Through cooperatives, farmers have been able to increase their incomes by substantial federal exemption from the antitrust laws prohibiting collusion among competitors.

Other government programs designed to increase farmer income by "guiding" the "invisible hand" of competition can be classified into four types: (1) price support

---

[26] J. K. Galbraith, *American Capitalism: The Concept of Countervailing Power* (Boston: Houghton Mifflin Co., 1956).

programs, (2) acreage control programs, (3) marketing control programs, and (4) promotion and research support programs.

Price support programs

During the depressions of the early twenties and the 1930s, when farm incomes declined sharply, the solution proposed was short-term storage to modify violent fluctuations in supply and hence stabilize prices. The first federal effort in this direction began in 1929 and was taken over in 1933 by the Commodity Credit Corporation (CCC), which undertook two programs of price supports.

In the case of storable commodities like grain and tobacco, nonrecourse loans have been used to the present time. Under this program, the farmer stores his crop and obtains a government loan at the support price. If the market price rises above the loan price, the farmer may sell and repay the loan. If the market price never reaches the loan price, the farmer defaults on the loan and fulfills his obligation by delivering the commodity to the government.

The other major program has been one of direct market purchase. In this case, the government buys the crop at the support price. The CCC then attempts to dispose of the commodities through foreign aid, commodity distribution to the poor, and school lunch programs. It may also store the commodity, as was done for a long period with butter, or destroy it.

In both cases, support prices were set with reference to farm income, with little regard for the demand side of the market. Over the years, amendments to these laws have placed increased emphasis on compulsory production controls when production exceeds a predetermined level. By the 1950s and 1960s, farmers had to agree to withdraw a portion of their land from production in order to secure price support protection. The current approach provides more direct income support to farmers and relies on the free market to determine price and resource allocation.

Acreage control programs

Production control programs also began in 1933, with the Agricultural Adjustment Act (AAA), but they were not very effective until the Soil Bank program of the 1950s. Partial or whole farms were rented for periods of up to 10 years and kept out of production. A similar program for grains was put into effect in the sixties. Rents on acreage can benefit the acreage but cannot benefit any but the current owner. Such payments raise the value of the land so that new buyers and renters are no better off than before.

Nonetheless, the experience since the thirties has shown that

the prices of farm products can be supported above open-market levels only if market supplies are reduced accordingly. . . . In cases where production has been reduced by acreage reduction, the benefit has naturally gone to [land]. But the fundamental purpose of agricultural policy is to benefit men. The purpose is to increase income per farmer. That requires a reduction in the number of farmers, not a reduction in the number of acres.[27]

---

[27] Shepherd and Futrell, *Marketing Farm Products,* p. 228.

Marketing: Principles and methods

Marketing control programs

While cooperative marketing would appear to be a key way for farmers to build countervailing market power, it has limitations. Lack of agreement between members and court decisions in the sixties, which found some cooperative activities in violation of the antitrust laws, are evidence that some other form of governmental involvement in collective action is necessary. One answer is the marketing orders and agreements which became possible under the Agricultural Marketing Agreement Act of 1937. Many states have passed similar legislation to cover growers within a single state. Farmers and assemblers are permitted to organize to control the quantity of a specific product which will be *marketed*, with immunity from antitrust laws. Such agreements are commonly used in marketing fluid milk and some 90 varieties of fruits and vegetables.

Agreements differ from orders in that they apply only to signers of the agreement. Orders, administered by a control board of growers and assemblers, apply to all producers and assemblers if two thirds of the growers and one half of the assemblers favor the issuance of an order. Noncooperative farmers are thus forced into the conspiracy.

Federal orders are intended to provide for an orderly flow of the commodity to market throughout its normal marketing season. They regulate the marketing of only fresh products and place no limits on production. State orders also may cover marketing to canners and freezers, and a few include production controls. However, a state order can be of little value if the crop is also raised in another state which does not regulate the quantity marketed. Both types of orders usually establish minimum quality standards.

The quantity to be marketed is established by forecasting how much will be demanded at a minimum "fair" price. The control board must be careful not to set the price so high that the primary demand for the product is eroded by close substitutes, e.g., peaches for apricots. In order to estimate demand, the enabling legislation almost always requires producers and assemblers to pay the cost of marketing research. The market should be capable of segmentation so that price discrimination can be practiced in different form, quality, time, and geographic segments. To be useful, the commodity covered by the order should not be storable, so there is no carryover product to the next season.

Marketing orders can provide legal collusive control over the quality and quantity of product brought to market. Like any monopoly, however, producers are still subject to the whims of consumer demand.

Promotion and research support programs

In addition to marketing order boards, many state legislatures have established commodity commissions for the purpose of grading, promotion, and research of key commodities within the state. Well-known examples are the Florida Citrus Commission, the Maine Potato Commission, and the Washington State Apple Commission. The commissioners are producers or assemblers appointed by the state executive branch. In 1965, the Agricultural Marketing Agreement Act was amended to enable producers under federal marketing orders to undertake advertising also.

These commissions, marketing order boards, cooperatives, voluntary producer groups, and state agencies spend over $90 million per year for the promotion of their commodities. This amount is no more than 4 percent of total annual food advertising expenditures. The object of this advertising is to maintain and enlarge the primary demand for the commodity in question. Promotional activities take the form of consumer advertising, dealer promotion, point-of-sale promotions, preparation of educational materials, and public relations activities. While most of this promotion mentions the state of origin and not a specific brand, funds may be contributed to processors or distributors for brand promotion. All producers and assemblers of the commodity are compelled to participate, through assessment, in payment for this promotion.

In this way, legal collusion is permitted in attempts to influence the demand side of the market. With some exceptions, the small size of the budgets and part-time management of the funds create many doubts as to the effectiveness of these efforts.

SUMMARY

Agriculture is well suited as an example of a complete marketing system because the performance of all the marketing functions is obvious and observable. This was particularly true in previous decades when specialized middlemen performed these functions. Government also plays an active role in the system through the performance of storing, shipping, standardization and grading, financing, information, and even selling and risk taking.

Chief among the constraints placed on the agricultural marketing systems is the small scale of the basic production unit, the farm. As the system has evolved through time, the functions of traditional middlemen have changed. The development of large urban and international markets has led to the development of a more decentralized and vertically integrated marketing system. Central markets and independent middlemen have declined in importance, while large integrated processors and distributors have gained in market power.

To offset this power, government has been active in helping farmers establish countervailing power. Three power groups have emerged: the producers, the manufacturers, and the distributors. Control of the system is now achieved through the competitive rivalry between these groups as regulated by federal and state governments. Producer power has been established through marketing cooperatives, marketing orders and agreements, and commodity commissions, which all enjoy partial immunity from antitrust laws.

Review the chapter to see if you can identify the objectives of the system, the important environmental factors, the structural characteristics of the system, the way various institutions in the system perform the marketing functions, and the methods by which the system is controlled. The review questions that follow will help you evaluate your knowledge of the material in this chapter.

REVIEW AND DISCUSSION QUESTIONS

1. Explain the major characteristics of agricultural production and their significant marketing implications.

2. "Wholesalers dealing in agricultural consumers' goods operate in one or two—sometimes three—different markets." Distinguish carefully among these markets.

3. Discuss the processes of sorting out, assembling, allocating, and assorting which take place in wholesale markets for agricultural products.

4. Explain the reasons for the decentralization taking place in commercial livestock slaughtering in this country.

5. Discuss the need for and types of storage facilities required for marketing agricultural products.

6. Prepare a short paper on the subject "Health Regulations in the Marketing of Selected Agricultural Products and Their Marketing Implications."

7. Provide specific illustrations to prove the truth of the following statement: "A high degree of nonuniformity at the producing end and a demand for uniformity at the consuming end make self-evident the importance of standardization and grading for agricultural products."

8. Prepare a concise statement outlining the marketing of fresh fruits and vegetables in this country.

9. Explain briefly the nature of cooperative marketing.

10. Distinguish carefully between the objectives of farmers' cooperative marketing associations and those of consumers' cooperatives.

11. Discuss the factors responsible for the growth of cooperative marketing associations in this country.

12. How do cooperatives hope to reduce the cost of marketing? How successful have they been in their efforts?

13. Distinguish between and cite examples of government price support programs, acreage control programs, marketing control programs, and demand stimulation programs in agriculture.

14. What are the causes and effects of decentralization and vertical integration in the marketing of agricultural products?

15. Account for the merger and consolidation of a number of cooperative associations. What have been the major motivating forces behind these actions?

SUPPLEMENTARY READINGS

Darrah, L. B. *Food Marketing.* New York: Ronald Press Co., 1967. Through a functional approach, the author considers various aspects of the problems involved in marketing foods and suggests methods of improvement. Chapters 19–22 are of special interest.

Kohls, R. L. *Marketing of Agricultural Products.* 3d ed. New York: Macmillan Co., 1967. The approach to this elementary treatment of the marketing of farm products, is partly functional, partly institutional, and partly by commodities. The behavioral systems approach is recognized also.

Manchester, A. C. *The Structure of Wholesale Produce Markets.* Agricultural Economic Report No. 45. Washington, D.C.: U.S. Department of Agriculture, 1964. The primary focus of this excellent treatment is on 52 markets at the wholesale level—their structure, behavior, and efficiency—but consideration is given also to the competitive process at the shipping point and the retail level.

Mortenson, W. P. *Modern Marketing of Farm Products.* Danville, Ill.: Interstate Printers & Publishers, 1963. Developments in agricultural marketing, including wholesaling, are discussed in this small volume.

National Commission on Food Marketing *Food from Farmer to Consumer.* Washington, D.C.: Government Printing Office, 1966. This report is the summary volume and includes recommendations of the Commission.

National Commission on Food Marketing *Organization and Competition in the Fruit and Vegetable Industry.* Technical Study No. 4. Washington, D.C.: Government Printing Office, 1966. The marketing student will find this analysis of value in understanding the nature and functions of the fruit and vegetable markets and the competition therein.

National Commission of Food Marketing *Studies of Organization and Competition in Grocery Manufacturing.* Technical Study No. 6. Washington, D.C.: Government Printing Office, 1966. An excellent description of modern grocery manufacturing with special study of the cereal and cracker and cookie industries.

Shepherd, G. S., and Futrell, G. A. *Marketing Farm Products: Economic Analysis.* Ames: Iowa State University Press, 1969. This text, which places more emphasis on economic analysis than others in the field, consists of three major parts: (1) the analytical approach to marketing, (2) overall marketing problems, and (3) commodity marketing problems.

Marketing: Principles and methods

Part VI *Marketing in special fields*

In considering the total marketing system so far, we have divided it into retailing consumers' products, wholesaling consumers' products, and marketing industrial products. Attention will now be given to two topics that are increasingly important in the marketing of both consumers' and industrial products. These are services in the marketing system and global marketing systems.

Services are often presumed to be marketed like products. Some services, however, have characteristics that call for the use of different marketing systems. Chapter 15 outlines these systems and focuses on the importance of the service sector in the United States. Over 40 cents of every consumer dollar and over half of the work force are devoted to providing services rather than products.

Chapter 16 discusses the importance of global marketing and the differences and similarities in them that are relative to marketing systems in the United States. Global marketing systems and multinational corporations have expanded rapidly in the past decade, and the years ahead portend even greater growth and change. In another decade it may not be possible to analyze meaningfully a strictly "domestic" marketing system.

15 Services in the marketing system

"Products and services" is a phrase commonly used in reference to marketing systems. Services however, are virtually ignored in the emphasis on products. This would seem to suggest that services are limited or unworthy of notice, that they are not different from products in significant ways, or that they are too difficult to explain. Such is not the case. Not only are services important, but there are differences in services which directly affect marketing systems. In promoting a better understanding of services, this chapter will examine the extensiveness and importance of services in marketing systems and explain how the marketing of services differs from the marketing of products.

SERVICES—WHAT ARE THEY?

If products are tangible goods, then services must be intangible. We could say that services are intangible, identifiable satisfactions or helpful activities that are of value to some buyers and that may be (but are not necessarily) marketed independently of tangible goods. If this definition is tried out on activities that are known to be services—car repair, tooth extraction, tailoring, legal representation, or baby sitting—it is found that in each case the focus is on some activity resulting in utility or satisfaction for the buyer. There may be an accompanying sale of a product, but the sale of the service can occur independent from the product or cause the product to be sold.

Tangible, in this situation, means real physical properties which can be seen, heard, tasted, touched, or smelled. Because services for the most part do not possess these physical properties, they are intangible. While this definition provides a basic notion of what services are and how they are different from products, it is not sufficiently broad to include all of the "things" that the Bureau of the Census includes in the service category.[1]

Consumer services

A look at one classification of consumer services that has been used by the U.S. Department of Commerce will help provide a better picture of what the federal government means by services.

1. Housing (includes rentals of hotels, motels, apartments, and houses and imputed values for owner-occupied houses).
2. Household operations (includes electricity, gas, water, telephones, house repairs, repair of equipment in houses, landscaping, and household cleaning).
3. Personal business (includes legal, financial, accounting, and advertising).
4. Medical and death care (includes dentists, physicians, private hospitals, medical and hospitalization insurance, morticians, and burial insurance).
5. Transportation (includes automobile repair, tolls, auto insurance, and purchased transportation, including car leasing).
6. Recreation (includes television and radio repair, admissions, club and fraternal organizations, pari-mutuel receipts).
7. Religious and welfare activities.
8. Private education and research.
9. Clothing and accessories services (includes shoe repair, clothes repair, and cleaning).
10. Personal care (includes such things as barbershops, beauty parlors, massage facilities).
11. Foreign travel.

This particular classification refers only to consumer (not business) services provided by private (not government) organizations. Businesses and other organizations buy not only some of these services but others such as marketing and management consulting. In addition, governmental units provide numerous services ranging from police and fire protection to education, recreation, and garbage collection.[2] Table 15–1 lists the selected services, including many business services, that are reported in the *Census of Business*. Note that only two kinds of service businesses decreased over the four-year period from 1963 to 1967.

Service/product mix

Many "things" that are partially services and partially products end up being called either services or products. In fact, few services occur without products, and vice versa. The *Survey of Current Business* has illustrated this point by partitioning selected personal consumption expenditures into service and product components, as shown in Table 15–2.

Note that consumer expenditures for food and tobacco are listed as being 100

---

[1] See J. M. Rathmell, "What Is Meant by Services," *Journal of Marketing*, 30 (October 1966), pp. 32–36; R. C. Judd, "The Case for Redefining Services," *Journal of Marketing*, 28 (January 1964) pp. 58–59.

[2] For a detailed review of government services, see U.S. Bureau of the Census, *Census of Governments, 1967*, Vol. I, *Governmental Organizations* (Washington: Government Printing Office, 1968).

Marketing: Principles and methods

percent product (clearly an overstatement because it includes food served in restaurants), while expenditures for personal business, private education and research, religious and welfare activities, and housing are listed as 100 percent service. These are only rough estimates, but they do illustrate that services and products are frequently marketed together and that we cannot consider only pure services.

THE IMPORTANCE OF SERVICES

Over the past 20 years personal consumption expenditures have increased faster for services than for products. In 1947 about 31 cents out of every dollar of consumer outlays went for services.[3] By 1960 almost 40 cents went for services and by 1970 this had risen to over 42 cents out of each dollar (see Table 15–3). Part of this increase reflects the faster rise in the prices of services than in the average of prices for all consumer purchases. Even after adjustment for price changes, however, purchases of services have risen more than those of products.

The proportion spent on services is likely to increase as consumers spend more on such services as travel, recreation, education, medical services, and motel and hotel accommodations. These expenditures tend to rise as a society becomes more affluent and has more "leisure" time.

Employment in services, defined in its broadest terms to include both private and public, accounted for over 50 percent of the labor force in 1969 in the United States. One expert has estimated that the demand for more services, coupled with the difficulty of increasing productivity, will increase service-related employment to 60 percent by 1979, and it may go as high as 80 percent by 1989.[4]

Rapidly growing services

Housing is by far the largest of the services (over 34 percent),[5] but in terms of marketing activities it is somewhat less important. Housing consists largely of the service provided by occupied dwelling units. The estimate for this service includes not only rent paid by renters[6] but also the imputed value for owner-occupied housing, which accounts for over 70 percent of this infrequently marketed service.

Electric, gas, and telephone utilities have grown rapidly in the past 20 years. Between 1950 and 1960, expenditures for these utility services increased two and one half times, while prices increased somewhat less than average. A similar pattern has also prevailed over the past 10 years. Greater use of these services has been related to the increase in the number of housing units and the popularity of new electric and gas appliances, particularly for heating and cooling. Many houses have also been converted from the use of coal and oil (classified as products) to natural gas and electricity, which are classified as services.

Other services that have increased dramatically since 1950 include education, nonmortgage loan services, orchestras and entertainers, foreign travel, car body repair shops, motels and motor hotels, medical and other health services, trailer parks, car

---

[3] For prior years, see W. J. Regan, "The Service Revolution," *Journal of Marketing,* 27 (July 1963), pp. 57–62.

[4] E. B. Weiss, "Marketers: Don't Ignore Our Growing Service-Oriented Society," *Advertising Age,* May 5, 1969, pp. 105–6.

[5] *Survey of Current Business,* (May 1971), p. 13.

[6] See Federal Reserve Bank of Chicago, "The Growth of Consumer Services," *Business Conditions,* November 1960, pp. 5–10.

TABLE 15–1
Selected services: Number of establishments and sales, 1967 and 1963

Kind of business	All establishments, 1967		All establishments, 1963		Percent change, all establishments, 1963 to 1967	
	Number	Receipts (in billions)	Number	Receipts (in billions)	Receipts	Payroll, entire year
Selected services total..........	1,187,814	60,542,218	1,061,673	44,586,261	35.8	43.7
Hotels, motels, tourist courts, and camps total....	87,006	7,038,890	84,706	5,049,255	39.4	38.3
Hotels............	23,625	3,823,158	22,692	3,005,692	27.2	22.9
Motels, motor hotels, and tourist courts.........	41,954	2,709,567	41,584	1,661,371	63.1	84.3
Trailer parks........	12,437	272,468	9,769	169,406	60.8	91.3
Sporting and recreational camps.........	8,990	233,697	10,661	212,786	9.8	25.2
Personal services total........	498,935	11,750,132	447,080	9,163,208	28.2	33.8
Laundry, cleaning, other garment services........	111,926	5,432,301	109,740	4,357,339	24.7	24.0
Coin-operated laundries and dry cleaning.........	29,551	557,364	26,153	372,721	49.5	84.3
Other laundry, cleaning, garment services......	82,375	4,874,937	83,587	3,984,618	22.3	22.2
Power laundries, family and commercial*........	*	*	10,313	1,042,497	*	−8.2
Dry cleaning plants, except rug cleaning*........	*	*	31,722	1,437,171	*	37.6
Laundry and cleaning services, N.E.C........	*	*	10,864	1,151,534	*	37.2
Garment pressing, alteration, and repairs......	*	*	30,688	353,416	*	43.0
Beauty shops........	179,209	2,354,398	151,720	1,617,959	45.5	64.7
Barber shops........	112,497	1,020,315	105,516	906,557	12.5	20.8
Photographic studios........	26,558	745,172	19,544	494,987	50.5	52.5
Shoe repair, shoe shine, and hat cleaning shops......	16,270	207,054	21,486	208,121	−0.5	32.5
Funeral service and crematories........	20,191	1,516,593	20,529	1,298,462	16.8	24.5
Miscellaneous personal services........	32,284	474,299	18,545	279,783	69.5	56.7
Miscellaneous business services total......	211,835	22,595,345	147,668	15,192,622	48.7	63.3

Advertising	20,124	8,341,629	12,896	6,384,147	30.1	28.4
Services to dwellings and other buildings	33,822	1,411,617	25,893	874,538	61.4	61.8
Business and consulting services	39,114	3,086,516	24,256	1,361,250	126.7	140.8
Other miscellaneous business services	118,775	9,755,583	84,623	6,572,687	48.4	57.1
Equipment rental and leasing services*	*	*	9,341	839,507	*	54.0
Miscellaneous business services, N.E.C.*	*	*	75,282	5,733,180		57.4
Automobile repair, automobile services, garages total	139,243	7,028,209	139,611	5,443,937	29.1	29.3
Automobile repair shops	109,946	4,085,540	114,459	3,588,120	13.9	21.2
General automobile repair shops	57,838	1,849,743	72,416	1,842,453	0.4	12.1
Top and body repair shops	20,828	824,206	16,207	561,169	46.9	46.9
Other automobile repair shops	31,280	1,411,591	25,836	1,184,498	19.2	18.4
Automobile parking	10,606	483,809	11,269	415,605	16.4	13.3
Car, truck rental and leasing, services, N.E.C.	18,691	2,458,860	13,883	1,440,212	70.7	62.9
Miscellaneous repair services total	138,014	3,826,754	146,776	3,021,988	26.6	40.5
Electrical repair shops	47,886	1,328,884	61,186	1,115,770	19.1	50.5
Radio and television repair shops	33,063	702,912	43,203	628,485	11.8	57.9
Other electrical repair, incl. refrigeration	14,823	625,972	17,978	487,285	28.5	45.0
Reupholstery and furniture repair	19,418	349,482	17,880	293,469	19.1	31.1
Other repair shops and related services	70,710	2,148,388	67,710	1,553,954	38.3	44.9
Motion pictures total	16,752	3,476,121	16,381	2,582,811	34.6	34.4
Motion picture production, distribution, services	4,565	2,183,086	3,729	1,520,079	43.6	45.9
Motion picture theaters	12,187	1,293,035	12,652	1,062,732	21.7	12.5
Amusement and recreation services, except motion pictures, total	96,029	4,826,767	79,451	3,990,286	21.0	28.3
Producers, orchestras, entertainers	27,698	873,514	14,280	590,162	48.0	50.7
Bowling alleys, billiard, pool establishments	15,497	1,010,591	15,927	1,016,228	-0.6	4.6
Other amusement and recreation services	52,834	2,942,662	49,244	2,333,896	26.1	32.1

*Data not provided.

Source: U.S. Bureau of the Census, *1967 Census of Business, Vol. V, Selected Services: Area Statistics* (Washington, D.C.: Government Printing Office, pp. 1–6, 1–7.

TABLE 15–2
Personal consumption expenditures by type of product

	1959 (percent)	1964 (percent)
Food and tobacco		
Goods...	100.0	100.0
Services..	0.0	0.0
Clothing, accessories, and jewelry		
Goods...	89.1	89.8
Services..	10.9	10.2
Personal care		
Goods...	55.3	56.8
Services..	44.7	43.2
Housing		
Goods...	0.0	0.0
Services..	100.0	100.0
Household operation		
Goods...	59.1	57.9
Services..	40.9	42.1
Medical care and death expenses		
Goods...	23.3	21.4
Services..	76.7	78.6
Personal business		
Goods...	0.0	0.0
Services..	100.0	100.0
Transportation		
Goods...	75.5	77.2
Services..	24.5	22.8
Recreation		
Goods...	66.4	68.5
Services..	33.6	31.5
Private education and research		
Goods...	0.0	0.0
Services..	100.0	100.0
Religious and welfare activities		
Goods...	0.0	0.0
Services..	100.0	100.0
Foreign travel and remittances (net)		
Goods...	50.3	39.5
Services..	49.7	60.5
Total personal consumption expenditures		
Goods...	61.4	59.2
Services..	38.6	40.8

Source: Derived from *Survey of Current Business*, 45 (November 1965), pp. 20–23.

and truck rental and leasing services, beauty shops, and photographic studios. In addition, two services which are exclusively business—building maintenance and business and consulting services—have had sizable increases. Between 1963 and 1967 the latter increased by almost 130 percent, the largest increase of any service. Computer-based services are another leading growth area. Data processing service centers, which have been around since IBM popularized punched cards, had total sales estimated at in excess of $1.40 billion a year in 1970. Computer software houses

Marketing: Principles and methods

TABLE 15–3
Expenditures for consumer services

Year	Services (in billions)	Personal consumption expenditures (in billions)	Services expenditure as a percent of personal consumption expenditures
1947	$ 49.8	$160.7	31.0
1950	62.4	191.0	32.7
1955	91.4	254.4	35.9
1960	128.7	325.2	39.6
1965	175.5	432.8	40.8
1967	204.2	492.3	41.4
1969	241.6	577.5	41.9
1970	262.6	616.7	42.4

Source: Data for 1947–67 from *Business Statistics: 1969* (biennial supplement to *Survey of Current Business*), p. 1; 1970 data from *Survey of Current Business,* 51 (May 1971), p. 13.

had annual sales estimated at about $1 billion in 1969, and computer communication systems are expected to gross over $1.5 billion by 1973.[7]

A concrete way to illustrate recent increases in services is to compare the statistics provided by the *1963 Census of Business for Selected Services* with those for 1967 (see Table 15–1 above). Though limited to the seven service categories shown in the table, sales increased in the four years by almost 36 percent and the number of establishments increased by about 12 percent (from 1,061,673 to 1,187,814).[8]

Decreasing services

Very few services have decreased in absolute sales in the past 10 or 20 years. Motion picture theater receipts did decrease during the 1950s, but between the 1963 and 1967 Censuses of Business they increased by almost 22 percent, even though the number of establishments decreased by about 4 percent.

Absolute decreases in dollar sales and number of establishments occurred between 1963 and 1967 for two categories: shoe repair, shoe shine and hat cleaning shops and for bowling alleys, billiard and pool halls. Each has shown about a 0.5 percent decrease in sales, although the decrease adjusted for price increases would be much larger. The *number* of shoe repair establishments had decreased by about 25 percent, while there has been only a 3 percent decrease in the second category.

Other changes in the number of establishments and sales of selected services between 1963 and 1967 can be observed in Table 15–1. Since the receipts are all listed in actual dollars, some of the growth is accounted for by price increases.

In addition to the seven service categories reported on in the census, other services include rental of homes, sales by public utility or transportation companies, sale of insurance and securities, radio and television broadcasting, educational services, medical and other health services, legal services, museums, art galleries, botani-

---

[7] "A New Industry's Wild Ride," *Business Week,* May 24, 1969, pp. 64–78.

[8] U.S. Bureau of the Census, *1967 Census of Business,* Vol. V, *Selected Services: Area Statistics* (Washington, D.C.: Government Printing Office) pp. 1–6, 1–7.

cal and zoological gardens, nonprofit membership clubs, and a catch-all category called miscellaneous services.

NATURE OF SERVICE ESTABLISHMENTS

Most commercial service establishments (about 70 percent) are small, whether measured in terms of sales or number of employees. These numerous small establishments have accounted for less than 15 percent of the sales among the seven service categories regularly enumerated by the *Census of Business,* while the largest 5 percent of the establishments have accounted for about 60 percent of total receipts.

There is considerable variation in size of operation by kind of service establishment. Personal services and miscellaneous repair services, for example, have had a larger than average percent of small establishments and a smaller than average percent of large establishments. Automobile repair service establishments tend to be of medium size, with only a small percentage being either small or large. Several types of services tend to be large, predominantly business services, amusement and recreation services, and hotels, motels, and camps.

Single-unit operations predominate among service establishments listed by the census. Multiunit operations are the strongest in the fields of amusement and recreation, but even here they account for less than 20 percent of the establishments and less than 50 percent of the receipts. Most of these are motion picture theaters; almost half of these establishments are multiunit operations which earn two thirds of the receipts.

CHARACTERISTICS UNIQUE TO SERVICES

The vast variety of services makes it difficult to describe overall marketing procedures in this area. Therefore, the best approach appears to be to: (1) examine the two major characteristics that make services different from products, and (2) explain the resulting marketing differences. The two major characteristics are: *intangibility* and the *simultaneous production and receipt* of services. How these characteristics result in marketing differences is the subject of the final section of this chapter.

Intangibility

Services are either intangible or much less tangible than physical products. A buyer of products normally has an opportunity to see, touch, hear, smell, or taste them before he buys. Services such as insurance, funeral arrangements, automobile repair, dental care, and legal advice are much less tangible, especially prior to purchase. A seller of products, such as bakery goods, can do little to either add to or alter prospective buyers' perceptions of his products. In contrast, an insurance salesman, a lawyer, or an advertising account representative can provide little opportunity for prospective buyers to see, touch, smell, taste or hear their services as they are attempting to sell them and must provide perceptions of their services instead.

Marketing implications. Sellers of services must be able to conceptualize their services and/or benefits for prospective buyers. They must provide mental pictures of what buyers can expect to receive because physical product features are not available to help them communicate. Picture a salesman selling a car if the buyer is unable to see, drive, hear, or kick actual vehicles. Such, though, is the problem and the opportunity, that confronts sellers of intangibles.

Marketing: Principles and methods

The less tangible a service and the benefits it offers, the more need there is for verbal two-way communications and the more conceptualization leeway there is within the seller's domain. Salesmen attempting to sell cars, houses, or dogs are confronted by the old adage—"You can't change a sow's ear into a silk purse." The minister or rabbi selling a set of beliefs, an admissions officer promoting a college, an orthodontist "recommending" braces for a child's teeth—these salesmen have far fewer physical blocks to overcome.

The less tangible the service, also, the less the physical distribution problem. Sellers of services have little physical inventory to store or deliver.

Simultaneous production and receipt

For many services, production and receipt occur simultaneously. A buyer of a haircut, a tax return, a car repair, or entertainment in a theater is a recipient of these services as they are being produced. Satisfaction may continue to flow, but the buyer receives the activity as it is being produced. In contrast, a buyer of a car, a comb, an adding machine, or a television set may become a recipient of these products long after they are produced.

Products can be produced for inventory—most services cannot. Services also cannot be produced prior to demand or in locations other than where demanded. Haircuts, college educations, car repairs, and live sports events cannot be produced prior to demand, placed in inventory, and shipped to points where there is demand.

Latent capacity to provide services, however, can be provided prior to need, can be inventoried, and can be transported. Facilities for physicians, barbers, and automobile mechanics can all be readied, held in reserve, and transported to various sites. However, all capacity that goes unused each day is forever gone. Empty airplane space, unrented motel rooms, undercapacity audiences at football games, unused electrical generating capacity—all perish because they cannot be stored. Since unused capacity is inefficient, a major quest in service areas is to operate at near capacity.

Marketing implications.   There are five major interrelated marketing implications to simultaneous production and receipt of services.

1. *Few physical distribution middlemen.*   Storage and physical distribution facilities and associated middlemen cannot be used in the marketing of most services. Services, as indicated earlier, cannot be stored in anticipation of demand or to gain efficiencies in production. Nor can they be produced at one location and transported to another. Discrepancy in assortments between suppliers and demanders, particularly in time, quantity, and location, cannot be equalized as they are for products. Consequently, institutions in the channel system for services provide less assortment than do sellers of products, and buyers must collect their own needed assortments.

2. *Customer queues.*   To be efficient in the production of services—to plan near-capacity, even production—customers must be placed in waiting lines to receive the services. A car wash that can wash a car every four minutes, to be most efficient, needs a car available every four minutes. An inadequate supply of dirty cars will cause the car wash to stand idle at times, and an excess supply will call for space for customer queues or increased facilities to produce the service. The same sort of situation prevails for dentists, surgeons, electric power companies, and many other service suppliers.

On the other hand, buyers have varying levels of tolerance for delays. A person having a heart attack has no tolerance for delay in receiving medical services, but one needing treatment of varicose veins may be able to wait several months or more.

Some people are willing to wait for an hour or more in a barber or beauty shop, while others will not tolerate more than a five-minute delay.

3. *Channel mechanisms to control demand.* If there is to be efficient production of services, there must be marketing channel mechanisms to *secure* and *maintain* a sufficient and orderly flow of buyers over both time and space. These mechanisms may be operated internally by the service supplier or may be extended through his agents.

A surgeon relies on other physicians (generalists and in other specialties) to refer patients for surgery. If a surgeon gets too large a backlog of patients, he can postpone operations on patients who can tolerate delays, request that his agents (referring physicians) refer fewer patients, or accept referrals from fewer agents. Price can also be used as a regulating mechanism. Over a period of time that is adequate for feedback to patients, he can increase his prices. Similar selling agents and mechanisms are available to orthodontists, accountants, lawyers, mechanics, carpenters, plumbers, and a large number of other service producers.

Demand can also be increased. The service producers in need of more customers or clients can engage in more public, political, and social events in order to get more exposure to more prospective clients and to referral agents (persons who will recommend him to prospective clients). In some service categories, service producers directly solicit and pay for the assistance of referral agents; in others, solicitation and payment are more subtle.

In the case of service suppliers who use advertising, some control in regulating flows can be achieved through advertising content and timing. Advertising can communicate information about such things as double trading-stamps days or lower or higher price days. In general, it can be used to remind customers of their needs and of the availability of services to fill them.

To market services efficiently the buyers must be segmented or partitioned according to their tolerance for delay. For services such as medical, segmentation is relatively simple because it relates primarily to the patient's diagnosed health condition. A barber cannot easily assess the delay tolerance of his clients unless he has a chance to observe their behavior, but he can establish an appointment chair to provide service to those who are least tolerant. Finally, for some buyers, tolerance for delay may be related to price. In such cases the seller can allocate buyers over time through price variations, with the lowest prices being available at the most slack periods.

4. *Scale of operation.* The fourth marketing implication of simultaneous production and consumption is that producers of services generally have smaller size operations than do producers of products, largely because the producer must travel to get the services to the buyer, or vice versa. When the producer travels to the buyer, time is taken away from the production of services and the cost of those services is increased. It also costs time and money for buyers to travel to producers of services. These diseconomies of time and travel provide incentives to locate more service centers closer to prospective customers, which results in smaller service centers.

5. *Change in risk.* In the marketing of services some risks are lessened in that services are not produced in advance of demand. All risks are not absent, however; only the risk of having finished products in inventory awaiting sale is removed. As an illustration, a boutique manager purchases a line of shirts in anticipation of demand by prospective customers. He faces the risk that market demand will change from stripes to prints or from collars to collarless and that he will not be able to sell his

shirts at a profit. A barber, in contrast, does not pile up an inventory of crew cuts or any other hair styles. As hair styles change, most of his shop and equipment can be adapted to the new demands. The barber's major risk is that his time will go unused.

The distinguishing differences between services and products and the resulting marketing differences are summarized in Table 15–4. Many of the differences are a matter of degree (more, fewer, less, greater) rather than of kind.

TABLE 15–4
Differences between the marketing of services and products

	Services	Products	Marketing implications: Services compared to products	
1.	Intangible	Tangible	a)	More conceptualization
			b)	More communication
			c)	More conceptualization leeway
			d)	Fewer physical distribution problems
2.	Simultaneous production and receipt	Production prior to buyer purchase	a)	Fewer physical distribution middlemen
			b)	Sellers provide less assortment
			c)	Greater need for orderly flows or sequencing of buyers
			d)	More channel mechanisms and concern to secure and maintain more orderly flows of buyers
			e)	Smaller scale of operation
			f)	Less risk due to absence of preproduced services

SERVICE MARKETING

While it is not feasible to examine the marketing of all types of services, some illustrations are given. A look at several categories will provide some idea of how the marketing of services and products differs.

Personalized services

Personalized services are those wherein the individual producer renders the service directly to the buyer or directly to a product which belongs to the buyer. These are the most labor-intensive services. Some producers of direct-to-the-buyer personalized service are barbers, beauticians, dentists, physicians, photographers, and morticians. Services rendered to products of buyers indicate shoe repair, sewer cleaning, laundry and dry cleaning, lawn care, automobile repair, baby care, and repair and maintenance services.

The personalized direct-to-buyer services only infrequently make use of middlemen (agents) and normally have very short distribution channels. Because the service is delivered directly from the producer to the buyer, however, does not mean that service producers do all the selling of their services. They frequently use sales agents or advertising agencies to aid in the selling function.

Marketing personal services. Photographic services, for example, are occasionally sold by independent sales agents who contract with a photographer (or other retailers of services and products) to sell his services through a coupon book. The agent sells the coupon books to consumers who, in turn, receive special prices for finished photographs.

Mortician services are sold in a number of different ways by independent sales companies. A popular plan is to sell "pre-need" services. The sales company contracts to sell funeral services and/or burial plots for a mortician or cemetery. Salesmen sell the service and collect for it (sometimes on an installment basis), retaining their sales commissions and remitting the balance to the mortician who, of course, performs the funeral service.

For advertising, smaller service firms usually buy directly from the local media, but larger ones, like International Funeral Homes (an ownership group), may employ advertising agencies. Thus even some of the personalized service producers employ agent middlemen or facilitating marketing agencies to assist them in marketing their services.

A few types of personal service firms—laundry and dry cleaning plants and franchised automobile repair shops—engage in considerable promotion of their services. More commonly, however, marketing programs for services consist merely of the selection of good locations, the provision of attractive facilities, and the skillful performance of the services. An on-site location sign (e.g., a barber's pole) and some local advertising, including a listing in the Yellow Pages, are normally all the formal promotion used.

Marketing professional services. Many of the professions offering personal services used by consumers—legal, medical, and accounting—discourage individual members from the direct solicitation of *new customers* (clients or patients) except for address change notices, nameplates (shingles), and listings in the Yellow Pages. Practically speaking, they discourage the use of advertising and "hard sell" personal selling.

Two pages (of four) regarding the promotion of accounting services from the *Code of Professional Ethics* of the American Institute of Certified Public Accountants are shown in Figure 15–1. Note that they prohibit designating fields of specialization.

Expansion of services to *present customers* through the use of personal selling, by contrast, is largely left to the discretion of the individual practitioner. Some accountants, for example, urgently suggest to their consumer tax clients that they should partake of estate planning or financial planning and other services. Accountants can solicit such business personally or through the use of form letters to their clients.

The individual service provider who is new to a geographical area or wants additional clients sometimes can be listed by his county professional organization. The organization will inform county residents that such a list is available and upon receipt of an inquiry will provide two or three names to the prospective customer.

Another approach is for the provider to join an established practice that already has more demand than it can service. He may later establish a separate practice when he has acquired sufficient customers.

All of the professional services make use of referrals. Specialized physicians, dentists, and lawyers look to the general practitioners to send patients or clients to them. While direct rebates or discount payments are frowned on by the professions, many expenditures are made (and listed on tax returns) to secure such favors. A similar situation prevails for accountants, but they receive most of their referrals from bankers and lawyers.

Extensive public and social contacts are also helpful in securing new customers. Consumers prefer to go to lawyers, dentists, physicians, and accountants they know or at least know about.

FIGURE 15–1
Advertising by public accountants

Advertising prohibitions relating to announcements, directories, business stationery, business cards, and office premises.

In the opinion of the committee on professional ethics, Rule 3.01 prohibits a member or associate from advertising his professional attainments or services through any medium. The rule clearly prohibits the publication of an announcement, also referred to as a "card," or advertising in the usual form in newspapers, magazines or other public media. It prohibits imprinting members' names, or the firm names of members, on tax booklets or other publications prepared by others. It further prohibits the association with a member's name of such phrases as "tax consultant," "tax expert," "management services," "bank auditor" and any other designations which indicate the special skills that a member possesses or particular services which he is prepared to render. It does not prohibit the use of the firm affiliation and the CPA designation in connection with authorship of technical articles and books, and it does not prohibit publicity which is of benefit to the profession as a whole.

The committee recognizes, however, that there are media, which may or may not be available to the public generally, in which it is both professional and desirable for a member's name to appear under certain circumstances. Such media include card announcements, directories, business stationery, business cards, and office premises. The committee's views on the uses of such media are as follows:

1. Announcements
    a) Announcements of change of address or opening of a new office and of changes in partners and supervisory personnel may be mailed to clients and individuals with whom professional contacts are maintained, such as lawyers of clients and bankers.
    b) Such announcements should be dignified, and fields of specialization are not permitted to be included in the announcements.
2. Directories
    a) General
        (1) A listing in a classified directory is restricted to the name, title (certified public accountant), address and telephone number of the person or firm, and it shall not appear in a box, or other form of display, or in a type or style which differentiates it from other listings in the same directory.
        (2) Listing of the same name in more than one place in a classified directory is prohibited, and, where the classified directory has such headings as "Certified Public Accountants," or "Public Accountants," the listing shall appear only under one of those headings. Each partner's name, as well as the firm name, may be listed.
    b) Yellow (or business) section of classified telephone directories
        Listings are permitted only in the classified directories which cover the area in which a bona fide office is maintained. Determination of what constitutes an "area" shall be made by the state societies in the light of local conditions.
    c) Trade associations and other membership directories
        (1) Listings of members in such directories are restricted to the information permitted in 2(a) and 2(a) (2) above, and, if classified, are further restricted to a listing under the classification of "Certified Public Accountants" or "Public Accountants."
        (2) Where the directory includes geographical as well as alphabetical listings, a member may be listed in such geographical section in addition to the listing permitted above.
3. Business stationery
    a) Information appearing on a member's stationery should be in keeping with the dignity of the profession. It shall not include a listing of areas of specialization of the member or his firm, and separate stationery for tax or management services, or other specialized departments of the firm, is prohibited.
    b) The stationery may include
        (1) The firm name, names of partners, names of deceased partners and their years of service, and names of staff men when preceded by a line to separate them from the partners.
        (2) The letters "CPA" following the name, the use of the words "Certified Public Accountant(s)," the address (or addresses) of office(s), telephone number(s), cities in which other offices and correspondents are located, and membership in professional societies in which all partners are members.

Source: American Institute of Certified Public Accountants, *Opinion No. 11:* "Advertising and Indication of Specialty Prohibited," in *Code of Professional Ethics,* December 30, 1969, pp. 20–21.

Individual providers generally use indirect or "soft" methods of marketing to secure new customers, rather than aggressive hard-selling methods. Because of the prevailing attitudes among members of these professions and the public, aggressive marketing methods probably would yield less, rather than more, results. Several of the professional associations, in addition to withdrawing membership from providers who violate their codes of ethics, have sufficient power to force such members to lose their state-granted licenses to practice the profession.

While advertising by individuals is discouraged, collective advertising by a county, state, or national association is commonplace. Bar groups typically advertise the advisability of consulting an attorney before buying real estate or signing a contract, and they urge the drawing of wills. Dentists attempt to "educate" the public to see their dentists twice a year. Physicians' groups promote annual physical examinations (and get immense aid in the effort from the pharmaceutical companies). In recent years they have also engaged in considerable advertising in attempts to improve the overall image of the medical profession.

Finally, both individually and collectively, service providers have worked at discrediting those persons and groups they view as being in competition with them. The American Medical Association and its individual members have battled both osteopaths and chiropractors before state agencies, through word of mouth, and even through advertisements for many years. Certified public accountants have been quite effective in gaining regulation of public accounting services and in establishing difficult entry requirements into the field. They have even been able to get telephone companies to list bookkeeping services (which incidentally are an important part of the services many certified public accountants provide) separate from accounting services in the Yellow Pages.

Marketing business services. Marketing activities of attorneys and certified public accountants (both of which offer business as well as consumer services) have been considered as professional services because marketing restrictions on them are more restraining than those on other business services. At the other end of the extreme in attempting to secure new clients are advertising agencies and some management consulting firms. While advertising agencies are free to advertise their own services, their major efforts are devoted to personal selling. Their salesmen (account executives) call on prospective clients (sometimes the clients of other agencies) and seek invitations to show advertisers what can be done for them.

Because management consultants typically do not have continuing relations with their clients, they use a variety of marketing methods to gain and retain favorable visibility among prospective clients and referral agents. Advertising is used in appropriate trade and professional journals (see Figure 15–2). Like accountants and lawyers, they seek speaking engagements before appropriate business groups and prepare articles and books for publication. It is also common for consulting firms to publish house organs and various brochures for the use of past and prospective clients as well as referral agents.

Most firms selling business services prefer to be invited to describe their offerings and to make specific proposals.[9] Some long-established firms that are widely and favorably known can limit their marketing prospecting practices to the indirect solicitation of invitations. Once an invitation to talk is secured, the personal selling begins.

Virtually all business services are both sold and rendered directly by the producer

---

[9] E. B. Turner, "Marketing Professional Services," *Journal of Marketing,* 33 (October 1969), pp. 56–61.

FIGURE 15–2

Example of advertisement used by management consultants in trade and professional journals

For your consideration...
...our full service concept

 National Mail Panel

 Advanced Computer Capabilities

 Telephone Research Center

 CENSTAT

 Personal Interviewing Capabilities

 Probability Sampling

 Test Marketing

 Marketing Consultant Services

 Insta–Vue

 DATA Services

 TvQ

 Full Service Agency

HOME TESTING INSTITUTE

DIVISION OF WESTAT INC

50 MAPLE PLACE • MANHASSET, NEW YORK 11030 • (516) 627–7510

410 NORTH MICHIGAN AVE.• CHICAGO, ILLINOIS 60611 • (312) 644–4777

PLEASE CONTACT EITHER OFFICE FOR A DESCRIPTIVE BROCHURE

Source: *Journal of Marketing Research, 8 (November 1971), p. 40*

to the buyer. No middlemen are involved, and very few facilitating agencies are used. However, within the firm there are salesmen whose job it is to sell and technicians whose job it is to deliver or render the service.

Financial services

Financial services are marketed to both business managers and final consumers. Rather than being personalized, they are often an organizational offering. Some of the major financial services are in the areas of banking, insurance, and securities.

Bank marketing. Until very recently, few banks have *practiced* the marketing concept. Instead, the typical banker has asked his customers to remember their account number, write it out on every transaction, come to his "store" only between 9:30 A.M. and 2:30 P.M. on only five days a week for anything more than routine money changing, and wait in four different lines for four different services. His trust or other service departments may not be upgraded from 1950 standards. Yet he has promoted his operation as a full-service bank.

Bankers do relatively little marketing of their services compared to other retailers and wholesalers, but they do engage in some advertising. Some banks use salesmen to seek and expand sales to commercial accounts although these activities are usually not well planned or integrated into overall bank programs.[10] The most meaningful marketing tools currently used by banks, particularly country banks, are not much different than they were years ago: high traffic, easy accessible locations, bank officers with broad bases of contact, and boards of directors consisting of prominent, influential customers.[11]

Insurance marketing. The insurance contract is a blend of indirect, future, and contingent services in connection with risk. The contract is about the only tangible aspect that can be presented to a prospective buyer, and it is difficult for prospects to comprehend. Consequently, sellers must describe both their services and the benefits they promise.

The marketing system for insurance has many facets. About two thirds is distributed on a voluntary (private) basis and the remainder on a social (government tax-supported) basis. Private insurance is marketed through four main channels: (1) direct selling, (2) agency, (3) brokerage and (4) group.[12]

1. *Direct selling.* The direct-selling channel exists when the insurer, through its employees, deals directly with the insured. State Farm Insurance and Allstate Insurance Company, which use their own retail outlets, are illustrations. Mutual of Omaha sells flight insurance directly to consumers through airport vending machines and over counters.

Direct-mail marketing of insurance is also important. Government Employee Group grew from one company with assets of only $296,000 in 1936 to a family of five affiliated corporations with assets of $647 million in 1970. While this group no longer limits itself only to direct-mail marketing, it claims its mail marketing has

[10] For views on bank marketing and the marketing concept, see R. H. Brien and J. E. Stafford, "The Myth of Marketing in Banking," *Business Horizons,* Spring 1967, pp. 71–78; and "Banks Are on Marketing Threshold," *Marketing Insights,* April 8, 1968, p. 17.

[11] L. H. Hodges, Jr., and R. Tillman, Jr., *Bank Marketing: Text and Cases* (Reading, Mass.: Addison-Wesley Publishing Co., 1968).

[12] D. L. Bickelhaupt, "Trends and Innovations in the Marketing of Insurance," *Journal of Marketing,* 31 (July 1967), pp. 17–22.

Marketing: Principles and methods

permitted it to offer insurance rates from 15 to 25 percent below those charged by others.[13]

2. *Agency channel.* The agency channel is composed of two parts—*independent* and *exclusive* agencies. Life insurance companies have long used a marketing system based predominantly on exclusive agents. These agents represent only one insurance company; the agent does not own the expiration records or other policyholder data, and the insurance company has the right to appoint a new agent to serve the policyholder if the existing agency relationship is terminated.

In contrast, the independent agent usually represents several insurance companies and controls his own records. He may retain his customers when he changes companies by placing the business with another of his insurers. Because he represents the offerings of several companies, the independent agent can serve his clients with a more complete assortment.

3. *Brokerage channel.* Brokers legally represent the insured rather than the insurer. The broker places the business for the insured, unlike the agency system where the agent technically is writing the insurance for the insurer. The brokerage channel is strongest in the commercial field, where the buyer is more concerned with the overall concept of "risk management."

4. *Group channel.* Under this channel the insurance is written mainly through employers, creditors, unions, or trustees for their employees or members. The employer (or other party) in effect is a middleman in that the insurer makes a contract with the organization to insure its members. The organization typically explains the contract alternatives that are available, enrolls members, and administers the insurance, including the collection of fees.

The group channel has been used for years in marketing health (Blue Cross/Blue Shield) and life (Bankers Life) insurance. While many states still limit group selling to life and health insurance, the sale of fire, automobile, and other types of insurance through the group channel is undergoing rapid expansion. The major advantage appears to be that the selling costs are greatly reduced. One insurer claims to have lowered its acquisition costs to less than 5 percent of the premium.[14]

Securities marketing. The marketing of securities is similar to the marketing of commodities. New securities (corporate stocks, bonds, and notes) originate with a corporation that wants to raise money. Arrangements for issuing and marketing or distributing securities usually are made through one or a syndicate of several security underwriting houses (investment bankers). They normally agree to purchase the issue at from 1 to 5 percent below the price they estimate the market will pay. This serves as their risk and service margin.

The underwriters are wholesalers in that they sell to banks and others not participating directly in the underwriting. They also do some retailing and sometimes will arrange private issues directly to large investors. The buying institutions serve as retailers by selling to ultimate investors, who may include institutional investors (insurance companies, trust funds, etc.), as well as individuals.

During the time when the issue is being distributed, the underwriters may support the market by buying the security at the initial retail price. This arrangement may tempt underwriters to underprice rather than overprice securities for which they guarantee a market.

---

[13] "Go Go Group," *Barron's,* April 19, 1971, pp. 5 and 23.

[14] Bickelhaupt, "Trends and Innovations in the Marketing of Insurance," p. 20.

The promotion of new securities is regulated by state and federal agencies. Federal regulations administered by the Securities and Exchange Commission tend to be more restraining than state regulations. Securities supposedly can be offered only through a written statement (prospectus) that describes in detail the corporation, its officers, and its financial status, which must be "certified" by a public accounting firm.[15]

Once issued, securities are traded on organized stock markets (the best known in the United States are the New York Stock Exchange and the American Stock Exchange), over-the-counter markets, and directly among individuals. The various stock exchanges are owned and operated by their members but regulated by the Securities and Exchange Commission. Trading in the exchange is limited to member firms called brokers, and stocks must meet specified criteria for listing. Brokers for the most part represent both buyers and sellers and are compensated by a schedule of regulated commissions paid by both. The market prices and the volumes of the exchanges are made public second by second as the market operates. Many of the brokerage houses maintain retail offices with "ticker tapes" and visual display boards reporting transactions as they occur and accepting various orders to buy and to sell securities. The selling function in these retail outlets is conducted by salesmen, sometimes called investment advisors.

Over-the-counter markets trade largely in unlisted (not listed on a formal exchange) securities. They are maintained by brokers and other interested parties by quoting "ask" and "bid" prices and by transacting the exchange of the securities. These markets, which are located in all the principal cities, are tied together through a network of cables, computers, and cathode-ray tubes to form an information system called NASDAQ.[16]

Those interested in the marketing of services in more detail or variety can find a wealth of material. One of the most penetrating studies is *Performing Arts: The Economic Dilemma.*[17]

SUMMARY

Services constitute a wide variety of activities, benefits, and "things" offered by public and private not-for-profit organizations as well as by profit-seeking enterprises. In general, they are less tangible than products, which may or may not accompany them.

We have considered services as constituting activities and satisfactions that can be rendered independently of products. Service activities like personal selling or gift wrapping, that occur only in connection with the sale of products have not been included. It is evident, however, that the marketing of many services and products is associated both by types of institutions and activities. Firms like Montgomery Ward & Company and Sears, Roebuck and Company in recent years have expanded their offerings of services to include income tax preparation, car rentals, automobile repair, and the sale of insurance.

Measured virtually by any dimension, services in the United States are important. Consumer expenditures for services account for over 42 cents out of every dollar.

---

[15] If this sounds like nobody can be bilked, see "Widow and Orphan," *Barron's*, June 21, 1971, p. 5.

[16] "Making a Market," *Barron's*, March 8, 1971, p. 3.

[17] W. J. Baumol and W. G. Bowen, *Performing Arts: The Economic Dilemma* (Cambridge, Mass.: M.I.T. Press, 1966).

Expenditures for consumer, business, and social services have been increasing proportionally faster than for products. Increased concern with ecology and the growing scarcity of resources may lead to a shift in emphasis away from physical products and toward services, both commercial and social. As one example, more widespread automobile leasing and use of public transportation (both services) should lessen the demand for automobiles and related products.[18]

Because services are less tangible and because production and receipt occurs simultaneously, many services are marketed through systems which are different from those used for products. There is no transportation or storage of services, and physical distribution functions and middlemen are rarely present in the system. Discrepancy of assortments for services must be managed by segmenting buyers by their tolerance for delay and by devising mechanisms for locating and sequencing them through service centers. Private service producers tend to be smaller than producers of products because either the consumer or the supplier of most services must be transported to the other.

A major function of government is to provide services. Governmental units are confronted with about the same marketing problems and opportunities that challenge private organizations as they seek to provide police and fire protection, education, research, medical care service, entertainment and recreation, and a vast array of other services.

REVIEW AND DISCUSSION QUESTIONS

1. What are services and how are they different from products?
2. List some services which to you appear to be more like products. Why are they listed as services and not as products?
3. Why have services been growing in importance in the past 20 years?
4. What are the major marketing implications that arise from the increased consumption of services?
5. What services will show the largest increases in the next five years? Why? Which services will show the largest decreases? Why?
6. What differences does intangibility make in the marketing of services?
7. What differences occur in the marketing of services because their production and receipt by customers occurs simultaneously?
8. Explain how a group of three certified public accountants new in a city should market the services of their public accounting firm.
9. Explain how an experienced, licensed barber, new in a city, could market the services of his barber–beauty shop.
10. Why are very few physical distribution middlemen used in the marketing of services? Why are relatively few middlemen of any kind used in the marketing of services?
11. Describe a bank that has fully adopted the marketing concept.
12. Why do several of the professions severely limit promotion of services to nonclients or nonpatients?

---

[18] L. P. Feldman, "Societal Adaptation: A New Challenge for Marketing," *Journal of Marketing,* 35 (July 1971), pp. 54–60.

13. What are the major similarities and differences in the marketing of services and products?

14. Are service organizations in general more customer oriented than product organizations? Explain.

15. Which type of insurance marketing channel—direct selling, independent agency, or exclusive agency—is likely to provide customers with the most satisfaction? Explain.

SUPPLEMENTARY READINGS

Baumol, W. J. and Bowen, W. G.   *Performing Arts: The Economic Dilemma.* Cambridge, Mass.: M.I.T. Press, 1966. Discusses in detail the nature of many of the performing arts (services), the factors affecting demand and earning, pricing practices, and financial support from outside sources.

Hodges, L. H., Jr. and Tillman, R., Jr.   *Bank Marketing: Text and Cases.* Reading, Mass.: Addison-Wesley Publishing Co., 1968. Good discussion and many illustrations of the marketing of financial services by banks.

Johnson, E. M.   *An Introduction to the Problems of Service Marketing Management.* Newark, Del.: Bureau of Economics and Business Research, University of Delaware, 1964. A basic introduction to some of the problems special to the marketing of services.

Parker, D. D.   *The Marketing of Consumer Services.* Business Study Series, No. 1. Seattle: University of Washington, 1960. This monograph explores some of the differences and similarities between the marketing of services and products.

16 Global marketing systems

While everyone knows that a Coke can be bought virtually anywhere in the free world, not all are aware that there are K-Marts in Australia or that Avon ladies call on customers in Venezuela, Mexico, France, Canada, Spain, Italy, and England. Singer sewing machine salesmen have been known around the globe since before 1880. Sears, Roebuck and Company extends throughout South and Central America, for years has been a partner with Canadian Simpsons-Sears, and recently opened its first store in Spain. Woolworth stores have dotted the landscape of Great Britain for a long time and also can be found in Canada, Germany, Mexico and, more recently, Spain.[1]

IBM, Inc., through its World Trade Corporation, operates in over 105 countries, employs about 100,000 foreign employees (about one third of their payroll), and makes over one third of its sales in foreign markets. Ford Motor Company has been selling about one fourth of its output outside the United States; in 1967 over 90 percent of Ford's net income came from foreign sales due to a domestic labor strike. International Telephone and Telegraph Corporation operates in about 70 countries and in recent years has been making 40 to 50 percent of its sales and about 35 to 50 percent of its net income overseas.[2]

The largest advertising agencies, almost without exception, have foreign offices —and not only in London. McCann-Erickson and Norman, Craig and Kummel have received over 50 percent of their billings in recent years from foreign markets, and five others at least 30 percent.[3]

---

[1] S. C. Hollander, "The International Storekeepers," *Business Topics,* Spring 1969, pp. 13–23.

[2] D. S. R. Leighton, "The Internationalization of American Business—The Third Industrial Revolution," *Journal of Marketing,* 34 (July 1970), pp. 3–6; and *Fortune,* September 15, 1968, p. 105.

[3] "Madison Avenue Goes Multinational," *Business Week,* September 12, 1970, pp. 48–58.

Table 16–1 shows the importance of global marketing to 25 U.S. companies in 1970. Relationships between net assets, sales, and profits from abroad for each company (for example, the differences in these factors for Hoover, IBM, and Koehring) can be noted.

TABLE 16–1
Foreign net assets, sales, and net earnings as percent of corporate totals for selected U.S. companies, 1970

Company	Percent net assets abroad	Percent sales abroad	Percent net earnings abroad
American Cyanamid	18	25	24
American Standard	n.a.	36	33
Anaconda	9	n.a.	2
Beatrice	23	15	20
Black and Decker	40	42	50
Charles Pfizer	47	47	55
Chrysler (excludes Canada)	27	24	Loss
Eli Lilly	15	28	27
Ford Motor	28	26	24
General Motors (excludes Canada)	9	19	19
Goodyear Tire and Rubber	37	n.a.	43
Gulf Oil	22	n.a.	21
H. J. Heinz	45	45	47
Hoover	82	59	35
International Business Machines	29	39	50
International Harvester	29	25	14
International Telephone and Telegraph	26	42	35
J. Walter Thompson	20	37	35
Koehring	24	18	50
Mobil Oil	45	59	49
National Cash Register	43	45	51
Procter and Gamble	16	n.a.	20
Standard Oil (N.J.)	48	n.a.	52
Xerox	24	30	38
Warner-Lambert Pharmaceutical	20	33	33

Source: *Business International,* July 2, 9, 23; August 27; and September 24; all 1971.

Global operations are not limited to U.S.–based companies. Unilever and Nestlé have placed their products in households throughout the world for years. Unilever, an English-Dutch company (Lever Bros. in the United States), has manufacturing plants in more than 50 countries and sells its products in over 70. Unilever sells more washing products than Procter and Gamble and more processed foods than General Foods. Nestlé, a Swiss company, has about 250 plants in about 40 countries and operates over 200 sales forces.[4] German-built cars, and more recently Japanese ones, are common on American streets and highways which are dotted by Shell service stations owned by the Royal Dutch/Shell Group.

Thousands of other multinational companies market their products and services

---

[4] For a comparative analysis of marketing by Unilever, Nestlé, and Beecham Group, see: J. C. Baker, "Multinational Marketing: A Comparative Case Study," in B. A. Morin (ed.), *Marketing in a Changing World,* conference proceedings, American Marketing Association, June 1969.

Marketing: Principles and methods

beyond their domestic borders. While U.S. companies engage in more global market-ing than those of any other country, organizations with home bases in Great Britain, Germany, France, Italy, Japan, and Switzerland, to mention a few, are also promi-nent.[5]

EXPORTS AND DIRECT PRIVATE INVESTMENTS

Exports

Global marketing operations partake of two basic formats. First, there are home-country-based operations which lead to exports from one nation to another. This is the situation when products produced in one nation are marketed in other nations. Canadian and U.S. wheat, for example, is sold to companies in Great Britain; Volkswa-gen cars and parts manufactured in Germany are sold in the United States. Exports include both raw materials, like coffee beans, crude oil, coal, and corn, and manufac-tured and processed products, like fabrics, transistors, cameras, camera lenses, and pumps, which may or may not need further processing or assembling prior to resale.

Direct private investments

Second, there are foreign-based operations and arrangements in which the predominate mode of operation is direct private investments in processing, manufac-turing, and marketing operations in foreign countries. Sears, Woolworth, Ford, IBM, and McCann-Erickson, for example, own and operate facilities in foreign markets. Companies like Ford and IBM market their foreign-produced goods for the most part in foreign markets, although they may export some to the United States. Firms with plants and/or marketing facilities located in more than one nation which are exten-sively engaged in global marketing have become known as multinational companies.

Alternatives and problems of firms who make direct investments abroad multiply rapidly. The firm can export from its overseas operation back to its own country or to third countries. The out-of-country operation also influences the nature of home-country exports. To start a tractor plant in South America, the John Deere Company, for example, exported virtually all of the manufacturing equipment. While they now export far fewer tractors to South America, they do export many more components to be used in manufacturing their tractors.[6]

As we shall see later in the chapter, there are a number of ways a firm can hedge making the total direct investment in an out-of-country operation. Licensing and technical assistance contracts, for example, drastically reduce the amount of direct investment required to establish foreign production.

Magnitude and expansion

Direct investments abroad by U.S. companies by 1970 were estimated at about $79 billion with sales of just over $157 billion. Total U.S. exports for the same year

---

[5] For some explanation of Japanese successes, see J. C. Abegglen, "Japan, Incorporated: Government and Business as Partners," in R. Moyer (ed.), *Changing Marketing Systems,* conference proceedings, American Marketing Association, Winter 1967, pp. 228–32.

[6] A lucid discussion of the effects of foreign investments on the U.S. balance of trade and payments is "Why the U.S. Must Sell More Overseas," *Business Week,* January 4, 1969, pp. 40–54.

were estimated to be about $43 billion.[7] While direct investments generated about 3.7 times the sales of exports, the more important point is that U.S. companies, as shown in Figure 16–1, were involved in global marketing to the extent of about $200 billion.[8]

FIGURE 16–1
Global sales by U.S. companies, 1970

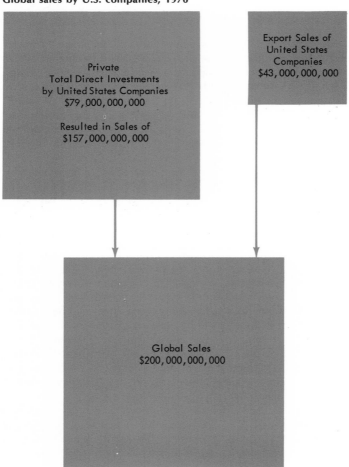

During the 1960s, direct private investment abroad by U.S. companies increased approximately 10 percent per year, while exports grew at about 7 percent per year. This level of expansion is expected to continue through the 1970s.

---

[7] "Current Business Statistics, Foreign Trade of the United States," *Survey of Current Business,* 51 (June 1971), p. S–21. This source also disaggregates the data by country and product category.

[8] N. W. Hazen, "Overseas High Stakes of Multinational Firms," in B. A. Morin (ed.), *Marketing in a Changing World,* conference proceedings, American Marketing Association, June 1969, pp. 47–52.

Importance of U.S. global marketing

How important are the global marketing activities of U.S. companies? The United States for many years has led the other nations of the world in exports, accounting in recent years for approximately 17 percent of the total. The second largest exporter has been Germany, with about 11 percent. Thus, in terms of total exports by all nations of the world, the United States leads.

Another measure of the degree of importance of exports to the total economy of a country is to compare them with its gross national product. Exports expressed as a percent of GNP for the United States have been between 4 and 5 percent in recent years. By comparison, comparable measures for West Germany and Great Britain have been 18–19 percent and approximately 25 percent for Switzerland. The world's highest has been approximately 36 percent for Belgium. Figure 16–2 helps indicate that the economic role of exports in the U.S. economy is not nearly so important as for many other nations of the free world.

FIGURE 16–2
Exports expressed as a percent of gross national product, selected countries, 1970

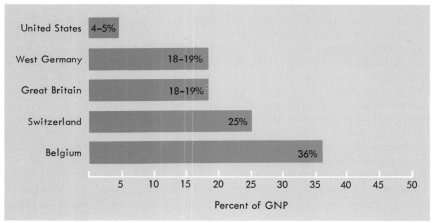

In terms of direct foreign investments, the United States accounted for an estimated $66 billion of the estimated world total of $90 billion at the end of 1968. Great Britain, the second largest investor, was estimated at about $15 billion, with the remaining investments spread among other European nations and Japan.[9]

The magnitude of U.S. investments abroad was illuminated by a French politician and journalist, Jean-Jacques Servan-Schreiber, in *Le Défi Américain* (*The American Challenge*), who feared that Europe was being turned into an American economic colony. He wrote, "Fifteen years from now the world's third greatest industrial power, just after the United States and Russia, may not be Europe, but American Industry in Europe."

---

[9] Ibid.

IS GLOBAL MARKETING DIFFERENT?

A general knowledge of marketing systems seems to indicate that global and domestic marketing do not differ markedly. Discrepancy of assortments is not limited to the United States but is present in all countries. The activities of the equalization process—sorting out, assembling, allocating, and assorting—are universal. There are far more similarities than differences between domestic and global marketing, and a good understanding of marketing systems is essential to understanding global marketing systems.[10] However, a *general* understanding of marketing systems, while necessary, is not sufficient. Global marketing requires additional inputs.

Gordon Miracle and Gerald Albaum, in their book on international marketing management, put it rather succinctly. To be qualified in global marketing requires: "(1) technical competence in marketing, (2) specialized knowledge of the factors in the international environment which are dissimilar or absent from the domestic environment, and (3) the ability to utilize such knowledge in working with others, at home or abroad, to develop and implement sound marketing programs."[11]

Item 1 can be examined extensively in this book. Item 2 requires somewhat more detailed knowledge of international trade theory, international payments, finance, money, banking, and political constraints on trade than that presented in this chapter. In addition it requires some knowledge of the comparative economic, resource, legal, and political environments in which global marketing must operate.

Item 3, concerning the cultural environment, is a more difficult task. Culture is the total social heritage of a people—their knowledge, beliefs, values, arts, customs, skills, technology, social institutions, and language. In discussing the role of culture as an exogenous variable in the buyer behavior model in Chapter 4, it was assumed that the seller was of the same or a similar culture. For the global marketer, that assumption does not hold. The international marketing references at the end of this chapter should be consulted for a complete discussion.[12] A key term to remember is *cultural empathy,* which Harry Evarts defines as being able to recognize cultural differences and to understand them sufficiently well to effectively communicate and direct human effort to implement marketing decisions.[13]

A starting place is to understand the basis of global marketing. With this as background, the major operational alternatives available to global marketers can be examined. Finally, attention will be focused on the environment for global marketing, particularly the economic and financial aspects.

BASIS OF GLOBAL MARKETING

All marketing is based on two factors. The first is that both individuals and organizations tend to specialize in areas of relative proficiency and to exchange

---

[10] R. Bartels, "Are Domestic and International Marketing Dissimilar?" *Journal of Marketing,* 32 (July 1968), pp. 56–61.

[11] G. E. Miracle and G. S. Albaum, *International Marketing Management* (Homewood, Ill.: Richard D. Irwin, Inc., 1970), pp. 8–9.

[12] For some illustrations both of cultural differences and the difficulty of providing useful classifications, also see J. L. Goldstucker, "The Influence of Culture on Channels of Distribution," in R. L. King (ed.), *Marketing and the New Science of Planning,* conference proceedings, American Marketing Association, Fall 1968, pp. 468–73; Y. Wind, "Cross Cultural Analysis of Consumer Behavior," in R. Moyer (ed.), *Changing Marketing Systems,* conference proceedings, American Marketing Association, Winter 1967, pp. 183–85; and S. P. Sethi, "Comparative Cluster Analysis for World Markets," *Journal of Marketing Research,* 8 (August 1971), pp. 348–54.

[13] H. Evarts, "Internationalization of Business Courses: Basic Assumptions," in L. G. Smith (ed.), *Reflections on Progress in Marketing* (Chicago: American Marketing Association, 1965), pp. 600–604.

surpluses. It is reasonable for oranges and grapefruit to be grown in Florida and Texas and for automobiles to be manufactured in Michigan made from steel processed in Indiana and mined in Minnesota. The second is that if labor and other cost conditions change, industry moves. When New England textile manufacturers and the Midwest poultry industry moved to the South, they faced no major state or national barriers.

Pooling of resources and the freedom to relocate encourage more efficient manufacturing and marketing. They help provide more and better goods and services at lower prices. Thus the rudiments of global marketing are merely extensions of those for all marketing.

Differences in natural resources, capital, and labor

Countries, like states, vary in their abilities to produce the products and services people want because of differences in combinations of natural resources, capital, and quality and quantity of labor. Some parts of the world are well endowed with coal, oil, iron ore, and other minerals that are essential for an industrial base. Some climates encourage the production of bananas, sugar cane, and coffee, while others are more favorable to wheat or cotton.

More advanced countries have accumulated capital, but capital deficiencies prevent economically deprived nations from developing capital-intensive industries. Consequently, a country like India may have the appropriate natural resources and the need for fertilizer plants, but it may not have the money to construct them. The bulk of the population of numerous countries faces the universal economic problem of the poor—they must expend all of their energy and income to sustain a meager level of subsistence. No capital is left over to invest for future returns.

The quality and quantity of labor also influence the goods and services a country will produce. In most of the Orient, unskilled labor is available in immense quantity, but skilled labor (particularly managerial skills) is in very short supply. Almost the opposite is true in the United States. Over the centuries certain peoples have also developed special skills. The Japanese, with a reputation for nimble fingers, have surpassed in the assembly of intricate items of manufacture. Norwegians have been seafaring, and Americans have been aggressive salesmen.

Finally, some countries have relatively inexpensive access to many markets. Japan can transport cars and steel to the heavily populated West Coast of the United States at less cost than producers in Michigan and Indiana. The mountainous, land-locked country of Switzerland has concentrated on the manufacture of watches, precision instruments, and other high-value products that can bear expensive transportation costs.

Differences in costs

The differences in combinations of natural resources, capital, and labor result in differences in the costs of producing various goods and services. Bananas and coffee beans can be grown in the United States, Japan, or Germany, but at nowhere near the low cost possible in Brazil. Cars can be manufactured in Brazil but at greater cost than in the United States, Japan, or Germany.

The cost structure of a country tends to remain rather permanent. Mineral resources can be developed only if they are present; labor supplies are not very mobile, particularly among nations; and there are often barriers to the free movement of capital. Consequently, nations tend to retain certain cost advantages and other disadvantages. Some changes do occur, however. Witness the industrial growth of modern-day Japan, whose labor costs have increased to the point where by 1969 some particularly labor-intensive products were being produced in other countries.[14] Such changes come slowly and usually stem from the movement of capital rather than of people or natural resources.

The relative permanence of international cost differences coupled with increasing demand for goods and services leads to international trade. Countries tend to produce those goods and services for which they have the lowest cost structure. They sell their surpluses to other countries and, in turn, buy needed goods and services. The advantages of such practices can be seen through some simple illustrations.

Absolute cost advantage. Let us look at only two countries and two commodities—beef and rum (Table 16–2). All productive factors will be put under the heading of labor.

TABLE 16–2
Absolute cost advantage

	Output	
	Rum (gallons)	Beef (pounds)
Country PR, labor of 1 manday will produce.................	12	or 3
Country A, labor of 1 manday will produce................	3	or 12

Country PR has an absolute advantage in the production of rum, and country A has an absolute advantage in the production of beef. If each country wishes to be self-sufficient and split its labor equally between the production of rum and beef, country PR will produce 6 gallons of rum and 1½ pounds of beef. Country A would produce 1½ gallons of rum and 6 pounds of beef. Combined output in the two countries would therefore be 7½ gallons of rum and 7½ pounds of beef. In contrast, if PR specializes in rum it can produce 12 gallons of rum while A specializes in beef and produces 12 pounds. The result is a gain over self-sufficiency of 4½ gallons of rum and 4½ pounds of beef.

Cases of absolute advantage are common. Our illustration could be Puerto Rican rum and Argentine beef.

Comparative cost advantage. In the real world one country is more likely to have absolute cost advantages in the production of many or even all products and services (Table 16–3). Is there a basis for trade in such situations?

If country PR splits its labor equally between the production of rum and beef it can produce 6 gallons of rum and 1½ pounds of beef. Country A doing the same thing can produce only 1 gallon of rum and one-half pound of beef. The joint production of both countries is 7 gallons of rum and 2 pounds of beef, less than if country PR specializes and produces 12 gallons of rum and country A specializes and produces 1 pound of beef. Country PR produces rum because it has the best comparative advantage over A (12:2) whereas in the production of beef its advantage is only 3:1.

---

[14] Hazen, "Overseas High Stakes of Multinational Firms," p. 50.

Marketing: Principles and methods

TABLE 16–3
Comparative cost advantage

	Output	
	Rum *(gallons)*	*Beef* *(pounds)*
Country PR, labor of 1 manday will produce................	12	3
Country A, labor of 1 manday will produce................	2	1

A, while at an absolute disadvantage in both, will produce beef because it has a *comparative* advantage where it has the smallest absolute disadvantage.

Both countries can still benefit from trade. Country PR will trade only within an exchange range of 4 gallons of rum for 1 pound of beef, since it can produce 1 pound of beef at the cost of 4 gallons of rum. Country A will offer no more than 1 pound of beef for 2 gallons of rum, since 2 gallons of rum can be produced at home for the cost of 1 pound of beef. Consequently, trade between the two countries will be beneficial to both between the ratio of 4 gallons of rum for 1 pound of beef and 2 gallons of rum for 1 pound of beef.

This illustrates the *law of comparative advantage,* which states that a country will gain economically by concentrating its production on those products and services in which it has the largest comparative advantage or the smallest comparative disadvantage. It will then trade with other countries.

The illustrations might be more meaningful if stated in money terms, because very few products are exchanged directly for other products. Assume that the exchange ratio settles at 3 gallons of rum to 1 pound of beef and that both countries use dollars. Then, if rum is priced at $1 per gallon (no tax), beef will be worth $3 per pound. One man laboring one day in country PR is worth $12, since he can produce 12 gallons of rum, but one man in country A is worth only $3, since he can only produce 1 pound of meat. In turn, the cost of production of rum is $1 per gallon in PR, but $1.50 per gallon in A (where labor costing $3 per day can produce only 2 gallons of rum). The cost of producing beef in country A is $3 per pound, but in PR it costs $4 per pound to produce it (where labor costing $12 per day can produce only 3 pounds of beef). Thus, considering prices and costs there is a basis for specialization and global marketing.

Some refinements

Two refinements in the illustrations are needed to make them conform to the real world.

All costs considered, not just labor. Throughout the illustrations cost differences were attributed to unequal amounts of labor that went into production of each of the products. In the real world, the final cost of production is actually the *combined* costs of the natural resources and capital as well as labor, which are not equally spread among the countries of the world and do result in different costs and prices. Therefore, the differences in product prices among countries is due, basically, to the relative scarcity (supply relative to demand) of the various factors of production in each country.

Japan, confronted with relatively few mineral resources and a shortage of capital, concentrates on the production of goods for which it can secure a cost advantage through the extensive use of its relatively cheap supply of labor. The United States, in contrast, with relatively high labor costs, tends to produce products whose costs can be decreased through the use of laborsaving capital equipment to increase the productivity of its expensive labor. To repeat, the cost advantages which accrue to one country compared with another are clearly the result of the cost of all the factors of production, not just labor.

Limits to specialization. If specialization yields such gains, why isn't it more widely practiced? The United States, Germany, Great Britain, France, and Japan produce and trade many similar products. Why don't the United States and Germany produce all the world's cars, Japan and the United States produce all the electronic products, Argentina, all the beef, Germany, all the beer, and so forth? The answer, of course, is that in the real world specialization faces some barriers which limit its application. Three of these are discussed below.

1. *Transportation costs.* Specialization costs may be offset by transportation costs. While one country might have production cost advantages over all other countries, they can be lost in the cost of transportation to distant markets.

2. *Diseconomies of scale.* There are limits to the quantity of output that can be produced without increased average costs. Argentina, for example, could produce more beef, but to do so it would need to use less productive or more expensive land or more feed supplements, and its long-run average costs would increase. Many countries meet demand for a product partly through production and partly through imports. France, for example, mines coal but also imports some; Cuba grows some rice, but imports some; the United States mines and imports iron ore. In each of these cases, the cost of the additional domestic production would be greater than the cost of the imported commodities.

3. *Barriers to trade.* Finally, many countries impose measures such as tariffs and quotas which restrict free trade. These may be to protect infant industries until they mature, to gain or retain critical defense industries, to protect certain industries (e.g., steel), to enhance national pride, or simply to protect certain industries which have lost their cost advantage. This is done to retain existing patterns of resource use, including employment. The restrictions that global marketers encounter are discussed in more detail in a later section of this chapter. The essence of global marketing is expressed in Figure 16–3.

FIGURE 16–3

Essence of global marketing

Differences in:
1. Natural Resources
2. Capital
3. Labor

Differences in:
1. Relative Costs Advantages
2. Absolute Costs Advantages

Restraints on Comparative Advantage Specialization
1. Transportation Cost
2. Operation at the Cost Limits
3. Barriers to Trade

Resulting Global Marketing

Marketing: Principles and methods

There are many routes a manufacturer can follow to reach foreign markets. Production can be located in either his home country or in a foreign country (or in both). Figure 16–4 depicts the major alternatives available to manufacturers but is also applicable to retailers and many sellers of services.

FIGURE 16–4
Multinational operating alternatives

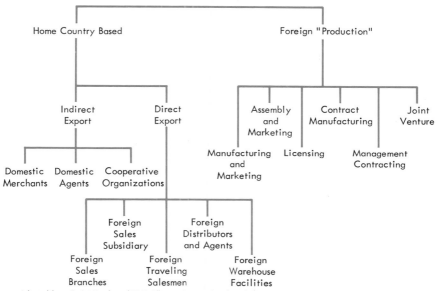

Adapted from G. E. Miracle and G. S. Albaum, *International Marketing Management* (Homewood, Ill.: Richard D. Irwin, Inc., 1970).

Home-country based

Typically, when companies first enter global marketing they prefer to test and probe foreign markets without the risk of heavy foreign investment in manufacturing or marketing facilities.[15] Retailers can start by operating only one or two stores, but with the exception of franchising or generating mail-order sales, they must virtually jump into foreign facilities and investment from the beginning. Manufacturers, on the other hand, can retain all or most of their operations in their home country. They can either export *indirectly* through domestic-based middlemen or they can deal *directly* with foreign-based middlemen.

Indirect export marketing. Indirect export marketing is similar to distributing through regular domestic channels. The export middlemen are the true exporters. They normally contact the foreign markets and handle all of the marketing activities associated with the foreign sales. There are several types of these middlemen.

---

[15] I. A. Litvak and P. M. Banting, "A Conceptual Framework for International Business Arrangement," in R. L. King (ed.), *Marketing and the New Science of Planning,* conference proceedings, American Marketing Association, Fall 1968, p. 460. They also hypothesize that there is a set of criteria that will help companies decide the types of distributive arrangements that are likely to evolve within different environments.

1. *Domestic-based merchants.* First, there are domestic-based merchants. They buy and sell for their own account and generally engage in both exporting and importing. Such merchants select their own foreign channels and perform the needed marketing functions. As elsewhere in the domestic market, there are limited-function as well as full-function merchant wholesalers who provide a variety of services for exporters.

2. *Domestic-based agents.* The more common varieties of export agent middlemen are the export commission house or export buying agent, broker, resident buyer, combination export manager, and manufacturer's export agent.

a) Export commission houses. These are agents who in the United States usually act as buyers for large foreign organizations (mines, wholesalers, retailers, and even governments). When commission houses are used by U.S. manufacturers to sell their products, exclusive sales rights may be specified.

b) Export and import brokers. These agents usually specialize in one or two staple products such as cotton and sugar or grain and cocoa. Brokers represent either buyers or sellers on a commission basis. They do not handle the commodities, but merely bring buyers' and sellers' offers together to form a transaction.

c) Resident buyers. These are not really middlemen but employees of foreign organizations who want to locate buyers directly in a seller's domestic market. Normally, they handle all export details.

d) Combination export managers. A CEM is "an international sales specialist who functions as the exclusive export department for several allied but noncompeting manufacturers."[16] He is to foreign markets essentially the same as the selling agent (described in Chapter 11) is to the domestic market. He takes the output for foreign markets (often on a buy-and-sell rather than a commission basis) and handles all marketing activities, conducting business in the name of each manufacturer he represents.

e) Manufacturer's export agents. This agent is similar to the combination export manager but operates in his own name and offers fewer marketing functions because he serves only as an agent. Some agents work on a *del credere* arrangement under which they assume foreign credit risks.

3. *Cooperative organizations.* These institutions actually are a cross between indirect and direct export. The two major types are piggyback marketing and export associations.

a) Piggyback marketing. Piggyback takes place when one manufacturer serves as a foreign wholesaler for another. The wholesaling-manufacturer usually broadens his own product line with complementary lines. Borg-Warner, to fill out its Norge line in South America, uses small appliances manufactured by Scoville Manufacturing Company (Hamilton Beach brand) and McGraw-Edison Company (Toastmaster brand). Many companies, including General Electric, Armco Steel Corporation, and Pillsbury Company, buy other U.S. companies' products outright and assume all export activities. Such companies may sell under the manufacturer's name, a private label, or their own name.[17]

b) Export associations. A grower or a manufacturer can also export cooperatively through membership in an exporting association. Cooperative associations have marketed citrus fruit and other agricultural products in both domestic and global

---

[16] R. G. Lurie, "CEMs Make Exporting Easy," *Clipper Cargo Horizons,* March 1965, p. 7.

[17] "Cooperative Exporting: An Easy Way to Sell Overseas," *Business Management,* January 1966, p. 44.

Marketing: Principles and methods

markets for many years. More unique are the export cartels organized solely for export marketing. The Webb-Pomerene Act enables competitive companies to form associations to engage in export marketing cooperatively.[18]

Direct export marketing. Direct exporting occurs when a company sells directly to another company located in a foreign market. The term "direct" here does *not* refer to selling direct to using consumers. The channel within various countries may be directly to the ultimate consumers or indirect.

There are several ways companies can sell direct to buyers located in foreign countries. They can use, singly or in combination: (1) foreign distributors or agents, (2) traveling export salesmen, or (3) foreign-located sales branches or sales subsidiaries. Foreign warehouse facilities and domestic-based export departments or divisions can also be used conjunctionally.

Direct investments in foreign nations can be held to a minimum when foreign-based wholesalers or domestic-based traveling salesmen are employed. The use of foreign-based sales branches and sales subsidiary calls for more extensive investments in foreign countries.

1. *Foreign distributors and agents.* As in the United States, distributor here refers to merchant wholesalers and agent refers to nontitle-taking wholesalers. Wholesalers who serve as manufacturers' direct export marketing middlemen usually have exclusive representation in a specified market area in which they sell and service the product line. They, in fact, are called "importers" when their imports represent a substantial share of their total operation. Such wholesalers in many respects are similar to wholesalers in the United States in terms of the activities they perform for manufacturers and they offer similar advantages and disadvantages.

2. *Traveling export salesmen.* These salesmen reside in their companies' home countries and travel to the foreign markets (in contrast, resident salesmen live in the foreign countries and usually work out of sales offices or branches). The traveling export salesman is used when an order-getter (not an order-taker) is needed and when infrequent calls will suffice.

3. *Foreign sales branches.* A branch usually handles all of the import activities, sales distribution, and promotion in a specified area. Its resident salesmen sell principally to wholesalers, retailers, and industrial users. The foreign sales branch, coupled with warehouse facilities, is typically a replacement or substitute for a merchant wholesaler.

4. *Foreign sales subsidiaries.* A sales subsidiary may function merely as a foreign sales branch. The subsidiary, however, is incorporated in the foreign country and often has broader responsibility. It may serve as both an operating company (manufacturing and/or marketing) and as a holding company. A survey of 107 U.S. companies indicated that the activities most frequently assigned to the subsidiaries were to: (1) serve as holding companies (ownership of other companies), (2) provide technical services for foreign subsidiaries and licenses, (3) handle imports of U.S. products, (4) manage foreign marketing activities, and (5) make foreign investments and handle foreign licensing arrangements.[19] A company that operates a group of retail stores in a foreign country or bloc of countries will also sometimes coordinate its activities through its foreign sales subsidiary.

---

[18] V. Travaglini, "Webb-Pomerene Act Overlooked by Exporter," *International Commerce,* December 28, 1964, pp. 13–14.

[19] E. B. Lovell, *Managing Foreign Based Corporations,* Studies in Business Policy, No. 110 (New York: National Industrial Conference Board, 1963), p. 29.

Foreign country "production"

Companies who find it advantageous to have facilities located in foreign countries have five major alternatives.[20] They can: (1) enter into licensing arrangements, (2) contract with foreign producers, (3) contract to manage foreign facilities, (4) establish and operate assembly and marketing operations, and (5) establish and operate manufacturing and marketing facilities. The first three approaches to foreign "production" call for limited investment of capital compared to the last two. A joint venture with foreign nationals under some arrangements *may* also greatly reduce capital investment.[21]

Licensing. A license is an agreement between two companies allowing the licensee to use the licensor's processes, trademark or name, patent, technical skills, marketing knowledge, and so forth. The agreement may require payment of an initial fee, an annual minimum, an annual royalty, or a percentage fee, plus fees for special services or activities.[22] The licensor may be called on to furnish some component ingredients or parts; Coca-Cola, for example, has a global network of licensed (franchised) bottlers whom they supply with syrup. A franchise is merely a special type of license. The licensor's brand name and marketing know-how are frequently more important than the other aspects of the agreement.[23]

Contract manufacturing. A domestic firm may contract for the manufacture or assembly of a product by a foreign company and may or may not retain marketing and distribution rights. Such a firm will want to ensure that finished products meet its quality standards and that marketing methods are appropriate for the markets served. Poor quality products or offensive marketing practices could give a poor test of market capacity and also could do long-run damage to product name and market acceptance.

Procter and Gamble entered the Italian market through contract manufacturing *and* marketing. They found an Italian soap manufacturer who had been contracting with Colgate and awarded him the Procter & Gamble contract for Tide when Colgate opened its own plant. Procter & Gamble used an independent selling agent to sell its products even after sufficient volume was attained for it to build its own manufacturing plant.[24]

Management contracting. Unlike contract manufacturing, management contracting calls for the global marketer to provide the know-how to manage the company for the foreign owner. Hilton International (a TWA subsidiary), for example, owns hotels and also manages a worldwide hotel network. Marketing as well as the physical operation of the hotels is included. It is not uncommon for the managing company to hold options to buy all or part of the operations they manage. Such arrangements mean less risk of losing operations once they become profitable.

---

[20] For discussion of decision making in multinational firms see W. J. Keegan, "Multinational Marketing: The Headquarters Role," *Columbia Journal of World Business,* January–February 1971, pp. 85–90; and R. J. Aylmer, "Who Makes Marketing Decisions in the Multinational Firm?" *Journal of Marketing,* 34 (October 1970), pp. 25–30.

[21] One expert suggests a marketing strategy for foreign markets should be to minimize risk, maximize control, and maintain flexibility. R. H. Holton, "Developing International Business," *Sales/Marketing Today,* January 1966.

[22] J. G. Myers, "Foreign Licensing—An Export Alternative," in I. A. Litvak and B. E. Mallen (eds.), *Marketing: Canada* (Toronto: McGraw-Hill Company of Canada Ltd., 1964), pp. 320–21.

[23] For some hazards of licensing see, "Does Foreign Licensing Pay?" *Dun's Review,* October 1969, p. 99.

[24] G. D. Bryson, *Profits from Abroad* (New York: McGraw-Hill Book Co., 1964), pp. 150–51.

Marketing: Principles and methods

Assembly and marketing operations. Assembly operations are a cross between an export operation and foreign-based manufacturing. The manufacturer may export many if not all of the parts assembled in the foreign country. This often affords generally lower costs, including those for transportation, custom duties, and assembly, while it allows quality control. Usually the firm desires to retain control over foreign marketing.

Assembly plants also may be built either because government discourages the importing of assembled products or for a better competitive position with local companies. Some of the reasons for making such investments in foreign manufacturing and marketing operations are discussed in a following section.

Manufacturing and marketing facilities. Manufacturing operations are different from assembly operations in that the majority of the component parts for manufacturing originate in the local country prior to assembly. A car manufacturer, instead of shipping engines, tires, fenders, windows, door panels, and so forth into a country for assembly, would either need to manufacture these items in the country or find or develop internal sources of supply for them. While this may be more costly to the manufacturer and increase his selling prices, developing countries prefer it because it usually provides more local employment, helps in the country's development, and reduces the purchases that must be made outside its borders.

A similar situation prevails in retailing. Mexico and other Central and South American countries have encouraged Sears and other retailers to establish and operate retail outlets. Mexico, in particular, has insisted that goods be of Mexican origin, and Sears has been instrumental in locating and aiding in the development of sources of supply. Mexico and some other nations also restrict the flow of profits out of their country (repatriation). Sears, which has reinvested its returns in its Mexico subsidiary, has realized larger long-run returns than would have resulted in investment in its U.S. operations.[25]

Joint ventures. Manufacturing (including assembly operations) and marketing facilities may be joint ventures—that is, a sharing of ownership and control—between two or more companies or between a company and a country. The host country partner may have a majority, equal, or minority interest.

Companies may enter into joint ventures in some countries because they offer the only alternative; by law, foreign nationals may not be permitted to have 100 percent ownership. In other countries, joint venture may simply appear to offer an alternative that is superior to either sole ownership or public ownership. Joint ventures generally do reduce the required investment, improve the political environment in the host country, and provide ready-made marketing facilities and market acceptance when one of the partners is established in the market. However, some firms have discovered that insufficient control to ensure the quality of their products or their marketing program results.

American Potash and Chemical Corporation entered into a 50–50 joint venture with Ugine to build a boric acid plant near Lyons, France. Each of the companies supplied about $1 million. The total amount was relatively low because the new plant was located adjacent to an existing Ugine plant with ready access to fuel, power, transportation, and other required facilities. The major advantage was in the realm of production, not marketing.[26]

---

[25] W. R. Fritsch, *Progress and Profits: The Sears, Roebuck Story in Peru* (Washington, D.C.: Action Committee for International Development, 1962), p. 65.

[26] *International Commerce*, May 30, 1966, p. 38.

Sears has a joint arrangement with Simpsons of Canada in the Simpsons-Sears retail outlets. It appears to work well for both parties, offering Sears a solid entry into the Canadian market and providing needed financing for Simpsons. Even for such experienced firms, however, joint ventures may not work well. Sears operated for four years with Walton's Ltd. of Australia under the Walton-Sears sign but then liquidated their interest. Walton has continued as a very profitable operation but quite different from the Sears way of doing business. Sears simply wanted to do business in the Sears way—new stores and Sears merchandise techniques—while Walton wanted to continue to buy up and operate existing stores.[27]

Channels within foreign markets

Some new terminology and slightly different institutions and activities have been introduced in our discussion of distribution between countries. For the most part, however, what was learned about domestic marketing in the United States has provided a good basis for viewing the global marketing scene. The same holds true for the distribution of goods *within* foreign countries.

Figure 16–5 indicates the major institutions and alternative channels in such distribution. While there are some differences in marketing practices within various countries of the world (as there are within individual countries), it is unnecessary to dwell on such details. The retailing and wholesaling operations that have already been

FIGURE 16–5
Internal channels in foreign countries

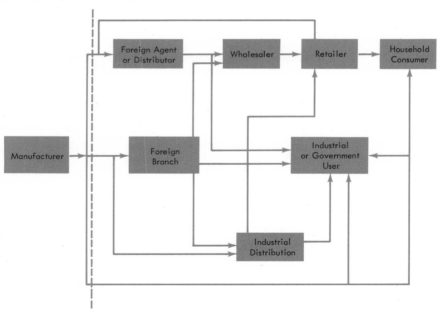

Adapted from G. E. Miracle and G. S. Albaum, *International Marketing Management* (Homewood, Ill.: Richard D. Irwin, Inc., 1970).

---

[27] "Sears Is Selling Its Entire Holding in Walton Sears," *Women's Wear Daily*, October 27, 1959.

discussed can provide a good understanding of retailing and wholesaling in foreign nations.[28] Instead we shall examine the economic-financial environment confronting global marketers.

Why do companies make foreign investments?

While we have not directly discussed the flow of direct private investments, we have pointed to some clues as to why they occur. The most important motives for a company to seek growth by out-of-country investment are:

1. A relatively immobile factor of production may be less costly in another country.
2. A potentially profitable foreign market may have erected import barriers to increase its domestic employment and conserve foreign exchange.
3. The bulk, density, or perishability of the product may make transportation costs exorbitant.
4. Foreign investments may offer higher expected returns than domestic investments.
5. Foreign customers may be more receptive to sellers who produce in their country than to those who import.
6. Domestic antitrust policy may restrict further internal growth.

Some of these motives are explored in more detail in Chapters 20 and 25.

ENVIRONMENT FOR GLOBAL MARKETING

A myopic view of global marketing is common. Some want absolute free trade where all of the nations of the world would be open to their own country's products, services, and marketing methods. Such views fail to perceive that developing nations have legitimate reasons for protecting and regulating flows of goods, services, money, and people. Others want many trade restrictions, particularly those that favor their own country or their own industry.

The global marketer operates in environments which differ from his domestic market economically, politically, socially, culturally, and in resources. The international money and banking system overlays these national and regional environmental differences as it operates under the pressures of ever-expanding world trade. The discussion here will be limited to two political-economic factors: the system of international monetary settlements and political restraints to free trade.

International monetary payments

The two key concepts involved in international payments are the *balance of payments* and the *rate of exchange.*

Balance of payments. The balance of payments of a country is a summary statement of all economic transactions completed between its residents and residents of the rest of the world during a period of time. The transactions are composed of: (1) merchandise trade, (2) services, (3) interest and dividends, (4) unilateral transfers (gifts, both private and public), (5) long-term investments, (6) short-term investments,

---

[28] Details on marketing institutions and activities can be found in Miracle and Albaum, *International Marketing Management;* C. R. Patty and H. L. Vredenburg (eds.), *Readings in Global Marketing Management* (New York: Meredith Corporation, 1969); and *Developing Distribution in Europe* (Geneva, Switzerland: Business International S.A., 1969).

(7) gold movements, and (8) currency shipments. The size of the various transactions indicates the way a country "pays its way" internationally, and the interrelationships of the transactions reveal the role a country plays in the world economy.

A country's balance of *payments* always balances, but its balance of *trade* may not. A country is said to have a "favorable" balance of trade when the value of its merchandise exports exceeds that of its merchandise imports. Such a "favorable" or "unfavorable" trade balance, while important, is not the only transaction that counts. The balance-of-payments concept is summarized in Figure 16–6. The individual components may not be of the same size, but the total of all of the components is the same.

FIGURE 16–6
Balance of payments

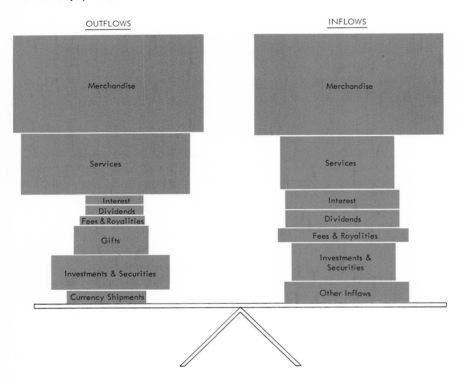

A country's current expenditures (the first four items in the figure) can exceed its current income without alarm that it is headed for bankruptcy. Such a deficit in current income can be offset by: (1) the receipt of long-term capital, (2) the receipt of unilateral transfers, (3) withdrawal of assets from abroad, (4) the export of gold, or (5) the use of short-term credit. Long-term capital being invested in a country from a foreign source can be quite favorable if it will give rise to future exports. The other four types of transactions, however, have no long-run implications; they can only be

Marketing: Principles and methods

viewed as nonsustainable.[29] Therefore, a country relying on these transactions to offset a large and persistent deficit which arises from an excess of imports over exports is headed for some changes that global marketers should be aware of.[30] Under free market conditions, if the country does not take corrective action, the price of its currency will decrease (that is, the rate of exchange residents will pay for other countries' currencies will increase) and the prices of its products and services to other nations will decline. On the other hand, in an attempt to lessen or reverse such a serious trade deficit, a country may instigate various measures such as tariffs, quotas, and exchange controls, which will be discussed below.

Foreign exchange market. Since there are over 50 currencies in the world, it is impractical for buyers and sellers to directly exchange currencies. The market in which claims to foreign moneys are bought and sold for domestic currency is known as the foreign exchange market. Its basic purpose is to transfer purchasing power from one country to another. Foreign exchange includes the credit instruments that give sellers of one country a claim on money in another country. A *bill of exchange,* for example, could be drawn by an American exporter (the seller) instructing the buyer, a British importer or his bank, to pay the exporter a certain amount. The bill of exchange received by the American exporter may in turn be purchased by an American importer who wishes to make payment in Great Britain. The American importer (a buyer) in effect pays dollars to the American exporter, and the British exporter (a seller) in effect collects sterling from the British importer. Actually, the bills of exchange are cleared through the foreign exchange market (in this case commercial banks in New York and London) much as are domestic checks in the United States.

The rate of exchange. Exporters and importers need to be aware of both the prices of the items they propose to purchase and the price of foreign exchange. For example, an American importing a Rolls Royce needs to know the price of the car and the dollar price of sterling. This second price, which must be paid in dollars to obtain one unit of foreign currency, is the rate of exchange. A New York rate of $2.55 on London means that one British pound costs $2.55 in New York or, expressed in reverse, the London price of $1 is 0.393 pounds. The rates of exchange tend to differ somewhat from the official rates and from one another. These differences are normally very small but this risk, like others, must be carried by someone in the marketing channel.

National and international controls and restrictions

While the merits of free trade might seem to be beyond question, country after country in one way or another manipulates its role in international commerce. In fact, no country practices absolute free trade. The primary tools of manipulation are tariffs, restrictive regulations, import quotas, exchange control systems, state-trading operations, and various forms of international combinations.

Tariffs. There is a wide variety of tariffs (a tax on imports), but all have as their purpose the provision of either revenue or protection. Revenue tariffs normally have relatively low rates of duty and are not intended to restrict imports. They are levied

---

[29] For an illustration see "Dollars at a Discount," *Barron's,* May 10, 1971, pp. 1 and 8.

[30] For a discussion of the balance-of-trade problems of the United States in 1967 and 1968 see "Why the U.S. Must Sell More Overseas," *Business Week,* January 4, 1969, pp. 40–54. For 1971 see "May to September," *Barron's,* July 19, 1971, pp. 3, 8, 10, and 12.

on merchandise of widespread domestic use, the supply of which may be entirely imported.

Protective tariffs, in contrast, are used to curtail imports which are competitive with similar domestic products or for some other reason are not wanted in the country. If the tariff is high enough to block all imports of the product, no revenue is yielded. Protective tariffs typically allow some units to enter and to yield some revenue.

Many arguments are used to support tariffs. The major ones are that they are needed to: (1) protect wages and the standard of living, (2) increase employment, (3) protect the home market, (4) keep money at home, (5) equalize the cost of production, (6) prevent chronic dumping, (7) bargain with other countries, (8) protect infant industries, (9) promote diversification and economic stability, (10) aid national defense, and (11) provide revenue.[31] Arguments 1 through 7, subjected to careful economic analysis, simply make little sense, particularly over the long run. They may help one group within a country, but they do not benefit the general welfare or the national interest. They arise largely from special-interest groups being heard, while consumers remain quiet.

Arguments 8 through 11 can be abused but do have merit for some countries at some times. The argument for infant industries is that some industries are economically justified as judged by their long-term prospects for survival in a free market, but must be protected from foreign competition during their early years.[32] The appeal of a diversified or balanced economy to gain greater economic stability has applicability only to "one-crop countries." The national defense argument goes that since wars do occur and since national survival is a goal of government policy, nations must protect industries that are essential in warfare. The abuse generally arises in the definition of essential (U.S. sugar producers have used this argument).

Experience shows that once tariffs come into being they tend to persist, and the removal of a tariff strips away a protection that special groups have come to rely on. Unless such removal is gradual, a quick and major economic readjustment may lead a country into political and social problems of gigantic proportions. Recognizing such problems, shortly after World War II the United States and 22 other countries adopted the General Agreement on Tariffs and Trade (GATT). This mechanism, designed in part to help reduce tariffs, now has more than 60 members and has had some influence on tariff reductions on more than 50,000 commodity items.

Export duties are "tariffs" levied against exports instead of imports. Such duties are common among countries that produce raw materials but are not often used by industrialized nations. They provide both revenue and protection for domestic industries. Latin American and Asiatic countries have been very dependent on revenue from export duties. A few years ago 80 percent of all government revenues in Chile came from this source.

Export duties provide protection for home industries when a raw material is in great demand in competing foreign industries and the supplying country can influence the price of the material. Norway and Sweden have used export duties on wood and timber in an attempt to encourage domestic pulp and woodworking industries.

Restrictive regulations. Administrative rules and requirements imposed by governmental bodies have the effect of protective tariffs and may be referred to as

---

[31] See almost any text on international economics. A particularly lucid presentation is W. Krause, *International Economics* (Boston: Houghton Mifflin Co., 1965), pp. 117–36.

[32] Japan, for example, protects its domestic automobile market with a 17.5 percent tariff plus a commodity tax of about 35 percent. J. Davenport, "Japan's Competitive Cutting Edge," *Fortune,* 48 (September 1, 1968).

"invisible" tariffs. For example, the United States requires that each single cigarette paper, rather than each package, is an individual article and must be marked with the name of its country of origin. Many Argentina cattle growers are certain that the exclusion of certain beef imports by the United States to "prevent the spread of hoof-and-mouth disease" is an invisible tariff.

Import quotas. Imports can be controlled by quotas as well as by tariffs. Quotas ("quantitative restrictions" or QRs) usually take the form of absolute limits on the physical volume of particular imports allowed to enter a country during a specified period. They may also be placed on the total value of all goods or administered as an import license with the license fee a percentage of the value of goods imported.

"Buy America" and similar restrictions have also been present in this country since 1933. These laws call for the exclusive purchase of American-made goods by government unless foreign-made goods are significantly less expensive (25 percent, later reduced to 6 percent).[33]

Exchange control systems. With exchange controls, the foreign exchange available in a country comes under the regulation of a government office. Foreign exchange must be sold to the authority for domestic currency, and prospective users of foreign exchange must make application to the authority.

This rationing of foreign exchange serves two purposes. First, when a country has an inadequate supply of foreign exchange, exchange control permits government to allocate scarce supplies of foreign exchange to fit national needs. Typically, an exchange control authority will rank various types of demand, eliminating nonessential expenditures. No foreign exchange, for example, may be allowed for speculative foreign investment, little or none for foreign travel, and little or none for luxury imports. In turn, foreign exchange may be allowed to finance imports of certain raw materials needed for domestic industry or for medicines or foodstuffs not available in the country. Such control may be coupled with import licensing to gain even more control over the volume and types of imports allowed to enter a country.

About half of the countries of the world currently use some form of exchange control.[34] The more advanced countries use it almost exclusively to lessen pressure on their balance-of-payments framework, underdeveloped countries use it to direct development into the right activities. Use by developed countries has merit to aid a short-run situation, but in that it offers no integral corrective action it fails to provide a lasting solution to a balance-of-payments difficulty. The case for its use in under-developed countries is much stronger.[35]

State trading operations. A portion of global marketing is done directly by government rather than private businesses, usually through state trading agencies.[36] This is common in communist-bloc countries but is also widespread among others, including the United States.[37] State trading permits the integration of global marketing

---

[33] "Local Barriers Crimp Growth of U.S. Trade," *Women's Wear Daily,* May 7, 1968, p. 2.

[34] Country-by-country information is available in *Report on Exchange Restrictions,* International Monetary Fund, Washington, D.C., issued annually.

[35] For detailed illustrations of the use of exchange control in Great Britain, Argentina, and the Philippines, see Krause, *International Economics,* pp. 175–95.

[36] For a view of companies trading with the U.S.S.R., see "Putting Supermarkets on the Steppes," *Business Week,* September 20, 1969, pp. 78–81.

[37] The U.S. engages in (1) the disposal of surplus commodities acquired under agricultural support prices, (2) purchases of goods and services under the "off-shore procurement" program, and (3) the purchase of strategic raw material for stockpiles.

with domestic planning. In extractive industries, the state has a responsibility for stewardship of the people's resources.

International cartels and commodity agreements. International cartels are usually private but may be government-sponsored agreements between companies producing and marketing similar products.[38] Cartels serve to control production, domestic and global marketing, and prices and ignore consumer interests.

Commodity agreements also attempt to control production, marketing, and prices. International commodity agreements arise because free market trade in the commodities is considered too unstable. Conditions range from surpluses to famine, with accompanying swings in prices. There are international commodity agreements on numerous products, including coffee, cocoa, sugar, and wheat.[39]

Regional common markets. International free trade areas have had mixed success in unifying many regions during the past two decades. The extent of union varies widely among regions. The least unification exists in the *free trade areas* such as the Latin American Free Trade Association (LAFTA), which is comprised of 11 countries, and the European Free Trade Association (EFTA), which includes Austria, Denmark, Iceland, Norway, Portugal, Sweden, Switzerland, Finland, and (as of this writing) the United Kingdom. The former association has had limited success in promoting free trade, while the latter removed the last tariffs and quotas from industrial products in 1966.[40]

The difference between a free trade area and a *customs union* is that the member countries are uniform in tariffs, quotas, and other control devices with nonmember countries. Each country, in other words, gives up its freedom to make special arrangements with nonmember countries. There are many customs unions; Benelux (Belgium, the Netherlands, and Luxembourg) is probably the best known.

Free internal mobility of the factors of production matched with the features of a customs union provides a *common market.* The best example of this form of regional market is the European Common Market (European Economic Community or EEC). By the end of 1968 the EEC, which was formed in 1957, had removed internal tariffs, created common external tariffs and achieved the free movement of workers. The EEC still has numerous goals as it attempts to integrate more fully the economic activities (particularly agriculture) of the member countries.

Even closer unions between nations are possible. Complete *economic union* would require all the features of a common market plus uniform currency, credit, government expenditures and taxation, and regulation of competition. A relatively high degree of political integration would be called for. *Political unions,* such as the British Commonwealth of Nations, are hybrid economic unions which have evolved from the days of the British Empire.

The marketing implications of a regional market union are clear. A multinational firm with one manufacturing plant within the regional market can gain relatively unrestricted marketing access to the other member countries. The future appears uncertain, however, because regional blocs have shown strong tendencies to put severe restrictions on imports. As they have lowered internal walls they have raised external ones. It is conceivable that sometime in the future regional blocs may require majority equity interest in all companies in their regions.

---

[38] A Japanese textile cartel regulates the quantity and allocation of firms shipping to the U.S. market. See "The World at Work," *Barron's,* July 5, 1971, p. 18.

[39] For illustrations of agreements on wheat and coffee see Krause, *International Economics,* pp. 245–52.

[40] *Building EFTA: A Free Trade Area in Europe* (rev. ed.; Geneva, Switzerland: EFTA Secretariate, August, 1968).

Marketing: Principles and methods

SUMMARY

As global travel, trade, and communication have brought the whole world in touch in recent years, "trade not aid" has become a major force in economic development. Direct private investments abroad by multinational companies has surpassed export marketing as the principal vehicle of global trade.

Many national restrictions on trade have given way, some on a worldwide basis and others limited to regional trading blocs. Foreign firms have been able to leap most of the restrictions and barriers of free market countries by expanding their manufacturing and marketing operations through the creation of subsidiaries within the protective walls. Most, but not all, countries have welcomed such "invasions."

While the advantages of global marketing to the people of the world are clear, national pride and self-interest remain dominant factors in decisions regarding who mines, manufactures, and markets what, where, and when. Some countries have grown concerned with the effect of foreign investments on exports and balances of trade and payments. Host countries have begun to express more concern about their "colonization" by foreign business firms, and some changes in the rules may be forthcoming. Cooperation between business and government to facilitate state trading also appears to be growing in popularity.

While the U.S. firm operating abroad may continue to find an unfriendly host, the future of the truly multinational firm looks bright. Affluence is becoming more widespread internationally; transportation and communication continue to improve; and it seems that nations may be learning to live in peace as the concept of "one world" becomes more of a reality. The business organization (corporation) is ahead of the political organization (government) in developing a multinational economy.

The goal of marketers today must be to encompass worldwide markets—not just national ones. The global market, like the domestic market, is in reality many dynamic markets. Success requires technical competence in marketing, specialized knowledge of the international environment, and the ability to utilize such competence and knowledge to develop and implement marketing programs.

REVIEW AND DISCUSSION QUESTIONS

1. What, from a marketer's point of view, are the basic differences between export marketing and direct private investments?
2. How important is global marketing to United States companies—to the United States; Japan; and other nations of the world?
3. Explain the major differences between *global* and *domestic* marketing.
4. Why does global marketing occur?
5. Explain and illustrate the concept of comparative cost advantage. On what products and services does the United States have the largest comparative advantage?
6. What are major advantages and disadvantages to a firm engaging in export marketing?
7. Under what conditions would a U.S. manufacturer be well advised to use a combination export manager?
8. If you were the product manager of McGraw-Edison Company's Toastmaster brand and the Pillsbury Company sought a piggyback marketing arrangement throughout South America (where you had no distribution) using the Toastmaster brand name, what would be your recommendation? Please explain.

9. Would you advise a bicycle manufacturer who wants to engage in global marketing to use (1) export marketing, (2) direct investments in facilities in foreign countries, (3) licensed arrangements for foreign manufacturing, (4) foreign manufacturers to make bicycles for him, or (5) undertake a joint manufacturing marketing venture in foreign markets? Please explain your choice.

10. What are the possible marketing advantages and disadvantages of *licensing* foreign companies to manufacture and market your product line?

11. Explain in detail why companies make direct foreign investments in manufacturing and marketing.

12. What is the difference between a balance of *payment* and a balance of *trade* deficiency? Which is more serious? Why?

13. What are the major restrictions or barriers to global marketing?

14. Would the standard of living be higher in virtually all nations of the world if there were no global trading restrictions or restraints? Explain.

15. Why do nations impose restrictions and restraints on the marketing of goods and services among countries?

SUPPLEMENTARY READINGS

Business International S.A. *Developing Distribution in Europe.* Geneva, Switzerland, 1969. A brief but detailed look at how to secure distribution in Europe that provides many illustrations.

Carson, D. *International Marketing: A Comparative Systems Approach.* New York: John Wiley & Sons, 1967. Emphasizes the impact of cultural, political, legal, and economic systems on international marketing.

Cateora, P. R. and Hess, J. M. *International Marketing.* Rev. ed. Homewood, Ill.: Richard D. Irwin, Inc., 1971. A basic textbook that provides coverage on most of the principal topics of global marketing.

Krause, W. *International Economics.* Boston: Houghton Mifflin Co., 1965. A readable textbook that discusses the major topics of international economics and some aspects of the economics of development.

Miracle, G. E. and Albaum, G. S. *International Marketing Management.* Homewood, Ill.: Richard D. Irwin, Inc., 1970. This good basic text in the area of global marketing discusses most of the more important topics and is particularly good on advertising.

Patty, C. R. and Vredenburg, H. L. (eds.) *Readings in Global Marketing Management.* New York: Appleton-Century-Crofts Educational Division, 1969. Contains a good representation of the articles on global marketing that have appeared in journals and magazines during the past 10 years.

Vernon, R. *Manager in the International Economy.* Englewood Cliffs, N.J.: Prentice-Hall, Inc., 1968. A leading text, with cases, in multinational business management.

Marketing: Principles and methods

Part VII   Policies and practices within marketing organizations

Part VII is different from all the other parts in that it employs a micro approach to examine marketing from *within* organizations. Preceding parts have taken a macro view of marketing systems as consisting of functions and institutions and have considered the ways in which they were joined together and operated, as well as their effectiveness and efficiency in meeting the needs of society.

To understand marketing, one must consider both macro and micro views of marketing systems. While the macro approach provides a comprehensive overview of the marketing system and subsystems and their roles in society, the micro approach penetrates the institutions to examine the marketing policies and practices of individual organizations that permit them to be viable in the marketing system. The principal focus is on the variables and subsystems within organizations over which managers have control.

A business manager can be viewed somewhat like the captain of an airplane or a ship. He is trying to get someplace—he has goals—and he must develop plans and strategies for reaching them. His challenge is that he must operate in an environment over which he has little if any control. He cannot change the legal environment, competition, the overall distribution system, technology, economic conditions, people, or other environmental variables. However he does have, within certain limits, control over the performance of his organization as it adapts to a dynamic environment and moves toward his goals. He must manage certain subsystems that together compose his total organizational system. These are normally considered to be marketing information, products and service offerings, channels of distribution, physical distribution, promotion by personal selling, advertising, and pricing. Along with planning and strategy formulation, these usually controllable subsystems constitute the topics discussed in this micro view of marketing.

Chapter 17 discusses marketing information systems. Chapter 18 examines product and service plans and policies. The selection and use of channels of distribution is the topic of Chapter 19, and Chapter 20 focuses on the available alternative physical distribution systems for a firm's products and services. Attention is turned in Chapters 21 and 22 to the promotion of an organization's products and services, with personal selling featured in the former and advertising in the latter. The final chapter in Part VII, Chapter 23, discusses pricing.

17 *Marketing information systems and research*

The dynamic nature of marketing activities requires manufacturers and middlemen to make almost continuous decisions on a variety of problems and opportunities. Large amounts of money depend on correct decisions being made by managers who must be able to make intelligent appraisals of alternatives and the consequences of their actions.[1] The decision-making task relies on the use of information about the environment, customers, competitors, and the activities of one's own organization. The role of marketing information systems and research is to obtain and analyze this information and aid managers to form intelligent appraisals. This role can be better understood by noting a few illustrations.

1. The manufacturer of a nationally advertised drug product was debating the advisability of a higher price. He hesitated to increase the price without more evidence as to what would happen to sales and net profit as a result of the change and turned to his marketing information manager for aid. To obtain the necessary *facts,* test marketing was employed, under which the higher price was made effective in California alone. During the test period the research staff made a careful *analysis* of the relationships between the new price and sales, between sales of this product and those of competitors, and between the new price and net profits. At the end of the trial period the information manager *recommended* that the higher price be adopted throughout the country.

2. A candy manufacturer was faced with a substantial increase in the cost of one of his important product ingredients. Although he knew of a lower priced substi-

---

[1] Bristol-Myers Company in 1967 and 1968 was reported to have spent over $21,000,000 on unsuccessful attempts to market Fact toothpaste, Vote toothpaste, and Resolve pain reliever. "Bristol-Myers Turns Out Parade of Clinkers," *Advertising Age,* August 2, 1971, pp. 1 and 50.

tute he hesitated to use it because it changed the color of his product slightly, and he was afraid of consumer resistance, based on long association of a specific color with his product. An independent marketing research organization was employed to test consumer reaction. This organization gathered its *facts* by placing the product made of the substitute ingredient on sale in selected stores throughout the country. During the period of the experiment the sales of these selected stores were *analyzed* and compared with those of other outlets. Moreover, sales figures for the product in the selected stores were compared with those for competing products in the same stores. As a final check, personal interviews were held with a sample of customers. Based on the analysis, it was evident that the manufacturer's fears were justified; the slump in his sales in the test stores was such that the research organization *recommended* against the substitute ingredient.

3. In the industrial goods market, sales of a small hand-truck manufacturer had remained stable for the past several years. Lacking definite information, he did not know whether this was a result of a limited market, an increase in competitors' sales, a poor product, an ineffective sales staff, or other factors. *Analysis* showed a substantial market and good customer acceptance of the product, but a disorganized and ineffective sales organization. It was *recommended* that a new sales manager be employed to rebuild this department.

4. A problem facing many large retailers which can be solved through careful research is that of locating branch or suburban stores. A department store in a downtown area found that its sales were showing a long-run falling trend. An analysis of possible causes indicated that the major factor was the gradual shift of retail sales to suburban areas. After a few weeks of gathering *facts* on alternative locations—facts as to traffic movement, population shifts, availability of parking facilities, and the like—a careful *analysis* led the research group to *recommend* a site in a suburban shopping center some 25 miles distant.

MARKETING RESEARCH AND INFORMATION SYSTEMS COMPARED

Some confusion arises over the differences and similarities of marketing research and marketing information systems. A frequently used definition of marketing research is "the systematic gathering, recording , and analyzing of data about problems relating to the marketing of goods and services."[2]

A marketing information system has been described as "A structured, interacting complex of persons, machines, and procedures designed to generate an orderly flow of pertinent information, collected from both intra- and extra-firm sources, for use as the basis for decision-making in specified responsibility areas of marketing management."[3]

A comparison of the two definitions suggests that the marketing research definition has been constructed from a researcher's point of view in that it describes the major activities. The information system definition places more emphasis on the fit and function of the activity within the larger marketing system. The implied objectives of both, however, are essentially the same.

This being the situation, why should marketing information systems be develop-

---

[2] R. S. Alexander, *Marketing Definitions,* American Marketing Association Committee on Definitions (Chicago, 1963), pp. 16–17.

[3] S. V. Smith, R. H. Brien, J. E. Stafford, *Readings in Marketing Information Systems* (Boston: Houghton Mifflin Co., 1968), p. 7.

ing while marketing research departments or offices are waning?[4] The explanation seems to be that in practice the scope of what has been called marketing research has fallen far short of the definition in many organizations, and management has been disappointed with marketing research results.

Marketing research shortcomings

Criticisms of marketing research[5] are that it has too frequently:

1. Produced data that are not relevant.
2. Been concerned with research on nonrecurrent problems but virtually ignored the regular collection, analysis, and dissemination of routine current-awareness information.
3. Failed to provide marketing information of sufficient relevance that its value exceeded its cost.

These shortcomings have arisen because marketing research has traditionally been principally a series of independent, uncoordinated organizational activities. Too frequently, it has not been organized as an internal system nor integrated into the larger marketing system.[6]

Marketing information systems, therefore, are often viewed as a substitute for unsatisfactory marketing research. The information systems approach promises to supply the features that too often are overlooked in marketing research: **integrated, analytical, systematic approaches which will identify, assemble, analyze, synthesize, process, and communicate relevant marketing information to decision makers.**[7]

The systems perspective can be used to learn about both marketing research and information system. It provides a total framework of an organization's marketing information needs. Thus an organization containing only a small marketing research function can be examined both in terms of what is present and what is missing.[8]

An overview: Marketing information systems

The relationship of a marketing information system to its organization and environment is symbolized in Figure 17–1, although there is no one unique system that will serve all organizations. The system shown in the circle is composed of three information subsystems: current-awareness, in-depth or special-problem, and unanticipated information. These subsystems are examined in more detail below.

The makeup of the system is shown by the three outlying layers of activities. For example, models and model building are used to provide pictures of problems, to

---

[4] L. E. Boone and D. L. Kurtz, "Marketing Information Systems: Current Status in American Industry," paper presented at 1971 Fall Conference, American Marketing Association.

[5] For a combination of both criticisms and recommendations, see J. G. Keane, "Some Observations on Marketing Research in Top Management Decision Making," *Journal of Marketing,* 33 (October 1969), pp. 10–15.

[6] See K. P. Uhl, "Better Management of Marketing Information," *Business Horizons,* 9 (Spring 1966), pp. 75–82.

[7] K. P. Uhl, "Marketing Information Systems," in R. Ferber (ed.), *Marketing Research Handbook* (New York: McGraw-Hill Book Co., in press), Chapter 4.

[8] For a more detailed comparison of marketing research and marketing information systems, see C. Berenson, "Marketing Information Systems," *Journal of Marketing,* 33 (October 1969), pp. 16–23.

FIGURE 17–1
Marketing information system

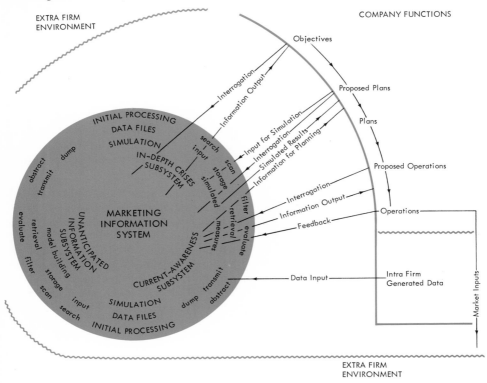

help frame analyses, and to help secure output for decision making through all three subsystems.[9] The next layer suggests that the prior activities require data inputs which must be stored, retrieved, transmitted, and discarded. Finally, the outside layer names some of the information securing-assembling activities. The principal ones are searching, scanning, filtering, evaluating, and abstracting.[10]

The information system interfaces with the major management activities of the larger organizational system—objective setting, planning, and operating. The lines between objectives and the information system suggest that management interrogates and gets information about proposed objectives from the information system. At the next stage, management gets information for planning and may also use the informa-

---

[9] For an illustration see G. D. Hughes and J. L. Guerrero, "Simultaneous Concept Testing with Computer-controlled Experiments," *Journal of Marketing,* 35 (January 1971), pp. 28–33.

[10] For other descriptions and discussions of marketing information systems, see D. B. Montgomery and G. L. Urban, "Marketing Decision-Information Systems: An Emerging View," *Journal of Marketing Research,* 7 (May 1970), pp. 226–34; J. N. Axelrod, "14 Rules for Building an MIS," *Journal of Advertising Research,* 10 (June 1970), pp. 3–11; M. McNiven and R. D. Hilton, "Reassessing Marketing Information Systems," *Journal of Advertising Research,* 10 (February 1970), pp. 3–12; and D. F. Cox and R. E. Good, "How to Build a Marketing Information System," *Harvard Business Review,* 45 (May–June, 1967), pp. 145–54.

tion system to simulate the outcome of proposed plans.[11] A similar relationship is indicated for operations. In a continuing process, the information system secures, assembles, and processes data on the organization, market results, and the environment (including competition) and provides managers with information feedback.

As you examine marketing information systems in more detail, keep in mind that they are *not* synonymous with *computer* systems. A marketing information system may use computer facilities, but a computer system is not an information system—it is merely a component part or tool (and a very useful one).[12]

OBJECTIVES OF MARKETING INFORMATION SYSTEMS

The fundamental objective of a marketing information system is to help managers make better decisions. Information systems must secure, assemble, process, and communicate *information* that can be *used* by managers to reduce uncertainty. Thus they help the marketing manager to devise strategies, follow plans, and reach goals in a harsh, competitive environment. This sounds pretty simple, but unfortunately too many systems provide too much noninformation as well as unused information, which is just as worthless.

Information means *relevant* data that can help managers reduce uncertainty. Nonrelevant data are noninformation. One brewery's information system kept track of sales of their brands of beer by package size, container type, container size, and color of bottle (brown or green). The first three items were used in making decisions about both production and promotion. The last item, while providing data, did not provide information. The brewery used all two-way bottles returned to them whether they were green or brown and based no production or promotion decisions on segregation of bottles by color.

To avoid collecting and providing noninformation and unused information, information systems must reflect business managers' needs.[13] They must know what decisions these managers must make and the information they need to make them. This calls for close interrelationships between information system managers and business decision makers. Each must be acquainted with the detailed needs and functions of the other.

OVERVIEW OF INFORMATION NEEDS

An immense variety of kinds of information is used by business managers, but there are three general classifications: (1) continually collected versus special-problem information, (2) internal versus external information, and (3) buyers' versus sellers' information.

Continually collected versus special-problem information

Information collected and used primarily for planning and decision making in recurrent marketing operations is called *continually collected* (or current-awareness)

---

[11] Some illustrations are given in G. C. Michael, "A Computer Simulation Model for Forecasting Catalog Sales," *Journal of Marketing Research,* 8 (May 1971), pp. 224–29; and L. Friedman, "Constructing a Media Simulation Model," *Journal of Advertising Research,* 10 (August 1970), pp. 33–39.

[12] P. Kotler, "The Future of the Computer in Marketing," *Journal of Marketing,* 34 (January 1970), pp. 11–14.

[13] R. L. Ackoff, "Management Misinformation Systems," *Management Sciences,* 14 (December 1967), pp. B–147–56.

information. An example is the information on the competitive position of existing products required to set marketing objectives, plan strategies, and evaluate the effectiveness of the current marketing mix.

In contrast, there are special situations that call for information in excess of, or different from, that required in the normal range of recurrent planning and decision-making situations. Needs for such *special-problem* (or indepth-crises) *information* arise because management can neither anticipate total future needs nor afford all wanted information on a continuing basis. An example is the product and market research required to develop and introduce new products. It should be noted that what may be special-problem information in one organization may be continually collected information in another.

If a subsystem of continually collected information can be compared to a fire prevention program, a subsystem of special-problem information is analogous to fire fighting. A good fire-prevention program can decrease both the cost of fire fighting and fire losses, but total fire-prevention programs are not feasible because it is not possible or practicable to prevent all fires from erupting.

Internal versus external information

Internal information is that which is both generated and available within the using organization. External information, in contrast, originates and is initially available only outside the using organization. Figure 17–2 shows some of the major kinds of each type.

The problems of searching, securing, and supplying external information are somewhat different from those of internal information. External information usually involves: (1) more extensive searching because of the multiplicity of sources, (2) securing information through or from outside independent organizations, and (3) more extensive involvement in collecting information.

FIGURE 17–2
Internal versus external information

Internal information

   Organization's sales   }   Both by various products,
   Organization's marketing costs}   territories, and functions

External information

   Other organizations' sales
   Other organizations' costs
   Measures of potential
   Customer behavior, patterns, and explanations
   Other environmental conditions, such as economic
      factors, legal restraints, political situations

Joint internal-external information

   Market share
   Market position
   Effort share
   Effort rank

Buyers' versus sellers' information

The buyers' side of a market represents all of the buyers for a particular product or service; for trail bikes it would include all current and prospective customers for all makes. The sellers' side is composed of all of the sellers of trail bikes that the buyers consider as alternatives. Information is available on both the buyers' and sellers' sides of the market, as indicated in Figure 17–3.

Sellers' side information. The left side of the figure, the sellers' side, contains the two categories of sales information and effort information.

1. *Sales information.* Sales information is separated into the firm's own sales and all sellers' (industry) sales. Information on the firm's sales that are made directly to consumers and into channels of distribution can normally be collected from internal sources. Because manufacturers often sell through thousands of independent middlemen, they also need to know their sales to consuming customers. A toy manufacturer, for example, sells and delivers most toys for Christmas sale by the end of October,

FIGURE 17–3
Major types of marketing information

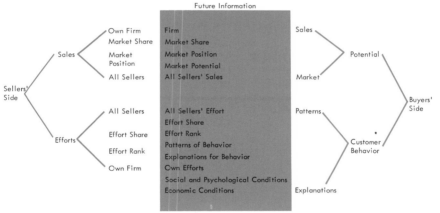

Source: K. P. Uhl and B. Schoner, *Marketing Research: Information Systems and Decision Making* (New York: John Wiley & Sons, Inc., 1969), p. 242.

yet most of them are not resold until December. Final sales information must be gathered from external sources—either from the final sellers or from the final buyers.

An organization's aggregate sales figures, such as appear on an income statement, are not very useful because they lack sufficient detail. The figures needed for analysis are sales by individual product lines or departments, by territories or by stores, by channels of distribution, and by other dimensions that are subject to control. Similar observations hold true for the sales of competitors.

Many kinds of sales information are collected and used on a continuing basis, by both manufacturers and middlemen. Retailers rely primarily on their own internal records. Manufacturers use a greater variety of sources, including returned warranty cards, tax or license reports, consumer purchase panels, audits of store sales, and middlemen sales reports.

Industry sales are relatively difficult to secure. Sometimes trade associations or governmental units release such information, but it normally is too aggregated. Marketers must usually buy such information from commercial sources or collect it themselves.

Market share, which is an organization's sales divided by industry sales, provides a measure of how well a seller is doing compared to competitors. For example, if Schlitz sells 900,000 bottles of beer in Milwaukee and total industry sales there are 4,500,000 bottles, Schlitz has a 20 percent market share (900,000 ÷ 4,500,000). Market position requires more information than market share because the sales of various sellers in a market must be ranked. These items of information are needed for each product line and for each market.

2. *Effort information.* Effort information (marketing cost information) has reference to expenditures by sellers to promote and distribute their products and services. An organization needs information about its own expenditures for personal selling, advertising, physical distribution, and other marketing efforts as well as those of other sellers. Ideally, organizations would like the same breakdowns on effort allocations as for sales. Detailed marketing cost information, even within the individual organization, is relatively expensive to collect, however. Detailed cost information on competitors—except for a few specific aggregate items—is even more difficult to secure and consequently is usually collected and used only on a special instead of a continuous basis.

Effort share and effort rank as shown in Figure 17–3 are computed in the same manner as are market share and market position except, of course, that selling expenditure figures are used. These measures are used to show sellers how much they are spending, compared to competitors, to gain their sales.

Buyers' side information. Information about the buyers' side of the market is divided into two parts, potential and customer behavior.

1. *Potential information.* Potential is a measure of the maximum capacity of a market to purchase or consume a product or a service. It is basically a quantitative measure or estimate of either the absolute or the relative number of units that a market has capacity to buy or use in a specified time.[14]

Market potential refers to the maximum capacity of the various segments or parts of a market to buy or use the goods or services from *all* of the sellers. *Sales potential* indicates the share of market potential for an individual seller.

While there are numerous uses of potential, one common analysis involves comparison, market by market, of relative market potential with actual sales and company selling efforts. This type of analysis helps spot weaknesses and strengths in the company's marketing program. For example, a company may note that only 3 percent of its sales occurred in a market in which it put 15 percent of its efforts but that had 10 percent of market potential.

2. *Customer behavior information.* Customer behavior information is concerned with the patterns of and explanations for behavior of customers. Marketers want to know *who* purchased *what, when, where,* and with what *frequency.* An important task is to identify heavy users and how to communicate with them. Marketers also attempt to discern *who* decides what products and brands are purchased. Housewives, for example, purchase most breakfast foods and beer in grocery stores,

---

[14] For a discussion of potential, see K. P. Uhl and B. Schoner, *Marketing Research: Information Systems and Decision Making* (New York: John Wiley & Sons, Inc., 1969), Chap. 14.

but the marketer must learn *how* various brands are selected and by *whom* (children, husband, jointly?). Purchasing agents in organizations frequently only place orders that are originated by others.

Explanations for behavior basically attempt to answer *why* various groups of customers act as they do. For example, why are certain groups of people heavy users of aspirin? Why do some consumers avoid the purchase of Texaco brand gasoline? Explanations are sought as an aid in predicting future behavior. Models of buyer behavior, such as the Howard-Sheth system discussed in Chapter 4, facilitate such understanding.

Almost all customer behavior and explanation information is external to the using organization. Some of this information is collected frequently (continually collected information) while other information may be collected only infrequently (special-problem information).

Explanatory information is generally more difficult to secure, analyze, and use than is information about behavior. Explanations cannot be observed, and individuals have little insight into their own behavior and even less interest and ability in explaining it. Would you be interested in explaining in a way that would be useful to a marketer why you do or do not like chocolate ice cream, beer, or Ford cars?

Future information. Future information, as shown in Figure 17–3, is merely information about future events and experience. Because any control a manager has is in the future, past information is collected on each event or activity that he wants to know about so he can "experience" it and use it as a basis for foreseeing the future.

A great variety of information can be made available to managers to help them make decisions. Individual situations vary immensely; the needs of, say, a supermarket manager are quite different from those of the product manager of the firm that supplies supermarkets with baby food or beer. The common factor is that all managers need information—some on a continual basis, some only now and then. The actual information needed and when it is needed are dependent on the decisions the manager makes.

MAJOR PARTS OF MARKETING INFORMATION SYSTEMS

Marketing information systems have been divided into the three subsystems shown in Figure 17–1 above: (1) current-awareness, (2) in-depth crisis, and (3) unanticipated information. Note, however, that each marketing information system is unique because as it evolves, management is confronted by different information needs, environments, and styles of management.

Virtually all marketing information systems are built one subsystem at a time and are managed in terms of subsystems. In mature systems, the major subsystems usually number two or three. Despite wide variation in titles, two common subsystems are frequently present. One of these is designed to handle continually collected current-awareness information and is called a current-awareness subsystem. A second typically handles in-depth information on special problems and problems of immediate high-priority concern to managers. This in-depth crisis subsystem is basically the one many companies have had under the title of "marketing research." When a third major information subsystem is present, it usually is designed to handle information and situations that do not fit into the other two subsystems but that do seem to warrant attention. This is designated as the unanticipated information subsystem.

Current-awareness subsystem

The current-awareness subsystem, designed to provide continuing flows of information, can supply periodic reports of company sales by products, territories, etc.; total annual sales to date; comparative past sales data, and future forecasted sales. It can also show changes in market share, competitive activities, costs expended along various dimensions, and other information on past and present factors and estimates of future conditions in reference to internal matters, competition, and the environment.

This type of subsystem is usually computer based, even in middle to small-size retail stores, and virtually requires access to extensive, meaningful sources and supplies (banks) of data.[15] In its operation, the subsystem must digest, analyze, match, and transfer information as managers need it.

FIGURE 17–4
Current-awareness subsystem

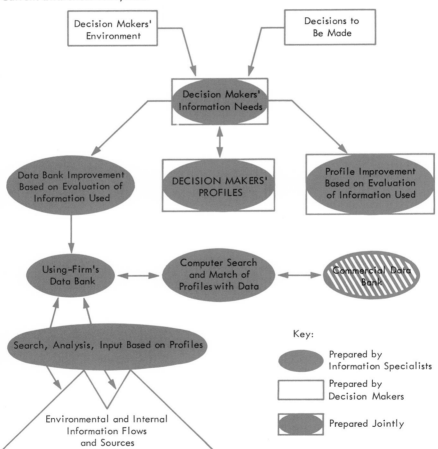

---

[15] For a description of a retail store control program (REACT), see: *General Information: React for Total Merchandise Control* (Dayton, Ohio: National Cash Register Company, n.d.).

A good current-awareness subsystem retains the bulk of its data in highly disaggregated form but is capable of providing it at almost any level of aggregation that is needed. For example, an individual salesman may need to know how many cases of each brand of his beer a specific tavern bought during July. The marketing manager may never want any more detail than brand sales by states.[16]

This subsystem can also provide information output soon after an event occurs. Some facets of some systems, in fact, operate on line, real time (OLRT). This means that as events occur they are communicated to the computer (on line) and managers use the information to control the operations within the short or instantaneous period (real time). Many airlines use OLRT passenger reservation systems to transmit each reservation request directly to a computer which either rejects or confirms it and adjusts the space-available figure in the computer memory unit accordingly. Some banks and savings and loans institutions with extensive branches use OLRT to keep accounts current, and department stores use it to inventory large or expensive items kept in a central warehouse but sold from floor models at downtown and branch stores.

In general, though, the nature of most marketing operations is such that OLRT systems are not efficient. Instead, most information moves and is processed and reported in batches. The important thing is that managers have the information when they need it—neither too frequently nor infrequently.[17]

A final crucial dimension of current-awareness subsystems is the transfer mechanisms used between the data sources and the information system and between the information system and the information users. Managers' needs are continually changing, as is the supply of information. Figure 17–4 sketches some of the details employed to make an information subsystem adaptive to changing conditions. Managers are asked what information they need, are told what is available, and are observed in terms of what they use—all on a continuous basis.

The types of linkage between the current-awareness subsystem and decision makers vary from direct interrogation by the information user to those where the users look to information specialists to provide the linkage. With the first type, the manager must have quite complete knowledge of the system, its content, and its language. With the second, he can get by with only a general understanding of the available data. Direct interrogation probably will become more common as more conventional computer languages and more advanced remote terminals become available.[18]

In-depth crisis subsystem

A subsystem designed to provide detailed information on special problems is an in-depth crisis subsystem. A company's current-awareness subsystem, for example, may indicate deteriorating sales and profits for a product line but fail to provide any insight as to the causes and needed corrections. In this situation an in-depth study of the problem may be required.

A predicament faced by a brewery provides a case in point. The brewery bought a small, but popular, regional brewery and integrated it into their current-awareness

---

[16] This and other key dimensions of information systems are discussed in A. E. Amstutz, "Market-Oriented Management Systems: The Current Status," *Journal of Marketing Research,* 6 (November 1969), pp. 481–96.

[17] For more information on this topic see Uhl and Schoner, *Marketing Research: Information Systems and Decision Making,* pp. 249–50.

[18] R. J. Kegerreis, "Marketing Management and the Computer: An Overview of Conflict and Contrast", *Journal of Marketing,* 35 (January 1971), pp. 3–12.

subsystem. About a year after the tie-in, the current-awareness subsystem reported declines in market share followed by declines in sales. These losses multiplied seriously within a few months. Management could not diagnose from the subsystem what caused the losses. A special-project task force was assembled within the in-depth crisis subsystem. After detailed market study the problems were isolated and recommendations for solution were made.

The success of this type of subsystem is largely conditioned by its ability to respond and adapt to unique problems that present severe time constraints, and often at inappropriate periods. The extensively staffed, routinized, computer-centered organization which works so well in the current-awareness subsystem is not well suited to these conditions, and another subsystem is called for.

A common approach is to formulate a specialized task force to handle specific, unique problems as they are identified. These groups may be composed solely of members of the subsystem or they may be made up of persons working in other areas of the company or even outsiders. The task force used by the brewery was composed of a brewmaster, a market planning expert, a sales manager, and an advertising research specialist and was coordinated by a marketing research project manager from the in-depth crisis subsystem. It is also common to turn virtually an entire project over to an outside consultant who assembles his own task force.

Incidental information subsystem

The two subsystems named above handle either identified types and sources of information or focus on specific problems. The incidental information subsystem does neither of these. This subsystem's *input* side facilitates the collection, assembly, analysis, and synthesis of unsolicited, unanticipated, and incidental data which may warrant the attention of decision makers. In a sense, it is akin to a giant jigsaw puzzle assembly.

The output side is concerned with the communication to decision makers of this unsolicited and incidental data that would not otherwise have shown up in other subsystems. It provides a means for the information manager to put business managers in contact with relevant but unsolicited information. For example, a patent search initiated by a firm's legal counsel may find product information of value, or a Congressional hearing may report on a marketing strategy employed by a competitor.[19]

A principal problem discourages firms from using this type of subsystem. Key personnel, who are the ones in frequent contact with relevant data, fail to recognize its value, to collect it, or to transmit it to those who can assemble it into useful information. This problem is somewhat common to all information subsystems, but it is particularly oppressive in this case because bits and pieces of data appear so inconsequential and because the input rests on numerous individuals who only incidentally collect information.[20] Formal incidental information subsystems are quite uncommon.

---

[19] For a more detailed illustration see Uhl and Schoner, *Marketing Research: Information Systems and Decision Making*, pp. 366–67.

[20] For some solutions to this problem, see G. Albaum, "Information Flows and Decentralized Decision Making in Marketing," *California Management Review* (Summer 1967), pp. 59–70; and K. P. Uhl, "Marketing Information Systems and Subsystems," in R. L. King (ed.), *Marketing and the New Science of Planning* (Chicago: American Marketing Association, 1968), pp. 163–68.

Marketing: Principles and methods

OPERATING PROCEDURES

Before any information is collected, whether on a continuing basis or for special problems, information managers must first establish their objectives (see Chapter 18). Then it is essential to ascertain exactly what information is to be obtained and in what manner it is to be used. Finally, plans and methods for collecting, analyzing, and communicating the information to users must be established. These procedures include the following: (1) identify and define the situation and problems, (2) formulate hypotheses, (3) plan the research design, (4) collect and tabulate the data, (5) analyze and interpret the data, (6) communicate the findings, and (7) follow up. For continually collected information, steps 4 through 7 recycle over and over, and steps 1 through 3 are repeated only periodically. Special-problem information involves all seven steps for each project. Such procedures can provide operational guidelines whether the information requirements involve experimental designs, survey research, or continuing store audits or the information is being secured by middlemen or manufacturers.

Identify and define the situation and problems

When an information manager meets a situation or problem, he rarely can identify it clearly. Instead he is confronted with conflicting bits and particles of symptoms, other people's ideas, and remnants of the past. The information manager cannot succeed by treating either symptoms or general problems. He must be able to make ample observations and gain sufficient knowledge of the situation to be able to identify and define specific opportunities and problems.

For example, an information manager may realize that the general problem confronting him is an ongoing evaluation of his organization's advertising program or the profitability of various product lines. He must move from these general and ambiguously defined problems of advertisement effectiveness and product-line profitability to a series of more specific problems whose dimensions can be carefully defined. For a minimum evaluation of advertising effectiveness, he must ascertain the media being used, the audience for these media, the proportion of each audience that views his company's advertisements, and the characteristics of this audience.

Formulate hypotheses

Once the investigator has a good grasp of the situation, he can start formulating hypotheses (tentative explanations) about the problems or opportunities. As a first stage, he must abstract the complex situation into relatively simple real-world models which he can comprehend and study.[21]

Hypotheses are used to direct the information plan. They suggest what information must be secured and, equally important, indicate what data are not relevant. For example, a driver observes that his car does not start. Many things could be wrong, and he cannot deal with everything at once. Based on his perception of the situation (the car and the environment), he is likely to formulate a tentative explanation (hypothesis) or two. Then he will secure information that will test these hypotheses. If the day is very cold and his car battery is old, he may hypothesize that the battery is dead.

---

[21] An illustration of using a model to select media is given in H. W. Boyd, Jr., H. J. Claycamp, and C. W. McClelland, "Media Models for the Industrial Goods Advertiser: A Do-It-Yourself Opportunity," *Journal of Marketing,* 34 (April 1970), pp. 23–27.

This directs him to collect information regarding the conditon of the battery—not information about the gas supply or the starter or some other element.

Similarly a manager may hypothesize that sales and profits are down because the firm's advertising program is ineffective. This hypothesis will require a far different set of information than if he would have hypothesized that one of the three marketing channels the company was using was clogged with competitive products.

One of the most difficult jobs facing managers is to formulate good hypotheses. These tentative explanations almost always arise from a clear picture of a situation accompanied by sufficient past experience to permit creative insight. A novice, or one who is unfamiliar with the situation, is not likely to develop relevant hypotheses. This is obvious when the success of a car mechanic attempting to diagnose the failure of a car to start is compared with that of an inexperienced driver.

Plan the research design

In planning the design that will allow testing of the hypothesis, the information manager must discern what information is needed. He must also discern the sources of this information and how to collect it. Units to be observed must be selected and appropriate collection instruments drawn up and tested. Procedures for analyzing and communicating the information must also be *planned* at this stage.

Above all, the information manager must ascertain that the called-for information, if collected and analyzed as planned, will yield benefits which justify the cost and effort. A marketing information system—for both continuously collected and special problem information—is maintained in order *to improve the quality of decision making.* The decision maker must believe that the payoff from improved decisions exceeds the cost of planning, collecting, and analyzing data. That is, **the value of the information must exceed its cost.** Every marketing information expenditure should be justified by this test. Much progress has been made in recent years in developing a method for this quantitative cost-benefit analysis. No research design is complete without it.

Collect and tabulate the data

Once plans are completed, an information manager must proceed to collect and tabulate information. This is the first stage, but not the last one, where a poor planner will be wallowing in empirical data. The information manager should have a perspective model in mind that will guide him in collecting and tabulating data. He must be certain that the data collection is appropriate, uniform, and always on schedule from all sources. Consistent measuring instruments and methods must be employed to make findings comparable.

Electronic data processing, while a great aid to tabulation and analysis, in no way will keep an information manager from bungling the data collection or from being swamped by the inflowing data. This seemingly innocent and simple stage, which has devastated many an information manager, is discussed in more detail in the section on data collection below.

Analyze and interpret the data

In analyzing and interpreting empirical data, the information manager is again faced with its "messiness." Data do not fit neatly into preconceived explanation patterns. As initially received and simply tabulated, they often display masses of nothingness. Occasionally, a suspected pattern will emerge almost on its own from a packet of data, but more frequently it must be analyzed and interpreted in order to provide fully useful information.

Analysis takes many forms and shapes ranging all the way from simple cross tabulations and comparisons to complex statistical analyses designed to display various features of the data. The key problem is determining how to examine the data to pull out its plausible relationships and explanations. This calls for familiarization with both the data and the tools of analysis.[22]

Intermediate interpretation is part of this stage. An information manager is continually looking at his data and asking what it means as he interprets it and moves into further analysis and interpretation. When all the findings are in and all analyses and intermediate interpretations are finished, the information manager must be able to relate these findings to the problem or situation.

Communicate the findings

Communication of the findings to prospective users is crucial to the successful completion of the process. Unused findings are useless findings.

Findings are presented in a number of different ways. In a computer-based current-awareness system, the new findings may be used to update the older data within the system or they may be presented separately. The more common transmission from the system is through page (table) printouts, sometimes at the users' option on an exception basis (when some information indicates a management problem), or on a specific time schedule (e.g., every Monday morning). Other forms of transmission include projection via cathode-ray tube and verbal briefings by information managers.[23]

When special-problem project information is to be communicated, a "popular" written and oral report is typically presented to the users which highlights the findings and recommendations. A technical report normally accompanies this report to explain the research design, important assumptions, detailed findings, and major limitations and supporting data. The popular report usually places considerable emphasis on communicating the findings and recommendations, while the technical report recites in detail what was done, why, and how and provides the supporting data.[24] The technical report allows managers to go into details of the findings and recommendations.[25]

Follow up

Final decisions regarding use of findings and reports are made by the prospective users. The information manager, however, has the responsibility to see that his findings are followed up and not "sidetracked" or discredited by intended users. The time,

---

[22] For a good perspective of multivariate analysis, see J. N. Sheth, "The Multivariate Revolution in Marketing Research," *Journal of Marketing,* 35 (January 1971), pp. 13–19; for a specific illustration, see H. E. Echelberger and E. L. Shafer, Jr., "Snow + (X) = Use of Ski Slopes," *Journal of Marketing Research,* 7 (August 1970), pp. 388–92.

[23] For several illustrations, see Kegerreis, "Marketing Management and the Computer"; and L. M. De Boer and W. H. Ward, "Integration of the Computer into Salesman Reporting," both in *Journal of Marketing,* 35 (January 1971), pp. 3–12 and 41–47.

[24] S. H. Britt, "The Writing of Readable Research Reports," *Journal of Marketing Research,* 8 (May 1971), pp. 262–66.

[25] A more complete description of each type of report is given in Uhl and Schoner, *Marketing Research: Information Systems and Decision Making,* pp. 259 and 260.

effort and expense of finding useful information will have been wasted unless the findings are used, which is especially difficult when they are contrary to the biases and beliefs of decision makers. The Ford Motor Company, for example, is said to have rejected its consultant's findings against marketing the Edsel automobile. Assuming adequacy and reliability of data and logic of interpretation, the information manager or consultant must be fully prepared to support his findings.

DATA COLLECTION

Subsystems that provide information output must have data inputs. These are of three types: construct data, secondary data, and primary data.

Construct data

Construct data are hypothetical data that are generated without specific measurement in the real world. Simulation models are constructed to help managers make marketing decisions. Data for an entire environment or a complete industry may be created in an attempt to simulate a sector of the real world. For example, an increase in prices and promotion by two firms in a multifirm industry may be simulated to determine probable results of decisions in that situation.

Secondary data

While the distinction between secondary and primary information is not always clear, primary information is that which is originated from the real world in view of specific needs. In contrast, secondary information is already in existence, having been previously searched, secured, analyzed, and stored. For instance, if the publisher of *Fortune* magazine collects information about his subscribers in order to orient the magazine to this audience, the survey would provide primary information to the publisher. This same information provided by *Fortune* to other users, however, would be secondary information to these secondary users.[26]

In a sense, secondary information is akin to a secondhand suit of tailor-made clothes. Because it can be found in many places other than tailors' shops, the first problem is to find it. Once it is found, the prospective user must examine it and try it on for fit. It may fit rather exactly and even justify a high purchase price, or the fit may be so poor that extensive (and expensive) alterations are required.[27] Finally, it may simply not fit his needs. In such cases, the information seeker must decide whether to search for other information, spend the money to secure primary information or do without the information.

Unfortunately, secondary information is too often relegated to a second-class category of importance.[28] With all that is occurring within each firm and within each firm's environment, no company can afford to ignore it. It is useful as general reference and as background information, and it may even provide specific solutions. A large dairy, for example, was prepared to run a field survey to ascertain the proportion of households that regularly purchased most of their milk needs from retail stores. A

---

[26] Secondary information can be collected from either the originating source or a secondary source. In general, the originating source is preferred because it is likely to be more accurate and provide greater detail.

[27] A useful guide for examining secondary research reports is "Evaluating Marketing Media Research Studies," Association of National Advertisers, 1968.

[28] See Uhl and Schoner, *Marketing Research: Information Systems and Decision Making,* pp. 393–99.

Marketing: Principles and methods

search for secondary information that cost about $100 provided the needed information plus much other useful data and saved the company over $3,000.

Finally, in numerous situations the only alternative to the use of secondary information is no information. No one company can marshal the resources to collect the federal census material or the mass of published state and local government information. Such secondary information provides the largest part of many firms' continuing information base.

Sources of secondary information. Secondary information is usually searched for by subject matter. When situations and problems give rise to needs for specific information, it is sought from various sources. Knowledge of the available sources can help searchers move more directly to find needed information. The major sources are: (1) within the company, (2) libraries, (3) trade publications, (4) government, (5) trade associations, (6) business firms, (7) research foundations, and (8) commercial information organizations.

1. *The company.* The information manager's own firm typically contains a wealth of data which have been collected for various purposes and are available as secondary information. The accounting and financial systems contain cost and sales data as well as detailed information on many customers.

2. *Libraries.* Some business firms have developed fairly extensive library facilities of their own. They may have accumulated files of the leading trade papers covering their fields of operation, reports of private studies made by research agencies and other firms, and outstanding books. Where such a company library is available, it represents a convenient information source. In practically all cases, however, the firm's library facilities are so limited that other libraries must be used. More specialized business school libraries or those maintained by publications are also useful. University libraries serve as depositories for many government as well as trade publications. Bibliographies,[29] card indexes, and publications that index books,[30] periodical articles,[31] and newspapers[32] help the researcher locate the needed material. Also of great aid are the "Book Reviews" sections of the *Journal of Marketing Research* and the *Journal of Marketing* and the "Marketing Abstracts" section of the latter publication.

3. *Trade publications.* Most trade papers go to great expense to report the facts available concerning their particular fields. Some even conduct detailed studies of subjects in which their readers are interested. In fields where responsible trade papers exist, they may constitute one of the most valuable secondary sources for many investigations. Those available are listed in such publications as the N. W. Ayer & Sons, Inc., *Directory of Newspapers and Periodicals.*

4. *Government.* Increasingly, publications and certain public records of the government—especially those of the federal government—are becoming a valuable source of information for marketing.[33] A comprehensive listing of all publications by

---

[29] Bibliographies on many subjects are prepared by the Library of Congress, Washington, D.C., and listed in the card files of many libraries. Prepared bibliographies are also listed in some of the periodical indexes.

[30] The *Cumulative Book Index* is issued monthly and cumulatively by the H. W. Wilson Co., New York. It includes all books published in the English language, except those issued by governments.

[31] The *Business Periodical Index* lists articles in business journals and periodicals. The *Readers' Guide to Periodical Literature* covers, both by subject and by author, the articles published by many periodicals of interest to the general public. The *Public Affairs Information Service* is particularly useful on public questions; it includes books as well as periodicals. The *Applied Science & Technology Index* covers technical trade publications.

[32] The *New York Times Index* is published twice a month. The London *Times* is also indexed.

[33] On July 4, 1967, a new federal law—termed "the nation's first real public information statute," opened the door to a vast storehouse of governmental information previously inaccessible to researchers.

departments and agencies of the federal government is available in the *Monthly Catalog of U.S. Government Publications;* a more limited listing is offered semi-monthly in *Selected United States Government Publications;* and selected federal publications relating directly to marketing are included in the monthly *Marketing Information Guide,* along with those of local and state governments, private business, professional groups, and institutions.[34] State government publications are also listed in the *Monthly Checklist of State Publications,* which is issued by the Library of Congress; and various state libraries maintain index cards through which a wide variety of publications can be located.

For the marketing of agricultural products, the U.S. Department of Agriculture issues a large number of periodic reports plus a great many special studies. For manufactured goods and, to some degree, agricultural products as well, valuable data are released by the U.S. Department of Commerce, the Federal Trade Commission, and the U.S. Department of Labor (especially through its Bureau of Labor Statistics). Special mention should be made of the *Census of Business* reports of the Bureau of the Census in the Department of Commerce. These broad tabulations of essential marketing data are invaluable to those engaged in marketing research. The Bureau also issues a catalog, *Bureau of the Census Catalog,* which lists all its publications. Also indispensable to the market researcher are the *Decennial Census of the United States, Census of Manufacturers,* and *Census of Agriculture.*[35] The nation's 866 zip code sectional centers and city units, when used in connection with other known facts about these areas, provide added power for the marketer to study local areas.[36]

In addition, the following publications of the federal government are helpful: *Statistical Abstract of the United States, Agricultural Statistics,* and monthly periodicals such as the *Survey of Current Business* and the *Monthly Labor Review.* On occasion, reports issued by congressional committees are of interest for special research projects.

5. *Trade Associations.* Trade associations have long played an important role in gathering information for their members, other businessmen, government agencies, and the general public. This role gained added significance during the National Recovery Administration era of 1933–35 and also during World War II and thereafter, when trade associations were called upon by the government to represent their respective industries in more or less official capacities. Some organizations increased their research activities in order to gain the information needed for presentations before governmental agencies. Through regular and special publications, these reports are made available to members and, in many cases, to the general public. But trade association services of a research nature are not limited to such activities. Statistical services in the form of financial and operating cost surveys, regular and special publications, educational activities, and others too numerous to mention constitute tasks currently being performed.

A list of trade associations, *National Associations of the United States,* is available from the U.S. Department of Commerce. Many are also listed in the annual volumes of the *Business Periodical Index.*

6. *Business firms.* Some information may be secured directly from business

---

[34] Since 1972 *Marketing Information Guide* has not been a government publication, but it is still published in a similar manner.

[35] For use of census material, see A. R. Eckler, "Profit from 1970 Census Data," *Harvard Business Review,* 48 (July–August 1970), pp. 4–16.

[36] See Martin Baier, "ZIP Code—New Tool for Marketers," *Harvard Business Review,* 45 (January–February 1967), pp. 136–40.

Marketing: Principles and methods

firms which have faced similar problems and have prepared printed material concerning them. For instance, Safeway Stores, Inc., has prepared a written statement of many of its policies. Such a report is of considerable value to a marketing study aimed at recommending policies for another chain of food stores. Data of interest to researchers are also issued by banks and insurance companies, in reports, often published periodically, covering general business conditions in specific markets, price trends, bank loans, and the like, or dealing with specific investigations. The Policy Holders' Bureau of the Metropolitan Life Insurance Company, for example, has released a number of specific marketing studies. The Household Finance Corporation has also issued numerous reports of value, particularly those relating to consumers. The researcher should also be aware of the Marketing Services Company, a division of Dun & Bradstreet, Inc., which has developed a Marketing Information System designed to provide a broad, factual base for marketing decisions. The system is based on the parent company's Marketing Data Bank containing more than 24 million items of marketing data from over 3.7 million business establishments.[37]

7. *Research foundations.* Several nonprofit foundations provide valuable marketing information. The Twentieth Century Fund has been responsible for such a monumental work as *America's Needs and Resources.* The American Management Association has issued a long list of material such as its *Guidelist for Marketing Research and Economic Forecasting.* Likewise, many of the reports of the Conference Board (formerly National Industrial Conference Board) are of value, such as *Using Marketing Consultants and Research Agencies* and *Research Support for Global Marketing.* Valuable reports also come from the Marketing Science Institute.

8. *Commercial organizations.* Numerous marketing research and consultant organizations, advertising agencies, management firms, and resident buying firms publish data of value. These organizations are also prepared to conduct investigations on a wide variety of problems. Although many of their studies are for clients only, others are given wide circulation, partly as a means of advertising the commercial organization.[38]

Primary data

When secondary information has been explored fully and additional data are still required, the marketing information manager turns to primary sources. He makes plans for the collection and use of specific material directly from "the field."

Sources of primary information. The more common primary sources of information are a company's own records, its salesmen, its dealers and prospective dealers, its competitors and other businessmen, and the users and potential users of its products.

1. *Company records.* It is natural for the information manager to turn to his own company for pertinent data. If a study is being made of customer acceptance of a particular product, for example, information on sales analyzed by various markets and on marketing expenditures will be very helpful.

2. *Salesmen.* A firm conducting research will find its own salesmen and those of its dealers or suppliers a productive source of data. Since they come directly into

---

[37] See the company's announcement in *Dun's Review and Modern Industry,* June 1966, p. 21.

[38] For a comprehensive list of organizations engaged in marketing research, see: E. S. Bradford (ed.), *Directory of Marketing Research Agencies and Management Consultants in the United States and the World* (13th ed.; Fairfax, Va.: E. S. Bradford, 1971).

touch with buyers, salesmen can report on their reaction to price and style changes and judge the impact of proposed policies concerning channels of distribution, exclusiveness of distribution, agreements with distributors, advertising, credit, and similar matters. Seeking the advice of the salesmen on such matters is more than a means of securing information; it also is an important morale builder.[39] Such action not only increases the knowledge of salesmen but aids in convincing them that their knowledge is valuable and is appreciated, that they have a part in establishing the firm's policies, and that their company deserves their best services.

3. *Dealers and prospective dealers.* Manufacturers or wholesalers find that their dealers constitute an important source of information. Dealers are in close contact with their customers and are able to supply firsthand knowledge regarding their views of the product and the marketing policies of their suppliers.

4. *Competitors and other businessmen.* On occasion, it is necessary to seek primary information from competitors. A food chain seeking to clarify the thinking of its top executives on future expansion policy may have its research department ask executives of chains in other areas about their policies on this particular issue. Or a manufacturer may seek information from a few of his rivals on credit policies. If the data desired are such that immediate competitors hesitate to release them, they may be obtained from comparable firms doing business in other areas, from suppliers, and from the "representative figures" collected by trade associations.

5. *Ultimate consumers and industrial users.* Since ultimate consumers or industrial users are the focal point of marketing activities, many marketing studies involve a direct approach to them. The customers' behavior, opinions, and attitudes may be sought through a one-time field survey (discussed later) or a consumer panel. Although the panel may be formed for a specific test, more often the group is established on a more or less permanent basis. Only an exceptional marketing firm can afford the permanent panel for its purposes alone, since the maintenance of a panel may cost from $10,000 to $30,000 or even more a year. When the services of such panels are desired, they may be obtained through advertising agencies or research organizations which maintain them for use by their clients.

Gathering primary information

Once the main primary sources of information are known they must be evaluated in the light of particular information needs. It is outside the scope of this book to discuss all the methods employed to obtain data from such sources, but attention will be given to business trips, informal counts, surveys, direct testing, experiments, and motivation research.

Business trips. Many business firms gather firsthand material during trips of their executives planned for this purpose. In other cases material is gathered merely as a by-product of buying or selling trips to central markets, and formalized planning may be unnecessary. For instance, the owner of a dress shop may be trying to decide on his price policy in the months immediately ahead. Shall he "clear out" a large part of his stock at sharply reduced prices, or may he count on the existing price level

---

[39] See L. W. Stern and J. L. Heskett, "Grass Roots Market Research," *Harvard Business Review,* 43 (March–April 1965), pp. 83–91. The authors argue in favor of using field sales personnel for some kinds of marketing research because doing so (1) encourages two-way communication between headquarters and the field, and (2) builds their knowledge and permits decisions to be made at the local level.

holding for some time? His judgment on this matter may be clarified by investigations while he is in the New York market to make purchases.

Informal counts. Nearly as informal as the research conducted as the by-product of the business trip is the simple enumerating type of research which often provides valuable data as a basis for marketing decisions. An example of this is afforded by the traffic count used by some chain stores in selecting locations for new units. An observer may be stationed near a proposed site to count the individuals who pass by at certain periods of the day. Based on previous experience with the type of people who patronize the kinds of stores operated by his company, his report may also contain comments as to the likelihood that those who pass by will become customers in the proposed store.

The style count is another illustration of this same research technique. In this instance an observer is asked to record data on women's shoes—noting the different styles, materials, and so forth—as women pass a particular location. The resulting information is of value in determining fashion trends. Another example of this technique is the "pantry inventory" used by observers who are sent from house to house in an effort to determine consumer buying habits for specific products.

A somewhat more formalized but related method is often put into practice by means of the telephone. Such is the case in many studies of television and radio listening habits, in which a number of homes are called to discover the programs tuned in at particular times. These latter studies usually make use of statistical procedures in obtaining adequate samples.

Surveys. The preparation of a list of questions which may be mailed to potential respondents or asked during a personal interview is the most common method of gathering firsthand data. Through this method a retailer may seek opinions from manufacturers, wholesalers, or other retailers as to future price trends in the industry; an advertising agency may inquire as to retailer reaction to a series of advertisements it has prepared for a manufacturer; a manufacturer may invite consumer reaction to the design or packaging of his product; or a retailer may discover how his customers appraise the various service features of his store.

1. *Preparation of a questionnaire.* Many studies make it clear that the validity of the respondents' replies to a questionnaire depend on the kinds of questions asked as well as the circumstances under which they are asked. To prepare a questionnaire which will encourage response and still provide trustworthy data is a most difficult task, and many a survey has failed in these respects. To minimize the possibility of failure, a definite series of steps is recommended. First, a general outline of the subjects about which information is needed is drafted. Second, with the outline prepared, a number of people are interviewed to determine their reactions. This process gives the researcher some appreciation of how people respond to various subjects contained in his outline, aids him in setting the order in which questions should be asked, indicates the best ways of phrasing questions and, in general, provides him with the "feel" of the project. Third, the questionnaire is drafted; and, fourth, pretested. The pretest usually consists of using the questionnaire on a small sample to be sure that all questions are understood, that the sequence and phrasing are satisfactory, that its length is manageable, and that the instructions to interviewers are clear and complete. Fifth, a final redrafting makes the questionnaire ready for use.

2. *Types of questionnaires.* The most common types of surveys are those prepared for (a) mailing to respondents, (b) personal interviews, and (c) telephone interviews.

a) The mail survey.   The well-prepared questionnaire distributed by mail has important advantages. Widely scattered people may be reached with less cost than by an interviewer. The researcher can be sure that the questions are asked in the same manner of all those from whom replies are sought, thereby minimizing interviewer bias. By mail, the questionnaire can be placed in the hands of many people who would not see an interviewer. Its anonymous nature encourages replies to personal questions related to age, income, and education. Moreover, a survey can be conducted from any point where post office facilities are available and by one or more persons, so that costly field research organizations are unnecessary. Finally, when properly developed, the mail sample is highly reliable.

The mail questionnaire is in widespread use. Experience has made it clear, however, that the mailed questionnaire is frequently a slow method of gathering data, since many persons may delay returning it. Also, nonresponse bias may be a serious problem unless the return is above 60 percent or a check of nonrespondents is conducted.[40] Moreover, although the cost of some kinds of answers is quite low, to take all the safeguards necessary to get quality answers in sufficient number may result in a cost per usable return that is as high as that resulting from personal interviews.[41]

b) Questionnaires used by interviewers.   Generally speaking, when the questionnaire is used as the basis for a personal interview with the respondent, a greater number of questions can be included, the sample of informants is easier to control, and information not obtainable with the mail questionnaire can be secured. However, the cost of data collection also is very much greater. Since it is essential that the sample is representative and that the interviews are carried on in an objective manner, problems of the determination of the sample and of personal bias on the part of interviewers are encountered.[42] In addition, many problems arise in connection with assembling and directing a staff of interviewers; so many, in fact, that frequently the actual interviewing is turned over to research organizations which have their own staffs of full-time or part-time interviewers.

c) Telephone surveys.   To an increasing extent in recent years, the telephone has been used to conduct interviews to obtain answers to questionnaires. Although the cost per reply may be reduced and the sample enlarged in a telephone interview as compared with personal interviews, the number of questions which can be asked is less, and the advantages of direct, personal contact are lost. For some studies, however, the telephone is a valuable medium. It is flexible, fast, and timely, and its use continues to grow as new methods are devised to reduce interviewing costs.[43]

Direct testing.   The research technique of direct testing involves securing information from those who have been asked to use the product or service and then to report their reactions. In some instances, it may be necessary for the user to write a brief report of his experience; but in most cases the report is prepared by a trained interviewer after consulting the person who has done the testing.

---

[40] Ways of correcting for nonresponse biases can be found in P. Ognibene, "Correcting Nonresponse Bias in Mail Questionnaires," *Journal of Marketing Research*, 8 (May 1971), pp. 233–35.

[41] For detailed instruction on mail surveys, see P. L. Erdos, *Professional Mail Surveys* (New York: McGraw-Hill Book Co., 1970).

[42] See H. W. Boyd, Jr., and R. Westfall, "Interviewer Bias Once More Revisited," *Journal of Marketing Research*, 7 (May 1970), pp. 249–53.

[43] Seymour Sudman, "New Uses of Telephone Methods in Survey Research," *Journal of Marketing Research*, 3 (May 1966), pp. 163–67. Also see S. L. Cooper, "Random Sampling by Telephone: A New and Improved Method," *Journal of Marketing Research*, 1 (November 1964), pp. 45–48.

The sample involved in the direct testing of a product or a service may be limited to a committee of the firm's executives, expanded to include others in the firm's employment, or enlarged to include, or consist entirely of, customers and prospective customers. A retailer, for example, may have the proposed additions to his stock tried out by his salespeople. A manufacturer may get opinions both from his salesmen and from people employed in his factories. Even better, however, is using a group of consumers for a direct testing project.

Experiments. Experiments, in simple terms, involve the selection of a small part of the total market for the conduct of certain tests, such as the drug manufacturer cited earlier who used California as the testing ground for a higher price on his product. Test units might also be one city or a small number of cities, a limited number of retail stores scattered throughout part or all of the country, a group of individual consumers, or—for an industrial good[44]—all accounts in the New England area. Likewise, the testing can apply to many variables—price change, a proposed new product, the type of packaging, the impact of an advertising campaign, or the type of retail establishment in which the product is sold.

The basis of a true experiment is that (1) a comparison is available between a test group (or groups) that receives the experimental treatment and a control group that does not receive the treatment but otherwise goes through exactly the same procedures and (2) experimental units are assigned to the test or control group by the *experimenter* in such a way that initial differences among the groups arise by chance alone.[45] Most test marketing, in the parlance of marketing information managers, does not constitute *true* experiments but instead is referred to as quasi experiments. This occurs because field conditions may make true experiments prohibitedly expensive.[46]

Motivation research. One of the most controversial marketing subjects of the past two decades is what is known as motivation research. Its merits and limitations have been widely discussed.[47]

Essentially, motivation research involves "the use of psychiatric and psychological techniques to obtain a better understanding of why people respond as they do to products, advertisements, and various other marketing situations."[48] Interest in it was stimulated by the long-recognized discrepancies between what people *say* they do, think, or like and what they *actually* do, think, or like. Experience indicates that the direct approach to a customer in which he is asked, "Why did you buy product X?" may not give the true answer. Instead, the respondent may answer what he thinks you want him to say. Thus a person may actually have "bought a house because it had nice red shutters and shrubs around it," but would not wish to admit to this reason

---

[44] See R. C. Nelson, "Why Industrial Marketers Need Concept Testing," *Industrial Marketing,* 50 (August 27, 1965), pp. 87–88.

[45] Contrary to much popular opinion, in a true experiment several variables can be manipulated at one time. See S. Banks, *Experimentation in Marketing* (New York: McGraw-Hill Book Co., 1965), and W. O. Barclay, "Factorial Design in a Pricing Experiment," *Journal of Marketing Research,* 6 (November 1969), pp. 427–29.

[46] K. P. Uhl, "Field Experimentation: Some Problems, Pitfalls, and Perspective," in R. M. Haas (ed.), *Science, Technology, and Marketing,* Fall Conference Proceedings, American Marketing Association, (Chicago, 1966), pp. 561–72.

[47] Perry Bliss, *Marketing and the Behavioral Sciences: Selected Readings* (Boston: Allyn & Bacon, 1963); Ernest Dichter, *Handbook of Consumer Motivations: The Psychology of the World of Objects* (New York: McGraw-Hill Book Co., Inc., 1964); and R. Ferber and H. G. Wales (eds.), *Motivation and Market Behavior* (Homewood, Ill.: Richard D. Irwin, Inc., 1958).

[48] L. C. Lockley, "The Use of Motivation Research in Marketing" in C. J. Dirksen, Arthur Kroger, and L. C. Lockley, *Readings in Marketing* (Homewood, Ill.: Richard D. Irwin, Inc., 1963), p. 439.

for rejecting "the more valuable and sturdier house next door. . . ."[49] Or the respondent may not truly know why he purchased a specific product or took a certain action. What motivation research attempts to do is to get at the underlying reasons for behavior.

Two major techniques from the field of psychology are used by motivational researchers. One of these is the long narrative interview, which is often referred to as the "depth interview." Under this technique, the questioner lets the respondent talk at will. He usually approaches his real subject in an indirect manner (so-called "nondirective questioning"). The other tool of motivational research consists of a number of projective techniques. This method involves the use of word association, response to pictures, and sentence completion—all used in an effort to get the respondent to reveal what he might cover up by direct questioning.

Whether depth interviewing or projective techniques lead the respondent unwittingly to divulge his real reasons for an act is not clear. Many researchers are convinced that these techniques have been "oversold" and that their true value, if any, has not been proven.

COMMERCIAL INFORMATION SUPPLIERS

Virtually any of the primary or secondary information that has been mentioned, whether it is continually collected or on a one-time basis, can be secured from or through commercial information and service firms, although company data are an exception. Some marketing organizations buy virtually all of their information and service needs from commercial sources; others buy nothing.

Information is available from commercial sources on a syndicated or custom basis. Syndicated reports are designed to fit the needs of many users. Duplicate reports are available to all who wish to purchase them. Custom information, in contrast, presumes a confidential relationship between the commercial supplier and the user, and the data are secured and supplied exclusively for one user. Many commercial sources offer information on both bases.

Types of commercial information

Information from commercial suppliers comes from four sources: (1) panels, (2) store or warehouse audits, (3) field enumerations, and (4) independent sample surveys. These are not mutually exclusive, but they do provide a reasonable perspective for viewing information from commercial information firms.

Panel information.   Panels are basically ongoing groups of persons who periodically answer the same questions regarding their buying behavior, intentions, attitudes, and motivation. Some panels cover a wide variety of products and activities (Market Research Corporation of America) while some relate only to a small bit of behavior (A. C. Nielsen Company's Radio-Television Households). Some panels are composed of ultimate consumers (MRCA), while some are made up of retailers, farmers, dealers or others. Most firms syndicate their panel information.

Store and warehouse audits.   The store audit is a periodic check to discern the sales of certain products and brands in specific outlets during specified time periods. Most store audits reflect the following equation: previous inventory *plus* store

---

[49] Ernest Dichter, "Seven Tenets of Creative Research," *Journal of Marketing,* 25 (April 1961), p. 4.

purchases (*minus* returns) *equals* stock available for sales *minus* present inventory *equals* consumer sales. In addition, information on couponing, price discounting, special promotions and other factors that may have influenced sales are reported. The warehouse audit is very similar to the store audit except it deals with *shipments* instead of sales and no promotional information is collected.

Numerous manufacturers of food and drug products subscribe to one or more syndicated services on a continuing basis. The data provide a measure of sales from the channel to the final consumer.

Field enumerations.   Some commercial information firms collect information from virtually all sources of specific types that will cooperate with them. The F. W. Dodge Corporation, Dun and Bradstreet, and R. L. Polk and Company are three of the firms that fit into this category. F. W. Dodge makes syndicated monthly reports to the building trades, collecting information from about 165,000 architects, engineers, contractors, public officials, and others associated with the building trades. Dun and Bradstreet collects information from more than 300,000 manufacturing firms in the United States and is probably best known for its financial credit rating information. One division of R. L. Polk and Company, through field-enumeration work, prepares household and business directories on more than 5,500 U.S. cities. Another division enumerates all car registrations in the United States.

Independent-sample survey.   This technique, in contrast to the panel technique, draws a new, or independent, sample for each new study. Some of the better known syndicated ones are the Starch Magazine Advertisement Readership Service and the Gallup Organization. In each case, they select a new sample and through personal interviews elicit answers to a set of questions.

Other commercial services

Commercial firms also do direct testing, collect field data, and provide consulting services on information problems. Few manufacturers or middlemen maintain their own field interview forces, but most use one or more firms that specialize in the service. Finally, special consulting help is available in technical areas ranging from design of samples to computer programming and data processing. Almost any information-service package is available to provide performance of a simple task or the complex handling of an entire information project.

THE FUTURE OF INFORMATION SYSTEMS

One of the few invariables in marketing is the process of change. This change, however, is not of the dramatic breakthrough type found in natural science areas where massive technological revolutions may occur. In marketing there are few barriers to dam up and then release a torrent of change. There is instead a slow constant evolution.

One of the most significant changes in process within the marketing system is in the manner in which it is managed. The nature of the practice of marketing is changing from intuitional management to management of marketing through information.

Formal marketing information systems, whatever the names under which they operate, are expanding in number, comprehensiveness, and usefulness. New managers are learning more about information, its management, and its application to decision making. A manager relying on 20 or 30 years of personal experience faces difficulty when confronted by one supported by a good marketing information system. He also faces difficulty if his marketing information system generates data unchecked. Modern data processing can easily overload the manager with data. The chief task for management in the 1970s may be to learn how to manage information—how to avoid overcollection of data, how to measure the value and cost of information, how to store what information, and how to retrieve and display the correct information at the correct time.

Judgment and experience, of course, cannot be replaced. Experience does come faster, however, when managers use information to learn more quickly and clearly the consequences of their decisions and to preplay alternative decisions in simulation exercises. Good judgment, particularly under pressure, remains a scarce talent. While it can be put to good use in marketing information systems, it in no way has been supplanted by them.

To use an analogy, a pilot can fly a small airplane by the seat of his pants when he has clear weather and daylight and few other aircraft are aloft. To haul more passengers longer distances, he needs a bigger plane and requires more instrumentation because he must traverse places he has not previously experienced, encounters more planes, and must fly under less ideal conditions. Marketing managers encounter similar circumstances. As the marketing environment becomes more complex, management's judgment must be supplemented with more complicated techniques of information planning, gathering, analysis, communication, and application. Measurement of their firm's operation and the marketing environment may not be as precise and reliable as for the pilot, but it is nonetheless essential both for planning and operating.

Continued expansion and increase of information systems can be foreseen. Monumental information management tasks are yet to be mastered, such as the development of practical distribution cost analysis programs, effort allocation models, and affordable simulation applications, to mention only a few. The major result of the use of marketing information systems is likely to be a more finely turned and more efficient marketing system. This system will be more responsive to customers' needs, because managers will know and understand them better, and more able to deliver desired products and services efficiently.

SUMMARY

This chapter has described a modern marketing information system as consisting of three subsystems, for current-awareness, in-depth–crisis, and unanticipated information. Classifications of information used in these systems include continually collected or special-problem information, internal or external information, and buyers' or sellers' information. Seven steps in the procedure for information planning, collection, analysis, and communication were discussed, and the major types and sources of secondary and primary data were described, with separate sections devoted to the major methods of gathering primary data and to commercial suppliers of information.

REVIEW AND DISCUSSION QUESTIONS

1. Explain the relationship of marketing research and marketing information to policy formation. Give specific illustrations.

Marketing: Principles and methods

2. Without reference to the text, formulate your own definition of marketing research and marketing information systems, giving particular attention to their nature, purposes, and differences.

3. What should be the objectives of marketing information systems? Why should a company have a marketing information system?

4. Assume that you are the director of marketing information systems for a large pharmaceutical manufacturer. The president has indicated his dissatisfaction with the present channel of distribution, which involves direct sale to prescription pharmacies, and wants your recommendations concerning one promising a higher sales volume. How would you proceed in carrying out this project?

5. What marketing information should an organization have available for its decision makers? Is there really a difference between information and data?

6. Explain what major subsystems are likely to be found in a marketing information subsystem and why each of them is likely to be present.

7. What is meant by "marketing research procedure"? Give two illustrations of sound procedure to clarify your answer.

8. Distinguish between secondary and primary sources of information, and indicate those you would use in carrying out the research involved in question 4 above. State your reasons.

9. Describe in detail four major sources of primary information and some conditions or circumstances under which they would probably be used.

10. Suggest criteria for evaluating the available secondary sources of information on a particular subject.

11. Compare the relative advantages and disadvantages of the mailed questionnaire with those of the questionnaire filled out by the interviewer.

12. a) Evaluate "test marketing" as a method of measuring consumer acceptance for products.
   b) What is your opinion regarding its usefulness for industrial products?

13. Based on library reading, prepare general rules which should be employed in the preparation of the questionnaire. Design a questionnaire illustrating these rules to determine consumer likes and dislikes for a specific product—for example, a brand of television set.

14. What are the major sources and types of commercial marketing information, and why do firms use commercial sources?

15. What is the relationship of marketing information systems to the marketing concept (Chapter 1)?

SUPPLEMENTARY READINGS

Ferber, R. (ed.) *Marketing Research Handbook.* New York: McGraw-Hill Book Co., in press. A users' guide which provides chapter-by-chapter discussion of over 50 different marketing research and information topics.

Frank, N. D. *Market Analysis: A Handbook of Current Data Sources.* New York: The Scarecrow Press, 1964. An excellent reference for sources of secondary data.

Green, P. E. and Tull, D. S. *Research for Marketing Decisions.* 2d ed. Englewood Cliffs, N.J.: Prentice-Hall, Inc., 1970. A basic text in marketing research techniques, data analysis, and information valuation with emphasis on quantitative methods.

Kotler, P. *Marketing Decision Making: A Model Building Approach.* New York: Holt, Rinehart, & Winston, Inc., 1971. Presents a systematic review of marketing analysis and decision making. Part IV is particularly devoted to marketing information systems.

Smith, S. V.; Brien, R. H.; and Stafford, J. E. (eds.) *Readings in Marketing Information Systems.* Boston: Houghton Mifflin Co., Inc., 1968. A general readings book on marketing information which includes many of the best articles through about 1967.

Uhl, K. P. and Schoner, B. *Marketing Research: Information Systems and Decision Making.* New York: John Wiley & Sons, Inc., 1969. A basic text in marketing research and information systems which gives emphasis both to recurring and nonrecurring information problems.

18 Product policies

The marketing concept holds that the firm should adapt its activities and resources to provide products and services to meet the needs of potential customers. To do so it must first identify needs of particular segments of buyers and then plan ways to *profitably* offer the products and services required. Since market needs and competition constantly change, both manufacturers and middlemen must continually adapt their activities and products. This adjustment of products to meet the needs of a market is called *product planning*.

Product planning is the concept upon which all other marketing planning and strategy should be based. Weak product planning policies are probably the greatest cause of waste in the marketing system. Millions of dollars are lost each year as companies doggedly try to market ill-conceived products to poorly defined markets in which competitive risks are high.

It is this important part of the competitive struggle within the marketing system which is the basic subject of this chapter. The viewpoint, as in all chapters in Part VII, is from within an organization rather than from the marketing system as a whole. Following definition of some concepts vital to an understanding of product policy decisions, the incentives and responsibility for product innovation are related to the overall growth strategy of the firm. A section on product-line policies considers strategies for growth, new-product development and introduction by manufacturers, development of a marketing plan, and product management by manufacturers and by middlemen. The remainder of the chapter is devoted to a discussion of brand policy and other product policy decisions, such as packaging, labeling, warranty, and service.

PRODUCT INNOVATION: NATURE AND SIGNIFICANCE

To understand the nature and processes of the product policies of the firm, it is necessary to have a clear understanding of the concepts of product, market, product life cycles, and the marketing mix.

Product

The concept of a product used in marketing is broader than just physical matter. **The product is that bundle of utility (satisfactions) which the buyer receives as the result of a lease or purchase. It includes the physical *good or service* itself (its form, taste, odor, color, and texture), the functioning of the product in use, the package, the label, the warranty, manufacturer's and retailer's service, after-sale service, the confidence or prestige received by the brand and the manufacturer's and retailer's reputation, and any other symbolic utility received from possession or use of the good or service.**

While the physical product itself is obvious to buyers, they see more than a "black box" when they look at one. Two automobiles may be similar in price and performance characteristics but far different in color and styling. The pleasant fragrance of a box of apples may make them more appealing than another box of apples that look the same but have no aroma. A dentist is considered to be a "better" dentist if he has a pleasant manner.

Goods are purchased to be used. Some, like apples, are consumed rapidly in use; others, like automobiles, slowly. The nutrition and taste provided by the apple and the transportation provided by the automobile are part of the product.

Utility can also be supplied by packages and labels. Covers sell books; jackets sell records; an attractive office, dental chair, and hygienist will help sell a dentist's services. In packaged food products, pictures of the product and instructions for preparation on the label provide consumer utility through indicating how the product can be expected to perform in use.

Not only do we expect a product to perform in use, but we expect a warranty, expressed or implied, that it will do so. The warranty and the buyer's confidence that the seller will stand behind his product, which come from both the manufacturer and the retailer, are also a part of the product.

For durable products, the ability to obtain reliable service and replacement parts is another aspect of the product. This service extension may be offered by retailers (Sears, Roebuck and Co. and Macy-Bamberger Stores) or by manufacturers (RCA and General Electric). Sometimes the service is not offered at all, as in the case of some imported electronic equipment. After-sale service is also an important product extension in industrial goods.

The purchase of branded merchandise provides the buyer with the utility of knowing he will receive a consistent level of quality. Apple marketers, for example, grade, package, and brand their products in order to assure uniform quality and build consumer preference for a brand.

The confidence that comes from selecting a name brand or the services of a particular manufacturer or dealer is a symbolic but important part of the bundle of utility we call "the product." Another type of symbolic utility is the prestige derived from owning and using a particular brand. One of the most conspicuous examples of the status utility received from product ownership is the automobile. The label of a high-fashion, high-quality garment is enough to provide status utility for some wearers, and premium beer is promoted for home consumption with the appeal that serving it to guests will increase the prestige of the host.

A large number of possible combinations or "bundles" of properties can be put together to form alternative products. Product planning is concerned with which properties can be profitably included in the alternative product assortments offered to various groups or segments of buyers.

Market

A key to product planning is the specification of the market segment that has the need for the product being designed. Too often manufacturers tend to define the market and the competition that exists in it incorrectly, by thinking in terms of specific types of services, products, manufacturing processes, or raw materials.[1] Railroads, for example, often see their competition as other railroads, when most of it comes from trucks, airplanes, and ships. Public transportation competes mainly with private automobiles and bicycles, not with other transit facilities. Sellers of glass containers compete with those of paper, steel, plastic, and aluminum.

Thus *markets are defined by buyers, not by sellers.* Products which buyers in a market perceive to be substitutable comprise the alternatives they will consider. The "goodness" of the substitution will vary between consumers and between points in time for the same consumer. For consumers with a college education, a visit to an art museum, a concert, a play, or a college football game might provide close substitutes for a Saturday afternoon's entertainment. For other consumers, close substitutes might include a football game, watching television, or playing pool. In some situations, a bicycle is a close substitute for a ride in an automobile or on the bus; in other situations it is not. Very different products may be substitutes. One may seek relaxation by a flight to Hawaii, a backpacking trip in the mountains, or the purchase of a new sports car.

The *closeness of substitution* of various products and services is measured by the cross elasticity of demand or by measures of distance between products in the consumers' perceptual map as derived by a new marketing research methodology called "nonmetric multidimensional scaling." For example, by asking a consumer a number of questions of a specific type about the similarities perceived among a group of alternative vacation spots, these spas can be plotted on a "map" which represents the way the respondent sees them. A backpacking trip or even a new car could be added to this map if the consumer perceives these things as substitute goods.

Product life cycles

A consideration that involves both the product and the market is the concept of the product life cycle. All *product classes* experience maturation with age, just as living things. The four stages in a typical product life cycle—introduction, growth, maturity, and decline—are shown in Figure 18–1 and discussed below.

It should be noted that the cycle applies to the entire product class (e.g., automobiles), not particular makes (e.g., Pontiac). Brands are subject to hazards which make the shape of their life cycles less predictable.

While the life-cycle concept is useful for planning, it is not an operational

---

[1] This tendency is usually identified with a term coined by Theodore Levitt—"marketing myopia." Levitt, "Marketing Myopia," *Harvard Business Review,* 38 (July–August 1960), pp. 45 ff.

forecasting tool. It is not known how high sales will go nor how long a stage will last. In consumer packaged goods some successful products, like enzyme detergents, may have a life cycle as short as 18 months. Automobiles, which have been a commercial product in the United States for almost 70 years, are approximately in their maturity but could face a long, slow decline. Profits are likely to be negative at introduction and reach a maximum before sales are at highest levels.

The marketing strategy of a product will be different in each stage. Such changes are motivated from both inside and outside the system. From outside, new discoveries constantly threaten to replace existing products with new ones, and consumer tastes and life styles change. From inside, competitive pressures force these changes.

The four stages in a product life cycle are as follows:

Introduction stage. During the first stage, only one or two sellers will have the technology, capacity, and know-how to offer the product commercially. The seller's

FIGURE 18–1

The product life cycle

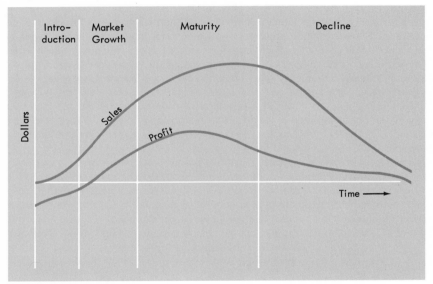

job in this stage, be he manufacturer or middleman, is to make buyers *aware* of the product, *knowledgeable* about its advantages, and *willing to try* it. The successful seller will have the competitive characteristics of a monopolist—more concerned with increasing primary demand than with battling competition.

Market growth stage. In the next period in the life of a successful product, tryers have been converted to repeat purchasers and a much larger number of potential customers is trying the product. Competitors have had the time to build the facilities and know-how to also offer the product and, seeing its success, emulate the innovator. In this stage, the innovator must be concerned with building a *selective demand* for his brand through promotion of its distinctive advantages rather than a general demand for the product class. The marketing activity required to fight off competition is the cause of the leveling of profit in this stage.

Maturity stage. It is hard to generalize behavior in this stage. The markets for some products quickly become competitive in the sense of classical economics—many sellers are offering a similar product at the same price. One source of new competition at this stage is likely to be the entry of distributors' brands. This competitive environment results in defensive promotion designed to hold market share. In addition, competition can drive prices down so that economic profit is near zero. Under such conditions, no funds are available to engage in new innovative activity.

For other products (soft margarine and prepared cereals in new shapes, for example) some spark sets off a series of product improvements. In this case the life cycle may enter a new substage called "innovative maturity."[2] Product differences and improvements reappear and an extended healthy period of competition may result.

It is during this stage that sellers in some product groups have been accused of "planned obsolescence." Annual model changes in consumer durables like automobiles are an example. Is this form of competitive rivalry bad for society? Probably not, unless improvements are held off the market so that something can be changed the following year or product quality is reduced so the product breaks down quickly. The competitive threat of being beaten to the market is probably too great for this practice to be common. A strategy of creative innovation or market expansion is a socially desirable form of competition.

Decline stage. Decline occurs when another product innovation, a new technology, or a new life style causes the entire product class to become obsolete. An example is laundry soap. While some soap is still on the market and is sold to a small, loyal band of customers, detergents have largely supplanted it. The seller's task is to try to reduce cost and keep the product profitable for as long as possible. Easily discouraged sellers will drop out and leave the remaining market to a few sellers. Eventually, the product will have no value to manufacturer or distributor.

The importance of the life cycle can be seen in Figure 18–2, which illustrates a number of life cycles for different products sold by the same firm. The firm must constantly seek new products to develop and introduce if it considers growth to be a major objective.

The marketing mix

In reaching decisions about marketing policies, there are certain factors over which the firm has some control and others over which it does not. The uncontrollable factors—government, the social environment, the existing channel structure, economic conditions, competition, demand, and technology—act as constraints on marketing decisions. The elements of marketing decisions over which the firm *does* have control are called the elements of the *marketing mix*. These are decisions relative to *product; channel* and *physical distribution; promotion,* including advertising and personal selling; and *pricing.* These four elements constitute the heart of the marketing decisions which must be made by the firm and are shown at the center of Figure 18–3, along with the other factors that constrain or influence these decisions. They also form the subject matter of the remaining chapters in Part VII.

---

[2] R. D. Buzzell and R. E. M. Nourse, *Product Innovation in Food Processing: 1954–1964* (Boston: Harvard Business School, 1967).

FIGURE 18–2
The effect of product life cycle on total sales growth

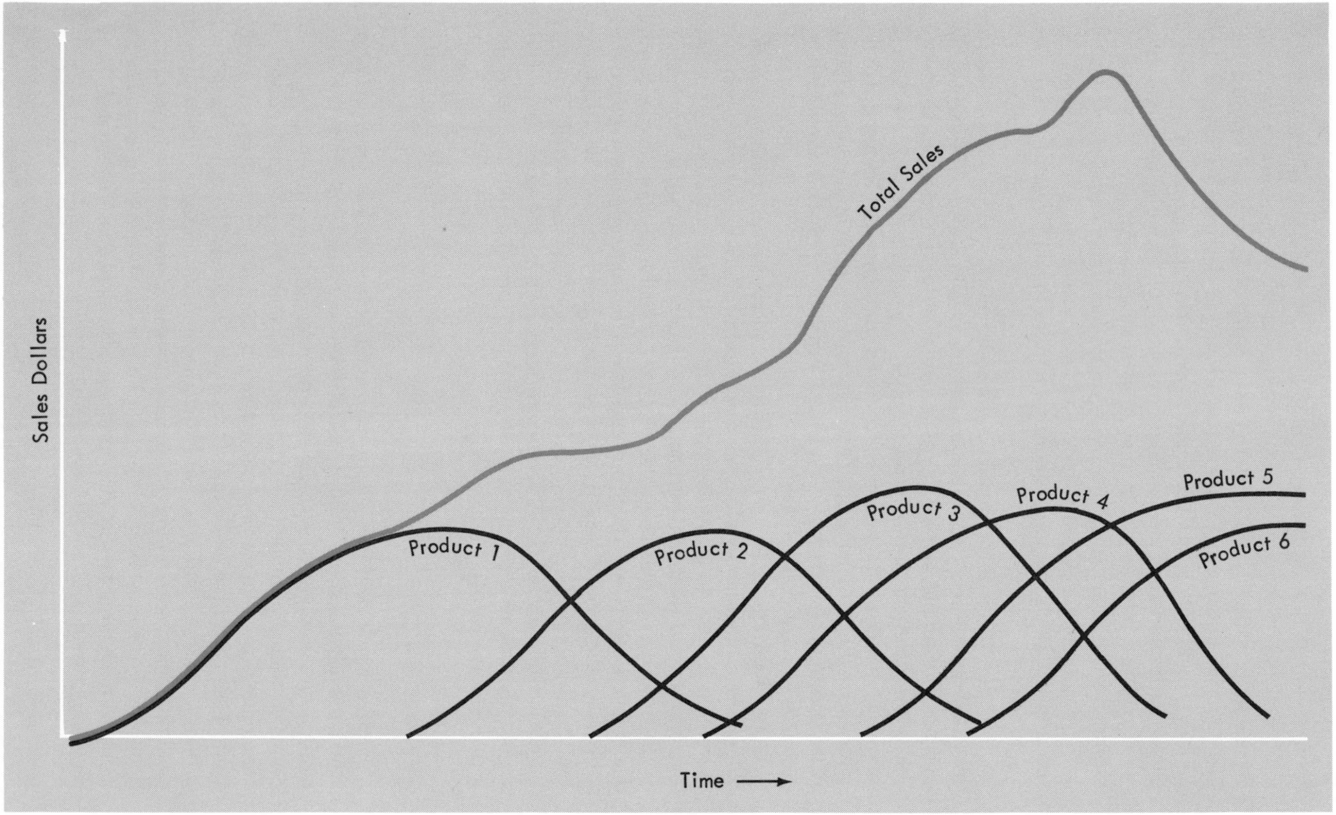

FIGURE 18–3
Factors for consideration in planning marketing strategies

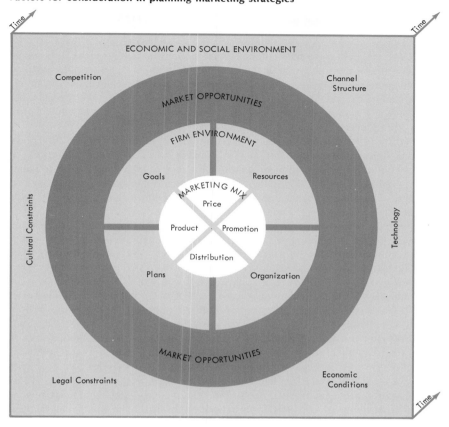

Marketing-mix decisions must be made within the constraints of the company goals, plans, resources, and organization, represented by the first ring in the figure. All marketing and company activities are directed toward identification of opportunities for profitable service of markets, the second ring. However, these marketing opportunities, like the firm's activities, are strongly influenced by the uncontrollable factors within the marketing system (competition and channel structure) and the environmental forces that operate on the system (technology, economic conditions, legal constraints, and cultural setting). Since the firm is a part of the marketing system, and that is not closed, it does have some opportunity to influence its markets, competition, distribution system, and the environment.

None of these factors is static. Because the system and its environment constantly change, marketing-mix decisions cannot be fixed. The marketing plan must be a dynamic one which anticipates marketing-mix change.

The elements of the mix come together more as a compound than as a mixture, for they are not mutually independent. When combined in the right proportions, their effect on sales is greater than the sum of their separate effects would be. They must be planned jointly. For example, the type of promotion, pricing, and dealer discounts for a trail bike must be compatible with the type of dealership planned.

Incentives and responsibility for product innovation

No seller would enjoy pure competition; in a purely competitive market he would have no control over his price or the demand he must serve. Instead he wants to achieve some degree of monopoly so he can raise his price and make economic profits, and he can do this if his product has no close substitutes. Thus the seller has an incentive to avoid homogeneous products and develop new ones or new assortments of products.

He strives for a monopolistic position by finding some *differential advantage* with which to customize an assortment for a unique *market segment,* by *positioning* a product in a unique way between existing products, or by a combination of these. Success will yield continued growth in sales, profits, and the value of the stock of the company. These new market opportunities can arise from two sources: scientific discovery and changing consumer wants.

Scientific discovery. The splitting of the atom, the harnessing of the laser beam, the development of the transistor and microintegrated circuitry, and a new chemical synthesis are all examples of inventions and discoveries which stemmed from basic scientific research in universities, government, or private research organizations. They have led to a host of commercial applications in medical care, power generation, communications, office equipment, apparel, and other products. The discoveries of basic research provide the incentive for firms to develop and introduce new or improved products.

Changing consumer wants. The incentive for product development in fashion goods such as popular music, hair styles, and apparel arises from the basic instability of consumer wants. Sellers know that failure to forecast new fashions continually will lead to a rapid and drastic decline in demand for their products. The same is true for nonfashion products, but at a somewhat slower pace. Sellers face fickle buyers. Changing life styles and consumer wants, products that reach the age of maturity, and the appearance of new technologies and discoveries provide the clever, creative marketer with never-ending opportunities for product innovations.

Responsibility for product innovation. While scientific discovery and changing consumer wants provide incentives for product development, only in special instances do scientists or buyers assume the responsibility for new product development and introduction. Most new industrial products and all new consumer products are developed by the marketing system. Firms in the marketing system have the responsibility of identifying areas of buyers' needs, developing the products and services required to fill these needs, planning methods of introducing new products and services to buyers and marketing institutions, and coordinating their introduction. These are the "premanufacturing" marketing functions introduced with the marketing concept in Chapter 1.

For products, these marketing functions usually fall to manufacturers. A physical product requires physical production (creation of form utility), which in turn requires capital equipment, technical know-how, substantial financial investment, a system for physical distribution, and a need to keep existing resources productive. Only manufacturers possess all of these properties. Thus *the chief responsibility for new product development falls to manufacturers,* and much of this chapter concerns the product planning and development activities of manufacturers.

PRODUCT-LINE POLICIES

Planning for growth

In striving for continued growth by seeking new ways to serve markets profitably, the firm attempts to establish a differential advantage in markets by: (1) increased market penetration, (2) vertical integration, (3) market expansion, (4) product development, and (5) diversification. These alternative growth strategies (see Figure 18–4) suggest the central role marketing plays.[3]

The *market penetration* strategy involves growth to increase market shares of existing products in existing markets. The *vertical integration* strategy involves growth through take-over of the functions or firms of other institutions in the channel of distribution (e.g., retailers performing wholesaling functions or purchasing their sources of supply). The *market expansion* strategy achieves growth by selling existing products to new market segments in the same market areas (e.g., selling college marketing textbooks to businessmen), in new domestic regions (e.g., expanding sales

FIGURE 18–4
Alternative strategies for growth

Product / Markets	Present	New
Present	Market penetration	Product development
	Vertical integration	
New	Market expansion	Diversification

Source: Adapted from H. Igor Ansoff, *Corporate Strategy* (New York: McGraw-Hill Book Co., 1965).

of a regional food product to other regions), or in foreign markets, either through export or foreign production.

The *product development* strategy for growth involves the development of new products (as defined in this chapter) for sale to present markets—the customers the seller knows best. A *diversification* strategy is one in which the firm grows by starting or acquiring businesses making products unlike its own and selling them in markets in which it is not known. Diversification strategies were very popular in the sixties. Such conglomerates as International Telephone and Telegraph, Textron, Inc., Gulf and Western Industries, and Loews Corporation have grown mainly through merger with firms in very different markets. Their structures are more like those of financial holding companies than of operating management.

Discussion of all of the factors that must be considered in choosing between these

---

[3] A *strategy* is the set of principles that guides the formation of a dynamic plan. Strategies for growth plans are discussed in this section, and marketing strategies, which are concerned with the principles to be used in determining how much of which marketing mix inputs are to be planned for future periods, are considered below.

five strategies is somewhat beyond the scope of this book. The chief considerations are the amount of investment required, the relative expected returns on each of the alternatives, the riskiness of each, and the impact of each on the stability of total company profits.

This chapter concentrates on the product-market alternatives of penetration, market expansion, and product development. A first step in choice among these alternatives is appraisal of the firm's strengths and weaknesses. It must be determined in which resources of the firm there is "excess capacity." If extra capacity is available in raw materials, by-products, or research and development, a product development strategy may be appropriate. If marketing or production capacity are in excess, market expansion may be the best route. Resources of a firm should be considered in broad terms. For example, a strong, young management team or a group of skilled craftsmen are a resource, just as is the productive capacity of a factory. The most flexible resource is capital, but manufacturing firms are seldom lucky enough to have an excess capacity of this one.

Hopefully, the analysis of strengths and weaknesses will constrain the breadth of alternatives the firm must consider. Within these constraints, the next task is to forecast the profitability and risk of alternative plans. Profitability should be expressed as return on invested capital over a planning period of a number of years. While this calculation is somewhat beyond the scope of this book, it is appropriate to mention a number of the factors that influence profitability and risk under each of the three growth strategies considered here.

Product development.   Product development is often undertaken in order to achieve an objective of stability in sales and profit, defined not as constant sales but as growth at a rate equal to that of the economy generally. Figure 18–2 above indicates that this is a difficult task if life cycles are short. It is hoped that ongoing developmental activity will make it possible to introduce successful new products at regular intervals and thereby to maintain a stable growth rate.

The development of additional products can often alleviate short-run instability created by seasonal demand patterns. On the other hand, since a product development strategy involves selling to the present market, the same seasonal patterns may exist for all products in that market. For example, cranberry growers have attempted to develop cranberry drinks in an effort to break the seasonal demand pattern for other cranberry products.

Market expansion.   A product development policy seeks to find products that complement or substitute for existing products and to achieve economies in marketing them to present markets. But compatibility in marketing and demand does not necessarily mean that the new product will be compatible with the firm in other respects. When it is not, market expansion strategies should also be considered.

Incompatibility occurs in at least one of six areas of the firm's activities. One of these is production. For example, Sara Lee Bakeries could find market compatibility in other dessert products, but the company's production is in frozen bakery products.

Raw-material requirements are a second cause of incompatibility. A trail bike company may find rubber rafts to be a compatible product in marketing, but the raw-material needs and technologies of metal and rubber are quite different.

Third, the quality level required for the new product may be different from that required for existing products. Producers of high-quality household furniture find they cannot use the same facilities to produce low-quality furniture at costs which are competitive with those of companies that specialize in it.

Fourth, end-use market compatibility does not guarantee channel compatibility.

A meat packer may sell soap or glue to ultimate consumers, but these products reach markets through very different channels of distribution than that for meat.

Fifth, the new product may have an after-sale service requirement which is not required for existing products. A producer of campers or camp trailers could not enter the market for self-propelled recreational vehicles without establishing a network of dealers who are capable of providing mechanical service.

Sixth, compatibility with marketing does not guarantee the marketing capacity to handle the product. A marketing organization responsible for a long line of products may simply not be able to promote and sell one additional product to their customers without neglecting some established product. This would be particularly true if the products had a seasonal pattern, such as a stationery supply house at back-to-school time. When the product line is too long to allow individual attention for the new item, the company may attempt to offer it as part of a balanced back-to-school assortment.

In all of these situations, the firm should consider increasing existing product sales by expansion into new markets instead of through product development. These sales may be: (1) through new channels (selling household appliances to builders as well as to consumers through appliance dealers), (2) to very different market segments (selling food products to institutions such as hospitals and the military rather than only to retail grocers), (3) to new areas of the country, or (4) to foreign markets. In all cases, the marketing functions may be performed by a new set of institutions, but the growth will complement activities in the other business functions.

The factors to be considered in choosing between strategies of product development or market expansion (as shown in Table 18–1) are similar but not identical. Whereas a strategy of product development attempts to achieve growth through economies in marketing, a strategy of market expansion attempts to achieve it through economies in production. Before either is undertaken, the firm should investigate whether it can grow and enjoy economies in *both* marketing and production through a strategy of market penetration.

Market penetration. A strategy of market penetration is appropriate if selling more of the same product to existing markets can be achieved at lower cost than would be incurred under either of the other strategies. A useful way to visualize this

TABLE 18–1

Compatibility factors influencing choice between product development and market expansion strategies

Product development	Market expansion
1. Profit growth	1. Profit growth
2. Company reputation	2. Company reputation
3. Company quality image	3. Company quality image
4. Marketing capability	4. Marketing capability
5. Sales force capacity	5. Sales force capacity
6. Existing channels of distribution	6. Existing channels of distribution
7. Promotion programs	7. Promotion programs
8. Production capacity	8. Production capacity
9. Seasonal stability of demand	9. Seasonal stability of demand
10. Service requirements	10. Service requirements
11. Technological capability	
12. Raw materials	

FIGURE 18–5
Marketing response function

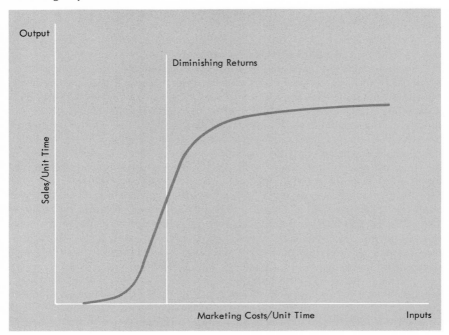

choice is through the concept of a "marketing response function " (Figure 18–5). This function is analogous to the production function studied in economics. As the quantity of marketing inputs (costs) is increased, output (sales) is expected to increase also. Sales response may initially be zero, increase first slowly and then more rapidly than costs, then increase more slowly than costs, and finally approach a zero increase in sales as costs are increased.

Market penetration is always the best strategy for growth up to some point when sales response per unit of input is no longer increasing as input is increased. The area in which this point is reached is shown in the figure as diminishing returns. Even in this area, market penetration may continue to be the best strategy for awhile. The decision between strategies will depend on which alternative use of inputs will cause the greatest increase in *profits,* not sales. Profits depend on *total* cost, not just marketing cost. Therefore, the profit-maximizing point cannot be determined with just the marketing response function. Because small increases in costs of a penetration strategy generate profit and the other strategies require much larger sums of money to do this, a penetration strategy should always be considered in deciding on new strategies for growth. In addition, the risks and uncertainty associated with penetration are usually lower than those for product development or market expansion.[4]

---

[4] For a more detailed discussion, see D. J. Luck and A. E. Prell, *Market Strategy* (New York: Appleton-Century-Crofts, 1968), Appendix A.

Product development and introduction by manufacturers

Manufacturers have had many product failures along with successes. Consideration of these failures as well as the successes has led to general procedures for new product development. Consequently, the role of the new product failure warrants attention along with new development procedures.

New-product failures. The introduction of new products has been characterized by many more failures than successes. Estimates regarding the proportion of new products that fail vary considerably, partly because of the difficulty of defining when a product fails. Booz, Allen & Hamilton, Inc. reported in 1968 that 58 new product ideas were required for each commercial success,[5] but only 2 of these actually reach commercial introduction. Their studies suggest a failure rate for commercialized products of about 33 percent. A study in 1970 by Marketing Communications Research Center, Princeton, N.J., found a 34 percent failure rate,[6] but a 1968 study of new supermarket products showed that 80 percent failed to reach their *sales goals*.[7] While failure of new products is an expected social cost of a market economy, marketing must work constantly to force the failure rate as low as possible. The loss by a large firm on a new consumer product failure will often reach $1 million.

Reasons for the high failure rate among new products center primarily around: (1) the failure of a new product to be really new or to offer a real user advantage, (2) overestimation in testing of the product's potential sales, (3) inadequate testing, and (4) lack of effective marketing at the time of introduction.[8] Competition is far down the list, while expecting advertising to "sell a fake new product" is at the top.

These reasons indicate that poor management of new-product development must be the chief cause of the problem. While it might be concluded, therefore, that large, well-managed companies do better than small ones, the evidence is not convincing. One expert estimates that 70 percent of new-product successes come from small companies, while 90 percent of development money is spent by large ones. Another estimates that the success rate of billion-dollar companies is half that of smaller firms.[9] Big companies too often plan products for small, subtle market segments which, in fact, do not exist. Others get tied up in their own bureaucracy and lose sight of creativity and hard work.

Yet the race to introduce new products goes on as firms constantly battle shorter product life cycles. Comments like "50 percent of our volume is in products which did not exist five years ago" are common, although they may be overstatements for most firms. "Creative destruction" is nevertheless an important element in the process which has made the United States economically successful, and the marketing student must understand the process of new-product development.

Steps in new-product development. The procedure a firm must go through to develop and introduce a new product can be divided into six steps, as shown in Figure 18–6. The time each takes and the mortality rate are also shown. The firm's management strategy in this procedure is to exclude as many poor product ideas as early in the process as possible. This is done because, as shown in Figure 18–7, the

---

[5] Management Research Department, *Management of New Products* (New York: Booz, Allen & Hamilton, Inc., 1968).

[6] *Conference Board Record,* June 1971.

[7] T. L. Angelus, "Why Do Most New Products Fail?" *Advertising Age,* March 24, 1969, p. 85.

[8] *Conference Board Record,* June 1971.

[9] T. L. Angelus, "New Products," *Marketing/Communications,* August 1969, p. 75.

investment the firm has in a product increases rapidly as it goes through the development process. Figure 18–6 shows a development time, averaged over a large number of firms and products, of three years after idea generation. The cost of an unsuccessful introduction can be so great that an investment of time and money in careful development is usually the course which will result in the greatest profit.

1. *Idea generation.* While some product ideas come from outside the firm, most are generated internally. In some industries, basic research is an important source. It is generally the responsibility of top management and marketing management to ensure that a mechanism for idea generation exists.

2. *Screening.* Preliminary economic analysis, the next step, considers compatibility of the new product with company objectives and resources, potential demand, costs, investments, and profitability. Because the objective of this step is to reject obviously poor ideas without investing large sums of money in them, it should be accomplished largely from secondary sources of information.

FIGURE 18–6

Mortality of new-product ideas, by stage of evaluation

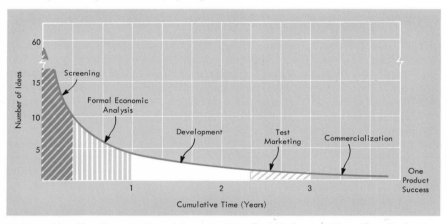

Source: Adapted from Management Research Department, Booz, Allen & Hamilton, Inc. © Booz, Allen & Hamilton, Inc., 1968.

3. *Formal economic analysis.* Product proposals that pass preliminary screening are next subjected to intensive study and evaluation. As in screening, the objectives are the qualification of demand, risk, investment, cost, and profitability. Any product passing this step will incur substantial sunk costs.

Products that pass are often assigned to small teams responsible for detailed product development, sometimes no more than project groups. Some firms organize almost complete mini firms called "venture teams" which remain responsible for the product after commercialization.

4. *Product development.* In the product development step, sizable sums of money must be sunk into the new product. The chief tasks to be accomplished in this period are: planning and scheduling of the development and testing phases,

specification of design features and constraints, engineering design and testing, prototype production, product testing, process design, procuring patents and trademarks, planning of pilot production, developing the marketing strategy and plan, legal department review, and recalculation of demand, risk, investment, and profitability.

5. *Test marketing.* "Test marketing" differs from "product testing" in that the former tests the production and marketing of the entire product in real conditions; the latter tests only the functioning of the product in artificial conditions. Test marketing is accomplished by introducing the product in two or more localized geographic markets. It usually takes at least six months in a test market, even for frequently purchased products, to determine if the product and its marketing are "right." When problem areas are discovered, this period may be extended to well over one year. The disadvantage of long test marketing is that the seller may lose his competitive advantage while at the same time he is incurring the costs of testing, but few consumer products are introduced into national distribution today without some form of test marketing.

FIGURE 18–7
Cumulative expenditures and time, all-industry average

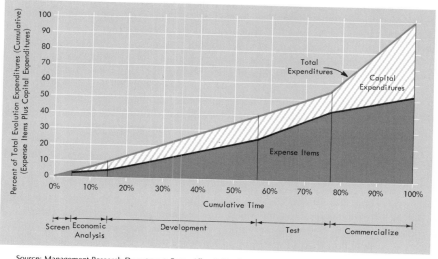

Source: Management Research Department, Booz, Allen & Hamilton, Inc., 1968. © Booz, Allen & Hamilton, Inc., 1968.

6. *Commercialization.* If test market results prove satisfactory, the full-scale introduction of the product can begin, either by "rolling-out" across the country from the test market areas or by simultaneous introduction in all markets. Careful studies must be conducted in order to monitor the sales success of a new product in both test marketing and commercialization. Information on the extent of distribution, promotion, trial, repeat purchase, and market share must get back to the company rapidly so that the introduction is kept on plan. Both commercial and company resources should be used in this monitoring effort (see Chapter 17). After introduction, the product development process is complete.

Developing a marketing plan

One step in the product development process is developing a marketing strategy and plan. The first marketing strategy decision which must be made for any new product concerns what the target market segment should be. Probably no product today should be designed for sale to "the total national consumer market." There are certainly limits to how far a firm should carry segmentation, however. A market segment must be (1) important, in terms of potential sales and profit, (2) a definable, homogeneous group, and (3) capable of being reached by the product and its promotion. It is likely that many new products will be easier to introduce and more profitable if they are designed to serve a broad market segment rather than one that is narrow and hard to reach.

After the target market segment is defined, the new product must be *positioned* between the other competing brands that serve the segment. Thus the product must have unique features of importance to buyers in the market segment. A new public accounting partnership may decide that its target market segment is the small businessman, but a package of services that will give it some differential advantage over other firms must be designed. Special expertise may be offered in cost accounting, inventory control, electronic data processing, or tax work, in addition to normal auditing duties. Positioning is important not only because it is the new product's differential advantage but also because it sets the initial specifications for all the elements of the marketing mix: promotional appeals, types and number of channels of distribution, and price.

After the initial marketing mix is decided, plans for introduction of the new product must be detailed. The introduction strategy is constrained by a firm's resources and by the structure of the marketing system for similar existing products. Product sampling, that is, sending large numbers of potential customers a sample of the new product, is an effective way of achieving new product trial for some products, but it is also very expensive. For consumer products, sending "cents-off" coupons is a less expensive alternative but currently is in danger of overuse. Neither of these techniques will be successful unless the seller has also persuaded retailers to stock the product before introductory promotion begins.

In general, the manufacturer's strategy is to make the introductory stage as short as possible and the growth stage as long as possible. By the maturity stage of the product life cycle, various competitive forces are at work reducing market share and profitability. The marketing mix at maturity must be geared more to holding share and fighting competition than to gaining trial by new customers.

Three general principles about the development of a marketing plan for a new product should be noted. First, because the marketing mix must change over the life cycle, these changes must be anticipated and built into the plan. Second, each element of the marketing mix is not a single variable but an entire set of variables and alternatives. Branding, packaging, quality level, labeling, warranty, and service decisions are all facets of the product decision, and many alternatives are available for each of them, as well as for the other factors in the marketing mix. Third, the product and its marketing mix require constant close management after a successful introduction.

Product management by manufacturers

In some consumers' goods companies and to a lesser degree in some industrial goods firms, products needing close marketing attention are assigned to a *product manager*. Product managers typically report to a marketing manager who is responsible for an entire line. In packaged goods, these men are often known as "brand managers."

The responsibility of product managers varies widely between firms—from responsibility for the entire marketing program (and profit) of the product to little more than liaison men with advertising agencies. Product managers seldom have line responsibility for field salesmen.

Because product management is often used as a training position for senior marketing positions, product managers are usually in their thirties and have been with their firms for only about five years.[10] Superiors are often reluctant to grant men in this stage of career development full authority for the great responsibility which goes with this position. Nonetheless, product management organization indicates the firm's recognition of the importance of product management and a marketing orientation.

Line simplification. A necessary job in product management is overseeing the decline and fall of products. It is important not to become so emotionally involved with products that efforts to save them drain resources from high-potential new ones. Carrying a large number of marginally profitable products can also so diffuse selling effort that profitable products do not receive the attention they deserve.

Existing products and lines should be subject to review at frequent intervals. In addition to sales of each product itself, the contribution which sales of a product can make to *total profit* must be considered. The total assortment of products and varieties in which each product is available can be very important to the sales of the entire product line. For example, a baby food manufacturer may have to sell fruits, vegetables, and meats in order to hold distribution, even though many of the fruit and vegetable items are not profitable.

Much can be gained from product-line review. To illustrate, a manufacturer of electrical "white goods" reduced his refrigerator models from 17 to 9, air conditioners from 23 to 11, and ranges from 8 to 6, thereby simplifying manufacturing and selling problems, as well as the inventory and sales problems of his retailers. By effective promotion of the remaining models, he substantially increased total sales.

Product management by middlemen

Middlemen have marketing-mix and product-line decisions to make just as do manufacturers. The existence of promotion and pricing decisions is perhaps more obvious than the existence of channel and product decisions. The product planning problems of middlemen differ from those of manufacturers because they are located differently in the marketing system. Whereas manufacturers are interested in *what to make,* the middleman's concern is *what to carry* in stock to meet the anticipated requirements of customers. Product management in retail and wholesale institutions is called "merchandising," and brand managers are called "merchandise managers," or in some cases, "buyers."

This difference between manufacturers and middlemen exists because manufacturers physically transform the goods they buy, and the customer is generally more concerned with the transformation than with the raw materials employed. Middlemen purchase for resale without physical transformation, and the customer is more concerned with the selling of the merchandise.

Both retailers and wholesalers commonly handle a wide diversity of lines repre-

---

[10] R. M. Fulmer, "Product Management: An Overview of a Youthful Art," *Sales/Marketing Today,* 14 (February 1968), pp. 8–11.

senting the products of many manufacturers. Whereas the middleman, like the manufacturer, should define his market and cater to it, some retail organizations handle merchandise appealing to a number of income groups. Thus a department store will operate both the "upstairs" and "downstairs" (basement) departments, and a shoe chain will open "low-price" stores under one name and "exclusive shops" under another. Branch stores often serve different socioeconomic markets.

Middlemen face a difficult task in fixing the limits on the kinds, sizes, qualities, and quantities of the goods they will handle. The growth in the number of food products and the resulting problems of shelf-space shortage in the supermarket is illustrative. Representatives of manufacturers are almost constantly bringing new items to the attention of middlemen and describing the forms of sales assistance that will be provided. In addition, visits to market centers reveal numerous varieties of available goods of all sorts. For many retailers, therefore, deciding what and how much to buy constitutes a continuing problem.

The management of inventories, including the fixing of appropriate limits and the establishment of controls to maintain them, is another product policy decision that must be made by middlemen. Many retailers make use of basic stock lists and model stocks, both of which are partly based on past sales, to aid their judgment regarding the kinds and qualities of goods to purchase. The former are commonly used for staple items, and the latter for fashion merchandise.[11] Some wholesalers also establish lists of items which serve them in the same way as the basic stock list helps retailers.

1. *The basic stock list.* A basic stock list usually consists of *(a)* a list of the items to be carried in stock, classified as to size and other important factors, such as color and material; *(b)* the minimum quantities to be reached before reordering; and *(c)* the quantity to purchase when reordering takes place.

2. *The model stock plan.* For fashion merchandise, it is not possible to draw up a definite basic stock list. The specific items that sold well during last year's winter season, for example, may not sell well this year. Past sales, however, can still aid the buyer, since they can help him to construct a model stock—a stock which in total dollar value and in its breakdown by sizes, types, prices, and other factors seems most likely to meet the customers' wants.

Among retailers, particularly the larger ones, rather elaborate methods and devices based on dollar values and physical units are employed to obtain the desired control. A balanced assortment of merchandise—that is, one that considers anticipated sales on the one hand and merchandise to meet these expectations on the other—is the goal. Electronic data processing equipment has made great advances in improving the inventory management position of middlemen, but even more improvement can be expected.

Differences exist in the product management of wholesalers and retailers, but the same governing influence—the demands of their customers—is the basic determinant. In judging whether to stock a particular item or a line of products, the fundamental consideration is: Will it sell in sufficient volume to justify the investment required and yield a satisfactory profit?

Wholesalers. Since wholesalers must solve problems peculiar to the market they serve and to their type of operation, wide variations exist in their merchandising procedures. Many of them rely on frequent careful analyses of such factors as past sales to retailers and industrial users, orders that have been received for goods not

---

[11] A rather detailed explanation of these topics can be found in D. J. Duncan, C. F. Phillips, and S. C. Hollander, *Modern Retailing Management: Basic Concepts and Practices* (Homewood, Ill.: Richard D. Irwin, Inc., 1972), chap. 10.

in stock, and complaints received as guides to product planning. They also maintain close contact with manufacturers to learn about new products and acquaint their customers with these developments.

Among wholesalers, product management is shared by buyers of related lines of merchandise, who are aided by the judgment of the general manager or president. A committee may decide on general merchandise policy, or the treasurer or controller may advise on the size of inventories.

Retailers. The product management policies of retailers involve two main problems: (1) what and how much to buy of the goods available and (2) preparing designs and specifications of merchandise to be "made to order."

The product function in retailing assumes greater importance as the size of the business increases and the responsibility for its performance becomes more significant. In small stores the proprietor remains in close touch with all phases of the business and performs the merchandising job along with other tasks. As stores grow in size, he must delegate this task to others. Thus, in department stores, which had been characterized by the grouping of similar commodities into departments but have recently undergone changes due to classification merchandising, responsibility is *shared* by the department manager or buyer; by the group or divisional merchandise manager, who exercises supervision over a number of related departments and assists the buyers; and by the general merchandise manager, to whom both buyers and group merchandise managers are accountable. In chain stores, in contrast, responsibility for merchandising is *centered* in head buyers—sometimes called "merchandise managers"—who purchase related groups of merchandise such as men's work clothing or women's inexpensive dresses.

BRAND POLICY

The importance of brands in both consumers' and industrial products continues to grow. Manufacturers and middlemen alike seek means of retaining and building customer patronage through better product and company images.

Meaning and types of brands

A brand is a word, mark, symbol, device, or a combination thereof used to identify some product or service. The term "trademark" is the legal counterpart of brand; the two are synonymous. When capable of being spoken, these marks constitute brand names. Examples in the automobile field are Oldsmobile, Ford, Pinto, and Fury. The brand may appear on the product itself, as when it is stamped directly on grapefruit, walnuts, and crackers, or placed on a name tag attached to products such as bed sheets, men's shirts, and women's dresses. Brand marks may also be placed on the container, as with toothpaste, or on a label, as with canned goods.

Brands may be classified in four ways: (1) ownership, (2) extent of geographic coverage, (3) use by the owner, or (4) number of products covered. Brands owned by manufacturers are *manufacturers' brands;* those owned by middlemen are *distributors' brands*. Brands sold nationally or internationally are called *national brands;* those sold in only certain areas are *regional brands*. High-quality brands that receive strong advertising support are called *primary brands;* those used for special purposes or to sell low-quality merchandise are called *secondary brands*.

The term *individual brand* is used for names reserved for one product only—for example, Tide. *Family brands* refer to names for groups of products—for example, Ivory is used for Soap, Flakes, Snow, and Liquid. A chain (Pathmark or the Kroger Company) places a wide range of products, including coffee, spices, tea, bread, milk, and canned fruits and vegetables, under the chain's brand name (Kroger or Pathmark). This practice is as efficient for the consumer as it is for the seller,. The store's brand indicates a consistent quality level, and there is little concern that bleach and bread carry the same name.

While a family brand involves several items under a single brand, all products of a middleman or a manufacturer seldom carry the same brand. It is common practice to use a number of family brands, one for each grade of merchandise. Automobile branding is an example. Some firms include only related merchandise under particular blanket brands. For example, Colgate-Palmolive Co. uses the Palmolive brand on more than five cleaning products but does not use it on eatable products. The obvious advantage of the family brand is that the advertising and goodwill developed for one item may carry over to others, with lower promotional cost per product as a result. If one product is unique from the group, however, the expenditure required to point up the distinction may be great enough that individual branding is preferred. Distributors find that family branding with the company name is particularly useful, since it is their reputation that stands behind the product. Quality distinctions can be made by use of color-coded labels and supplementary descriptive words such as "economy grade." Family branding is often useful in introducing and gaining distribution for products which are followers to the marketplace. Thus, Lux Liquid was selected for a dishwashing liquid that followed the introduction of similar products by competitors.

The terms "national brands" and "private brands" are commonly used to connote manufacturers' brands and distributors' brands, respectively. These terms are unsatisfactory, however, because a manufacturers' brand need not be national, while many private brands (e.g., A & P and Safeway) are.

All registered brands are private property, and their rights as such have been protected by common law since medieval times, when trade guilds used signs to communicate craftsmen's skills. These rights for registered brands are currently codified in the United States by Public Law 489, the Lanham Act of 1946.

Advantages and disadvantages of branding for buyers

The protection of the property rights of trademarks is believed to be an appropriate responsibility of government because branding provides not only aid to sellers but social benefits through advantages for buyers. A brand can be an efficient communication device. If consumers understand its meaning and sellers are honest in its use, it is a shorthand message containing a great amount of information. The brand provides: (1) an assurance of uniform quality level, either high or low; (2) the identification of the warrantor in case the product is unsatisfactory; (3) an implicit summary statement of product specifications; (4) the psychological utility of confidence that the product will perform in the manner expected; and (5) social prestige. An example of the last point is Le Sueur Early Peas, which are packaged in cans with a distinctive silver label, no picture, and only the minimum information required by law. Yet many consumers know that the Le Sueur brand implies the highest quality canned peas from the Green Giant Company, and may derive status from buying the brand.

Extensive use of branding has also led to some consumer disadvantages. First, for standardized commodities, the presence of brands may preclude the use of standards and grades which would communicate more information than the brand name. "Choice U.S. Grade Beef" communicates more to most consumers than "Swift's Premium Beef."

Second, heavy promotion of a brand may lead to consumer confusion rather than information. Bayer aspirin promotion, for example, has permitted the sale of a standardized product at a premium price for many years, although it is difficult to find any consumer advantage which could justify it. Thus consumers pay a premium to buy branded merchandise, assuming the brand implies higher quality, when, in fact, no difference in quality exists.

Third, very successful brand promotion may lead to such consumer loyalty that it is very difficult for new brands to enter the market. For example, a few cola companies have enjoyed lower levels of distributor and regional brand competitive incursion than other products with similar life-cycle and technical characteristics. A key reason for this success in holding market share has been the impact which massive cola promotion has had on consumer brand choice even though, in blind-taste tests, consumers generally cannot differentiate among brands.

Benefits of branding for sellers

Manufacturers and middlemen brand their products because it is believed to increase sales, provide assistance in the conduct of sales programs, and improve profits. These convictions are based on a number of benefits which flow from successful branding and can be summed under the heading of control over the marketing of the product. Brand names can provide the following specific benefits:

1. *Simplify sales promotion.* Effective sales promotion depends heavily on branding or identifying the product. Although some advertising is general in character, as in promoting the sale of a type of product or service, most of it seeks to sell a specific brand.

2. *Encourage repeat sales.* Branding may encourage sales even for the manufacturer or middleman who does not wish to advertise, since the brand name makes it easier for the consumer to repurchase a specific product which has proved satisfactory. This is an advantage to both the consumer and the manufacturer.

3. *Provide protection against substitution.* By preventing the substitution of the products of one manufacturer for those of another, brands afford protection against loss of sales. Most customers who wish to repurchase unbranded sheeting, for instance, are entirely at the mercy of the retail salesperson. Is the sheeting of the same quality as that purchased previously, which gave satisfactory service? In such situations the customer must accept the salesperson's word and knowledge (or lack of knowledge), and substitution is relatively easy. When the sheeting is branded to specify a particular quality or manufacturer, substitution is more difficult.

4. *Minimize price comparisons.* Retailers' brands make price comparison between items sold in competing stores very difficult, since the customer is never sure that exactly the same quality of merchandise is being compared. Consequently, retailers with private brands are under less pressure to meet the price cuts on other brands sold by competing stores. This factor is especially important to high-cost firms. It explains why some independent retailers prefer to "push" the private brands of wholesalers instead of well-known manufacturers' brands. It also suggests why some retailers have turned to private brands as a defense against the discount house.

5. *Aid in segmentation.* Brands aid in customizing products for sale to different

market segments. For example, Green Giant sells canned peas to four different market segments—gourmet, manufacturer brand, distributor brand, and institutional—under different brand names for each.

6. *Aid selective distribution.* Manufacturers who can develop buyer preferences for their brands (that is, build a consumer franchise) can use this asset to organize a corps of aggressive distributors to carry the brand on a selective basis. For example, Benjamin Moore or Pittsburgh paints are often desired by retailers because of the reputation of these brands and the promotional help given by their manufacturers. Some manufacturers develop more than one brand name so that more retailers can have "exclusive" dealerships.

7. *Facilitate the introduction of new items.* Use of a well-known brand is of much value in the introduction of new products. By placing the new products under the familiar brand, some of the customer goodwill for the old products may be transferred to them.

8. *Aid in maintaining resale prices.* The relative advantages and disadvantages in the manufacturer of resale price maintenance are analyzed in Chapter 23. We will note here only that some manufacturers establish resale prices for their products and the establishment of such prices is legal only for commodities identified by the trademark. Consequently, manufacturers who wish to practice resale price maintenance must brand their merchandise.

9. *Afford greater price stability.* It is generally accepted that widely advertised brands of products achieve a greater degree of price stability than do unbranded ones. During periods of falling prices, branded goods show less tendency to decline, with the result that the inventory losses of manufacturers and middlemen are lower. It is the desire for increased price stability that has encouraged some manufacturers to develop their own brands.

10. *Branded merchandise preferred by many middlemen.* Although numerous large middlemen frequently prefer to develop their own private brands, most of the smaller ones, and even some of the larger ones, prefer to handle well-known manufacturers' brands. Customer acceptance is high for such brands, so less selling effort is required. Although unit profit may sometimes be less than for unbranded goods, more rapid turnover and a larger sales volume may result in greater total profits. Thus self-service retailers often favor highly advertised manufacturers' brands.

11. *Afford greater profits at lower prices.* Distributor brands offer some middlemen the opportunity to put quality products on the market to be sold for less than competing manufacturers' brands and still provide a wider gross margin. Distributors can buy merchandise for their label at prices below those for branded goods of similar quality. Although the distributor may incur greater selling expenses than if he handled manufacturers' brands, he is usually able to sell at lower prices and still leave himself a greater net profit.[12]

Branding by middlemen

Although manufacturers were the first to use brands, middlemen have discovered that private brands provide a means of gaining the countervailing power to hold customers and become marketing channel leaders (see Chapter 3). Thus the "battle

---

[12] See the report of the National Commission on Food Marketing, *Food from Farmer to Consumer* (Washington, D.C.: Government Printing Office, 1966), p. 75.

of the brands" between manufacturers and distributors has played a decisive role in the "war" for channel control.

Among middlemen using their own brands are wholesalers; such retailers as chain stores, department stores, mail-order houses, and voluntary and cooperative chains; farmers' marketing cooperatives; and consumers' cooperatives. Distributor labels account for 60 percent of department store sales, 90 percent of Sears, Roebuck's volume, and 10 to 20 percent of supermarket volume,[13] and this business is on the rise.

Middlemen, like manufacturers, have brand problems. If the private brand is heavily promoted, for example, considerable money and executive effort are involved. Moreover, the middleman must assume responsibility for quality and must give attention to such matters as product specifications, packaging, and labeling.

For many distributors the reaction of the "branding" manufacturer constitutes a real problem. For instance, one factor encouraging manufacturers to circumvent the wholesaler has been the latter's development of his own brands. This problem, however, is less serious for the retailer having brands of his own, since few manufacturers have been able to develop programs to eliminate him from their trade channels. Another difficulty in connection with distributor brands is the sales volume of the middleman. Unless sales are sufficient to enable him to buy in large quantities and to promote his brands effectively, he will be at a competitive disadvantage.

Sources of supply for distributor brands. Although some large food chains, drug chains, and mail-order companies make a substantial portion of the items they sell in their own bakeries, dairies, canneries, coffee roasters, etc., the distribution-oriented channel leader usually lacks the technical know-how to make a majority of the items he sells. For other products, the economies of large-scale production dictate that a "buy" decision is preferable to a "make" decision. Thus most purchases by retailers for their own brands are made from manufacturers who produce such goods in addition to merchandise sold under their own brands. For example, Del Monte and Libby pack Kroger's private brands of canned fruits and vegetables; General Electric produces J. C. Penney's kitchen and laundry appliances; and the Goodyear Tire & Rubber Company manufactures Penney's private label automotive tires. Other manufacturers produce private brands exclusively, usually for more than one customer. This situation is a source of conflict for both manufacturer and distributor.

From the manufacturer's point of view, there is danger that: (1) the dual branding will become known to the public and hurt the image of the manufacturer's brand; (2) the manufacturer will create a new source of low-price competition for his own brand and his own distributors; or (3) the middleman will decide to make the product himself, go to another source of supply, or bargain for a lower price by threatening to take the business elsewhere.

From the distributor's point of view, the problems are all connected with identifying a source of supply that will be reliable in terms of providing a constant and ready supply that is consistent in quality. Although some distributors may seek special buys of merchandise of marginal quality, the modern distribution-oriented channel leader has too much invested in his own reputation to sell substandard merchandise under his own brand. For this reason, distributors usually buy private-brand merchandise to specifications written in their own laboratories and maintain elaborate quality control programs to ensure that suppliers are meeting them. The nature of these specifications varies with the product. In agricultural products, they are often estab-

---

[13] "The Public's Crush on Private Labels," *Time,* October 4, 1971, p. 79.

lished grades. Drugs and paint must meet chemical specifications. Soft goods and appliances are specified as to material, design, tolerances, and often performance characteristics. Such organizations as Consumers' Union, the National Bureau of Standards, and the American Society for Testing Materials have encouraged the development of performance standards for consumer products.

OTHER PRODUCT POLICY DECISIONS

Packaging and labeling

Packaging, labeling, and branding are closely related. Before self-service was the rule and many products were shipped to retailers in bulk, packaging was not a significant element of consumer goods marketing, but today prepackaged products are the rule. The consumer often cannot see the product and must base her decision only on the package. Thus a completed sale depends on the package doing a selling job. The package must protect the product and make it harder to pilfer, easier for the consumer to see on a crowded store shelf and more convenient for middleman and consumer handling. In addition it must carry a label with brand and product identification; promote the product through appealing design, graphics, and copy; and help alleviate solid waste pollution.

Faced with rapidly changing technology in packaging materials and machinery and a high level of consumer complaints, many firms, such as General Foods Corporation and National Biscuit Company, have established corporate packaging staffs to maintain control over this area of product policy. The cost of packaging alone justifies this attention. About four cents out of every dollar of retail sales goes for packaging. The total amount, $15 to $16 billion, is nearly as great as the amount spent on advertising. About 45 percent of all packaging materials are for grocery products.[14]

Many products, such as men's and women's cosmetics and aerosol products, sell so much package that it is difficult to ascertain if the product or the package is of greater value. It also is sometimes not clear which of the two contains the greater consumer appeal. Coordinated graphics in packaging across a product line in both industrial and consumer packaged goods are considered to be an important element in selling a complete line. Graphics must make the product visibly outstanding and appealing.

Labeling is not a significant part of the product's total cost, but it requires careful planning and policy formulation. While eye-catching graphics are important—particularly if the label covers a large portion of the package—*the label's primary purpose should be to inform buyers by fairly representing the contents of the package.* Both the vignette (illustration) and the copy should accurately describe the contents of the package and guide the consumer in its use.

Social concerns in packaging and labeling. Perhaps the most important consumer concern during the resurgence of the consumer movement in the last half of the 1960s was packaging and labeling. This concern centers around packaging pollution, plus deception, confusion, and inadequate information on product quantity, quality, and contents, and possible health and safety hazards. Most of these problems were discussed in Chapter 6.

---

[14] These statistics, for 1966, are from "Packaging Wraps up the Future," *Fortune,* 75 (February 1967), p. 123; and D. W. Twedt, "How Much Value Can Be Added through Packaging?" *Journal of Marketing,* 32 (January 1968), pp. 58–59.

It is estimated that each American family discards roughly a ton of empty packages each year, all of which must be either destructible or recyclable. The beer and soft drink industries had just about completed a shift to nonreturnable bottles in 1969 when the public began demanding that glass and aluminum containers be returned rather than discarded.

The responsibility to respond to consumer demand and to eliminate deception and confusion in packaging and labeling falls to the packager. If he does not rise to this challenge, the government will step in to impose regulations on package sizes and descriptions of product quantity and quality. (See Chapters 6, 14, and 25.)

Warranty

A warranty is the assumption of responsibility by the manufacturer and his distributors for the clear title, quality, character, and suitability for intended use of products sold. A warranty may be *expressed* (by an affirmative statement by the seller) or *implied* (recognized by law to exist even if no statement is made by the seller or on the product).

In the past, many expressed warranties were valueless promotional statements or attempts to limit implied warranties, but such is not the case today. Congress, the courts, and the federal regulatory agencies have made it difficult for a seller to deny his implied warranty. Warranties now "run with the product"; that is, manufacturers are held liable for product failures even though they did not enter into a purchase contract with the buyer and their negligence has not been proved. *Caveat emptor* has been replaced by *caveat venditor* as the law of the marketplace. Thus a seller must ensure that his products will meet the provisions of implied warranties. The cost in money and goodwill of an adverse court or Federal Trade Commission decision can be tremendous.

The warranty sometimes becomes a part of the firm's promotional strategy. Mail-order sellers must offer "full satisfaction or your money back" in order to gain sales. For products with low unit value, the cost to the customer of returning the product can easily exceed its value. Returns are low, although prestige retail stores accept them without question. However, as automobile companies have learned, the cost of service warranties for repairs of durables covering periods beyond expected normal life can make them a costly promotional expenditure. Competition on warranties started with the 1963 models. By 1969, the outlays to dealers for warranty work at Ford had risen to over $200 per car.[15] The aggregate amount was almost equal to the cost of retooling for the new model year. Since 1968, auto makers have been reducing the generosity of their warranty provisions.

Postsale service

The problems of automobile, appliance, and television manufacturers in providing adequate postsale service have been discussed above. As durable products have become technically more complex, consumers and retailers have been unable to service them locally. Increasing consumer dissatisfaction has led to state and local licensing and regulation of service companies in many fields. To solve this problem, many manufacturers and chain retailers have taken over the service function. They can reap promotional benefits from an efficient service organization and even from an occasional recall to correct a production or engineering mistake.

---

[15] "Detroit Tries a U-Turn on Warranties," *Business Week,* July 25, 1970, pp. 44–48.

SUMMARY

This chapter is one of seven in this part of the book which views the marketing system from inside the firm. In considering product policies of individual firms within the system, important elements of the marketing system have been developed.

The term "product" encompasses the good or service proper, the use received from it, distributor services like credit and delivery, the package and label, warranty, postsale service, and the prestige received through possession of the good or service. The competitive market system provides the incentive to search for new products which can serve society. By developing new products to market, sellers hope to grow and to earn monopoly profits. If they do not succeed, society will pass them by.

Firms can grow through market penetration, vertical integration, market expansion, product development, and diversification. The best strategy for growth can be determined by an analysis of the firm's strengths and weaknesses—where it has excess capacity and where it is vulnerable. An analysis of the marketing response function for present products will help in deciding if market penetration is the best strategy. If excess capacity exists in marketing and untapped market segments can be identified, market expansion may be more desirable. Consideration of the stage in the life cycle of existing products will also help determine the need for new-product development.

Because of the high probability and high cost of new-product failure, care is taken in product development and introduction. A part of the development process is to plan the marketing mix, or the combination of product, channel, promotion, and pricing decisions necessary to market the product. Among the product elements to be planned are brand, package, label, warranty, and postsale service.

The ownership of brands between manufacturers and distributors and their coverage between an individual product and a family of products can be distinguished. Branding is necessary for a seller to promote the product, and it is useful to the consumer as an efficient communication device. Intense competition, however, has led sellers in some markets to engage in practices in branding, packaging, labeling, warranty, and service that are not in the best interests of society. When this has occurred, government has taken action to protect buyers.

REVIEW AND DISCUSSION QUESTIONS

1. Given the many opportunities for market penetration, market expansion, and product development, should a firm choose a diversification strategy only as a last resort?

2. If new-product failure rates are high, why don't firms devote more time to development and testing?

3. In about 500 words, define carefully what planned obsolescence is and what it is not.

4. If a company were going to pursue a strategy of product development, would it look only for products which complement its present line rather than for substitutes for the existing line? Explain your answer.

5. Plot the sales of a typical consumer product over its life cycle. Using the same horizontal axis, plot the path of price, expenditures on dealer aids per dollar of sales, and advertising expenditures per dollar of sales that you would expect to find. Explain why you believe this to be a sound marketing strategy.

6. Distinguish precisely between a marketing response function and a production function.

7. Based on articles in current periodicals, prepare a paper of about 1,000 words on the topic "The Product Manager as Executor of the Marketing Concept: Successes and Failures."

8. Compare and contrast the duties of a product manager in a consumer packaged-goods firm and a merchandising manager in a major department store in your area.

9. Define the marketing mix in your own words. Describe, in outline form, the marketing mix used for Schwinn bicycles.

10. Some cigarette producers family brand their menthol cigarettes, while others use individual brands. Using specific firms as examples, try to explain this difference.

11. List the advantages and disadvantages of brand names which:
    a) Imply a characteristic of the product—Golden Grain Noodles.
    b) Are a proper name with little meaning—Hellman's Mayonnaise.
    c) Are a descriptive name—Best Foods.
    d) Are initials—CPC International.

12. Is there an inconsistency in the statement, "The primary objective of package design should be to sell; the primary objective of label design should be to inform"?

13. Demonstrate with drawings and calculations of volumes how package shape, proportions, and slack fill could be used to increase shelf facing area.

14. Argue the case for and against the proposition that "In product development and acceptance, the package is more important than the product."

15. Prepare a paper of about 1,000 words on the topic "Truth in Packaging and Labeling: Its Aims and Its Problems."

SUPPLEMENTARY READINGS

Alexander, R. S.; Cross. J. S.; and Hill, R. M.   *Industrial Marketing,* 3d ed. Homewood Ill.: Richard D. Irwin, Inc., 1967, chap. 6, "Product Planning and Development." Both text and cases treat product planning for industrial goods.

Ansoff, H. I.   *Corporate Strategy.* New York: McGraw-Hill Book Co., Inc., 1965. An excellent and readable volume on planning for growth.

Applebaum, W. and Goldberg, R. A.   *Brand Strategy in United States Food Marketing.* Boston: Harvard University, Graduate School of Business Administration, 1967. Both a historical perspective and an analysis of the profitability of private and national brands are included in this valuable volume.

Berg, T. L.   *Mismarketing: Case Histories of Marketing Misfires.* New York: Doubleday and Co., Inc., 1970. Contains case histories of marketing failures, in the introduction of five new products.

Berg, T. L. and Shuchman, A.   *Product Strategy and Management.* New York: Holt, Rinehart & Winston, Inc., 1963. A complete volume on the topics covered in this chapter.

Booz, Allen & Hamilton, Inc.   *New Product Management.* New York, 1968. An excellent guide to new-product evaluation programs, company acquisitions, and managing the new-product function.

Duncan, D. J., Phillips, C. F.; and Hollander, S. C.   *Modern Retailing Management: Basic Concepts and Practices.* Homewood, Ill.: Richard D. Irwin, Inc., 1972. Chapters 10–17 discuss the buying and merchandising functions from the retailer's point of view.

Eastlack, J. O. (ed.)   *New Product Development.* Chicago: American Marketing Association, 1967. Number 13 in the Marketing for Executive Series, "this monograph studies the development and introduction of new consumer goods in the last 20 years."

Lorsch, J. W. and Lawrence, P. R.   "Organizing for Product Innovation," *Harvard Business Review,* 43 (January–February 1967), pp. 109–22. The importance of organization in product development is emphasized in this article.

Mackenzie, G. F. "On Marketing's Missing Link—The Product Life Cycle Concept," *Industrial Marketing,* 56 (April, May, June, 1971). This three-part article shows that the life-cycle concept is more than an abstract idea and can be used as an operational planning tool.

Pessemier, E. A. *New Product Decisions: An Analytical Approach.* New York: McGraw-Hill Book Co., Inc., 1966. How analytical tools may be used to evaluate proposed new products is the subject of this volume.

Phelps, D. M. and Westing, J. H. *Marketing Management.* 3d ed. Homewood, Ill.: Richard D. Irwin, Inc., 1968. Concerned mainly with the manufacturer's marketing problems, such as product development, testing of the product, branding, packaging, and labeling.

Wingate, J. W. and Friedlander, J. S. *The Management of Retail Buying.* Englewood Cliffs, N.J. Prentice-Hall, Inc., 1963. A standard college text on buying from the retailer's point of view, this volume continues to be the best available on this subject.

19 Channels of distribution: Selection and evaluation

One of the most important decisions a seller must make is to determine the channels of distribution he will use in marketing his products. Decisions in this area are particularly important because, unless the seller is willing to undertake vertical integration, he must use external organizations to establish a channel structure. These organizations become an integral part of his marketing program for the product, and poor choices will cause it to falter, if not fail.

This chapter will view channel decisions principally from the standpoint of a manufacturing-oriented channel leader. Management policies toward distribution are reflected in decisions on three basic matters: (1) the *type* of middleman to use; (2) the number of each type of outlet to use; and (3) how to plan, lead, and control the activities of these middlemen. The dynamic nature of our economy requires that channel policies be reviewed almost continuously.

Another set of policy decisions relating to physical distribution: how to ship, where and how much to store are the subject of Chapter 20.

SELECTING THE TYPE OF CHANNEL MEMBERS[1]

Although no two companies will proceed in exactly the same way to select and evaluate the type of members making up their channel systems, practically all, in the

---

[1] One of the best sources of information on the factors affecting the choice and appraisal of distributive outlets is R. M. Pegram, *Selecting and Evaluating Distributors,* Studies in Business Policy No. 116 (New York: National Industrial Conference Board, 1965). Although the term "distributors" is used in the title, the discussion covers a wide range of resellers.

TABLE 19–1

Nine steps for selecting and reviewing channel system members

1. Analyze the product to determine its characteristics and uses.
2. Examine the firm itself.
3. Investigate the nature and extent of the market and competition.
4. Review existing channels, particularly competitors'.
5. Evaluate the merits of using more than one channel structure.
6. Appraise each channel system for potential sales, costs, and profits.
7. Secure customers' and middlemen's opinions about various channels.
8. Determine the cooperation expected from various channel members.
9. Formulate plans about the assistance to be provided to various channel members.

course of their deliberations, will take the steps presented in Table 19–1 and discussed below.

Analyzing the product

A thorough analysis of the nature of the product, including its classification as a consumer or industrial good and its subclassification within these two broad categories, is the first step to be taken in choosing and evaluating channel systems. In the case of consumer goods, classifying the product as a convenience, shopping, or specialty good may dictate the types of members that should be used to reach the ultimate consumer and may also assist in determining the number of such members to employ. The same holds true for industrial products, although not to the same extent. Heavy machinery or installations are nearly always sold directly to the user, whereas operating supplies may be marketed through mill supply houses.

Several additional product considerations have extensive influence on channel system selection and management.

Perishability. Products and services that are perishable or change often need channel systems which will move them rapidly from time of production to time of transfer to users. This is equally true of products like orchids and fresh bakery products that are subject to rapid physical deterioration; high fashion which deteriorates because of shifts in a style cycle; and services such as new hair styles which barbers and beauticians must learn while their customers want them. In general, highly perishable products and services require short (direct) channels. In addition, special middlemen (e.g., freight forwarders) and channels which offer certain facilities (e.g., refrigeration) may be required.

Physical dimensions. Products which are costly to store, handle, and ship relative to their value normally will be distributed through channels that help minimize these costs. Much lumber and coal, for example, is assembled and sold in carload or truckload quantities by drop shippers. The General Electric Company built Appliance Park to concentrate manufacturing and storage facilities for many of its appliances so it could assemble mixed carload and truckload quantities for their dealers. This, in turn, changed some of their needs at the wholesale level.

Price/quantity relationship. Products with low prices sold in small quantities cannot bear much channel expense and normally move through long channels which emphasize low cost per unit handled. Pencils, paper clips, and toilet tissue are examples. Low-price, high-volume items tend to have shorter, more direct channels. Manufacturers of lock washers, for example, frequently sell directly through their salesmen or sales agents to large industrial users, but for the household trade, they may use two to five middlemen. High-price items, whether sold singularly or in larger quantities, usually require the seller to convey product and use knowledge or provide extensive service and are best offered by short channel systems.

Extent of technical assistance and after-sale service required. Products that are technically complex or custom designed, such as machinery, require close liaison between customer and producer and call for short channels of distribution. Products which need custom installation, after-sale service, and rapid availability of replacement parts also require different activities of middlemen than those for which no service is necessary.

Product line. The extent of a firm's product line helps determine the channel members with which it will work. When the Maytag Company, with its limited line, was not able to maintain adequate representation at the wholesale level, it assumed this function. Retail outlets handling their products are a bit different from those handling, for example, General Electric products. More Maytag dealers specialize in washing and drying appliances, and Maytag products are more frequently coupled with other noncompetitive short-line manufacturers like Zenith. By contrast, General Electric has more full-line dealers.

Finally, some manufacturers find they must use sales representatives, because their limited product lines will not support their own salesmen, or wholesalers, because resellers want more complete assortments.

Examining the firm itself

The company considering the use of various channel systems is well advised to analyze its own financial resources, distribution costs, managerial experience and ability, and need or desire to command various channels.

Financial resources. A financially strong firm has more channel alternatives than a weak one, which must sell its products quicker and get other channel members to carry the bulk of the inventory and to perform many marketing functions. The channel system requiring the least marketing effort on the part of the manufacturer arises when it produces and sells to order all of its output under private labels (the buyers' brand names). In this situation marketing is largely limited to finding and negotiating contracts with private label buyers.

A firm with financial strength can seriously consider the alternative of investing funds in the acquisition of all or parts of channel systems. The Singer Company sells most of its sewing machines through its retail stores, and Sears, Wards, and A & P own some of the manufacturing and processing plants that supply them. The overall return on company funds provides the main criterion for considering channel investment versus other forms of investment.

Many reasons have already been given why manufacturers decide to integrate vertically or to bypass wholesalers. These reasons are summarized in Table 19–2. Because cost has a direct bearing on the return the firm will receive on its investment in distribution facilities, the question of cost savings merits more attention.

The cost of wholesale functions. Some manufacturers bypass the service wholesaler in an effort to reduce total distribution cost. If such a reduction is reflected in lower prices to the consumer, increased sales for the manufacturer will result; and insofar as the reduced cost results in higher manufacturer profits, the advantage to the manufacturer is evident.

Adequate information is lacking on the question whether economy is achieved

TABLE 19–2
Eight reasons why manufacturers bypass wholesalers

1. Dissatisfaction with wholesalers' performance.
2. Direct competition from wholesalers' brands.
3. Lack of aggressive promotion.
4. Large retailers will not buy through wholesalers.
5. Less need for wholesalers in urban, concentrated, or important markets.
6. Desire to be closer to and know more about retailers and users.
7. Availabilitiy of alternative marketing facilities.
8. Opportunity to reduce marketing costs.

TABLE 19–3
Operating expenses of merchant wholesalers and manufacturers' sales branches (with stocks), 1967 (net sales = 100 percent)

Kind of business	Merchant wholesalers	Manufacturers' sales branches (with stocks)
Paint and varnishes..25.5%		18.4%
Footwear...15.1		16.3
Groceries and related products..10.5		11.6
Electrical appliances, TV and radio sets............................12.9		9.8
Hardware...19.7		14.1
Home furnishings and floor coverings...............................17.9		9.3
Jewelry, diamonds, and precious stones 16.4		15.2

Source: U.S. Bureau of the Census, *1967 Census of Business*, Vol. IV, *Wholesale Trade* (Washington, D.C.: Government Printing Office, 1970), Table 2.

through bypassing the service wholesaler. For those products manufacturers market to retailers through their own branch houses, however, some evidence is available. Table 19–3 presents data showing operating expenses as a percentage of sales for a number of product categories for merchant wholesalers and manufacturers' sales branches with stocks.[2] In all fields except two (footwear and dry groceries) the advantage is definitely with the sales branch, representing a shift since the census year of 1939. This advantage seems to provide a factual base for the claim that bypassing the wholesaler results in economies in distribution. The manufacturer considering direct sale to retailers should not accept this claim without question, however, but should make a careful cost analysis to be sure that reduced costs are possible in his specific situation.

Managerial experience and ability. Managers will normally not plunge into new channel systems without experience. When a product or service new to them requires marketing, they generally prefer to turn it over to experienced middlemen with proven records. The large retail grocery chains, for instance, allowed rack jobbers to market hardware, cosmetics, records, and other products in their stores until they gained the needed experience to do the job themselves.

Need to control a channel system. A company's managers may be convinced

---

[2] Both service and limited-function wholesalers are included, but the former are so important that they largely determine the cost figures for both kinds of wholesalers.

they must control their channel systems in terms of various crucial dimensions. Sears, Roebuck discontinued its association with Walton-Sears of Australia because, while profitable, it simply was not the "Sears" way of acquiring additional retail outlets. Some firms need to control promotion, pricing, services, product quality, or other aspects in the channel. Others will not sell through private label (distributor brand) channels because they cannot control them. This consideration of control is an important influence on channel selection for many firms.

Investigating the market and competition

Marketing-minded managements choose channels designed to serve the preferences of their present and prospective customers as demonstrated through past buying habits and ascertained by organized research. Since products are made to sell to potential buyers and users, no factor is more important in selecting and managing a channel of distribution than a clear understanding of the nature and extent of this market. The manufacturer must find answers for such questions as: Who are the potential buyers and users of my product? How many are there? Where are they? How do they now satisfy the wants my product satisfies? What are their likes, dislikes, preferences, and prejudices? And he must understand the buyer's decision-making process, as explained in Chapter 4.

When a manufacturer has decided where buyers will expect to find his type of product, he must provide for *adequate distribution* to such locations. A manufacturer may know that users of his product prefer to buy it from a retail drugstore. Since he cannot sell directly to *all* such stores, provision must be made for distribution among the wholesalers from whom these retailers buy. Similarly, a manufacturer of an industrial product with customers who commonly buy from mill supply houses because they require prompt service on replacement parts should be sure that his product is available there, although he might also establish sales branches to furnish the required service. Marketers who use channels which make it possible for users to find the product with their normal purchasing habits will realize better sales and profits. Thus frequently purchased, low-priced consumer convenience products with broad markets are usually marketed with considerable reliance on mass-media promotion, many outlets, and long channels. Marketing of infrequently purchased, high-value shopping products is more likely to rely on personal selling, selective retail outlets, and short channels.

There are two other market considerations which have a strong influence on the selection and management of channel systems.

Number of customers. A large number of small customers for a product (e.g., hair combs) calls for the use of numerous middlemen to fan the products out to them. With only a few customers, there is greater likelihood of using short channels. An industrial product such as rubber rollers can be sold direct, while floor-sweeping compound has too many customers to permit direct sale.

Geographic concentration. A geographically compact market encourages short channels more than a widespread one does. A manufacturer can locate closer to more of his customers in a compact market, thus simplifying storage, distribution, and selling and making it more feasible to provide and supervise these functions. Sparse markets without enough buyers to support company salesmen and nearby storage facilities may call for sales or selling agents carrying many products and shipments moving from distant warehouses. Other alternatives are to sell only through wholesalers or to solicit sales via phone or mail.

Reviewing existing channels of distribution

The main distribution channel structures, as discussed in Chapters 3 and 13, are summarized in Figure 19–1. Each should be thoroughly appraised *in relation to the objectives being sought.*

FIGURE 19–1
The main channels of distribution

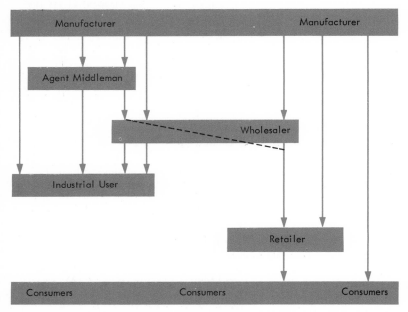

The problem of selecting a channel system may seem easy to solve. You may reason that a grocery item should be sold through wholesale and retail grocers, a hardware item through hardware middlemen, and so forth. Although this is generally true, a recent trend toward "scramble merchandising" has complicated the situation. The growth of the supermarkets and discount houses, with their broad lines of merchandise and constantly changing product mix; the widespread handling of drugstore items by food stores and vice versa; and the changing competitive position of department stores are all indications of the dynamic nature of the trade channels for consumer products. Wise selection of distribution channels necessitates familiarity with current developments in marketing.

As an illustration of a field in which significant channel changes are taking place, consider toilet goods and cosmetics. Among the dynamic factors are these: (1) mergers among cosmetics companies which permit small firms to increase their marketing potential and improve their distribution methods; (2) the increasing interest of men in toiletries of various kinds; (3) the drop in the starting age for cosmetics consumption, now down to 12 years;[3] and (4) a sharpened interest in toiletries among young adults. Table 19–4, which shows the shifting importance of various retail outlets for toilet goods, suggests the importance of careful review of distribution channels by marketers of these products.

TABLE 19–4
Retail sales of toilet goods by type of outlet, 1950 and 1966

Type of outlet	Percentage of total retail sales of toilet goods	
	1950	1966
Chain and independent drug stores	37.0	26.8
Department and specialty stores	27.0	14.1
Food stores	6.1	23.8
House-to-house selling	14.0	20.7
Limited-price variety stores	11.0	9.1
All other outlets	4.9	5.5
Total	100.0	100.0

Source: "Toilet Goods Top $3 Billion," *Oil, Paint and Drug Reporter*, June 26, 1967, p. 47.

Using more than one channel structure

The task of selecting trade channels is frequently complicated because different channels are necessary for some of the firm's products. Two channels are used by a manufacturer of children's wear—its best-quality line is sold direct to large retailers, whereas its lower price line goes through wholesalers who develop sales with smaller stores. Producers in many fields use both independent and company-owned outlets at the retail level. Thus, Goodyear Tire & Rubber Company has some 600 company-owned stores, and more units are being added "at an accelerated rate . . . placing them particularly in areas where existing dealerships are not capable of securing the proper share of the market for Goodyear."[4] Goodyear products are also sold through some 70,000 independent gasoline stations, tire shops, garages, automobile supply stores, and general stores. A typical channel system for tires is shown in Figure 19–2.

The petroleum industry is another example of dual distribution. Gasoline is sold both under the refiner's brand by their own and independent stations and to independent distributiors for resale under their own brands.

Dual distribution has created considerable criticism from independent middlemen and government antitrust agencies because the manufacturer is inclined to favor his captive retailers in periods of downward price pressure or short supply. By charging relatively high prices or restricting supply, the manufacturer places the independent at a competitive disadvantage which could force him out of business.

Before engaging in dual distribution the manufacturer should consider the potential disadvantages of government complaints or poor relations with distributors, as well

---

[3] "Toiletry Makers Now Tapping the 'Under Sixteen' Market," *Oil, Paint and Drug Reporter*, July 5, 1965, p. 29. In the same issue also see "Cosmetics and the 'Young Market,' " p. 39.

[4] Victor Holt, president, "The Goodyear Story," an address before the San Francisco Society of Security Analysts, April 7, 1966, p. 13.

FIGURE 19–2

Set of channels used by tire manufacturer

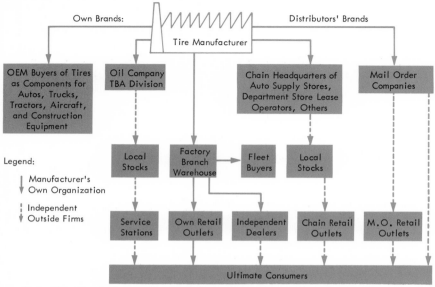

Source: Adapted from D. Wasson and D. McConoughy, *Buying Behavior and Marketing Decisions* (New York: Appleton-Century-Crofts, 1968), p. 198.

as the advantages of complete market coverage and additional business which can accrue.

Appraising sales, costs, risks, and profits

It is axiomatic that every firm should use the channels of distribution that will produce the combination of sales volume and cost yielding the maximum amount of profit. But the sales volume attained with a particular channel is often not the greatest possible, and the "best" cost is not necessarily the lowest possible unit or percentage cost. Moreover, since both the short-run and the long-run points of view must be considered, appraising sales, costs, and profits is not a simple task.

Volume of sales. The sales volume obtained through any channel of distribution will depend not only on the potential of that channel but also on the care with which marketing plans are made, executed, and followed up. It would be illogical to compare a well-conceived and properly executed plan of selling directly to retailers with a poorly conceived and managed plan of selling only to wholesalers. Assuming other things to be equal, sales volume will vary in direct relation to the channel capacity and the thoroughness and foresight of management in formulating and carrying out its sales efforts.

Costs. Evaluation of a specific trade channel may reveal that it has the greatest sales potentialities but the costs involved are so high that profits will be jeopardized. Manufacturer-owned retail stores may provide maximum retail sales promotion but be too costly to operate, thus forcing the firm to use a lower cost channel.

Marketing: Principles and methods

The most costly channel systems are generally those involving direct sales to household consumers and industrial users. When manufacturers distribute in this manner, therefore, they expect to obtain advantages which offset these increased costs. This method of distribution is expensive because of such factors as the skilled salesmen required and the long period of negotiation necessary to consummate sales. Direct contact with potential customers, however, is sometimes essential if sales are to be made.

To reduce the costs inherent in direct sale to industrial users (or to thousands of retail stores in the case of consumer products) many manufacturers use wholesale middlemen who sell in turn to retailers or users. By selling to a reduced number of customers, the manufacturer achieves a reduction in his selling force and in the time necessary to supervise and administer his sales organization. Such a practice may also enable him to decrease the amount of capital invested in his inventory and accounts receivable and to reduce the interest charges thereon as well as the credit risk involved. Often, however, the manufacturer offsets these savings by adopting practices that increase other costs. For example, he may make extensive use of missionary salesmen or assume some of the wholesalers' warehousing functions.

The analysis of costs for different channels is a difficult task which requires considerable knowledge of cost allocation. Arriving at valid policy decisions based on such analysis is equally difficult, necessitating answers to such questions as: What is the best time to make the changes suggested by the cost analysis? Are the potential savings great enough to justify the risks of shifting from a tried channel to an untried one? Even though the cost analysis supports a change to a different channel, do the trends in customer buying habits indicate that the present channels are proving satisfactory? The cost survey is simply an aid to executive judgment; how much it will contribute to the success of the firm depends upon the validity of the decisions to which it contributes.

Profits. The primary objective of a firm's economic activity is to maximize profit and returns on invested capital. Choosing the channel systems that will achieve these goals is not simple. Vertical integration requires invested capital and thus increases both the numerator and the denominator (investments) of the profit rate. Even hiring a sales force to sell directly to large retailers can convert a variable cost (wholesaler margin or agent commission) into a fixed cost, unless salesmen are paid only commission. The dynamics of competition and changing consumer wants make it difficult to forecast long-range profits.

Only in rare instances is there any one choice which gives superiority over all others, as far as profits are concerned. All the firm can do is consider the problem carefully on its merits, weigh all the pertinent payoffs and risks, and make the decision.

Securing customers' and middlemen's opinions

Helpful information in selecting and managing a marketing channel system may be gained from surveying opinions of customers and prospective customers who have purchased similar goods. This step, which is closely related to determining the nature and extent of the market, is concerned primarily with customers' impressions as to the availability of products in question. The survey should also include interviews with officers of typical outlets used by competitors, who can furnish information about their operations, and with bankers, credit bureaus, and lawyers, who can suggest promising dealer prospects.

Oliver Corporation, a manufacturer of farm equipment, uses the market survey as one of two major steps in selecting outlets, the other being interviews with community leaders. The market survey (by the territorial manager) involves a minimum of 100 farm calls (and up to 200 in larger markets). According to the company,

These are necessary to get a cross section of most trade areas, and to give the territorial manager the necessary confidence and conviction to present the merits of the Oliver franchise and convince the prospect that he should accept it. The success of the dealer will depend in large measure on an accurate knowledge of customer requirements, which can only be had with an inventory of potential sales prospects. It means visiting the farmer, learning his conditions, and building a sales program to fill his needs.[5]

Determining the cooperation expected from the channel members

Adequate appraisal of a channel system is impossible without considering the ability and the willingness of each member to cooperate in the sale of the product. Effective sales assistance is based upon a clear-cut recognition by members of what is expected of them and what they expect of others. The responsibility for providing this knowledge rests with the channel leader.

Middlemen may provide many forms of assistance to the manufacturer, although important differences exist in the fields of consumer and industrial products. Perhaps the major support furnished by the middleman is that of promotional assistance. The financial condition of some manufacturers is such that they have to "purchase" promotional aid from their outlets by allowing larger discounts. Another form of assistance is servicing the merchandise after sale, which is expected for such consumer durable products as household appliances and automobiles, and installing and repairing such industrial products as heavy machinery and accessory equipment. Other aids consist of financial assistance through advancement of funds, setting up window and interior displays, and giving demonstrations of the product in actual use.

Planning the forms of assistance to channel members

Once the manufacturer has defined the various forms of cooperation he expects from his trade channel, he should formulate plans detailing the assistance he will provide the middlemen involved. As a general rule, his chances of getting and keeping desirable outlets for his product are proportional to the help he agrees to furnish. It has been noted that

in dealing with independent resellers manufacturers find that the shoe is often on the other foot, with the supplier being subjected to even greater scrutiny from the order side of the desk. The manufacturer is constantly looking for better distribution outlets; the distributor is not always seeking more products. In short, selection is a two-way street.[6]

Table 19–5 indicates the major factors of interest to distributors.

Examples of assistance given by manufacturers. Among manufacturers of consumer products a wide variation prevails in the kinds and amounts of assistance extended to outlets. Probably the most common aid is dealer displays adapted to the particular product, together with advertising and miscellaneous sales promotional

---

[5] Pegram, *Selecting and Evaluating Distribuitors,* p. 19. This source lists the kind of information collected in the market survey and explains the purposes and conduct of the community leaders' meeting.

[6] Ibid., p. 92.

TABLE 19–5
Factors of interest to distributors in deciding on sources of supply

1. The manufacturer's record of financial capacity and stability.
2. Market potential for the supplier's product in the territory.
3. Major industries to be served by virtue of carrying the line.
4. National and local sales position and reputation of the product line.
5. National and local sales position of the supplier's major competitors.
6. Information on other distributors and dealers handling the line.
7. Sales policies of the company (terms, discounts, minimal inventory requirements, and total initial investment required).
8. Gross margin expectations.
9. Estimated annual sales volume and profits for the first and succeeding years should the line be added.
10. Warehousing requirements.
11. Packaging requirements for the products.
12. Advertising and sales promotion assistance.
13. Field sales assistance and training available from the supplier.

Source: R. M. Pegram, *Selecting and Evaluating Distributors* (New York: National Industrial Conference Board, 1965), p. 93.

devices. Some companies provide missionary salesmen, and others conduct formal training institutes and workshops to train dealers' salesmen. Johnson & Johnson, for example, operates an extensive sales training program for salesmen in drugstores which sell its products.

In some markets, General Electric and Westinghouse do not require dealers to carry appliance inventory. Instead they loan him display samples and then make delivery direct to the customer from stock in a factory branch. This program enables the manufacturer to achieve a broader display of his merchandise in the dealer's display room, provides better installation and postsale servicing, and reduces storage and delivery costs. The Maytag Company, recognizing that dealers needed help in handling trade-ins, has a program for reconditioning and selling them at a profit. To keep customers satisfied with their purchases, many appliance firms conduct schools for dealers' repairmen. Rexall Drug and Chemical Company provides its retail outlets with assistance on such matters as fixtures, operating methods, and expense control, as well as financial backing when required. The major tire manufacturers use their company-owned retail outlets as training centers for independent retailers selling their products, thereby aiding them in layout problems, stock keeping, and stock control.

Manufacturers are sometimes unable to obtain the desired cooperation from their chosen outlets because their plans and programs have been "unrealistic." A few years ago, for example, Smith, Klein & French Laboratories devised a plan to win the cooperation of beauty-supply wholesalers through a detailed plan of discounts and incentives. It proved unworkable, partly because it "tampered with traditional discount systems" and expected more cooperation than was obtainable.[7] This experience points up the importance of careful planning of programs designed to provide assistance and to gain cooperation from channel members to recognize the mutual expectations and obligations involved.

Among the many aids provided by industrial goods manufacturers to their outlets

---

[7] See E. B. Weiss, "You Can Lead a Horse to Water, but . . . ," *Advertising Age,* March 1, 1967, p. 92; and his "The Horse Wouldn't Even Sip the Water," *Advertising Age,* April 10, 1967, pp. 76, 78. Also see "How Motorola Solved a Tough Dealer Problem," *Marketing Insights,* February 13, 1967, pp. 16–17.

are training programs for distributors, engineering and technical assistance, personal calls on outlets by executives, industrial advertising, and missionary salesmen. Many producers send company bulletins or newsletters to their distributors' salesmen as a means of keeping them up to date on products and to give them selling points. Others supply information designed to improve purchasing and inventory management. SKF Industries uses a panel of its distributors to develop programs which will be helpful to all those handling its products.

Marketing strategy, segmentation, and channel choice. The manufacturing-oriented channel leader plans his marketing strategy by first identifying the target segments to which he wants to direct his product and then developing marketing plans for each segment. Because these market segments will usually be homogeneous with regard to the type of retail outlets preferred by customers, the types of channels used to serve a segment will also be homogeneous.

Each channel member has an important role to play in implementing a marketing strategy. The leader depends on the channel to perform the various functions of stocking the correct assortment, displaying, informing, financing, selling, servicing, pricing, and promoting which together make up the total marketing plan. For the plan to be executed correctly, each channel member must know in detail what is expected of him, and the leader must make clear exactly what assistance he is willing to provide. All members in the system must be committed to a single channel strategy designed by the leader; the individual channel member should *not* develop his own *independent* strategy.

While the importance of correct channel choice is recognized, the risk from an incorrect channel choice may not be. A poor advertising campaign is costly, but it can be stopped in a matter of days or weeks. A poor choice of channel members may take years to undo, and in the meantime the entire marketing effort may be completely ineffective.

Assistance related to promotion. The extent of assistance to be given to middlemen can be arrayed along a continuum of their participation in the promotion function.

1. *Push promotion.* At one end of this continuum is a "push" strategy in which each member places primary emphasis on persuading the member below him in the channel to carry the product and place strong promotional effort behind it. This strategy is usually characterized by the presence of a large and effective manufacturer's sales force, relatively high middleman margins, little reliance on national advertising, limited retail distribution, large retail product assortments, and strong display, promotion, selling, and consumer service at the retail level. It is common for shopping goods such as household furniture and women's wearing apparel. Because emphasis is laid on promotion at the retail level, the leader must provide assistance in these activities.

2. *Pull promotion.* At the other end of the continuum is a "pull" strategy in which the manufacturer attempts to force the product through the channel system by establishing a demand for it among ultimate consumers. If this demand is strong enough, retailers will find the shelf space to carry it. This strategy is usually characterized by heavy media advertising, relatively low middleman margins, and broad distribution, as in the marketing of packaged foods and personal care products. Manufacturers often employ a detail sales force to work with retailers on display of the item because they do not expect it to be of such importance to the retailer that he will perform point-of-purchase selling functions.

SELECTING THE NUMBER OF EACH TYPE OF OUTLET TO USE

Along with decisions as to the types of channel members to be used, the number of various types of members to be included in each channel system must be determined.[8] A channel captain can choose from among four major distribution policies: (1) intensive distribution, in which the product or service is offered for sale in as many as possible of the outlets in which potential customers would expect to find it; (2) selective distribution, in which a limited number of outlets, chosen according to a definite plan designed to reduce selling costs, is utilized; (3) exclusive distribution, in which only one outlet in a particular geographic area is employed; and (4) franchising, which includes the area-limitation aspect of exclusive distribution but adds certain significant obligations on the part of both manufacturer and outlet.

Intensive distribution

Intensive distribution—i.e., maximum exposure to sale—is generally required for convenience products and services because customers will not go out of their way to purchase them. Since consumers will often accept substitutes if their preferred products are not readily accessible, it is to the advantage of the manufacturer to have "100 percent distribution." Bayer aspirin and coin telephones are examples of goods found in practically every drugstore (and many other kinds of stores, as well) in the United States.

The increase in the number and variety of products offered for sale in most kinds of retail stores and the number of competing lines carried have caused the inventory investment of many middlemen to increase faster than their sales. Consequently, they are more cautious in stocking new items, which complicates the marketing problem for the manufacturer and may cause him to accept more restricted distribution or to expand his sales promotional program. In many drugstores, for example, the numerous lines of cosmetics competing for the consumer's dollar have created an inventory problem for the retailer and the wholesaler which makes it very difficult for the manufacturer to obtain entry without substantial, costly sales promotional efforts. This type of situation is more prevalent with consumer products than industrial products.

Selective distribution

A policy of selective distribution may be followed in the marketing of all kinds of consumer and industrial products, although the degree of selectivity of customers will vary according to the specific types of each class of products in a particular situation.

Once a channel leader is assured that he can get adequate market coverage and penetration, he is in a position to reduce the number of middlemen used in a particular geographic area. The principal advantages of selective distribution are that the manufacturer can offer the distributor some reduction in competition from sellers of the same brand and thus gain from him more aggressive promotion, agreement to carry a complete line, willingness to engage in after-sale service, a defense against distributor branding, an interest in maintaining retail prices, and a more cohesive channel organization.

---

[8] For a quantitative approach to this decision, see S. K. Gupta and C. Maier-Rothe, "A Note on the Partitioning of a Single Product Market into Territories of Outlets," *Journal of Marketing Research,* 6 (May 1969), pp. 232–36.

The experience of the Amprobe Company, a marketer of electrical measuring devices, suggests some of the reasons why a growing number of companies is adopting this policy. Annual volume requirements for selected distributors and the stipulation that they "must stock broadly and deeply, promote and sell actively, and cover the market completely" resulted in significant sales gains. Although the new policy caused 37 percent of the company's distributors to discontinue handling the firm's products, total sales increased 38 percent, average annual sales per distributor quadrupled, average size of order advanced significantly, delivery time was cut from four or five weeks to six days, and paper-work costs were reduced by 15 percent.[9]

While volume of business, improved cooperation, and size of order are major considerations in selecting customers under a program of selective distribution, other factors are also involved. Some customers may be eliminated because they demand too much of the "free" service offered by the manufacturer or wholesaler; others may return too much of what they order. The credit standing of some may not be satisfactory, or they may not cooperate fully with the seller's sales program. By eliminating or reducing selling effort to such customers, the manufacturer's selling cost may be reduced, cooperation from other dealers increased, sales expanded through more calls on profitable customers, morale of salesmen improved, and total profits enlarged.

The dangers of selective distribution to the manufacturer are that market coverage may be inadequate, the remaining dealers in the area may not be the best ones, consumers may not be able to locate a dealer who carries the brand or product, and it may be difficult to change dealers when such action becomes necessary.

Exclusive distribution

Exclusive distribution arrangements between manufacturers and their outlets covering both consumer and industrial products and services have been used in this country for many years. Some of the major forms these arrangements have taken, drawing upon both business experience and legal terminology, are discussed below.

Distinguishing between exclusive selling and exclusive dealing. An *exclusive distributorship or dealership,* also known as an *exclusive selling agreement,* exists when a manufacturer or other supplier agrees with a particular wholesaler or retailer not to sell to other wholesalers or retailers in the same area. Under an *exclusive dealing* arrangement the distributor or dealer agrees to refrain from handling competing products in consideration of being supplied with the manufacturer's goods. Some exclusive arrangements also involve a consignment agreement, although this is not essential to the exclusive arrangement. In such cases the manufacturer or other supplier furnishes products to the distributor or dealer as his agent but continues to hold title to the goods until they are sold by the agent under prescribed terms and conditions.

Examples of exclusive distribution. Perhaps the best-known examples of exclusive agencies in the United States are in the automobile industry, in which in effect "the dealer is the factory's point-of-sale representative." Similar arrangements also exist in the marketing of such products as shoes (Florsheim), clothing (Hart Schaffner & Marx), pianos (Steinway), television sets and radios (Magnavox), and numerous others in sporting goods, furniture, and farm implements—to mention a few. Manufacturers and wholesalers alike are interested in the advantages this plan of distribution

---

[9] "Distributor 'Weeding Out' Nets Healthy Sales Rise," *Industrial Marketing,* 52 (May 1967), pp. 67–69.

Marketing: Principles and methods

affords but, as noted in a subsequent section, they are concerned about its legal implications.

Merits and limitations of exclusive distribution. Whether or not a manufacturer (or a wholesaler) uses exclusive agreements as a part of his marketing program will be determined by his appraisal of the merits and limitations of such an arrangement both from his point of view and from that of the middlemen involved. Some of the more important of these are discussed below. It should be emphasized, however, that, once a decision has been made to employ this device, details concerning the size of the area to be served, the product or line to be carried, and the manufacturer's and middleman's obligations are usually set forth in a written contract.

1. *The grantor's point of view.* Exclusive agreements offer certain advantages to the manufacturer or wholesaler using them. Knowing that he will be the only retailer in the area to gain from his advertising of the manufacturer's product, the dealer is much more likely to undertake promotion and encourage his salespeople to push the product. The dealer *sells the manufacturer's product more aggressively,* is more willing to *carry a complete stock* of the manufacturer's line, since his own success is tied to a considerable degree to that of the manufacturer, and has more incentive to *maintain a service and repair department. Resale price maintenance is easier* because the number of outlets is limited and, because there are fewer accounts for his salesmen to call on and to whom credit must be extended, the manufacturer may find that his *cost of marketing is reduced.*

Despite the advantages of exclusive arrangements, not all manufacturers and wholesalers use them. For many products and services, in fact, they are clearly not suitable. Many consumer goods require extensive distribution, as do those industrial products classified as operating supplies. Even if a manufacturer of convenience products carried on an extensive advertising program, he would find his sales limited if his products were not handled by a large number of middlemen. Moreover, many shopping products require sale through more than one store in a given trading area. The loss of an exclusive dealer in a certain section is a matter of great importance to the manufacturer, especially since it may take some time to replace him satisfactorily. In contrast, when a producer has several representatives in an area, the loss of any one is relatively unimportant. Thus sellers of consumer products and services find exclusive outlets more satisfactory for specialty items, and sellers of industrial goods find it advantageous for installations and accessory equipment. This form of selling is also desirable for products requiring the rendering of special services by those handling them, such as automobiles, tractors, and furnaces, and for products requiring a large investment in stock, such as men's clothing.

2. *The dealer's point of view.* The dealer under an exclusive agreement may discover that his contract has certain disadvantages—its possible withdrawal after much effort has been spent in promoting a product, its requirements for carrying a complete stock and rendering certain services, and (if exclusive dealing is also involved) loss of sales on competing lines which might otherwise be carried.[10] It also offers important advantages, however. The advertising of the seller and the dealer will aid only the dealer in that area. Price cutting is minimized. Elimination of duplicate brands may increase stock turnover. More cooperation may be forthcoming from the manufacturer. And the complete stock and the repair department required enable the

---

[10] For such items as automobiles, washing machines, and refrigerators, the contract may forbid the dealer to deal in competing brands, although this provision has been modified somewhat in recent years. In contrast, few sellers of cosmetics, foods, and men's clothing can induce dealers to sign such contracts.

dealer to render better service to customers, thus creating goodwill for his firm. These advantages help explain why exclusive arrangements are sought by many dealers as well as wholesalers.

Legality of exclusive distribution agreements. The history of court interpretations of the antitrust laws with regard to exclusive selling and dealing is long and somewhat confusing. Reciprocal exclusive selling and dealing agreements are probably always illegal. The area of uncertainty today centers around when an exclusive selling agreement which limits *intrabrand* competition but not *interbrand* competition is illegal. A more detailed discussion of this area of antitrust concern is reserved for Chapter 25.

Franchising

Franchising, which has become the fastest growing distribution arrangement in recent years (see Chapter 8), is an extension of exclusive distribution. Virtually all franchise agreements purport to grant a degree of exclusive selling area.[11] In addition, the agreements usually stipulate that the franchisee can engage in the business in a specific location provided he follows the established pattern. The franchisee buys these rights and the franchiser provides a set of services (and sometimes merchandise). It is these mutual obligations that move franchise systems beyond the normal exclusive distribution agreement.

CONTROLLING AND EVALUATING CHANNELS

The management process involves planning, organizing, leading, and controlling. The manufacturing-oriented channel leader usually recognizes and accepts responsibility for managing the marketing of his product. He must also accept the responsibility for performing these management functions for the entire channel—even though many channel members may be outside his own firm. The acceptance by channel members of extraorganizational leadership is dependent on how well the leader does his job as a marketing manager.

The final management process involves control, which must provide answers to a number of questions. How can a nationwide coalition of independent firms be controlled? What kinds of feedback information are required? How can it be obtained? What performance criteria should be applied?

The scope and frequency of evaluation should conform to the situation in a particular company. Some reviews are designed merely to keep management currently informed regarding the channel member's success with its products. Others may involve the overall performance of the dealer or distributor as an aid in judging his suitability. Among the decisive factors in such a broad analysis are sales performance and selling capabilities, inventory maintenance, attitude, competition, growth prospects, financial status, customer opinion, and character and reputation.[12] All of these, of course, are also vital considerations in selecting members for a channel system. Frequency of channel evaluation is commonly determined by such considera-

---

[11] It has been suggested that the future importance of cooperative contractual channel ties will be greatly influenced by the extent to which closed (exclusive) territories can be granted under the antitrust laws. See D. F. Dixon, "The Impact of Recent Antitrust Decisions upon Franchise Marketing," *MSU Business Topics*, 17 (Spring 1969), pp. 68–79.

[12] These factors are discussed in detail in Pegram, *Selecting and Evaluating Distributors*, pp. 108–28.

tions as the kinds and number of middlemen used; products involved; previous experience in appraising the efforts of resellers; shifts in competitors' channels; and the development of new channels.[13] In the years ahead channel structures should continue to change as marketing institutions adjust to new methods of transportation and communication, electronic data processing, integration in retailing, and the impact of the megalopolis.[14] One method of evaluating channels, distribution cost analysis, is described in Appendix A of this book.

Even without changes in the marketing structure, frequent evaluation of channels is necessary because what may have been the best channel when a product was introduced may not continue to be when the product is well established. Even though the manufacturer of a new product may wish to sell through wholesalers, he may find them reluctant to add another item and may be forced to sell direct to retailers, or even house to house, to establish his product. Once it is firmly established in the market, a gradual shift can be made to wholesalers. The nature and extent of cooperation to be given to the wholesaler and the nature of the control techniques to be used in evaluating his performance are quite different from those used with other methods of distribution.

SUMMARY

In conclusion two points should be emphasized. First, the maintenance of satisfactory relationships between the manufacturer and members in his channels of distribution is essential if sales and profit possibilities are to be maximized. Astute marketers will view their channels of distribution as extensions of their own formal organizations, the only difference being that instead of hiring their own sales forces, they have hired independent sales forces to do the job. The marketing tasks, in all cases, must still be performed.

The second point is that mutually profitable manufacturer-distributor relationships do not develop automatically. From the manufacturer's points of view,

The attack must start with a careful study of his channel members' methods of operation and of the factors that enhance or retard their success. The success of the . . . manufacturer in capturing the cooperation of individuals and firms that comprise his marketing channel depends in no small degree on the extent to which he is able to develop methods for making the achievement of his objectives promote their welfare. . . . Good manufacturer-outlet relationships begin in the attitude that governs their administration.[15]

Most channel systems today are integrated or managed by one institution in the system which has established the power to lead the channel and which may have either a manufacturing or a distribution orientation. This chapter explored the problems of the selection and evaluation of channel structures from the viewpoint of the manufacturing-oriented channel manager. Three management questions were discussed: how to plan the type of channels to employ, how to determine the number of each type to employ, and how to control these channels.

---

[13] See L. W. Stern, "The Concept of Channel Control," *Journal of Retailing,* 43 (Summer 1967), pp. 14–20, 67.

[14] A new channel system is developing for the recycling of solid wastes. See W. G. Zinkmund and W. J. Stanton, "Recycling Solid Wastes: A Channel of Distribution Problem," *Journal of Marketing,* 35 (July 1971), pp. 34–39. Also W. R. Davidson, "Changes in Distributive Institutions," *Journal of Marketing,* 34 (January 1970), pp. 7–10.

[15] R. S. Alexander, J. S. Cross, and R. M. Hill, *Industrial Marketing* (Homewood, Ill.: Richard D. Irwin, Inc., 1967), p. 294.

In arriving at a decision as to the type of channel, the manager should focus on: (1) the characteristics of his product line, (2) the strengths and weaknesses of his company, (3) the characteristics of the market, (4) the characteristics of his competitors and their channels, (5) the present and future investments, costs, risks, and profits of alternative channel structures, (6) the suitability of potential channel members, (7) the tasks which channel members will be expected to perform; and (8) the forms of assistance to be given channel members.

The answer to the question of number of outlets is usually determined by the degree of selectivity in distribution which is appropriate for the total marketing strategy. Control can be achieved through continuing evaluation.

REVIEW AND DISCUSSION QUESTIONS

1. Explain briefly the fundamental considerations in the choice of a manufacturer's trade channel policies.

2. Distinguish between a manufacturing-oriented channel leader and a distribution-oriented channel leader. Give examples of each.

3. In choosing a channel of distribution, what part is played by each of the following: (a) a wide variety of uses for the product, (b) high frequency of purchase, (c) high-fashion element, (d) need for maintenance service, (e) substantial seasonal sale cycle, and (f) low unit price?

4. Name some circumstances within his firm which might persuade a manufacturer not to bypass wholesalers even though he is convinced the performance of his current wholesalers is unsatisfactory.

5. Explain the relationship, if any, between middleman margins and channel strategy.

6. What is the relationship between the market segmentation strategy and the channel strategy of a manufacturer of household furniture?

7. Explain the various ways in which risks can vary between alternative channels of distribution.

8. A few years ago, a large manufacturer of an apparel accessory discontinued selling to wholesalers and introduced a program of selling directly to retailers by mail. "By eliminating the jobber, we squeezed out a lot of the air between manufacturers' and retail prices," said the president of this firm. In your opinion, what chief factors should dictate such a policy change?

9. Summarize in parallel columns: (a) the main factors the manufacturer should consider in selecting a distributor (or other reseller) for his product, and (b) those the particular outlet should take into account in appraising the manufacturer's proposition.

10. Explain the distinction between a "push" strategy and a "pull" strategy for gaining distribution for a manufactured product. Under what circumstances is each appropriate?

11. How does the strategic decision as to a push or pull approach to gaining distribution relate to the selectivity of distribution a manufacturer may employ?

12. Distinguish among intensive, selective, and exclusive distribution and franchising, providing illustrations of each.

13. List the information you would like to have in order to evaluate the performance of independent wholesalers who are distributing your product. How could this information be obtained?

14. List the information you would like to have to evaluate the performance of retailers who carry your product under a program of selective distribution. How could this information be obtained?

15. In what ways are the problems of extraorganization channel managers different from those of normal intraorganization management?

SUPPLEMENTARY READINGS

Alexander, R. S.; Cross, J. S.; and Hill, R. M. *Industrial Marketing.* 3d ed. Homewood, Ill.: Richard D. Irwin, Inc., 1967. Chapters 9 and 10 discuss marketing channels for industrial products. Among subjects covered are the available outlets for such products and the selection and supervision of trade channels.

Bowersox, D. J. and McCarthy, E. J. "Strategic Development of Planned Vertical Marketing Systems." In L. P. Bucklin (ed.), *Vertical Marketing Systems.* Glenview, Ill.: Scott, Foresman & Co., 1970. An excellent development of the strategic considerations of channel selection.

Kelley, E. J. and Lazer, W. (eds.) *Managerial Marketing: Perspectives and Viewpoints.* 3rd ed. Homewood, Ill.: Richard D. Irwin, Inc., 1967. The eight readings included under the heading of "Distribution Mix" in this source book are helpful in connection with this chapter.

Lewis, E. H. *Marketing Channels: Structure and Strategy.* New York: McGraw-Hill Book Co., 1968. Chapters 4, 5 and 6 of this short, comprehensive volume cover channel management.

Mallen, B. E. (ed.) *The Marketing Channel: A Conceptual Viewpoint.* New York: John Wiley & Sons, Inc., 1967. Both the structure of the channel and the relationships among its elements are emphasized in this book of readings.

Moller, W. G., Jr. and Wilemon, D. L. *Marketing Channels: A Systems Viewpoint.* Homewood, Ill.: Richard D. Irwin, Inc., 1971. An excellent new collection of writings on channels. Parts VI, VII and VIII are concerned with the issues discussed in this chapter.

Pegram, R. M. *Selecting and Evaluating Distributors.* New York: National Industrial Conference Board, Studies in Business Policy No. 116, 1965. This excellent study reviews the chief considerations involved in the choosing and keeping of industrial distributors. Numerous company practices are described.

20 *Physical distribution*

Problems of the physical transport of products have been among the most basic encountered in the development of societies. They remain important today, as exemplified by recent problems in the transportation of oil—major oil spills at sea, the closing of the Suez Canal, developing methods to deliver the bounty from Alaska's North Slope.

In terms of cost, it is difficult to determine just how much of the total marketing bill goes for physical distribution. Some writers suggest that it may make up half of the total marketing bill for products, although this figure is probably high for the total marketing system. Because no functional breakdowns of marketing costs are available and because the marketing costs of manufacturers' shipping and storing of finished products are not separated from the production costs of shipping and storing raw and in-process materials, the exact percentage is unknown. Since middlemen perform physical distribution functions themselves, the input-output tables which record purchased transportation and storage services are of little value. The National Commission on Food Marketing did report that in 1954 transportation costs made up only 11.1 percent of the cost of marketing domestic farm foods. A study of all available evidence suggests that, for the total marketing system, physical distribution makes up more nearly one fourth, rather than one half, of the total cost of marketing.

Physical distribution is defined as including the activities of transportation, storage, materials handling, protective packaging, inventory control, storage location, order processing, information processing, and production planning concerned with the movement of raw materials and finished goods from production line or extractive site to consumers or industrial users. Some experts make a distinction between physical distribution and *logistics,* which includes plant location and in-process shipping and storage.

This definition suggests not only the organization of this chapter but also the approach which should be used in the analysis of physical distribution problems—a systems approach. Perhaps no other aspect of marketing lends itself so well to systematic analysis as physical distribution. The activities noted in the definition above suggest that equal levels of time and place utility can be achieved through many alternative arrangements, or trade-offs, between the costs of production set-up and run length, handling, storage and transportation. To optimize the use of these inputs requires an analysis of the total system.

Thus the appropriate system for analysis is not a single firm but the total inputs, outputs, and performance of the physical distribution system over an entire channel of distribution. Two individual firms seeking their own goals without realizing that they are interdependent may well develop high-cost distribution systems that will yield less than satisfactory levels of utility. A current situation illustrates this. Grocery manufacturers and distributors both use item codes to identify products within their own inventory management systems. They have argued for years over how to develop a system of universal codes which would be compatible with both distribution and manufacturer data processing systems. Suboptimization of the problem by each channel member has resulted in a coding system which does not minimize costs for the total channel.

This chapter is organized around the physical distribution functions which the marketing system must perform rather than around the institutions which perform them. The first section provides an overview of these systems; the second discusses management of inventory. The third and fourth sections consider the location of field stocks and public warehouse facilities, and the final section is devoted to the topic of transportation.

THE PHYSICAL DISTRIBUTION SYSTEM

The *objective* of a physical distribution system should be to provide high, competitive levels of customer service at the lowest possible cost. A system which gets fall fashions to Kansas City in December, provides refrigerators in four colors but only after a three-month wait, or delivers spoiled lettuce to the consumer, even inexpensively, is not performing well for buyers or sellers. However, it is not easy for the system or the individual firm to measure the level of customer service and then to try to achieve some optimum balance between increased service and the cost of providing it. Almost any level of service is obtainable if one is willing to pay the price. Therefore, it is usually preferable to specify the level of service to be provided in terms of the costs of *not* providing that service and then to express the objective of the system as performance of physical distribution functions at the lowest possible total cost.

Measures of performance

Total cost, rather than the physical distribution costs of manufacturers, wholesalers, or retailers, can be the measure of performance for the system. Figure 20–1 shows the physical distribution system for a consumer durable product. Raw materials are distributed to a steel producer, and the finished steel is distributed to a parts producer and to the plants of the manufacturer of the product. This steel and the

FIGURE 20–1
Physical distribution system for a consumer durable

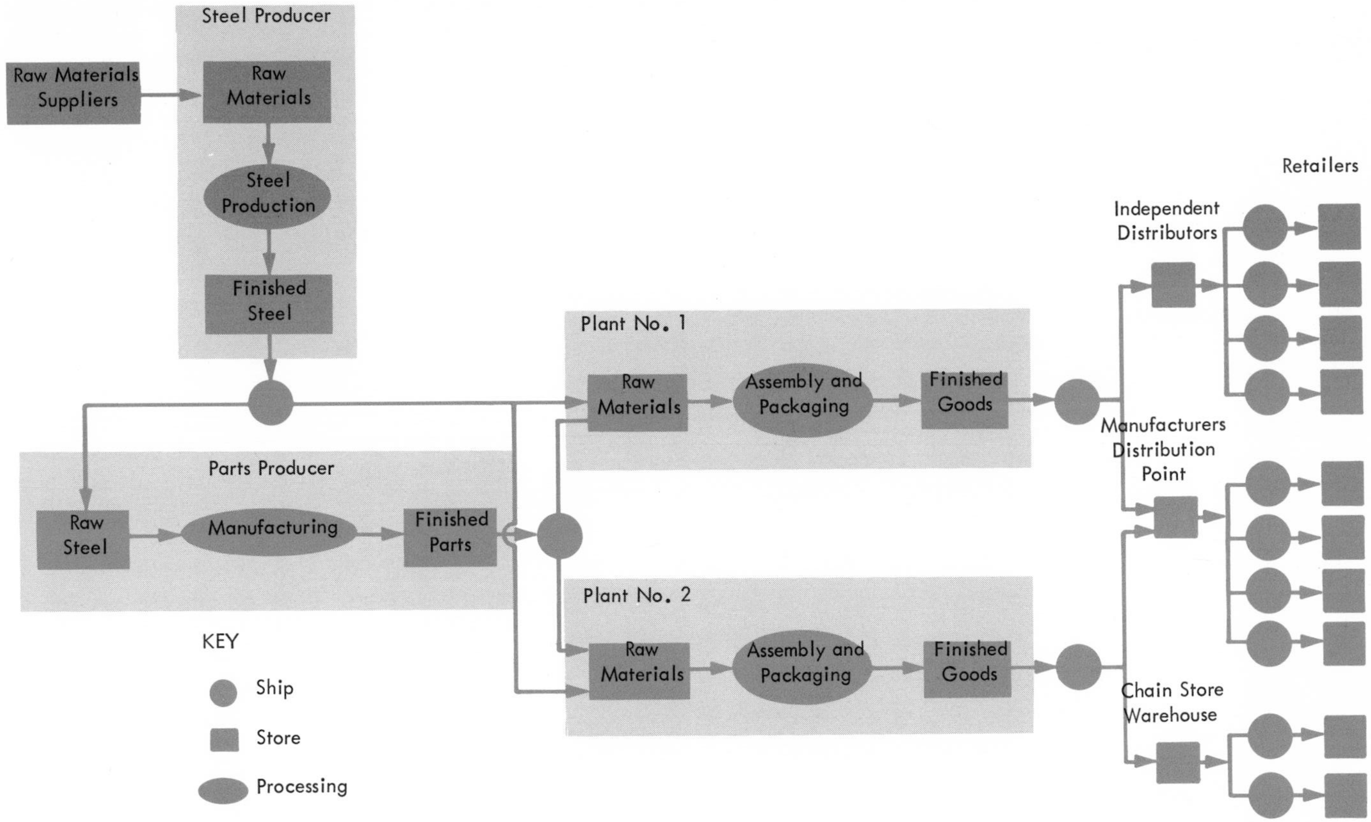

finished parts become the raw materials for the manufacturer, who assembles the product in two plants and distributes it to retailers through three different types of channels: direct through chain store warehouses, through his own regional field stocks, and through independent distributors. Note that each factory in the system also stocks finished goods.

From the standpoint of the firm, the figure emphasizes that performance should not be measured by the cost of the traffic department, the warehouse department, or the factory manager, but by the total cost of all physical distribution functions. The elements which go into this total cost and some of the trade-offs between them are discussed below.

Cost of unsatisfactory services. The cost of providing unsatisfactory or noncompetitive customer service may be expressed as a constraint or as a cost function. When expressed as a constraint, the system is required to meet some specified level of service; for example, all retailers are to receive overnight delivery. Such constraints are specified as the minimum consistent with the total marketing mix for each product. Of course, all products may not require the same service.

Constraints should be expressed in terms of both time and consistency—acceptable performance might be overnight delivery in 90 percent of all orders. A consistency component is important because without it the cost of a "stock-out" is implicitly considered to be infinitely large. The cost of achieving overnight delivery for the last 10 percent of all orders may be very great indeed. It might require a transcontinental shipment by air when a truck shipment could make the delivery with an additional one-day delay.

When the level of service is expressed as a cost function, it is necessary to relate slow delivery to the probability of a lost sale. The cost can then be expressed as the expected profit lost as a function of delivery time or of the expected number of stock-outs. While these costs and probabilities may not be easy to estimate, they do determine how much penalty would have to be paid in lost profit by a reduction in the costs of performing physical distribution functions. The implicit costs of the constraint approach become explicit in the cost function approach.

Cost of information. While information costs are often considered to be simply the administrative costs of order processing and inventory control, it is more meaningful to consider them as including expediting, communication, data storage and retrieval, forecasting, and production planning. Costs of such an information system increase with the complexity of the distribution system, but they also have a salutary effect on the costs of poor customer service, inventory obsolescence, transportation, and inventory carrying.

For example, an accurate production forecast and plan can reduce the carrying cost of finished and raw materials, help to level production, and reduce obsolescence in finished goods. A comprehensive and accessible system of storing and retrieving summaries of past purchases of retailers can help distribution points to keep stocks that will fill the needs of retailers. A rapid system of retailer order entry and order processing can reduce delivery time and the quantity of buffer stock required in the channel.

Materials handling costs. The costs of handling include the cost of protective packaging, including pallets, strapping, etc.; freight charges to ship this protective packaging, as well as the product; and the costs of materials handling equipment and of goods damaged in handling. The most important cost is for labor associated with picking, packing, loading, and unloading inventory. Because labor costs are high when warehouses and order size are small and when the number of items carried is large, it might be expected that if retail orders could be filled at the factory and shipped, handling costs would go down. However, the cost of picking and shipping many small orders and the time required for delivery usually result in higher total costs than would be the case with field distribution points.

Use of mechanized and automated materials handling equipment has been adopted slowly but is increasing. Old multistory warehouses in the inner city are no longer competitive because of the difficulty of truck access and the inability to handle goods efficiently within them. The need today is for single-story flexible buildings with railspurs and easy truck access from freeways. Flexibility may be the key to successful warehouse design, since demand requirements, product assortments, product characteristics, and materials handling technology are changing so rapidly that a warehouse which cannot be easily rearranged will rapidly become obsolete.

Materials handling equipment can be divided into that used for in-plant movement and for storing and picking orders. Movement equipment includes hand or power trucks and tractors, conveyors, and towlines. Automated power lines or towlines, which move continuously, can be placed in the floor of all aisles to power tow trucks that are programmed to switch to spur lines. Heavy and bulky items must be stored on pallets and moved by forklift truck. Rapid-movement equipment is vital since the modern warehouse may cover a quarter million square feet on a single story.

Mechanical order picking has proved to be a much more difficult problem. Even systems that automatically program trucks to travel to a sequence of bins have not solved the problem of reaching into the bin and selecting a specified number of items of a variety of shapes and sizes. A new lift truck device by Mobility Systems, Inc., of Santa Clara, California, is driven around the warehouse by a computer, stops at programmed locations, and lifts the cab to the level of the shelf where the item is stored, but it requires an operator in the cab to lift the item from the shelf. Mechanical order pickers of other designs, such as overhead crane systems, have had some application in manufacturing plants with a static or limited product mix but have been less successful in distributor warehouses.

Fixed warehouse cost.   Requirements for quick delivery, large shipment size in long hauls, and a mixture of assortments from different factories have created the need in many channels for regional wholesale middlemen or factory branches to carry finished inventory. The costs of maintaining a warehouse building are largely fixed and independent of the amount of stock they hold or the amount of handling required. These fixed costs include land, building cost, light, heat, maintenance and administrative personnel, office and materials handling equipment, insurance, and taxes. They can be transformed into variable costs by storing in a central location and paying higher transportation charges, using public warehouses, or shifting storage functions to other channel members and receiving lower margins.

Inventory carrying cost.   The ownership of inventory entails costs for the money thus invested, insurance on its value, inventory taxes, pilferage and deterioration losses, and obsolescence, in addition to the occupancy costs noted above. Depending on the products involved, they may range between 12 and 30 percent of the average value of the inventory. Thus if the quantity of inventory in raw or finished stocks can be reduced through better planning, slower deliveries, or alternative transportation media, savings in total cost may be possible.

Transportation cost.   Transportation is so vital to economic activity that it has become the focal point of those concerned with physical distribution. Almost all firms designate a traffic manager early in their growth. Because of the many alternative ways to ship, the complex nature of freight rates, and the possibility of trade-offs of freight costs with other distribution costs, there are no simple formulas for determining optimum transportation systems.

Transportation costs can be divided on the basis of whether shipment is performed by common carrier, contract hauler, the seller's own transportation fleet, or the buyer. The costs of private carriage, for example, include the costs of owning or leasing equipment, maintaining and providing terminal facilities for it, and operating it. The main elements of operating cost are labor, fuel, insurance, and taxes. Local delivery costs must sometimes also be considered as an element of transportation cost.

Components of the system—opportunities for conflict

The large number of components in the physical distribution system, within the firm and the channel as a whole, provides considerable opportunity for conflict over which distribution policies are optimum. Marketing, production, and finance groups attempt to achieve different objectives which are in conflict with one another. Marketing would like to maximize customer service because this policy provides them with the greatest competitive advantage. Production would like to maximize the stability of production because this policy results in the lowest average production cost. Finance would like to minimize the capital invested in the system (inventories, warehouses, equipment) because this policy is believed to be the one which will maximize return on investment. In some firms the objective of the traffic department is erroneously identified as minimizing freight cost per ton-mile.

Of course, all of these policies influence the profit returned. The design of the total physical distribution system can only be optimized by viewing the entire channel as a whole. This can be illustrated by the classic example of air freight. Table 20–1 shows a cost comparison between air freight, one of the highest cost transportation methods, and ocean freight combined with finished inventory stored at the destination. The comparison is for a product manufactured in California and sold in Hawaii. The level of customer service provided by both systems is the same. When total costs are calculated, it can be seen that with air freight it is possible to reduce inventory investment, use less protective packaging, make one local destination delivery rather than two, and eliminate a warehouse. These savings more than offset the higher freight rate for air shipment, although it should be emphasized that this would not always be the case. Only through an analysis of total cost can the optimum system be

TABLE 20–1
Cost analysis between air freight and ocean freight plus destination warehouse (San Francisco–Hawaii for a three-month period.)*

	Air		Ocean	
Packaging and handling	$ 30,000		$100,000	
Delivery to terminal	30,000		30,000	
Intercity freight charges	600,000	($6/cwt.)	100,000	
Destination local delivery	40,000		60,000	
Inventory carrying cost	130,000	(10 day)	400,000	(30 days)
Warehouse costs	—		300,000	
Total cost	$830,000		$990,000	
Total cost/cwt.	$8.30		$9.90	

*Average sales are 100,000 cwt. per quarter.

determined. Once the level of customer service and proper cost accounting analysis have been established, a variety of alternative distribution systems can easily be evaluated.

Systems control

Whether a firm uses its own distribution facilities, public carriers and warehouses, or shifts a part of the distribution functions to other channel members, the channel

FIGURE 20–2
Organization structure in which physical distribution activities are divided among several individuals

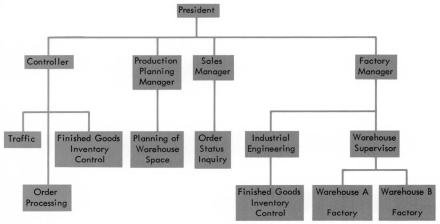

Source: Prepared by P. F. Cannon, Barrington Associates, Inc.

FIGURE 20–3
Organization structure with centralized physical distribution responsibility

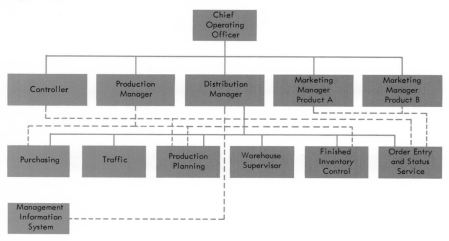

Marketing: Principles and methods

leader can evaluate performance and control the system by organizing both people and information for a total system analysis.

The modern firm can bury itself in a mountain of data. The challenge is to collect data on all aspects of physical distribution, to store them so they can be retrieved when needed, and to organize reports from them which will lead to timely corrective action when the system is out of control (see Chapter 17). A management information system which will accomplish these tasks itself requires an organizational structure to provide a "distribution nerve center."

The classic organization structure for physical distribution, shown in Figure 20–2, is not likely to be effective. The modern approach to organization, however, as shown in Figure 20–3, typically establishes a central corporate responsibility for the total physical distribution activities of the firm. Note that responsibility formerly shared by four men is now centralized in one.

INVENTORY MANAGEMENT

The objective of inventory management is to minimize the investment tied up in inventory while achieving an established level of customer service and reliability. Computerized inventory control systems are one of the most productive uses for the computer in the entire firm. It is standard practice to program the computer for a warehouse operation to automatically write a purchase order for a specified order quantity when the inventory level for an item reaches a preset reorder point. Some industrial distributors even place terminals of their computers at customers' plants so that orders generated by customers' computers are automatically transmitted to the distributor's. In some chain store operations, all retail outlets have terminal connections, sometimes at each cash register, to a central computer which services the warehouse or a network of warehouses. Every incoming order, by data phone or by mail, must be rewritten as an order for the distributor. This one writing through the computer can generate the warehouse packing list, a program for automated order picking, the shipping ticket, retail price tags, and the invoice, as well as updating warehouse inventory records. These data then provide the current demand and inventory update information required for the wholesaler's inventory management system. Such automation in communications and data processing shortens the time required to fill an order and thereby reduces the safety stock which must be held.

While advances in information processing obviously increase productivity and improve inventory management for repetitive items, the record of computer inventory management systems has not been spectacular. Fluctuations in total inventories are less violent with these systems, and total stock-to-sales ratios are somewhat lower. However, it is difficult for inventory management to improve as fast as the increase in the rate of introduction of new products and new fashions.

Increased use of on-line, time-sharing computers with which buyers can interact more easily may provide the answer to this difficulty. While computers can store information and do arithmetic, only people can manage. The success of the manager today is largely determined by his ability to cope with change in the environment—in this case, in demand, the price level, and production. On its own, a computer can do only repetitive operations; the manager must do the creative thinking. All techniques for determining what, when, and how much to order and hold assume some stability (not constancy) in the environment. The success of inventory control systems is never better than the ability to forecast when and what changes will take place in the environment. Thus the newest information systems for physical distribution management provide greater capability for man-machine interaction through random access to information and rapid display of answers to inquiries.

Reasons for inventory

The primary reason for holding inventory is to adjust supply and demand through the creation of time utility. Through storage, goods are made available at the time needed and in the proper condition.

The major reasons why storage is necessary are as follows:

1. Many goods are produced seasonally and are consumed the year around—for example, most farm products.
2. Some goods are consumed seasonally and are produced regularly. In the case of items such as athletic equipment, Christmas toys, and woolen blankets, manufacturers find it economical to produce on a year-round basis to prepare for high seasonal volume.
3. Products may be stored as a hedge against expected price advances and as a protection against later scarcities. This situation prevails during periods of emergency such as labor strikes in transportation agencies and the conflict in Indochina.
4. Storage may be made necessary by purchases of quantities larger than those needed to meet immediate requirements because of the desire to obtain quantity discounts on purchases and lower transportation rates.
5. Many products require special storage facilities while being transported to market. Fresh fruits and vegetables, eggs, and butter, for example, need refrigerator cars or trucks. Other commodities require heated cars to avoid exposure to extreme cold during the winter months.
6. Between the time of production and consumption, certain commodities, such as meats, cheese, tobacco, and some liquors require "conditioning" to improve quality and make the products more suitable for consumption.
7. Goods are stored by producers to obtain more favorable market prices.

These seven reasons can be reduced to three classifications for the purposes of inventory management: (1) basic stock, (2) safety stock, and (3) promotional or seasonal stock.

Basic stock and the economic order cycle. The basic stock is the assortment required to serve the average level of demand. It forms the bulk of the inventory. Once the items in the basic stock are agreed upon, the problem is to determine the quantity to order and when to reorder. The object is to minimize the cost of acquisition plus the cost of carrying the inventory. Buying large lots may reduce the price and the cost of placing the order, shipping it, and receiving it, but it also increases all of the inventory carrying costs. This problem, one of the classics in industrial engineering and operations research, is known as the economic order quantity (EOQ) problem. Solving it requires estimates of costs described above, the distribution of expected usage rate, and the distribution of expected delivery time.

Safety stock. Safety stocks are intended to absorb unexpected variations in supply (e.g., wildcat strikes) or demand (e.g., a sudden surge of orders). They can be thought of as a buffer layer of inventory which is held at relatively constant levels throughout the year. The amount of safety stock held depends on: (1) the time required for an order to be processed and filled, (2) the extent of variation in normal demand, (3) skill in forecasting changes in normal demand, and (4) the service reliability or consistency expected of the system (which is often measured as the number of stock-outs per unit of time or the proportion of orders not filled from stock). If there is low variance in normal demand, if forecasting is successful, and if service consistency constraints are not great, safety stocks can be reduced to levels where real savings in carrying costs can be achieved. Safety stocks are the aspect of inventory that provides the greatest potential savings in inventory investment and can benefit most from man-computer interaction.

Seasonal and promotional stock. Fluctuations that arise when demand is subject to seasonal patterns, or supply sources shut down for vacations, can be made a part of the automated control mechanism *without* reflecting as a part of the *natural variation* in *basic stock* requirements. In seasonal consumer goods of almost all types, seasonal fluctuations are reflected in seasonal promotion programs. When this is true, seasonal inventory policies are more easily expressed in dollars rather than physical units, and buyers, product managers, and merchandise managers should be given the freedom to make those purchases that will generate the greatest promotional impact.

WAREHOUSE LOCATION

The problem of where to locate finished stocks requires consideration of: (1) geographic distribution of demand for each product; (2) distribution of order size at each location; (3) location of the production point or points for each product; (4) transportation facilities between production point and market; (5) freight rates charged; (6) level of service constraints placed on the system for each product; and (7) cost of maintaining a warehouse and the inventory in it.

Probably there will never be a situation when a firm is free to make decisions on all of these factors. The geographic configuration of demand is fixed by the location of customers, the task being to create time and place utility for them, given their locations. The level of service to be provided is largely determined by competitive conditions and, unless truck transport only is to be used, the firm has limited influence over the transportation facilities available to it.

Plant location considerations

At best, the firm is able to begin formulating a distribution system design with plant location. If locations are fixed, the problem can be stated simply as where to locate distribution centers for storing finished inventory and filling orders, as visualized in Figure 20–4. Plant location decisions are often based on proximity to raw materials rather than markets and on considerations of the fact that all plants may not produce the complete product line. Therefore, distribution centers must be located between plants and markets in such a way that carrying, handling, and shipping costs are minimized, given the constraints of the level of service to be provided.

The design is complicated by the production characteristics of plants, the demand and service characteristics of markets, and the freight-rate structure between plants and markets. Often, as shown in the figure, the optimum solution does not involve storing finished inventory either at each plant or in each market. It may be best to service large customers, such as chain stores, that buy large quantities of all products by direct shipments from production centers. If a marketing strategy calls for increasing the amount of time utility provided (that is, shortening delivery time), field stocks

FIGURE 20-4
Representation of the warehouse location problem

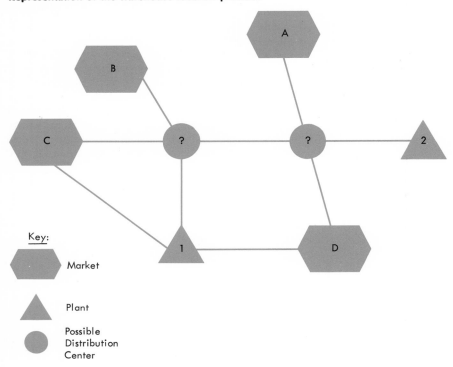

Key:

▬ Market

▲ Plant

● Possible
Distribution
Center

may be located closer to a market even though transportation costs increase. If the product is bulky, perishable, or has low value per unit of weight, transportation facilities and rates can weigh heavily in the decision.

Much attention has been given to analytical techniques for solving this complex problem during the past 20 years. Many multiproduct firms in household appliances, such as the Whirlpool Corporation, and in grocery products, such as H. J. Heinz Company, have used the techniques of simulation and mathematical programming to rearrange and reduce the number of locations where finished stocks are stored.

Warehouse operation considerations

The decision on location of a warehouse distribution center cannot be finalized without also giving consideration to the operation of the warehouse. Property values, wage rates, and local labor union requirements, for example, have a direct bearing on the costs of performing warehouse functions.

Distribution centers are concerned with the marketing processes of allocating and assorting, which involve the functions of *receiving* bulk quantities, *handling* them for *storage, picking* assortments to fill customer orders, and *shipping* or local delivery to customers. For some products, distribution centers may also perform the functions of product service and repair, complaint settlement, and technical service.

Methods of transportation must also be decided. If, for example, water transportation is to be used, minimizing unloading and delivery costs from the vessel must be considered. A rail spur is usually required, and truck or trailer loading and unloading facilities must be designed.

Estimation of warehouse size and space requirements must also be made before an investment decision is possible. The need for future expansion and the extent of seasonal fluctuations in the inventory to be held must be considered. The amount of warehouse investment is directly related to the number of square feet of space required. Only after all of these decisions are made can the task of site selection begin.

Warehouse alternatives. A manufacturer or middleman should not jump into investment in privately owned warehouses at the sites selected until he has considered the available alternatives. Available funds might return a greater profit if invested in ventures other than physical distribution facilities. The alternatives are: (1) shifting the storage function to customers by reducing the level of service provided, (2) having other channel members (suppliers or distributors) perform the storage functions and thus earn additional margin, (3) using private leased warehouses, (4) using public warehouses, and (5) some combination of these.

The objective is to find the warehouse system that will maximize the profit on total investment. A distributor might be selected to perform the storage function in one geographic area, while a private warehouse is constructed or purchased in another. Real estate developers may have leased warehouse space available at attractive rates, or arrangements might be made for the use of public warehouses, an important facilitating marketing institution which requires more detailed attention.

PUBLIC STORAGE FACILITIES

The role of public storage facilities as facilitating marketing institutions was introduced in Chapters 11 and 14. There are six main types:

1. General merchandise warehouses, in which a wide variety of goods is stored for manufacturers and others, usually for short periods of time until delivery to middlemen and industrial buyers.
2. Bonded warehouses, a specialized form of the general merchandise warehouse used for products on which a tax must be paid before the goods are released —e.g., whiskey, some imported goods.
3. Special commodity warehouses for the storage of agricultural commodities such as cotton or tobacco.
4. Household goods and furniture warehouses for the storage of personal property.
5. Field or custodian warehouses, located on the premises of the owner but are controlled by an authorized custodian who issues warehouse receipts which make the products collateral for loans.
6. Cold-storage or refrigerated warehouses, which are used for the storage of perishables.

Developments in public warehousing

Significant developments in public warehousing are taking place. These include: (1) more accessible locations, (2) larger space to accommodate containerized shipments, (3) the merger or formation of associations of public warehouses in a number of cities, (4) automated handling equipment, and (5) the addition of invoicing and local delivery services. Thus a public warehouse company can now serve as the complete "distribution center" for a seller. To do so it must be prepared to perform four specialized services: (1) stock spotting, (2) complete-line assortment, (3) break bulk, and (4) in-transit mixing.[1]

Stock spotting. The idea behind stock spotting is to locate finished stock near large markets or a single large customer rather than at production plants. Delivery time and transportation costs are reduced when consolidated carload shipments are made to public warehouses located near key customers. The public warehouse must then fill the customer's orders upon receipt and make local delivery.

Complete-line assortment. The distinction between stock spotting and complete-line assortment is one of degree. If the seller ships a broad line to the public warehouse and the warehouse services not just key customers but the entire market area, it is performing complete-line assortment. In this case, the warehouse must be equipped to pick customized assortments of products for each order as well as make local delivery. Complete-line assortment services are essentially all those performed by a company distribution center.

Break bulk. Break bulk service is for local delivery rather than storage. A manufacturer can combine orders for a number of different customers located in a market area into a single carload shipment and send the pooled shipment to a public warehouse, where individual orders are separated and delivered. In this way the seller gains the advantage of consolidated freight rates and consolidated control over local deliveries.

In-transit mixing. In-transit mixing is a long-haul version of break bulk which grows out of special transportation tariffs that permit stopovers for processing or mixing of carload quantities between production points and market without loss of the through carload freight rate. In-transit mixing usually involves shipments from more than one plant to a central public warehouse that serves as a mixing point. The warehouseman receives the carload lots of the single products, mixes them into combined carload lots, and ships them to specific markets or customers. In order to ship correct assortments, the warehouse usually gains some storage business in the process.

Regulation of storage facilities

Storage facilities are regulated through state and federal laws which attempt to protect consumers from unscrupulous operators as well as to guarantee the integrity of warehouse receipts. Two major regulatory measures are discussed here.

The United States Warehouse Act of 1916 provides for the licensing and bonding of public warehouses storing certain agricultural commodities under conditions intended to establish the integrity of warehouse receipts and make them generally acceptable as security for loans. The act is designed to establish a uniform system of warehousing certain farm products (i.e., cotton, grain, wool, and tobacco), to facilitate their financing while in storage through warehouse receipts of acceptable quality, and to effect reductions in marketing costs. It should be made clear, however, that no compulsion is involved. The act simply provides for federal supervision through the U.S. Department of Agriculture of warehousing practices on a voluntary basis.

---

[1] The discussion of these services is based on D. J. Bowersox, E. W. Smykay, and B. J. LaLonde, *Physical Distribution Management* (New York: Macmillan Co., 1968), pp. 265–67.

The Uniform Commercial Code (see Chapter 24) sets forth the fundamental law relating to public warehousing. It applies to warehousemen of all types and establishes their obligations as the custodians of the property of the public. The act increases the value of warehouse receipts as evidence of ownership to those storing goods and as collateral for loans. Stored goods are not subject to attachment.

Storage costs

Accurate information on the total cost of performing the storage function is not available. To prepare even a reasonably accurate estimate would be extremely difficult, since it would have to cover so many categories of cost—including physical facilities, interest on investment in stored products, costs for quality deterioration, shrinkage or fashion changes, and risk of price change during the storage period. Further, the emphasis should be on the *total cost* of physical distribution rather than on the cost of storage alone. The experience of the Pillsbury Company is illustrative. At one time, this company had

. . . 125 small warehouses under the control of 33 branch sales offices that also performed accounting and order processing functions. . . .

Now its 33 branch offices have grown to 52 regional offices concentrating on sales. Orders and accounting are all handled by a huge computer center in Minneapolis. And instead of having 125 little warehouses, Pillsbury has 13 big ones at key transportation centers. Interestingly, the company did not shift its transportation methods in this change; it's still mainly a rail shipper.

Pillsbury maintains it would be impossible to come up with meaningful numbers on how much money has been saved, because while it was revamping its distribution it was also adding products. Nevertheless, it says its service is improved and its business has grown, largely because it has kept pace with the changing needs of food wholesalers and grocery chains.[2]

Storage cost reductions may be a result of changing from one type of storage to another. A steel company discovered that savings were possible by using low-cost outdoor storage, contrary to industry practice. Some manufacturers and wholesalers with small stocks at some points have switched from private to public warehouses, with savings; some with large stocks have achieved lower costs by moving from public to private facilities. Continuous evaluation of the storage problem facing each businessman is necessary if the lowest cost is to be achieved.

TRANSPORTATION FACILITIES

Transportation's job is to move goods from points of production and sale to points of consumption in the quantities required, at the times needed, and at a reasonable cost. The transportation system adds time and place utilities to the goods handled and thus increases their economic value. To achieve these goals, transportation facilities must be adequate, the service regular and dependable, and the costs equitable in the light of the facilities and service provided.

The transportation function pervades the marketing system. The necessity of moving equipment, raw materials, and operating supplies to the manufacturer, of finished goods to middlemen, and of their subsequent movement to other middlemen and to consumers indicates the scope of transportation in the economy. The movement of agricultural products to markets is also essential.

---

[2] "The Next Place for Paring Costs," *Business Week,* May 1, 1965, pp. 134, 136.

TABLE 20–2
Volume of intercity freight traffic, by type of transportation: Selected years, 1930 to 1969 (millions of ton-miles)

	1930	1940	1950	1960	1969 (preliminary)
Total traffic volume	524,350	651,204	1,094,160	1,329,995	1,898,200
Railroads (electric, express, and mail)					
Volume	389,648	411,813	628,463	594,855	780,000
Percent of total	74.30	63.24	57.44	44.73	41.09
Motor vehicles (private, contract, and common intercity carriers but not all local delivery)					
Volume	20,345	62,043	172,860	285,483	404,000
Percent of total	3.90	9.53	15.80	21.46	21.28
Inland waterways (Great Lakes and Alaska for all; Hawaii beginning 1960)					
Volume	86,453	118,057	163,344	220,253	300,000
Percent of total	16.50	18.13	14.93	16.56	15.80
Oil pipelines (only regulated ones)					
Volume	27,900	59,277	129,175	228,626	411,000
Percent of total	5.30	9.10	11.81	17.19	21.65
Air (domestic revenue service only— express, mail, and baggage)					
Volume	4	14	318	778	3,200
Percent of total	0.001	0.002	0.029	0.058	0.169

Source: U.S. Bureau of the Census, Statistical Abstract of the United States, 1971 (Washington, D.C.: Government Printing Office, 1971), p. 525.

To fulfill these obligations, a variety of transportation facilities has been developed in the United States. The major ones include railroads, boats and barges on inland waterways (the Great Lakes, rivers and canals), trucks, pipelines, airplanes, and express facilities.

The relative importance of these facilities is indicated by the distribution of commercial traffic in the United States during recent decades, as shown in Table 20–2. The table reveals several significant facts:

1. Railroads have increased their ton-miles and still carry nearly twice the freight tonnage of trucks, despite their loss in relative position.
2. Pipelines have moved into second place and are likely to maintain it.
3. The ton-miles of freight carried on inland waterways have increased and their relative importance has remained about the same.
4. Despite a tremendous growth rate, air freight still handles a small fraction of the commercial traffic in this country.

Railroads

Railroads move 41 percent of all the ton-miles of freight in the United States. For each of the several modes of transportation—rail, truck, water, pipeline, and air—there is an area in which it has an inherent natural advantage. For the railroads, it is their ability to handle heavy bulk products and to interchange cars with other roads without generating additional paperwork for the shipper.

Marketing: Principles and methods

Raw natural materials make up over 70 percent of the revenue freight tonnage originated by the railroads, while manufactured products comprise less than 30 percent. The average railroad haul is about 500 miles and costs less than 1.4 cents per ton-mile. Low-grade freight (ore, coal, timber) goes at lower rates and produces a smaller proportionate revenue than high-grade freight.

Improved technology in assembling trains and controlling traffic has resulted in increasingly faster and longer trains. However, new special services for shippers have been the main reason railroads have been able to maintain a stable position as the heart of the transportation system. Some of these special services are discussed below.

Pool cars. Most rail tariffs specify rates for each commodity or class of product. Pool cars permit a single shipper to mix the products in a car and ship at carload rates if the car is loaded at a single point of shipment. The receiver must arrange for local delivery. In some cities, operators of several retail stores have banded together to form a shippers' association which sponsors a periodic (some as often as daily) pooled car to their city from a major shipping point.

A variation of this practice is for a number of shippers to "make up a car" and have it moved to a designated location at carload rates. This may be done by one or more of the shippers but is commonly the work of a "freight forwarder," who is paid for his service by collecting the difference between less-than-carload and carload rates. Freight forwarders are themselves facilitating marketing institutions which are also regulated by the Interstate Commerce Commission. In recent years they have assumed more importance in air freight, but in the aggregate, they have enjoyed little growth since 1950.

Milling in transit. A tariff provision similar to that which permits in-transit mixing of products is milling in transit. Under this arrangement, which is designed to equalize the advantage of competing industrial locations, wheat may be dispatched to a certain destination, unloaded and ground into flour at a mill en route, and moved on to market at the through rate applicable from point of origin to destination. Since this rate is less than the rates on the wheat to the mill and on the flour from the mill to the market, the advantage is clear. Similar privileges are granted on many other commodities, such as fabrication in transit on steel.

Diversion in transit. Another privilege extended by railroads to shippers of carload lots is diversion in transit. This permits shippers to move goods in the general direction of the market without specifying their exact destination, and later, at so-called "diversion points," to designate the particular city to which they will be sent. A nominal charge is made for this reconsignment privilege, but the shipper pays only the through rate to the actual destination. To illustrate: Sunkist Growers, Inc., of California may ship 10 carloads of oranges to Chicago. During the movement of the oranges eastward, the shipper may find that St. Louis offers the best market for them at that time. Consequently, when the oranges reach Omaha—a diversion point—they are rerouted to St. Louis. Fresh fruits and vegetables, grain, cotton, and other products are often diverted in this manner.

The unitized train. Originally, the unitized train consisted of 100 or more cars carrying coal on a shuttle basis between mines and a utility company. The use of modern loading and unloading facilities, full-time operation of the train, and the avoidance of switching at yards allows excellent service at substantial cost savings. In recent years unitized trains have been used for transporting grain, iron ore, and other commodities, and their use continues to grow.

"Piggyback" service. Also known as trailer-on-flat-car service (TOFC), piggyback refers to the hauling of loaded truck trailers over railroad lines on specially designed flatcars. Combining greater speed with flexibility, piggyback has shown a tremendous growth in recent years. In 1965 piggybacking reached the million-car mark for the first time, continuing a succession of annual highs since statistics were first compiled in 1955. Shippers fighting higher transportation costs have demonstrated increasing interest because it affords substantial savings in freight handling. Since it costs less per mile to transport a trailer on a flatcar than over the road, lower rates can be charged. Further advantages are reduction of damage while enroute and decrease in delivery time. Railroads have developed various piggyback plans to provide services demanded by shippers. These plans permit the use of trailers owned by the railroad, a freight forwarder, a common carrier, or the shipper. In most cases, the entire shipment can be made on a single bill of lading.

Piggyback service is also available on waterways and seaways. Under this arrangement, loaded trailers or vans are moved by ship between designated points, again at important savings in transportation costs. This service was probably used first in moving freight between East Coast and Gulf of Mexico ports. The completion of the St. Lawrence Seaway gave new impetus to this service, which allows old carload-handling methods to be replaced with more efficient ones.

Containerization. Piggyback service has led to the development of a completely new concept, "containerization," which is expanding into all modes of transportation. The concept refers to the design and use of filled van or trailer-size containers (or smaller ones) which may be moved interchangeably between various types of carriers without breaking bulk. For example, a shipment may be moved from truck to rail or from truck to ship, thus reducing handling charges, damage, and losses from pilferage, as well as speeding up the movement of shipments. To increase the speed of delivery further, some railroads are running special trains devoted entirely to containerized freight. Even air freight forwarders are finding containerization to be an efficient method of handling cargo.

The greatest use of containers has been in ocean freight. Ships and port facilities have been constructed exclusively to handle containerized cargo. The standard container is a reinforced aluminum box 8 feet square and 10 or 20 feet long. The shipper seals the container, and it remains sealed until it reaches the consignee. The products in the container may be mixed in any way desired. The costs for the shipper are 10 to 20 percent under those for break bulk shipment. A new concept in container ships is to load about 24 containers in a barge which is loaded and unloaded as a unit from the ship to the water. The ship is then free to load other barges and move back out to sea.

Inland waterways

The movement of raw materials, supplies, and manufactured goods to market over inland waterways is of considerable importance in this country. By means of many thousands of cargo ships, barges, and miscellaneous types of vessels, goods are transported over the 29,000 miles of waterways maintained at public expense and considered as "public highways," open to anyone. This situation is in sharp contrast to railway transportation, where roadbeds are maintained by private enterprise and use is restricted.

The inland waterways of the United States, which form a system unmatched by any other country, are commonly grouped into the five major systems indicated by Figure 20–5: (1) the Great Lakes system, (2) the Mississippi River system, (3) Atlantic

FIGURE 20–5
Inland waterways of the United States

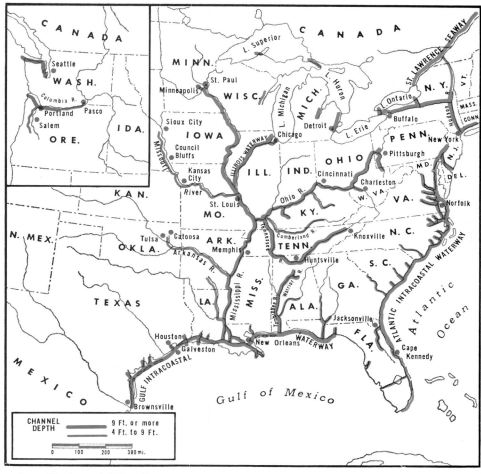

Source: *Time,* January 4, 1963, p. 63.

Coast rivers, (4) Gulf Coast rivers, and (5) Pacific Coast rivers. The Great Lakes and Mississippi River systems are most important, carrying about 80 percent of the total ton-miles. The bulk of this traffic is raw materials—40 percent of all domestic intercity petroleum, 68 percent of coal, 86 percent of grain, and 75 percent of all chemicals.[3]

The major advantage of water transportation is its low cost. When compared with rail shipment, the saving is often substantial. The average length of a water haul is about the same as that for rail (just under 500 miles), but the rate is much less—about 0.4 cents per ton-mile, one third that for rail. Against the economy factor, however,

---

[3] "Now: Traffic Jams on U.S. Rivers," *U.S. News & World Report,* September 20, 1971, p. 66.

must be weighed the disadvantages of slowness, the seasonal character of the service, the risk of delay caused by drought or floods, the unavailability of service in many areas of the country, and the lower liability for loss and damage as compared with the railroads.

Mark Twain once mistakenly remarked that "Mississippi steamboating was born about 1812; at the end of 30 years it had grown to mighty proportions; and in less than 30 more it was dead. A strangely short life for so majestic a creature."[4] Although the type of transport vehicle has changed, transportation on the Mississippi and other rivers is far from dead. In fact, it is likely that the ton-miles of freight moved over our inland waterways will continue to increase.

Motor transportation

That motor transportation, also known as "highway transportation," has gained in importance with the development of improved vehicles and the expansion of the highway system of the country is evident from the data of Table 20–2. Truck trailers become larger and more numerous each year. Motor transport is characterized by the ability to move small shipments economically, to move shipments of varying sizes short distances, and to deliver shipments to any point in the country that is served by roads and highways.

While the average cost of motor transport is over 7 cents per ton-mile, the total cost for short hauls is lower than on the railroads. For longer hauls, it is difficult to forecast when rail transport will be less costly than motor transport. Rate-making mechanisms and rate structures for all carriers are complex.

Motor carriers of goods for the market are commonly classified into three types: common, contract (also known as "for-hire"), and private carriers. *Common carriers* serve the public at large, moving goods of all types to any part of the country. In practice, however, certain carriers restrict their operations to the handling of one line of goods or closely related lines. *Contract carriers* enter into rather formal arrangements to transport goods for selected customers, usually for definite periods of time. *Private carriers,* also known as "exempt" carriers, are operated by business firms and individuals for the transportation of their own goods.

The truck is used for the transportation of nearly all kinds of goods, particularly manufactured products such as textiles, machinery, rubber, and plastic products. Trucks dominate in the movement of household goods, small packages, and shipments under 50,000 pounds.[5]

Pipelines

In terms of ton-miles, pipelines represent the second most important mode of transportation in the United States. This is an amazing record given the limited number of pipelines and the limited kinds of freight they can handle—any product that can be put in a fluid state. While most pipelines are used to transport liquid petroleum products, other products shipped by this method include natural gas, chemicals, coal, minerals, sulphite pulp, asphalt, wood chips, and as many as 30 other nonliquid products.

---

[4] As quoted in "Transportation: New Life on the River," *Time,* January 4, 1963, p. 62.

[5] U.S. Bureau of the Census, *Statistical Abstract of the United States, 1971* (Washington, D.C.: Government Printing Office, 1971), p. 548.

Pipelines are an extremely economical mode of transport, the average cost being about 0.3 cents per ton-mile. Most pipelines are owned by or affiliated with major oil companies or gas transmission companies. When the services of these lines are sold to others, the rates are regulated by government. Future growth of pipeline transport should be at least as rapid as the growth in pipeline mileage. In 1950, this figure was 129 thousand miles; in 1960, 152 thousand miles; and in 1969, 171 thousand miles.[6]

Air transport

In recent years significant growth has taken place in the air transportation of freight, although total air freight volume is still small as compared with movement by railroads, waterways, motor trucks, and pipelines, comprising less than 1 percent of the total transportation of goods in the United States. For some products, however, it is of considerable significance. Women's wearing apparel, machinery and machinery parts, drugs, printed matter, cut flowers, fresh seafood, and early-season perishable foods are among the products shipped by air.

The primary advantage of air shipment, of course, is the speed with which the traffic moves between air terminals. Some of this advantage, however, may be lost by delays at terminals and during local delivery. The chief disadvantage of air freight has been its high cost. All-cargo jets such as the Boeing 707 permit a cost of about 13 cents per ton-mile, and it is hoped that the Boeing 747 can cut that to about 10 cents.[7] Until such jumbo jets are more common in cargo applications, the buyer of air transportation service must also consider restrictions on the size and shape of shipments as a possible limitation.

Express

Perhaps the weakest links in the U.S. transportation network are the facilities available to ship a 75-pound package. Discounting independent mail services, which concentrate on deliveries of packages weighing under one pound, a shipper has four or fewer choices for small shipments: independent freight forwarders, REA Express, United Parcel Service, and the U.S. Postal Service parcel post.

Freight forwarders usually specialize in either surface or air express, since the two are regulated by different federal agencies (ICC and CAB, respectively). They primarily serve commercial sellers with regular needs for shipping less-than-truckload lots and also provide local delivery service. The use of surface freight forwarders has not grown in recent decades.

REA Express is the major small-shipment freight forwarder in the United States. It began as a joint venture of the railroads, which carried its cars on every passenger train. As passenger trains declined, so did REA service. The railroads sold the company in 1969, and it has become truly intermodal. Over half of its shipments move over highways, about 20 percent by rail piggyback, and 25 percent by the airlines. REA has great flexibility to handle any size shipment. It provides local pickup and delivery and caters to personal shipments as well as commercial ones. As of 1970, however, the company was not profitable.

---

[6] Ibid., p. 550.

[7] "Air Transportation Technology," *Handling and Shipping,* 10 (January 1969), p. 53.

United Parcel Service, a well-established local delivery service for retailers, has gone into the long-haul express business in 28 states where it operates locally. UPS uses its own fleet for local pickup and delivery, and long-distance hauls are by truck or the airlines—much like REA. The company is trying to develop an initial market with its existing apparel and textile customers. No packages over 50 pounds are accepted, making UPS service more nearly competitive with parcel post, which has a 70-pound weight limitation.

Although express and parcel post are competitive, express shipments are not subject to the same limitations concerning size, weight and perishability that are placed on users of the parcel post system by the U.S. Postal Service. Consequently, although more favorable rates on shipments are available via parcel post on short distances, this advantage is offset to some extent by limitations on acceptable shipments.

Adoption of the federal parcel post system in 1912 greatly stimulated the shipment of goods by mail and brought about large increases in the sales volume of mail-order companies. Establishment of the system was also welcomed by many other organizations as well, who took advantage of the opportunity to ship goods at the reasonable rates provided. In 1970, revenues from this class of mail were $680 million.[8]

Transportation rates

Although it is outside the scope of this book to present detailed information on freight classifications and rates, reasons why transportation rates vary among different products and among different points should be understood if one is to appreciate why transportation costs constitute such a substantial part of the overall costs of marketing.

Factors determining rates among different commodities. The chief factors influencing the rates charged for transporting different commodities are as follows:

1. The loading characteristics of the article. Wide differences exist, for example, among such commodities as wheat, lumber, canned goods, and pharmaceuticals.
2. The risk of loss and damage. Note the difference in the nature of the risk for cement, perishables, dynamite, and liquors.
3. The amount of liability assumed by the carrier. Is this liability partial or complete?
4. The volume in which the traffic moves. When volume is large, better organization of operation and handling methods is possible.
5. The regularity with which the traffic moves. Generally speaking, the more regular the movement, the greater the economy.
6. The type of equipment required. Goods requiring refrigerator cars are more expensive to transport than those needing only boxcars or flatcars.
7. The special services required. Livestock, fruits and vegetables, and meat products, for example, need various special services to insure proper care during transit.[9]

Factors determining rates among different points. Transportation rates vary among particular places for these major reasons:

1. The distance involved. Generally speaking, the longer the haul, the greater the cost of the service provided, although these costs do not increase proportionately.

---

[8] *Statistical Abstract of the United States, 1971,* p. 480.

[9] D. P. Locklin, *Economics of Transportation* (6th ed.; Homewood, Ill.: Richard D. Irwin, Inc., 1966), pp. 410–17.

Marketing: Principles and methods

2. The differences in operating conditions along the route of travel. Heavy grades, snow removal, and washouts caused by heavy rains are examples of such differences.
3. The number of railroad lines over which the goods are carried. Switching and loading problems—the latter for less-than-carload shipments—all affect the rates charged.
4. The density and balance of traffic. Broadly speaking, the denser the traffic, the lower the rate. Moreover, the extent to which return business is available and the movement of empty cars in one direction which is necessary are considerations of importance.
5. Empty-car movement. Since the unbalanced condition of the traffic necessitates the hauling of empty cars, rates are lower in the direction of the empty-car movement.[10]

Although these factors serve to explain the variations in rates for transporting different commodities, they do not include important demand factors related to what the traffic will bear. These are the value of the commodity, its general nature (whether it is a raw material or a finished good), the use to which it will be put, and the demand for service reflected by the conditions prevailing within a given industry.

The determination of equitable transportation rates for various commodities, particularly those in interstate commerce, is a complicated process. There are three basic types of rates: (1) class, (2) commodity, and (3) exception. All three are quoted in carload or truckload and less-than-carload (LCL) or less-than-truckload (LTL) quantities. Minimum charges are also specified. Class rates are those covering manufactured goods classified into over 10,000 different groups. Commodity rates cover raw materials and agricultural products. Exception rates are established to cover special services or to meet intermodal competition.

While the topic is widely debated, it is not likely that the structure of transportation rates will be simplified in the near future. Surface and water transportation is currently regulated by the Interstate Commerce Commission, a regulatory agency which is now a part of the Department of Transportation. The Commission has come under repeated attack in recent years for its inability to develop a rational and comprehensive national transportation policy, but positive progress in this direction is difficult to achieve.

SUMMARY

The operations through which time and place utility are created by a channel for physical distribution of goods are an integral part of the total marketing system. From the viewpoint of society or the firm, the objective is to design a distribution system that will provide high levels of time and place utility for customers at the lowest possible cost.

The performance of a distribution system may be measured by an objective function of minimization of the total cost of the system under the constraint of a specified level of customer service. In addition to the costs associated with poor service, those which must be considered in the solution to this problem are associated with the physical distribution subfunctions: shipping, storing, handling, information,

---

[10] Ibid., pp. 435–38. Some special rate considerations are discussed on pp. 438–41 of this source.

and physical distribution management. Many cost trade-offs are possible between, as well as within, each of these activities.

The facilitating institutions for storage and transportation of goods within the marketing system were considered in detail.

REVIEW AND DISCUSSION QUESTIONS

1. How do you account for the increasing attention being given to physical distribution by marketers?
2. If a firm were able to reduce inventory levels by 10 percent, what costs would you investigate to determine how total costs had changed?
3. Explain why a company's controller, factory manager, and marketing manager might have frequent conflicts over problems of physical distribution. Give examples.
4. What are the costs connected with the information required to run an efficient physical distribution system? Could one trade off information costs with carrying costs? How?
5. What types of stock should a computerized purchasing system never be permitted to reorder?
6. Specifically, what are the ways in which a computerized inventory management system should be able to reduce the average level of inventories?
7. From outside reading, write a short paper explaining the approach for calculating economic order quantities.
8. What is meant by the "reliability" of a service policy?
9. In a distribution system from a single existing plant, what factors must be considered in determining where to locate distribution centers?
10. What are the advantages and disadvantages of public warehouses as compared with privately owned warehouses?
11. Visit the office of a local intercity motor cargo company and obtain a few examples of truck tariff schedules.
12. Explain the necessity of storage in our economic system and distinguish among the main types of storage facilities in this country.
13. Explain briefly the significant changes in the handling of intercity freight traffic by the various transportation agencies since 1940.
14. Summarize the relative advantages and disadvantages of moving products by rail and by motor transportation.
15. Through supplementary reading, prepare a brief report summarizing the latest developments in water transportation and in pipeline transportation of nonpetroleum products.

SUPPLEMENTARY READINGS

Bowersox, D. J.; Smykay, E. W.; and La Londe, B. J. *Physical Distribution Management.* New York: Macmillan Co., 1968. An excellent and up-to-date text covering all aspects of the logistics problems of the firm.

Bowersox, D. J. Smykay, E. W.; and La Londe, B. J. *Readings in Physical Distribution Management.* New York: Macmillan Co., 1969. A collection of 36 important articles covering

Marketing: Principles and methods

all aspects of physical distribution which is designed to expand on the text materials in the previous reference.

Constantin, J. A. *Principles of Logistics Management.* New York: Appleton-Century-Crofts, 1966. Well-described by its subtitle, a "Functional Analysis of Physical Distribution Systems," the book covers transportation, storage, materials handling, order processing, and related aspects of such systems.

Heskett, J. L.; Ivie, R. M.; and Glaskowsky, N. A. *Business Logistics.* New York: Ronald Press Co., 1964. A comprehensive text in the field of physical distribution.

Locklin, D. P. *Economics of Transportation.* 7th ed. Homewood, Ill.: Richard D. Irwin, Inc., 1972. Covering the whole field of transportation, this standard textbook affords an excellent reference.

Magee, J. F. *Industrial Logistics.* New York: McGraw-Hill Book Co., 1968. An introduction to the concepts and elements of a logistic system and the techniques of analysis that can be helpful in the design and management of such a system.

Taff, C. A. *Management of Traffic and Physical Distribution.* 5th ed. Homewood, Ill.: Richard D. Irwin, Inc., 1972. A leading text in transportation and traffic management.

21 *Promotional systems and personal selling*

Advertising and personal selling are blamed for many of the ills of society. The man of the cloth laments that booze, sex, tobacco, and material greediness keep man from spiritual salvation; the devil called promotion is responsible. Economists for years virtually ignored promotion by assuming it away. Confronted by its persistence, they claimed it reflected imperfect or monopolistic competition. More recently, promotion has been accused of misdirecting resource allocation from the "natural" public sector of education, health care facilities, and so forth into the private sector of cars, color television, and other "contrived" wants.[1] Governmental agencies and spokesmen have accused promoters of inaccuracy and misrepresentation and have begun to supervise claims of performance and superiority and to restrain advertisers.[2] Consumers crotchety about practices in retail selling and advertising have found spokesmen in their behalf.[3]

In response to these criticisms, company executives and media people have become more defensive about their promotional practices. They have also reemphasized, with considerable fervor, the role of promotion in a marketplace economy.[4]

In this setting, in which there is more heat than light, we will examine the *basics* of promotional systems. This chapter will consider (1) the composition of promotional systems and their relationship to the communication process; (2) the relationship of promotion to the process of buyer decision making; (3) the major promotional system decisions that must be made within organizations; and (4) the role of personal selling both in the economic system and as a part of an organization's promotional system.

---

[1] J. K. Galbraith, *The Affluent Society,* (Boston: Houghton Mifflin Company, 1958).

[2] For current commentary on enforcements, proposed new regulations and actions, see the weekly publication, *Advertising Age.* For example, the July 19, 1971, issue reported on over six enforcement situations.

[3] The foremost are probably Ralph Nader and Colston Warne, president of Consumers Union.

[4] For example, see P. C. Harper, Jr., "A Fireside Chat with Commissioner X," address to the Advertising Lodge of B'nai Brith, Freedom House, New York City, September 22, 1971.

Promotion is a subset of communication; that is, it is only one facet of communication, specifically that part with the objective of gaining and retaining acceptance by others of the views, products, or services of the originator of the message. Promotion, of course, is not limited to marketing. It is used by lawyers, ministers, policemen, politicians, and virtually every individual.

As a topic of study, promotion has received considerable attention in many fields, from both academicians and practitioners. It has been considered under such titles as attitude change, persuasion, propaganda analysis, promotion, advertising research, and communication.[5] You may have studied some aspects of promotion in psychology, sociology, social psychology, political science, communication, or even English or rhetoric, and you have surely been a practitioner of persuasion virtually from the day you were born.

Components of promotion

The concern in this book is with the promotional systems of business and other types of organizations. Promotion in business is typically found under four labels: personal selling, advertising, sales promotion, and publicity. In addition, consumer product labels and containers, which were discussed in Chapter 18, also are promotion agents. Definitions of the four terms are:

1. Personal selling is the oral presentation in conversations with one or more prospective purchasers for the purpose of making sales.
2. Advertising is any paid form of nonpersonal presentation and promotion of ideas, goods, or services by an identified sponsor.
3. Sales promotion includes those marketing activities other than personal selling, advertising, and publicity that stimulate consumer purchasing and dealer effectiveness. They include point-of-purchase displays, shows and exhibits, demonstrations, and other nonrecurrent selling efforts.
4. Publicity is nonpersonal stimulation of demand for a product, service, or business unit that is obtained by planting commercially significant news about it in a published medium or obtaining favorable presentation of it through other media. It is not paid for by the sponsor.[6]

A promotional system

The activities defined above are effectively integrated in many organizations into a promotional system, the objective of which is to *inform and persuade*.[7] Such a

---

[5] A. Shuchman and M. Perry, "Self-Confidence and Persuasibility in Marketing: A Reappraisal," *Journal of Marketing Research,* 6 (May 1969), pp. 146–55; C. I. Hovland and I. L. Janis, (eds.), *Personality and Persuasibility* (New Haven, Conn.: Yale University Press, 1959); D. K. Berlo, *The Process of Communication* (New York: Holt, Rinehart & Winston, Inc., 1960); and C. I. Hovland, I. L. Janis, and H. H. Kelley, *Communication and Persuasion Effects of Mass Communication* (Urbana, Ill.: University of Illinois Press, 1954).

[6] *Marketing Definitions: A Glossary of Marketing Terms,* Committee on Definitions of the American Marketing Association, R. S. Alexander, Chairman (Chicago: American Marketing Association, 1960).

[7] Textbooks devoted to the overall promotional area are relatively new. The first one in recent times was E. L. Brink and W. T. Kelley, *The Management of Promotion* (Englewood Cliffs, N.J.: Prentice-Hall, Inc., 1963). Also see J. F. Engel, H. G. Wales, and M. R. Warshaw, *Promotional Strategy* (Rev. ed.; Homewood, Ill.: Richard D. Irwin, Inc., 1971); R. Tillman and C. A. Kirkpatrick, *Promotion: Persuasive Communication in Marketing* (Homewood, Ill.: Richard D. Irwin, Inc., 1968); and J. B. Kernan, W. P. Dommermuth, and M. S. Sommers, *Promotion: An Introductory Analysis* (New York: McGraw-Hill Book Co., 1970).

system, however, is not particularly easy to implement and maintain even in large organizations with specialists in sales force management, advertising, sales promotion, and public relations.[8] Each specialist is inclined to maintain that his activity is more effective than the others and therefore should receive more of the total dollars budgeted for promotion. These experts also often are personally competing for the opportunity to advance to marketing manager. This competition tends to increase the difficulty of maintaining an integrated promotional system.

Effective promotional system integration is dependent on a well-defined set of overall corporate or organization goals and objectives plus a set of promotional objectives. The goals and objectives serve as a framework in which to make promotional decisions, as discussed in more detail below.[9]

Promotional activities are formally integrated in organizations in a variety of ways. A common arrangement in a limited-line manufacturing company is to integrate them through a manager of marketing to whom each activity manager (advertising, sales, public relations, and promotion) is responsible. Companies with numerous products frequently coordinate promotion activities at individual product levels by making product managers responsible for the total promotional programs of their products. In large retail outlets, buyers frequently coordinate the available promotional efforts (as well as buying and other activities), while in smaller retail stores, the store manager controls all of these activities.

Promotion by both sellers and buyers

Because promotional activity in business situations is largely instigated by sellers, most of the discussion below will be directed to sellers' promotion programs. However, buyers—industrial customers, middlemen, and final consumers—also instigate and engage in promotion when they attempt to communicate their wants to sellers and to gain favorable terms on prices, qualities, delivery dates, and so forth. A city or school district, for example, will advertise for bids on products and services it seeks to buy. Individual consumers will often get prices from various car dealers and use an assortment of information to negotiate (promote) prices and other terms. Thus both sellers and buyers utilize promotion as a subset of communication.

THE COMMUNICATION PROCESS

To communicate is to convey a sense of commonness. The communicator shares an idea, attitude, or some other kind of information with a receiver through verbal or nonverbal symbols. For the communications process to be completed, what is common must come to the attention of the receiver.

A communication has four essential ingredients: a message, a message vehicle (medium), a sender, and a receiver. The basic problem of communication is that the prospective receiver may not receive or understand the message as intended because of the nature of the message, the message vehicle, or the communication environment. The sender typically has many message and media alternatives available to him, and he is confronted with a variety of environments. For example, if a man wants

---

[8] For an illustration of how Continental Airlines failed to coordinate its advertisements with its sales personnel, see "Deceptive Airline Ad," *Advertising Age,* August 23, 1971, p. 8.

[9] For a detailed view of one company's promotional mix, see "How Nabisco Keeps Its Cookie Crown," *Business Week,* May 10, 1969, pp. 64–66.

Marketing: Principles and methods

to let a woman know he loves her, how many messages and media are there that will transmit this feeling?

Selection of messages and media

The message forms and media that are selected by the sender will be conditioned by the environment as well as by the sender's knowledge of the prospective receiver. The sender seeks to encode (express) his thoughts in a message and send it in such a way that the prospective receiver will receive it, will decode (decipher) the intended meaning of the message, and will respond to it in the manner intended by the sender.[10]

The environment makes a lot of difference in the perception of messages. The noise of an airplane may drown out an audio message, or a competitor's argument may lead the receiver to forget or reject the sender's messages. These disruptive influences from the environment are commonly referred to as the *noise* in the communication process.

FIGURE 21–1

How experience overlap aids communication

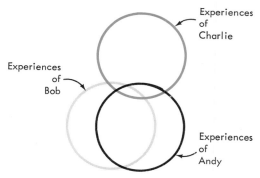

The familiarity with or knowledge of the receiver that the sender has is of fundamental importance. The more the sender and the receiver have in common, the less difficult it is to communicate. In the communication between three individuals illustrated in Figure 21–1, Andy and Bob will be able to communicate much more easily with one another than with Charlie. Similar goals, objectives, and symbolic understandings help the communication process; for example, people with a common language (code) can communicate more readily than those with different languages.

Common experiences also help bring understanding to words and actions, because most of these relate to what we have learned, through experience or otherwise. "Expensive theater tickets," for example, connotes different things to people of different income and geographical backgrounds. A low-income farmer in rural America is accustomed to movie theaters, and to him expensive tickets mean those over $2.50. A New York banker familiar with prices for live theater will think of expensive tickets

---

[10] W. Schramm, "How Communication Works," in Schramm, (ed.), *The Process and Effects of Mass Communication* (Urbana, Ill.: University of Illinois Press, 1960), p. 13.

as over $15. The word "stoned" provides another type of illustration. To most parents who were teen-agers in the 1940s and the 1950s, stoned means drunk (very drunk) from consumption of liquor. To most college students of the 1970s, it means affected by dangerous drugs.

Communication and promotion

Salesmen who are more like their prospective customers in age, income, outlook, and behavior will in general realize greater selling success than those who are far different from their customers. In the communication process, we do not all perceive all things the same.[11] We may have a high degree of agreement on a few objects (e.g., trees, chalk, and pencils), but mention of such objects as the Catholic Church, unwed mothers or fathers or the Republican Party evokes varying responses.

The communication process is depicted in Figure 21–2. The sender encodes his thoughts into a message and selects the appropriate medium for transmitting it in view of his knowledge of the receiver, the environment, and the noise therein. The receiver decodes (deciphers) the meaning of the message if it comes to his attention and may in turn encode and return a message to the sender.

FIGURE 21–2
The communication process

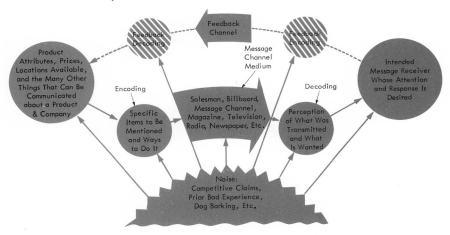

In personal selling, the seller has an opportunity to engage in initial probing activity to gain knowledge about the buyer's attitudes, interests, and abilities. This permits him to select the way to encode his message. For example, if he perceives that a prospect is quality conscious, he can emphasize the high quality of his product or service. If he detects a price consciousness, he can emphasize this and explain why his product or service is a good buy compared to alternative units.

---

[11] F. B. Evans, "Selling as a Dyadic Relationship," *American Behavioral Scientist,* 6 (May 1963), pp. 76–79; M. S. Gadel, "Concentration of Salesmen on Congenial Prospects," *Journal of Marketing,* 28 (April 1964), pp. 64–66; and H. L. Tosi, "The Effects of Expectation Levels and Role Consensus on the Buyer-Seller Dyad," *Journal of Business,* 39 (October 1966), pp. 516–29.

Throughout the personal selling process, the salesman can adjust and redirect his messages and clear up misunderstandings in view of the responses (feedback) from the prospect until the point is reached where a sale is made or the parties disengage, either temporarily or permanently. Such response activities are not immediately available with the other promotional techniques, but feedback is nevertheless needed in order to evaluate the extent and quality of the communication effort as well as to determine the nature of further communication.[12] Sometimes only rough estimates of the effects of promotion on sales are used. Other feedback mechanisms include redemption of coupons and surveys of prospective customers to discern awareness of various advertisements.

RELATIONSHIP OF PROMOTION TO BUYER BEHAVIOR

The communication process and promotion relate directly to the buyer decision-making process that was discussed in Chapter 4. Figure 21–3 is virtually the same as the final comprehensive figure that was studied at the close of that chapter. Now, though, the former rectangle in the lower left-hand corner has been developed as the first part of the communication process in which several sellers attempt to communicate with the prospective buyer.

From the large amounts of available information, sellers attempt to select and encode messages. These are matched with the media they believe are the most likely to receive the attention of the prospective buyer and to get through his perceptual processes in a favorable way.

Prospective buyers engaged in overt search are more receptive to information than are other buyers. However, if there is a large number of sellers, it is not likely that all of them will get their messages into the buyer's evoked-set comprehension. Further, while it is very difficult to change motives, a seller may be able to get his product or service into the buyer's evoked set by working on his decision-making process at a number of other points. He may be able to get his product or service recognized as an appropriate goal-object for an existing set of motives. He may also be able to influence the buyers' choice criteria so they more closely coincide with his offering. Finally, of course, sellers may be able to intensify or renew buyers' motives to priority levels that will lead to buying decisions.[13]

PROMOTION DECISIONS

The starting place for an organization attempting to plan a promotional program is with its overall goals and objectives. *Goals* are the achievements the organization wants to attain. *Objectives* are the benchmarks or reference points that must be reached along the way if the goals are to be achieved. For example, management's goals may be to build net worth to $45 million within 10 years, retain family ownership and management, and provide $20 million in cash payout to family management during the 10-year period (see Figure 21–4).

The company's objectives to achieve the three-prong goal may be to double sales during each of the next five years and increase profits by 30 percent each year. These company objectives in turn provide the framework for the marketing objectives,

---

[12] For a critical discussion of communication research in advertising, see D. L. Kanter, "Communication Theory and Advertising Decisions," *Journal of Advertising Research,* 10 (December 1970), pp. 3–8.

[13] If this brief discussion is not sufficiently clear, reread Chapter 4, "A System of Consumer Behavior."

FIGURE 21–3

Relationship of promotion to buyer behavior

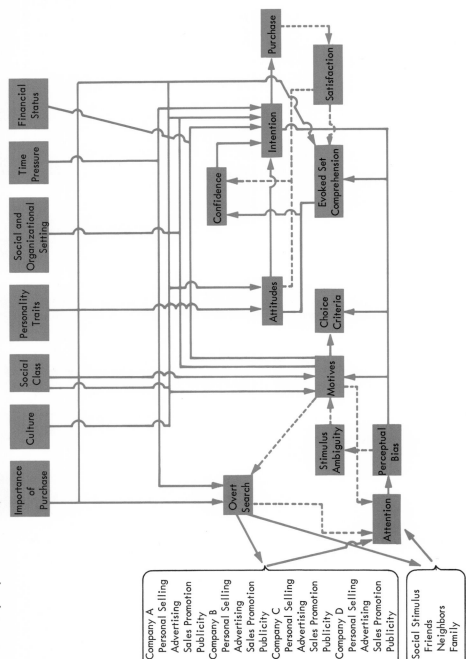

Adapted from J. H. Howard and J. N. Sheth, *The Theory of Buyer Behavior* (New York: John Wiley and Sons, Inc., 1969).

FIGURE 21–4
Goals and objectives hierarchy of a promotional program

which might be to double sales each year, limit marketing expenses to no more than 30 percent of sales, and gain 20 percent in market share for each of the company's five major product lines.

The marketing mix for each product is formulated on the basis of these marketing objectives. For example, to achieve a marketing objective of 20 percent gain in market share, the marketing strategy might center around upgrading the quality image of products and services so they will generally be perceived to be at least commensurate with the best available. This strategy would involve far more than merely making changes in the products and services, which might be redesigned or repackaged. New-product additions to the line might also be made and new distribution channels added to gain access through more prestigious outlets. Weak distributors and dealers that relied principally on price promotion might be weeded out. The firm might also develop a new warranty program and institute an information feedback channel direct from users to a quality maintenance office, and so forth.

For established products, the product itself and the channels of distribution can change only slowly. Therefore, the key strategic elements in the marketing mix for established products are promotion and price. Discussion of pricing strategies is delayed until Chapter 23.

The task of promotion is to help change the product's image by communicating to the distribution system, ultimate consumers, and prospective customers that changes have been made in product, channels, or price and that these changes are to the benefit of middlemen and buyers. Since it is no simple matter to communicate even a simple message to a small group of people, a coordinated plan for promotion involving advertising, personal selling, sales promotion, and publicity must be devised. The task assigned to a promotional system is dependent on the organization's goals and objectives and related to the tasks assigned to the other controllable variables in the marketing mix.

There are six essential stages in preparing a promotional plan: (1) identify the target market segments, (2) choose messages to be communicated, (3) determine competitive positioning, (4) select an overall marketing mix, (5) select the mix of communication channels (media) to be used, and (6) decide the amount of money to be spent on promotion. These stages, however, are not mutually exclusive or independent; each extends into and influences the others.

Identify target market segments

The target market (the prospective message recipients) must first be identified. It must be determined who the prospects and customers are, how many there are, where they are located, why they are customers or likely prospects, and what characteristics identify them as customers or prospects. These data facilitate identification of the target market and provide information for partitioning the total market into more homogeneous segments for promotional activities.

In each market segment, the appeals of competing products must next be determined. A manufacturer of trail bikes may observe, for example, that in his target market there are three separate groups: male teen-agers not old enough to be licensed to drive cars, adult males who are outdoor enthusiasts, and farmers and ranchers who use trail bikes in their work. While there is some overlap, it will probably be advantageous for the manufacturer to develop different messages and use different media for each of the three segments.

Choose messages and determine competitive positioning

In this stage management must decide rather precisely what it is they wish to communicate to various members of the channel system and to ultimate users in order to demonstrate how its brand is superior to competing ones. To appeal to large mass markets, relatively few relevant but simple product messages communicated repeatedly are usually most effective. These messages attempt to *position* the brand among competing brands. Procter & Gamble's promotion of Crest toothpaste (cavity prevention), Head and Shoulders shampoo (dandruff control), and most of their other consumer-good products provide illustrations of product positioning. H & R Block Company (low-price income tax services) and State Farm Insurance ("all you need to know about insurance") illustrate positioning in the promotion of services. Promotion by Volkswagen of America ("the dependable bug") illustrates that such an approach is not limited to convenience goods. Some communication experts express this approach as the KISS formula—KEEP IT SIMPLE AND SHORT.

Organizations promoting their offerings to a limited market with few prospects and customers have more opportunity to adapt and change their messages. Even in these situations, however, a basic theme (appeal) is typically maintained over a long period.

Select a media mix

Next, relevant means of transmitting the messages to the channel members and to the segments of the target market must be selected. The major media, as noted above, are personal selling, advertising, sales promotion, and publicity (and for packaged products, containers). There are numerous alternatives within each of these

Marketing: Principles and methods

categories, and most often some combination of message carriers is used. The communications mix problem presents one of the most difficult decision stages in marketing.

Selection decisions must also be made within each of the media. If a firm determines that its marketing mix is to be 60 percent personal selling, 30 percent advertising, 8 percent sales promotion, and 2 percent publicity, it still must decide within each medium the specific vehicle to be used. For example, will printed advertisements be used and, if so, in which publications should they appear? Will the company use their own salesmen or sales agents, and will they be order-takers, order-getters, or supportive salesmen?

In the mix decision stage, two major factors—the nature of the product or service and the capabilities of the available media—are very influential. Their consideration entails examination of such related factors as the nature of the market, the availability of funds, and the costs of various media.

Promoting products and services. Frequently purchased, low-priced consumer goods like toothpaste, gum, gasoline, and canned peaches are promoted most efficiently through the use of advertising and display pieces (sales promotion).[14] Favorable publicity is also helpful, but, as many a publicist has discovered, canned peaches or toothpaste do not command much public attention unless something detrimental can be said. Personal selling receives some use in the sale of convenience goods, but its principal task is to sell the products to the channel members.

Shopping and specialty goods require more extensive personal selling than do convenience goods. While advertisements and publicity can gain consumers' attention and interest in such products as automobiles, pianos, and boats, a salesman is normally needed to answer specific questions, demonstrate the products, negotiate the prices and terms of sale, and close the sale.

Professional services, as well as many personal services, utilize extensive personal selling and publicity but make limited use of advertising and sales promotion, which may be prohibited by professional "ethics." Many personal and financial services, which are of a convenience nature, are extensively advertised, however.[15]

Industrial products and services—particularly installations, made-to-order parts and services, and large-quantity transactions—are extensively promoted through personal selling. Advertising, when it is used, is normally limited to gaining the attention of the prospect in order to create awareness of products and services and their vendors.

Media capabilities. Managers could easily make promotional mix decisions *if* they had inexpensive and accurate measurements of the marginal profits resulting from each mixture. Lacking them, some managers place great reliance on the average cost per contact. Each television viewer may cost 4 cents, while each *Life* reader may cost 3 cents and each sales call, $30. Such an approach is obviously not very satisfactory, even within media categories, because it provides virtually no consideration of benefits.

It is difficult to generalize about promotional mixes. With this in mind, the buyer decision-making model which views target customers as moving from a state of unawareness through to buying action can help explain the selection of message

---

[14] The classification of goods and services (Chapter 4) can be reviewed in conjunction with the marketing strategy discussion (Chapters 18 and 19).

[15] For further discussion about the promotion of services, a review of Chapter 15 is recommended.

vehicle mixes. These stages or steps can be remembered as AIDA—Attention—→ Interest—→Desire—→Action—or as the psychological *hierarchy of effects* model. Advertising, sales promotion, and publicity are considered more efficient for gaining target customers' *attention* and *interest* than is personal selling. Personal selling, however, is generally thought to be more efficient in securing buying *action* (except for convenience goods) than are the other forms of promotion. *Desire* can be influenced through each of the message vehicles, depending on the specific product or service being promoted.

The optimum promotional mix, while influenced primarily by the product or service and the available media, is also affected by the nature of the buying process, the extent and nature of competition, and the nature of the market. As a more detailed view of personal selling, advertising, and the other media is presented in the second half of this chapter and in Chapter 22, some aspects of the mix decision should become clearer.

Amount to spend on promotion

The final issue is to determine the total amount of funds that should be spent for promotion. A conceptual answer is easy to arrive at—an organization should spend up to that amount where the resulting marginal revenues (the additional sales) just equal the marginal (additional) costs of gaining those sales. This is the amount that will produce the maximum return on the promotional dollars. Unfortunately, both cost and revenue measurement problems beset this solution. Most sellers do not have (nor can they get) appropriate marginal revenue or marginal cost measures or estimates. The major alternatives are to spend (1) all the firm can afford, (2) some percent of sales, (3) some proportion of the amount competitors spend, or (4) the amount needed to reach objectives.

All the firm can afford. Some firms, unable to measure the benefits of promotion but knowing that it helps generate sales, simply allocate as promotional expenditures whatever funds can be pulled out of the total budget. With this approach, expenditures for personal selling tend to remain relatively constant for each decision period, because it is difficult to quickly decrease or increase the size of a sales force. Advertising and sales promotion expenditures, however, tend to fluctuate violently because they can be terminated or increased rather quickly.

This method of allocating promotional funds is not uncommon. Many an advertising agency executive has witnessed such client behavior. A short-line farm equipment manufacturer told one of the authors that his advertising expenditure for fiscal year 1970 was $112,000, but he had decided in the face of a sales decline of about 15 percent to cut his advertising to the bare bones. In 1971 his advertising expenditure was only $12,000, while he maintained personal selling at the 1970 level. Based on his prior reasoning he may need to cut back his personal-selling efforts, because he cannot cut back much further on advertising and his sales declined by almost 36 percent in 1971. Such an approach is ludicrous in the sense that promotion is supposed to cause sales, not vice versa. It is also incompatible with long-range planning for marketing efforts.

Percent of sales. More firms probably use the percent-of-sales approach to determine their promotional budget than any other method. For example, a firm may allocate 2 percent of sales for advertising and sales promotion and 8 percent of sales for personal selling. The sales figure on which the promotion budget is based is often for the previous period—not the forecasted period during which the promotional dollars will be spent.

This approach does encourage stability in market position if all firms in an industry use it and their promotions are equally effective. In such a situation each seller bases his promotion expenditure on his past sales, and market shares remain relatively constant. It may be a safe approach in industries for which the *total* demand schedule is quite inelastic (total demand is not price responsive) but for which there is high cross-price elasticity among brands (individual brand demand is very price sensitive). Such a demand situation prevails in gasoline for automobiles in individual markets.

The disadvantages of the percentage method are about the same as for the "all the firm can afford" approach. Both methods are based on macro views and discourage an examination of the promotion needed to achieve specific sales objectives for various products and territories. They fail to recognize the causal relationship between sales and promotion and discourage attempts to stimulate sales through promotion by saying, in effect, that whatever pushed sales down must pick them up. The percentage method, however, frequently has the support of financial managers because they can readily respond by decreasing expenditures to match decreased sales.

Competitive parity. With the competitive parity approach, promotional budgets are set in proportion to what firms believe one or more major competitors will spend. A distributor of lawn mowers and snowmobiles is an example. Twice a year, as he prepares promotional budgets for the two lines, he "goes fishing" with his two major competitors. They apparently have some sort of meeting of the minds because their total promotional budgets are quite similar year after year. (While meetings such as these are probably illegal under U.S. antitrust laws, all parallel action by competitors does not imply collusion.)

Some companies follow the competitive parity approach because they believe their competitors are good marketers. Even if they are (and such an assumption often is dubious), what is the correct amount or proportion for one company to spend is not likely to be so for another. Like the other methods discussed above, such an approach leads a company to ignore their product-line and territory objectives and plans.

Objective-and-task method. When management first determines the objectives and then decides the promotional effort needed to reach them, it is said to be using the objective-and-task approach. The steps in this method are: (1) determine promotional objectives, (2) outline the tasks necessary to reach them, and (3) estimate the promotional costs of performing the tasks. The sum of these costs, from all dimensions of the business, constitutes the promotional budget.

This method is based on better logic than the others. Recognizing that promotion should influence sales, it attempts to ascertain in some detail the amount and kind of promotion needed for each product line in each market. Success is dependent on careful evaluation of the objectives and good estimates of the associated costs of the tasks required to achieve them. Using this approach, only those objectives with "reasonable" price tags should be included in the promotional budget.

Most large companies use this method. The product-by-product, market-by-market buildup of this micro approach facilitates the overall management of promotion as a system. The major difficulty is lack of information regarding the effectiveness of the available promotional tools.

Other approaches. Some quantitative models are being built to help handle small facets of some of these decision areas. And, of course, some quantitative techniques are very helpful for specific analyses.[16] In general, though, the major promotional decisions still remain much more of an art than a science.[17]

PERSONAL SELLING

Personal selling, which involves direct personal contact between the seller or his representative and the buyer, is the oldest and most important method of promotion. It is "a unique, hard-to-replace force in modern marketing because it makes possible two-way communication of ideas between a seller and a buyer. It is the only form of sales promotion that can encourage and make immediate, on-the-spot use of responses from buyers."[18]

Importance of personal selling

The Census Bureau indicates that almost 10 percent of the United States labor force is engaged in sales work, an understatement because many who are principally salesmen are listed in other occupational categories. To cite two cases, sale engineers are listed as engineers and retail store owners and managers are listed as owners and managers. In absolute numbers, more than seven million people in the United States are primarily engaged in personal selling. Advertising, by comparison, is not nearly so large as a direct employer; less than one-half million people or far less than 1 percent of the labor force are engaged in advertising. Expenditures for personal selling far exceed those for all other promotional activities combined, accounting for from 8 to 15 percent of net sales in many companies, whereas advertising expenditures normally range from 1 to 3 percent.[19]

The importance of personal selling in the overall marketing system and society as a whole is so obvious it warrants little discussion. However, if you think marketing or society would be better off without personal selling, you should review the equalization process—sorting out, assembling, allocating and assorting—as presented in Chapter 2. Then ask the question, "How well would this process work without personal selling?" If you can visualize that it would function at all, ask, "Would it be more or less efficient without personal selling?" Finally, if you still fail to see the importance of personal selling, ask yourself, "Why is it that personal selling remains a major function in all marketing systems?"

Skepticism concerning personal salesmanship. Some observers do maintain that the "creative salesman" is less needed today than he was, say, 50 years ago. It is especially argued that personal selling is not needed by low margin retailers such

[16] L. Friedman, "Constructing a Media Simulation Model," *Journal of Advertising Research*, 10 (August 1970), pp. 33–39 and D.S. Diamond, "A Quantitative Approach to Magazine Advertisement Format Selection," *Journal of Marketing Research*, 5 (November 1968), pp. 376–87.

[17] For insight on the state of the art in this area, see P. E. Green, P. J. Robinson, and P. T. Fitz Roy, "Advertising Expenditure Models: State of the Art and Prospects," *Business Horizons* (Summer 1966), pp. 72–80; R. M. Fulmer, "How Should Advertising and Sales Promotion Funds Be Allocated" *Journal of Marketing*, 31 (October 1967), pp. 8–11; and D. C. Marsehner, "Theory versus Practice in Allocating Advertising Money," *Journal of Business*, 40 (July 1967), pp. 286–302.

[18] S. J. Shaw and C. M. Gittinger, *Marketing in Business Management* (New York: Macmillan Co., 1963), p. 350.

[19] *A Graphic Guide to Consumer Markets: 1968–1969* (New York: Conference Board, 1968), pp. 80–81. States one manufacturer: "Personal selling is still the most important element in our marketing mix. We don't have anything that sells itself." "Company with a Heart: Even Miraculous Merchandise Cannot Sell Itself," *Dun's Review*, August 1967, p. 49.

Marketing: Principles and methods

as discount houses, where major emphasis is placed on open displays, low prices, and rapid turnover.

A number of other developments have contributed to a growing skepticism regarding the importance of personal salesmanship today. These include:

1. Customers are presold by national advertising.
2. A growing part of the selling task can be assigned to merchandise displays, packaging, and labeling.
3. Buying committees are being developed which depend less on the salesman and more on the buyer's judgment.
4. Electronic data processing is providing increased and more rapid flow of information to the buyer.
5. Self-service and self-selection stores, such as the supermarket and the discount house, are increasing.
6. Some observers believe that the automated store is the store of the future. A few see the end of the retail store as we know it, with the customer "shopping" at home over a television set or ordering by telephone from an outlet like a warehouse with no floor traffic.

Further, critics of personal selling maintain that much of it is so ineffective that it is hardly worth management's time to seek ways to improve it.

Continuing need for personal selling. Although recognizing that recent developments may have lessened the importance of personal selling in *some* stores and for *some* manufacturers and wholesalers, most experts are of the opinion that personal salesmanship is still essential for the vast majority of business enterprises. This conclusion is supported by a comprehensive survey undertaken by one of the authors which revealed that personal selling constituted the most important single factor in the marketing mix of the responding companies and had grown in significance in recent years.[20] Major reasons for such emphasis were the expanding needs of the economy, the large increase in the number and variety of new products, and the concomitant sharpening of competition in the marketplace. The study also discovered that:

1. Almost 99 percent of the respondents voiced strong disagreement with the argument that personal selling holds few opportunities for college graduates.
2. Detractors of personal selling have had only a limited effect on the ability of companies to recruit new salesmen and on the performance of present salesmen.
3. More company presidents have had experience in personal selling than in any other area of primary activity. Even those without such experience were practically unanimous in agreeing on its desirability as preparation for their jobs.

It is in view of the foregoing facts that many firms at all levels of the marketing structure are devoting an increased amount of time and money to the improvement of their sales staffs and selling techniques, especially through better application of the basic principles of personal selling.

Variety of personal selling jobs

The variety of forms that personal selling may take are too numerous to list, but in the main they include: (1) across-the-counter selling, such as is carried on in all

---

[20] D. J. Duncan, *Top Management Attitudes toward Salesmen and Salesmanship* (New York: Klein Institute for Aptitude Testing, Inc., 1967). Also see V. A. Adams, "Is the Salesman Ahead of His Image?" *Sales Management,* January 15, 1965, pp. 21–23.

retail stores except those operating on the self-service plan; (2) house-to-house selling, as exemplified by the representatives of the Fuller Brush Company; (3) salesmen employed by wholesalers to call upon retailers, such as those used by wholesale grocers or druggists; (4) salesmen used by manufacturers to call upon other manufacturers, wholesalers, and retailers; and (5) calls made upon important customers by executives to effect sales, as is often done in selling to chain stores and large industrial accounts. In addition, there are nonorder-taking salesmen employed by manufacturers to perform such functions as introducing new products, setting up displays, reviving retailers' interest in old products, and giving advice and assistance to the customers.

The differences in various personal selling jobs can be seen more clearly by dividing salesmen's activities into: (1) *order-taking*, (2) *order-getting*, and (3) *supporting*. All three are essential and are performed by almost all salesmen, but the amount and importance of each activity in a selling situation will largely determine the nature of the salesman's job. That is, some salesmen are principally order-takers, some are principally sales-getters, and some are not order oriented.[21]

Order-takers. The order-taker is a salesman who basically notes which of his company's products his customers want or need, helps his customers choose the desired items and quantities, and writes up the orders. In addition, he frequently makes adjustments and attempts to handle most complaints, conveys prices and other general information, places or arranges merchandise and display pieces (in the absence of prohibiting labor union agreements) and makes collections from customers. He is normally not expected to engage in the type of "creative" selling required of order-getters, but he must be regular, diligent, and attentive. Order-takers are extensively employed as retail salesmen (clerks) and as manufacturer and wholesale salesmen to call on wholesalers and retailers.

When the order-taker is involved in the introduction of a new product, his role is normally limited to a perfunctory explanation of the details. Manufacturers will typically set up the entire game plan to pull the products through the channel or use a special introductory sales team.[22]

Order-getters. The order-getter is more concerned with seeking out prospective customers and creating and developing them as customers. His selling job is creative. He must be able to convince prospective customers that, through him, his company's products and services can fulfill certain of their needs better than any available competitive products and services. In many situations he must know enough about prospective customers to be able to show them both their needs and the fulfillment capabilities of his products and services.

An order-getting salesman places considerable emphasis on concepts, ideas, and benefits, whether he is selling products or services.[23] A salesman of computers is not going to make many sales featuring only his hardware. He must help prospective customers see that they need a new or revised set of systems and that his hardware-

---

[21] A more detailed breakdown divides order-takers into driver or delivery salesmen, inside order-takers, and outside order-takers; order-getters into product order-getters and service order-getters; and supporting salesmen into: goodwill/educators and service consultants. See R. N. McMurry, "The Mystique of Super-Salesmanship," *Harvard Business Review,* 39 (March-April 1961), p. 114.

[22] For two detailed examples, see "How Nabisco Keeps Its Cookie Crown," *Business Week,* May 10, 1969; W. F. Funkhouser, "Wholesale Drug Salesmen Need Knowledge, Understanding," *Marketing Insights,* March 18, 1969, pp. 17–20.

[23] See I. Barmash, "Old-Time Drummer a Vanishing Breed," *New York Times,* February 15, 1970, pp. F1, 13.

software system provides just the right benefits (perhaps including increased personal prestige) and capabilities.

A salesman of life insurance or encyclopedias is confronted by a similar situation. Few customers want these items to the point of seeking out the sellers. Typically, the salesman must prospect among the many eligible buyers and identify the most likely prospects. He must examine the personal situations of these prospects sufficiently well to identify specific needs and persuade them that these needs are of sufficient importance and that his products offer all of the needed benefits. Customers do not buy an insurance contract or a set of books; they buy expected benefits.

Supporting salesmen. Supporting salesmen assist and support order-oriented salesmen but do not concentrate on securing on-the-spot orders themselves. Two principal types are detail or missionary salesmen and consulting engineers.

1. *Detail or missionary men.* Such salesmen, frequently employed by manufacturers of drug products, building supplies, and college textbooks, and are called "detail men," "missionary men," and "travelers" or "field editors," respectively. In general, they are used in selling situations where products and services are purchased by the users because they have been prescribed by physicians, architects, or some other expert. Detail men employed by drug companies, for example, call on physicians, veterinarians, dentists, drug wholesalers, and pharmacists in attempts to get their brands prescribed, stocked, and displayed.

2. *Consulting engineers.* These supportive salesmen may be called "consulting," "service" or "technical" engineers. Sales engineers for Portland cement manufacturers, for example, help prospective cement-batch plant operators design plants and troubleshoot problems in batching operations and specific cement applications. They also call on cement-using contractors and other large-scale customers to advise them on special applications, solve problems, and provide designs for improving cement-processing systems. These salesmen are crucial in this industry because, along with physical delivery and credit terms, they provide the only difference among competitive offerings. Portland cement is no different whether it comes from Northwestern Cement Company, Lehigh Portland Cement Company, or Dewey Portland Cement Company. It is manufactured to rigid industry specifications (at most, there might be a slight color variation), and the price schedule available to a given buyer is the same from all sellers, almost without exception.

Basic principles of personal selling

Productive selling efforts are dependent upon familiarity with and conformance to certain principles well established through long experience. These principles relate primarily to four topics: (1) adequate preparation, (2) finding buyers, (3) making the sale, and (4) developing goodwill after the sale.

Adequate preparation.[24] Preparation is related to the knowledge required to ensure satisfactory results from selling efforts. Salesmen need information on the market in which the goods will be sold, present and prospective customers, the products to be sold, and the basic principles of salesmanship.

Finding buyers. Some retail and wholesale order-taking salesmen serve only those prospects who contact them. Others use the retail or wholesale store principally as a base for action. In many markets, for example, car salesmen will be assigned to the selling floor only three to four days per week. During slack time on the floor,

---

[24] See the excellent discussion of this subject in C. A. Pederson and M. D. Wright, *Salesmanship: Principles and Methods* (5th ed.; Homewood, Ill.: Richard D. Irwin, Inc., 1971), part III.

they are expected to engage in prospecting (via phone). On their "off days," they are expected to be fully engaged in establishing and contacting their "birddogs" (barbers, bartenders, car mechanics, gasoline station attendants, and others who "know" when their customers are contemplating a car purchase), following up on prior contacts with prospects, and establishing new prospects through "cold turkey" routines (e.g., notes on car windshields indicating car trade-in values and calling persons mentioned by news media as newly promoted, graduated, married, a gift recipient, etc.). Such selling activities are not limited to car salesmen, but are practiced in many types of retail and wholesale establishments.

Some firms employing outside order-taking salesmen formerly allowed them almost complete freedom in choosing the prospects and customers they called upon, the territory they covered, and the frequency of calls they made. Today, however, practically all firms carefully define territories, arrange routes, and specify frequency of call to ensure that all desirable prospects are reached. Because marketing executives appreciate the importance of cultivating their markets properly in order to obtain maximum benefits, it is common practice to set market potentials for each territory, establish quotas as measuring sticks of performance, and require frequent reports on sales efforts. Close overall supervision of the salesmen's work is thus exercised.

Order-getting salesmen are permitted somewhat more leeway in prospecting. An important part of their task is to secure and develop new customers, and this cannot be as routinized as order-taking activities. Order-getting salesmen are usually assigned to specific territories and estimates of potential, price quotes, and sales forecasts are prepared. Prospect lists may even be supplied. The more creative and order-getting the selling task is, the more leeway is granted the salesman to manage his territory.

Making sales. Making sales is the major job of the salesman and the heart of the selling process. Although situations under which sales are made vary widely and it is necessary for the salesman to adapt his selling efforts accordingly, certain steps or stages are common to most of them. These are: (1) approaching and greeting the prospective customer, (2) determining the prospect's needs, (3) presenting the merchandise or service effectively, (4) meeting objections, (5) closing the sale, and (6) selling additional items through pertinent suggestions.

Building goodwill after the sale. A sale should be mutually satisfying for both buyer and seller. If conducted properly, the buyer will be helped to obtain products or services suited to his requirements, and the seller will benefit and perhaps find a continuing customer. Mutual goodwill develops from such a sale: The buyer is disposed to buy again from the salesman who has treated him well, and the seller gains a sense of appreciation of the buyer's needs and is better able to serve him.

In addition to the goodwill developed from the sale itself, there are frequently specific postsale services a salesman can render to the buyer. Shipments may be expedited, the buyer's inventory may be watched to keep it at a proper level, retailers' merchandise displays may be provided and perhaps actually set up by the salesman, and the buyer's employees instructed in the use of resale of the product.

Management of the sales force[25]

Although the preceding analysis of the salesman's job has been brief and incomplete, it should have made it clear that in a competitive economy personal selling is

---

[25] *Sales Management* and *Marketing/Communications* (formerly *Printers' Ink*) are good sources of current information on this topic, especially for sales staffs selling consumers' goods; *Industrial Marketing* and *Industrial Distribution* may be consulted for comparable information in this field.

no easy job. Selling calls for a person who is well trained, has initiative and determination, and is not easily discouraged and whose personality is such that buyers enjoy dealing with him. Business firms develop successful sales staffs only by the careful selection, training, compensation, and supervision of their salesmen. These tasks and the responsibility for all personal selling functions are usually assigned to a "sales manager."

Selecting salesmen. A few years ago the director of sales training for a major company said: "The big problem is recruitment of salesmen. Careful selection of those candidates with the most potential is the key to better selling. We find that you can't change a man very much after you've hired him. You have to choose the right one in the first place."[26] Today some sales executives might disagree with the emphasis this statement gives to the significance of sales personnel selection, but all would agree that proper selection is essential.[27]

Sound selection procedure should begin with a careful analysis of the sales task. This should permit preparation of a comprehensive list of the qualifications required for satisfactory salesmanship, which are much the same as those necessary for success in any line of business: hard work, honesty in all matters, confidence in one's company and one's merchandise, courage to meet disappointment and defeat, judgment, discrimination and good sense, creative imagination or the capacity to develop ideas (particularly for order-getting situations), a talent for getting along with one's associates and superiors, and knowledge of the job to be done. The salesman should also be willing to accept guidance from his supervisors and appreciate the need for self-development to meet the challenges and opportunities that will confront him. Such qualities as a genuine interest in people, enthusiasm, the ability to instill confidence, and some flair for showmanship contribute much to his success.[28] Since it is the salesman's job to overcome causes for hesitation, he must be positive and self-confident. Finally, he must also be a good loser. It is not possible to close every sale attempted, but if the salesman leaves the prospective buyer with a favorable impression, there is much more likelihood that he will make a sale the next time he calls.

With the qualifications determined, the marketer has a yardstick against which to measure candidates and is ready to proceed with the task of hiring the type of salesman needed. He must recruit qualified candidates and make final selections based on information obtained through application blanks and references, interviews, and tests.[29]

1. *Locating qualified sales candidates.* Candidates for sales positions may be found through such means as recommendations of employees, advertisements, campus placement officers, and employment agencies. Many candidates take the initiative

---

[26] M. L. Van Dagens of Chrysler, quoted in H. W. Boyd, Jr., and R. M. Clewett (eds.), *Contemporary American Marketing: Readings on the Changing Market Structure* (rev. ed.; Homewood, Ill.: Richard D. Irwin, Inc., 1962), p. 320.

[27] For a list of 11 factors to be considered when recruiting and appraising sales candidates, see J. Hudig, "Appraising Sales Talent," *Sales/Marketing Today,* March 1966, pp. 8–9. Also see "How Do You Evaluate Sales Candidates?" *Sales Management,* July 1, 1967, pp. 39–41. A study of the sales manpower division of the New York Sales Executives Club revealed that machinery manufacturers "anticipate spending more than $68.4 million, exclusive of salaries, to locate and train 7,750 new salesmen over the next year." "Developments to Check," *Industrial Marketing,* 52 (August 1967), p. 37.

[28] Writes G. S. Carlin in his *The Power of Enthusiastic Selling,* "A top salesman has what we call emotional stamina. He has what many sports writers refer to as 'heart.' The courage and stamina to keep going when the going gets tougher! The determination to fight even harder when defeat seems so near." Quoted in *Sales/Marketing Today,* February 1963, p. 26.

[29] A report on the relative use of each of these tools is in T. R. Wotruba, "An Analysis of the Salesmen Selection Process," *The Southern Journal of Business,* 5 (January 1970), pp. 41–51.

and make direct application to selected firms. Some companies attempt to recruit their salesmen from particular sources or with specified backgrounds. A firm selling technical goods, for example, may be interested only in men who have worked in its production division, who have been employed by comparable firms, or who have an engineering degree. At the other extreme are those concerns that want to employ men who have never sold before, in the belief that they have "less to unlearn." Some employers follow a policy of selecting only college men while others avoid hiring them or look upon a college background with indifference.[30] In view of the wide range of abilities called for by the variety of selling jobs offered by different companies, the existence of such divergent policies is not surprising.

2. *Application blanks and references.* Application blanks are widely used as devices for screening salesmen, as they are for other employees. They can provide a considerable amount of data concerning the applicant's background. The information requested will depend on the preferences of the employment executive and the needs of the particular concern. References, which are commonly requested on the application form, can be the source of additional information. Some firms use rating scales to judge the answers to application-blank questions, and applicants not scoring a predetermined number of points are not employed.

3. *Interviews.* Interviews afford the prospective employer his best opportunity to judge the applicant's personality and to obtain information on his interests, experience, and similar factors. They should be carefully planned, however, or they may be worthless. Interviewers should be chosen with discretion and supplied with lists of points to cover, interviewing guides, and rating sheets. A multiple-interview system usually gives improved results.

4. *Psychological tests.* Although there are wide differences of opinion among companies as to the value of psychological tests,[31] a growing number of firms is using tests of various kinds to supplement the judgment of interviewers. Such tests minimize mistakes in the attempt to select men best suited to a company's particular needs. Intelligence, personality, sales aptitude, and other tests may be employed, often combined in a test battery.

Application blanks, interviews, and psychological tests may be looked upon as screens through which candidates for selling positions must pass, usually in the order in which they have been discussed. As useful management tools, they play an important part in any well-balanced program for selecting salesmen.

Training and developing salesmen. After salesmen have been selected, their training in the performance of sales tasks should be continuously developed.[32] The

---

[30] The Sales Executives Club of New York reports that "only 39 percent of employers seeking either experienced salesmen or sales trainees through . . . the Sales Manpower Division . . . of the club . . . insist on a college diploma . . . The other 61 percent would . . . be happy to get college men but don't feel that such education is absolutely necessary for their success." Of those insisting on college degrees, 53 percent did so "because an *engineering* degree was necessary for the work to be done." "Do Salesmen Really Have to Be College Graduates?" *News about the Sales Executives Club of New York,* February 20, 1967, p. 1.

[31] W. L. French, "Psychological Testing: Some Problems and Solutions," *Personnel Administration,* 29 (March-April 1966), pp. 485–87; L. Rich, "Can Salesmen Be Tested?" *Dun's Review and Modern Industry,* 87 (March 1966), pp.. 40 ff. (examines the question "Are those hosts of new tests really worth the money in discovering who can sell and who cannot?"); and "The Pre-Tested Failures," *Sales Management,* 98 (June 1, 1967), pp. 69–70. On the use of psychological tests in the selection of industrial salesmen see R. Burnon, "Psychological Tests: How Valid Are They?" *Industrial Distribution,* 56 (July 1966), pp. 49–52.

[32] Although the discussion is restricted mainly to "outside" salesmen, the necessity of also training retail salespeople is apparent. For excellent suggestions on this topic see W. B. Logan, *Training Retail Salespeople,* Small Business Bibliography No. 23 (Washington, D.C.: Small Business Administration, 1966). Also "Rexall's New Sales Training Program," *Training in Business and Industry,* May 1967, pp. 38–40.

Marketing: Principles and methods

training provided will depend, of course, on the specific selling job and the salesman's background and abilities. Thus firms selling highly technical products such as textile machinery, which is purchased by skilled buyers, will require better trained salesmen than those selling standardized consumer goods. Firms recruiting college men who have never sold before must devote more attention to the training problem than those who seek new salesmen from the trained staffs of competitors. Although the nature and amount of training will vary from firm to firm and even among trainees, most firms will find it desirable to provide some kind of training program and to adapt it to changing conditions.[33]

1. *The training program.* Although the actual content of the training program will depend upon the particular circumstances in any company and on the experience and preferences of the sales executives responsible for this function, certain basic factors characterize most, if not all, training programs. As Professor H. R. Tosdal wrote two decades ago:

Every well-planned training program will take into account at least four divisions of knowledge and skill which the salesman must possess if he is to perform satisfactorily, as follows:
1. The salesman should know the sales proposition, that is, the product or service which he is to sell, and should have a thorough knowledge and understanding of the policies and practices of the selling organization of which he is a part.
2. He must know how to study his market. Specifically he must know who the prospective buyers are and develop skill in finding them. He must also either know or be able to find out their requirements.[34]
3. He must know how to sell. This involves the development of skill in presenting his sales proposition to prospective buyers in such a way as to make sales, develop customers, and build good will, so that costs are reduced and repeat sales facilitated.
4. Finally, he must be trained in sales management and in his nonselling tasks. Such training will show him how to plan and manage his own work effectively and to perform satisfactorily the various types of nonselling tasks which may be required of him.[35]

The methods employed to accomplish these goals may be as informal and as cursory as a trip through the firm's plant, interviews and talks with headquarters executives, and the assignment of a regular salesman to take the new salesman around his territory and "show him the ropes." Or it may involve more formal training, given through organized classes on the product, sales policies, and markets.[36] Tools for sales training may include sales manuals, printed materials, visual aids of several types, and teaching machines.[37]

A company can conduct its own training program or employ one of the growing number of outside organizations for this purpose. Leading organizations use either or both types of these training methods.[38]

---

[33] The need for such revisions is well illustrated in the ethical drug industry. See E. B. Weiss, "Time Is Running Out for the Ethical Drug Detail Man's Old-Fashioned Ways," *Advertising Age,* April 3, 1967, pp. 92, 96.

[34] See John Vollbrecht, "Are You Leaving the Customer Out of Your Sales Training?" *Sales Management,* August 15, 1967, pp. 29–31 ff.

[35] In C. f. Phillips (ed.), *Marketing by Manufacturers* (rev. ed.; Homewood, Ill.: Richard D. Irwin, Inc., 1951), pp. 415–16.

[36] M. J. Riordan, "The Dynamics of Education in Selling," *Sales/Marketing Today,* July 1967, pp. 13–15.

[37] Jack Wertis, "Sales Training: New Tools, Methods Do a Faster Job," *Industrial Distribution,* 56 (September 1966), pp. 70–72. The Quaker Oats Company uses programmed instruction to train its own salesmen and those of its retailer customers. See "PI Goes to the Supermarket," *Training in Business and Industry,* December, 1966, pp. 33 ff. On the failure of some training programs, see "Many Sales Training Courses a 'Waste of Time' Exec. Grumbles," *Marketing Insights,* October 17, 1966, p. 14.

[38] L. Rich, "The Ins and Outs of Sales Training," *Dun's Review and Modern Industry,* August 1966, pp. 35, 67–69.

2. *Sales training: A continuing task.* In view of the dynamics of each of the four areas in which a salesman should be trained, the training function must be a continuous one. Consider the third area listed above—how to sell. Whereas many years ago the selling task was often a relatively simple one with certain steps to be followed as directed by standardized sales presentations, today the salesman should be, in the words of a General Foods marketing vice president,

part home economist—part advertising man—part merchandising and promotion man—part creative idea man—part materials handling expert—and part financial analyst.

Salesman? Well, hardly! He is more accurately described as "an account manager." No longer is he in charge of a geographical area known as a territory. He is, instead, the manager of his company's total business relationship with one or more important accounts.[39]

The net result: Salesmen must be retrained to cope with the new situation. As products, markets, and management methods change, retraining in these areas is equally essential.

Compensating salesmen.[40] An adequate compensation plan is essential in building and maintaining a successful sales organization because salesmen are vitally interested in the monetary rewards provided, and their employers are interested in plans which produce the best results in relation to the selling costs. As far as possible, the compensation plan any particular firm adopts should meet the requirements of both salesmen and employer.

1. *Requisites of a good compensation plan.* Salesmen usually want a plan (a) that is simple and understandable, (b) that provides earnings comparable with those obtained for similar work, (c) that is fair and equitable among salesmen and is considered to be` such, (d) that yields ample rewards for extra effort, (e) that supplies payments at regular intervals and rewards for extra effort without undue delay, (f) that does not penalize them for conditions outside their control, and (g) that they have had a part in developing.

From the point of view of the company, a compensation plan should (a) meet the requirements of a good plan from the salesmen's point of view, as far as possible, (b) minimize the selling costs, (c) enable the firm to obtain and keep the type of men needed, (d) provide incentives to call forth the latent energies and abilities of the salesmen, (e) maintain reasonable stability of real income during variations of business conditions, (f) furnish sufficient flexibility to enable prompt revisions to be made where advisable, and (g) allow salesmen ample time to sell by minimizing reports and other clerical work.

No compensation plan, of course, can meet all the desirable characteristics from both the salesman's and the company's point of view. Consequently, the plan adopted will represent a compromise that will vary from firm to firm.[41] There is no one best compensation plan for all companies under all conditions!

2. *Compensation methods.* Although the numerous types of compensation methods are varied to meet particular needs, they may be classified into four major groups: (a) straight salary; (b) basic salary plus incentive payment; (c) straight commis-

[39] E. B. Weiss, "The New, Expanded Role of Salesmanship Rolls On," *Advertising Age,* June 13, 1966, p. 86. Also see J. J. Breen, "The Marketing Manager," *Sales/Marketing Today,* July 1964, pp. 12–15.

[40] For the suggestions of six sales executives on "What Is the Best Way to Compensate Salesmen?", *Sales Management,* August 1, 1967, pp. 30–31. Also, D. A. Weeks, "Changing Patterns in Salesmen's Compensation," *Conference Board Record,* February 1966, pp. 37–42.

[41] A "method for developing a rational compensation plan" which represents the best compromise of the salesman's and company's points of view is given in F. E. Webster, Jr., "Rationalizing Salesmen's Compensation Plans," *Journal of Marketing,* 30 (January 1966), pp. 55–58.

sion, with or without drawing account;[42] and (d) profit sharing.[43] Many firms selling both industrial and consumer goods use a straight-salary compensation plan. Despite the advantages of such a plan—simplicity, provision of stable income, and encouragement for the salesman to make goodwill calls that do not produce immediate sales—the trend is clearly toward a plan with some kind of incentive payment. Firms using such payment plans provide a salary plus a commission on sales (or on sales above a pre-determined amount) or give a bonus for the accomplishment of a certain sales volume or specific promotional work. Other companies depend entirely upon a commission plan, without coupling it to a basic salary.[44] However, the great fluctuation in earnings which may result has encouraged the establishment of drawing accounts, which in many instances become, in effect, a basic salary. Some payment plans involve profit sharing and other various combinations of methods. In general, however, few profit-sharing plans have been used for salesmen, since their effectiveness is in doubt.

Supervising the sales force. Carefully selecting, training, and compensating salesmen does not complete management's responsibility in connection with the sales force. Salesmen need to be well supervised if they are to perform effectively. Some executives believe that more failures among salesmen are caused by inadequate supervision than by lack of sales ability. And, despite the care taken in selecting and training, some salesmen are unable to produce the results expected of them. The sooner these men are detected, the sooner appropriate remedial measures can be taken.[45]

1. *Techniques of supervision.* Skillful direction of a sales force is a continuous task which involves an understanding of salesmen's motivations[46] and the maintenance of close relations with sales personnel in the field or in the place of business. It includes such matters as planning and readjustment of sales territories, sales routes, sales contests, and sales quotas;[47] the establishment of the supervisory organization; the development of a flow of reports, bulletins, and correspondence, both to and from the salesman—to keep him informed of developments at headquarters, and so that headquarters can watch his progress; and, frequently, the use of meetings and conferences as methods of communication and stimulation.

One observer has suggested that we should

---

[42] A drawing account is money a company provides a salesman prior to the time he earns it and later subtracts from his commissions.

[43] See Philip Salisbury, "Compensating Salesmen," *Sales Management,* January 21, 1966, pp. 45–54, for a report on current compensation practices. Also see R. C. Smyth, "Financial Incentives for Salesmen," *Harvard Business Review,* 46 (January–February 1968), pp. 109–17.

[44] Relating the compensation of salesmen to the sales volume is not always a satisfactory way to encourage profitable selling, since there is a wide variation in the profitability of items sold. The increased use of computers may make it possible for a company to give its salesmen more information concerning the profitability of various items and to base salesmen's compensation on the resulting profits. See L. H. Robertson, "Profitability Commission Plans Relating Sales Compensation to Profitability," *Management Accounting,* 49 (June 1968), pp. 39–45.

[45] Some of the newer techniques used for locating poor salesmen are discussed in "How to Find the Weak Links in Your Sales Force," *Sales Management,* August 15, 1967, pp. 32–33. Also see Bruce Williams, "Distributor Salesmen Don't Sell," *Industrial Distribution,* 56 (August 1966), pp. 67–72, for a critical look at industrial selling.

[46] See J. M. Briggs, "31 Ways to Motivate Your Salesmen and Yourself," *Sales Management,* August 6, 1965, pp. 31–32; and *The New Motivation,* an 11-page booklet by the Research Institute of America, New York.

[47] M. A. Brice, "The Art of Dividing Sales Territories," *Dun's Review,* May 1967, pp. 47–48 ff.; and L. Rich, "The Controversy in Sales Quotas," *Dun's Review and Modern Industry,* May 1966, pp. 47–48 ff.

Pity today's embattled sales manager. In a highly prosperous but also highly competitive economy, he must not only wage a constant battle to hold his own against all comers, but must try to carve out for his company a bigger share of the ever-growing U.S. market. To serve the needs of customers who are more knowledgeable and more demanding than ever, he must see to it that his salesmen are trained and equipped to do a more sophisticated job than in the past.

But as business increases and his staff expands, he faces a sharp dilemma: Does his first duty lie with the reports, questionnaires, and other administrative red tape piled high on his desk, or should he toss them aside and get out where the action is? How can he be a competent manager if he is forever bogged down in a mass of paperwork? Yet how can he keep up with the demands of his job if the paperwork lies undone?[48]

2. *Maintaining morale: Motivation and leadership.* Effective sales performance is impossible without proper morale and enthusiasm. Consequently, it is management's responsibility to provide an "atmosphere" conducive to the development and maintenance of a high morale among its sales force. Although there is no simple explanation for any given state of morale, certain factors are important in building the spirit of the sales force, such as: (a) a simple and relatively informal organizational structure which offers a high degree of freedom to the salesman, utilizes a large measure of his capacities, requires the exercise of his personal judgment and initiative, and encourages the development of his native abilities; (b) a high order of administrative effectiveness; and (c) a favorable attitude of top management toward its employees.

In a study one of the authors reports as follows:

Every experienced work supervisor—including the sales executive—is aware of the difficulties involved in motivating a group effectively. The complexity of human behavior and the wide variety of hopes, fears, and attitudes prevalent among the individuals comprising the group is responsible for this situation. Moreover, some individuals are motivatable and others are not. But even among motivatable individuals no single stimulant, or group of stimulants, applies with equal force to all. Yet, if the supervisior is to obtain satisfactory productivity from members of his staff, he must understand not only the factors that motivate employees to work most effectively, but also those which contribute to their dissatisfaction.

In fulfilling these obligations, he should not lose sight of the fact, as one psychologist has so well expressed it, that "the supervisor's job—at any level of the managment hierarchy—is people. His success, or lack of it, depends chiefly on his ability to work through people." He needs to recognize, also that the behavior of a person acting alone may be quite different from that individual's behavior as a member of a group. This responsibility carries with it the necessity of having some knowledge of individual psychology and group dynamics if he is to perform satisfactorily as an administrator and a leader.[49]

An effective sales force needs above all:

strong, imaginative, aggressive—even ruthless—leadership at the top of the sales organization. . . . Nearly every dynamic and productive sales organization mirrors the drive of one man, its sales manager. It is he who sets the group's objectives; it is he who structures the activities of everyone below him; and it is he who often relentlessly applies continued pressure for superior performance. . . . He is liberal in his recognition for missions well accomplished, but he demands results—and gets them.[50]

---

[48] M. A. Brice, "The Sales Manager's Alter Ego," *Dun's Review and Modern Industry,* November 1966, pp. 59, 111–14.

[49] D. J. Duncan, *Some Basic Determinants of Behavior in Industrial Purchasing* (Berkeley: Institute of Business and Economic Research, University of California, 1965), p. 3.

[50] R. N. McMurry, "The Mystique of Super-Salesmanship," *Harvard Business Review,* 39 (March–April 1961), p. 122.

TELEPHONE SELLING

An increasing number of marketing executives in this country is turning to telephone selling to improve the productiveness of sales efforts. This method of selling may be employed on a consistent, year-round basis or in a "blitz" type of campaign. When, through careful planning, its major disadvantages are minimized—including high merchandise returns, expense of telephoning, training salesmen to sell over the telephone, inability to see facial reactions during the sales presentation, and difficulty in describing the product—the telephone is an effective device for increasing sales and, by reducing sales expenses, improving profits. In addition, to quote one enthusiast for this selling method, it may result in "faster and easier selling, greater results from advertising, bigger returns from the same selling effort, extra sales from hard-to-get-to places without traveling, lower selling costs, and better customer relations. . . ."[51]

A few examples suggest the possibilities of telephone selling:

1. An Illinois company producing rolled steel employs 18 salesmen to telephone 20–25 prospects per day. Most of its $8.5 million annual sales comes from this selling method.
2. An independent tire dealer, selling directly from factory to fleet owners, expanded his annual sales volume to $10 million by using 40 telephone salesmen. Averaging one sale from three calls, this company has no travel or other sales costs and has never met its customers face to face.
3. A manufacturer of toiletries has placed its products on the shelves of fifty thousand retailers throughout the country entirely by telephone. Product placement amounts to $3.41 per account against an estimated $11 through distributors' salesmen.[52]

Various plans have been developed to integrate telephone selling with personal selling. Two such plans are known as the "skip stop" and the "key town." Skip stop is simply a method of routing calls in a territory in such a manner that a salesman *visits* one half of his customers and *telephones* the other half on each trip around his sales area. Key town is a technique designed for companies having many customers in the metropolitan areas of major cities. Under this plan, salesmen make personal calls on those customers within the city proper and then telephone those who are located in nearby smaller cities. This method provides a low-cost coverage of now-and-then buyers and small-volume customers.

It is probable that additional attention will be given to telephone selling in the years ahead as marketers seek ways of reducing costs and meeting the competition of a growing number of new products. Manufacturers of both consumer and industrial products are presently increasing their solicitation of customers by telephone.

SUMMARY

Components of a promotional system include advertising, sales promotion, publicity, and personal selling. For packaged products containers and labels are also promotional devices, particularly in self-service settings.

---

[51] T. A. Johnson, *88 Ways to Make the Telephone Work for You* (Englewood Cliffs, N.J.: Prentice-Hall, Inc., 1962), p. 32.

[52] For additional illustrations, see Johnson, op. cit., and Robert Moon, "Telephone Selling Solves Lakeside's Profit Problem," *Industrial Marketing,* 51 (January 1966), pp. 72–73.

All forms of promotion are subsets of communication, which has four essential ingredients: a message, a medium, a sender, and a receiver. The basic problem of communication is to get one or more persons to understand the meaning of what the sender wishes to convey. Generally, the more common the backgrounds and experiences of individuals, the less difficult it is to communicate.

Organizations preparing promotional plans must identify or select six factors: target market segments, competitive positioning, the messages to be communicated, an overall marketing mix, the mix of communication media, and the amount of money to be spent. This chapter gave greatest attention to the last three of these stages.

Personal selling, which was discussed in the second half of the chapter, can be a fascinating and rewarding career. In the United States well over 10 percent of the labor force is engaged in personal selling, and salesmen are an essential part of the marketing system. While many salespeople function only as order-takers who do not command large paychecks, order-getter salesmen and saleswomen can realize income levels that equal or exceed those of any of the professions. Further, creative selling is needed by all types of organizations, not just business firms.

Successful personal selling requires at least the following ingredients. Salesmen must have adequate preparation and knowledge of their products and services, of markets, and of the basic principles of salesmanship. They must also have knowledge of present and prospective customers and be able to find buyers, to make sales, and to build goodwill after each sale.

Sales force management requires special skills; good salesmen do not automatically make good sales managers any more than good athletes make good coaches. A sales manager who has been a salesman does have more empathy for and knowledge about those on his staff, but his activities are quite different from those of a salesperson. A sales manager spends most of his time selecting, training, and supervising salespeople. He also must devise appropriate compensation and other motivational programs and develop plans for effective market coverage.

The brief treatment of personal selling and sales management in this chapter provides only an introduction to an essential aspect of marketing. This should not be taken as an indication that personal selling is unimportant. Some of the books listed in the supplementary reading section can provide the next learning phase on this subject.

REVIEW AND DISCUSSION QUESTIONS

1. What benefits, from the social point of view, flow from efficient promotion?
2. What is a promotional system, and why is it often difficult to establish and maintain one?
3. Why should a person who is interested in promotional activities be interested in the communication processes? Explain the difference and similarities between communication and promotion.
4. Explain the essential relationships of the buyer decision-making process to effective promotion.
5. Explain why overall organization goals and objectives are important to making promotional decisions. Please provide several illustrations.
6. Distinguish the differences among personal selling, advertising, sales promotion, and pub-

licity. Give an illustration of how one organization might use all four of these promotional tools.

7. Explain briefly the main factors to be considered in selecting a particular promotional method or combination of methods.

8. What kinds of organizations would you expect to rely exclusively on personal selling and, in turn, make virtually no use of other message vehicles. Why?

9. Assume that you have been asked to justify the necessity of personal selling in the American economy. Present the arguments you would use to support your position and also provide answers to the criticisms of this activity.

10. Explain the types of information the salesman needs to do an effective selling job. Suggest sources for obtaining this information.

11. "Although situations under which sales are made vary widely and it is necessary for the salesman to adapt his selling efforts accordingly, certain steps or stages are common to most of them." What useful purpose is served by these steps or stages? Illustrate, using two different types of products.

12. Although there is no pattern of selecting salesmen which is foolproof, through a combination of various techniques it is possible to minimize selection errors. List and evaluate the various techniques which may be used to select salesmen.

13. Prepare an outline of the major points you would include in a training program for a college graduate employed as a "trainee" by a manufacturer of consumer goods. What changes in the program would you make if the new salesmen had previously been employed by a competitor?

14. Explain the more important compensation methods used for salesmen in this country. Are any trends evident with respect to the plan or plans employed?

15. What do you consider to be the most significant developments in sales force management in recent years? Defend your answer.

SUPPLEMENTARY READINGS

American Telephone and Telegraph Co. *A Blue Print for Telephone Selling.* New York, n.d. *A Formula for Profit.* New York, n.d. These two pamphlets provide suggestions for improving selling efforts through use of the telephone.

Aspley, J. C. and Harkness, J. C. (eds.) *The Sales Manager's Handbook,* 10th ed. Chicago: Dartnell Corp., 1966. Designed as a reference work for the sales manager, this volume contains considerable practical information for the marketing student.

Baker, R. M., Jr. and Phifer, G. *Salesmanship: Communication, Persuasion, Perception.* Boston: Allyn & Bacon, Inc., 1966. Stresses perception and persuasion in the selling process and develops a philosophy of salesmanship.

Barnhill, J. A. *Sales Management: Contemporary Perspectives.* Glenview, Ill.: Scott, Foresman & Co., 1970. A good collection of 42 articles discussing aspects of personal selling through administration of the sales force.

Bearden, J. *Personal Selling: Behavioral Science Readings and Cases.* New York: John Wiley & Sons, Inc., 1967. The contents of this volume are well indicated by its title.

Dun & Bradstreet, Inc. *Successful Sales Managing.* New York, 1967. Analyzes the knowledge and skills required for success in sales management.

Engel, J. F.; Wales, H. G.; and Warshaw, M. R. *Promotional Strategy.* Homewood, Ill.: Richard D. Irwin, Inc., 1971. Built "on a rigorous base of consumer psychology," this basic text for courses in sales promotion (including advertising) also offers case materials.

Kurtz, D. L. and Hubbard, C. W. (eds.) *The Sales Function and Its Management:*

Selected Readings. Morristown, N.J.: General Learning Press, 1971. A good readings book containing almost 50 articles on the selling function and personal selling which have appeared in various journals and magazines over the past few years.

National Industrial Conference Board   *Incentives for Salesmen.* New York, 1967. Sixteen executives discuss how to design and administer an incentive program for salesmen. Also see **Elliott, J. G.,** "Sales Incentives: Beyond Money," *Sales Management,* December 15, 1967, p. 30.

Pederson, C. A. and Wright, M. D.   *Salesmanship: Principles and Methods.* 5th ed. Homewood, Ill.: Richard D. Irwin, Inc., 1971. This standard textbook in the field of salesmanship also contains valuable case materials.

Phelps, D. M. and Westing, J. M.   *Marketing Management.* 3d ed. Homewood, Ill.: Richard D. Irwin, Inc., 1968. Chapters 19 through 32 treat fully the sales management topics discussed in this chapter.

22 Advertising

Early to Bed,
Early to Rise,
Work Like Hell,
and Advertise.

It's an incontestable fact that a lot of money is spent on advertising. Procter & Gamble spent $265 million for national advertising during 1970; General Foods Corporation, $170 million; Sears, Roebuck and Company, $130 million, and General Motors Corporation, almost $130 million. Four other companies—Warner-Lambert Pharmaceuticals, Colgate-Palmolive, Bristol-Myers Company, and American Home Products—each spent over $100 million in national advertising in 1970. Expenditures of national advertising were at least 30 percent of sales for three drug and cosmetics companies while 19 of the 100 largest national advertisers spent at least 10 percent of sales. The largest 100 advertisers, collectively, spent over $4.6 billion on national advertising, and over $20 billion was spent for national and local advertising by all advertisers in 1970. One minute of commercial time on the Super Bowl (football) telecast for 1972 carried the price tag of $200,000.[1]

The purpose of this chapter is to see *why* and *how* these dollars are spent and just how significant advertising is relative to the promotional, marketing, and economic systems. The major questions addressed are: (1) Advertising—what is it? (2) What are the purposes of advertising? (3) How important is advertising? (4) What is the structure of the advertising industry? (5) How is advertising managed?

ADVERTISING—WHAT IS IT?

In the preceding chapter advertising was defined as **any paid form of nonpersonal presentation and promotion of ideas, goods, or services by an identified sponsor.** Its key elements are that it is:

---
[1] "100 Leading National Advertisers," *Advertising Age,* August 30, 1971.

1. Impersonal. Unlike personal selling, advertising is not a personal face-to-face situation where two-way communication occurs but instead is a medium-to-face relationship.
2. Concerned with communication of ideas, goods or services. Its purpose, like other forms of promotion, is to communicate.
3. Presented by an identified, paying sponsor. Unlike publicity, which usually is not paid for (at least directly), or propaganda, which usually does not identify the sponsor, all advertising is paid for by an identified sponsor.

Advertising, of course, is not all of one type. It can be categorized by any of a number of varieties: primary, pull, national, cooperative, direct, industrial, and print. Each of these categories is useful in studying the scope of advertising.

Primary/selective

Advertisements that feature principally specific brands or makes of product or service are said to be *selective*. They try to get their audiences to select specific brands from among the available alternatives. *Primary* advertisements are those that feature a class of product, service, or idea without featuring a specific brand or vendor. A somewhat more descriptive word for this type of advertising is *pioneering*.

Primary advertising has been extensively used to promote the sale of oranges, bananas, color television, mobile homes, attorney services, dental work, and the Christian religion, to mention a few examples. Four basic situations give rise to its use. First, products, services, and ideas that offer new experiences for prospective customers when first introduced typically can be most efficiently promoted in their generic state. The purpose is to allow prospects to perceive the new offering and the ways in which it can satisfy some of their needs (goal-objects). The subtle differences between brands or makes, at this stage, would add more clutter than clarity. It would have been foolish, for example, for the United Fruit Company to advertise in the 1930s and 1940s that "The seal on the peel tells you it's a Chiquita brand banana." People needed to know about bananas and their uses, not why or how Chiquita brand was superior to another.[2]

Second, firms that have monopolies (regardless of the reason) have little need to use selective advertising. When it was the sole producer of color television sets, RCA did not need to advertise its brand. Most telephone companies and electric generating companies do not need selective advertising. When no close alternatives are available, all advertising resources can be directed to increasing demand for the total offering.

Third, some suppliers—for example, physicians and lawyers—are not permitted to engage in selective advertising. They use primary advertising jointly in the hope of increasing total demand for their offerings or getting audiences to accept ideas that are favorable toward them.

Fourth, suppliers of undifferentiated goods who are convinced that differentiation tactics (e.g., branding) are not profitable will frequently group together to promote increased consumption of their offerings. This has been done by producers (producer cooperatives) of cattle, hogs, milk, and numerous other agricultural goods.

---

[2] "Chiquita Banana Shifts U.S. Portion of Account to Y&R," *Advertising Age,* August 9, 1971, p. 35.

Pull/push advertising

As discussed in Chapter 19, advertising can be directed principally to the ultimate buyers or to the resellers in the distribution channels. When the concentration is on the ultimate buyer, the seller is using *pull*-type advertising. The seller hopes to build buyer demand and have them pull the offering through the channel by asking the retailer for it. This type of advertising is extensively used by food, beverage (including beer), toy, automobile insurance, and other manufacturer-marketers who distribute largely through consensus channels. (See Chapter 3.)

Push-type advertising, in contrast, is directed principally at channel members and is designed to encourage them to propel or push the offering through the channel. This type of advertising and promotion is used extensively by clothing (particularly less well-known brands), shoe, hardware, life insurance, and other producers who have not established strong brand preferences. It also finds extensive, but not exclusive, use where the seller owns or controls the channel, perhaps because he is in a better position to tell members what to do.

Some combination of pull- and push-type advertising can usually do a more adequate selling job than one type alone. Retailers must be encouraged to provide as many shelf facings as possible; however, to be able to maintain the in-store exposure, consumers must keep the brand flowing through the check-out counter. For example, General Foods Corporation spent about $3,000,000 in pull-type advertising in 1970 for their Jell-O puddings.[3] In addition, they directed advertisements directly to various channel members informing them about their program of pull advertising and, in general, encouraged them to promote the Jell-O pudding lines.

National/local advertising

National contrasted with local advertising is a somewhat fuzzy distinction. In a general sense, *national* has reference to advertising sponsored directly by producers (even though in only one market) or appearing in national media, whereas *local* advertising is placed by individual retailers usually in one market. The Sears advertisements, for example, that appear in *Life* magazine—along with all other advertisements in *Life*—are national. Sears' sale advertisements placed by local Sears stores in local newspapers are local advertisements. Some media, however, contain both national and local advertising. If Ford Motor Company, for example, places a general advertisement in a local newspaper featuring their cars or their viewpoint on an issue like safety, it is considered national advertising, and the local newspaper bills it at its national rate. When a local Ford dealer places advertisements featuring his dealership, it is a local advertisement billed at the local rate, even though some portion of the cost is paid by Ford Motor Company.

The distinction between national and local advertising is meaningful in that most local newspapers, radio, and television stations have two different rate structures. Local advertising rates generally are considerably lower but do not allow advertising agency discounts. National advertising rates generally exceed local advertising rates (by considerably more than 15 percent) but do allow a 15 percent discount to advertising agencies.

---

[3] "General Foods Corp.," *Advertising Age,* August 30, 1971, p. 110.

Cooperative advertising

When manufacturers or other sellers share the media expense of individual local advertisements with resellers, the result is called cooperative advertising. A common arrangement is for the manufacturer (in addition to supplying film strips, advertising mats, and other media materials) to match the dealer's advertising expenditures dollar for dollar up to a maximum amount (e.g., 2 percent of the dealer's sales). The dealer normally must provide proof that the advertising actually occurred in order to gain reimbursement.

Manufacturers make extensive use of cooperative advertising programs. Many firms feel that it more than doubles the efforts and results they put into cooperative programs (on a 50/50 basis) because: (1) dealers (retailers) must spend an equal amount of their money in behalf of the company's products, (2) the dealer placing the advertisement can get the lower local rate, and (3) the involvement of dealers with their own dollars and placement ensures their interest in the coordination of all selling efforts.[4]

Direct/institutional advertising

Direct advertisements feature the products, services, or ideas the vendor is promoting. For example, Goodwill Industries advertisements may appeal directly for contributions of used clothing and furniture, money, and/or individuals' time, or the New York Life Insurance Company might use an advertisement that describes the central features of one or several of its available policies. In both situations the advertisements are direct. In the case of Goodwill Industries the advertising focuses directly and principally on the organization's specific needs, and the New York Life Insurance Company advertisement seeks fairly direct action and response to a specific policy.

In contrast, advertisements that feature principally the organization or its viewpoint or general situation but do not specifically focus on more immediate market responses for the firm's offerings are institutional advertisements. The New York Life Insurance Company, in another advertisement, for example, may stress that it is so many years old, has assets of over so many dollars, and has the integrity of the Pope. Such an advertisement helps to remind people of the company and to maintain or create a more favorable long-term image. Similarly, Goodwill Industries uses institutional advertisements to tell about the roles it hopes to play in communities.

Institutional advertisements, however, are not used solely to build long-term goodwill. Many a funeral home and bank, for example, uses extensive institutional advertising because it does not believe it possesses service or product features that can be advertised to generate direct action; at least it feels that the integrity of its institutions is of greater importance. Institutional advertising is also used by firms to help market its stocks and bonds by making more people more favorably aware of the company, diffusing the stock more broadly and at higher prices, and making it possible to borrow money at lower rates.

Finally, established public utilities use institutional advertising to encourage a big-brother type of friendliness. Utilities are interested in relatively high levels of

---

[4] "Co-op Ad Allowances," *Marketing Insights,* January 19, 1970, pp. 1 ff.; R. L. Hicks, "Can You Buy Distribution with Your Cooperative Advertising?" *Sales Management,* September 5, 1958, p. 58; D. D. Sorenson, "Three Views of Cooperative Advertising," *Journal of Advertising Research,* 10 (December 1970), pp. 13–19.

constant consumption, high rates (prices) for their services, and renewal of their franchises as exclusive suppliers. Institutional advertising is particularly useful in helping to secure the last two objectives by regular use of the appeals: "We are good neighbors and friends—look at how clean we are, how much tax we pay, how we support the community betterment, and how much employment we provide." Then, at rate-increase or franchise-renewal time, direct advertising may be used to tell the consumers explicitly what "big brother" needs in order to retain his stance. Such a combined use of direct and institutional advertising is not unusual.

Industrial/trade/consumer advertising

Advertising in behalf of industrial products, services, and ideas that is directed to industrial buyers is simply called *industrial* advertising. Advertising directed principally to a group of middlemen, advertising people, or other facilitating agencies is called *trade* advertising, while that directed principally to consumers is referred to as *consumer* advertising.

The differences in the three markets, in general, are reflected in some differences in media and copy. Industrial and trade advertising tends to be directed more specifically to recommenders and buyers via special-market magazines, such as *Advertising Age, Progressive Grocer,* and *Iron Age,* and via direct mail. Mass or broad media such as newspapers, radio and television broadcasting, mass-media magazines such as *Life,* and billboards are used almost exclusively for consumer advertising—and for obvious reasons.

Print/electronic/outdoor/specialty/direct mail advertising

The various media used as vehicles to communicate messages to prospective receivers form another classification of advertising. *Print* generally has reference to advertisements in newspapers and magazines; *electronic* covers both radio and television, *outdoor* has reference to billboards and posters; and *specialty* advertising includes a variety of gift objects, usually low priced such as matches, pencils, pens, and calenders, which usually carry the donor company's name. *Direct mail* is advertising sent by mail directly to prospects. In addition, there are other categories of advertising based on the vehicle or conveyer used. Transit advertising, for example, is the bulletins, posters, and signs in and outside busses and other mass-transit vehicles and stations.

WHAT ARE THE PURPOSES OF ADVERTISING?

A long list of purposes of advertising can be developed—to make target groups aware of a product, service, or company; to cause receivers to remember something over time; to create favorable associations and attitudes, and so forth.[5] However, ultimately the purpose of advertising for the business firm is to help influence its sales.

Neil H. Borden and, more recently, Lee Preston have pointed out rather concisely how advertising tries to accomplish such a purpose.[6] An individual firm selling in a

---

[5] See L. Bogart, B. S. Tolley, and F. Orenstein, "What One Little Ad Can Do," *Journal of Advertising Research,* 10 (August 1970), pp. 3–13.

[6] N. H. Borden, *The Economic Effects of Advertising* (Homewood, Ill.: Richard D. Irwin, Inc., 1942); L. E. Preston, *Markets and Marketing: An Orientation* (Glenview, Ill.: Scott, Foresman & Co., 1970), pp. 194–98.

market with undifferentiated demand faces a horizontal demand schedule (Figure 22–1A). In such a situation the firm is merely one of many small sellers; its products and services are very similar to those of other sellers, it cannot offer enough product units to reduce the market price, and there is no reason why any buyers would pay more than the market price for the firm's products and services. A major purpose of advertising and other nonprice promotion by individual firms to is get out of this type of market situation—to get free of the market and gain meaningful discretion over price and other marketing variables.

Many a firm has attempted to shift the entire demand schedule up and to the right, as shown in Figure 22–1B. This, however, is likely to occur only where there

FIGURE 22–1
Demand schedules for advertising purposes

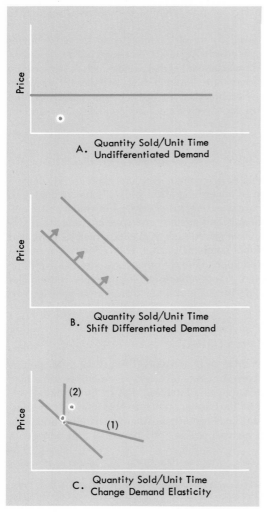

A. Quantity Sold/Unit Time
   Undifferentiated Demand

B. Quantity Sold/Unit Time
   Shift Differentiated Demand

(2)

(1)

C. Quantity Sold/Unit Time
   Change Demand Elasticity

Marketing: Principles and methods

already is differentiated demand. If demand is not already differentiated, the increased sales must have come either from a total increase in market demand in which the firm retained its share or from sales taken away from competitors. In both of these cases, however, the firm in all likelihood will lose its sales increase readily via the same route it was gained.

A second purpose of advertising is to make segments of the demand schedule facing the firm more elastic or less elastic (Figure 22–1C). If a firm seeks to increase prices or thinks its competitors are about to reduce theirs it may want to decrease the elasticity of the relevant range (i.e., make buyers less price sensitive; segment 2). However, if the firm is contemplating reducing its prices, it will want a large response to its decrease, so it will attempt through advertising to make the relevant section of the demand schedule more elastic (segment 1). It might do this by advertising 10 cents off standard prices or calling the price reduction to the buyers' attention in other ways.

Finally, a firm may use advertising to help stabilize demand. Advertising that attempts to increase brand loyalty, for example, also attempts to stabilize demand.

None of these purposes is mutually exclusive nor necessarily appropriate for a specific company. However, they do provide a good basis for planning advertising campaigns.

One problem with the classical demand-curve approach to analyzing the effects of advertising is that, with all sellers attempting to differentiate their offerings so as to separate their demand functions from those of other sellers, it becomes difficult, if not impossible, to define what is meant by a market or a product group. How does one define the trail bike market? Does it include motorcycles? bicycles? Jeep-type vehicles? snowmobiles? When one attempts to use broad definitions, the market rapidly becomes a worldwide market for all consumer goods. A partial solution to this problem can be found in the demand analysis suggested by Kelvin J. Lancaster.[7]

HOW IMPORTANT IS ADVERTISING?

It is an unusual business firm that does not advertise. Many, if not most, not-for-profit organizations (churches, the Girl Scouts, American Red Cross, the Consumers Union), also advertise, as do agencies of the federal and state government. For some years the Hershey Chocolate Company was an example of a business firm that engaged in virtually no consumer advertising. Even then, however, it advertised extensively to the trade and used in-store promotional displays.[8] The typical local church limits its advertising to a listing in the Yellow Pages of the phone directory and a weekly listing of services in one or more local newspapers. However, there are churches that publish (particularly above the local level) their own newspapers and magazines, operate their own radio stations, and devote substantial space or time to advertising their own ideas and services. The Department of Defense through the U.S. Army spent almost $11 million in advertising in four months in 1971 trying to gain recruits. The Air Force budget for advertising was about $6 million in 1972.[9] In addition, in both cases considerable free time and space was donated by media. The U.S. Postal Service expects to spend about $5 million per year on advertising.[10]

---

[7] K. J. Lancaster, "A New Approach to Consumer Theory," *Journal of Political Economy,* 74 (April 1968), pp. 132–57.

[8] "Hershey's Sweet Tooth Starts Aching," *Business Week,* February 7, 1970, pp. 98–104.

[9] "Army to Seek More Free Air Time This Fall," *Advertising Age,* September 6, 1971, p. 39.

[10] "Post Office Picks Burnett, NH&S," *Advertising Age,* August 9, 1971, p. 1.

TABLE 22–1
Advertising revenue by medium, selected years, 1947–69

		ADVERTISING REVENUE BY MEDIUM									OTHER	
Year	Total	Newspapers	Magazines	Business Publications	Farm Publications	Television	Radio	Direct Mail	Outdoor	Point of Purchase Displays	Agency Income	Expenditures
1947	4,241	1,192	434	150	41	2	365	566	113	187	265	926
1948	4,907	1,410	482	163	42	9	408	671	115	194	309	1,104
1949	5,331	1,503	463	162	43	34	415	724	115	199	338	1,335
1950	5,864	1,641	481	164	42	106	444	749	132	202	373	1,530
1951	6,497	1,747	545	182	44	236	450	833	137	235	414	1,674
1952	7,161	1,879	592	210	46	324	470	907	145	262	459	1,867
1953	7,784	2,002	650	220	48	432	476	1,003	158	290	501	2,004
1954	8,080	2,059	646	228	48	593	449	1,040	172	288	520	2,037
1955	8,997	2,320	668	250	50	745	453	1,229	176	311	597	2,198
1956	9,674	2,476	680	275	53	897	480	1,308	189	345	675	2,296
1957	10,313	2,510	695	319	56	943	517	1,324	201	318	737	2,693
1958	10,414	2,459	652	302	55	1,030	523	1,419	219	344	757	2,654
1959	11,358	2,705	718	354	58	1,164	560	1,597	223	362	815	2,802
1960	11,900	2,821	769	383	55	1,269	598	1,658	242	387	859	2,859
1961	12,048	2,818	774	384	53	1,318	591	1,687	232	405	870	2,916
1962	12,919	2,930	797	378	50	1,486	636	1,758	230	416	955	3,283
1963	13,639	3,087	832	413	47	1,597	681	1,760	229	490	1,005	3,498
1964R	14,824	3,411	873	451	47	1,793	732	1,890	241	554	1,085	3,747
1965R	16,175	3,658	924	475	47	1,965	793	2,057	251	574	1,194	4,237
1966R	17,511	4,130	997	528	47	2,203	872	2,277	270	597	1,305	4,285
1967R	17,986	4,175	990	545	46	2,273	907	2,323	279	666	1,317	4,465
1968R	19,001	4,446	1,020	560	46	2,521	1,023	2,434	310	706	1,441	4,494
1969P	20,455	4,793	1,065	582	42	2,831	1,100	2,507	327	777	1,564	4,867

RRevised   PPreliminary

Source: *Advertising Age*, March 30, 1970.

Illustrations drawn from many additional types of organizations could be presented. It should be obvious even to the casual observer that both private and public, both profit-seeking and not-for-profit, organizations allocate funds to advertising.

Importance of expenditure levels

The total expenditure for advertising in the United States in 1969 was estimated at $20.455 billion dollars. This is an increase of almost 65 percent since 1959, and the expenditure expected by 1976 is $30 billion.[11]

The total annual volume of advertising and the volume by major media in the United States for selected years starting with 1947 are indicated in Table 22–1. To help give the total advertising dollar figures more meaning, they can be compared with the U.S. gross national product (GNP) for each of the years (Table 22–2). In 1969, total advertising expenditures were only 2.19 percent of GNP, which is less than it was in 1963. While the total volume of advertising increased each year, some media did not increase as rapidly as others. Note particularly the statistics for magazines and radio in Table 22–1.

TABLE 22–2
Advertising as a percent of GNP

	GNP (in billions)	Advertising expenditures (in millions)	Advertising expense/GNP ratio (percent)
1963	$590.5	$13,639	2.31
1964	632.4	14,824	2.34
1965	684.9	16,175	2.36
1966	749.9	17,556	2.34
1967	793.5	17,986	2.27
1968	865.7	19,001	2.20
1969	923.3	20,455	2.19

Note: All estimates in current dollars.
Source: *Advertising Age,* March 30, 1970.

Importance to individual firms

Total advertising dollars also need to be disaggregated in order to consider the importance of advertising to the overall budgets of individual organizations. While no one best comparison base is available, the most widely used is sales. One firm, J. B. Williams Company, spent about 36 cents out of every dollar of sales on national advertising in 1971. Some of the brands they advertised heavily were Geritol, Sominex, Aqua Velva, Pro Slim, Lectric Shave, and Serutan.

Alberto Culver Company, another cosmetic firm, had a *national* advertising to sales ratio in 1971 of 30.6 percent. In addition to the $52 million spent on national advertising of such brands as FDS, Command, Dry and Natural, VO5, Born Free, Calm, Shimmy Skins, and New Dawn, the firm is reported to have spent another $36 million for local advertising, selling, and general expenses. Thus with a total of almost

---

[11] Jules Backman, *Advertising and Competition* (New York: New York University Press, 1967), p. 179.

$88 million for advertising and $170 million in sales, Alberto Culver had an actual advertising to sales ratio of almost 52 percent.[12]

The five largest firms in the soap, cleanser, and allied products field ranged from a low ratio of national advertising to sales for 1971 of 8.3 to 22.4 percent, with the median at 15.3 percent. The range in the drug and cosmetic field for the top 20 firms was from 3.1 to 36 percent, with the median at about 12 percent. The 16 largest national advertisers of food products ranged from a low of 1.5 percent (Borden Incorporated) to a high of 14.1 percent (Nabisco), with the median at about 5 percent. Only two major automobile sellers—Volkswagen of America (2.2 percent) and American Motors Corporation (1.7 percent)—spent as much as 1 percent of sales on advertising. These ratios are for national advertising, however, and additional dollars were devoted to cooperative advertising programs by many automobile manufacturers; much automobile advertising is placed through dealers or dealer associations. Sears, Roebuck and Company, as another example, spent $130 million for national advertising in 1971 (1.4 percent of sales) and another $200 million in local advertising for a total advertising ratio of about 3.9 percent of sales.[13]

A more representative picture of the expenditures on advertising by U.S. companies is provided by a Conference Board report that found that manufacturers of consumer goods and services spend on the average of 3 percent of sales for advertising, and industrial goods manufacturers spend under 1 percent (Figure 22–2). Putting together all manufacturers, service suppliers, and retailers, the average amount spent on advertising was under 2 percent of sales. Note, however, that the variance between industries is large. Remember also that the ratio is expressed as a percent of sales, and very few of the companies listed had profits expressed as a percent of sales in excess of 4 percent.[14] Advertising is of great importance to many firms, and it is of some importance and concern to almost all.[15]

Importance compared to other promotion

Despite the example of Alberto Culver's promotional program and those of some other drug and cosmetic companies, most companies spend far more on personal selling than they do on advertising. Rough estimates seem to indicate that the only industries that spend as much or more on advertising as on personal selling are proprietary drugs and cosmetics (toiletries); soap, cleanser and allied products; tobacco (with about 8 cents per carton); and beverages, soft and hard. Advertising in most industries runs from 1 to 3 percent of sales, while personal selling, whether the firm uses its own salesmen or agents, averages from about 8 to 15 percent of sales.[16]

Virtually all retailers, including so called self-service outlets, and wholesalers spend far more promotional dollars on personal selling than on advertising. Retailers, for example, typically spend from 7 to 20 percent on personal selling. The wholesale trade overall spends just under one half of 1 percent on advertising, while the retail

---

[12] "Alberto Culver Company," *Advertising Age,* August 30, 1971, pp. 21–22.

[13] "100 Leaders' Advertising as Percent of Sales," *Advertising Age,* August 30, 1971, p. 22.

[14] S. A. Greyser and B. B. Reece, "Businessmen Look Hard at Advertising," *Harvard Business Review,* 49 (May–June 1971), pp. 18–27.

[15] See "Industrial Ads: The View from the Top," *Business Week,* May 30, 1970, pp. 92–96.

[16] D. Houghton, "Marketing Costs: What Ratio to Sales?" *Printers' Ink,* February 1, 1957, p. 24.

Marketing: Principles and methods

FIGURE 22–2

Advertising expenditures as a percentage of sales for selected types of manufacturers, retailers, and service industries, 1964

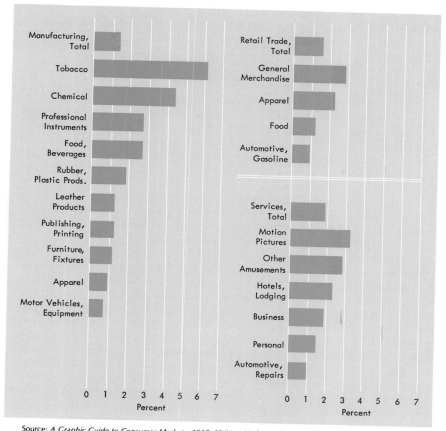

Source: *A Graphic Guide to Consumer Markets: 1968–69* (New York: Conference Board 1968), pp. 80–81. Original data source, U.S. Treasury Department.

trade averages about 1.6 percent of sales for advertising. Mail-order houses, of course, are a major exception.[17]

Employment

Advertising is not labor intensive. Most of the estimated $20 billion annual expenditure goes to media, not to people considered to be employed in the advertising industry. There are around 4,000 advertising agencies in the United States. They employ from 70 to, at most, 80 thousand people.[18] Add to this figure all of the people

---

[17] *Advertising Age,* December 29, 1969, pp. 32–33.

[18] The *1967 Census of Business* reported 74,199 employees in advertising agencies.

working in advertising activities in manufacturing, wholesaling, retailing, government, trade associations, and all those working in advertising activities for all media and, at most, there are no more than 400,000 persons working directly in advertising. To help put this in perspective, you may recall that there are estimated to be about 7 million people working in personal selling and that the total civilian labor force in the United States in recent years has been over 80 million.

Importance to the economic system

Those who would dismiss the importance of advertising in the marketing system and in the larger economic system typically point to how little direct employment it provides and what a small part of GNP it represents. Such a basis used as the sole consideration of advertising's importance is quite inappropriate. Instead, the role of advertising in the marketing and economic systems must be considered in terms of the activities it performs in the total system and how less (or more) efficient each of the systems would be without it.

You may recall from Chapter 2 that whenever there is specialization, discrepancy of assortments arises and that the marketing system's reason for being is to perform the equalization process. That is, the marketing system is present only to equalize the gap or differences in form, time, location, quantity, and value between production and consumption. It brings supply and demand together through the activities of sorting out, assembling, allocating, and assorting.[19] Processors, manufacturers, middlemen, facilitating agencies, and customers—all of whom perform these activities—do so on the basis of information and persuasion. For example, manufacturers attempt to determine the wants and needs of prospective customers, but they also must inform customers about the products and services they have available, when and where and at what prices. To inform customers, they can inform various wholesalers, who, in turn, inform retailers who inform the ultimate customers (push promotion); they can directly inform prospective customers about offerings (pull promotion); or they can use both approaches to inform customers. The information function of advertising is essential because information does not issue automatically to those who need it as a basis for performing marketing activities or consumption. Only one person in the past 2,500 years has been widely credited with being omniscient, and many people reject even that one. Consequently, the information portion of promotion is absolutely essential.

This should not suggest that the persuasive aspects of advertising that are not informative are useless. Remember that efficiencies in production and marketing are dependent on mass production and mass marketing. The result is that the precise products and services to suit each individual's taste are not produced, and products and services are not made available to each individual just when, where, how, and at the prices desired. Individuals must be *persuaded* that the products, services, and ideas, their availability, and their prices are close enough to their needs and wants to warrant their acceptance. Consequently, both information and persuasion are needed in the marketing system. To yield effective communication, a message must be attractive to receivers. It is not possible to define a line which separates an informative message from a persuasive one.

As a part of the promotional system, advertising is simply the most efficient form

---

[19] See the second section of Chapter 2.

Marketing: Principles and methods

to use when simple messages are appropriate for informing or persuading a large number of people. When the information to be communicated to a large number of people is not too complicated and the individual differences are not too great, advertising can inform and help persuade more people per dollar spent than can other forms of promotion.

Finally, the objective of a marketing system is compatible with the objectives of our economic system—to efficiently allocate scarce resources in such a way as to satisfy to the greatest extent possible the needs of man. With advertising as a form of promotion, the marketing system is more efficient than it would be without it. Our economic system is also more efficient in terms of inputs required to produce desired outputs with advertising than it would be without it.[20]

WHAT IS THE STRUCTURE OF THE ADVERTISING INDUSTRY?

The advertising industry consists of three principal components: (1) advertisers, (2) advertising agencies and departments, and (3) advertising media. In the advertising buying mechanism, the advertisers are the buyers and the agencies and media are the suppliers. Methods by which organizations function as advertisers are discussed in another section. Here attention is devoted to brief views of advertising agencies and departments and advertising media.

Advertising agencies, house agencies, and departments

Advertising agencies. Advertising agencies are present in a variety of types, sizes, and locations. The latest *Census of Business* indicated there were 5,618 advertising agency establishments in the United States. Because each office was listed as a separate establishment, however, the total number of separate advertising agencies is probably closer to 4,000. Some 208 agencies had total billings of $5.3 billion and accounted for around 70 percent of the total receipts for all of the agencies. There are wide differences among agencies.[21]

The larger agencies for the most part are located in the metropolitan areas. New York City has 943 agencies (many of which are located on Madison Avenue), Chicago has 415 agencies (Michigan Avenue is the popular location), and Los Angeles has 381 agencies. While 10 cities host almost half of all the advertising agencies in the United States, the remainder is scattered throughout the country. Virtually every city of business importance has at least one agency listed in the *Standard Directory of Advertising: The Agency List.*

Agencies vary in the amount of in-house service capabilities they have available for clients. In general, the larger the agency the more in-house creative, copy, media, research, and marketing services they will have.[22] The smaller agencies, on the other hand, either limit their services or "hire out" many more activities and serve more to coordinate the activities of outside specialists in behalf of their clients. Virtually all

---

[20] This is not to say that advertising is as efficient as it could be; there are, of course, inefficiencies in advertising. The relative efficiency of advertising is examined in Chapters 6 and 24.

[21] Note that agency size is based not on their volume of sales to clients but by the "billings" they place with media. The J. Walter Thompson Company, which has been the largest in recent years, has had billings of over $600 million, but their sales have probably been closer to $100 million.

[22] For insight on a very large agency, see Ralph Leezenbaum, "JWT: Mystical Melding of the Swinging and the Staid," *Marketing/Communications,* March 1970, pp. 22–30.

22 / Advertising

agencies, however, make some use of outside specialists in creative work, media selection and buying, photography, and so forth.[23]

House agencies. The ownership and management at most agencies are independent of the advertisers they serve. Agencies that are under the control of one of their advertisers, even if they serve additional clients, are known as house agencies. Only a few major advertisers currently use house agencies. Among them in 1970 were the Quaker Oats Company, Hunt-Wesson, Inc., Monsanto Company, John Deere and Company, Jeno's, Inc., Warner-Lambert Pharmaceutical Company, Melville Shoe Corporation, Hystron Fibers, Inc., and the Lane Company.[24]

To advertisers that use house agencies the major advantage is some combination of lower prices, quicker responses, and better advertising. The price break, where it is important, comes about because traditionally the single largest source of payment to most advertising agencies is the 15 percent discount allowed by media on national advertising.[25] An advertiser who feels this discount overpays the agencies for the services rendered or that he, as a client, is being charged too many fees for additional services that should be covered by the discount may set up his own agency and receive the discount himself. This house agency may be fully staffed like Warner-Lambert's Lambert and Feasley or it may be like Melville Shoe Corporation's, which is staffed by only a handful of people who supervise the work done by outside specialists. A Melville spokesman has said that they buy their advertisements from different "creative boutiques" and free-lancers and use an independent production house and an independent media-buying company to get into print and on the air. The advantages he claims are that it "saved 'a considerable amount of money, a substantial amount,' but also is buying better advertising." Another advertiser claims his house agency is much more responsive, ". . . the typical agency takes four weeks to solve a problem. . . . We've found out that we can cut that time to a few days."[26]

Advertising departments. Well over half of the advertising dollars are *not* spent through advertising agencies. Most retailers and other heavy users of newspaper advertising or other local media either create and place their own advertisements or work closely with media representatives to develop advertisements.

Further, most companies that do use advertising agencies also have advertising departments. In some companies such departments serve primarily as liaison between their companies and the agencies to see that they receive appropriate (1) creative skills (such as campaign planning and appeal planning), (2) media information and the best possible media buys, and (3) supporting research. Such departments are also usually in on the firing and hiring of advertising agencies (a not uncommon occurrence).[27] Other advertising departments, at the other extreme, are almost fully staffed and use agencies only for limited activities. A broad range of activities is performed within advertisers' organizations by their own advertising departments, and there appear to

---

[23] For a discussion of likely changes in advertising agencies, see J. J. Johnston, "It's Time for Major Revamp of Outdated Agency System," *Advertising Age,* April 13, 1970, pp. 98 and 100.

[24] "Advertisers Do It Themselves," *Business Week,* July 18, 1970, p. 66.

[25] For discussion about agency compensation, see W. R. King, "A Conceptual Framework for Ad Agency Compensation," *Journal of Marketing Research,* 5 (May 1968), pp. 178–80; and "The Sacred Cow Needs a Vet," *Industrial Marketing,* 54 (June 1969), pp. 65–66.

[26] "Advertisers Do It Themselves," *Business Week.*

[27] For a report on relating and working with advertising agencies, see *Industrial Marketing,* 53 (April 1968), Section 2.

be few useful guidelines. Management must decide the best arrangements for each situation.[28]

Advertising media

Many media are available to advertisers. The principal ones are:[29]

1. Newspapers—dailies, weeklies, shopping news.
2. Magazines—consumer, business, professional, and farm.[30]
3. Radio—local, national spot, network.
4. Television—local, national spot, network.
5. Direct mail—letters, postcards, circulars, booklets, and leaflets.
6. Outdoor—billboards and signs.
7. Specialty—pencils, pens, blotters, etc., imprinted with the advertiser's name.
8. Transit—bus, taxicab, and suburban station and train cards.
9. Theatrical films.
10. Handbills and package inserts.
11. Classified columns in telephone directories, buyers' directories, and newspapers.

Each of the media has a combination of characteristics that make it somewhat unique and particularly appropriate or inappropriate for use as a communication vehicle in various situations. The outstanding characteristics of the first seven media are discussed below. More detailed information is available in some of the books noted in the references at the end of this chapter.

Newspapers. The outstanding characteristics of newspapers are that they are flexible and timely, offer general and intensive local market coverage, and are read in detail for current news. Advertisements of virtually any size and with any composition of words and pictures can be inserted or changed within one or two days of when they are to appear. Papers have intense coverage because most adults read at least one daily and, while they may first learn about events elsewhere, they expect current, detailed newspaper coverage. Finally, newspapers normally remain available for reference a day or two before they are discarded.

Magazines. The outstanding characteristics of many (but not all) magazines are that they offer advertisers prestigious, broad, multimarket coverage to either mass general or selected audiences, and they permit high-quality color print reproduction. A general magazine like *Life* provides regional sections in which space can be purchased, as well as total national coverage. Magazines like *Playboy* and *Sports Afield* deliver selected audiences because they appeal to and get read by only special-interest groups. Magazines are less timely and flexible than some other media in that advertise-

---

[28] D. A. Newton, "Advertising Agency Services: Make or Buy?" *Harvard Business Review,* 43 (July–August, 1965), pp. 111–18.

[29] Newspapers carry about 80 percent of all retail advertising. P. C. Hauck, "Local Stores Turn Increasingly to TV Ads as Their Costs Drop, Color Sets Multiply," *Wall Street Journal,* February 2, 1967, p. 24.

[30] Magazines that accept advertising and are distributed free to selected readers, such as *American Machinist, Plastics World, Modern Materials Handling,* and *Holiday Inn,* are classified as "qualified circulation." See P. H. Dougherty, "Advertising: Magazines that Nobody Buys," *New York Times,* May 14, 1967, p. F14.

22 / Advertising

541

ments must be inserted long before publication dates and many magazines appear only monthly.[31]

Radio. Radio, like newspapers, is flexible and timely and can be quite selective geographically as well as by audience characteristics, according to programming and the time of day. It does, of course, communicate through sound, which permits a personal and dramatic word-coloring impact, but not visually, and it is not available for rehearing until repeated, but it can be repeated frequently. It usually lends itself to brief rather than long or detailed messages.

Television. Television is unique among mass media in that it communicates through moving, visual impressions and sound simultaneously. Because the sound permits personal and dramatic word-and-situation inflections and the picture can show action, television can provide a very natural setting. While network television requires extensive advertising lead time, local television can be quite flexible and timely. Television advertising on some programs can be purchased for only local markets, or packages of markets can be purchased that allow certain portions to be excluded. In addition, while television is generally considered to be a general-audience medium, some audience-characteristic selection is possible through buying time on programs like "American Bandstand," "Captain Kangaroo," and "As the World Turns." As in radio, an individual advertisement is available to the audience only when it is being broadcast.

Direct mail. Direct mail can be more personal and selective than other media. Partitioning of the market into various segments for which messages can be tailor-made is limited only to the availability of mailing lists with prospects' characteristics. Thousands of mailing lists (of varying quality) of different types of groups (dog owners, new car purchasers, high school seniors, etc.) are available for purchase. Cost per reader contacted is relatively high compared to the other media.

Outdoor. Outdoor advertisements generally are big and hard to avoid seeing. They can provide local or almost any other market coverage for any required exposure period. Normally, the messages must be brief and contain few words. This medium is excellent for reminders, short announcements, or location directions. Most outdoor advertising offers very little audience selection.

Specialty advertising. Calendars, pens, pencils, key chains, change holders and a variety of novelty items imprinted with the advertiser's name and a brief message can keep prospective customers aware of the advertiser for a considerable time. The major difficulties are getting distribution to the appropriate prospects so they can appreciate the item as a gift and retain it as an announcement or reminder.[32]

HOW IS ADVERTISING MANAGED?

Enough of the essentials in the structure of advertising have been covered that the major decisions that organizations must make in order to use advertising effectively can be determined. Some of these decision areas have already been discussed in the preceding chapter under the rubric of promotion.

The starting place for an organization attempting to plan an advertising program is with its overall goals and objectives. From these goals flow a set of annual company,

---

[31] For an excellent overview of magazines prior to the collapse of *Look,* see P. H. Dougherty, "What Future for Magazines," *New York Times,* April 27, 1969, pp. F1, 13.

[32] For a more precise definition and many illustrations, see *Specialty Advertising Report,* published bimonthly by the Specialty Advertising Bureau, Chicago, Illinois.

marketing, promotion, and advertising objectives, as illustrated in Figure 22–3. Each level of objectives in the hierarchy would be based on the objectives in the prior set as well as on the capabilities of the particular activity—e.g., advertising.

FIGURE 22–3

Goals and objectives hierarchy for an advertising program

Company Goals

Company Objectives

Marketing Objectives

Promotional Objectives

Advertising Objectives

Campaign Objectives

Individual Advertisement Objective

Advertising objectives

The basic question which must be asked in order to formulate advertising objectives is: *What can and should advertising accomplish in view of the hierarchy of objectives?* Without going into detail on what the intervening company, marketing, and promotional objectives are, in view of its goals, some of the general advertising objectives might be to:

1. Tell prospective customers about new products.
2. Increase market share.
3. Assist in securing new dealers.
4. Make prospective customers more familiar with the company's brands.
5. Make more buyers accessible to the company's salesmen.
6. Increase the middlemen's knowledge about the profitability of the company's products.

Specific advertising objectives. These general objectives, to be more useful, should be recast into more specific objectives, such as:

1. Secure at least a 30 percent awareness of prospective customers for new products in the Standard Metropolitan Statistical Area (SMSA) markets.
2. Increase in-store customer inquiry for brands by at least 30 percent.
3. Get at least 500 new dealer inquiries through the use of trade advertising.

4. Increase market awareness of leading brands to 35 percent and of weaker brands to at least 8 percent.
5. Secure at least 100 inquiries and invitations from buyers for salesmen to call.
6. See that at least 70 percent of the middlemen know that the 45 percent gross margin offered is the largest of any seller.

The recast specific objectives do not lose any of the thrust of the general objectives, but they do provide the advertising group with more explicit guidance. They also indicate that the degree of objective attainment will be subject to measurement. This in itself is a good way to improve performance.[33]

Plans

With the objectives fairly well formulated, advertising management must prepare plans. Typically, plans are for one-year periods and are prepared for each distinct product or service line (unless these are advertised together). A manufacturer like the Mennen Company, with well over 50 products, typically uses a group of brand or project managers to prepare the advertising plans. Such managers work with their company's information resources and advertising agencies to prepare tentative sets of marketing and advertising plans for each major product line or brand. These tentative plans are scrutinized and modified by a merchandising or marketing manager and must often win the approval of top management.

With a short-line manufacturer like the Maytag Company, the advertising manager and the company's advertising agency are likely to prepare the first or tentative set of advertising plans. Then the marketing vice president, followed by other top managers, gets involved in finalizing the plans.

The major planning tasks are to decide: (1) how much of the total promotion budget will go into advertising, (2) what central messages or themes will be used, (3) what media will be used, (4) when the advertising will have its impact, and (5) where the advertising will have its impact geographically. Because the first item was discussed in the preceding chapter, attention here will be devoted principally to copy strategy, media strategy, and where and when the advertising should impact. An advertiser seeks to mold these components into what is known in advertisers' parlance as an *advertising campaign*—more specifically, an *effective* advertising campaign.

Advertising campaign decisions

A company may conduct only one campaign over a long time, it may sequence campaigns by selling seasons, or it may have several running at one time (but not usually to a single market segment). Each campaign objective must be in keeping with the company's overall advertising objective.

Copy strategy. Formulation of a campaign begins with the determination of a basic copy approach. Advertisers typically ask, in essence, "What is it that must be communicated to our target prospects to achieve the advertising and campaign objectives?" Two major lines of questions are useful in probing for the central or keynote theme. One is: "What is unique or different about our offering that would lead prospects to buy it rather than competing brands?" It could be "Never a Rough

---

[33] Case histories and a discussion of managing advertising by objectives are given in *Setting Advertising Objectives,* Studies in Business Policy No. 118 (New York: National Industrial Conference Board, 1966).

Puff," "Longer . . . yet milder," "With the Famous Micronite Filter," "Come to Where the Flavor Is," "Beachwood Aging," "Brewed by an Old World Formula," "Rocky Mountain Spring Water," or "Brewed in Milwaukee." Frequently in a retail campaign it is the price or the assortment or, quite often, something ambiguous called "quality." Infrequently an advertiser will have the opportunity to use the appeal that he really has a "now" product. An excellent example is reproduced in Figure 22–4.

The other question that is often asked is: "What is attractive and common to the people we want as customers?" The thought is that the advertiser can feature customers or their desires with, at best, only vague reference to his product or service attribute. That is, the advertiser associates his product with the desirable. Themes that could have been developed out of this approach include, "You only go around once," "If you've got the time, we've got the beer," "They're not for everybody," "You've got a lot to live. Pepsi's got a lot to give."

1. *Copy themes need to be simple.* These short and simple central themes should not suggest that advertisers think prospective customers are all simple or stupid. If you will recall the communications model presented in the preceding chapter and the models of buyer behavior discussed in Chapters 4 and 12, you probably will appreciate what advertisers are attempting to do and why they are doing it. The message must get exposed to prospective customers so they both perceive the offering and receive it favorably. Remember, the seller is attempting to get or keep his product, service, or idea in the evoked set (the considered alternatives) of prospective customers. Furthermore, the seller wants customers to prefer and buy his offering.

Just to communicate is difficult; to communicate favorably is even harder; to get a product or service included in a large number of buyers' evoked sets is exceedingly difficult. Thus, to repeatedly be the first choice of a large number of buyers, an organization must engage in myriad marketing activities (including advertising) better than their competitors do.

2. *Possible misunderstandings.* Two major misunderstandings may have arisen. First, because we have considered only the central or key themes that help achieve advertising objectives, this does not mean that nothing else is necessary. Ford Motor Company, for example, has used many words and pictures in its consumer advertising, all of which are basically trying to communicate one central theme favorably. In recent years, it has been to the effect that "Ford has a better idea." This theme provides a favorable umbrella under which Ford can communicate some of its better ideas (car features) to prospective buyers. Similar illustrations could be Procter & Gamble's Crest brand toothpaste (what is their central theme?) or almost any of their other successful products.

Retailers also use the central theme concept. Because the typical retailer offers so many different products and services, his keynote theme relates to the institution. Retailers, large and small, for years have maintained that successful stores have personalities, which advertising is used to help develop and convey. Sears, Roebuck and Company used as a central theme the fact that Sears had changed; it was no longer only a farmers' store for work clothes and hardware. Of course, they said it quite differently: "You've changed a lot lately. So has Sears." In the same continuing campaign Sears advertisements talked about the "Italian Renaissance—Sears-style," "Rajah—Sears fresh translation of the Far East," and so forth. In addition, Sears makes extensive use of sale advertising.

There may also be a misunderstanding over the fact that central themes can change over time. Copy themes should not be changed simply because they are old, but rather because a new one can meet the hierarchy of objectives more effectively.

New see-thru roasting wrap revolutionizes cooking!

1 ...**because** when you wrap in see-thru REVEAL,™ you can keep an eye on things from start to finish. It's a whole new way to roast the juiciest, most flavorful meats.

2 ...**because** REVEAL'S unique Sure-Seal strips lock in the flavorful juices all the while the meat is roasting. You can see meats continuously basting *inside the wrap*. Watch meats deliciously browning *right through the wrap*. Pans and ovens stay clean as a whistle.

3 ...**because** you can wrap everything you roast in REVEAL. Juicy roast beef . . . a golden, plump bird . . . lots of yummy chops. Put what you like in see-thru REVEAL, and take out something you'll love.

Source: Colgate-Palmolive Company, New York, N.Y.

Procter & Gamble has not changed the Crest theme in years. In contrast, some firms have changed, or at least transitioned, central themes frequently.

3. *Creating copy.* Developing copy for the selected theme is difficult and calls for considerable creative effort. While there are hundreds of rules for copy writing—"keep human interest high, keep it fresh, keep it easy to read"—there really is no detailed formula to guide the copy editor. Years ago, Victor O. Schwab captured the essence of good copy. He proposed five basic guides: (1) get attention, (2) show people an advantage, (3) prove it, (4) persuade people to grasp this advantage, and (5) ask for action. The big question in each of these steps, of course, is "How?"[34]

Within recent years the advertising industry has acknowledged that some of the best copy has been coming out of the Doyle Dane Bernbach agency. An example of their work is the well-known Volkswagen campaign.[35]

Media strategy. The basic question which underlies the formulation of media strategy is: "What media should be used, and when, to carry our messages to our target audiences?" Answers require knowledge about the available media and the capabilities of each, particularly in terms of their coverage and reach. In addition, it is necessary to identify the intended audiences, including where they are located and when they should be contacted. The essence of media strategy is to match target audiences and available media. Media strategists cannot function properly with limited knowledge of media dimensions or audience characteristics; they must have detailed comprehension of both areas.[36] In preceding chapters, particularly Chapter 17, acquisition of information about consumers was generally discussed. Some aspects of media evaluation need more attention, however.

Media strategists can use a great variety of alternative media. The general capabilities among the types of media—newspapers, magazines, television, etc.—are quite different, and within any one medium there are also large differences. *The New York Times,* for example, offers something far different from the *Des Moines Register.* An appropriate media mix is essential because for good copy to have its intended effect, it must get conveyed to the target prospects. Media-selection decisions depend principally on (1) *coverage,* (2) *reach,* (3) *effectiveness,* and (4) *cost.*

1. *Media coverage.* The ideal geographical coverage is offered by media whose boundaries coincide with the advertiser's target audiences. The coverage that extends beyond the intended audience is "spillover." It must be paid for, but it cannot produce meaningful benefits.

Because advertisers find it difficult to obtain just the right coverage, they frequently end up buying spillover or adjusting their marketing coverage. An illustration concerns a wholesaler (distributor) of snowmobiles who had an exclusive franchise for all of Iowa. His real market and dealer organization, however, was limited to the substantial snowfall area, which, at best, included the northern half of Iowa. A statewide newspaper offered three regional advertising sections, but the divisions were east, middle, and west. With each regional buy, almost half of the coverage would be spillover. Local-market newspapers did not have the disadvantage of spillover, but

---

[34] For some details on this, see "Advertising's Creative Explosion," *Newsweek,* August 18, 1969, pp. 46–51.

[35] "Nader Rips 'Clever' VW Ads for Promoting 'Unsafe' Auto," *Advertising Age,* September 13, 1971, p. 1. Also see C. H. Sandage and V. Fryburger, *Advertising Theory and Practice* (8th ed.; Homewood, Ill.: Richard D. Irwin, Inc., 1971), and S. W. Dunn, *Advertising: Its Role in Modern Marketing* (2d ed.; New York: Holt, Rinehart & Winston, Inc., 1969).

[36] See C. W. King and J. O. Summers, "Attitudes and Media Exposure," *Journal of Advertising Research,* 11 (February 1971), pp. 26–32.

22 / Advertising

neither did they offer very complete rural coverage. Television use presented some interesting problems. Some stations were so located that most of their prime viewing areas were within the distributor's market area. The only station, however, that provided coverage into several key counties also provided extensive coverage in Minnesota. In order to relieve the spillover problem, the Iowa distributor shared the cost of the coverage with the Minnesota distributor. On the western border, the only adequate Iowa coverage also provided coverage into eastern Nebraska. In this situation, the Iowa distributor was able to secure distribution rights to the Nebraska television coverage area. This is not all there was to his media problem, but the example does point out some of the problems of securing appropriate coverage.

The coverage problem is usually more severe for local marketers than for regional or national marketers simply because there are relatively few media. The regional marketer can always aggregate the local media into regional coverage, and the national market can aggregate the local and regional media into national coverage. Local campaigns must usually be conveyed by local newspapers, local radio, local television, billboards, and other local media—and many of them spill over. Single- and limited-outlet stores, particularly convenience goods stores, in metropolitan markets often must buy coverage they cannot use. Large retailers like K-Mart, Woolco, Safeway, and Kroger that rely on extensive advertising strive to establish sufficient retail outlets to serve the advertising coverage area.[37]

2. *Media reach.* Another concern is determining the media that can actually *reach* the target customers within coverage areas. Various market segments, by definition, have different compositions. The total target market for trail bikes may be composed of three major segments—persons too young to have drivers' licenses, farmers or ranchers, and outdoor enthusiasts. The prospects within a segment tend to be somewhat alike but quite different from those in the other two segments. In turn, a hard-rock radio program that may reach the teen audience would not reach the other two segments, and while the *Farm Bureau Spokesman* or *Progressive Farmer* would reach the farm segment, it would not reach the other two.[38]

The media strategist, to help gain the appropriate reach, must know the profiles or characteristics (e.g., age, income, location, occupation, education, etc.) of his various market segments. Then he must match this data with like information about media audiences. A shortcut is to discover directly the media that reach the prospects. Unfortunately, sufficiently current and detailed information of this nature normally is not available.

3. *Media cost.* The cost of the various media needed to attain specific coverage and reach are compared by media strategists. When several media are believed to provide near equal coverage and reach, the lowest priced medium is likely to be selected. Unfortunately, while the cost figures are very explicit, the necessary coverage and reach figures tend to be not directly comparable from one medium to another and are often imprecise estimates.

Media sellers often state their prices on the basis of a cost per thousand—the dollar cost required to reach one thousand of their audience. Of course, not every

---

[37] K-Mart, for example, operates about 14 stores in the Chicago area, 35 in Los Angeles, and 19 in Detroit. It is going into the Maryland-Virginia suburbs of Washington, D.C., and hopes to open with 5 stores but to have 16 by 1974. "K-Mart Heads for Record $2.5," *Discount Stores News, Discount Census '71/'72,* August 23, 1971, pp. A50 and A53.

[38] See, for example, "The Hot Magazines Aim at Special Targets," *Business Week,* May 2, 1970, pp. 14 and 74; "More Magazines Offer a Chance to Aim at a Specific Group," *Wall Street Journal,* March 17, 1970, pp. 1 ff., and "Playboy Puts a Glint in the Admen's Eyes," *Business Week,* June 28, 1969, pp. 142–46.

magazine reader or television viewer sees every advertisement, nor does each medium have the same effect on its audience. An advertisement may be perceived and quickly forgotten, or it may at the other extreme influence a favorable buying decision.

4. Media duplication. There is another complicating consideration. Multimedia buyers are confronted with problems of duplication—the overlap of media audiences. If a media buyer is attempting to reach Iowa farmers once a month, he will not buy both the *Wallace Farmer* and the *Farm Bureau Spokesman* because it would be duplication; over 50 percent of the Iowa farmers subscribe to both journals. However, if he is attempting to reach Iowa farm women, he may have difficulty unless he buys considerable duplication. The best medium may reach only 50 percent of the women; a second best might reach 40 percent but provide only 20 percent new reach. Thus to reach 70 percent of the women the advertiser may need to buy 20 percent duplication. And of course, as he tries to reach a higher proportion, his duplication is likely to soar.[39]

5. Media models. The selection of the most appropriate set of media is difficult, at best, because of media and audience measurement problems. Even with reliable and precise information, the number of alternative media combinations is very large. Thus, the best available media mix is likely to be a compromise—that is, it will not be an ideal, but rather, in view of the available media, it will represent a possible mix which is clearly superior to a large number of other possible mixes.

Some media-selection models have been developed and are being used. Their state of development is limited at this time, and they are normally used together with a media buyer, or a media buyer evaluates their output and, as necessary, modifies it. Media selection is still an art in which media strategists play key roles.[40]

Media schedules. In creating and managing an advertising campaign, decisions must be made as to *when* and *how often* the advertisements must impact. In advertising parlance, this is referred to as preparing the media schedule. Three basic alternatives are available: (1) level-expenditure method, (2) big-early, little-late method, and (3) snowballing or crescendo method.

1. Level-expenditure method. Under this approach near equal amounts of advertising appear during each of the time periods during the campaign. Many food supermarkets employ this pattern, with each calendar week constituting a time period. There may be double advertising allowances just prior to certain holidays, but for the most part, the total advertising expenditure in any two months is likely to be very similar.

This approach is used principally by organizations that are established and whose sales tend to be fairly constant throughout the year. It certainly would not be appropriate for a brewer with highly seasonal sales nor for a car manufacturer with major annual model changes.

2. Big-early, little-late method. Under this approach, relatively large amounts

---

[39] For discussion of duplication on television, see G. J. Goodhardt and A. F. C. Ehrenberg, "Duplication of Television Viewing between and within Channels," *Journal of Marketing Research,* 6 (May 1969), pp. 169–78.

[40] R. D. Buzzell, *Mathematical Models and Marketing Management* (Boston: Graduate School of Business Administration, Harvard University, 1964) chap. 5; D. B. Montgomery and G. L. Urban, *Management Science in Marketing* (Englewood Cliffs, N.J.: Prentice-Hall, Inc., 1969), pp. 137–53; D. B. Brown, "A Practical Method for Media Selection," *Journal of Marketing Research,* 4 (August 1967), pp. 262–69; H. W. Boyd, Jr., J. H. Claycamp, and C. W. McClelland, "Media Models for the Industrial Goods Advertiser—A Do-It-Yourself Opportunity," *Journal of Marketing,* 34 (April 1970), pp. 23–29; and Philip Kotler, *Marketing Decision Making: A Model Building Approach* (New York: Holt, Rinehart & Winston, 1971), pp. 428–68.

22 / Advertising

of advertising appear early in the campaign, with lesser amounts appearing later. This approach has been used by the car manufacturers to provide massive advertising exposure at the time new models are introduced. A few years ago, for example, Ford Motor Company contracted with one television network for all of their commercial time during prime hours the evening before the cars were introduced in dealer showrooms. In addition, they concentrated exposure in newspapers and magazines immediately before and after the introduction date.

In general, organizations that have *new* products, services, markets, or outlets use this approach to ensure that the news reaches the awareness threshold of a majority of the target prospects. Various patterns of "follow-up" advertising exposure are used. Some firms will gradually taper off their advertising until it reaches a minimum level late in the campaign. Firms with new retail outlets, like K-Mart, after their huge initial exposure often go to a virtually level expenditure pattern, making exceptions only for certain peak seasons or promotional events. Other firms, after their initial blast-off advertising, will have periodic but lesser massive advertising exposures as the campaign progresses.

3. *Snowballing or crescendo method.* Under this approach the advertising exposure is small at the beginning but continues to grow until it reaches a maximum or climax level late in the campaign. This approach has been used in a variety of situations. Some organizations simply are not ready for a rush of sales because their products or services are available in only limited supply. As the available supply increases, they increase their advertising exposure. The crescendo method is also used when organizations are still learning how to advertise their offering. They may need to learn the messages, media, and the magnitude of exposure needed to reach prospects' threshold levels. Or it may be used when firms want previous sales to finance following advertising; adequate funds for another type of approach simply may not be available. Finally, this approach is used for teaser campaigns—a campaign to arouse curiosity and interest but tell little about the product. A Washington state brewer, for example, initiated a successful campaign by starting with a few teaser newspaper advertisements. These were followed by limited billboard exposure, more newspaper advertising, and increasing advertising exposure, until the big tease was released. This final level of advertising exposure was maintained throughout the remainder of the campaign.

The three basic media schedule methods are shown in Figure 22–5. Keep in mind, however, that there are a variety of departures from these methods which may be appropriate for specific situations.

4. *Other schedule explanations.* In addition to the explanations for the preference of the various schedules that have been presented, there may be no clear-cut reason other than the particular style of a company's management. Two national breweries, for example, have used two opposite advertising and promotional approaches to introduce their beer brands into new markets. Anheuser-Busch has used an exaggerated form of big-early, little-late method to introduce its Busch-Bavarian brand in individual markets. Their philosophy apparently has been to attempt to gain maximum exposure and trial use in order to grab off a large initial market share, then gravitate the advertising back to a normal level and let the market share digress to its "natural" level. Carling Brewing Company, in contrast, has used limited advertising in the introductory stages and advertised more as larger market shares have been gained. Their philosophy has been expressed as securing and slowly building a market of loyal customers. They apparently see little advantage in people who have tried but dropped the use of their brands.

Marketing: Principles and methods

FIGURE 22–5
Media scheduling over time—Three alternatives

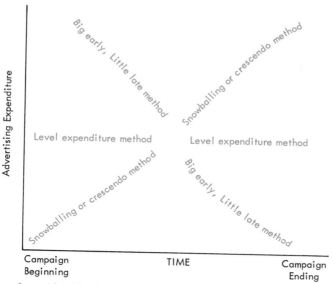

Source: Adapted from R. S. Alexander and T. L. Berg, *Dynamic Management in Marketing* (Homewood, Ill.: Richard D. Irwin, Inc., 1965), p. 382.

Regardless of the initial battle plan, it is common for advertisers to retain some uncommitted funds for contingencies. The marketplace for many sellers is a dynamic, vacillating place as customers' tastes and the marketing environment change, and competitors are continually on the alert to make changes that must injure their competitors' sales to help their own. Consequently, advertising plans written to include open dollars for contingencies are the order of the day. The advertiser must decide on: (1) the basic time pattern of his media schedule, including the frequency of impact; (2) the actual media that are to be used in various markets; and (3) the copy the media are to convey to the target prospects.[41]

Evaluating advertising effectiveness

In advertising, as in other activities, management not only must establish objectives and prepare plans but they must also know what their experiences have been. Hence they need feedback information. The ultimate purpose of most advertising in business firms is to make sales or profits larger than they would be otherwise. The contribution that advertising makes to either sales or profits, however, is generally very difficult to assess. In most situations, advertising works jointly with the other promotional tools in conjunction with the products, services, prices, and other variables in an ever-changing environment. What causes what is usually difficult to discern. Measurement and evaluation of advertising is therefore not often in terms of sales or

---

[41] Maxwell Ule provides a rundown on myths in advertising in "Advertising Tenets—Are They Gospel or Old Wives' Tales?" *Advertising Age,* June 29, 1970, pp. 1 and 82.

profits, but instead is done in terms of intermediate events that advertising must accomplish if it is to influence sales or profits.[42]

Readership, viewership measurements. A person must be exposed to an advertisement to be influenced by it. In one attempt at measurement, target prospects are asked if they saw a particular magazine, newspaper, or program. If they indicate they did, they are asked what advertisements they recall. And if they can recall the appropriate advertisement, they are asked if they can recall the brand or the company —and so forth to see if they can recall the essence of the copy. The assumption is that the more a person knows about the advertisement, the more likely he is to be favorably influenced by it. This, of course, is a long way from having been influenced to purchase the advertised product or service.[43]

Measurement through response rates. In both industrial and consumer marketing, advertisements are used to urge prospects to inquire about various products and services. These inquiries often serve to notify salesmen about prospects, but they also are used to help evaluate the effectiveness of the advertising. The assumption is that the more inquiries received, the larger the advertising coverage and reach and the greater the interest in the offering.

A somewhat different double-function approach is to provide a redeemable money-off coupon or deal as a part of a print advertisement. The more that are redeemed, the more successful the advertisement is assumed to be.

Store audits and diary panels. For products like toothpaste and deodorants that are dependent almost exclusively on advertising to create sales because the channel merely makes them physically available, store audits and consumer diary panels are used. The purpose of these techniques is to obtain current measures of retail sales to consumers. In the retail audit measurements the investigator audits the store's inventory, compares it with the previous inventory, and adds to it shipments received to discern how many units have been sold during the time period. Consumer diaries do about the same thing, except individual consumers record their purchases.[44]

In both situations the covariations between the retail sales or consumer purchase and the impact of advertisements and advertising campaigns is examined. Presumably if sales are related to advertising, they were caused by the advertising, and hence the investigator has an evaluation of advertising effectiveness.

There are other ways of evaluating advertising. Like those already illustrated, however, they measure either intermediate events—rather than sales or profits—or they provide quite vague rather than precise and reliable estimates of the effects of advertising.

Preadvertising measurement. Because of these measurement problems, some advertisers or their agencies engage in testing (measuring) various facets of their advertising campaigns before they are put into broad use. Some of the simpler tests involve exposing groups of people to an advertisement or a set of advertisements and soliciting their comments about what they like or dislike. This assumes that their attitudes will be favorable and will be reflected in resulting behavior and that the reviewers are representative of target prospects.

---

[42] For a study that purports to measure advertising effects on sales, see "Westinghouse Study Proves Ads Influence Buyers," *Industrial Marketing,* 55 (April 1970), pp. 14–15.

[43] J. B. Haskins, "Factual Recall as a Measure of Advertising Effectiveness," *Journal of Advertising Research,* 4 (March 1964), pp. 2–7.

[44] For a study utilizing the diary approach, see C. McDonald, "What Is the Short-Term Effect of Advertising?" Marketing Science Institute, Cambridge, Mass., 1971.

Another and somewhat more sophisticated procedure was referred to earlier as test marketing. Various advertisements, along with other controllable variables, are actually manipulated in a limited number of markets before the product is introduced elsewhere, and the differences in outcome are examined and analyzed. In two markets, for example, the company may use television to the exclusion of all other media. In a second set of two markets, they may use only newspapers, and so forth. Obviously, the influence of measurable variables like population must be removed. A variety of experimental designs and statistical techniques, particularly analysis of variance, also receives extensive use in measuring the effectiveness of advertising.[45]

Many firms (although not even a majority) attempt to measure the effects of their advertisements and advertising campaigns. Measurements tend to be quite vague, but even these can be useful to managers of advertising programs.[46]

SALES PROMOTION

In the preceding chapter, sales promotion was defined as those marketing activities—other than advertising, personal selling and publicity—that stimulate consumer purchasing and dealer effectiveness, such as point-of-purchase displays, shows and exhibits, demonstrations, and various nonrecurrent selling efforts not in the ordinary routine. Sales promotion is a phrase that covers a multitude of activities ranging from direct and immediate sales help (such as point-of-purchase displays) to indirect, long-range building of goodwill (such as publishers providing cocktail receptions for college professors at conventions or banks providing calendars or matches for all who wish to pick them up.)

Sales promotion should not be dismissed as a miscellaneous part of promotion. To some sellers, it may be the single most important type of promotion. Almost all sellers make some use of sales promotion.

Point-of-purchase display material, for example, has become increasingly important as self-service has increased. Sales display pieces that have been made familiar to prospective buyers through advertising frequently serve as a major link between advertising and in-store purchasing.[47] Displays, exhibits, and demonstrations can be particularly useful in introducing new products and services. They can provide means to bring a large number of interested prospective buyers together in one place to view sellers' offerings. A new manufacturer of boutique shirts, for example, rented a display booth at a clothing trade show and wrote more orders for merchandise in two days than he could have sold through sales calls in over three weeks.

Sales promotion can be complementary to advertising and personal selling. Because it has accompanying costs, decisions to use it, as well as how to use it, must be based on the belief that it can provide certain activities that will give greater benefits than would an equal expenditure for other forms of promotion or other sales activities.

---

[45] See for example, K. K. Cox and B. M. Enis, *Experimentation for Marketing Decisions* (Scranton, Pa.: International Textbook Co., 1969).

[46] For discussion on measuring advertising effectiveness, see R. H. Campbell, *Measuring the Sales and Profit Results of Advertising: A Managerial Approach* (New York: Association of National Advertisers, Inc., 1969); D. A. Schwartz, "Measuring the Effectiveness of Your Company's Advertising," *Journal of Marketing,* 33 (April 1969), pp. 20–25; and J. E. Morrill, "Industrial Advertising Pays Off," *Harvard Business Review,* 48 (March–April 1970), pp. 4–14 ff. For a discussion of why advertising measurement is often not used, see "Advertising Really Pays—What's Your Proof?" *Media/Scope,* June 1969, p. 35.

[47] For a discussion of use of point-of-purchase displays, see B. C. McCammon, Jr., "The Role of Point of Purchase Display in the Manufacturer's Marketing Mix," in T. W. Meloan and C. M. Uhitto (eds.), *Competition in Marketing* (Los Angeles: University of Southern California Press, 1964) pp. 75–92.

The planning and administration of sales promotion are quite similar to those for advertising and personal selling. The manager evaluates the appropriateness of various types of sales promotion activities along with other controllable resources in view of the firm's hierarchy of goals and objectives. It is out of this kind of planning that programs involving use of sales promotion should be developed.[48]

CONCLUSIONS AND SUMMARY

This chapter has not begun to cover advertising and sales promotion comprehensively. Together with the preceding chapter on promotional systems, however, it has provided at least cursory insights into most of the central issues. There have been two exclusions in the coverage—social criticisms of advertising have not been advanced very far, and the regulation of advertising has not been mentioned. Neither topic allows for adequate discussion when only advertising is being considered. The major social criticisms of advertising and promotion were discussed in Chapter 6, and more will be said about them in the final two chapters of the text. It is also in the final two chapters that the regulation of advertising (both by competition and government), along with the regulation of other marketing activities, is examined.

The widespread use of advertising and sales promotion by manufacturers and middlemen of both consumer and industrial goods and services, along with government and other not-for-profit organizations, plus the many forms of advertising have complicated the problem of precisely defining the purposes of advertising and sales promotion. In general, however, they are used to accomplish six major objectives in marketing. They (1) aid in the introduction of new products, services, and ideas, (2) assist in the expansion of already existing markets, (3) help to obtain desirable channel member assistance, (4) help prepare the way for other forms of communication, particularly salesmen, (5) help explain new applications for existing products, services, and ideas, and (6) afford the promoter representation even when he is not physically present. All these uses, of course, are ultimately concerned with informing and/or persuading persons so they will behave or think in ways that are favorable toward the advertiser. For the business firm this usually spells "sales," to churches it may spell "belief structure support," and so forth.

Finally, although advertising and sales promotion are important selling aids, some users expect far too much from them. They assume that an expensive advertising campaign will make up for a poorly selected channel of distribution or that it will sell a product that is poorly made, overpriced, or not even desired by many customers. Another assumption that is frequently not valid is that advertising and promotion will result in great increases in sales even if used only for a short period.

Such expectations are unrealistic, as experience has revealed. Advertising and sales promotion are each single factors in a successful marketing program. They give best results when used in connection with products, services, and ideas that customers want, that are well designed, packaged, and priced, and that are sold through properly selected trade channels. Neither advertising nor sales promotion will contribute its share *unless* it is carefully planned in advance, proper appeals are presented, the right types of media are selected, the cost is not excessive and, in most cases, it is used continuously.

---

[48] A detailed discussion of sales promotion is presented in J. F. Luick and W. L. Ziegler, *Sales Promotion and Modern Merchandising* (New York: McGraw-Hill Book Co., 1968).

REVIEW AND DISCUSSION QUESTIONS

1. What is advertising and how is it different from personal selling? How is it different from sales promotion?

2. Provide three illustrations of organizations that are currently using principally primary rather than selective advertising. Explain their likely reasons.

3. Talk to two or three retailers that use cooperative advertising and find out both what they like and dislike about several of their cooperative programs.

4. Why should or should not utility firms with market monopolies be permitted to expend as much as they desire on advertising?

5. What are the major purposes for organizations expending funds for advertising? Explain.

6. Why is it important for a seller in a competitive market to be able to favorably differentiate his products and services from competitors?

7. Why might a seller want a market to be more sensitive to price (a more elastic demand schedule)? Less sensitive to price (a more inelastic demand schedule)?

8. How important is advertising in the United States? Please explain.

9. Why have advertising expenditures continued to increase in the United States every year over at least the past 25 years?

10. Indicate the role of advertising in our economic system. Could our economic system operate better and more efficiently without any advertising?

11. Why must advertising campaigns be based and conducted on hierarchical sets of objectives that extend beyond the promotion and even the marketing area?

12. Select an advertising campaign that has been particularly noticeable to you. Analyze it in terms of (a) what you believe the advertiser is trying to accomplish, (b) how he is trying to accomplish it, and (c) the weak and strong points in the campaign.

13. Indicate an ideal situation in which to use the level-expenditure method for allocating advertising dollars: the big-early, little-late method; the snowballing or crescendo method.

14. Discuss the methods used to evaluate the effectiveness of advertising. Why is there considerable concern with the measurement of advertising effectiveness?

15. Provide five or six illustrations of sales promotion activities. What kinds of organizations or what set of circumstances might result in greater use of sales promotion than other forms of promotion?

SUPPLEMENTARY READINGS

Advertising Age   This weekly trade paper of the advertising industry provides an excellent source of current affairs and the industries' position.

Backman, J.   *Advertising and Competition.* New York: New York University Press, 1967. After a careful examination of advertising's place in our economy, Professor Backman arrives at four major conclusions (among others): (1) Advertising is not anticompetitive; (2) It does not generate excessive profit; (3) It does not set up barriers against new companies entering an industry; and (4) It does not contribute to price increases.

Bogart, L.   *Strategy in Advertising.* New York: Harcourt, Brace & World, Inc., 1967. In this excellent volume based on the conviction that advertising can be scientifically measured but not created, the author emphasizes media strategy and the characteristics of effective mass communication in successful marketing.

Borden, N. H.   *The Economic Effects of Advertising.* Homewood, Ill.: Richard D. Irwin,

Inc., 1944. This is one of the early and comprehensive reviews of the economic implications of advertising.

Boyd, H. W., Jr. and Levy, S. J. *Promotion: A Behavioral View.* Englewood Cliffs, N. J.: Prentice-Hall, Inc., 1967. Presents a behaviorally oriented approach to sales promotion organized around the communication process.

Corden, W. *A Tax on Advertising?* Research Series 222. London, The Fabian Society, 1961. This monograph provides a penetrating and critical discussion of advertising. Presents the opposite point of view to the Backman book cited above.

23 *Pricing*

The discussions of the formulation of marketing strategy in the chapters on product policy, channel policy, and promotion policy emphasized the interdependence of decisions in these areas with each other and with those in price policy. The marketing man views all four of these controllable decision variables as being equally important and requiring virtually simultaneous solution.

Pricing is not treated this way in economics. Economists have made "price theory" the center of focus in their analysis of firms and markets and have ignored vertical channel relationships and promotion. It is helpful to see why they have followed this approach. With money as the universal medium of exchange, price is the only measure of individual value and utility, and money is the only measure which can be aggregated to establish market values. The individual economic unit, household or firm, sells its products and services in a market for money and uses this money to buy other products and services in other markets. Thus, as David A. Revzan has noted, "the price structure is the integrating force through which the exchange of goods and services takes place within a mass marketing system. . . . Ultimately, all prices in a business economy are continuously influencing one another."[1] In an economy working through individual exchange in a system of markets, the price structure is a useful concept for analyzing and evaluating performance.

However, from the viewpoint of a firm within the system, price is just one decision element in the determination of marketing strategy. The firm does not have complete freedom to set any price it wishes. Pricing decisions are constrained by

---

[1] D. A. Revzan, *Perspectives for Research in Marketing* (Berkeley: University of California, Institute of Business and Economic Research, 1965), pp. 34, 38.

competitive forces in the market and by the value buyers assign to the products or services offered.

Thus, this chapter begins with a section on the constraints a competitive market structure places on pricing decisions. The analysis of demand has been discussed extensively in previous chapters. The central section of the chapter deals with the methods by which manufacturers and middlemen determine their pricing policies. The final section discusses some important topics of price administration: tactics, discounts, geographic variation, and resale price maintenance.

PRICING DECISIONS AND MARKET STRUCTURE

It is important to recognize the way in which the competitive structure of the market influences the degree of control over price that sellers are able to exercise. Much of the behavior of sellers is motivated by the desire to have more control over their prices.

A three-way classification of market structure based on the number of sellers, the number of buyers, and the degree of product homogeneity is shown in Table 23–1.

TABLE 23–1
Classification of competitive market structures

Number of buyers	Number of sellers		
	One	Few	Many
One	Bilateral monopoly	Monopsony	Pure monopsony
Few...	Monopoly	Bilateral oligopoly	Oligopsony
Many, homogeneous product.........	Monopoly	Homogeneous oligopoly	Pure competition
Many, differentiated product..........	Monopoly	Differentiated oligopoly	Monopolistic competition

Most of these 12 situations (cells) are discussed in terms of pricing freedom and the opportunities to increase it. This serves as a background to help understand how sellers determine pricing policies. They also form the background for the next two chapters, which examine how the competitive structure and government regulation control and coordinate the total marketing system.

Pure competition is said to exist when, first, there are a large number of small sellers and buyers and, second, the products offered for sale by all sellers are identical in the minds of all buyers and are sold under similar conditions. Both these conditions need to be fulfilled. The first results in each seller having such a relatively small supply for sale that he is unable to exert any significant influence on the total supply regardless of whether or not he offers his goods for sale. The second condition results in price

Marketing: Principles and methods

becoming the only factor of importance in determining from which seller any buyer will make his purchases.

Under these two conditions, all the individual seller can do is accept (or refuse) the price in the market; he cannot change it. If he holds out for more, buyers will make their purchases from other sellers; and he need not take less, since he can sell his relatively small supply at the going price. Under pure competition, price determination is taken out of the hands of the individual seller. He is powerless to set a price above the going price, and it is foolish to set a lower price. But we still need to face the question: What determines the market price the seller may accept or refuse, but not change?

The answer is that the going price is the one that equates supply and demand. As prices are reduced, the number of buyers who are willing to pay the price increases and the number of sellers who are willing to sell at that price goes down. Others, perhaps because they are not covering their costs of production, will withhold their goods from the market. We can picture the intersection of the supply and demand schedules as in Figure 23–1. A price of 25 cents per unit is the price at which the market is "cleared." Sellers who wait for higher prices sell nothing. It is this market price of 25 cents, then, as determined by the amount all buyers are willing to take and all sellers are willing to sell, that fixes the price at which any individual seller will sell under conditions of pure competition. The pricing problem is quite beyond the control of the individual.

FIGURE 23–1
Industry supply and demand in a purely competitive market

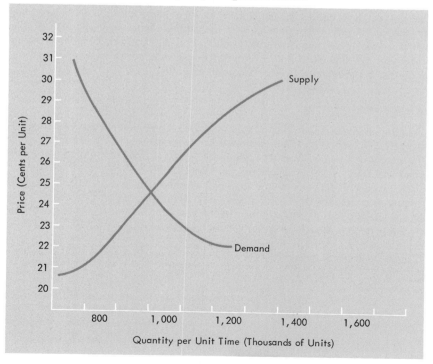

Over a period of time, it is obvious that a firm will not continue to sell at a loss—that is, at a price below its cost of production.[2] The decision is one of how much, if anything, to produce—not at what price output will be sold. Thus one consequence of pure competition is that if price remains below the cost of production for a long period, sellers will exit from the business—they have no other alternative.

A second consequence of pure competition is that any seller can increase his total income (number of units sold multiplied by the price per unit) *only* by selling more units. A farmer with 2,000 quarts of strawberries for sale cannot possibly receive more from any smaller number of quarts—for example, 1,000 of them—than he could for the whole 2,000. If the market price happens to be 40 cents a quart, he could sell the 1,000 quarts for 40 cents each and receive $400, or he may sell the 2,000 quarts and receive $800. When conditions of pure competition are not present, as we shall see below, it may be possible for the total income to be increased by the sale of a smaller number of units.

One should also question the social desirability of a system in which all markets are purely competitive. This discussion is reserved for the next chapter.

In actual market situations, "there has never been a time when the economists' model of pure and perfect competition was actually operative."[3] Or, as the late Wroe Alderson expressed it, ". . . the perfectly homogeneous market . . . is only a convenient fiction adopted by economists who want to think about the economic problems of price. . . ."[4] Yet as a "convenient fiction" or an analytical reference point, the foregoing analysis provides a useful approach to an understanding of pricing fundamentals.

Moreover, the market does offer some fairly close examples of pure competition—such as the bituminous coal industry, with many mines producing an undifferentiated product; the commodity and stock exchanges; and some agricultural products. Even with these products, however, pure competition is the exception rather than the rule. In markets for manufactured products, conditions approaching those of pure competition are difficult to find. Even retail markets do not fit the requirements of homogeneous product and service assortments.

Pricing under monopoly

At the other extreme from conditions of pure competition are those of complete monopoly. Such conditions are illustrated by a company which has control of the entire supply of a certain product—a situation which at one time was approximated for cash registers, nickel, magnesium, and basic aluminum.

The pricing objective of the monopolist is essentially the same as that of the seller operating in conditions of pure competition—the maximizing of *total* profits in the long run. In fact, the important difference between the monopolist and the firm in pure competition is the nature of the demand curve (average revenue)[5] he faces and

---

[2] In the phrase "cost of production" the so-called "wages" of management are included. This inclusion means that management obtains not only enough from its product to cover the cost of hired labor, raw materials, rent, etc., but also enough more to leave it as much as it could get in wages from the firm offering it the highest wage.

[3] C. B. Hoover, *The Economy, Liberty and the State* (New York: Twentieth Century Fund, 1959), p. 262.

[4] W. Alderson, *Dynamic Marketing Behavior* (Homewood, Ill.: Richard D. Irwin, Inc., 1965), p. 30.

[5] As noted in economics, the demand schedule is also called the "average revenue curve" and represents price.

$$P \cdot Q = TR, \ AR = \frac{TR}{Q} = \frac{P \cdot Q}{Q} = P.$$

Figure 23–3 illustrates these concepts.

Marketing: Principles and methods

the consequences of this difference. In pure competition, the demand curve faced by the *firm* is a horizontal line when plotted against output per period. Price is fixed by the market; thus the average revenue (demand schedule) is the same regardless of the quantity sold by the firm.

The demand curve faced by the monopolist is downward sloping. It is the industry demand curve in Figure 23–1, for the monopolist is the industry. While the monopolist has the power to set his price anywhere along this curve, his sales are still determined by the quantity that buyers in the market are willing to take at that price. For most products buyers will take more at lower prices than at higher prices. If he held his price too high, his sales would be insignificant. In order to sell additional units of output, he must reduce the price to *all* customers—even those who would have purchased at a higher price.[6] The net addition to the monopolist's revenue resulting from the lower price is called *marginal revenue*. It is equal to the revenues generated from the sale of the additional units, minus the change in price required to secure the new sales, multiplied by the number of units which would have been sold without the price reduction.[7]

The monopolist must always sacrifice something to gain the additional business; the marginal revenue will always be less than market price. Further, since the demand curve (price curve) is downward sloping with increasing output, *marginal revenue will be less than price and decreasing*. In fact, the marginal revenue curve will fall faster than price as output is increased.

For profit maximization, then, the monopolist will expand output (decrease price) only as long as the additional (marginal) revenue exceeds the additional (marginal) cost of producing and marketing the additional output. The monopolist's profit-maximizing policy is the same as that for the firm in pure competition—the aim is to market and produce at the rate where marginal revenue equals marginal cost. However, for the monopolist, price exceeds marginal revenue, while for the competitive firm they are equal.

The monopolist's price, therefore, exceeds his marginal cost. Do not conclude, however, that the monopolist's price will necessarily exceed his long-run *average cost* per unit and that he thereby makes a pure profit. Fear of government regulation and entry into the market by other sellers may prevent him from holding average price above average costs. In fact, a fear of competitive entry may cause him to engage in promotional activities in an attempt to "shift the demand curve to the right" and to build the confidence and loyalty of buyers. Such promotion may be profitable in the short run and actually increase his market power in the long run. In contrast, a seller under pure competition never uses promotion, for it is never profitable.

Pricing under homogeneous oligopoly

Oligopoly pricing presents some striking contrasts with the analysis for pure competition and monopoly. First, even homogeneous oligopoly (few sellers of homogeneous products) is not so rare a market structure as the other two. This structure is typical of capital-intensive extractive and manufacturing industries which produce

---

[6] This assumes that the seller is not able to segment his market so as to sell at different prices in different markets. The ability to practice price discrimination is just one of the benefits of market segmentation.

[7] For example, if the old price is $.75 and the new price is $.65, and if 100 units would have been sold at $.75 and 130 will be sold at $.65, then the marginal revenues from the 30 additional units will be $MR = P_1 \cdot \triangle Q - \triangle P \cdot Q_1$, or ($.65) (30) minus ($.10) (100), or $9.50.

standardized commodities such as steel and its products and cement and its products.

Second, there is no single general, theoretical solution as in the other two structures. Because the number of sellers is few and the products are homogeneous, sellers realize that their decisions are interdependent. Their best marketing strategy depends on the choices made by their competitors. Each firm's price, promotion, channel, and output decisions influence the sales and profits of competitors. An important change in one firm's policies is likely to elicit change in the policies of competitors. Each firm makes predictions of each rival's decisions and reactions and arrives at its own decisions in light of these predictions.

Thus, general solutions require many specific assumptions about the nature of the firms, the product, the market, and even the personalities of the decision makers. The analysis must focus not only on the *structure* of the market but on the *behavior* of the competitors. All of the models of oligopoly pricing which credit the decision makers with cooperative reasoning ability reach results which anticipate that oligopolistic markets will exhibit a tendency toward maximization of the total profit of all sellers. Further their prices are not far below those of the monopolist.

Conditions conducive to cooperation include equal size of firms or an obvious single-firm price leader, ease of communication between competitors, standardized products sold to a stable group of buyers, and rapid competitive response to price cutters. In addition, they include willingness by sellers to forgo maximum price advances in times of short-run shortages, to compete on a nonprice basis, and to make adjustments in capacity designed to maintain stability in supply.

Overt collusion is useful but not necessary for achievement of these conditions. Collusive agreements are difficult to maintain and are illegal. While most government action against collusion is not so dramatic as the cases against the electrical equipment industry in the early 1960s, the frequency of conviction and the penalties in such cases are great.

The stability through time of prices in homogeneous oligopoly is also a delicate matter. Price wars and "squeeze plays" by some competitors against others may prove devastating to the losers.

Thus the firm in homogeneous oligopoly does not have the pricing freedom enjoyed by the monopolist and is motivated to seek a way to gain more pricing freedom and more market power. He may try to gain these advantages by: (1) policies which attempt to drive competitors into extinction (which is illegal), (2) horizontal merger with competitors (which is very likely to be illegal), (3) vertical integration (discussed in previous chapters), or (4) fleeing from homogeneous oligopoly into differentiated oligopoly (few sellers offering products which are different from one another but are close substitutes). This structure was discussed in Chapter 18.

Pricing under differentiated oligopoly and monopolistic competition

How does the firm flee from homogeneous oligopoly? By engaging in a number of activities we have already discussed: (1) segmenting the market for existing products by serving new distributors, new geographic areas, or new groups of customers not served by competitors; (2) offering new-product and service variations which are desired by customers but not offered by competitors; and (3) differentiating existing products and services through increased promotional expenditures aimed at building a preference for the firm's brands over competitors' brands. All attempts to segment

Marketing: Principles and methods

markets or to differentiate the bundle of utilities offered by a particular seller in order to induce buyers to prefer his products and services over those of others are efforts to escape from the joint industry demand curve and to build some degree of monopoly power.

The practice of product differentiation is practiced by sellers in more than one of the types of market structure. One structure is differentiated oligopoly, which is characterized by a few well-known giant firms with very large advertising budgets and perhaps a number of very small regional firms. Examples in the United States include manufacturers of automobiles, cigarettes, drugs, soaps, and detergents. In these industries, prices move in parallel, but the prices and offerings of all sellers are not identical. Each firm looks at the marketing tactics of his competitors, plans his moves in light of their actions, and expects that his competitors are doing likewise.

The second market structure for which there is strong motivation to follow a policy of differentiation is that of monopolistic competition. This structure is characterized by a large number of small firms and ease of entry into the market by even more firms. Each firm, however, has some differential advantage over his competitors which provides him with a small degree of monopoly power. The most common situation is the advantage of a key location held by a retail store. Most retailing can be classified in this market structure. Many small manufacturers with a unique product or a unique approach to marketing it likewise fall into the monopolistic competition category. All attempts to offer additional services in connection with a sale—such as product installation by a manufacturer and credit and delivery services by the retailer—represent attempts at differentiation. Consequently, the retailer who tries to gain trade by means of attractive window displays and courteous salespeople is practicing differentiation, and so is the manufacturer who, through his brand advertising, tries to achieve not just consumer acceptance of his product but consumer preference and—if possible—consumer insistence on his brands.

In both differentiated oligopoly and monopolistic competition, the intent of the seller is to use differentiation, convenience, promotion, and other marketing variables to attempt to produce a downward-sloping demand curve like that of the monopolist so that he can charge more than the lowest priced competitor and still retain market share. This, not the polar opposites of pure competition and pure monopoly, is the competitive "game" which is played in the large majority of real-world markets.

Reaching a long-run equilibrium price structure. The analysis of price under the market structures of differentiated oligopoly and monopolistic competition requires consideration of the dynamics of how firms reach equilibrium points in their competitive struggle. To begin with, assume a firm has just successfully differentiated its product and now holds a position much like that of a monopolist. The demand curve slopes to the right, and the marginal revenue falls faster than the selling price. Marginal cost will fall to the point of diminishing returns and then rise. As long as marginal cost is below marginal revenue (that is, the added cost for a unit is less than the added revenue from the unit), output will be expanded. Given the demand curve and the cost curves of Figure 23–2, the seller will produce OA units and sell at a price of OF (or AE), thus giving the total profit represented by $GCEF$. These profits represent the largest possible gains under the given conditions.

It should now be clear that price under imperfect competition resulting from product differentiation would be the same as under monopoly *if we assume that the demand curve facing the individual seller remains constant.* But in the long run, this assumption is not true, since the profits being made will attract competition.

A firm may believe, and correctly so, that with no competititive reaction its

FIGURE 23–2
Demand and cost curves for a firm with a differentiated product

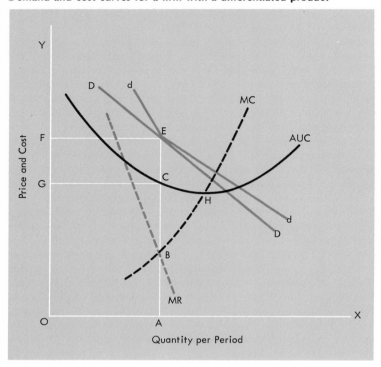

demand curve is actually *dd*. That is, demand is elastic with price decreases and inelastic with price increases. However, possible competitive responses cause the firm to decide it is not more profitable to lower its price. If the structure is one of monopolistic competition, new firms, seeing the pure profit being earned by this firm, will squeeze into the market and push its demand curve to the left and its price downward until its demand curve is tangent to the average-cost function, *AUC*. Now, even though the demand curve is still downward sloping, there is no monopoly profit. If the firm is in differentiated oligopoly, competition will retaliate by meeting any price reduction so that the quantity sold does not increase along *dd* but along *DD*. The firm, anticipating competitive reaction, will see that its profit will not increase if price is changed or output expanded.

Therefore, the firm does not change its price but attempts to achieve a goal of shifting *dd* to the right of *DD* and becoming more of a monopolist by further differentiation. These attempts have the effect of raising the average-cost curve (*AUC*), since increases in product variations, product quality, market coverage, and promotion all cost money. Even worse, the new entrants, attracted by the pure profits, and existing competitors are also increasing their advertising and differentiating their offerings. These efforts hold *dd* to *DD* and push the original firm's demand to the left! Its own efforts at differentiation are now required simply to maintain its existing market share.

This competitive struggle continues between new entrants and existing competi-

FIGURE 23–3
The same firm in long-run equilibrium

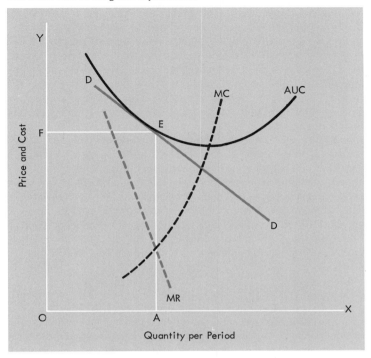

tors. The weapons are price, promotion, product or firm differentiation, and segmentation. In the long run, firms are able to adjust their scale of plant or leave or enter the industry. The long-run equilibrium position, shown in Figure 23–3, is the point at which there is no more motivation to change price or marketing expenditure, all monopoly profit is eliminated, and long-run average cost is tangent to the demand curve. If all firms are in this same position and do not change their marketing expenditures, there is no motivation for any seller to change his strategy.

Implications of this result. This result is one of the most important in this book, for it goes a long way to explain just how our competitive marketing system operates. Six of the most important of the implications of this analysis merit reviewing.

First, nonprice competition has been successful. Many of the firms with the greatest level of spending for promotion and new-product development are the most profitable in our economy. It appears that well-managed firms are able through smart marketing management to prevent a leftward shift in their demand curves. These firms are able to charge a premium price for some of their brands and still build and hold customer loyalty. Zenith Corporation, Gillette, Coco-Cola, and Procter & Gamble are examples. The toll of firms who cannot keep up in this competitive struggle far outnumbers the list of long-term winners.

Second, firms in this structure spend more money on promotion than would firms in pure competition, where it never pays to advertise. Thus, there appears to be a cost penalty to the society if only *static* measures of performance are considered.

Third, the cost in this market structure is probably a price well worth paying, for differentiation confers great benefits on the consumer. Providing a "carrot" of monopoly profit results in a burning desire on the part of sellers to innovate and provide products and services that are better adapted for customers' needs. The vast majority of consumers, at least all but the most disadvantaged in American society, are far better served than if sellers offered homogeneous products in pure competition.

Fourth, the emphasis placed on price competition in economic theory does not match with the marketing facts of life. Sellers have a kit of tools—product, distribution, promotion, and price—which can be arranged into that assortment of utility bundles that is most demanded by buyers.

Fifth, because a price decrease is the one tactic a competitor can immediately follow in most situations, sellers prefer to compete on a nonprice basis, i.e., to alter their cost structures before they alter their price structures.

Sixth, in product categories where product innovation and differentiation is difficult, the competitive struggle can result in heavy spending for defensive advertising, which is dysfunctional for society. Cigarettes provide an example. In 1971, after the ban on cigarette television advertising, the profits of cigarette producers went up markedly. A forced reduction of defensive advertising by all competitors simply removed a layer of cost from each producer.

Pricing when the number of buyers is small[8]

The growing importance of the distribution-oriented channel leader means that a student of marketing should be familiar with the pricing problem in market structures where the number of buyers is small: bilateral monopoly, bilateral oligopoly, monopsony, and oligopsony.

The three methods of gaining channel control discussed in Chapter 3—vertical integration, contractual agreements, and consensus—are all either the cause or the result of monopsony (buying) power in the hands of distribution-oriented channel leaders. Because this power influences prices in intermediate markets, it can also influence them in final markets. The question that needs to be answered is, how? The answers can be provided in a single short section not because the analyses are similar or simple, but because the number of general principles which can be presented are few.

There is no general solution to the pricing problem in bilateral monopoly or bilateral oligopoly which will indicate the price resulting from negotiations between buyers and sellers. It could be lower than the price which would result in a purely competitive market, but it could be as high as the price in pure monopoly. Also, it is not clear if the monopsonist (only one buyer) will pass fruits of his negotiations on to his customers in his resale prices.

The large buyer (Safeway Stores or Walgreen Company) may be able to play one large seller against another in such a way as to extract a series of price concessions. Oligopolists, by segmenting markets by type or size of account, may be able to grant price concessions to powerful buyers without lowering prices to smaller customers.

---

[8] This discussion owes much to F. M. Scherer, *Industrial Market Structure and Economic Performance* (Chicago: Rand McNally & Co., 1970), Chap. 9.

On the other hand, the oligopolists may soon find that such concessions are destructive and refuse to bargain with monopsonists. When this occurs, the large buyers may integrate backward, or threaten to, and take the business from all the oligopolistic sellers. Thus it should be clear that powerful buyers have the *ability,* in the long run, to counter the market power of monopolists and oligopolists.

As for large buyers purchasing from many small sellers, their power will dominate so that price will be at least as low as that in pure competition. Such behavior may lead small sellers to combine in one way or another to gain more market power.

Implications. In summary, the price in oligopsony will be at least as low as that in pure competition; the price in bilateral oligopsony could likewise be that low but is not guaranteed to be. Morris Adelman's study of A&P may be useful here as an illustration.[9] Except for cost savings associated with efficiencies in procurement and physical distribution, A&P did not purchase unbranded agricultural commodities below competitive prices because there was no motivation for the atomistic agricultural producers to sell their small outputs at less than prevailing market prices. The chain did not purchase dominant national brands below competitive prices because the dominant sellers did not have to grant price concessions to gain sales to A&P. The manufacturer's brand was the one with the "consumer franchise." A&P *was* successful in obtaining preferential treatment from producers of moderately differentiated products, who had to compete aggressively for the distributors' business to hold or increase their market shares. The large distributor could therefore play off these sellers against one another and gain price concessions.

What are the implications of such price concessions on the prices paid by final buyers and on the efficiency of the entire channel system for the products involved? Price concessions and price discrimination can lead to instability and misallocation of resources. But in the short run, such instability in the system is not necessarily bad.

The determining factor is whether or not the dynamic trend in the instability is toward higher or lower efficiency within the system. John Kenneth Galbraith advanced the notion that power on one side of a market (for example, manufacturing-oriented channel leaders in grocery products) will inevitably lead to the formation of countervailing power on the other side of the market (for example, supermarket chain channel leaders), and that this countervailing power will lead to efficiency in the total system.[10] Joseph Spengler suggests that the efficiency problems can be resolved through the evolution of vertically integrated channels (or at least well-defined channel leaders).[11] Unfortunately, both of these conclusions are probably somewhat optimistic.

It is not clear that the fruits of this efficiency will not become trapped in the channel instead of being passed on to final buyers *unless the final markets are competitive.* If retailers face intensive competition which forces them to adjust their prices and output decisions so that their demand is tangent to their average-unit-cost curve, they will be motivated to seek price concessions and to pass them along to consumers. A retailer with a steep demand curve will not be so motivated.

---

[9] M. A. Adelman, *A&P: A Study in Price-Cost Behavior and Public Policy* (Cambridge, Mass.: Harvard University Press, 1959), pp. 207–20.

[10] J. K. Galbraith, *American Capitalism: The Theory of Countervailing Power* (Boston: Houghton Mifflin Co., 1952), pp. 117–20.

[11] J. J. Spengler, "Vertical Integration and Antitrust Policy," *Journal of Political Economy,* 59 (August 1950), pp. 347–52.

PRICING POLICIES

A seller seeks to arrive at sound and stable pricing objectives early in his planning of marketing strategy. Over the long term, these prices should maximize the profit return on investment.

Every price decision should result from the balancing of a number of price and nonprice factors. Because strategy decisions are plans for an entire planning period, often over the life cycle of the product, initial profit planning may involve different prices at different points in time. In some periods, a company's marketing, and hence price, objectives can be expressed in such terms as target market share or minimum cash flow. (Marketing goals and objectives and marketing strategy were discussed in Chapters 18 and 21.) These considerations may result in a pricing strategy which does not maximize profit in the short run. However, in the long run, all but not-for-profit manufacturers, wholesalers, or retailers should have as their goal the maximization of return on invested capital.

Price determination by manufacturers

"Target" rate of return. There is a growing tendency to aim at a predetermined or "target" rate of return on investment. Thus it is reported that General Motors Corporation's goal is a 20 percent pretax return on its investment when operating at its "standard" output and that Genesco, Inc., and Campbell Soup Company aim at 25 percent, these rates falling to approximately 10 and 12.5 percent after taxes.[12] To illustrate, if we assume $5 million are invested in the business and 20 percent is selected as the desired pretax rate of return, the firm needs to earn $1 million. With a "standard" output of one million units, the amount of profit to be included in the price of each unit is $1. Supposedly, a new product which could not be sold at an average price over its life cycle to return a profit of at least $1 per unit would be dropped.

The relationship between this minimum acceptable return and price can be seen in the following equation:

$$\text{Rate of return } (r) = \frac{\text{Profit}}{\text{Investments}} = \frac{Q\,(p - v) - F}{A}$$

where:

Q is the quantity demanded, a function of price and marketing costs.

p is price.

v is the unit cost, assumed constant per unit. These costs are variable with output, that is, go up or down directly with the quantity produced.

$p - v$ is often called the "contribution to fixed costs and profits."

F is the total fixed costs per year, that is, those costs, such as salaries and rents, which do not change with the quantity produced in the short run.

A is the amount of fixed and liquid assets invested in the product.

---

[12] "What's the Key to GM's Success?" *Business Week,* May 8, 1965, p. 25; "Genesco: The High Style in Management," *Dun's Review and Modern Industry,* June 1967, p. 38; and "Campbell's Recipe for Growth," *Dun's Review and Modern Industry,* August 1966, p. 30. Appendix A contains an additional discussion of cost as a function of volume.

This expression can be solved for p:

$$p = \frac{rA + vQ + F}{Q}$$

but the question is whether values for each of the quantities in the equation can be determined. The rate of return (r) is established by general company policy. The variable costs per unit (v) are largely production costs, but they are strongly influenced by marketing. The quality level of the product, the expensiveness of packaging, any selling margins that are fixed per unit sold, and the cost of each physical and functional characteristic of the product are largely marketing-determined costs.

The fixed costs include fixed production costs associated with machinery, buildings, and land, as well as executive and marketing salaries and the great bulk of promotional expenditures, including advertising. Thus in order to establish a minimum acceptable price, it is necessary to establish first a positioning for the product, the product design, a promotion strategy, and a distribution plan.

With this planning complete, all quantities are now known except Q and p. It is possible to calculate a schedule of quantities and prices which satisfy the equation, that is, prices that would incorporate a planned marketing strategy (and its costs) which would have to be obtained over a relevant range of possible sales in order to achieve the minimum acceptable rate of return. Such a schedule is plotted as rr in Figure 23–4.

Estimation of demand.   The next task for the manufacturer in his *first attempt* to establish his price is to estimate the demand curve for his product. It is possible to estimate the demand curves for most products by one of a variety of methods based on: (1) the price and sales of products that are close substitutes; (2) asking potential

FIGURE 23–4

Estimated prices and quantities demanded and necessary for acceptable rate of return

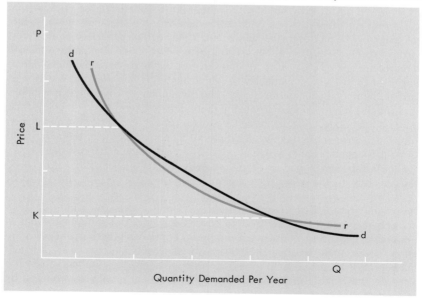

customers how much they would purchase at a series of prices asked in decreasing order; (3) asking distributors how many units they think they could sell at a series of prices asked in decreasing order; (4) econometric studies of the past prices and demand of substitute products. In general it can be said that the demand curves of individuals are downward sloping and that market demand curves, made up of the sum of the quantities demanded by each individual at each price, will also be downward sloping but with a much smaller absolute slope. In Figure 23–4, this estimated demand schedule is plotted as *dd*.

In this example the expected demand equals or exceeds the acceptable rate of return over a range of prices from *K* to *L*. Of course, this would not always be true—particularly in the first attempt to plan a strategy. If the two curves were to touch in only a very narrow range, as may be the case when many close substitute products exist, the price decision would be settled by the price of competitive products.

If there were no price on the demand curve which met the rate-of-return criterion, then the entire strategy would have to be reviewed and questioned. Does a market segment really exist where we thought it did? Is our product really unique? Should some less expensive channels of distribution be considered? Can promotional expenditures be reduced?

When a range of prices like *LK* in Figure 23–4 exists, more pricing choices remain to be made. Decisions among these choices depend primarily upon competitive strategy. Since these considerations are similar for manufacturers and middlemen, how price determination by middlemen may differ from that by manufacturers is discussed first.

Price determination by middlemen

Two differences in the cost structures of middleman operations make their pricing problems different from those of manufacturers. First, middlemen operate establishments in which space is used to store, display, and sell merchandise. The amount of heat, light, rent, property taxes, and labor required for the operation of 100 square feet of space in one part of the establishment, if they can be separated at all, differs little from those same costs in another 100 square feet of space. The entire establishment represents a fixed cost which must be covered by the profit on the merchandise moving through it. The only variables are the value of the merchandise which must be carried, the rate at which it turns over, and the number of square feet it requires.

Second, most middlemen carry many more different items (i.e., a much greater assortment) than does a manufacturer. These two factors have led most middlemen to employ a cost-oriented method of simply marking up the cost of the goods sold by a "normal" percentage to arrive at price. The percentage markup is determined by dividing the amount of markup—the amount by which the selling price of an article exceeds its cost—by the selling price and multiplying by 100 percent (see Appendix A).

In pricing according to a normal markup, a seller will ordinarily aim to establish a markup percentage sufficiently large to cover the cost of doing business—that is, total operating expenses—and leave a net profit. For goods where markdowns are common—for example, seasonal, fashionable, or perishable merchandise—the original markup must be sufficient to meet these requirements after the markdown has been taken. The markup used should vary by products or groups of products, by sellers, and according to the conditions of the time, although a few retailers have tried—usually unsuccessfully—to operate an entire store on a single markup. In addition to providing aid in pricing, the percentage markups used by the middleman can also serve as a negotiating tool with the vendor, as a control and planning device, and as a decision-making tool.[13]

The basis for altering markups from normal are the space products require, their turnover, and competition. While cost accounting methods have been employed to reflect other differences in the middleman's cost of handling each line, simpler approaches remain in favor with merchants. In a department store, for example, furniture should carry a higher margin than panty hose because the sales per week per square foot of space required for the former is lower. However, it is unlikely that a store would find it profitable to make fine distinctions in the operating costs between bedroom and dining room furniture. (Table 7–4 shows that the operating expenses of furniture stores were 38 percent of sales, while those of general department stores were 27 percent of sales.)

The final important reason for deviation from "normal" markup is competition. At times certain products become favorites for price competition between retailers. Some sellers believe it so important to meet competition that they adopt this as a specific price policy. The president of a supermarket chain has stated to the authors: "Although we know what markup we would like in each product category, our actual prices are determined by our policy of matching competitors' prices." The units of the Federated Department Stores group meet competitive prices even if it means operating a whole department at a loss. Firms following this pricing policy usually move rapidly to meet competitors' prices, since there is some evidence that any appreciable delay decreases the effectiveness of the move in holding customers. In recognition of this fact, most large stores employ one or more comparison shoppers specifically to compare merchandise and prices, as well as various aspects of service, in competing stores.

Pricing strategy

Pricing calculations usually will result in a range of feasible prices for the manufacturer and feasible normal markups for the wholesaler and retailer. Within this range, the seller will select his price on the basis of the competitive strategy he plans to employ.

It should be clear from the previous discussion of market structures that competitive strategies should consider not only the probable reactions of buyers to a particular price but also the reactions of competitors. Six major pricing strategies that consider these reactions are examined below.

Skimming the market. A high-price strategy that assumes the market can be segmented so that the seller is able to isolate a group of consumers who are willing to buy the product or service at a high price is termed "skimming the market." For example, in Figure 23–4, L would be a skimming price. It generates far fewer sales, but it does generate an acceptable rate of return.

There are a number of situations in which this strategy may be sound. One is the case of a new product for which production capacity is limited and a big demand could not be served—Disney World provides an illustration. A second is a monopolist who feels it would be some time before competitors will enter the market (e.g.,

---

[13] These additional uses of the markup are developed in Roger Dickinson, "Markup in Department Store Management," *Journal of Marketing,* 31 (January 1967), pp. 32–34.

Polaroid Land cameras and film). A third is a price leader who is trying to reduce price cutting in the industry (Schwinn in the bicycle field). A fourth is the pricing of a novelty or fashion with an expected short life cycle. Finally, a skimming strategy is reasonable for a merchant who feels he can do a better job of serving this segment than can his competitors.

The seller who consistently overprices his competitors must follow supporting policies and practices, or his price policy will fail. Thus the high-priced women's apparel shop must offer fashionable quality garments in a fine store setting and provide many services.[14] The Zenith Radio Corporation can get from $3 to $20 more for its television sets because of its emphasis on quality and service, plus a carefully controlled channel of distribution. Careful attention to quality is also an important factor in the success of the Green Giant Company, a packer of foods, in carrying out an above-average pricing policy.

Sliding down the demand curve. A longer run strategy that starts as a skimming policy but includes plans to reduce price as time goes on and the market expands is called "sliding down the demand curve." In Figure 23–4, the seller plans to introduce the product at L and slide down to K as time goes on. This strategy is a good one for a new product when entry by competitors is not expected to be rapid. The initial high price permits a more rapid recovery of development costs and still allows retention of a large market share by reducing price in advance of competition. If the product is accepted, the demand curve will actually shift to the right. With this strategy the seller plans to reduce his price faster than he would be forced to by competitive entry. Most really unique consumer durables and apparel items introduced today employ this strategy.

Penetration pricing. In the opposite strategy to skimming, called "penetration pricing," the product is priced at the minimum that will generate an acceptable return—price K in Figure 23–4. The objective of such a plan is to open up a dominant position in a large market as rapidly as possible and thereby to fight off or discourage competitors.

Clearly there is an assumption that a large potential market exists and that it will respond to a low price. There is also usually an assumption of potential economies of scale in production. Henry Ford made this strategy famous in the 1920s when he priced the Model T in such a way as to introduce the mass-produced automobile to the mass market.

This strategy is also observable in retailing by sellers who determine their normal margin by noting what is being charged by competitors and then setting their prices still lower. The assumption is that the response of consumers will be great enough to increase turnover to a point where the return on investment is satisfactory. A&P successfully employed this strategy in opening new stores during the period of its fastest growth.

Leader pricing. Prices placed on specific items by manufacturers or middlemen who market several products are significantly influenced by the seller's desire to maximize his *total* profit rather than to maximize his profit on any specific product. Retailers often find that by pricing certain items at very low levels, they attract large numbers of extra customers to their stores, thereby expanding their sales of higher

---

[14] How the retailer may support his policy of "price above competition" through such factors as service, prestige, location, store hours, private brands, and arrangements with manufacturers is suggested in D. J. Duncan, C. F. Phillips, and S. C. Hollander, *Modern Retailing Management: Basic Concepts and Practices* (Homewood, Ill.: Richard D. Irwin, Inc., 1972), pp. 391–93.

margin items and adding to their total profits. This strategy is known as "leader pricing." The heavily promoted leaders are usually sold for 25 to 50 percent below the usual price—near the cost of the merchandise and hopefully below the cost of competing retailers. In some discount stores with food departments the entire food department has been operated at a loss in an effort to attract traffic for other departments.

Likewise, a manufacturer may price one product relatively low in the hope that this will give his salesmen a means of "getting to the buyers" to sell other products carrying more satisfactory profit margins. Or a product which cannot be operated without other products (a razor which needs a supply of blades; a camera which must have film; or a mimeograph machine which requires ink and paper) may be sold without profit or at a very low profit margin simply to create a market for the more profitable items. It is the *total* profit which is important to the seller, not the profit on any specific product.

Variable leader pricing. At least until "discount supermarkets" became a popular competitive strategy in 1969, the most popular pricing strategy for supermarkets was a dynamic version of leader pricing called "variable leader pricing." This strategy requires changing leaders not only with regard to one's own previous leaders but with regard to those promoted by competitors. These weekly advertised "specials" attract and hold patronage by *differentiating* leaders from those of competitors.

Most competition between specials is confined to a relatively small number of high-volume items such as coffee and some cuts of fresh meat. Each week the seller initiates an "upward and downward manipulation of prices . . . for the purpose of drawing attention to its market offerings and maintaining or increasing its share of total market sales."[15] With big volume leaders, even slight price reductions may cut deeply into total profits. To protect profits, careful planning of the price mix is necessary. In setting up and adjusting their price mixes some sellers go so far as to estimate the sales of each featured item. This step allows the calculation of the "cost" of any price change before it is actually made, and the accuracy of each estimate is carefully checked against actual sales at the end of each promotion. By cumulating these data over a period of time and using them systematically, a seller may be able to maintain the necessary gross profit and still meet or beat competition on many items of merchandise.

Producing to a price. Although in periods of rapid inflation it is difficult to find much empirical support for the concept, some retailers do believe that certain prices, like $5.95, and certain price lines, like $3, $5, and $7 ties, are more attractive to consumers than others. The 5-cent candy bar is an example of such a pricing policy which is rapidly vanishing. Apparel stores still buy dresses to sell for $29.98 and $39.98. Variety chains such as F. W. Woolworth Co., some shoe stores, and many women's apparel stores will only purchase merchandise that is designed to sell at preselected prices.

Odd pricing at 39, 49, 69, and 98 cents is another example of pricing which retailers feel appeals to consumers, although only in some food lines is there research support for this belief. Inflation and state sales taxes also create questions as to the merits of this concept. Nonetheless, odd prices like $199.99 and $1,995 continue to appear on new as well as old products. Sears, Roebuck & Company currently offers five models of trail bikes with prices all ending in $4.95 or $9.95.

---

[15] P. E. Nelson and L. E. Preston, *Price Merchandising in Food Retailing: A Case Study* (Berkeley, Calif.: University of California, Institute of Business and Economic Research, 1966), p. 98.

If retailers want to carry merchandise to sell at particular price points, manufacturers must design products so that they can be sold at these prices and still allow middlemen the necessary margins. Increasingly, when a seller moves away from an established price, especially if the move is upward, he tests the new price in a limited market to determine consumer reactions. And, even after testing, the manufacturer may move very slowly to make the change. One pencil manufacturer, after suggesting a 5-cent retail price for many years, gradually moved to 6 cents, then to two for 15 cents, and finally to 10 cents—with each advance accompanied by widespread promotional efforts.

Price lining represents price-quality combinations which make more sense from a consumer and manufacturer point of view than odd pricing does. For example, General Motors offered brands of cars at various levels of price, size, and quality. Only as big cars became less popular and dealers demanded a wider assortment has it been necessary to expand the number of lines within a single brand. Now the Chevrolet dealer, like the dress retailer, can meet the needs of his customers and still limit his size, style, and color assortment to three price ranges which give him low-, medium-, and high-price quality groups. Manufacturers of luggage and hi-fi equipment also concentrate on three price lines, while a popular-priced women's sportswear chain has selected four price groups. By price lining, manufacturers and retailers hope to gain lower inventories, increased turnover, and reduced markdowns, although they face the same problems of adjusting price line to price-level changes. Consumers may also find quality comparisons easier to make when price lines are distinct.

PRICE ADMINISTRATION

Four areas of price administration will be discussed here: (1) pricing tactics, (2) discounts, (3) geographic pricing, and (4) resale price maintenance.

Pricing tactics

A strategy was defined in Chapter 18 as "the set of principles which guide the formation of a dynamic plan." Tactics differ in that they are concerned with shorter run competitive maneuvers. Hence,

Space

does not permit a complete discussion of all pricing tactics unique to middlemen,[16] but a few are discussed below.

Price promotions. Short-run variations in price are an essential part of most sellers' competitive strategy. A market in which sellers were able to maintain a single price in all markets for long periods of time would probably not be doing a satisfactory job of efficient resource allocation. The common reasons for short-run price variations are to:

1. Meet or overcome an aggressive competitor in one or all geographic market areas.
2. Reduce seasonal variations in demand.
3. Relieve an out-of-balance inventory situation.
4. Provide an incentive for aggressive selling in a particular channel.

---

[16] See Duncan, Phillips, and Hollander, *Modern Retailing Management,* Chaps. 16 and 17; and D. A. Revzan, *Wholesaling in Marketing Organization* (New York: John Wiley & Sons, Inc., 1961).

5. Win a very large order from a particular customer.
6. Provide a positive promotional surge designed to increase market share.

If merchant middlemen are used in the channel of distribution, any change in price, suggested retail price, or discounts will almost always cause a corresponding change in the other two pricing elements.

Price promotions are designed in such a way that all customers and middlemen recognize them as being temporary promotions designed to create immediate buying action. Without this characteristic, a promotion will not achieve its desired impact and can also be difficult to withdraw. A distinction can be made between promotions primarily directed at the trade and those designed to appeal directly to consumers although they may be used in combination with one another. Some distributor promotions which are popular today are straight price reductions, free goods, promotional allowances, and full-line discounts.

1. *A simple price reduction.* A straight price reduction to the trade may provide the motivation for distributors to run their own promotions featuring the manufacturer's brand. On the other hand, the decrease in price may result simply in higher margins and no extra promotion.

2. *Free goods.* "Bakers' dozens" and related free-goods deals are trade deals intended to gain distributor support through increasing the effective margin without altering the published manufacturer's price or discounts.

3. *Promotional allowances.* Another trade deal designed to create distributor support by providing extra margin which is, at least nominally, intended to be used for consumer promotion is promotional allowances. Sellers often insist on proof that the allowance is used for this purpose before paying it, for these allowances have a history of wide abuse.

4. *Full-line discounts.* These discounts, similar to the one above, are given as a consideration for a distributor buying a minimum order size of a complete assortment of the seller's line. Back-to-school supplies are often offered as complete assortment deals with attractive margins.

Examples of consumer price promotions include cents-off promotions, coupons, premiums, and additional- or combination-product deals.

1. *Cents-off promotions.* This is the most direct and most efficient of all price promotions. The manufacturer simply prints the amount of the reduction on the package and reduces his price to the trade by an equal amount. The result is a consumer bargain and a higher percentage markup for the distributor at a low cost to the manufacturer.

2. *Coupons.* Coupons for discounts on a particular product are probably the most common promotion used today. These may be sent to consumers through the mail, printed in newspapers and magazines, distributed at the store, or enclosed in packages of the product. Coupons are used to gain trial or repeat purchase.

3. *Premiums.* Premiums are not clearly price reductions but unrelated merchandise (e.g., novelities packed in a cereal box), or a price reduction on unrelated merchandise (e.g., "Send cereal box top and 25 cents for . . ."). The effect is to provide a consumer value in goods, not cash as with cents-off deals or coupons.

4. *Additional- or combination-product deals.* Sometimes a price is reduced by maintaining the shelf price at its regular level and increasing the size of the container so it includes "bonus product." The effect is a reduction in the price per unit. Variations are the "two-for-the-price-of-one" deal and the "one-cent" sale. If the combination deal is on another product from the same manufacturer, the objective

is usually to gain trial for the second product, not to run a price promotion on the first one.

Price wars. Although price competition is often effective with customers, it does not make those practicing it popular with competing retailers. In fact, the policy may lead to a price war, that is, a "head-on conflict between (or among) vendors . . . [which] is characterized by successive moves and countermoves with resulting downward spiraling of prices."[17] Usually confined to a single product or to a limited number of fast-moving items, price wars can bring prices to a relatively low point. They are one of the most fascinating aspects of economic competition.

Many price wars end after a short preliminary skirmish—a period in which the competitors make downward price adjustments and, finding that their reductions are matched by others, quickly retire from the battle. On other occasions, a specific retailer will attempt to check the downward spiraling of prices. During a Los Angeles milk war, which reduced the price of a quart of milk to one cent, one retailer gave pennies to his customers and urged them to "go across the street and buy the one-cent milk from his competitor." In the majority of cases, however, some kind of joint action by retailers or manufacturers is required before the upward price move takes place. Perhaps a group of retailers other than the warring principals will send in "employees . . . to buy stocks of goods at prices lower than their own wholesalers could provide." Persuasive committees of retailers may call upon the price cutters, or the latter may be invited to a meeting for a discussion of the evils of price wars.

Guarantee against price decline. An always difficult problem of price administration concerns the type and extent of protection to be given distributors, dealers, and users in case of a price decline. The method of handling this problem must be different in the case of price wars, regular price decreases, and promotional pricing "deals."

In some price wars, notably gasoline, a decrease in the wholesale price motivated by an excess supply is usually the cause. For this reason, suppliers try to share price cuts with their retailers so they can remain competitive. However, if retail wars continue after supplies are back in line with demand, a refiner may refuse to share the cost of the price war with his wholesalers and retailers. Such actions inevitably generate charges from independent dealers that the refiners are trying to discriminate against them. The competitive complexities of this maneuvering are such that federal antitrust agencies have been unable to explain the implications of these charges and activities after over 30 years of study and litigation.

A decrease in the list price of an item can create serious problems with buyers, particularly if they have been caught with large inventories purchased at higher prices. The administration of this problem differs between types of products—notably between raw materials and manufactured products for resale. In the former situation, the price may be the one in effect at time of order, at time of shipment, or even for some period after shipment. The justification for a guarantee of price protection after shipment must be based on the seller's desire to smooth production in the face of buyer speculation that prices will decline further. However, such guarantees can actually lead to increased speculation, wider swings in orders, and bad feelings between buyer and seller. A policy of price in effect at time of shipment is usually better in the long run.

---

[17] All quotations in this section from R. Cassady, Jr., "Price Warfare—A Form of Business Rivalry," in R. Cox, W. Alderson, and S. J. Shapiro (eds.), *Theory in Marketing* (Homewood, Ill.: Richard D. Irwin, Inc., 1964), pp. 356–71. See also Cassady's "The Price Skirmish—A Distinctive Pattern of Competitive Behavior," *California Management Review,* Winter 1964, pp. 11–16.

For sales of finished goods by manufacturers to distributors, the rationale for price protection is dependent on who holds the power in the channel. If the manufacturer is the channel leader, he should not "load" his distributors with high-cost merchandise unless he is prepared to offer them a "barn burner" promotion to help them clear out his merchandise. If the distributor is the channel leader, the manufacturer dare not refuse to grant price rebates if he wants the continued support of the distributor.

Policies for handling price deals are the most easily resolved because of established procedures within the channel and government regulations concerning such deals. The merchandise must be clearly identified, distributor margins must be at least as great as on regular merchandise, and the length and frequency of deals are restricted so that regular-priced merchandise in distributor warehouses does not become obsolete.

Discount policy

In pricing their goods, many sellers allow the buyer certain discounts or reductions from a list price. The most common are the quantity discount, based on the quantity purchased; the trade discount, based on the trade status of the buyer; and the cash discount, allowed for prompt payment. In addition, a discount or allowance is sometimes given for promotional services rendered by the buyer. A seller may use all four of these kinds of discounts and still follow a one-price policy, as long as he gives similar discounts to comparable buyers.[18]

Quantity discounts. Reductions in price granted to buyers based on the quantity purchased are termed "quantity discounts." When the discount is determined by the quantity purchased at a given time, it is known as a "noncumulative quantity discount." When based on the quantity purchased over a period of time, regardless of the size and number of individual orders, it is termed a "cumulative quantity discount." In either case the discount may refer to the quantity of a specific item or to the quantity of several different items purchased.

1. *Noncumulative quantity discounts.* This type of discount is illustrated by the manufacturer of dolls who adopts the following schedule of quantity discounts:

	Price
Orders for—	per dozen
Less than 5 dozen	$12.75
5–10 dozen	12.50
11–20 dozen	12.25
21–50 dozen	12.00
Over 50 dozen	11.75

It is evident that the seller may achieve lower costs because of the large orders encouraged by noncumulative quantity discounts. Selling cost is reduced when the small-order customer adopts a policy of placing one large order every two months. Packing, transporting, and collecting costs are also decreased; and under certain circumstances, large orders may aid in cutting production cost because they facilitate production planning. Insofar as savings in cost can be traced to large orders, noncumulative quantity discounts seem justified.

---

[18] In some instances so-called "brokerage" discounts or allowances and seasonal discounts are also granted. See Duncan, Phillips, and Hollander, *Modern Retailing Management,* pp. 287–88, and B. J. Mezines, "Brokerage—When is it Permitted under the Robinson-Patman Act?" *Boston College Industrial and Commercial Law Review,* Summer 1966, pp. 821–45.

2. *Cumulative quantity discounts.* This type of discount, which is also known as a "deferred," "patronage," or "volume" discount, is sometimes used for perishables, replacement tires and tubes, and the products of the rayon industry. In the latter industry a common discount is 1 percent on annual purchases of over $100,000 but less than $200,000, with the discount gradually increasing to 5 percent on purchases in excess of $500,000.[19]

The cumulative quantity discount does not offer the possibilities of cost reduction that may result from the use of noncumulative discounts. Under the former the goods may still be shipped in small lots at a number of times, thus involving higher billing, packing, transporting, and collecting costs. Likewise, unless the whole order is placed at one time (an exceptional case), with parts of it to be shipped on certain specific dates, there is no saving in selling cost or in production. In fact, the cumulative discount is offered largely as a means of encouraging concentration of purchases and rewarding customers for their patronage.[20]

Cumulative quantity discounts also suffer from certain practical difficulties. Toward the end of the discount period, buyers are inclined to place large orders to qualify for higher discounts. This practice may disrupt the production schedule of the manufacturer, so that his costs are actually increased. At the same time, such orders will reduce sales at the beginning of the following period. Thus, instability of the production schedule is encouraged. Moreover, it is often difficult to deal with those buyers who fall just short of the quantity needed to obtain the next higher discount. They may argue that they are so close that they should receive it. Finally, some authorities believe that the cumulative discount does not even achieve its aim of encouraging concentration of purchases by buyers—or at least, that the degree of concentration which is obtained could be secured at lower cost through various methods of sales promotion. In view of these difficulties and the fact that their legality, discussed in Chapter 25, is in serious question, cumulative quantity discounts are used infrequently today.

Trade discounts. A trade discount (sometimes referred to as a "functional discount") is a reduction in price given to certain classes of buyers, usually to compensate them for the performance of particular marketing functions. Thus a manufacturer selling to both wholesalers and retailers may offer wholesalers a discount of 50 percent off his list price, whereas retailers are given only 30 percent off list. When goods are sold through the wholesaler, this middleman, in effect, receives both the wholesale and the retail discount; he then passes the latter discount on to the retailer. Note that the trade discount bears no relationship to the quantity purchased at any given time. It may be given in addition to a quantity discount.

Trade discounts are often justified on the grounds that they offer an easy way of suggesting resale prices. In the example of the preceding paragraph, assuming a $1 list price, the manufacturer is suggesting that the wholesaler resell to the retailer at 70 cents and the retailer to the customer at $1. Trade discounts also help a seller to keep his prices secret, (if he can keep his discount schedule from the hands of his competitors), and minimize the need for revising prices in catalogs (he merely issues

---

[19] Additional examples of cumulative quantity discounts will be found in R. A. Lynn, *Price Policies and Marketing Management* (Homewood, Ill.: Richard D. Irwin, Inc., 1967), p. 204, and in R. L. Knox, "Competitive Oligopolistic Pricing," *Journal of Marketing,* 30 (July 1966), pp. 48–49.

[20] R. C. Brooks, Jr., argues that the concentration of purchases which results from the cumulative quantity discount may produce "Market effects similar to those of exclusive dealing and tying arrangements." "Volume Discounts as Barriers to Entry and Access," *Journal of Political Economy,* 69 (February 1961), p. 63.

a new discount sheet). But the main reasons for trade discounts are twofold: a cost argument and the desire for extensive distribution.

The cost argument is simply that the discount represents the cost of the marketing functions which the various middlemen perform. In practice, however, this argument is losing some of its validity with the disappearance of the fairly sharp lines which existed earlier between wholesalers and retailers. Many retailers have grown so large that they order direct from manufacturers in quantities as large as or larger than those of the wholesaler. Moreover, some of the earlier assumed functions of the wholesaler have gradually been pushed back onto the manufacturer. Therefore, whatever validity the cost argument has today applies only in those instances where the manufacturer has carefully analyzed his sales costs through various middlemen and classified the latter into trade discount groups based on this analysis.

Middlemen discounts which cannot be cost justified arise when a manufacturer needs the support of a particular channel and can find no other way to gain it except by paying excessive functional discounts. This practice, known as "buying distribution," can be justified easily by the manufacturer, as the cost may be low compared to alternatives. However, from the point of view of general social welfare, this practice is an example of the trapping of inefficiencies in the distribution channel, criticized earlier in this chapter.

Cash discounts. A cash discount is a reduction in price allowed the buyer for the prompt payment of his bill. For example, a manufacturer may quote a price of $12 a dozen on a specific item, with a 2 percent discount if the bill is paid within 10 days. If not paid within this period, the buyer loses the 2 percent cash discount, but he may be given 20 days more before the bill actually becomes due. Such terms of sale are conveniently stated as 2/10, n/30; that is, the bill is subject to a 2 percent discount for 10 days after the invoice date, but the total net amount is due in 30 days. A 2 percent charge for 20 days is equivalent to a simple interest rate of 36 percent per year. When trade or quantity discounts are included in the invoice, these deductions are made before the cash discount percentage is applied to the balance.

The cash discount terms granted by sellers differ appreciably from one industry or trade to another. Whereas 2/10, n/30 is common in the food field, a textile mill quotes n/10/60 extra—the net amount being due in 10 days, but it may be delayed for an additional 60-day period (a total of 70 days in all). In the dress industry the traditional cash discount is 8/10 E.O.M.—meaning that an 8 percent cash discount period extends to 10 days following the end of the month in which the purchase was made. Cash discounts may also vary over time within an industry or trade.

Cash discounts have not always been used simply to encourage prompt payment. Some manufacturers and wholesalers have varied their cash discounts as a means of giving what amounted to discriminatory prices. One buyer, for instance, was given terms of 2/10, n/30; whereas another buyer, after exerting pressure on the manufacturer, obtained 4/20, n/90. The second buyer (assuming the two buyers to be comparable in other respects) was obviously being favored. He could take advantage of the discount and thus get a lower net cost of merchandise, or he might use the credit extended by the seller for the whole 90 days. Such a perversion of the cash discount was considered by Congress as unfair competition and was declared illegal under the Robinson-Patman amendment to the Clayton Act. To be legal at the present time, comparable cash discounts must be offered to all competing comparable buyers.

Promotional discounts or allowances. Promotional or advertising allowances constitute a reduction in price allowed the buyer as compensation for specific and direct forms of sales promotion. They are given by manufacturers to wholesalers and retailers, especially the latter. Some manufacturers feel that their advertising in newspapers is more effective if it is incorporated in the advertisements of well-known retail stores. Consequently, they make such arrangements with various retailers and pay for the space used through advertising or promotional allowances. There is also some economy in this practice, since local advertising rates are usually lower than national rates. Other manufacturers obtain window and interior displays for their products in a similar manner. Finally, some producers have used the promotional allowance as a means of getting retail salespeople to "push" particular products. These promotional services are of special importance to a company introducing a new product.

Promotional allowances therefore are not intended to reduce merchandise cost but are payments for a service, like the payments for any other advertising a manufacturer might undertake. As such, they do not necessarily have anything to do with the quantity of goods bought. One retailer may buy in carload lots and get no promotional allowance, whereas another retailer, buying in smaller quantities but operating in an area in which the manufacturer desires to do advertising, may get a large allowance.

For many years prior to the Robinson-Patman Act of 1936, some promotional allowances were undoubtedly used in a discriminatory manner. That is, they were given to certain favored customers, with little effort to secure effective promotional services in return. In recent years the government has been vigorous in its attempts to ensure that promotional allowances are made available to large and small customers on proportionately equal terms. (See Chapter 25.)

Geographical pricing policies

Every seller, regardless of whether he is a manufacturer, a wholesaler, or a retailer, must establish a policy as to the price differentials he will charge because of the locations of different buyers. Of the many possibilities open to him, five call for some discussion: (1) f.o.b. factory, (2) freight equalization, (3) freight allowed, (4) zone pricing, and (5) basing-point pricing.

F.o.b. factory. When prices are quoted "f.o.b. factory" (free on board), the buyer is responsible for paying the cost of transportation. Title and risk transfer to the buyer after loading at the shipper's dock. Consequently, although comparable buyers will pay identical prices to the seller, their delivered prices will vary with the transportation charge.

We usually think of "f.o.b. factory" as a manufacturer's price policy, but it is also widely used by wholesalers and retailers. A cash-and-carry wholesaler will have some customers who are located close to his warehouse, whereas others are at a considerable distance. Regardless of the location of the customer, he pays similar prices at the warehouse and is then responsible for the cost of transporting the goods to his place of business. Similarly, the cash-and-carry retailer prices on an f.o.b. factory (store) basis.

Freight equalization. The seller who quotes a uniform price to all buyers at his factory or warehouse frequently finds that his market is limited to nearby customers. If he has a competitor 100 miles away who is charging the same f.o.b. factory price, a potential customer located just across the road from that competitor will achieve a lower delivered price through buying locally.

To overcome the disadvantage of distance, many sellers adopt a freight equalization policy. The distant buyer is quoted a delivered price, which consists of the f.o.b. factory price plus the delivery cost from the competitor located closest to the customer. Through such a policy a manufacturer or wholesaler located in Boston may still compete successfully for business in Pittsfield, Massachusetts, against a competitor located in Albany, New York, even though Pittsfield is only 37 miles from Albany and is 137 miles from Boston. Although the seller receives a lower net (after transportation) price on the business done at a distance, the additional business will still be profitable if the price exceeds direct costs. Since abandoning multiple basing-point pricing in 1948, the steel industry has practiced freight equalization.

Freight allowed, or postage-stamp pricing. Instead of computing delivery costs from competitors located close to potential customers, many sellers simply price their goods f.o.b. the customer's place of business. The seller quotes a price which includes delivery cost regardless of the buyer's location. Essentially, this is the policy being followed by the milk dealer who delivers milk at a uniform price to families located across the street from his plant as well as to those living on the opposite side of the city. Department stores usually follow a similar policy on merchandise sold to families within the area in which deliveries are made. Manufacturers of drugs and cosmetics frequently employ postage-stamp pricing.

In addition to making it possible to sell customers over a broad area—perhaps the whole country—and who are located closer to competitors, a freight-allowed policy has other advantages. The seller can advertise a single price throughout his entire market. It is easier for the buyer to compare prices of competing sellers. The quoting of prices is simplified. Fewer complaints are received from customers who, under an f.o.b. factory policy, resent the lower prices obtained by customers located close to the factory.

Zone pricing. For sellers with bulk products, such as heavy electrical appliances, paints, and furniture, the cost of delivery to distant points is such an important part of the delivered price that a freight-allowed policy to all customers cannot be followed. In these circumstances the advantages of that policy can be obtained within a given area by zone pricing. Under this policy the company's marketing area is divided into zones. Although delivered prices may vary from zone to zone, within a zone all customers pay the same delivered price.

Basing-point pricing. Prior to 1948, when most such systems were ruled to be illegal, the basing-point pricing system was widely used by the metal, cement, lumber, sugar, and plate-glass industries. It is not commonly used today. In a basing-point pricing scheme, all competitors price their products at a base price plus freight from the same location—whether or not the seller happens to ship from that point. All too frequently, this method of geographical pricing has been adopted as a method of minimizing price competition among competing firms. The effect is that a buyer is quoted the same price regardless of the location of the plants quoting prices. All buyers do not pay the same price, as they do under a freight-allowed scheme, but all buyers at one location pay the same price regardless of where the product originates.

The government has been more critical of basing-point pricing than of freight equalization or zone pricing because the latter two may be independently operated logically by a seller to meet the price of known competitors. Basing-point systems are usually complex and do not make sense either competitively or costwise for any seller. The only reasonable conclusion is that such schemes constitute evidence of price collusion between sellers.

Resale price maintenance policy

Resale price maintenance refers to the policy under which manufacturers establish and attempt to enforce the prices at which their products are resold to consumers. In practice, this policy applies primarily to consumer goods. Some manufacturers and retailers believe the maintenance of retail prices is important because price cutting:

1. Encourages some "regular-price" retailers to practice substitution, that is, to urge the purchase of another brand.
2. Leads other regular-price retailers to discontinue the brand or to "put it under the counter."
3. Encourages regular-price retailers to urge the manufacturer to reduce his price to them so that they can better meet the prices of cut price retailers.
4. Results in an alleged loss of prestige for the brand, since some consumers might believe that the cut price represented its "real value."
5. Reduces the attractiveness of full-service retailers.

The most talked about technique for achieving this policy is through state and federal "fair trade" laws which permit sellers to fix the minimum retail prices of their products. These and a related type of state law, the "unfair trade practices acts," are discussed in Chapter 25. Here the discussion will be restricted to five techniques that do not require enabling legislation: (1) list prices, (2) advertised list prices, (3) franchising, (4) selling on consignment and (5) vertical integration.

List prices. The mildest attempt at resale price maintenance is simply to publish, sometimes on the product, a list or suggested retail price. This is the price from which middlemen deduct their functional discounts. Wholesalers and retailers are ,not required to follow these prices and discounts, and they do provide a benchmark from which price cutters can work. If price cutting becomes common practice, the list prices have no value and will even be considered deceptive by the Federal Trade Commission.

Advertised list prices. A manufacturer spending his own promotional budget to advertise the list price of a brand can have the effect of making retailers reluctant to cut price. However, it can have the reverse effect of making a price cut more obvious and significant to consumers. It is difficult to generalize about the merits of this approach. In some cases it has been a successful technique for resale price maintenance; in others it has not. The posting of price stickers in new cars provides an interesting situation of government-imposed list price marking which neither dealer nor manufacturer expect will be enforced. Yet the government in 1969 issued complaints that these list prices were deceptive because they did not reflect the prices for which automobiles were actually sold.

Franchising. A more successful policy for maintaining resale prices has been to franchise dealers, using contractual agreements covering mutual aid, and to refuse to sell to middlemen who consistently cut price. This policy can be followed successfully only by manufacturers with strong brand names who are willing to support their dealers, police them, and terminate those who do not perform. Put another way, a selective distribution policy must be appropriate if franchising is to be practical. The manufacturer must also minimize the retailer's desire to cut prices by discouraging overstocking, establishing competitive list prices, providing vigorous promotional support, and settling consumer and retailer claims promptly.

Selling on consignment. The alternative of selling on consignment is a costly one which has been used successfully in only a minority of situations—notably General Electric's policy of selling light bulbs on consignment. By consignment selling we mean that the manufacturer retains title to the products in the retailer's store and thereby has an absolute private property right to establish the price at which they are sold. Note however, that he also has the obligation to take back unsold merchandise. This risk and investment is great.

Vertical integration. The most extreme technique for resale price maintenance is for the manufacturer to operate his own wholesale and retail outlets. For Baldwin pianos, Allied "Radio Shack" hi-fi stores, some shoe companies, Singer Company, and even Charles of the Ritz cosmetics, this approach has been successful. However, this is a costly and extreme approach to resale price maintenance. It is probably only undertaken if there are other motivations for vertical integration.

Restrictions on pricing freedom

In concluding this discussion of pricing, the growth of restrictions on the seller's pricing freedom should be emphasized. In practice, this freedom has never been so complete as envisaged by much of the theoretical analysis of introductory textbooks in the field of economics. But our pricing system has long been dominated by competitive considerations. Today the scope of such considerations is appreciably reduced. The fair-trade acts and some of the unfair-sales laws discussed in preceding paragraphs severely limit the pricing freedom of many retailers. Discount practices of manufacturers are influenced by federal regulations. Parity price controls for agricultural products play a major role in the pricing of many of the raw materials used by industry.

Since competitive price setting is the very heart of our free enterprise system, it is questionable how far we can go in placing restrictions on the pricing freedom of individual business firms and still retain our type of economy. But it is clear that at some point—if we want the advantages of freedom and the high standard of living which our system affords—we must be willing to accept the rigors of price competition and not try to protect everyone from its impact. And there is a very encouraging aspect of these restrictive laws: after a careful evaluation of their history, Professor Hollander concludes that "if we take a long enough view . . . these restraints seem to lose much of their force."[21] Apparently (and fortunately) it is difficult to remove the impact of competitive factors in the business world.

SUMMARY

Several basic facts have been established in this discussion of pricing: (1) for all market structures except pure competition, demand curves are downward sloping; (2) for all market structures except pure competition and homogeneous oligopoly, the firm does have some discretion to set price within a range where demand will not dry up or profits become negative; (3) a large percentage of all U.S. markets have structures other than pure competition, monopoly, or homogeneous oligopoly; (4) sellers can alter their demand curves and cost structures through changes in all marketing mix variables—not just price. Therefore, it is important for the marketing decision maker to develop techniques for analyzing demand in such a way that he can determine the mix of product, channel, promotion, and price variables which will maximize profit in the long run.

---

[21] S. C. Hollander, *Restraints upon Retail Competition* (East Lansing: Michigan State University Graduate School of Business Administration, 1965), p. 84.

Classical demand analysis does not fully fill this need because it assumes all variables are fixed except price. In fact, all the variables of all sellers in a market are free to change. And, in fact, most competitors are differentiating their offerings and attempting to extend their offerings into other markets.

Within the constraints imposed by market structure, pricing must be managed in terms of the firm's goals in concert with the other controllable variables. Manufacturers must be able to gain good estimates both of their costs and the demand schedules that confront them. This, in turn, lets them determine general price ranges for various products. Middlemen, in contrast, carry so many different types of products and have so many joint costs that they usually seek their general price ranges by adding some percentage to their costs.

Within the generally established price ranges, firms seek specific price strategies. These strategies usually are designed to reflect the likely reactions of both prospective buyers and competitors. Price strategies considered included (1) skimming the market, (2) sliding down the demand curve, (3) penetration pricing, (4) leader pricing, (5) variable leader pricing, and (6) producing to price.

Policies concerning four areas of price administration also were discussed: (1) pricing tactics—such as price promotions, price wars and guarantees against price declines; (2) discount policies—such as quantity discounts, trade discounts, cash discounts, and promotional discounts; (3) geographical pricing policies—such as f.o.b. factory, freight equalization, freight allowed, zone pricing and basing-point pricing; and (4) policies for attempting to maintain resale prices.

Finally, it is appropriate to caution that this chapter was only intended to provide an introduction to pricing. Pricing is a complex topic. A "correct" price is correct in view of its mix with the other controllable variables (product, promotion, and channel) and the market and competitive reactions. As the controllable variables or the market or competitors change, prices need to be changed. Not only is pricing very complex, it is also quite dynamic.

To help you learn more about pricing, we encourage you to use the review and discussion questions and to examine some of the material listed in the supplementary readings at the end of this chapter.

REVIEW AND DISCUSSION QUESTIONS

1. From your experience or from library reading, give two examples of products sold under conditions approximating each of the market structures in Table 23–1.
2. Carefully explain the relationship between the ease of product innovation and the social role and value of advertising.
3. Explain the conditions under which the concentration of market power in the hands of large distributors may be beneficial or not beneficial for the marketing system.
4. Explain the difference in the way marketing analysis of price and nonprice competition differs from that of traditional economic analysis.
5. Discuss the statement that "virtually every differential advantage possessed by a seller tends to erode; its value in generating exceptional sales or profits declines." Give examples.
6. "From the consumer point of view, monopolistic competition may give more satisfactory results than pure competition." Evaluate.

7. How should corporate income taxes be added to the calculation of the price schedule that will return the target rate of return?

8. Show how a retailer can use this same expression to estimate his normal markup on a class of merchandise.

9. Give three specific illustrations of pricing which recognize that maximizing total profit does not necessarily mean maximizing the profit on a specific product.

10. What is meant by "penetration pricing"? From your reading or observation cite two illustrations of such pricing other than those mentioned in the text.

11. Explain the price strategy followed by the Ford Motor Company in the early days of the automobile industry. What strategy does it use today? What factors have led to any change in strategy you note?

12. Explain the difference in supermarket pricing strategy between discount pricing and variable leader pricing.

13. Compare and contrast the objectives of a manufacturer in using a trade deal and a consumer deal.

14. Prepare a 10-minute report on price wars including causes, examples, impact on buyers and sellers, and termination.

15. From the seller's point of view, why are quantity discounts granted?

16. "Price leadership tends to result in greater price stability. Price stability leads to greater profits. Increased profits lead to industrial activity and prosperity. Can anyone doubt that the practice of 'following the leader' as regards prices should be encouraged?" Discuss.

17. What do you believe are the factors which have led quantity discounts to become more popular and trade discounts less popular in the past two decades?

SUPPLEMENTARY READINGS

Alderson, W. *Dynamic Marketing Behavior.* Homewood, Ill.: Richard D. Irwin, Inc., 1965. Chapter 4, "Negotiated Price, Price Leadership, and Market Prices," develops "a point of view for grappling with price problems in heterogeneous markets."

Cassady, R., Jr. *Competition and Price Making in Food Retailing: The Anatomy of Supermarket Operations.* New York: Ronald Press Co., 1963. The early chapters of this volume present an excellent analysis of price and nonprice competition in a specific field of retailing.

Cohen, K. J. and Cyert, R. M. *Theory of the Firm.* Englewood Cliffs, N.J.: Prentice-Hall, Inc., 1965. Chapters 4–14 offer a more complete treatment of many of the subjects covered by this chapter.

Duncan, D. J.; Phillips, C. F.; and Hollander, S. C. *Modern Retailing Management: Basic Concepts and Practices,* 8th ed. Homewood, Ill.: Richard D. Irwin, Inc., 1972. Chapters 16 and 17 discuss price policy from the retailer's point of view.

Grether, E. T. *Marketing and Public Policy.* Englewood Cliffs, N.J.: Prentice-Hall, Inc., 1966. In connection with the present chapter, see pp. 22–24, which discuss product differentiation and brand promotion, and Chapter 4, "Environment and Goals of the Enterprise."

Hollander, S. C. *Restraints upon Retail Competition.* East Lansing, Mich.: Michigan State University, Graduate School of Business Administration, 1965. In this study "of the forces that tend to limit competition in retailing," Professor Hollander discusses (among many other subjects) resale price maintenance, unfair practices acts, and price wars.

Lynn, R. A. *Price Policies and Marketing Management.* Homewood, Ill.: Richard D. Irwin, 1967. Chapter 3, "Insights from the Theory of Price," offers an introductory analysis of pure competition and monopolistic competition, together with a discussion of the practical usefulness of price theory.

Mansfield, E. *Microeconomics: Theory and Applications.* New York: W. W. Norton & Co., 1970. This textbook on intermediate microeconomic theory covers in far more detail many of the topics on market structure discussed here.

Marting, E. (ed.) *Creative Pricing.* New York: American Management Association, 1968. A collection of articles which survey pricing methods and policies.

Nelson, P. E. and Preston, L. E. *Price Merchandising in Food Retailing: A Case Study.* Berkeley, Calif.: University of California, Institute of Business and Economic Research, 1966. This study of retail prices for food suggests the absence of consistent and strong price leadership and the existence of "followers" in "the frequent upward and downward manipulation of prices on selected items. . . ."

Phelps, D. M. and Westing, J. H. *Marketing Management.* Homewood, Ill.: Richard D. Irwin, Inc., 1968. Chapters 10, 11, and 12 provide an excellent discussion of pricing and the pricing environment.

Scherer, F. M. *Industrial Market Structure and Economic Performance.* Chicago: Rand McNally & Co., 1970. Chapters 2 through 14 provide an excellent and comprehensive treatment of market structure, pricing practices, and social welfare.

Part VIII Coordination of the marketing system

The final part of this book considers the mechanisms that coordinate marketing systems in the United States. You have learned that this country has a marketing-oriented type of economy. In Chapter 1, we used the words "manage and control" to describe how the marketing system is "governed." The intent of society in this regard, however, might be better expressed by the word "coordinate," which means to bring into common action.

Unlike some other types of economic systems, a marketing-oriented economy is not affected greatly by governmental planning and regulation. Competition, far and above anything else, is the major mechanism that coordinates this marketing system. Chapter 24, "Competition," focuses on the marketing aspects of the topic.

There are other systems for resource allocation, as was also noted in Chapter 1. Economic planning, for example, serves as the allocator in command-based systems. In this country some resources are allocated in this manner—that is, there are a number of situations in which the government must replace or supplement the market. For example, most private utilities are legal monopolies in which government regulators are substituted for market control. We will not discuss these control mechanisms here.

In some situations markets have been deemed unable to do the complete job of maximizing consumer welfare. In these situations, although market mechanisms perform the bulk of the coordination function, some government intervention occurs. As a result, a considerable amount of federal, state, and local legislation has been designed to augment competition in coordinating the marketing system. Part of this legislation, but certainly not all of it, has been designed to help improve the competi-

587

tive situation or to serve where competition is inadequate. These attempts by government to supplement market coordination are discussed in Chapter 25.

The two topics of competiton and governmental legislation go hand in glove and provide meaningful material with which to conclude the book.

24 *Competition*

Now that the environment of the marketing system, the structure and functions of its component institutions, and some of the policies and practices about which marketing decisions must be made have been explored, we can direct our attention to how this complex system is coordinated in a market where sellers seek profits. Competition among sellers for the favor of knowledgeable buyers is the major coordinating mechanism in a marketing-based economy; the market provides a self-controlling mechanism which causes the system to operate for the general good. Competition as a coordinating mechanism, therefore, is the subject of this chapter.

Outline of the chapter

The analysis of how the market mechanisms operate to produce consumer benefits can be gained through a study of "industrial organization" which focuses on three sets of variables: (1) competitive structure, (2) competitive conduct, and (3) market performance.[1]

Competitive (market) *structure* is concerned with such things as the number of buyers and sellers in a market, the relative size of these firms, the barriers to entry by new firms into the market, and merger activity which alters the competitive structure. *Competitive conduct* has reference to variables such as pricing behavior, nonprice competitive behavior, implicit and explicit agreements between institutions designed to control conduct, and the strategies and tactics of competitive behavior. *Market performance* is the result of competitive activity and is generally discussed

---

[1] For a more complete discussion of the history and model of industrial organization, see F. M. Scherer, *Industrial Market Structure and Economic Performance* (Chicago: Rand McNally & Co., 1970), chap. 1.

in terms of efficiency and effectiveness of resource allocation, innovativeness, allocation of benefits, and sometimes in terms of external environmental effects. Study of
these three topics should provide a good understanding of competition and how it
serves in our marketing-type economy as a coordinating mechanism.

MARKET STRUCTURE

Table 23–1 in the preceding chapter provides a quick review of competitive
market structures in terms of number of buyers and sellers and extent of product
differentiation. Other important structural characteristics that you need to be familiar
with to understand how competition serves as a market mechanism are: (1) the size
distribution of firms, (2) vertical channel structure, (3) economies of scale, and (4)
barriers to entry.

Size distribution and concentration of firms

The sheer size of firms may not be a particularly satisfactory measure of market
power. However, the implications of bigness for concentration of employment power,
financial power, and political power have concerned many who are aware that the
concentration of economic power is substantial and is growing. For example, the share
of all *manufacturing assets* held by the 100 largest manufacturing firms rose from
about 36 percent in 1929 to about 50 percent in 1966.[2] The *value added domesti-
cally* by the 100 largest manufacturing firms increased from 23 percent of total value
added in 1947 to 33 percent in 1967.[3]

Measure of concentration. The simplest and most often used measure of
concentration is the "concentration ratio." This is the percentage of total shipments
by sellers in a particular market accounted for by the largest four, eight, or some other
number of firms. The four- and eight-firm concentration ratios for selected manufacturing industries are shown in Table 24–1.

Most economists argue that the greater the concentration ratio in an industry,
the less competition there is among sellers and the greater the likelihood that the
conduct and performance of the industry is not satisfactory to consumer well-being.
This is because a high four-firm ratio is an indication of either considerable monopoly
power or of a structure of firms producing homogeneous (alike) products.

The four-firm concentration measure is not, however, a particularly reliable
measure of performance in resource allocation. It is too much of a summary measure.
To see the real market structure and the working of competition, we must look behind
the concentration ratio. For example, an industry with a four-firm ratio of 80 percent
may yield very competitive results if each of the 4 sellers has a 20 percent market
share and is aggressive in competitive behavior. This situation is approximated in the
case with soybean oil mills (SIC 2092). Even in a situation with four uneven size firms
and a ratio of 80 percent, aggressive competition founded in innovative product
research and development may provide an adequate market mechanism.

However, we must look behind concentration ratios to determine if the various
firms in an industry really produce competitive products. For instance, the four firms
that sell 69 percent of aircraft (SIC 3721) *might* so differentiate their products that

---

[2] The sources and analysis of the statistics in this section may be found in Scherer, *ibid.,* pp. 39–47.

[3] U.S. Bureau of the Census, *Census of Manufactures, 1967,* Vol. I, *Summary and Subject Statistics*
(Washington, D.C.: Government Printing Office, 1971), p. 9–6.

TABLE 24–1

Concentration ratios (percent of value of shipments) for selected manufacturing industries, 1967

SIC code and industry	Number of companies	4-firm ratio	8-firm ratio
3741. Locomotives and parts	26	97	99
3334. Primary aluminum	10	n.a.	100
3211. Flat glass	39	94	98
3711. Motor vehicles	107	92	98
3641. Electric lamps	72	91	95
2043. Cereal preparations	30	88	97
2073. Chewing gum	19	86	96
3672. Cathode-ray picture tubes	95	84	98
2824. Organic fibers, noncellulosic	22	84	94
2111. Cigarettes	8	81	100
3275. Gypsum products	55	80	93
3633. Household laundry equipment	25	79	95
3331. Primary copper	15	77	98
2072. Chocolate and cocoa products	27	77	89
3632. Household refrigerators	31	73	93
3411. Metal cans	96	73	84
3011. Tires and innertubes	119	70	88
2841. Soap and other detergents	599	70	78
3861. Photographic equipment and supplies	505	69	81
3721. Aircraft	91	69	89
3722. Aircraft engines and parts	205	64	81
3221. Glass containers	39	60	75
2052. Cookies and crackers	286	59	70
2092. Soybean oil mills	60	55	76
2095. Roasted coffee	206	53	71
3651. Radio and TV receiving sets	303	49	69
3621. Motors and generators	320	48	60
3312. Blast furnaces and steel mills	200	48	66
2221. Weaving mills, synthetics	272	46	54
3522. Farm machinery	1,526	44	56
3531. Construction machinery	578	41	53
2082. Malt liquors	125	40	59
3357. Nonferrous wire drawing and insulating	206	39	55
3461. Metal stamping	2,564	39	44
2844. Toilet preparations	628	38	52
2911. Petroleum refining	276	33	57
2211. Weaving mills, cotton	218	30	48
2631. Paperboard mills	276	27	42
2051. Bread, cake, and related products	3,445	26	38
2011. Meatpacking plants	2,529	26	38
3561. Pumps and compressors	480	26	37
2834. Pharmaceutical preparations	791	24	40
2721. Periodicals	2,430	24	37
2026. Fluid milk	2,988	22	30
3541. Machine tools, metal-cutting	865	21	33
2751. Commerical printing, except lithography	11,955	14	21
3441. Fabricated structural steel	1,865	13	18
2511. Wood household furniture	2,934	12	18
2331. Women's and misses' dresses	5,008	7	9

Source: U.S. Bureau of the Census, *Census of Manufactures, 1967*, Vol. I, *Summary and Subject Statistics* (Washington, D.C.: Government Printing Office, 1971), pp. 9–9 to 9–40.

they hardly compete with one another. If such a situation prevailed, there would be relatively little competition to regulate the market. It could also be that firms in different industries may actually make products that are highly competitive with each other. For example, although the metal cans (SIC 3411) and glass containers (SIC 3221) industries each appear quite concentrated, in reality there is far more competition to allocate resources because the two industries compete for many of the same customers. Unfortunately, the SIC codes are based on manufacturing processes and material inputs, not on customers' perceptions of the manufacturers' outputs. This is one of the serious shortcomings of concentration ratios as a measure of market structure.

To discern the impact of competition as a market mechanism, we also need to look beyond concentration ratios to the geographical market coverage of the sellers. A seller could have a near monopoly in a number of large regional markets and still not have a large national market share. In contrast, he could have a large national market (because he was present in so many markets) but fail to have a dominant position in any of the regional markets.

The geographic market becomes an even more complex problem for multinational companies. In some countries—notably France—the public policy seems to be to let sellers enjoy domestic monopoly in order to make them strong enough to meet competition in foreign markets. In this country, conversely, many firms are forced to compete in foreign markets because public policy prevents them from substantially increasing their domestic market share. IBM and General Motors are illustrations of U.S. companies which would face government opposition to domestic growth. These interrelationships among domestic and international markets have a significant bearing on the competitive performance of the firm in any one market. A multinational company, for example, may offer more product or price competition in certain markets because it can subsidize such a strategy from its other more profitable markets.

A similar problem arises because most firms sell more than one product and brand, raising a question as to whether the firm's share of the market for all of its brands should be considered jointly. A second brand might be used to engage in aggressive price cutting in order to protect the profit margin and market share of the primary brand, or it might simply be an attempt to offer a broader assortment of product variations to the market. Procter & Gamble uses both these tactics with their various toothpaste brands, and the so-called soap companies (SIC 2841) offer a more general example with their marketing of detergents.

Thus simple market structure analysis is hardly adequate. An understanding of industry concentration and its influence on competition as a market mechanism should go beyond concentration ratios.

Vertical channel structure

Vertical channel structure is another major dimension of market structure that greatly influences the working of competition as a market mechanism. Figure 24–1 and Table 24–2 bring together many of the considerations necessary to analyze the competition brought about by vertical channel structures. The large number of possible structures suggested by Figure 24–1 should indicate that the analysis of conduct and performance of a channel system is more complex than that indicated by a classification of market structures at a single level such as that shown in Table 23–1

Marketing: Principles and methods

FIGURE 24–1
Classification of vertical market structures

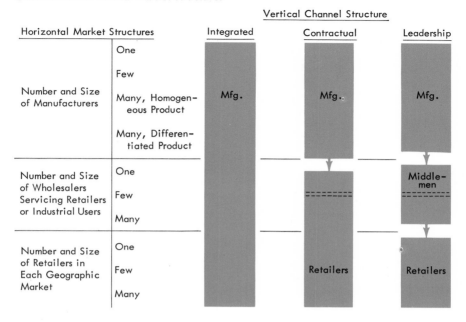

in the preceding chapter. Some of the possibilities for undesirable competitive conduct are suggested in Table 24–2.

In arriving at desirable public policies, structure and conduct must be analyzed jointly. For example, a vertically integrated channel does not provide the opportunity to exhibit exploitation of weak channel members by the channel leader, but neither does it *guarantee* desirable conduct or performance in final markets.

A firm integrates vertically because it believes this can enhance its profit potential. The increased profit may come from increased efficiency, either through integration of production and physical distribution facilities or through elimination of the uncertainty and fluctuations of resource allocation through the market. Neither of these efficiences is guaranteed to occur, however. Many "logical" mergers have failed because management skill was insufficient to make the necessary linkages of the two operations. Vertical integration could also provide the market power to trap the gains in efficiency so they are not passed on to subsequent markets; "too much" success can produce the power required to block entry and prevent competitors from cutting prices.

There will be greater competitive rivalry (1) the larger the number of market levels, (2) the more channel members there are at each level, and (3) the greater the geographic complexity of the channel of distribution. Because these conditions are likely to increase the number of transactions which must take place, however, this increased competition could lead to decreased channel efficiency. The point is that vertical channel structure influences the amount and kinds of competition that are present as market mechanisms.

TABLE 24–2
Competitive conduct considerations under three different vertical channel structures

1. Integrated channel structures
   - *a)* Extent of use of dual (nonintegrated) channels.
   - *b)* Tactics used in final market competition.
   - *c)* Extent of research and development.
   - *d)* Undesirable discrimination against nonintegrated middlemen.
   - *e)* Collusion with final market competitors.
   - *f)* Horizontal mergers designed to reduce competition at any market level.
   - *g)* Attempts to block entry of competitors at *any* market level.

2. Contractual channel structures
   - *a)* Exploitation by leaders of other channel members.
   - *b)* Exclusive dealership arrangements which reduce competition at any market level.
   - *c)* Threats to eliminate other channel members for reasons other than unsatisfactory performance.
   - *d)* Contracts designed to maintain resale prices or otherwise restrain competition in *any* market level.
   - *e)* Shifting of risk to weaker channel members.
   - *f)* Extent of research and development in the *total* vertical structure.
   - *g)* Horizontal or vertical mergers which reduce competition in the *total* vertical structure.

3. Leadership channel structures
   - *a)* Exploitation of members by the channel leader.
   - *b)* Unfair competitive tactics at *any* market level.
   - *c)* Extent of research and development in the *total* vertical structure.
   - *d)* Collusion in restraint of trade at *any* market level.
   - *e)* Resale price maintenance at *any* market level.
   - *f)* Refusal to deal for the purpose of eliminating competition at *any* market level.
   - *g)* Horizontal or vertical mergers which reduce competition in the *total* vertical structure.
   - *h)* Attempts to block entry of competitors at *any* market level.

Economies of scale

A third market structure characteristic that influences the amount and type of competition is termed "economies of scale." As the size (scale) of the operation increases, average unit costs decrease to some minimum level. The characteristic of interest is the minimum investment in the operation that is required to achieve a scale which permits operations at a level close to where average costs are minimum. In capital-intensive industries such as primary aluminum (SIC 3334), flat glass (SIC 3211), and basic steel (SIC 3312), this economic size may be very large relative to the size of total potential demand. Thus, in such industries, public policy must try to determine the relative advantage of a *competitive* market served by a large number of inefficient firms or an *oligopolistic* market served by a small number of efficient firms. In general, the public policy in the United States in this situation has been to settle for a small number of firms (but certainly more than one), the *conduct* of which is carefully monitored by the government.

Economies of scale are not limited to production efficiency. They extend to—and, in fact, are probably more meaningful in—marketing activities such as buying and physical distribution, personal selling, and advertising. For example, relatively large firm size permits specialization in the buying function and allows firms the efficiencies of both buying and receiving carload lots. Whereas the cost of a company sales force is virtually prohibitive to a small company, a larger one may be able to add several new products to its line and gain increased productivity from its sales force without added cost. The same sort of situation tends to prevail for advertising. The larger advertiser appears to gain benefits much faster than costs, compared to the small advertiser.

Like the other two facets of market structure—concentration of firms and vertical channels—economies of scale influence the amount and types of competition that will be present to help govern the operation of markets.

Barriers to entry

The fourth characteristic that has a major influence on the amount and types of competition present in the market structure is termed "barriers to entry." These are the advantages that existing firms have over potential rivals. They can stem from any of the economies of scale, possession of patents or technical know-how, ownership or control of raw materials, ability to obtain capital in greater amounts or at lower cost than new entrants, and goodwill and loyalty with distributors and buyers. When such barriers exist, potential entrants are either unable to begin to compete or can do so only at a loss.

Blocked entry permits existing sellers to behave in ways that yield profits greater than those that would exist if more sellers were present. Insofar as these "excess" profits result in a misallocation of resources in the economy, barriers to entry are an undesirable structural characteristic. Three aspects of the barriers problem are important: (1) the effect of barriers to entry on innovation, (2) their effect on pricing, and (3) the barriers to entry created through marketing.

Effect on innovation. High barriers to entry can influence sellers not to invest in research and development or to innovate because they are currently making satisfactory profits, are not threatened, and see no need to spend the money to innovate. Very low barriers to entry can also deter sellers from investing in research and development because prices are held close to that of pure competition, they do not have the size nor money to innovate, or they fear their innovations will be too easily followed by competitors.

Markets with moderate barriers to entry—i.e., where some capital investment is required for optimum scale and some degree of product differentiation—are typically those in which spending for development is greatest per dollar of sales. Apparently this is because sellers in this structure see new-product innovation as their best method of staying ahead of existing and potential competitors. (See the discussion of strategies for growth in Chapter 18.) Such thinking is probably well founded, for there is overwhelming evidence that the success rate of new firms is greatest among those that have really new and important product innovations. Thus we can generalize that some modest barriers to entry appear to be a desirable market characteristic. They provide the promise of some monopoly profit to existing firms in return for innovation and new-product development. At the same time, these barriers must be kept low enough that new competitors with significant innovations can successfully enter the market.

This conclusion has direct implications for U.S. patent law, which grants 17 years of protection to the owners of a new invention. This law was intended to encourage new entrants in a market by providing some protection from imitation. The Polaroid Land Camera offers an example. However, if the required technical know-how is significant or the invention belongs to an established firm in a market with high entry barriers, then exclusive 17-year patent protection is probably not required as a spur to innovation.

24 / Competition

Effect on pricing behavior. When barriers to entry are high, skimming is a likely pricing strategy; when moderate, "sliding down" is likely; when low, penetration is appropriate. An existing seller could set his price so that it provided a barrier to entry by making it *just below the estimated minimum average cost of potential entrants.* Polaroid followed such a strategy when it introduced the low-priced "Swinger."

The existing firm may also be able to threaten potential entrants by demonstrating a willingness to cut price below that which would yield any profit to the new entrant. Such threats might take the form of short-term price cuts. In these situations, the threat of entry has the effect of reducing price. Thus, if we view pricing strategy in terms of socially desirable market structures, we reach a general conclusion that low or moderate barriers are preferable to high barriers.

Marketing barriers to entry. Advertising and price are the two marketing barriers which have received greatest public attention. Advertising as a barrier is discussed in the next section. Two other items in the marketing mix—product and distribution—which, if managed successfully, can provide barriers to competitive entry will be considered here.

Advertising cannot create durable barriers unless the brand has significant advantages of importance to consumers. Thus, the more important barrier is the *product's differences,* not the advertising used to communicate these differences to buyers.

Similarly, advertising cannot be effective unless distribution has been achieved. Of course, it can be used to gain distribution, but if ample distributors were available, new entrants could do the same. Distribution barriers to entry occur in situations where there are more brands than distributors. These situations are common: qualified distributors for high-priced, high-technology durables like automobiles and most industrial equipment are hard to find or develop; merchant wholesalers and industrial distributors often handle so many lines that they are not able to promote a new item effectively; supermarkets allocate their limited shelf space among a fraction of the total brands available to them. For example, in a recent antitrust action against the largest manufacturers of prepared cereals (SIC 2043), the FTC charged that the dominant manufacturer had gained control of cereal department shelf space and allocated it among the largest firms, thereby blocking the entry of new competitors.

In such an instance, the courts could find that the barriers to entry have become too high. But in most markets, the existence of moderate barriers to entry through marketing is the carrot which causes sellers to work hard to serve buyers better than they are served by other sellers. When kept in moderation and in the presence of aggressive competition, product innovation, pricing, promotion, and distribution barriers usually work to the buyer's advantage—not disadvantage. A more likely hypothesis in today's market is that the carrot works too well; considerable social waste is created by unsuccessful attempts of sellers to differentiate their offerings.

COMPETITIVE CONDUCT

Market structure, the topic of the prior section, encompasses the number of players and constraints on their movements in the game of competition. Competitive conduct refers to the alternatives, strategies, and actions of the players. Structural constraints such as barriers to entry have implications for the conduct of players because it is this conduct that leads to good or bad performance. Much public policy discussion concerning competition centers around the identification of conduct believed to lead to unsatisfactory performance or to be patently undesirable in itself.

Marketing: Principles and methods

Discussion of this subject is divided into five sections: (1) anticompetitive effects of advertising, (2) mergers, (3) pricing behavior, (4) agreements in restraint of trade, and (5) unfair methods of competition. Some conduct characteristics, such as the amount of innovation and research undertaken, were discussed in the previous section on structure. Other conduct variables are listed in Table 24–2 above.

Anticompetitive effects of advertising

The pervading presence of advertising raises many questions in the minds of the public regarding its desirability for society and for competition. The possibly undesirable social effects of advertising on consumers were discussed in Chapter 6. Here we will analyze some of the arguments as to when and why advertising may constitute a form of undesirable business conduct.

An inefficient and unnecessary cost of marketing. A somewhat imprecise charge often voiced by those not trained in economics is that advertising is an inefficient and unnecessary cost of marketing which increases prices without benefiting consumers. This complaint is more easily justified in markets where unadvertised, low-priced alternatives are not available. Where such alternatives are available, the charge must be based on one or more of the following assumptions: (1) the advertising is ineffective, (2) psychological benefits of advertising are socially undesirable, (3) average unit costs are increasing, or (4) primary demand cannot be increased.

Under the first assumption that advertising is ineffective, the criticism is based on the notion that the advertising cost is simply added on to other production and marketing costs but has no influence on sales. Thus, the cost of the advertising results in higher prices or lower profits or both. Were this the case, a seller would soon discover it and either change his advertising or eliminate it. There would be no motivation to continue an unsuccessful campaign.

The second assumption of socially undesirable results raises some of the issues developed in Chapter 6. It is felt that buyers should not find utility in the assurance of quality or the prestige received from buying an advertised brand. In the case of some brands where advertising expenditures are perhaps too high, such as in analgesics, deodorants, and hair products, the charge is that they would perform just as well without advertising. Although one may criticize personal values, the marketing system cannot be criticized on this basis unless it is creating or altering the values of members of the society.[4]

Reference to Figure 24–2 will be helpful in understanding assumptions 3 and 4, which concern the nature of costs and demand. This figure shows three average-unit-cost curves for a firm: one for all costs but advertising, one for advertising, and one for the total unit cost, including advertising. The latter is simply the vertical sum of the first two. If a firm is selling an output of *N* or less, the cost of advertising adds a layer of cost which lowers profits or must be absorbed by higher prices. However, if the amount of advertising added can generate sales in a range from *P* to *Q*, then total unit costs have been reduced *even if prices are not increased*. Note, however, that the criticism that advertising raises costs could be based on assumption 3, above. That is, if the firm without advertising is operating near *O*, rather than near *N*, advertising would raise unit costs rather than reduce them.

Assumption 4, concerning the extent to which primary demand may be in-

---

[4] For a more complete development of these and related issues, see P. Doyle, "Economic Aspects of Advertising: A Survey," *Economic Journal*, 78 (September 1968), pp. 570–602.

FIGURE 24–2
Average costs with and without advertising

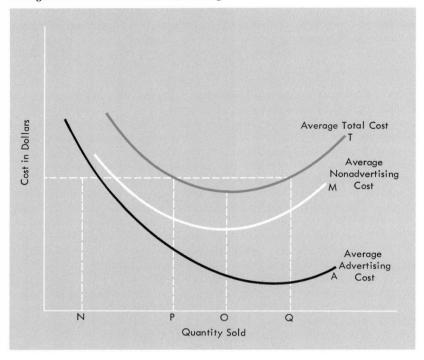

creased, assumes that all firms serving the market are operating in the area of decreasing average costs, say between *N* and *P,* but that the total demand in the market
cannot be increased through advertising. Now, if one firm advertises, its market share
may increase enough to reduce its total average cost, but competitors will lose sales
back toward *N.* The competitors would, in turn, advertise and successfully regain their
previous market shares. In the end, all firms are selling the same amounts as previously
(since industry sales did not increase), but with higher costs. If the advertising itself
does not increase the utility of buyers (by being entertaining or because it reduces
the price of the media), then assumption 4 does represent a situation in which
advertising is likely to reduce the efficiency of the marketing system.

Detracts from real innovation. A second economic criticism of advertising is
that sellers often find it is easier to differentiate their products through advertising than
through research and development. The result is that creative competitive efforts are
directed to innovative advertising rather than to innovative product improvements.
The advertising of products for which evaluation is difficult or where technological
breakthroughs come infrequently, like gasoline, deodorants, and analgesics, is subject
to this criticism. Such criticism might also be extended to product development. The
automobile industry, for example, is often criticized for its reliance on annual model
changes which prove very costly for both the smaller producers and the consumer.

Fortunately for most products, an advertised consumer advantage, unless proven valid through use of the product, will result in trial but not repeat purchase and thus is not a permanent source of new customers. In the final analysis, value is determined by the buyer through use of the product. If one brand is found to be no better than the rest, there are many advertisements to induce trial of a competing brand next time. Although advertising can probably cause a purchase through emphasis of an insignificant product advantage, it is this sale which is the easiest to lose. A real product improvement is, and is likely to remain, the goal of the marketing strategies of all successful sellers. Probably the most useful function of advertising is to inform buyers that a significant new improvement is available. There is seldom criticism of such informative advertising.

The special problem of homogeneous oligopoly. The market structure of homogeneous oligopoly is usually present along with the characteristics which cause advertising to increase cost and detract from real innovation. In this structure, the following conditions hold:

1. Since the number of sellers is few, low-priced alternatives are not available.
2. Technological progress and important differentiations are difficult or, by definition, the oligopoly would not be homogeneous.
3. The scale of operations can be adjusted quickly enough to avoid increasing average unit costs.

Even under these conditions, however, advertising may enhance competition and not increase prices as long as primary (total) demand is increasing. When it is not, these structural conditions will produce poor conduct and poor performance. Examples of industries in which this occurs include cigarettes, motor vehicles, and cereal preparations (find those industries in Table 24–1). This situation can be illustrated in more detail by considering the available marketing strategy alternatives.

Differentiating the product for specific market segments (for example, a cigarette for women) appears to be a logical strategy and works to the advantage of the firm and of buyers for some time. Eventually, however, the total market is divided into segments too small to justify the cost of customized product variations. And, since primary demand is not growing, the firm finds competition in even small market segments.

Competition for distribution is also important. However, once the product is in the maturity stage of its life cycle and channel relationships have become established, independent middlemen are unlikely to do anything extra for one brand (e.g., give it more promotion) unless it can be done without injury for other profitable brands.

Price is not likely to be an important strategic variable unless the firm has significant cost advantages or primary demand is very price-elastic. Price cuts are too easily followed.

Thus the marketing manager frequently turns to creative advertising to find the help he needs to gain market share. If he is successful in this, he can gain market share through a new consumer appeal which his competitors either cannot follow at all or can follow only after months of delay. The creative advertising man and the dollars to support his output are "the answer to the brand manager's prayer." Some brand managers are successful in finding an appeal that increases market share; those who are not change advertising agencies or try to replace lack of creativity with more advertising dollars.

The difficulty in reaching equilibrium in this battle stems largely from *the central role which creativity plays in the competitive struggle.* Very large increases in advertising expenditures are not common because either a creative campaign deserving of support is not available or the response to continued repetition of the same message diminishes rapidly. Thus competitors more often tend to stabilize advertising expenditures (dollars per year) or advertising/sales ratios (5 percent of forecast or of last year's sales). Attempts to gain competitive advantage take the form of finding new appeals to advertise with the same level of spending, which often involves finding new creative groups to develop it. The combination of these stabilizing and destabilizing elements can lead to increasingly higher levels of advertising which become reflected in prices but do little except cancel out one another. For example, sales and profits reported by cigarette producers since the ban on broadcast cigarette advertising show clearly that advertising spending was above the level required either to maintain demand or to maximize joint profits of all producers. Some empirical evidence even suggests that competitive rivalry of this type may not only lead to poor performance but also feed back to produce even greater structural concentration.[5]

Advertising as a barrier to entry. Another possible anticompetitive effect of advertising returns to the earlier discussion of marketing barriers to entry. Three possible ways in which advertising could create barriers to the entry of new competitors into a market are discussed below.

1. *Accumulated goodwill.* The goodwill argument assumes that past promotional activities have been successful in differentiating a brand, that is, giving it some degree of monopoly position (Bayer or St. Joseph's aspirin). Once established and appreciated by a group of loyal customers, this distinctiveness is hard for new entrants to overcome, because (1) customer habit patterns are hard to break, (2) past advertising has some carryover effect that generates current period sales, and (3) the current promotion of the established seller in the short run is likely to be about as effective as the current promotion of the entrant. Critics of advertising often use "advertising" as a symbol for all marketing effort. It should be remembered that in addition to advertising goodwill, an established seller has a further competitive advantage over a new competitor in that he has established channels of distribution and a stock of goodwill among distributors.

In short, the goodwill barriers argument is like the game, "King of the Mountain." When you are on the top of the mountain, you have an advantage which permits you to ward off attacks from many directions. The seriousness of the problem from the standpoint of the performance of the marketing system is simply a question of the steepness of the mountain—the extent and importance to buyers of the brand's distinctive features.

2. *Cost advantages.* The argument of cost as a barrier to entry is somewhat more complex. It could be a valid criticism if one or both of two conditions held: (1) the prices established advertisers pay for advertising messages are lower than those paid by new advertisers; (2) the response of buyers to the advertising messages of established advertisers is greater per message than the response to those of new advertisers.

The first advantage would be true if established advertisers could obtain discounts in the prices they pay for time and space, advertising production costs, or advertising agency services. In all three of these markets, some price competition does exist, but there is little evidence suggesting that the age of the competitive firm or the size of the advertising budget will provide *very much* help in obtaining substantially lower prices for any of these services. The new entrant may also pay higher prices if he must use local media while established sellers are buying network television.

---

[5] For a review of this evidence, see Scherer, *Industrial Market Structure and Economic Performance,* pp. 125–30 and 341–43.

The second advantage can be discussed by reference to Figure 24–3. (This figure is like Figure 18–5, except that the measure of output has been generalized to "response" to advertising rather than sales produced, and inputs are expressed in messages rather than dollars.) If prices paid for a message are the same for established and new sellers, then the response per message will be the slope of the curve. For the response to the message of an established seller to be greater than that of a new seller, the latter would have to be advertising to the left of the threshold level required for advertising to be noticed, or to the right of the established seller in the area of

FIGURE 24–3
Advertising response function

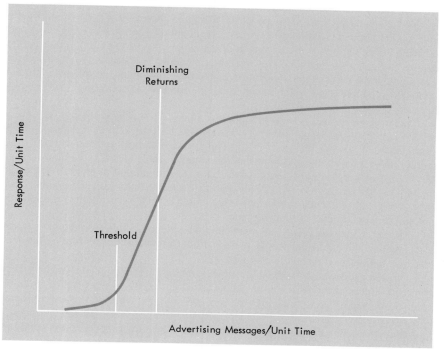

diminishing return. Because it is not rational for the old or new seller to hold advertising below the area of diminishing returns, it is likely that both will advertise near the point where returns begin to diminish, but established sellers will be to the right of a new seller.

3. *Absolute scale barriers.* The absolute size of advertising expenditures required to reach the area of diminishing returns is very large, and the inability of potential competitors to raise this amount may bar them from the market. A lender or investor would consider the high entry fee as greatly increasing the risk of the new venture and hence would be reluctant to supply the funds unless expected profit rates were much above average. Thus, in industries where annual advertising expenditures are very high (for example, cereals and beauty aids), advertising may constitute a capital requirements barrier to entry.

The urge to merge

Like advertising, mergers in themselves are not undesirable business conduct. They are only undesirable if they lead to poor performance. Mergers, which can affect the performance of the marketing system positively or negatively, are generally classified into three types: horizontal, vertical, and conglomerate.

Horizontal mergers. A horizontal merger is a combination between two firms that are at the same level of the channel and are competitors in the same market. An example is a merger between two public accounting firms in the same region in which the objectives are to eliminate a competitor, to gain new clients, to gain know-how possessed by the competitor, and to gain additional production capacity without increasing industry capacity, perhaps at a bargain price. It is possible that a merger between two small, perhaps failing, firms may increase the competitive rivalry in a market. However, in all other cases, competition would achieve the same end as merger and without an increase in concentration. Thus, since 1968, public policy toward horizontal mergers has become very restrictive, so that no two competitors can merge if the result is the elimination of a viable competitor. Both theory and the increase in concentration which has occurred in recent decades suggest the soundness of such a policy.

Vertical mergers. A vertical merger is a combination between a buyer and a seller—that is, between two firms serving the same final market but at different levels of the channel. An example is a shoe manufacturer who buys a chain of retail shoe stores. The motives and possible desirable and undesirable effects of vertical integration to channel and system performance have been discussed at length. While it is recognized in the case of horizontal integration that competition can achieve the same economies and efficiency in the marketing channel, with vertical integration this is not so obvious, at least in the short run.

Merger is one way to integrate vertically. The potential for significant economies in production and marketing processes from proper balancing, linking, and rationalization of functions and resources is great.

Offsetting these potential benefits for performance are the possible ways in which vertical mergers can produce undesirable structural consequences which, in turn, could produce poor performance. Such mergers could result in: (1) a vertical combination which creates such a vast, efficient system as to constitute substantial barriers to competitive entry, (2) the power to cut price and selectively squeeze out competition, or (3) foreclosure of some market. Competitors would be foreclosed in a supply market if a firm merged with an important supplier, and they would be foreclosed in an output market if a firm merged with an important distributor which currently handles many lines. Thus vertical mergers have the effect of reducing the number of buyers or sellers at another level of the channel. Vertically integrated firms can also foreclose markets by practicing reciprocity.

The tradeoff between apparent efficiencies through integration and possible anticompetitive effects makes the formation of public policy toward vertical mergers somewhat more difficult than in the case of horizontal mergers. However, a policy of "preventing elimination of an independent business entity . . . likely to have a substantial competitive influence in [*any*] [emphasis added] market" is a sound beginning.[6]

---

[6] U.S. Department of Justice, *Merger Guidelines* (Washington, D.C.: Government Printing Office, May 30, 1968), p. 7. Also see p. 13 of these guidelines.

Conglomerates. A classification of merger types corresponding to the classification of a firm's growth strategies (see Figure 18–1) can be formulated.

horizontal mergers	provide	market penetration
vertical mergers	provide	vertical integration
market expansion mergers	provide	market expansion
product expansion mergers	provide	product development
true conglomerate mergers.	provide	diversification

Until recently, the last three types of mergers were all considered conglomerate. The diversification merger involves two firms which were not previously involved in serving the same markets, either vertically or horizontally. Diversification is a sound strategy for growth if it can spread risk to a larger number of markets or produce more profit or faster growth in profit than could product development or market expansion. A chief concern of society is whether or not this growth should be achieved through merger.

From the standpoint of performance evaluation of a single product market or of a vertical channel system, the true conglomerate merger is of little concern. However, many mergers which may appear to be diversification are really product or market expansion. An illustration is the case involving the attempt by Procter & Gamble to acquire the Clorox Company. The products of both firms are sold through grocery store channels and with considerable consumer advertising.[7] This merger could more appropriately be considered a horizontal product-expansion merger because Procter & Gamble was a likely *potential entrant* into the bleach market. The firm enjoys economies of scale from product developments (line extensions) sold through existing channels to markets it now serves. Viewed in this way, the line-extension merger results in the potential for poor performance through poor structure because the acquiring firm is a potential competitor.

The other route of reasoning that conglomerate mergers (or, more accurately, diversification and large size generally) result in poor market performance are only slightly more direct. Three will be mentioned here.

1. *Reciprocity.* Each division of the conglomerate firm can bring pressure on its suppliers to purchase the products of other divisions. Thus, the opportunity for reciprocal buying pressures is increased. Often referred to as "trade relations," this is the practice of buying from actual or potential customers and using this as an argument for selling to them. Trade relations activities in some companies become very involved. They may include establishing separate departments for the purpose of compiling records of purchases by suppliers for use by the sales department.

A single reciprocal arrangement may involve as many as four firms, but simple two-way reciprocity is most common and more easily arranged. A manufacturer of metal office furniture uses steel, available from many sources; steel producers buy much metal office furniture, also procurable from many sources. Both companies could appear in the dual role of supplier and customer. The opportunity for a reciprocal claim for patronage will be obvious to the sales departments of both firms. Particularly for the large firm with a broad product line and an organized trade relations department, the practice is not at all like doing business with your friends. It is an attempt to use economic power to conspire with suppliers to restrain trade.

2. *Extinction pricing.* The conglomerate firm, by shifting resources between

---

[7] *FTC* v. *Procter & Gamble Co.,* 386 U.S. 568 (1967).

divisions, can operate one division at a loss for a longer period than can independent competitors. The significance of this power for marketing is that a seller with conglomerate support can cut its price or increase its promotion to a point where it and all competitors who follow are losing money. This practice is known as a "predatory" or "extinction" pricing policy. Such a strategy will force competitors out of business and leave the conglomerate with a dominant market position from which it can then increase its price to the monopoly level and recover its past losses.

3. *Capital allocation.* Because of its accumulated assets and large cash flow, the conglomerate firm is able to allocate investment funds between markets as it sees fit without recourse to capital markets. Those who fear giant conglomerate firms argue that such allocations will not be in the general good and that free capital markets can do a better job of allocating investment funds. Those who run conglomerates argue that they are much closer to end-use markets than are investors or investment bankers. Hence, they are in a better position to allocate funds to various product markets than are the capital markets.

Pricing behavior

Pricing behavior can result in unsatisfactory market performances by producing high prices and high profits (for example, resale price maintenance agreements) or such low prices that competitors lose money and exit, leaving a more concentrated structure. The extinction (or predatory) pricing policy discussed in the previous section is an example of the latter. By pricing below one's competitor's average total unit cost, a large market share—and perhaps monopoly—could result. Such a policy might be considered as the next lower price policy to the "penetration pricing" discussed in Chapter 23.

Price discrimination. Price discrimination is a topic that has received much attention in economics.[8] It means selling the same product (identical in quantity, quality, and place) to different customers at different prices. Practicing such a policy requires that customers can be segmented so that secondary markets do not undermine the discrimination. Movie theaters, for example, attempt to discourage secondary markets when they practice price discrimination by issuing identification cards for lower student prices.

Price discrimination can improve the efficiency of resource allocation by permitting sellers to set prices at many points along the demand curve instead of just one. As shown in Figure 24–4, buyers who will pay high prices do so, and those who will not are sold at the prices they are willing to pay. Both revenue and output are maximized. If these lower prices just cover marginal cost, the seller could not afford this sale if he were required to charge a single price (because marginal cost is greater at lower levels of sales). Price discrimination is regularly practiced by electric utilities (industrial customers and off-peak-hours customers pay low rates; households and peak-hour customers pay high rates), airlines, and by many sellers of consumer goods (a packer may pack similar products for his high-margin line and his high-volume, low-margin, distributor-branded line).

Undesirable price discrimination may occur in intermediate markets when the

---

[8] The best introduction to this topic for the marketing student is two articles in Vol. 11 of the *Journal of Marketing* by Ralph Cassady, Jr., "Some Economic Aspects of Price Discrimination Under Non-Perfect Market Conditions" (July 1946), pp. 7–20; and "Techniques and Purposes of Price Discrimination" (October 1946), pp. 135–50.

FIGURE 24–4
Revenue with a single price and with price discrimination

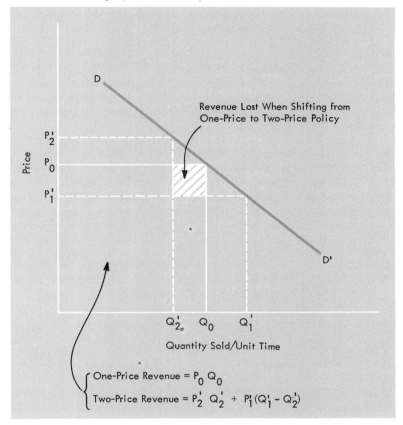

One-Price Revenue = $P_0 Q_0$

Two-Price Revenue = $P_2' Q_2' + P_1' (Q_1' - Q_2')$

same products or services are sold to two buyers in competition with one another at different prices which do not reflect differences in cost. The reasoning is that one customer will be operating at a competitive disadvantage and will eventually have to exit from the market, leaving consumers less well served and other competitors with larger market shares. Of course, the objective of the marketing system is to improve performance—not to save competitors. Thus, the undesirability of the discrimination is not proved until the impact of alternative pricing policies on performance is analyzed.

As a more detailed illustration, suppose that the Kansas City Cement Company sells cement to the Kansas City Paving Contractor Company, the Omaha Cement Company sells cement to the Omaha Paving Contractor Company, and the two paving contractors are in competition. Then suppose that the Kansas City Cement Company decides to attempt to gain business from the Omaha Paving Contractor Company. To do this, he must pay freight on his product to Omaha and also cut his price below that of the Omaha Cement Company. Obviously, the Kansas City Cement

Company is discriminating in price between its two customers, yet competitive rivalry for the business of the Omaha Paving Contractor Company is greater than before. Next, assume that the Omaha Cement Company is unhappy with this turn of events and, to win back business, cuts its price to the Omaha Paving Contractor Company, but not to the St. Jo Paving Contractor, who is in competition with the other two paving contractors. The St. Jo Paving Contractor and the Kansas City Paving Contractor will be at a competitive disadvantage to the Omaha Paving Contractor. On the other hand, if the three paving contractors were not in competition with one another, a favorable market performance could have resulted from the price discrimination in that competitive rivalry for sale to the Omaha Paving Contractor Company was greater than before.

Legally, the price discrimination problem is confusing today because of some provisions of the Robinson-Patman Act of 1936 and the large number of companies selling through dual channels of distribution. For example, if a manufacturer sells to both merchant wholesalers and retailers, should any price differences exactly reflect differences in cost? The answer should be based on the impact of the discrimination on the performance of the entire channel system—not solely on the desire to protect an independent competitor whose efficiency may be subject to question. The price discrimination problem will be discussed further in the next chapter, and the sections on "Discount Policy" and "Geographical Pricing Policies" in the previous chapter can also be reviewed.

Agreements in restraint of trade

Competitive conduct involving collusion or agreements designed to restrain free competitive rivalry almost certainly stems from motives designed to increase the private gain of sellers at the expense of buyers. Three of the most common types of such agreements are (1) resale price maintenance, (2) tying agreements, and (3) collusive agreements.

Resale price maintenance. A seller would like to sell his products and have distributors sell them for the maximum price possible. A number of techniques for maintaining the prices charged by resellers were discussed in the previous chapter. Some of these are unilateral; others involve bilateral agreements, such as a requirement in a franchise agreement between a manufacturer and a distributor that the franchisee will sell only at the prices suggested by the manufacturer. Still others are made possible by state "fair trade" laws (Chapter 25) or through agricultural marketing orders controlling supply (Chapter 14). Even where such agreements have been legalized, there is considerable debate as to whether there is any situation in which an agreement to fix price or maintain resale prices helps to improve the performance of the marketing system.

Tying agreements One major point of uncertainty arises because agreements between buyer and seller in the same channel (as contrasted with agreements between competing sellers) clearly can generate substantial efficiencies in distribution which are often greater than any advantages of a channel led by the "invisible hand" of competition. Further, a seller can achieve these efficiencies without interfirm agreements, through vertical integration. The criteria for evaluation of any agreement between channel members concerning price or any marketing function must focus on channel performance rather than on conduct itself. Yet, as we learned in Chapter 19, the judicial law regulating exclusive dealerships has become very restrictive in recent years.

Other kinds of agreements which have caused concern are (1) dealer territorial restrictions, (2) full-line requirements, and (3) tying requirements. Contracts which limit the geographic area in which the dealer can sell are designed to increase his competitive effectiveness in one area while not permitting him to compete against sellers of the same brand in other areas.

Full-line requirements which have been common in contracts between oil companies and gasoline station lessees, are designed to give the refiner control over the tires, batteries, and accessories (TBA) offered by the retail station. Such requirements could block some manufacturers of TBA from access to important retail outlets and thereby reduce price rivalry and the number of alternatives available to consumers.

Tying requirements are similar but are imposed by a dominant seller on users rather than dealers. For example, for some years IBM forced lessees of its machines to purchase punch cards from it.[9] Such restrictions almost always require that the seller have considerable monopoly power. Thus the tying requirement is an excellent example of poor structure causing undesirable conduct which results in poor performance.

Collusive agreements. Collusive agreements between competitors at the same level of the channel (horizontal agreements) that are designed to restrain trade or competitive rivalry constitute conduct which is very likely to result in poor performance. An example would be an agreement between two manufacturers to stay out of one another's territories. An exception would be an agreement between oligopolists to reduce destructive competitive tactics that are likely to cut the number of sellers still more. An agreement to stop spiraling defensive advertising expenditures would be an example; the patent pool among U.S. automotive manufacturers is another.

Restrictive agreements may take many forms. Among the most commonly tried are agreements to restrict production, fix price, block entry, or assign customers or orders. The electrical equipment conspiracy of the 1950s is one of the most spectacular examples of collusion to contain all of these elements.[10] All such agreements are subject to breakdown when one competitor feels he can do better by independent action. But when they exist, the goal of such agreements is to support prices above competitive levels or to reduce product innovation.

Unfair methods of competition

A final aspect of undesirable competitive conduct involves unilateral conduct which is "unfair." In U.S. law, the definition of what is unfair began with the Norman Conquest of England and developed into the law of persons, the law of property, the law of torts, and the law of contracts. Common law against monopoly dates from 1624—before the Industrial Revolution or the Sherman Act. This body of common law provided the rules for the conduct of trade, primarily through contract law; the protection of the rights of buyers; the right to compete; the rights of property, including the right to refuse to trade; and noncriminal wrongs (torts) such as slander, deceit, and negligence against traders.

Common law over the centuries became very complex, and attempts to reduce common commercial law to statutory law began in the United States before the Civil War. Success was not achieved until after 1955, when the Uniform Commercial Code

---

[9] *International Business Machine Corp.* v. *United States,* 298 U.S. 131 (1936).

[10] A number of excellent articles and books describe this conspiracy in detail. One is R. A. Smith, "The Incredible Electrical Conspiracy," *Fortune,* 63 (April and May 1961).

first began to be used by the states. Today it provides nearly uniform statutory practices for *all* areas of commercial activity, including sales contracts, title, commercial paper, credit, collection, physical transfer, warehouse receipts, bills of lading, securities, and stock transfer.

Aside from fairness in the conduct of the millions of marketing transactions conducted among producers and middlemen each year, the marketing man is concerned with three types of "unfairness": (1) conduct that is unfair to buyers, (2) torts that are likely to be illegal under criminal or common law, and (3) conduct that is designed to drive competitors out of business.

The first category includes conduct such as deception and sale of unsafe products, which was discussed in detail in Chapter 6. The second is concerned with such practices as business espionage (theft), dissemination of untrue, derogatory information about a rival's firm or product (slander), and fraud against another firm. The third category is the one in which enforcement is often difficult, for it requires a determination of whether the intent is predatory or simply healthy competition. The undesirability of the act is not always direct but is due to its effect on market structure and, hence, subsequent conduct and performance. Regulatory orders by government agencies are not common in this area and are frequently reversed on appeal. Examples include bribing employees of competitors or distributors, refusal to deal (buy or sell) with another firm for the purpose of driving it from the market, and engaging in litigation where the intent is only harassment. The practice of providing retail sales people with push money (PM's) to favor one brand over those of competitors is an example of a practice which has long created a problem for the Federal Trade Commission because of the difficulty of defining "fairness."

MARKET PERFORMANCE

In considering measures to be used in determining how well the marketing system allocates scarce resources for the satisfaction of man, it was emphasized in Chapter 2 that satisfaction is a multidimensional construct, and a measure of performance on any single dimension is therefore unsatisfactory. Three sets of dimensions on which to measure the performance of the system were suggested: (1) static efficiency, (2) dynamic efficiency, and (3) quality of life. While space does not permit a discussion of how to measure each of these dimensions, we can summarize some of the dimensions of market performance that have been encountered in the text as each chapter has provided more detail on how the marketing system works for the satisfaction of man. *Identifying* the dimensions of performance and *measuring* them are separate tasks, however.

Static efficiency

The efficiency of both buyers and sellers in performing each function can be measured, as noted in the following outline.

1. Supply considerations
   a) The level of profits. Are profit rates so high as to misallocate resources or so low that needed supplies are disappearing?
   b) The level of information provided to the market by sellers.

Marketing: Principles and methods

c) Efficiency in production.
d) Utilization of existing plant capacity. Is excess or a shortage of capacity a chronic problem?
e) Efficiency in physical distribution.
f) Efficiency in promotion.
g) The level of performance of products and services.
h) The number of alternative product and service offerings.
2. Demand considerations
a) The level of buyer knowledge and use of information. Do buyers help make the market work?
b) The effectiveness of buyer feedback to suppliers.
c) The level of consumer complaints.

Dynamic efficiency

The time trend of all of the dimensions of static efficiency is important. In addition, some other dynamic dimensions of efficiency should be considered.

1. The rate of real aggregate growth. Is the marketing system contributing to the growth of national wealth after allowances for increases in population and price level?
2. Progressiveness. What is the rate of introduction and the success rate of new innovations in products, services, and process technology?
3. The rate of entry of new competitors into the market.
4. The extent and frequency of supply/demand imbalances. How quickly does the market mechanism bring supply and demand back into balance?
5. The speed with which sellers respond to shifts in values, life styles, and technology in their markets.

External effects: The quality of life

The set of dimensions concerned with external effects attempts to measure the impact, both direct and indirect, that a marketing system has on its environment and on the quality of life generally.

1. The availability of healthy and challenging job opportunities within the system.
2. The availability within the system of employment, training, and advancement opportunities for the disadvantaged.
3. The effectiveness of pollution-abatement activities.
4. The effectiveness of contributions to improved education, health, and recreation.
5. The effectiveness of the system in providing society with exposure to art, culture, and beauty.
6. The effectiveness of the system in promoting ethical behavior and values.

IMPLICATIONS FOR PUBLIC POLICY

To a large extent, competition among individuals and business firms is relied on as the major regulatory force in coordinating the marketing system. If one firm over-prices its products, competitors with lower prices will take away its customers—thus forcing a reduction in the price of the first firm. Or if a company does not constantly strive to improve its product and services, it will lose out to competitors who engage in product and services research.

Stated briefly, competition works to the benefit of society by:

1. Promoting the flow of new products, services, and product and service improvements.
2. Offering consumers adequate choices and alternatives of both goods and services.
3. Organizing production—that is, determining the quantities and quality of what products and services to be produced by whom and the allocation of inputs to the producers.
4. Expanding output and consumption and, at the same time, "clearing the market"—that is, keeping supply and demand in balance in all regional markets.
5. Passing on to customers the results of research in the form of lower prices or products and services which offer better consumer satisfaction.
6. Improving real wages, together with shorter hours and better working conditions.
7. Providing opportunity for indivduals to launch new enterprises and to make capital investments.
8. Giving the individual freedom to select his own career.
9. Providing the economic conditions which are in harmony with the individual's desire for freedom of assembly, for freedom of religion, and for freedom of speech.[11]

When the marketing system operates to these ends, we say that the market has *workable competition* or *effective competition.* One authority defines competition as workable when there is no public policy change which would result in greater social gains than social losses.[12] The task of regulation of the system is no simple matter when the definition of effective competition is so general. Society, through government, must (1) ensure that the system has a *structure* which will let the market perform its self-regulating magic; (2) ensure that competitors *conduct* their functions honestly, fairly, and according to rules that ensure a competitive structure; and (3) monitor the *performance* of the system to ensure that the self-regulating control mechanism is indeed working for social gain.

Just as it is generally easier to identify undesirable performance than desirable performance, it is easier to identify structure and conduct which *could* lead to undesirable performance than it is to show that poor performance is inevitable. It is also easier to identify unacceptable performance on a single dimension than to build a unidimensional scale of desirability. If a market is performing acceptably on 6 measures, marginally on 10, and unacceptably on 2, how much of what kind of public action is required? The government's regulatory strategy for solving this dilemma seems to be to rank actual structure and conduct in order of decreasing undesirability and then to identify markets near the top of this priority listing where existing legislation provides a means for changing conduct or structure in order to yield a net social gain.

---

[11] On this point, see Milton Friedman, *Capitalism and Freedom* (Chicago: University of Chicago Press, 1962); John Davenport, *The U.S. Economy* (Chicago: Henry Regnery Co., 1964; and D. A. Revzan, *A Marketing View of Spatial Competition* (Berkeley, Calif., 1971), chaps. 2 and 3.

[12] J. N. Markham, "An Alternative Approach to the Concept of Workable Competition," *American Economic Review,* 40 (June 1950), pp. 349–61.

SUMMARY

As a summary to this chapter, it is useful to suggest how a strategy that ranks desirability of market structure and conduct might be operationalized.[13] We began with a classification of market structure by: size distribution of firms, including number, extent of differentiation, and relative size; vertical channel structure; economies of scale; and barriers to entry. Since no structure in itself is undesirable, only two public policy guidelines emerged from this discussion:

1. Monopoly is to be avoided.
2. While modest barriers to entry may provide the incentive for superior performance, the existence of very high barriers to entry is undesirable because monopoly can form behind them. Barriers may be created by large capital investment required to reach an efficient scale of operation, technological know-how overly protected by patents, the power to control channels of distribution, or an accumulation of buyer goodwill maintained by very large advertising expenditures.

The number of policy guidelines suggested in the analysis of competitive conduct was far greater.

3. Predatory conduct designed to drive viable competitors from the market and hence gain monopoly is undesirable.
4. Horizontal mergers are undesirable if a viable competitor is eliminated.
5. Vertical mergers are undesirable only under specific circumstances. These are when the expected future gains in efficiency are less than the expected future drop in performance caused by the monopoly power created when: (a) the vertical merger creates sizable barriers to entry, or (b) a viable competitor is eliminated from some market in the channel system.
6. The undesirability of conglomerate mergers is not proved without extensive analysis of the subsequent conduct that may result.
7. Homogeneous oligopoly may be a very unsatisfactory market structure if it results in the following types of conduct:
   a) Price equilibrium near the monopoly level.
   b) Collusion between competitors to bar entry or price competition.
   c) Ineffective research and development activity.
   d) Large defensive advertising expenditures which have little effect on consumer information, primary demand, or market share.
8. Theft, slander, and fraud in competitive conduct should not be tolerated.
9. Horizontal collusive agreements are undesirable since they are likely to be designed to increase private gain at public expense.
10. Agreements between members of the same vertical channel may be undesirable if the resulting efficiencies become trapped as profit by some channel member and do not result in an increase in total channel efficiency.

The performance of independent channel members is likely not to be as efficient as the performance of a coordinated or integrated channel structure, but unsatisfactory performance can seldom be inferred in items 5, 6, 7, and 10 of this priority listing. Performance must be empirically measured, a task which is not well done in the U.S. economy. The role of public policy, therefore, is to attempt to maintain effective competition with very imperfect information on performance.

---

[13] For a more detailed attempt at ranking desirability of competitive conduct, see A. G. Papandreau and J. T. Wheeler, *Competition and Its Regulation* (New York: Prentice-Hall, Inc., 1954), chap. 13.

REVIEW AND DISCUSSION QUESTIONS

1. Outline the key elements of the control mechanisms used in command-based economies and in regulated monopolies in this country. Compare these elements with those in our competition-controlled economy.

2. Using examples, trace the logic of the argument that poor structure causes poor conduct which causes poor performance. Cite examples of actual markets in which this two-step cause-and-effect relationship breaks down.

3. Under what circumstances is a structure of homogeneous oligopoly most likely to provide unsatisfactory performance?

4. Under what circumstances would you imagine homogeneous oligopoly among manufacturers could result in satisfactory channel performance?

5. In evaluating the structure of a market at one level in a channel, about what characteristics of the firms would you seek information?

6. In evaluating the structure of a vertical channel system, about what characteristics of the system would you seek information?

7. If you were the first to market a new product requiring considerable know-how to manufacture, how could you reason that a price of average cost at capacity plus normal industry markup is a pricing policy which not only considers potential competition but may also be profit maximizing in the long run?

8. Why is the height of barriers to entry, rather than their existence, so important in evaluating market structure?

9. In what situations could a well-established distribution system constitute a barrier to entry?

10. Write a short essay arguing either side of the proposition that an established advertiser is likely to have cost advantages over potential entrants which constitute significant barriers to entry.

11. What is the relation between an advertising response function and the average advertising cost curve?

12. What determines the effectiveness of a dollar expended for advertising?

13. How could one argue that a conglomerate merger is, in fact, a form of vertical integration in investment banking?

14. If price discrimination is likely to increase the revenue and profit of the firm and the efficiency of the channel system, how can price discrimination constitute undesirable conduct?

15. Select any one of the dimensions of market performance listed in the chapter and write a report not to exceed 1,500 words on the availability of data of measuring this dimension.

SUPPLEMENTARY READINGS

The references to Cohen and Cyert, Grether, and Scherer at the end of Chapter 23 also provide excellent supplementary information for this chapter.

Bain, J. S. *Industrial Organization.* New York: John Wiley & Sons, Inc., 1968. This is the best known of the texts in industrial organization. Professor Bain places more emphasis on structure and less on conduct than do most other authorities today.

Caves, R. E. *American Industry: Structure, Conduct, Performance.* Englewood Cliffs, N.J.: Prentice-Hall, Inc., 1967. Another leading text—perhaps the easiest going for the beginning student.

Mansfield, E. *Monopoly Power and Economic Performance.* New York: W. W. Norton

& Co., 1968. The focus of this book is the performance of the large corporation in imperfect markets.

Mueller, W. F. *A Primer on Monopoly and Competition.* New York: Random House, 1970. A book for the layman written by the former chief economist of the Federal Trade Commission.

Papandreou, A. G. and Wheeler, J. T. *Competition and Its Regulation.* New York: Prentice-Hall, Inc., 1954. An interesting, nonclassical, behavioral approach to the regulation of competition.

Phillips, A. and Williamson, O. W. *Prices: Issues in Theory, Practice and Public Policy.* Philadelphia: University of Pennsylvania Press, 1967. Newer than the previous reference, this collection of papers also places emphasis on competitive behavior.

Schumpeter, J. A. *Capitalism, Socialism, and Democracy.* New York: Harper & Row, 1942. This is a classic in the dynamics of modern competition which should be read by every student of marketing.

Simon, J. L. *Issues in the Economics of Advertising.* Urbana, Ill.: Universitiy of Illinois Press, 1970. In this area, where much empirical research is now taking place, this is the most up-to-date and complete book-length treatment.

Sosnick, S. H. "Toward a Concrete Concept of Effective Competition," *American Journal of Agricultural Economics,* 50 (November 1968), pp. 827–53. A thoughtful and operational approach to defining effective competition.

Vernon, J. M. *Market Structure and Industrial Performance: A Review of Statistical Findings.* Boston, Mass.: Allyn & Bacon, Inc., 1972. An up-to-date review of empirical studies on the issues raised in this chapter, with some particular emphasis on advertising.

25 *Government regulation*

Governments attempt to control their marketing systems in one of two ways: through formal planning in command-based systems or through regulation of competition in market-based systems. This chapter will focus on the techniques used by the U.S. government to regulate competition and marketing operations in our marketing-based system. We will not consider government planning efforts in other countries or the control of legal monopolies, such as utilities, and public enterprises, such as mass transit, in this country.

The most important legislation enabling our government to conduct market regulatory activities came into being years before the principles of industrial organization were developed or the theories of monopolistic competition and oligopoly were devised. Thus regulatory agencies are hampered by a patchwork of legislation which surely would be organized differently if a new start were to be made.

The chapter begins with an overview of the legislation controlling the competitive marketing system. While some state legislation is included, the overview is concerned mainly with federal legislation. The remainder of the chapter is divided into two main sections: the regulation of structure and the regulation of conduct.

GOVERNMENT LEGISLATIVE CONTROLS OF MARKETING

"Marketing is the process . . . by which the demand structure . . . is (changed and) satisfied . . ." By our definition of marketing, government influence is as pervasive as government activity itself. The discussion, here, however, will be limited to government *control* of the process. Not included is the most important legal control of all—the Uniform Commercial Code, which was introduced in Chapter 24. Also excluded is legislation designed to achieve aggregate economic stability. Even without direct controls over production and the use of materials such as those adopted in wartime, fiscal and monetary policies designed to stabilize the rate of economic growth, maintain full employment, and control wages and prices have a direct influence on the marketing system. Such policies affect costs through wage controls and price levels, prices through controls, and demand through taxes, interest rates, and consumer confidence.

Even with these exclusions, the list of government regulations of marketing enumerated in Table 25–1 is not comprehensive. The tables show only the major statutes which: (1) regulate market structure, (2) regulate competitive conduct, (3) protect consumers, and (4) concern special-interest groups within the marketing system.

Special interest group legislation

Aids to agriculture. Since 1862, when Congress established the Department of Agriculture, passed the Homestead Act, and established the land-grant colleges through the Morrill Act, government has been deeply involved in agricultural marketing. Some agricultural legislation, like that concerned with irrigation, crop insurance, and rural electrification, is not, of course, central to marketing. Other agricultural legislation, concerned with research support and the regulation of organized markets for livestock, crop commodities, and commodity futures, does affect marketing directly. Perhaps most significant and controversial are laws designed to increase farm income by: (1) cooperative marketing, (2) orderly marketing, and (3) direct income payment for restricting production.

The major legislation in the area of cooperative marketing (discussed in Chapter 14) includes:

1. Section 6 of the Clayton Act (1914), which states that nonprofit agricultural organizations without capital stock are not conspiracies in restraint of trade.
2. The Capper-Volstead Cooperative Marketing Association Act (1922), which extends this exemption to capital stock agricultural cooperatives and federations of such cooperatives (e.g., Land O'Lakes Creameries, Inc.), even when they achieve monopoly control over supply.
3. The Cooperative Marketing Act (1926), which gives cooperatives or other producer groups the right to exchange the information required to prevent excess production and promote orderly marketing.
4. The Fishermen's Collective Marketing Act (1934), which extends the rights of cooperatives to fishermen.

The key federal legislation in the category of orderly marketing is the Agricultural Marketing Agreements Acts of 1937 and 1946. A number of abortive attempts to control agricultural prices with and without effective production controls have also been made.

Effective land retirement had its beginning in the Eisenhower "Soil-Bank" program of the 1950s. It has not been established whether such programs lead to equitable income distribution.

Government control of agricultural marketing is detailed in Chapter 14.

Regulation of international marketing. The regulation of foreign trade is far too complex a subject to summarize here. While a general discussion of the topic can be found in Chapter 16, it should be noted that the marketing system has moved farther toward a one-world concept than has the political system. Trade has already

TABLE 25–1

Partial listing of government regulation of marketing

Laws regulating market structure

1. *Sherman Antitrust Act* (1890), Section 2.
2. *Celler-Kefauver Antimerger Act* (1950), amends Section 7 of the *Clayton Act* (1914).

Laws regulating competitive conduct

1. *Sherman Antitrust Act* (1890), Section 1.
2. *Federal Trade Commission Act* (1914).
3. *Clayton Act* (1914), Section 3.
4. *Clayton Act* (1914), Section 8.
5. *Robinson-Patman Act* (1936), replaces Section 2 of the Clayton Act.
6. *State Fair Trade Acts* (1931–38), as expanded by;
    a) *Miller-Tydings Resale Price Maintenance Act* (1937), amends Section 1 of the Sherman Act.
    b) *McGuire-Keogh Fair Trade Enabling Act* (1952), amends Section 5 of the Federal Trade Commission Act.

Laws designed for the protection of consumers

1. *Federal Trade Commission Act* (1914), as amended by:
    a) *Wheeler-Lea Act* (1938). (See Chapter 6.)
2. *Materials labeling acts* (1939–67). (See Chapter 6.)
3. *Hazardous Substances Act* (1960, 1969).
4. *Wholesome Meat and Poultry Inspection Acts* (1907, 1967, 1968).
5. *Perishable Agricultural Commodities Act* (1930).
6. *Food, Drug, and Cosmetic Acts* (1906 and 1938). (See Chapter 6.)
7. *Automobile Information Disclosure Act* (1958).
8. *Fair Packaging and Labeling Act* (1966). (See Chapter 6.)
9. *Traffic and Motor Vehicle Safety Act* (1966).
10. *Truth-in-Lending Act* (1968).
11. *State and local legislation* (See Chapter 6.)

Laws concerning the marketing activities of special-interest groups

1. *Packers and Stockyards Act* (1921).
2. *Alcohol Administration Act* (1935). This law and the one above contain "little Clayton Acts" directed at specific industries.
3. *Patent Laws* (Constitution and Act of 1836 as amended). Provides legal monopoly as a spur to invention.
4. *Lanham Trademark Act* (1946). (See Chapter 18.)
5. *Labor Law* (Beginning 1932). This date marks the beginning of authority for labor to organize and bargain collectively.
6. *Interstate Commerce Act* (1887). This is the beginning of the Interstate Commerce Commission for the regulation of transportation.
7. *Civil Aeronautics Act* (1938). This act begins regulation of air transportation.
8. *Merchant Marine Act* (1920). This act marks the beginning of direct government activity in the ocean shipping market.
9. *Federal Communications Act* (1934). This act established the FCC for the regulation of communications media.
10. *Automobile Dealer Franchise Act* (1956). This act prevents an automobile manufacturer from canceling a dealer's franchise without due process.
11. *Armed Services Procurement Act* (1947).
12. *Defense Production Act* (1950).
13. *Renegotiation Act* (1951). These three bills provide the ground rules for marketing the Department of Defense. (See Chapter 13.)
14. *Aids to Agriculture.* (See Chapter 14.)
15. *Regulation of International Marketing.* (See Chapter 16.)

Marketing: Principles and methods

outstepped regulation by a single nation. Regulation by either a nation or a trade block (e.g., common market), however, encourages exports and is a mild restraint for imports. In this country, for example, the first antidumping law was the Revenue Act of 1916. The Tariff Act of 1930 attempted to ensure that imports would not injure a domestic industry, while the Webb-Pomerene Export Act of 1918 exempted export trade associations from the Sherman Act conspiracy provisions.

From World War II until at least 1970, the U.S. foreign trade posture has been expansionistic. This country has generally sought reduction of trade barriers through the multinational General Agreement on Tariffs and Trade (GATT). However, there has been a definite increase in the popularity of protectionism in recent years.

Discriminatory restrictions on marketing. A wide variety of special-interest groups have sought legislative relief from the rigors of competition.[1] As supermarkets and discount houses added packaged drugs to their stocks, the National Association of Retail Druggists unsuccessfully sought an amendment to the Federal Food, Drug, and Cosmetic Act which would require that these products be sold in licensed pharmacies and by licensed pharmacists; and several state pharmacy boards went so far as to refuse licenses to operate drugstores if such outlets were not owned by pharmacists.[2]

Many states taxed margarine until World War II, and in Wisconsin the dairy interests were able to keep on the books until 1967 a law which forbade the sale of margarine colored to resemble butter.

Another form of special-interest legislation consists of the discriminatory chain store tax laws which, over the years, have been adopted by 29 states. Fortunately, however, the special-interest aspect of these laws has gradually been recognized, with the result that they have been repealed in many states and exist today in only 14.

Under most of the existing laws the tax rate is graduated upward with the number of stores. In Louisiana the tax begins at $10 for the first store and gradually increases to $550 for the 501st and all additional units. Such taxes are collected regardless of the physical size of the store, its sales, or its profits. A unit of a food chain doing a $10,000 business a day may pay the same tax as a chain unit in the discount field with sales of $20,000 a day, and both pay more than an independent department store with daily sales of $50,000. Because such laws have as their real object the protection of less efficient retailers and wholesalers from the competition of the chains, their gradual repeal in the 14 states still having them would be in the interests of the public.

The widespread use of the trading stamp to attract customers has led some retailers to seek legislative action against this particular form of sales promotion. Although some retailers oppose the stamp plan as too expensive a form of promotion, others argue that it is really an unfair form of competition. In general, those taking the former position are quite willing to let the stamp battle be fought out in the market-place, while those supporting the latter argument have turned to legislatures for aid. In response to their urgings, legislative bodies have developed various types of regulations. Some of these laws merely seek to avoid possible abuse, such as those which set up reasonable requirements for the bonding of stamp companies to ensure

---

[1] Far more illustrations than can be given here will be found in S. C. Hollander, *Restraints upon Retail Competition* (East Lansing, Mich.: Michigan State University, Bureau of Business and Economic Research, 1965).

[2] The legal struggles against such requirements in Michigan and Minnesota are related in *Super Market Merchandising,* March 1965, pp. 10–11. Also see the editorial by A. D. Friedman, "There Oughta Be a Law," in *Chain Store Age* (Supermarket Executives Edition), January 1966, p. 45.

redemption and require the stamp company to give ample notice if the redemption right is to be terminated. However, Kansas completely prohibits the issuance of trading stamps; and Washington, Wisconsin, and Wyoming require that stamps be redeemed in cash. Moreover, over 700 antistamp bills have been introduced in the legislatures of other states during the past 20 years.[3] As with discriminatory taxes levied on the chain store, discriminatory regulation of this form of sales promotion is not in keeping with the philosophy of a competitive economy.

THE REGULATION OF STRUCTURE

Figure 25–1 contains excerpts from the Sherman Act and the Clayton Act. Of interest here are Section 2 of the Sherman Act, the basic antimonopoly law, and Section 7 of the Clayton Act as amended by the Celler-Kefauver Act, the antimerger law.

The enforcement of the Sherman Act is exclusively the responsibility of the Antitrust Division of the Department of Justice. The Clayton Act is enforced by both the Department of Justice and the Federal Trade Commission. The Department of Justice can bring action in court as either a civil or criminal proceeding, the latter resulting in possible prison sentences. Under both the Sherman and Clayton Acts, persons injured by antitrust law violations may sue to recover triple the amount of damage sustained following any antitrust judgment, even that resulting from a government-initiated case. Since World War II, such judgments have been substantial. While the maximum fine in the Sherman Act is only $50,000 per count, the triple damage claims in the electrical conspiracy mentioned in Chapter 24 probably exceeded $500 million.

The antimonopoly law

The wording of Section 2 of the Sherman Act is clear—monopoly or attempts to monopolize are illegal. Since there are few real monopolies, however, the opportunities for simple decisions are rare. Early cases won by the government focused on predatory practices designed to drive competitors out of business. These cases attacked *unreasonable conduct,* not structure, as the test of legality.[4] However, in the U.S. Steel decision of 1920, the court forged the "rule of reason" which discouraged the Justice Department from further serious antitrust enforcement for 25 years.[5] This decision said that mere size or power is not an offense; the Sherman Act requires overt monopolistic acts. Further, the courts stated that the act does not require a market to be competitive—only that it not be a monopoly.

Most authorities feel that the Alcoa decision in 1945 marked a change in judicial interpretation of Section 2 because Alcoa was a monopoly with 90 percent of aluminum ingot production, including imported ingots.[6] The decision was based largely on a finding that this share of production constituted a monopoly and that Alcoa worked to maintain its monopoly position. Monopoly power, no matter how acquired and

---

[3] *Answers to Some Frequently Asked Questions About the Sperry and Hutchinson Company and S & H Green Stamps* (New York, 1967), p. 23.

[4] *U.S.* v. *Standard Oil Co. of New Jersey et al.,* 221 U.S. 1 (1911).

[5] *U.S.* v. *U.S. Steel Corporation et al.,* 251 U.S. 417 (1920).

[6] *U.S.* v. *Aluminum Co. of America et al.,* 148 F.2d 416 (1945).

FIGURE 25–1

Excerpts from the Sherman Act and the Clayton Act, as amended by the Celler-Kefauver Act

SHERMAN ACT

Sec. 1. Every contract, combination in the form of trust or otherwise, or conspiracy, in restraint of trade or commerce among the several States, or with foreign nations, is hereby declared to be illegal. Every person who shall make any such contract or engage in any such combination or conspiracy, shall be deemed guilty of a misdemeanor, and, on conviction thereof, shall be punished by fine not exceeding fifty thousand dollars, or by imprisonment not exceeding one year, or by both said punishments, in the discretion of the court.

Sec. 2. Every person who shall monopolize, or attempt to monopolize, or combine or conspire with any other person or persons, to monopolize any part of the trade or commerce among the several States, or with foreign nations, shall be deemed guilty of a misdemeanor, and, on conviction thereof, shall be punished by fine not exceeding fifty thousand dollars, or by imprisonment not exceeding one year, or by both said punishments, in the discretion of the court.

CLAYTON ACT, AS AMENDED

Sec. 3. That it shall be unlawful for any person engaged in commerce, in the course of such commerce, to lease or make a sale or contract for sale of goods, wares, merchandise, machinery, supplies or other commodities, whether patented or unpatented, for use, consumption or resale within the United States or any Territory thereof or the District of Columbia or any insular possession or other place under the jurisdiction of the United States, or fix a price charged therefor, or discount from, or rebate upon, such price, on the condition, agreement, or understanding that the lessee or purchaser thereof shall not use or deal in the goods, wares, merchandise, machinery, supplies or other commodity of a competitor or competitors of the lessor or seller, where the effect of such lease, sale, or contract for sale or such condition, agreement, or understanding may be to substantially lessen competition or tend to create a monopoly in any line of commerce.

Sec. 7. That no corporation engaged in commerce shall acquire, directly or indirectly, the whole or any part of the stock or other share capital and no corporation subject to the jurisdiction of the Federal Trade Commission shall acquire the whole or any part of the assets of another corporation engaged also in commerce, where in any line of commerce in any section of the country, the effect of such acquisition may be substantially to lessen competition, or to tend to create a monopoly. . . .

This section shall not apply to corporations purchasing such stock solely for investment and not using the same by voting or otherwise to bring about, or in attempting to bring about, the substantial lessening of competition. Nor shall anything contained in this section prevent a corporation engaged in commerce from causing the formation of subsidiary corporations for the actual carrying on of their immediate lawful business, or the natural and legitimate branches or extensions thereof, or from owning and holding all or a part of the stock of such subsidiary corporations, when the effect of such formation is not to substantially lessen competition.

Sec. 8. That no person shall at the same time be a director in any two or more competing corporations engaged in commerce where one of them has a capital and surplus of more than $1 million and where the elimination of competition . . . between them would constitute a violation of any of the provisions of the antitrust laws.

---

whether exercised or not, whether "good" or "bad," is now condemned under Section 2.

While this decision has permitted the existence of monopoly power through structure to be condemned, the absence of monopolies as obvious as Alcoa's on the American scene has provided few opportunities for the Justice Department to use this decision to *improve* competitive structure. In all subsequent Sherman Act Section 2 cases, the decision has been made on market conduct which was predatory or blocked entry, not on the existing structure. For example, in 1967 the government dropped its Section 2 suit against General Motors Corporation's diesel locomotive division due to insufficient evidence. (See SIC 3741 in Table 24–1.)

Perhaps more interesting is the success the government has had in using Section 2 to break up vertically integrated companies on the basis that the integration foreclosed certain markets. In 1944 the Pullman Company was required to sell its car-operating branch.[7] In the late 1940s, motion picture studios were required to sell their theater chains because they prevented independent theaters from obtaining first-run films.[8] Similar actions against Eastman Kodak color-film-processing plants, RCA patents in television technology, and United Fruit Corporation's banana operations were settled out of court in the government's favor.[9] Thus, Section 2 does appear to provide an adequate vehicle to prohibit and deter monopoly, predatory practices, and barriers to entry.

An antioligopoly law? Those who feel the government should have more power to regulate structure have proposed with increasing frequency a law which would outlaw oligopoly or "shared monopoly." The reasoning is that Section 2 adequately prevents monopoly, and recent court decisions have adequately blocked undesirable mergers. However, a review of Table 24–1 will show that much oligopoly still exists. It is not difficult to criticize the performance in some of these markets: the equilibrium achieved, either through collusion or "conscious parallel action," is very close to that of a monopolist; innovation is often lacking; advertising emphasizes unimportant product characteristics; and sellers are not responsive to consumer desires. In short, it is alleged that the special problems of homogeneous oligopoly described in the last chapter exist in all too frequent numbers, and there is no legislative power to change this structure.

In a 1972 cereal complaint, the FTC tried to attack such structure through another law (Section 5 of the Federal Trade Commission Act). Their approach appeared cumbersome; perhaps a new law is required. If so, it would have to require proof of unsatisfactory performance, for oligopoly structure alone need not be undesirable. Such a provision would indeed be a novel approach for antitrust lawyers, who seem to prefer to work with rules of conduct and simplistic notions of structure which are conjectural and probabilistic.

The antimerger law

Section 7 of the Clayton Act, as it was rewritten in 1950 by the Celler-Kefauver Antimerger Act, says that no corporate merger, accomplished in any way, is legal "where in any line of commerce in any section of the country, the effect . . . *may* . . . lessen competition, or . . . *tend* to create monopoly" (emphasis added). This law makes clear the point that growth through merger, unlike internal growth, will eliminate a competitor or potential competitor. The government must prove only that such elimination is likely to reduce competition. An actual lessening is not required.

The passage of the 1950 amendment did not immediately stop the merger trend, which is shown since 1951 in Figure 25–2.[10] In terms of numbers of firms acquired,

---

[7] *U.S.* v. *Pullman Co.,* 55 F. Supp. 985 (1944).

[8] *Loew's Inc.* v. *U.S.,* 339 U.S. 974 (1950).

[9] *U.S.* v. *Eastman Kodak Co.,* CCH 1961 Trade Cases, Para. 70,100; *U.S.* v. *Radio Corporation of America,* CCH 1958 Trade Cases, Para. 69,164; *U.S.* v. *United Fruit Corporation,* CCH 1958 Trade Cases, Para. 68,941.

[10] An excellent summary of the merger activity in these earlier periods may be found in F. M. Scherer, *Industrial Market Structure and Economic Performance* (Chicago: Rand McNally & Co., 1970), pp. 103–12.

Number of mergers in manufacturing and mining, 1949–70

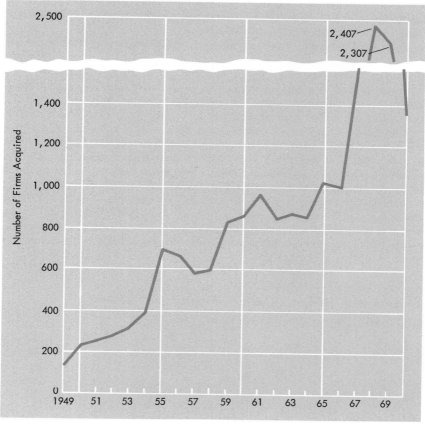

Source: U.S. Federal Trade Commission, *Current Trends in Merger Activity, 1970* (Washington, D.C.: Government Printing Office, March 1971).

the number grew at an increasing rate during the 1950s and 1960s and reached record proportions in 1967 and 1968.

However, unlike the mergers at the turn of the century, the recent merger wave is characterized by giant firms buying small firms rather than mergers between giants. Most of the mergers have been largely of the conglomerate type rather than horizontal or vertical, which the government has discouraged. Thus the recent merger wave has increased aggregate concentration (which the antitrust laws do not address at all) but has had far less impact on concentration in individual markets. The change in types of mergers is shown in Figure 25–3.

It took the government and the courts about 15 years to forge the legal precedents required for tight enforcement. Supreme Court decisions on Section 7 cases during the 1960s provide a strong, almost dramatic, barrier to deterioration of market structure by merger. The precedents established by the courts on the definition of "relevant

25 / Government regulation

market" and of the importance of a "potential competitor" in product and market expansion cases are interesting. However, the present merger guidelines are so different from those of 10 years ago that a review of the important case decisions is not required. Because most of the key issues were discussed in Chapter 24, we will only summarize present public policy toward mergers.

Horizontal mergers. While an exception is possible if it can be shown that a firm must merge to avoid bankruptcy, no efficiency arguments provide acceptable justifications for a horizontal merger. In concentrated industries, a merger involving a firm with as little as a 2 percent market share is likely to be challenged; in less concentrated industries, a 10 percent share for the acquiring firm and 5 percent for the acquired firm are the approximate maximum limits.

A special problem in public policy toward mergers arises in the case of regulated industries (gas, electric, and telephone companies). Generally, the legislation establishing the regulation and, in some cases, the Celler-Kefauver Act suggest that the regulatory agency has considerable authority to approve a merger which will result in an increase in efficiency. In some industries (for example, utilities producing power), it is the efficiency of legal monopoly which led to the regulation of price and output in the industry to begin with. Hence the notion of preserving competition at the expense of obvious efficiency has no merit. However, in other industries, such as banking, competitive markets still play a major role in determining price and product

FIGURE 25–3
Types of mergers expressed as a percentage of total assets acquired

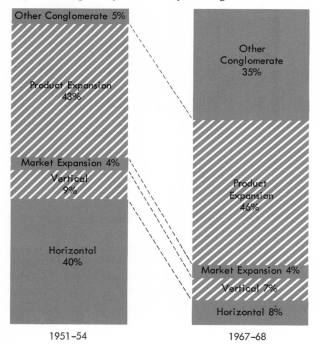

Source: Federal Trade Commission, *Current Trends in Merger Activity, 1968* (Washington, D.C.: Government Printing Office, 1969).

Marketing: Principles and methods

offerings. In these industries, the application of the Celler-Kefauver Act may have considerable merit. Congress, by the Bank Merger Act of 1966, seemed to give authority to the Controller of the Currency to approve bank mergers. However, in 1967 the Supreme Court ruled that the Celler-Kefauver criteria should still apply.[11]

Vertical mergers. The guidelines for vertical mergers are only slightly less stringent than those for horizontal ones. A merger between a supplier with more than a 10 percent share and a buyer with 6 percent or more of any geographic market is likely to be challenged. The tests are whether or not markets are foreclosed, barriers to entry are raised, or nonintegrated competitors in either the suppliers or buyers market are disadvantaged. Efficiency in distribution is not generally considered.

Conglomerate mergers. The law concerning conglomerate mergers is much less clear than that concerning horizontal or vertical mergers. One of the most important guidelines concerning product or market expansion mergers stems from the 1964 El Paso Natural Gas Co. case in which the Supreme Court said that a merger would violate Section 7 if it reduced *potential* competition.[12] Since then, the government has successfully challenged a number of mergers, including Procter & Gamble–Chlorox, on the grounds that the acquiring firm would likely enter the market through internal growth were it not for the merger. The status of the precedent for joint ventures is not clear, but it appears that if both partners in a joint venture are potential entrants, the venture will be in violation of Section 7.

Perhaps in even more doubt is the question of when a market or product extension merger becomes true diversification. In a merger between Sterling Drug Co. and Lehn and Fink, the FTC seemingly has determined that cosmetics and toilet preparations are not in the same market as over-the-counter drugs. The question of definition of relevant market is certainly one of the most difficult to answer in all antitrust matters. The courts are probably wise to study the product-market configurations of each set of firms rather than writing general guidelines on the definition of relevant market.

Mergers have also been challenged because of the opportunity they provide for reciprocal dealing. In 1965 the Supreme Court climaxed eight years of litigation against the purchase by Consolidated Foods Corporation of Gentry, Inc., a supplier of garlic and onions.[13] The Court said that it was not necessary or desirable to wait and see if Consolidated used its position to pressure other suppliers into buying Gentry onions. If one partner in the merger has substantial market position and the possibility of reciprocal buying pressures exists, this is sufficient evidence to block the merger.

U.S. public policy statements on pure conglomerate mergers are charged with emotion, contradiction, and politics. The large number of such mergers (see Figure 25–3 above) has led the government to seek new ways to attack them. The reciprocity and predatory-pricing arguments have been used successfully, but a frontal attack on bigness has met with little success. Even the reciprocity argument has occasionally been rejected by district courts. It is going to require a Supreme Court decision and possibly even new legislation to determine to what extent our public policy places limits on aggregate corporate bigness. Public, legal, and economic opinion is certainly not unanimous in favoring a prohibition of bigness. A rigid policy against conglomerates seems particularly questionable in this age of multinational business. Not only is the United States staggering from foreign competition, but no other industrial nation in the world has an antitrust policy as tough as ours.

---

[11] *U.S.* v. *First City National Bank of Houston et al.,* 386 U.S. 361 (1967).

[12] *U.S.* v. *El Paso Natural Gas Co. et al.,* 376 U.S. 651 (1964).

[13] *F.T.C.* v. *Consolidated Foods Corp. et al.,* 380 U.S. 592 (1965).

This section is concerned with the regulation of: (1) collusive practices through enforcement of Section 1 of the Sherman Act (Figure 25–1), (2) price discrimination through the Robinson-Patman Act, (3) resale price maintenance through fair-trade laws and similar state legislation, and (4) distribution through Section 3 of the Clayton Act (Figure 25–1). The Federal Trade Commission is the independent regulatory agency responsible for regulating competition.

The Federal Trade Commission

The Federal Trade Commission Act was passed in 1914 when Congress, which was not happy with the job the courts were doing interpreting the Sherman Act, felt a commission of specialists should have broad powers to deal quickly and effectively with the many detailed and technical aspects of competitive rivalry. Therefore, it gave the commission broad authority in Section 5 with a statement that declared unlawful "unfair methods of competition . . . and unfair or deceptive acts or practices in commerce." Congress did not attempt to frame a definition of unfair competition.

The procedure provided in the act for the Commission to check unfair methods and practices of competition is of considerable interest.[14] In the majority of cases the machinery of the Commission is set in motion by a complaint made by a competitor or a consumer group, but action may be initiated by the Commission itself. After a study of the matter to determine whether or not the Commission has jurisdiction, the case is assigned to a staff member for an investigation. During this fact-gathering period the person (or firm) complained against is given a chance to present his side of the case. If the facts developed by this investigation convince the Commission that the case should be followed through, it typically proceeds in one of two ways.

First, a complaint may be issued setting forth the practices from which the respondent is to cease and desist. Sometimes it is accompanied by the form of the proposed cease-and-desist order, thus informing the respondent exactly what the Commission has in mind and subjecting him to "bad" publicity just once rather than twice (when the complaint is issued and again when the order is released). The respondent is given 20 days in which to file a formal answer to the charges, either denying or admitting them. If he wishes to accept a cease-and-desist order, he may do so without admission of guilt—and the case is closed. Otherwise, the next step is an open hearing before a trial examiner, at which the party complained against is given full opportunity to state his case. The examiner's written opinion becomes final unless either the respondent or the Commission's counsel appeals to the Commission itself. Upon appeal, there is a filing of briefs with the Commission, a final argument before that body, and the issuance of the final order. Assuming that the final order is one requiring the respondent to cease and desist, he is given a stated time within which to comply with the order and to report to the Commission.

Throughout this entire procedure the Commission's emphasis is upon voluntary compliance with its orders. In fact, the Commission cannot force compliance directly; but if at the end of a 60-day period the respondent has not complied with the order, the Commission may appeal to the courts for enforcement.

A second, shorter procedure involves issuing a consent order. In this case, the respondent is merely notified that the Commission intends to issue a complaint unless

---

[14] For further details see the latest edition of the Commission's *Rules of Practice, Procedures and Organization.*

its proposed cease-and-desist order is accepted. Prior to mid-1967 such consent agreements were negotiated confidentially between the respondent and the Commission, but now the agreement is made public for a 30-day period during which the Commission accepts comments from other interested parties on the fitness of the settlement. Once issued, the consent order has the same legal standing as a decision reached under full adjudicative proceedings.

The Commission also attempts to increase the efficiency of its operations by providing businessmen with guides for proper competitive conduct. Some of the published guides include shoe labeling, deceptive pricing, guarantees, and advertising allowances.

Some of the Federal Trade Commission's most effective work has been through the trade practices conferences held with representatives of various industries to encourage the elimination of unfair methods of competition. At such conferences, under the chairmanship of a commissioner or a staff member, unfair practices are discussed openly, and business is allowed the initiative to establish its own advisory rules of business conduct, subject to the approval of the Commission. The trade practices conference has been especially valuable to groups of businessmen who wish to take the initiative in removing dubious activities from their industry or trade. It is a more logical method than the issuance by the Commission of a large number of complaints against individual business firms. Up to the present time, such conferences have resulted in rules for over 300 manufacturing, marketing, or industry groups.

The Commission also follows the practice of giving advance rulings on the legality of proposed advertising, promotional, pricing, and labeling campaigns by business organizations. No publicity is involved in seeking such rulings. In adopting this program of advance rulings in 1962, the Commission's goal was to prevent unlawful practices *before* they took place; and, since the overwhelming number of businessmen wish to abide by the law, the program was favored by the business community. However, it places such a burden on the staff and resources of the Commission that its future is uncertain.

The FTC regularly uses its general authority under Section 5 to attack any unfair practice that it fears may be enjoying judicial protection from narrow interpretations of the Sherman, Clayton, and Robinson-Patman acts. For example, the FTC generally attacks conspiracy with Section 5 because it does not have authority to enforce the Sherman Act. Section 5 also provides the flexibility to halt predatory practices which are not specifically mentioned in other antitrust laws. In 1938 Congress passed the Wheeler-Lea Act which extended Section 5 to include protection of consumers as well as injury to a competitor. The 1972 complaint against the cereal industry, in which the Commission attempted to use Section 5 as an antioligopoly law, may provide a test of how far this provision can be extended.

Section 5 has been used as authority to regulate such activities as "push money" as inducements to middleman sales personnel, commercial bribery of disc jockeys in the "payola" investigations of the 1960s, and reciprocity.[15]

Collusive practices

Collusion in restraint of trade may be attacked by the Justice Department under Section 1 of the Sherman Act or by the FTC under Section 5. While price-fixing

---

[15] The Justice Department used Section 1 of the Sherman Act in similar reciprocity actions against U.S. Steel in 1969 and General Tire and Rubber Co., settled in 1970. See, *U.S.* v. *General Tire & Rubber Co. et al.,* CCH Trade Cases, para. 73,303 (1970).

agreements have received the greatest attention, other collusive arrangements which have been successfully attacked include production controls and allocations; allocation of customers, big orders, or geographic markets; agreements to destroy certain competitors; discriminatory patent pools; and agreements to limit the design of products. In many major decisions, the courts have ruled that the existence of such agreements is per se illegal, that is, their reasonableness is not to be considered.

During the Great Depression the government encouraged the formation of trade associations for the purpose of what was later ruled to be illegal collusion. This effort has resulted in a larger number of trade associations which continue today legally to gather and disseminate price, cost, and volume information; to lobby; and to provide information on their industry to the public. It is difficult to generalize on the desirability of these associations. While they provide some opportunity for collusion, they sometimes have pushed their members into more socially desirable behavior than would have resulted from free competition. Price reporting among association members is the information activity which has received the greatest attention from the courts. Many of these cases date back to the 1920s when price sharing was more common. Over the years a policy has developed which suggests that sharing of prices on *individual orders,* particularly in oligopolistic industries, is illegal. However, periodic reporting of the average price of a large number of transactions is probably a legal practice.[16]

Conscious parallel action. Perhaps the most difficult policy issue in the collusion area concerns the remedy for the case of homogeneous oligopoly where, without collusion, the competitors are able to establish an equilibrium close to the monopoly price level. In the antitrust field the resultant behavior is known as the *conscious parallelism* doctrine. Since the government has no antioligopoly law to attack such structure directly, it has tried to attack the behavior as being an implicit conspiracy, illegal under Section 1.[17]

It is clear that for Section 1 to apply, a conspiracy must exist. However, the courts have been very liberal in accepting circumstantial evidence of conspiracy. If competitive prices move together in a complex way and at profit levels well above the purely competitive price, more than one judge and jury has been willing to accept this as evidence of conspiracy even though *no* evidence of an overt conspiratory act or communication was introduced.

Price discrimination

The Robinson-Patman Act. In 1936, the debilitating effect of the Great Depression on small business led Congress to pass the Robinson-Patman Act as a revision of Section 2 of the Clayton Act. The major provisions of this act are given in Figure 25-4.

The FTC is responsible for enforcement of the Robinson-Patman Act. Its intent can be seen in the name it was commonly known by at the time of passage, "The Price Discrimination Chain Store Act." The major policy change in this act is that it

---

[16] An interesting recent decision is *U.S.* v. *Container Corporation of America et al.,* 393 U.S. 333 (1969).

[17] For some of the most entertaining of these cases, see W. H. Nicholls, "The Tobacco Case of 1946," *American Economic Review,* 39 (May 1949), pp. 284–96; U.S. Department of Justice, *Report of the Attorney General's National Committee to Study the Antitrust Laws* (Washington, D.C.: Government Printing Office, 1955), pp. 30–42; *Theatre Enterprises, Inc.* v. *Paramount Film Distributing Corp.,* 346 U.S. 537, 540 (1954); *U.S.* v. *Eli Lilly and Co., et al.,* CCH Trade Cases, para. 69,536; *U.S.* v. *Charles Pfizer & Co., Inc., et al.,* 281 F Supp. 837 (1968).

FIGURE 25–4
Excerpts from the Robinson-Patman Act, amending Section 2 of the Clayton Act

SEC. 2(*a*) That it shall be unlawful for any person engaged in commerce, in the course of such commerce, either directly or indirectly, to discriminate in price between different purchasers of commodities of like grade and quality, where either or any of the purchases involved in such discrimination are in commerce, where such commodities are sold for use, consumption, or resale within the United States or any Territory thereof or the District of Columbia or any insular possession or other place under the jurisdiction of the United States, and where the effect of such discrimination may be substantially to lessen competition or tend to create a monopoly in any line of commerce, or to injure, destroy, or prevent competition with any person who either grants or knowingly receives the benefit of such discrimination, or with customrs of either of them: *Provided,* That nothing herein contained shall prevent differentials which make only due allowance for differences in the cost of manufacture, sale, or delivery resulting from the differing methods or quantities in which such commodities are to such purchasers sold or delivered: *Provided, however,* That the Federal Trade Commission may, after due investigation and hearing to all interested parties, fix and establish quantity limits, and revise the same as it finds necessary, as to particular commodities or classes of commodities, where it finds that available purchasers in greater quantities are so few as to render differentials on account thereof unjustly discriminatory or promotive of monopoly in any line of commerce; and the foregoing shall then not be construed to permit differentials based on differences in quantities greater than those so fixed and established: *And provided further,* That nothing herein contained shall prevent persons engaged in selling goods, wares, or merchandise in commerce from selecting their own customers in bona fide transactions and not in restraint of trade: *And provided further,* That nothing herein contained shall prevent price changes from time to time where in response to changing conditions affecting the market for or the marketability of the goods concerned, such as but not limited to actual or imminent deterioration of perishable goods, obsolescence of seasonal goods, distress sales under court process, or sales in good faith in discontinuance of business in the goods concerned.

(*b*) Upon proof being made, at any hearing on a complaint under this section, that there has been discrimination in price or services or facilities furnished, the burden of rebutting the prima facie case thus made by showing justification shall be upon the person charged with a violation of this section, and unless justification shall be affirmatively shown, the Commission is authorized to issue an order terminating the discrimination: *Provided, however,* That nothing herein contained shall prevent a seller rebutting the prima facie case thus made by showing that his lower price or the furnishing of services or facilities to any purchaser or purchasers was made in good faith to meet an equally low price of a competitor, or the services or facilities furnished by a competitor.

(*c*) That it shall be unlawful for any person engaged in commerce, in the course of such commerce, to pay or grant, or to receive or accept, anything of value as a commission, broker-age, or other compensation, or any allowance or discount in lieu thereof, except for services rendered in connection with the sale or purchase of goods, wares, or merchandise, either to the other party to such transaction or to an agent, representative, or other intermediary therein where such intermediary is acting in fact for or in behalf, or is subject to the direct or indirect control, of any party to such transaction other than the person by whom such compensation is so granted or paid.

(*d*) That it shall be unlawful for any person engaged in commerce to pay or contract for the payment of anything of value to or for the benefit of a customer of such person in the course of such commerce as compensation or in consideration for any services or facilities furnished by or through such customer in connection with the processing, handling, sale, or offering for sale of any products or commodities manufactured, sold, or offered for sale by such person, unless such payment or consideration is available on proportionally equal terms to all other customers competing in the distribution of such products or commodities.

(*e*) That it shall be unlawful for any person to discriminate in favor of one purchaser against another purchaser or purchasers of a commodity bought for resale, with or without processing, by contracting to furnish or furnishing, or by contributing to the furnishing of, any services or facilities connected with the processing, handling, sale, or offering for sale of such commodity so purchased upon terms not accorded to all purchasers on proportionally equal terms.

(*f*) That it shall be unlawful for any person engaged in commerce, in the course of such commerce, knowingly to induce or receive a discrimination in price which is prohibited by this section.

attempts to give greater equality of opportunity to small business by giving consideration to individual *competitors* as well as to the vitality of *competition* in a market.

The language of the law is cumbersome, but its main thrust is to prohibit discrimination in price between *competing* purchasers of products of like grade and quality in interstate commerce where the effect *may* be to lessen competition. Four possible defenses are specified, and each has been the subject of considerable legal controversy over the years. Discrimination may be justified if: (1) the goods are perishable or distressed, (2) there can be no possible injury to competition, (3) the differences in price reflect no more than differences in cost in serving the two customers, (4) the lower price was made in good faith to meet an equally low price of a competitor. (It may be useful to review the discussion of price discrimination in Chapter 24.)

Like grade and quality.   What appeared to be a straightforward determination of fact in Section 2(*a*) became an important issue to the marketing man in 1966 when the government charged the Borden Company with price discrimination for selling unbranded evaporated milk at a lower price than that sold under the Borden label when, in fact, the milk was identical. The net of two decisions in two different courts in this case was that the goods were indeed of like grade and quality but that there was no possibility of injury to competition, since both brands were offered to all sellers and the middleman margins for both were roughly equivalent.[18]

Quantity discounts.   Section 2(*a*) of the act specifically gives the FTC the authority to establish quantity discount schedules when existing discounts could provide to very large buyers prices which were so low as to promote monopoly. The Commission has not been successful in exercising this authority, although it has successfully challenged a number of quantity discount schemes. Discounts which are not related to cost savings are clearly illegal. An example is a cumulative discount which increases with the accumulation of orders over an extended period of time (e.g., 5 percent discount on purchases of $100,000 to $200,000 in any calendar year and 10 percent discount on any purchase over $200,000) rather than the size of an individual order or shipment.

The cost defense.   The quantity discount issue has been the trigger for some of the most interesting attempts to use the cost justification mentioned in Section 2(*a*) as a defense. The FTC and the courts have insisted that differences be justified by careful allocations of *full* costs (including overhead costs), not just marginal costs, which would be the correct cost from a rational managerial point of view. Marketing as well as production costs must be included in the analysis. The standards imposed for admissibility are so high that the cost defense may be illusory if the seller attempts to reconstruct costs after the fact. However, companies may well head off a complaint by careful cost data collection and analysis before the fact. The FTC will probably not issue a complaint if it feels the firm has kept good cost records.[19] Also, the seller may find some solace in the knowledge that the Commission's attempt to set an upper limit on a quantity discount schedule even when it has a justification in cost has been overruled by the courts.[20]

Delivered pricing.   The steel industry began quoting delivered prices which

---

[18] *FTC* v. *Borden Co.,* 383 U.S. 637 (1966) and 381 F.2d 175, 181 (1967). For a discussion of the marketing implications see M. L. Mayer, J. B. Mason, and E. A. Orbeck, "The Borden Case—A Legal Basis for Private Brand Price Discrimination," *MSU Business Topics,* 18 (Winter 1970), pp. 56–63.

[19] For a review of the cost-justification defense see B. J. Linder and A. H. Savage, "Price Discrimination and Cost Defense—Change Ahead?" *MSU Business Topics,* 19 (Summer 1971), pp. 21–26, and H. F. Taggert, *Cost Justification* (Ann Arbor: University of Michigan Bureau of Business Research, 1959).

[20] *FTC* v. *B. F. Goodrich Co.,* 242 F.2d 31 (1957).

used Pittsburgh as a basing point as early as 1880. The first formal complaint was issued in 1924 under Section 5 of the Federal Trade Commission Act but it was 1945 before the government won a case against the basing-point system, and those cases were initiated under Section 2(a) of the Robinson-Patman Act. It was 1948 before the government won a decisive Supreme Court decision on this issue under Section 5.[21]

The 1945 decisions concerned A. E. Staley Co., of Decatur, Illinois, and Corn Products Refining Co., of Chicago and Kansas City, both large producers of corn sugar (glucose). Both used the Corn Products plant in Chicago as a basing point. The Court ruled that differences in delivered prices from mills at Decatur and Kansas City could not be cost justified, since they included freight from Chicago. For example, a customer in Missouri or southern Illinois paid more than a customer in northern Illinois, even though each was equidistant from the mill which produced his glucose—hence, a clear violation of Section 2(a). Staley attempted a Section 2(b) "good faith" defense saying that it was merely meeting the delivered prices of its Chicago competitor. The Court ruled against Staley saying that the defense could not apply because the prices being met were illegally discriminatory.[22]

Functional discounts. Section 2(c) of the Act prohibits a particular type of price discrimination—that of paying brokerage commissions, allowances, or discounts except to middlemen actually performing the functions of an independent broker. None of the four defenses apply to this section.

This provision was aimed specifically at the large food chains who had established their own buying offices to purchase the products of farmers and small processors and then charged the latter a brokerage fee as if they were independent middlemen serving the sellers. The problem is a real one, for the large chains clearly have more market power than the small sellers. Despite the clear wording, the FTC has found it necessary to continue to issue cease-and-desist orders under this section.

Of course, brokerage commissions are just one form of payment for the performance of middleman functions. In this age of vertical integration, it is often difficult to know just what functions a middleman performs, based on his title. Thus it is not unusual for a seller to find himself in the position of selling to two competitors and honestly granting only one of them a functional discount, even though such sales constitute price discrimination. The act gives no specific mention to functional discounts the way it does to quantity and brokerage discounts. Thus, whether or not the price discrimination is illegal depends on a finding as to whether such discrimination lessens competition or tends to create monopoly. The cost defense or the meeting-of-competition defense also may be available.

Many sellers today find that functional discounts are not workable and similar results can be accomplished with quantity discounts, since large middlemen performing wholesale functions will buy in large quantities. However, a seller is free to decide whether or not he wishes to use functional discounts. Specifically, this means that a manufacturer may classify his buyers into wholesalers, chain stores, department stores, independents, and so on, and offer different trade discounts to each group. Within each group, of course, the trade discount must be identical.

It should be emphasized, however, that the seller cannot adopt just any arbitrary classification of accounts. Thus, while the U.S. Supreme Court has held that price

---

[21] *FTC* v. *Cement Institute, et al.,* 333 U.S. 683 (1948).

[22] *Corn Products Refining Co.* v. *FTC,* 324 U.S. 726 (1945) and *FTC* v. *A. E. Staley Manufacturing Co., et al.,* 324 U.S. 746 (1945).

differentials among *appropriate* classes of customers are justified, it has also ruled that homogeneity of members within each class is required. As a test of such homogeneity the court suggested that the members of a class should have "such selfsameness as to make the average of the cost of dealing with the group a valid and reasonable indicium of the cost of dealing with each specific group member."[23] Moreover, the Federal Trade Commission has disapproved trade discounts granting one class of buyer a different net price than that allowed another class of buyer who purchases in similar quantities. The courts seem to be moving toward the position recommended by the Attorney General's National Committee to Study the Antitrust Laws: that the law should be interpreted to "focus on actual marketing functions, not 'ambiguous labels,' so as to recognize genuine functional discounts while exposing subterfuge."[24]

The thorniest area for carrying out this recommendation is the manufacturer who uses dual distribution. The manufacturer may compete with his customers, or two customers purchasing at different prices in different channels may compete with one another. The Commission has to be very careful not to enforce the law so as to force sellers to integrate vertically or to prevent a manufacturer from rewarding an efficient integrated middleman with a functional discount he deserves.

The good-faith defense. The functional discount problem has been involved in a number of the more interesting decisions which have established the current rulings on the use of the good-faith defense.[25] Price discrimination in good faith to meet an equally low price of a competitor is a complete defense under Section 2(*b*) of the act if: (1) the competitor's price is a lawful one, (2) the price and quality offered meet, not beat, that of the competitor, (3) the competitor is at the same level of the channel as the seller accused of discrimination, and (4) the competitor's price offer is substantiated.

Promotional allowances. Sections 2(*d*) and 2(*e*) prevent offering promotional allowances in money, goods, or services except on proportionally equal terms to all buyers. No proof of injury is necessary for a violation of these sections. The problem of administration has been to obtain clear judicial interpretation of "proportionally equal terms to all buyers."[26] The current legal situation may be summarized as follows:

A vendor should not offer, nor should a buyer accept, a promotional allowance unless (1) it is a reasonable payment for the service; (2) it is made for a service which competing dealers in this product similarly and proportionally furnish to the vendor; and (3) it is proportionalized among the dealers furnishing a similar service. Likewise, a buyer should not accept a merchandising service, such as store demonstrators, from a vendor unless the service is similarly and proportionally furnished to competing buyers. "Equal" means of equal cost to the seller. "Proportionally" means the allowance may be based on any reasonable index of sales, such as dollars or quantity ordered. "Similarly" means that each offer must include enough alternative services

---

[23] *United States.* v. *The Borden Company, et al.,* 82 S. Ct. 1309 (June 1962). For another case involving this principle see *General Auto Supplies, Inc., et al.* v. *Federal Trade Commission,* CA–7 (April 1965). Also the discussion of "Qualify for the Functional Discount of the Wholesaler," in J. W. Wingate and J. S. Friedlander, *The Management of Retail Buying* (Englewood Cliffs, N.J.: Prentice-Hall, Inc., 1963), pp. 287–88.

[24] *Report of the Attorney General's National Committee to Study the Antitrust Laws* (Washington, D.C.: Government Printing Office, 1955), pp. 208–9.

[25] For example, *FTC* v. *Standard Oil Co. of Indiana, et al.,* 340 U.S. 231, 238 (1951) and 355 U.S. 396, 404 (1958). This case involved a price war in 1938 which resulted in 20 years of litigation.

[26] In 1969 the responsibilities of the manufacturer to notify all buyers of the availability of promotional aids and the liability of buyers who induce illegal allowances were increased. See the latest FTC *Guides for Allowances and Services.*

that all buyers can find one which is suitable for their use. "Is available" means that the seller is responsible for notifying all buyers that an offer of promotional aid has been made.

Buyer's liability. Section 2(*f*) makes it illegal for a buyer to knowingly induce or receive an illegally discriminatory price. This provision reflects the belief in the 1930s that the market power of large buyers had to be checked. While enforcement experience under this section has been limited, the FTC has issued complaints under it in recent years. Proof of guilt requires that the illegal price concession has been received and that the buyer knows enough about market conditions to know that he is receiving a price lower than that paid by his competitors. The seller may even be able to use the good-faith defense if he can prove he sincerely tried in negotiations to "meet" and not "beat" the competitive offer. The buyer, on the other hand, is guilty if he used his size to force the seller into the illegal low-price offer.

Despite the limitations placed on price bargaining by this section, the buyer still has ample opportunity to negotiate for lower prices. There is nothing in the act to prevent a buyer from buying at the lowest lawful prices that sellers are willing to offer or accept. To this end, he should take advantage of all savings (other than brokerage) which sellers realize by reason of the buyer's methods of purchasing and the quantities he buys. Likewise, he should attempt to benefit from all lawful fluctuations in market prices and from the best trade discount classification and seasonal discount he can get. By making up his own specifications and thus receiving a product that is not of "like grade and quality" with the vendor's other goods, the buyer also opens the way for price concessions. The buyer has the right and obligation to seek the lowest prices given to competitors of his class. He should not assume that every seller is serious about maintaining a one-price policy.[27]

Summary: The Robinson-Patman Act. An excellent case can be made that the Robinson-Patman Act is inconsistent with the principles of a competitive economy.[28] Through its emphasis on cost as the basis of price differentials and on "proportionately equal terms" for advertising allowances, it inhibits a seller from achieving the best possible competitive "mix" of price and nonprice strategy and has "the effect of limiting the decision-making freedom of businessmen."[29] As E. T. Grether points out, action taken under the act has "often [been] contrary to the purposes of antitrust enforcement."[30]

The events leading to the passage of the Robinson-Patman Act suggest that its goal "was to prevent large concerns from using their market power to secure unfair price advantage over their competitors."[31] Actually, the real purpose of those who sponsored the bill was probably to protect the small independent retailer by curbing the growth of multiunit retail operations. It is doubtful if this purpose has been achieved.

It should be emphasized that the act is the most controversial antitrust law on

---

[27] For a current interpretation of Section 2 *(f)*, see L. X. Tarpey, Sr., "Buyer Liability under the Robinson-Patman Act: A Current Appraisal," *Journal of Marketing*, 36 (January 1972), pp. 38–42.

[28] This case is well presented by Philip Elman, a member of the Federal Trade Commission, in "The Robinson-Patman Act and Antitrust Policy: A Time for Reappraisal," *University of Washington Law Review*, 42 (October 1966), pp. 1–31. For alternative approaches, see D. A. Revzan, *Spatial Competition* (Berkeley, Calif., 1971), chap. 8.

[29] L. X. Tarpey, Sr., "The Woman's Day Case and Cooperative Advertising," *Journal of Marketing*, 29 (July 1965), p. 39.

[30] E. T. Grether, *Marketing and Public Policy* (Englewood Cliffs, N.J.: Prentice-Hall, Inc., 1966), p. 59.

[31] R. L. Kohls, *Marketing of Agricultural Products* (3d ed.; New York: Macmillan Co., 1967), p. 194.

the books. It may be that a fresh legislative start is required to undo the inconsistencies in enforcement that have developed over the years. A strong law to discourage predatory discrimination would certainly have to take its place. Congress has not heeded suggestions for repeal and may not during Representative Patman's lifetime. The original act is still the law, and it must be taken into account in establishing and administering price policies.

Resale price maintenance

"Resale price maintenance" or "fair trade," as it is popularly (and erroneously) called, refers to that price policy under which the manufacturer of a branded product in open competition establishes the price, or the minimum price, at which such product shall be resold to the consumer. In practice, this policy applies primarily to consumer goods. As an example, some years ago, R. H. Macy & Company sold the then popular novel *Gone with the Wind* at a price much below the $3 retail price suggested by the publisher—at times as low as 87 cents. As a result, the publisher of the book took advantage of New York's fair-trade law, the resale price was fixed at $3 and it immediately became illegal for Macy or any other New York State retailer handling this book to sell it for any lower figure.

Until the 1930s it was illegal for manufacturers to sign contracts with retailers under which the latter would be required to resell at manufacturer-established prices. To some degree the same result was secured by refusing to sell to price cutters, if the manufacturer did not go too far in his efforts to discover those who cut prices.[32] He was also allowed to establish resale prices on consigned merchandise and on goods sold through his own stores or by his house-to-house salesmen.

Fair-trade laws. Beginning with California in 1931, however, 46 states—all except Alaska, Missouri, Texas, and Vermont plus the District of Columbia—passed so-called "fair-trade" laws which make it legal for the manufacturer of a branded good in open competition to sign a contract with the retailer to assure maintenance of the retail price. These laws contain a "nonsigner's" clause which makes them binding upon other retailers as soon as they are notified. Such clauses are important because although in any state it is easy to find one retailer who will sign a contract, getting the signatures of all retailers handling a particular product is an impossible feat. Thus, the nonsigner's clause is practically a "must" from the point of view of a resale price maintenance program.

Under the state laws resale price maintenance was limited to intrastate commerce. By passing the Miller-Tydings Act of 1937, Congress legalized this practice in interstate commerce. Then the Supreme Court delivered what looked like a death-blow to fair trade: in the Schwegmann decision of May 1951, the nonsigner's clause was ruled illegal under federal law.[33] Consequently, the manufacturer who wanted to fair trade his product was required to sign contracts with all his outlets, an act which was quite impossible for practically all producers.

The Schwegmann decision restriction on fair trade did not last long. In 1952 Congress passed the McGuire amendment to the Federal Trade Commission Act, and once again the nonsigner's clause was legal in interstate commerce. However, state

---

[32] The courts made it clear that refusal to sell did not extend so far as to allow the manufacturer to use his customers or special agents as a means of getting information on price cutters, or to use a package-numbering system so that the source of merchandise sold by price cutters could be traced.

[33] *Schwegmann Bros.* v. *Calvert Distillers,* 341 U.S. 384.

Marketing: Principles and methods

court decisions against the constitutionality of the nonsigner's clause and state legislative action have gradually reduced to about 20 the number of states in which resale price maintenance is legally effective.

Legal situation today. As a result of the foregoing legal developments, it is now possible for a manufacturer of a branded good which is in competition with other goods to fix the retail price of his product within any one of the states in which retail price maintenance is legal by signing a contract with a single retailer in that state and notifying other retailers or merely by notifying retailers of the resale price.

It should be noted, however, that not all manufacturers who sell within these states can fair trade their products. This privilege is given only to manufacturers and distributors of products that carry "the trademark, brand, or name of the producer or distributor" and that are in "free and open competition with commodities of the same general class produced or distributed by others."[34] Moreover, the manufacturer's influence over price must be in a vertical line only, that is, from manufacturer to wholesaler to retailer. Any attempt to effect horizontal price agreements among manufacturers, among wholesalers, or among retailers is still illegal.

Under some circumstances a retailer may still sell below the fair-trade price. Court decisions grant pricing freedom on mail-order sales from a nonfair-trade state to a buyer in a fair-trade state. Even within fair-trade states, the retailer may undersell the established price if the trademark, brand, or manufacturer's name is removed from the product. Closing-out sales are exempted from the established price, although in some states the manufacturer must be given an opportunity to buy back his merchandise at cost. Likewise, damaged or deteriorated merchandise may be sold without pricing restrictions, usually after public notice has been given as to the condition of the merchandise. But for the great majority of his sales of products for which fair-trade prices have been established, these prices are binding on the retailer.

The enforcement provisions under the state fair-trade laws are quite clear—and unsatisfactory, so far as fair-trade advocates are concerned. In general, those who "knowingly and wilfully" sell under the fair-trade price may be sued for damages. In addition, court injunctions may be obtained to enjoin such price cutting. But note that selling below the fair-trade price is not a statutory offense against which the state will take action. In other words, it is up to the manufacturer, wholesaler, or retailer to police those selling fair-traded goods and to institute action; and, increasingly, court decisions have limited the action which may be taken to enforce fair-trade agreements. In view of court decisions as well as the expense and executive time required, the majority of manufacturers do a poor policing job, with the result that many retailers complain about the present enforcement situation.

Manufacturers attempting to follow a resale price maintenance policy are mainly in such fields as drugs, toilet goods and cosmetics, photographic supplies and equipment, books, sporting goods, and liquor. As a practical matter it seems doubtful if more than 5 percent of all retail volume in fair-trade states is covered.

The decline of fair trade. Since 1945, resale price maintenance has increasingly been under attack both abroad and in this country. In Canada, Sweden, and Denmark the practice is now specifically prohibited, and it is severely restricted in Finland.[35] In Britain, where as recently as 1964 "one quarter of all personal consumer

---

[34] These limitations, stated in the Miller-Tydings Act of 1937, were not changed by the Schwegmann decision or the McGuire amendment.

[35] L. A. Skeock, "The Abolition of Resale Price Maintenance: Some Notes on Canadian Experience," *Economica,* 31 (August 1964), pp. 260–69; *Journal of Marketing,* 29 (April 1965), p. 85; and B. S. Yamey (ed.), *Resale Price Maintenance* (Chicago, Ill.: Aldine Publishing Co., 1966).

expenditure [was] price maintained,"[36] resale price maintenance has been banned by Parliament, except for those manufacturers who can convince a Restrictive Practices Court that free pricing would be detrimental, that is, because of such possible results as lower quality goods, unnecessary services, or higher prices in the long run.[37]

In the United States, government, consumers, and professional economists have consistently recommended the repeal of the Miller-Tydings Act. Not only has fair trade been losing ground in its legal battles, it has suffered even greater defeats on the economic front. Many manufacturers have gradually come to realize that their resale price maintenance programs contain the seeds of their own destruction. That is, by creating such a wide margin between wholesale and retail prices, manufacturers have encouraged the growth of discount houses and the spread of discounting among "legitimate" retailers; in turn, these developments have made it impossible for the manufacturers to enforce resale price-control contracts against other retailers. The net result is that fair trade has been abandoned for all or part of their products by many of its strongest and oldest supporters—W. A. Sheaffer Pen Co., General Electric Co., Sunbeam Corporation, and Eastman Kodak Company, to name just a few.

Aggressive manufacturers have found they can overcome some of the disadvantages of having prices cut on their brands by other methods; in fact, the problems created by resale price maintenance are so great that today's manufacturers are only lukewarm, rather than enthusiastic, in its support. For the consumer the policy means higher prices. For the high-price retailer the immediate benefits of price maintenance are so significant that he remains the main advocate of this pricing policy; but his gains are obtained at the expense of higher prices to the consumer and reduced sales by more efficient retailers. To the low-price retailer, price maintenance means giving up some of his operating advantages in order to subsidize his high-price competitors. Consequently, a broad policy of price maintenance seems contrary to the interest of the general welfare.

Despite the strength of the antifair-trade forces and their considerable success to date, it seems doubtful that the attack will lead to the total elimination of resale price maintenance. Abandoned by many manufacturers, it is still strongly supported by others. It is still lawful in about 20 states, including such heavily populated areas as California, Illinois, and New York. Within the past 10 years, a national fair-trade law (named the "Quality Stabilization Act") very nearly passed in Congress.

The United States has gone far down the road toward extending protection to many groups who wish to escape from the impact of a competitive economy. As long as we have tariffs to protect producers and subsidy programs to aid farmers, we may expect fair-trade laws in some form to remain on our statute books.

State unfair-trade practices acts. Despite the general negative feeling toward fair-trade laws, it may be desirable to have a law prohibiting predatory price cutting among middlemen. A law which makes illegal those prices below net purchase cost of the goods (marginal cost) may represent a step in the right direction. Twenty-six states currently have laws, known as unfair-sales acts, unfair-trade-practices acts, or sales-below-cost laws, with provisions like this. Unfortunately, they usually require

---

[36] Christina Fulop, *Competition for Consumers* (London: Institute of Economic Affairs, 1964), p. 55.

[37] That the shift to free pricing has stimulated price competition to the consumer's benefit is reported in "British Consumer Gets First Taste of Unfixed Prices; More to Follow," *Business Week,* March 13, 1965, p. 118; "British Shoppers Get Spate of Price Cuts as 'Fair Trade' Fades," *Wall Street Journal,* March 4, 1965, p. 14; and "Britain's Candy Shops Cut Prices as Much as 33 1/3%," *Wall Street Journal,* July 26, 1967, p. 9.

some standard markup to be added to cost in order to arrive at minimum price.[38] Most of these statutes are aimed at price-cutting activities where the intent is to injure or destroy competition. In contrast with fair-trade laws which apply to branded merchandise and are permissive,[39] these laws apply to all goods and are mandatory. For example, Minnesota's Unfair Sales Act requires retailers to add at least 8 percent to their invoice cost of goods and wholesalers to add at least 2 percent, the only exception being that lower prices may be charged if necessary to meet the legal prices of competitors. Since the minimum costs of retailing for practically all merchandise necessarily involves a margin in excess of 8 percent of sales, this addition is probably not unreasonable. Only in a few states has the "floor" been defined as the cost of merchandise without the addition of a small markup.

Some states have adopted acts that may have less favorable results than those growing out of the Minnesota act. In Arizona the retailer must take a markup of at least 12 percent. Since this is in excess of the markup required for the retailing of some goods, it may result in higher prices to the consumer. In California, the law forbids sales below cost except to meet competition, but then defines cost as "the invoice or replacement cost, whichever is lower, of the article or product to the distributor and vendor, *plus the cost of doing business by said distributor and vendor.*"[40]

The California type of statute has at least two serious faults: an administrative difficulty and an economic fallacy. The administrative difficulty is that it involves the determination of the cost of operation of every retailer accused of violating the law. The economic fallacy is that it seems to require each product sold to carry a markup equal to the merchant's average cost of doing business. Since many items can be sold on a margin considerably under the average cost of doing business, there seems no sound reason for raising the prices of such merchandise. Yet, in the states where these laws exist, the retailer must take them into account in establishing the markup on his goods.

No administrative agency has been established with the special responsibility of administering or enforcing the majority of these laws.[41] Although violations are statutory offenses against which the attorneys general of the various states may take action, in practice aggressive enforcement programs have not been followed. As a consequence, in certain states wholesalers and retailers have formed associations, partly for the purpose of bringing alleged violations to the attention of the attorneys general and of encouraging the enforcement of the laws. In some instances these associations have themselves been prosecuted on the grounds that they were encouraging horizontal price fixing contrary to both state and federal laws.[42] Using these laws for horizontal price fixing is one of the two basic objections to them; the other is that even though instituted without a markup requirement or with a very low one, pressure may be exerted on the state legislatures to raise it—to the point that it eliminates price cutting which is justifiable as well as that which is predatory.

---

[38] These laws are summarized in Technical Study No. 10, National Commission on Food Marketing, *Special Studies in Food Marketing* (Washington, D.C.: Government Printing Office, 1966), pp. 223, 227–28.

[39] In 11 states the liquor laws provide that resale price maintenance shall be compulsory. For many years (but not now) the New York State Liquor Authority applied this principle "to promote temperance and provide for more orderly distribution of alcoholic beverages."

[40] Statutes of 1935, chap. 477.

[41] There are exceptions. For example, Connecticut has a Commissioner of Consumer Protection who may raise complaints "whenever he has reason to believe" a retailer has violated the state's sales-below-cost law. See *Journal of Marketing,* 30 (January 1966), p. 71.

[42] Hollander, *Restraints upon Retail Competition,* p. 39.

Section 3 of the Clayton Act deals with illegal conduct in distribution. The language of Section 3 (see Figure 25–1) says that a contract between a seller and a buyer which limits the ability of the buyer to buy the goods of the seller's competitor, where the effect is to lessen competition or tend to create a monopoly, is illegal. Agreements with agent middlemen are not covered, since agents do not take title or lease the product. The current status of enforcement under Section 3 is discussed here under two headings: exclusive dealerships and tying arrangements.

Exclusive dealerships. The degree of selectivity of distribution (see Chapter 19) is one of the most important strategy decisions a seller has to make. The state of the law on the legality of exclusive distributorships is changing so rapidly that you would do well to check the latest decisions on the matter rather than accepting the following summary as remaining currently accurate.[43]

An agreement *among dealers* of a brand, with or without the involvement of the manufacturer, not to compete against one another is a classic conspiracy in violation of Section 1 of the Sherman Act.[44]

Similarly, mutually exclusive arrangements (agreements calling for the manufacturer to sell only to a particular dealer in some specified geographic region and the dealer to buy the product in question from no other manufacturer) are clearly illegal since they are conspiracies in restraint of trade.[45]

The status of requirements or exclusivity contracts in automobile dealerships has to be treated as a special case. Automobile manufacturers have succeeded in avoiding definitive Supreme Court decisions, and dealers have been successful in obtaining special legislation which, in fact, protects *their* interests, rather than competition, at both the federal and state levels.[46]

The greatest difficulty in interpreting the courts is in the situation of a unilateral, intrabrand geographic limitation placed on the area which a dealer is to serve (e.g., a truck dealers franchise which stipulates that he may solicit business only within his county). In 1963, the Supreme Court ruled that the restriction of *interbrand* competition may be justified if it is done in order to more effectively engage in *interbrand* competition.[47] This, of course, is precisely why a manufacturer would engage in selective distribution. The minority opinion, though, is surprising. Justices Warren and Clark wrote that suppression of intrabrand competition is still suppression of competition and ought to be illegal per se.

This concept reappeared in the 1967 opinion in the Schwinn bicycle decision, which states that once the manufacturer has transferred title, any effort to restrict

---

[43] For the most recent court cases refer to each new issue of the *Journal of Marketing*, "Legal Developments in Marketing," particularly the subsection, "Regulation of Channels of Distribution."

[44] *U.S.* v. *General Motors Corp., et al.,* 384 U.S. 127 (1966).

[45] In *F.T.C.* v. *Brown Shoe Co.,* 384 U.S. 316 (1966) the Commission used Section 5 of the FTC Act rather than the Clayton Act to restrain the defendant from using a franchise agreement in which only dealers who agreed to carry no other manufacturers' shoes received promotional materials, sales training programs, and low-premium group insurance.

[46] The Automobile Dealers Franchise Act was passed by Congress in 1956. In 1971, according to the National Automobile Dealers Association, 17 states had effective laws regulating automobile manufacturer-dealer relationships, and such laws were proposed in 15 more states. In at least one, Texas, the law gives the dealers the right to prevent the entry of new dealers.

[47] *White Motor Co.* v. *U.S.,* 372 U.S. 253 (1963) and *Snap-On Tool Corp.* v. *F.T.C.,* 321 F.2d. 825 (1963).

freedom of distribution is a per se violation of Section 1 of the Sherman Act.[48] The decision goes on to suggest that a small firm can fight a vertically integrated giant by selling on consignment to franchised dealers and spells out the circumstances under which consignment selling is legal.[49] In our opinion this decision is not a proper one but is so internally inconsistent that the courts can still ask for proof of whether or not a franchise agreement helps or hinders competition before ruling it to be illegal.

Tying arrangements. Contracts to tie the sale of a product which a customer does not want to the purchase of one he does want and requirements that the purchaser buy only from a single source of supply have both been held illegal under Section 3. However, as presently interpreted, the law is less severe here than in the case of price-fixing agreements. The government is required to show that such a requirement has the effect of lessening competition or that it tends to create monopoly. On this point, the Supreme Court has suggested that structural considerations should be used as a basis of proof. The courts are reluctant to engage in a weighing of anticompetitive effects versus gains in efficiency. Violation will not be found unless there is foreclosure of a market or the seller is large and powerful.[50]

A current debate on this point centers around whether tying contracts by sellers of newspaper advertising are legal in those cities where morning and evening papers have been allowed to publish jointly in order to avoid bankruptcy. The courts have been tolerant of such contracts by small firms or by new firms who are trying to establish themselves as viable competitors. Thus, an early community television system firm was permitted to tie five-year maintenance contracts to purchase of the system when it was new and trained independent repairmen were not available. However, the contracts were found to be illegal after other firms in the industry had become established.[51]

SUMMARY: THE ROAD AHEAD

The best summary of this chapter could be a review of the first section, "Government Legislative Controls of Marketing," to see if the pieces of this regulatory patchwork have now fallen into place. The following summary observations about attempts to control the marketing system through government regulation also seem warranted:

1. It is a complex undertaking.
2. There is no sharp distinction in our complex society between private enterprise and public enterprise. "Free" enterprise is clearly a misnomer today. Over 10 percent of our gross national product is produced in either regulated monopolies or in industries where the influence of regulation on price, quantity, and quality is greater than the influence of competition. All global marketing is shaped as much by political as economic influences.

---

[48] *U.S.* v. *Arnold Schwinn and Co., et al.,* 388 U.S. 365 (1967).

[49] For a more detailed discussion of this decision, see S. P. Bridges, "The Schwinn Case: A Landmark Decision," *Business Horizons,* 11 (August 1968), pp. 77–85, and B. Bock, *Antitrust Issues in Restricting Sales Territories* (New York: Conference Board, 1968).

[50] The leading case decisions are: *Standard Oil Co. of California, et al.* v. *U.S.* 337 U.S. 293 (1949); *U.S.* v. *Richfield Oil Corp.,* 99 F. Supp. 280 (1951), affirmed per curiam, 343 U.S. 922 (1952); *Northern Pacific Railway Co.* v. *U.S.,* 356 U.S. 1 (1958); *Tampa Electric Co.* v. *Nashville Coal Co.,* 365 U.S. 320 (1961).

[51] *U.S.* v. *Jerrold Electronic Corp.,* 187 F. Supp. 545, affirmed per curiam, 363 U.S. 567 (1961).

3. The cost in terms of the efforts of competitors, lawyers, and expert witnesses; the operation of regulatory agencies; and the maintenance of the judicial system itself is not insignificant. If a complaint cannot be settled by a consent decree, there is no such thing as "quick justice" in the antitrust field.
4. Special-interest groups seek protection from the risks of competition by urging additional regulation. Businessmen under regulation have found that it is often easier to manipulate a regulatory agency (a political institution) than a market (an economic institution).
5. Even in the judicial arena, political considerations often make it desirable for the government to settle out of court rather than to fight for bigger stakes in a Supreme Court decision.

Government control does not seem to be a likely replacement for competition as the coordinating mechanism in our marketing system. If the costs of market imperfection per transaction could be compared to the costs of a regulated system per transaction, the cost of a few market imperfections would likely be relatively small. But note that this conclusion requires that we be constantly on the alert to ensure that the structure and conduct of markets is providing efficiency and progress in performance.

Businessmen sometimes have difficulty in distinguishing between the need for efficiency of the system and efficiency of the individual firm. Any careful survey of business in this country or abroad will disclose a shockingly wide divergence between business rhetoric and business behavior. Businessmen may preach the benefits of competition but in practice try to entice legislative bodies to enact laws which serve their special interests to the detriment of society. Yet, to an important degree, the maintenance of an effective competitive system based on private property depends on the continued existence of business leaders who are truly competition-minded in both thought and action. In fact, such leaders need to be so aggressive that they are willing to enter into competition with the government by undertaking activities which have been assumed by government agencies—e.g., slum clearance, planned cities, pollution control, or innovations in education.

The American people, too, are somewhat inconsistent in their attitudes toward competition. On the one hand they favor their choice in the marketplace and enjoy the fruits of competition. On the other, they are willing to tolerate the practice of big business and big labor negotiating wage and price increases which distort values and lead to prices and products that cannot meet the test of competition in international markets. They look to government when a market does not perform satisfactorily—not for more competition, but for more regulation.

The people have reason to be confused, for our choice is not a simple one between a market economy versus a planned economy. In fact, our choice is not between existing alternatives. In our advanced, industrial, affluent society we are forced to create new and untried techniques for coordination of economic activity. We also do not have the choice of standing still. With change mandatory and risks great, we can expect to make mistakes. The real concern is whether we can distinguish when we are moving forward from when we are moving backward.

As one who now knows a little about the marketing system, you may now be in a better position to ask the right questions and make valid analyses of exactly what mix of competition and regulation will permit our marketing system to move forward in providing a rising standard of living with increased individual opportunities and freedom to all members of our society.

REVIEW AND DISCUSSION QUESTIONS

1. Make a comparison of the provisions of the basic antitrust laws of the United States, Japan, United Kingdom, and the European Economic Community.

2. Do you believe the United States needs a new law to block conglomerate mergers? If no, explain why not. If yes, what provisions would you suggest such a law contain?

3. Do you believe the United States needs a new law to attack a market structure of homogeneous oligopoly? If no, explain why not. If yes, how do you feel such a law could be framed?

4. Explain the role of the following in FTC procedures: hearing examiner, the Commissioners, complaint, consent decree, cease-and-desist order, federal district courts.

5. What is the significance in Section 2(a) of the Robinson-Patman Act of the provision, "nothing herein contained shall prevent persons engaged in selling . . . from selecting their own customers. . . ."?

6. Prepare a concise report on conglomerate mergers challenged by the federal government during the past two years. Include a discussion of the extent of enforcement, the success of the challenges, the impact on the trend toward big business, and any suggestions for improving this area of public concern.

7. Discuss: "Few of those who believe in a competitive system object to the principle of governmental action against unfair methods of competition."

8. "The failure of the Federal Trade Commission Act was inherent in the failure of Congress to define 'unfair methods' of competiton." Would you agree? How would you define the term?

9. Review the list of conduct considerations for contractual and leadership channel structures in Table 24–2. If you were a member of the FTC staff, under what provision of the law would you bring a complaint of unsatisfactory conduct under each item in the list?

10. Evaluate from the points of view of (1) the Federal Trade Commission and (2) a respondent, the Commission's procedure as summarized on pages 624–25.

11. You have been appointed executive director of a nationwide consumer organization dedicated to the elimination of special-interest legislation which discriminates against consumers and other businessmen. How would you proceed with your assignment?

12. Give three examples of agreements between two institutions at different levels of the same channel which would be legal if the firms were vertically integrated but would probably not be if the firms were independent. What is the logic which has led to the development of this apparent double standard?

13. Argue either for or against whether the following types of agreements *should* constitute a violation of Section 1 of the Sherman Act: (a) a franchise from a manufacturer to his distributors awarding them exclusive rights to sell the brand in a specified geographic area only; (b) a clause in the franchise that if the distributor wants to sell Brand X, he must also sell Brand Y; (c) a clause in the franchise that the distributor may not also sell a competitor's brands; and (d) a clause that fixes the prices at which the distributor is to sell the brands.

14. Review the past year's issues of Commerce Clearing House, *Trade Regulation Reporter* or Bureau of National Affairs, *Antitrust and Trade Regulation Report* and list the nature of all complaints brought under Section 5 of the Federal Trade Commission Act.

15. Discuss the advantages and disadvantages of resale price maintenance from the point of view of (a) the manufacturer, (b) the retailer, and (c) the consumer.

SUPPLEMENTARY READINGS

The references to Chapter 24 also are appropriate here.

Grether, E. T. *Marketing and Public Policy.* Englewood Cliffs, N.J.: Prentice-Hall, Inc., 1966. Written by a long-time student of both marketing and public policy. Dr. Grether's discussion of maintaining the rule of competition (chapters 3 to 9) is especially pertinent to the present chapter.

Hollander, S. C. *Restraints upon Retail Competition.* East Lansing, Mich.: Michigan State University, Bureau of Business and Economic Research, 1965. In this study "of the forces that tend to limit competition in retailing," chapter 5 deals with limitations imposed by law.

Howard, M. C. *Legal Aspects of Marketing.* New York: McGraw-Hill Book Co., Inc., 1964. This excellent little volume covers all of the topics discussed in this chapter but is now somewhat in need of revision.

Kaysen, C. and Turner, D. F. *Antitrust Policy: An Economic and Legal Analysis.* Cambridge, Mass.: Harvard University Press, 1959. Economics, legal training, and practical experience are combined to make this an excellent volume that suggests some changes in our antitrust policy.

Kintner, E. W. *An Antitrust Primer.* New York: Macmillan Co., 1964. A former chairman of the Federal Trade Commission draws on his experience to provide, in the words of the book's subtitle, "a guide to antitrust and trade regulation laws for businessmen." Special attention is given to the Robinson-Patman Act.

Kintner, E. W. *A Primer on the Law of Deceptive Practices: A Guide for the Businessman.* New York: Macmillan Co., 1971. Does an excellent job of explaining the present status of deception under Section 5 of the FTC Act.

Lynn, R. A. *Price Policies and Marketing Management.* Homewood, Ill.: Richard D. Irwin, Inc., 1967. Chapters 10 through 14 include excellent coverage of the legal aspects of pricing.

Preston, L. E. (ed.) *Social Issues in Marketing.* Glenview, Ill.: Scott, Foresman & Co., 1968. Part III of this volume of readings is pertinent to this chapter.

Scherer, E. M. *Industrial Market Structure and Economic Performance.* Chicago: Rand McNally & Co., 1970. Chapters 18 through 21 provide more detail on all of the topics discussed in this chapter.

Scott, J. C. *Antitrust and Trade Regulation Today.* Washington, D.C.: Bureau of National Affairs, Inc., 1969. An excellent updating which analyzes 43 recent developments covering a variety of antitrust actions.

Singer, E. M. *Antitrust Economics: Selected Legal Cases and Economic Models.* Englewood Cliffs, N.J. Prentice-Hall, Inc., 1968. This textbook is unique because of its dual economic and legal approach to the subject.

Wilcox, Clair. *Public Policies toward Business.* Homewood, Ill.: Richard D. Irwin, Inc., 1966. The classic text in the field of regulation of business for the business, economics, or political science student. It covers more depth and breath than the present chapter in a very readable fashion.

Yamey, B. S. (ed.) *Resale Price Maintenance.* Chicago: Aldine Publishing Co., 1966. The leading scholar on resale price maintenance has brought together seven studies covering Canada, United States, Sweden, Denmark, Ireland, United Kingdom, and the European Economic Community.

Appendixes

A *Numerical concepts for marketing analysis*

It is easier to study marketing with some knowledge of quantitative analysis. This appendix is intended to provide a review and reinforcement of some fundamental numerical concepts from accounting and economics that are particularly useful in the analysis of marketing problems.

The discussion is divided into six sections: (1) analysis of income statements, (2) retail arithmetic, (3) the classification of costs, (4) break-even analysis, (5) profit planning, and (6) distribution cost analysis. Chapter 23, Pricing, contains discussions on the important quantitative concepts of price theory, simple return on investment, discounts, and terms of sale.

ANALYSIS OF INCOME STATEMENTS

The income statement is one of the most basic accounting reports. Its purpose is to show, for some period of time (4 weeks, 13 weeks, or 1 year are common), the impact of revenues and expenses on the value of the enterprise. While it may be released to stockholders and outsiders, it is also used as a managerial tool for planning and control. In this use, the income statement may be for a single "profit center" such as a division, product line, product, or new-product proposal rather than the whole firm.

Figures A–1 and A–2 show income statements covering a one-year period for a retailer and a manufacturer. The main difference in the two is in the section on cost of goods sold. The manufacturer will show more detail here, because he is concerned with managing the elements of cost that go to make up the *manufacturing cost* of the product. The middleman purchases the finished product and thus is not concerned with the elements of manufacturing cost.

FIGURE A–1
Retailer's one-year income statement

OFF-THE-ROAD VEHICLES DEPARTMENT
INCOME STATEMENT, YEAR ENDING JUNE 30, 197_

Gross sales		$104,000
Less: Returns and allowances		(4,000)
Net sales..		$100,000
Cost of goods sold		
Beginning inventory, at cost	$ 8,000	
Purchases...$56,000		
Less: Cash discounts received................................... (1,200)		
Plus: Freight-in... 6,700		
Purchases at net delivered cost	56,500	
Cost of goods available for sale..................................	$64,500	
Less: Ending inventory	(4,500)	
Cost of goods sold		60,000
Gross margin		$ 40,000
Expenses		
Sales salaries and commissions	$15,000	
Advertising, less allowances by suppliers	4,000	
Other promotion expenses...	1,000	
Building occupancy charges..	1,400	
Administrative salaries	8,000	
Office expense charges	2,200	
Bad debts...	300	
Insurance	100	
Total operating expenses		32,000
Operating income (before taxes and		
extraordinary items)...		$ 8,000

Operating ratios

In other respects, the statements are very similar. They show *sales* (perhaps broken down into specific products), *costs* (broken down by the function or department of the business that generated them), and the *operating income* that results. Costs are incurred in order to generate sales and, to some extent, some costs can be substituted for others. Thus the manager is interested in analyzing not only how much sales have been generated and how much profit has resulted, but also the *relative amount of the costs to sales and to one another.* The calculation of ratios between items on the operating statement can be used for this purpose.

Some of the most useful operating ratios are those that express key cost and profit items to sales. These can be illustrated with reference to Figure A–2:

$$\frac{\text{Cost of goods sold}}{\text{Net sales}} = \frac{\$22,500,000}{\$50,000,000} \times 100 = 45\%$$

$$\frac{\text{Marketing expense}}{\text{Net sales}} = \frac{\$20,450,000}{\$50,000,000} \times 100 = 40.9\%$$

$$\frac{\text{Total operating expense}}{\text{Net sales}} = \frac{\$21,600,000}{\$50,000,000} \times 100 = 43.2\%$$

TRAIL MANUFACTURING COMPANY, OFF-THE-ROAD BIKE MODELS
INCOME STATEMENT, YEAR ENDING JUNE 30, 197_

Gross sales..			$52,000,000	
Less: Returns and allowances.................			2,000,000	
Net sales....................................			$50,000,000	(100%)
Cost of goods sold				
Beginning finished-goods inventory.......		$ 2,000,000		
Cost of goods manufactured				
Cost of materials used in production ..	$12,000,000			
Direct labor.................................	5,000,000			
Manufacturing overhead				
Indirect labor $1,500,000				
Supervisory salaries 1,000,000				
Operating supplies 650,000				
Depreciation, plant and equipment. 1,150,000				
Occupancy charges.................... 700,000				
Total manufacturing overhead........	5,000,000			
Total cost of goods manufactured......		22,000,000		
Less ending finished-goods inventory.....		(1,500,000)		
Cost of goods sold............................			22,500,000	(45%)
Manufacturing margin			$27,500,000	(55%)
Marketing expenses				
Sales salaries and commissions $7,000,000				
Salesmen's expenses........................ 6,500,000				
Media advertising............................. 1,200,000				
Cooperative advertising allowances....... 300,000				
Other promotional materials............... 400,000				
Transportation expenses 4,500,000				
Warehouse charges 300,000				
Order processing expenses................. 100,000				
Losses on bad debts.......................... 150,000				
	$20,450,000			(40.9%)
Administrative expenses				
Executive salaries.............................. $ 180,000				
Office salaries 125,000				
Office supplies and expenses............... 195,000				
Office space charges......................... 90,000				
Insurance 1,000				
Interest 9,000				
Other administrative expenses 550,000				
	1,150,000			(2.3%)
Total operating expenses			21,600,000	(43.2%)
Operating income, before income taxes....			$ 5,900,000	(11.8%)

$$\text{Gross (manufacturing) markup} = \frac{\text{Net sales} - \text{Cost of goods sold}}{\text{Net sales}} \times 100$$

$$= \frac{\text{Gross margin}}{\text{Net sales}} \times 100$$

$$= \frac{\$27,500,000}{\$50,000,000} \times 100 = 55\%$$

A / Numerical concepts for marketing analysis

Manufacturing management is often interested in the components of cost which go into the cost of manufactured goods. These can be calculated simply from the income statement in Figure A–2, as shown below:

Cost of goods manufactured		
Cost of materials used in production	$12,000,000	54.5%
Direct labor	5,000,000	22.8
Manufacturing overhead		
Indirect labor	$1,500,000	6.8%
Supervisory salaries	1,000,000	4.5
Operating supplies	650,000	3.0
Depreciation, plant and equipment	1,150,000	5.2
Occupancy charges	700,000	3.2
Total manufacturing overhead	5,000,000	22.7
Total cost of goods manufactured	$22,000,000	100.0%

Marketing managers are also interested in the impact on sales of altering the amount of money spent on various elements of the marketing mix. The first step in such an analysis is to look at the relative size of the marketing budget, as abstracted from Figure A–2:

Marketing expenses		
Sales salaries and commissions	$ 7,000,000	34.2%
Salesmen's expenses	6,500,000	31.8
Media advertising	1,200,000	5.8
Cooperative advertising allowances	300,000	1.5
Other promotional materials	400,000	2.0
Transportation expenses	4,500,000	22.0
Warehouse charges	300,000	1.5
Order processing expenses	100,000	.5
Losses on bad debts	150,000	.7
	$20,450,000	100.0%

We see that 66 percent of the marketing budget goes for personal selling, 7.3 percent for media advertising, 2.0 percent on other types of promotion, 24 percent for physical distribution, and 0.7 percent for losses on sales to accounts who did not pay their bills. The manager is now in a position not only to ask which of these expenses can be reduced without lowering efficiency but to investigate whether, for example, the strong reliance on personal selling in this firm is necessary. It might be that sales could be increased by shifting some personal-selling expense to media advertising or promotion. The analysis can be extended by comparing the ratios for various times and for organizations with comparable accounting systems.

RETAIL ARITHMETIC

In most industries, trade associations and trade publications provide operating ratios for a large sample of firms in that industry. The definitions used in organizing these statistics are reasonably standardized by accounting convention. The marketing manager should be familiar with the most common of these, particularly those used by middlemen. The most elusive concern pricing and inventory valuation in retail trade.

Cost of goods sold

The accounting problem in the income statement is to match with revenues the expenses incurred in generating those revenues. Thus it is necessary to determine the cost of the goods sold. The accounting problems in this task center around *what goods* and *what cost*. If a firm sells only one product, the question of what goods to include is not difficult. But most retail firms sell a broad assortment of different goods, and certain estimation procedures are often used to determine the cost of goods sold.

The calculation of costs included is shown in Figure A–1. Purchased value is the invoiced price of the goods, less cash or other discounts received, plus all the costs of physical distribution of the product to the retail store. When this *net delivered cost* is added to the value of the inventory at the beginning of the period and the cost of the ending inventory is subtracted, the result is the cost of the goods sold.

Valuation of inventory

The chief problem in inventory evaluation is to determine the value to be placed on the ending inventory. Different firms use different methods of inventory valuation.

Where it is not feasible to maintain inventory and sales records by items and to take physical counts of inventory at frequent intervals, the *retail method* of inventory valuation is often used. In this method, records are kept of the retail value of the inventory, and the sales for the period are deducted to produce an estimated ending inventory at selling price. The cost of goods sold is calculated by reducing the inventory valued at selling price by applying the *average ratio of cost to selling price* for all goods passing through the establishment. It is then necessary to reduce the value of the ending inventory by an *estimate* of the amount of pilferage and breakage that took place during the period. For the retail method to be reliable, it is necessary for the distribution of markups on the mix of products sold and the inventory shrinkage rate to remain the same from period to period. Since mistakes in the ending inventory in one period become mistakes in the beginning inventory in subsequent periods, errors in inventory valuation cumulate and can lead to substantial errors in operating income. Thus physical inventory counts must be made from time to time.

Gross margin

As indicated in the example of operating ratios above, gross margin is defined as the *difference between net sales* and the *cost of goods sold.*

Markup

Gross margin is expressed in dollars. If we express gross margin as a percentage of net sales, the result is usually referred to as *markup.* Thus in Figure A–1, the gross margin is $40,000, and the markup is 40 percent.

Confusion sometimes arises over this term because some middlemen use a target markup percentage in establishing selling prices. But, since they are trying to determine price, it is necessary to express the ratio as a *percentage of cost* instead of price. This is referred to as *markon.* There is a simple relationship between the two.

Let:

p = price in dollars
c = cost in dollars
mp = percentage markup on price
mc = percentage markon to cost

Markup on price is defined as

$$mp = \frac{p - c}{p} \cdot 100. \qquad (1)$$

By algebra, one can express price in terms of markup on price as

$$p(100 - mp) = 100c$$

$$p = \frac{c}{1 - mp/100}. \qquad (2)$$

Markon to cost is defined as

$$mc = \frac{p - c}{c} \cdot 100. \qquad (3)$$

Substitute (2) into (3); this will determine the relationship of markon to markup:

$$mc = \left(\frac{c}{1 - mp/100} - c \right) \frac{100}{c}.$$

This expression can be simplified:

$$mc = \left(\frac{mp}{1 - mp/100} \right) \cdot 100$$

$$mc = \frac{mp}{100 - mp} \cdot 100. \qquad (4)$$

The relationship of markup to markon follows directly from (4):

$$100\,mc - mc\,mp = 100\,mp$$
$$mp\,(100 + mc) = 100\,mc$$
$$mp = \frac{mc}{100 + mc} \cdot 100. \qquad (5)$$

To illustrate these relationships, consider an item selling at retail for $5 and costing that retailer $3. From (1), the markup,

$$mp = \frac{p - c}{p} = \frac{\$5 - \$3}{\$5} = 40\%.$$

With this markup, one can calculate price from (2),

$$p = \frac{c}{1 - mp/100} = \frac{\$3}{1 - .40} = \$5.$$

The markon to cost can be calculated from (3) and (4),

$$mc = \frac{p - c}{c} \cdot 100 = \frac{\$5 - \$3}{\$3} \cdot 100 = 66.7\%,$$

Marketing: Principles and methods

$$mc = \frac{mp}{100 - mp} \cdot 100 = \frac{40\%}{100\% - 40\%} \cdot 100 = 66.7\%.$$

To calculate markup from markon, use (5):

$$mp = \frac{mc}{100 + mc} \cdot 100 = \frac{66.7}{100\% + 66.7\%} \cdot 100 = 40.0\%.$$

Markdown

Retailers frequently reduce the price of their merchandise for a sale or because the original price was too high, the items are not selling, or the merchandise has become soiled or damaged in handling or display. Such price reductions, which are due to marketing errors in buying, handling, or pricing, *do not reflect in the operating statement* because they are simply a price change made before a sale transaction. Markdowns are an expected part of the retailer's operation, but he is interested in knowing the extent of markdowns as a management control tool. Most retailers maintain markdown records by department or line of merchandise. They provide a guide as to how much markdown to anticipate in establishing the original markup on an item, as well as a tool in evaluation of the performance of buyers and merchandise managers. Careful recording of markdowns is necessary to the retail method of inventory evaluation.

The markdown ratio is computed on *net selling price,* not on the original price. Thus, for a group of items or a department,

$$\text{Markdown percent} = \frac{\$ \text{ Markdown}}{\$ \text{ Net sales}} \cdot 100.$$

For example, if a retailer purchased an item for $3 and marked it up 40 percent, the original selling price would be $5. If the item did not sell and the price were reduced to $4, the retailer could advertise that it was reduced 20 percent $\left(\frac{\$1}{\$5} \times 100\right)$, but he would calculate the markdown percentage as:

$$\text{Percent markdown} = \frac{\$1}{\$4} \times 100 = 25\%.$$

Stock turnover

Stock turnover refers to the number of times within a given period, usually a year, the average stock (or inventory) of merchandise is sold. Assume that a wholesaler has an average inventory[1] of $200,000 (at cost) and that the cost to him of all the goods he sold during the year was $1 million. His stock turnover would be computed as follows:[2]

$$\text{Stock turnover} = \frac{\text{Cost of goods sold}}{\text{Average inventory (at cost)}}$$

$$= \frac{\$1,000,000}{\$ \ 200,000}$$

$$= 5$$

---

[1] In practice, the average inventory is usually computed by averaging the year's opening and closing inventories. Sometimes a midyear inventory is also included in the average; and in a few cases, monthly inventories are averaged.

[2] Sales and inventory figures, of course, may be at selling prices. The important point is that both sales and inventory figures must be comparable, i.e., both at cost or both at selling prices.

When a policy of buying is followed that leads to a better balanced relationship between stocks and sales and to increased turnover, a direct increase in profit on invested capital can result. For example, if the $1 million of goods sold in the example above results in $50,000 profit, the profit on the $200,000 investment would be: $50,000 × 5 = $250,000 per year. On the other hand, if $1 million in goods sold required an average inventory of $300,000, the stock turnover would be:

$$\frac{\$1,000,000}{\$\ \ 300,000} = 3.33,$$

and the profit would be

$$\$50,000 \times 3.33 = \$166,500 \text{ per year.}$$

Other advantages of rapid turnover to the middleman are: (1) "fresher" stocks are maintained—a consideration which is of special importance in the case of perishable and fashion merchandise and which may result in larger sales despite smaller inventories; (2) smaller interest, insurance, and tax charges are paid on funds tied up in the inventory, and (3) where less space is used and that released is put to other productive uses, the result is a lower rent in relation to sales. Offsetting these advantages in the eyes of some middlemen, however, are the possible disadvantages resulting from (1) loss of quantity discounts; (2) loss of sales and customer goodwill if desired goods are out of stock when needed or assortments are inadequate; and (3) the greater cost of placing, transporting, and receiving a large number of small orders.

THE CLASSIFICATION OF COSTS

A great portion of management is concerned with the allocation of resources or the analysis of costs, that is, deciding how much to spend on various inputs of the organization in order to generate the desired revenues and profits. Costs can be classified on a number of different dimensions which are not alternative classification schemes; each cost can be classified on each dimension. Which dimension is important depends on the purpose of the analysis. The most important classifications for our purposes are by time period, controllability, traceability to an activity, and relationship to volume.

Matching costs to time periods

The accounting process is largely concerned with matching costs with revenues in specific time periods in order to determine if any residual income has been generated. Marketing managers are also concerned with the evaluation of new marketing opportunities. In both cases, it is important that costs be assigned properly to the time period in which they are incurred and also that they be matched against the revenues they are intended to generate.

Controllability

It is useful to identify the extent to which a manager can control the current level of use of each input. Although the use of all inputs can be altered to some degree, the manager may want to focus on those costs he can change quickly and in substantial amounts. Thus, he may dichotomize costs into those that are *unavoidable* and those that are *discretionary*.

Examples of unavoidable costs would be the direct labor of the operator of the machine making a product, the depreciation on that machine, the electricity it takes to run it, or the occupancy cost to the space it occupies. Although any of these costs may be changed some in the short run, the manager cannot make major changes in them on an annual basis.

Discretionary costs, on the other hand, are usually decided by management as a part of an annual plan. Almost all promotion expenditures fall into this category. While the sales force probably cannot be eliminated for a year, a 20 percent reduction or increase is often possible.

Traceability

Costs can also be dichotomized into *direct costs*—those directly attributable to a particular unit of production or to a particular sale—and *joint (or common) costs* —those incurred to produce a number of groups of products or sales. The latter costs cannot be allocated to a particular product or sale except by some questionable and arbitrary allocation basis.

This distinction is most useful in making pricing decisions and in distribution cost analysis (discussed below).

Costs as a function of volume

In classifying how costs change as a result of changes in the level of activity, the usual practice is to divide costs into *fixed costs*—such as executive salaries that do not change as production or sales go up or down, and *variable costs*—such as the material in the product that varies directly with the number of units produced. Note that fixed costs may vary with time, but not with the level of operations, and that fixed cost *per unit* produced changes with the level of operations but variable cost per unit is fixed.

There are two other possible points of confusion regarding how variable costs vary with volume. One is simply the question of how to measure the level of activity. In organizations where production activities are separated from marketing activities and substantial finished inventory exists, sales is not a good measure of activity for the production departments, and units produced is not a good measure of activity for the sales department.

The second common confusion concerns *how* variable costs change with volume. The usual assumption is to assume a linear relationship. However, away from ideal levels of activity, costs may exhibit curvilinear or even step relationships with volume. Both these situations are illustrated in Figure A–3. The graph shows variable costs rise quite rapidly at less than 10 percent and more than 90 percent of capacity. There is a similar linear relationship between 10 percent and 67 percent, but a step occurs when the plant goes from one to two shifts and from two to three shifts. Between 67 and 90 percent, variable costs are still linear, but with a greater slope.

Variable costs as a function of plant capacity

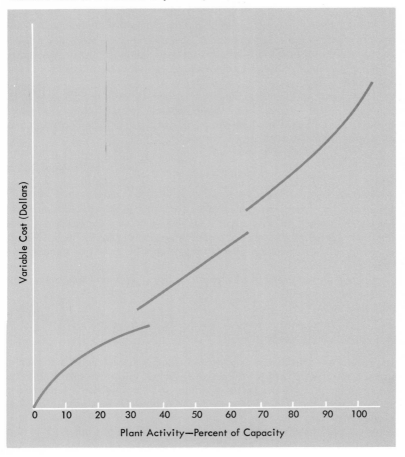

BREAK-EVEN ANALYSIS

A useful tool in the examination of marketing problems is break-even analysis, which considers the concepts of revenues, variable costs, unavoidable fixed costs, and discretionary fixed costs and their influence on profit. Such an analysis is useful in the review of past performance and in planning future competitive moves. In our description of this tool, it is assumed that the volumes being considered are in a range where fixed costs are constant and variable costs are linear.

Figure A–4 is a graphic depiction of break-even analysis. If dollar sales are used as the measure of output rate, the revenue line becomes a 45° diagonal, since sales dollars are being plotted against dollars. Other measures such as percent of capacity or units of output could be used instead of sales. However, it is important to recognize the analysis does not consider inventory accumulation—everything produced is sold.

The total cost line is drawn in such a way that its intercept is total fixed cost and

Marketing: Principles and methods

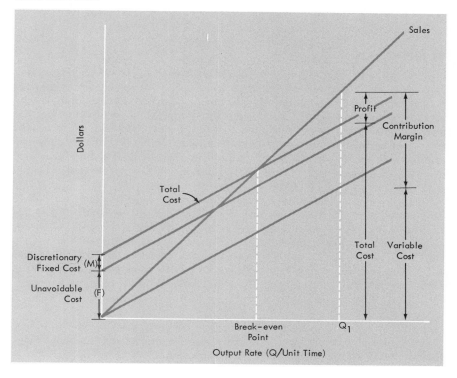

its slope is the variable cost per unit. The break-even point is where revenue just covers total cost and profit is zero—that is, where sales equal total cost. At levels of operation above this point, profit is positive. These relationships can be shown algebraically.

Let:

Q = units sold
P = selling price
v = variable cost per unit
F = unavoidable fixed cost
M = discretionary fixed costs
π = operating profit

The definition accounting equation is sales equals cost plus profit,

$$PQ = vQ + F + M + \pi. \tag{6}$$

The revenue line is simply a graph of PQ, and the total cost equation is $C = vQ + F + M$. The break-even point is that output where profit is zero,

$$Q = \frac{F + M}{(P - v)}. \tag{7}$$

A / Numerical concepts for marketing analysis

653

The profit at any level of output can be calculated by

$$\pi = (P - v)Q - F - M. \tag{8}$$

PROFIT PLANNING

The first term, $(P - v)Q$, is shown on the chart and is the contribution generated by sales at level Q to cover fixed costs and profit. $P - v$ is known as the *unit contribution*. These relationships provide enough background to demonstrate why break-even analysis is such a fundamental tool in marketing decision making. The marketing manager must determine the price (P) at which his product is to be sold and how much discretionary promotional expenditure to use to sell it (M). He may even be able to alter the quality of the product some by adding more expensive materials, accessories, or packaging to it (v). Equation (8) shows the effect that changes in P, v, and M will have on profit if Q does not change.

For complete profit planning, the marketing manager must also know what effect his changes in P, M, and v will have on the number of units sold, Q. For this information, he must attempt to estimate his *demand curve* and *response function* for the various marketing inputs. These two functions and their estimation are discussed in Chapters 18, 21, and 23. The mathematical form of the classical function is $Q = f(P)$, but the modern marketing approach is to make price just one of the elements in the marketing mix and, thus, just one factor in the response function,

$$Q = f(P, M, v), \tag{9}$$

where we consider M to be the discretionary marketing costs in promotion and distribution, and v to be the variable marketing costs in product and distribution (sales commissions are an example).

Substituting (9) for Q in (8) gives,

$$\pi = (P - v)Qf(P, M, v) - F - M, \tag{10}$$

a profit equation expressed in terms of marketing variables. If marketing research can provide estimates of the parameters of the response function, the marketing manager could then find that level of P, M, and v that maximizes profit.[3]

In addition to the problems of estimating the response function and assuming linearity of costs, the break-even model has other limitations for many marketing decisions. These are largely associated with the evaluation of new marketing ventures where investments of new funds are required and the venture must be evaluated over a number of years rather than the single planning period considered in the break-even analysis.

If the marketing project being planned requires the investment of additional funds that are not recovered in the first year, the correct criterion to maximize is return on investment rather than dollar profit, as in Equation (10). A common situation, discussed in Chapter 18, is the decision as to if and how a new product is to be produced and marketed. This is the approach adopted in the section on "Price Determination by Manufacturers" in Chapter 23.

---

[3] Although data limitations cause most marketing managers to use trial-and-error techniques to find optimum levels of P, M, and v, theoretical solutions have been known for some years. See K. S. Palda, *Economic Analysis for Marketing Decisions* (Englewood Cliffs, N.J.: Prentice-Hall, Inc., 1969), chap. 1 and 2.

With or without additional investment, marketing plans should be made in a dynamic framework. Response functions, costs (F and v), price (P), and discretionary marketing expenditures (M) will and should change in most years. The break-even model looks just one year ahead. Multiperiod analysis will show that even if investment occurs only in one year, the return (operating income) on that investment will vary from year to year and, as one looks further into the future, the uncertainty as to the amount of this return increases. The correct model for analyzing such situations requires an estimation of investment, revenues, and costs in each future period—something like the solution of Equation (10) for each period—and then summing these results for a number of planning periods. The method of summing and of explicitly considering the return on investment is called the *present-value,* or *discounted cash-flow model.* This model involves an understanding of compound interest and is beyond the level of this book.

Uncertainty about the future can be brought into the present-value model by estimating not just a single value for revenues, costs, and investment, but a *probability distribution* of possible values for each of these variables in each period. Again, this refinement is beyond the scope of this book. It is mentioned only to introduce these concepts and to emphasize that formal analytical techniques for marketing planning can be developed to the point where they are useful to marketing managers.

DISTRIBUTION COST ANALYSIS

When profits are unsatisfactory, one way to attempt to improve them is to analyze which existing inputs (costs) can be reduced without reducing demand. Put another way, how can efforts or the quantity of each input employed be reallocated so as to increase profits? This reallocation can be either among the elements of the marketing mix (products, distribution channels, promotion, and price) or among the market segments to which these marketing efforts are directed.

Marketing-mix allocation models

The reallocation of the elements within the marketing mix is usually accomplished by use of an analytical model which is an expansion on Equation (10). Specifically, these models consider each type of expenditure within each element of the marketing mix and also the marketing mix used by major competitors. Such models have proved most effective when they are constructed as a computer simulation. In this way it is possible to consider many possible reallocations within the firm's marketing mix, many possible reactions by competitors, and the effect of these changes on profits. The level of complexity and uncertainty in such models is such that trial-and-error solutions are easier and more useful than models which seek unique profit-maximizing solutions as does Equation (10).

Distribution-cost-analysis model[4]

Reallocations of marketing effort among market segments involves a model from cost accounting which investigates whether there are: (1) products, (2) channels of distribution, (3) order sizes, (4) territories, (5) customers, or (6) salesmen who do not

---

[4] For more complete discussions of distribution cost analysis, see D. R. Longman and Michael Schiff, *Practical Distribution Cost Analysis* (Homewood, Ill.: Richard D. Irwin, Inc., 1955); and C. H. Sevin, *Marketing Productivity Analysis* (New York: McGraw-Hill Book Co., 1965).

make satisfactory *contributions* to fixed costs and profit. The steps in the analysis will be briefly outlined.

Determine the marketing functions to be included. This step involves simply ensuring that all the firm's departments that are engaged in marketing activities are included in the analysis. As shown in Figure A–2, these include personal selling, advertising, cost of servicing distributors, warehousing and shipping, transportation, order processing, and collections. The exact title of these departments will vary among companies. The important point is to include all departments performing marketing functions.

It may well be that the accounting control procedure in the firm may allocate all of the expenses in one marketing function to other functions. This is typically the case if some budget units are line operating units organized around products or territories and others are staff service units whose entire function is to service the line units. For example, a marketing research department or promotion group may be required to "sell" the full cost of their services to the product groups they service. If this reallocation of staff services has been done on a "real" basis—that is, on the basis of the cost of services performed for a product, territory, or customer—then it will be satisfactory to pick up these costs in the line unit. However, if the reallocations have been made on an arbitrary basis, the natural expenses of the staff department should be analyzed just like those of any other department.

Assign expenses to marketing departments. The allocation of natural expense items like salaries, space charges, and supplies is a normal part of the department's budget and expense-control process.

These first two steps are usually supplied on a monthly basis as a normal accounting function to provide data as the input to the distribution cost analysis. Market segments that are the subject of the analysis—products, channels, orders, territories, customers, or salesmen—must next be divided.

Calculate the gross margin for each segment. If, for example, it is territories that are being analyzed, this next step involves determining the gross margin on the sales made to each territory. Whether the firm is a manufacturer or a middleman, the costs of goods sold are accounted for by item or lot as a part of the normal accounting procedure. Thus these gross margins are easily determined. Table A–1 provides illustrative data for a territorial cost analysis for a distributor. If the markup in each territory is calculated, it can be noted that the differences in the product mix purchased by the customers in the various territories cause the markup among districts to vary from 6 to 19 percent.

Allocate functional expenses to segments. This step is typically the most difficult one in the analysis. The task is to allocate the expense of each marketing function to the segments that are the subject of the analysis, for example, to allocate all shipping expense to the territories being analyzed. If functional expenses are allocated, there must be a direct or causative basis for the allocation. The expense of shipping to particular territories, for example, can be allocated quite directly, but expenses of a new-product development group might be difficult to allocate to territories unarbitrarily. On the other hand, if the group works on projects which come from suggestions of customers or salesmen in specific territories, the source of these ideas could become a basis for allocation. If the new-product group is working on projects unrelated to current products, there is no basis for allocation, and the expenses *should not be allocated* at all.

The criterion to be used in allocating functional expenses is whether there is a direct cause between the segment being analyzed and the incurring of the cost. If the costs are common to all segments and no basis for allocation exists, the functional expense should be omitted from the analysis. The sources in the footnote at the beginning of this section will provide help in deciding how various marketing expenses can be allocated. In Table A–1, the basis of the allocation of each function is shown.

Calculate the contribution of each function. Subtracting the allocated costs from the gross margin yields the contribution of each segment to cover indirect costs and profits. The results are very revealing. As shown in Table A–1, Long Beach is the best territory in terms of gross margin, contribution, and contribution margin. The Los Angeles Basin performs less well almost entirely because customers in that territory purchase products that carry low gross margins. Thus an analysis of the products sold in this district may be in order.

The Ontario territory yields a lower contribution than Long Beach, partially because the gross margin is lower, but more because shipping charges are greater and selling costs are high relative to the quantity sold. The same can be said about the San Fernando territory, but to an even greater extent. Both San Bernadino and Orange County show negative contributions, primarily because they produce very little volume, but the cost of serving these territories is high.

Determine and test possible methods of corrective action. The analysis has pointed out which territories are weak and why. It is quite another matter to determine

TABLE A–1
Analysis of contribution to fixed costs and profit of sales territories (thousands of dollars per year)

	Los Angeles Basin	Long Beach	San Fernando Valley	Ontario area	San Bernadino	Orange County
Sales	112.50	207.69	27.50	49.50	10.00	10.00
Cost of sales	105.75	168.64	23.60	41.70	9.00	9.30
Gross margin	6.75	39.05	3.90	7.80	1.00	0.70
Expenses						
Personal selling (actual cost of salesmen in territory).............	.30	.30	.45	.35	.35	.35
Sales management ($150 per salesman)	.05	.05	.05	.05	.05	.05
Mail promotion ($2 per mailing to each territory)........	.10	.20	.04	.08	.04	.05
Shipping (actual transportation cost)	.25	.35	1.00	.85	.70	.30
Handling ($60 per order shipped)	.30	.30	.60	.45	.30	.20
Order processing ($1 per order line)	.18	.10	.06	.02	.01	.01
Media advertising (not allocated)	—	—	—	—	—	—
Inventory costs (not allocated)	—	—	—	—	—	—
Total expenses............	1.18	1.20	2.20	1.80	1.45	.96
Contribution	5.57	37.85	1.70	6.00	(.45)	(.26)
Contribution margin	4.95%	18.2%	6.18%	12.1%	—	—

what to do about it. For example, the distant territories of San Bernadino and Orange Counties could be dropped, or the salesmen could be withdrawn and the customers serviced by telephone, or perhaps the salesmen should be directed to try to develop more customers in these areas. An analysis of products sold to Los Angeles Basin customers may suggest that the prices on some items should be increased or the items dropped. However, the firm may not want to do this if they feel it would cause the loss of valuable customers.

We learned early in the text that a small proportion of customers usually account for a large proportion of the business. The problem is to determine exactly how to operate on the margin so that all customers contribute something to overhead and profit. The distribution cost analysis will not do this. The analyst must arrive at alternative solutions and try to recast the analysis under each alternative in order to find the one that will maximize profit in the long run.

REVIEW AND DISCUSSION QUESTIONS

1. Construct an operating statement from the following data:

Purchases at billed cost	$31,000
Net sales	40,000
Salaries	4,000
Rent	4,000
Other operating expenses	4,000
Shipping expense of merchandise sold	1,000
Freight on merchandise purchased	3,000
Beginning inventory, at cost	7,000
Ending inventory, at cost	12,000
Sales returns	200
Cash discounts allowed	600
Cash discounts received	300

2. Calculate the markup, net operating income, and operating expense ratios to sales for the operating statement development from the data above. Also, calculate markon to cost and stock turnover.

3. What are the selling prices for items that have the costs and percentage markups on selling price shown below?

   (a) $14.50   20%   (c) $1.49   40%
   (b) $45.00 $33^1/_3$%   (d) $50.00   50%

4. What are the percentage markons to cost that correspond to percentage markups given in Question 3?

5. What net sales volume is required to maintain a stock turnover of five times a year on an average inventory that costs $300,000 with a gross markup of 30 percent?

6. A stationery store purchased a gross of pens designed to sell at retail for $1.49 each and yield a markup to the retailer of 45 percent. The merchant sold 100 pens at this price but rebated the full purchase price on six of them because they were defective. The remainder were marked down to $.99 and sold at that price. What was the markdown percentage on this lot of pens?

7. Construct a break-even chart for a new product venture where the selling price is planned for $1.49, unit variable costs are $.88, and total annual fixed costs are $61,000. Assume plant capacity is 200,000 units per year.

Marketing: Principles and methods

8. For the venture in Question 7, calculate (*a*) the break-even point, (*b*) the profit with sales of 120,000 units per year, and (*c*) what you would want to know before you could evaluate a proposal to increase advertising expenditures by $10,000 per year.

9. A small automobile dealership has been approached with a proposition to add a new Japanese automobile to its line. Experience of other dealers has shown that the dealer can expect to make only about $100 net profit on a $3,000 car and that the investment necessary to take on the dealership is about $100,000. How many cars must he sell per year to return the 12 percent he currently receives on the capital he has invested in the business?

10. If a distribution cost analysis by order size showed that any order under a certain size yielded a negative contribution margin, what action might the company take?

11. What is the relevance of the discussion in Chapter 17 to the discussion of "profit planning" here?

12. Compare and contrast the items in each of the following pairs:
    (*a*) Operating income and net profit.
    (*b*) Markup and gross margin.
    (*c*) Discretionary costs and fixed costs.
    (*d*) Joint costs and fixed costs.
    (*e*) Variable costs and fixed costs.
    (*f*) Variable costs and direct costs.
    (*g*) Discounted cash-flow model and simple return on investment.
    (*h*) Marketing-mix allocation problem and distribution cost analysis.
    (*i*) Natural-expense categories and functional costs.

A / Numerical concepts for marketing analysis   **659**

B The commodity exchange as a facilitating marketing institution

The commodity futures exchange facilitates marketing of major agricultural products and raw materials by providing a vehicle for shifting the risk associated with price changes. A commodity exchange is an organization or association of individuals which promotes the interests of those dealing in a particular commodity and provides a place for trading conducted under uniform rules, with facilities for the adjustment of disputes among members and for the collection and dissemination of market information.[1] Because the facilities of the exchanges are used mainly for dealing in contracts for future delivery, they are often called "commodity futures exchanges."

Commodity exchanges do not themselves deal in commodities. All dealings on the "floor" are made by members, who may buy and sell both for themselves and (for a standard commission) for nonmembers. Admission to membership usually requires the purchase of an already existing membership (called a "seat"), since the number of members is limited by the charter of incorporation. Moreover, new members are admitted only after a two-thirds vote (in some cases only a majority) of the existing members. Exchanges are not profit-making institutions but collect dues and service fees to cover their costs of operation.

Commodity exchange in the United States

There are several dozen active commodity futures markets in the United States and a much larger number in the rest of the world. On about 18 of these exchanges, "futures trading" is conducted in 21 different commodities under regulation of the

---

[1] There are a few exchanges that provide market information and other services but no place for trading in a commodity. The Boston Fruit and Produce Exchange is a nontrading exchange. The word "exchange" is also often used to designate just the facilities provided by the members of the exchange; the Chicago Board of Trade building is referred to as the "Exchange."

U.S. Department of Agriculture's Commodity Exchange Commission through the Commodity Exchange Authority.

Futures in grain have been traded in Chicago since 1848. Because of their value in protecting the farmer and marketer of agricultural products against price declines, the government has regulated futures markets in domestic agricultural products since 1916. The Authority's objectives are the maintenance of fair and honest practices in the futures markets, the prevention of price manipulation and corners, and the protection of hedgers and traders against improper brokerage practices.

To accomplish these objectives, the Commodity Exchange Authority has responsibility for:

1. Market licensing—designating commodity exchanges as "contract markets."
2. Broker registration—requiring brokers on contract markets to register each year.
3. Audits of brokerage firms to insure "trust fund" treatment of traders' funds and to prevent their misuse.
4. Trading surveillance and market analysis—supervision of trading through a system of daily reports by all traders on special forms provided for this purpose.
5. Establishing and enforcing speculative limits such as (a) the two-million-bushel limit applicable to daily trading in wheat futures, (b) the amount of speculative trading done by any individual, and (c) the maximum price advance or decline allowed in any one day.
6. Investigating possible violations revealed by surveillance of trading or based on complaints by traders and the public.
7. Making market surveys and preparing reports based on them.
8. Publication of market information of value to the public, traders, and the Commodity Exchange Authority.

The current legislation, the Commodity Exchange Act of 1936, was last amended in 1968 when frozen orange juice concentrate and livestock were included in the regulations.

About 15 commodities (such as lumber, metals, rubber, sugar, coffee, and cocoa) are actively traded in the United States but are not regulated. Table B–1 lists the major U.S. exchanges and the commodities they handle. About 60 percent ($460 million per day) of the total volume of contracts is traded by the two Chicago exchanges. For comparison purposes, the volume of trading on these two exchanges represents about three fourths that of the two major New York *stock* exchanges.

Types of trading

The dealing in any commodity which takes place on the larger exchanges is of two types: cash and futures. "Cash dealing" (or "spot dealing"; in practice, the terms are used interchangeably), refers to all transactions in real product and contemplates actual delivery, usually immediately. "Futures trading" involves a contract providing for delivery in a future month and permits any one of a number of approved grades of grain to be delivered. Although the holder of the contract can insist on delivery in the specified future month, actually very little product is delivered to settle futures contracts.

The more important differences between cash and futures contracts have been summarized by G. H. Hoffman.[2]

---

[2] G. W. Hoffman, *Future Trading upon Organized Commodity Markets* (Philadelphia: University of Pennsylvania Press, 1932), p. 109.

	Cash Contract		Futures Contract
1.	Used to market or merchandise the commodity	1.	Used to speculate on or hedge against price changes
2.	Executed at exchange tables or privately	2.	Executed only by open auction on a central exchange in a ring, known as the "pit"
3.	Trades in irregular amounts (car lots, cargoes, any number of bales)	3.	Trades in round lots (5,000 bushels for grain).
4.	Varying lengths of time used for delivery	4.	A future month used for delivery
5.	May or may not not have optional period of delivery	5.	Seller's option of day of delivery
6.	Usually calls for specific grade	6.	Seller's option of grade to be delivered

TABLE B–1
Major commodity futures trading in the United States

Commodity	Chicago Board of Trade	Chicago Mercantile Exchange	Kansas City Board of Trade	Minneapolis Grain Exchange	New York Cotton Exchange
Wheat	x		x	x	
Corn	x		x		
Oats	x			x	
Rye	x				
Soybeans	x				
Soybean meal	x				
Soybean oil	x				
Cattle (live)	x	x			
Broilers (iced)	x				
Pork bellies		x			
Hogs (live)		x			
Eggs		x			
Potatoes		x			
Sorghum			x		
Cotton					x
Orange juice					x
Wool					x
Cottonseed oil					
Fishmeal					
Copper					
Hides					
Lead					
Mercury					
Palladium					
Platinum					
Propane					
Rubber					
Silver	x				
Tin					
Zinc					
Plywood	x				
Lumber		x			
Cocoa					
Coffee					
Sugar					

Marketing: Principles and methods

Cash or spot transactions on the exchange. Cash or spot sales typically take place at tables located in one section of the trading floor of the exchange (Figure B–1) where samples of the grain are displayed. Buyers inspect these samples and then negotiate purchases (Figure B–2). Consummating transactions on the exchange has many advantages for dealers as compared with trading privately in their offices. When many buyers and sellers meet at one place and at one time, buyers save time in finding sellers, and sellers can quickly locate possible buyers. The trend of prices may be judged quickly and accurately, as the effects of demand and supply forces tend to be concentrated at one point. Actual prices at which transactions take place are openly established and can be quoted in the press, thus providing exact information on the price that wheat is bringing in open competition. Because the exchange serves many members, it can also gather a great amount of market information at a low cost

New York Produce Exchange	Commodity Exchange, Inc. New York	New York Mercantile Exchange	New York Cocoa Exchange	New York Coffee and Sugar Exchange
x				
		x		
x				
x				
	x			
	x			
	x			
	x			
		x		
		x		
	x			
	x			
	x			
	x			
	x			
		x		
			x	
				x
				x

FIGURE B–1
Floor plan of the Chicago Board of Trade

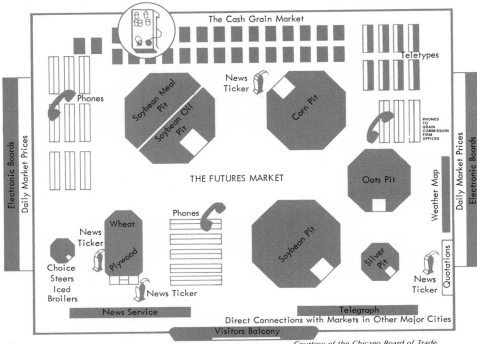

Courtesy of the Chicago Board of Trade

per member.[3] Since many members do not wish to limit their trading to grain represented by samples shown on the floor but prefer to buy and sell by grade, exchanges often take the lead in standardization. An exchange can draw up and enforce (through its power of expulsion) rules of trading and can provide settlement machinery for all disputes that may arise among members.

Futures trading. A recognition of the advantages of cash trading through exchanges led to their early establishment in the United States. With the passing years, trading has gradually shifted from cash contracts to standardized contracts for future delivery. Today, trading in such contracts exceeds by many times the volume of trading in the physical commodity itself.

Why would a buyer desire to purchase a contract calling for the delivery of wheat three months in advance? The obvious guess might be that the buyer—a flour miller, for example—might be expecting orders for flour in the future so that he would be interested in buying ahead to cover such possible orders rather than in buying cash

---

[3] Market data gathered by exchanges can include government reports on the size of the crop farmers intend to plant; monthly reports on actual plantings, condition of the growing crop, and crop estimates; and intermediate reports on warehouse and elevator supplies. Private reports on the size of crops forecast by leading crop reporters and estimates of supplies on hand are also compiled. In addition, the exchange serves as a news-making agency by publishing daily, weekly, and yearly reports on market price movements and receipts and shipments to various markets. News gathered which has sufficient merit can be flashed over the entire country by wire.

Marketing: Principles and methods

Samples of cash grain are available for traders' inspection

Courtesy of the Chicago Board of Trade

grain and holding it until the orders materialized. But a glance at the futures trading statistics of any large exchange will show that this reasoning is false: The delivery of grain against futures contracts is practically nil, despite the fact that the contracts are valid and enforceable at law; less than 1 percent of the futures contracts in grain is settled by delivery of the physical commodity.[4] Futures contracts, therefore, are not bought in order to have grain delivered against them as a method of closing them out. The main business use of futures trading lies in another direction—to make possible the practice of hedging, in which no delivery is contemplated when the contract is made.

Hedging

Hedging consists of the simultaneous purchase and sale of equal amounts of a commodity, with the expectation that the loss (or gain) on one set of transactions will

---

[4] G. S. Shepherd and G. A. Futrell, *Marketing Farm Products: Economic Analysis* (Ames: Iowa State University Press, 1969), p. 147.

be offset by a gain (or loss) on the other when the hedge is closed. It is a means of getting some degree of protection against inevitable price changes. In wheat dealings a hedge involves the purchase of a certain quantity in one type of contract—cash or futures—and the sale of a similar quantity of the opposite type. When the hedge is closed, a similar, though opposite, type of transaction is necessary.

Although a considerable amount of hedging is done by country grain elevators as protection against price changes while the wheat is in storage or on the way to a market, most hedging is practiced by owners of grain or grain products who operate in the terminal markets. One of the more important of these operators—the flour miller—can be used as an example which, while oversimplified as compared with the hedge in actual operation, accurately illustrates the basic principles involved.[5]

Opening the hedge. Assume that on July 10 of a certain year a flour miller lacked specific orders for flour but wished to keep his mill busy and bought 10,000 bushels of wheat at $1.65 per bushel to grind into flour. Since he was well aware of the wide fluctuations which might take place in the price of wheat, as well as the fact that wheat and flour prices move together, he wished to take steps to protect himself. He was willing to forgo any profits he might receive through an advance in price if he could escape any losses he might incur through a fall in price. His function was milling, and he was satisfied with a milling profit. This protection against price fluctuations could be provided by a hedge in the futures market. Therefore, when he bought his 10,000 bushels of cash grain at $1.65, he sold a futures contract calling for delivery of 10,000 bushels of contract grade wheat in December of the same year at $1.73. These transactions can be summarized as follows:

I. July 10 transactions:
Bought 10,000 bu. cash wheat @............................ $1.65 bu.
Sold 10,000 bu. December wheat @ .... 1.73 bu.

Net gain... $0.08 bu.

Closing the hedge on a falling market. Assume further that early in August the price of spot wheat declined 6 cents a bushel, accompanied by a proportionate fall in the price of flour. On August 8 the miller accepted an order for flour (the flour for this order having been ground out of the cash wheat purchased on July 10 at $1.65 per bushel) at a price which would give him his milling profit *only if he could consider that the wheat cost him but $1.59 per bushel.* Although he had actually paid $1.65 for the cash wheat, December futures had suffered a decline (along with the decline in the price of spot wheat), having fallen from $1.73 as of July 10 to $1.67 as of August 8, when the order for flour was received. Hence, on the day that the miller sold the 10,000 bushels in the form of flour, he bought a December futures contract to cancel the one he had sold in July. In brief, his August 8 transactions were as follows:

II. August 8 transactions (decline in cash price):　⎧ plus milling
Sold 10,000 bu. wheat (as flour) @ .... $1.59 bu.　⎬ cost and
Bought 10,000 bu. December wheat @ ...... 1.67 bu.　⎩ profit

Net loss.............................. $0.08 bu.

---

[5] For illustrations of hedging in wheat by terminal elevators and in cotton by cotton merchants, see R. L. Kohls, *Marketing of Agricultural Products* (3d ed.; New York: Macmillan Co., 1967), pp. 338–39.

The net result of the transaction is that the miller made his milling profit on the flour he sold. This follows from the facts that (1) he priced his flour so that he would make money if the flour had cost but $1.59 per bushel and (2) his wheat actually cost him but $1.59 per bushel. A glance at the transactions for these two days will show that this latter statement is true. Although the miller actually paid $1.65 for his cash wheat on July 10, he had a 6-cent profit on his futures transactions.

Closing the hedge on a rising market. But what if the price of spot wheat had advanced by August 8 to $1.70 per bushel? If the miller had not hedged his July 10 purchase, this advance of 5 cents per bushel would have resulted in his obtaining not only the milling profit but also an additional speculative gain. Since the miller did not choose to speculate, however, and *since we assume that the futures price changed in line with the cash price,* the 5-cent rise would have made no difference.

The August 8 transactions would have appeared as follows:

II. (a) August 8 transactions (rise in cash price):
    Sold 10,000 bu. wheat (as flour) @ . . . . $1.70 bu.   ⎱ plus milling
    Bought 10,000 bu. December wheat @. . . . .   1.78 bu.   ⎰ cost and profit
    Net loss. . . . . $0.08 bu.

The miller would have gained 5 cents per bushel on his cash wheat but would have lost an equal amount on his futures. Put another way, his wheat would have cost him $1.70 per bushel, since he actually paid $1.65 a bushel and then lost 5 cents per bushel on his futures. Because any order he received for flour on August 8 for immediate delivery would have been based on the cash price of wheat for the day, he would have made merely his milling profit. This example should bring out the fact that the perfect hedge in itself gives neither profit nor loss (except for commission fees). Any profit the hedger makes comes from the performance of grading, cleaning, mixing, milling, or some other service. The hedge simply protects his normal profits, and the hedger forgoes either losses or gains from unforeseen price changes.

Hedging in actual practice. In practice, hedging is a much more complicated procedure. The net result of these complications is that the hedge is not the perfect form of protection it seems to be from the foregoing discussions. The basic assumption of the hedge is that the cash and the futures prices will change equally and in the same direction. This comparable movement is the factor which gives the protection from price changes, since the loss in one contract is offset by the gain in the other, or vice versa. In general, there is good reason for assuming that these two prices will move together (that is, that the spread will remain fairly constant) because the factors influencing one price tend to influence the other,[6] and there is the possibility of shifting from one market to the other. Yet, at any given time, two sets of forces are at work which tend to change the spread.

The first force is quite predictable and arises out of the cost of carrying cash grain to meet a futures contract. It should be obvious that the spread cannot remain greater than this cost. If it becomes wider, operators in the market will sell futures and buy cash, thus increasing the supply of futures and driving down their price, and increasing

---

[6] Both cash and futures prices are determined by fundamental conditions of supply and demand. Neither determines the other. Holbrook Working, a long-time student of futures markets, notes that "Future prices tend to be highly reliable estimates of what should be expected on the basis of *contemporarily available information* concerning present and probable future demand and supply. . . ." See his "New Concepts concerning Futures Markets and Prices," *American Economic Review,* 52 (June 1962), p. 432, and Shepherd and Futrell, *Marketing Farm Products,* pp. 159–61.

the demand for cash grain and raising its price. Hence the maximum amount by which the futures price for any month can exceed the cash price is the amount of the carrying charges. As the number of months which must elapse before the date of the futures gradually decreases, the carrying charges—and therefore the maximum spread—also decrease.[7]

Unfortunately, although the carrying charges set the maximum by which the futures may exceed the cash price and operate as an automatic check to increased spreads, there is no factor which can be definitely forecast to act as a check when the spread becomes less than the carrying charges. And, as a second force tending to change the spread, there is a group of irregular influences which may cause it to be considerably less than the carrying charges. In fact, these irregular forces are sufficient at times to cause the cash price to exceed the future price.[8] This situation might occur, for example, if a scarcity of grain for immediate delivery developed while the prospects for the oncoming crop were good. Another irregular factor is the heavy buying of spot grain by the government, which forces the spot price up without a corresponding rise in futures. During such periods, hedging itself inevitably involves a considerable element of risk, and some traders even speculate by attempting to secure a profitable change in the spot-futures relationship. Still another force upsetting normal price relationships is found in the international commodity agreements which have been concluded from time to time for such commodities as coffee.

Thus a hedge is not a perfect means of protection against price changes, for the spread can change in unpredictable ways. Moreover, hedging itself entails two basic costs. One is the brokerage charge. If the miller did not own a seat on the exchange, he would have to pay a commission of under $30 per 5,000-bushel contract on the complete buy-and-sell transaction. The second is the cost of the margin funds which must be deposited, commonly about 5 to 10 percent of the contract value.

Because of the imperfections, the costs, or because they want to speculate as well as hedge, processors, producers, and middlemen will often hedge only a part of their inventories. Despite these limitations, hedging still retains a high degree of effectiveness in the reduction of risk. A study of the hedging operations of 45 terminal grain merchants on 76 million bushels of futures discloses a loss of less than one-quarter cent per bushel plus commissions—a cheap price to pay for insurance.

Short selling and price stability. There is some ground for the belief that futures trading tends to stabilize prices by making possible the practice of short selling. Assume that the cash price of wheat is advancing and that a large number of speculators feel the price is too high. All they can do (with no short selling) to make their convictions known is to refuse to buy. But if there are people still willing to buy—such as millers who need wheat to fill orders for flour—the price may continue to advance until it has reached such heights that a considerable drop is necessary to bring it in line with underlying supply and demand conditions.

With the short selling which futures trading makes available to the speculator, however, when the cash price reaches levels above that at which the speculators feel it will remain, they can show their feelings in a positive way by selling short in the futures market; that is, they can sell contracts calling for the future delivery of wheat with the idea in mind that the price of wheat will fall before they have to deliver.

[7] The nature and use of carrying charges are well explained in R. J. Teweles, C. V. Harlow, and H. L. Stone, *The Commodity Futures Trading Guide* (New York: McGraw-Hill Book Co., 1969), pp. 157–59.

[8] The cash price for wheat has exceeded the futures price during much of the post-World War II inflationary period.

If the price does fall, they will make a profit on their transactions; if it rises, they will suffer a loss. It is true that all such short selling does directly is to influence the price of futures; but since the tendency is for cash and futures prices to move in the same direction, the weakness in futures will influence the cash price. Hence the peak is taken off the rise in cash prices. Furthermore, as the price begins to fall, the shorts begin "to cover" (to buy) their short sales, so that the decline is not so great as it might be if short selling did not exist. Considered from this point of view, futures trading may indirectly result in greater long-term price stability and may also result in quicker adjustment to supply and demand conditions.

Not everyone accepts the foregoing price stability argument for futures trading. One authority, after stating that "futures trading on the large terminal markets merits neither the blame that has been heaped upon it for causing large [price] fluctuations, nor the praise that has been bestowed upon it for its alleged stabilizing force," goes on to conclude that it has "perhaps . . . accentuated small, short-time fluctuations."[9]

Speculation on commodity exchanges

The benefits of futures trading cannot be realized without encouraging speculation—the attempt to make a profit from price changes. First, futures trading make possible short selling, so that the trader may speculate on both sides of the market. Second, it provides for the purchase and sale of contracts, and speculation in contracts is easier than buying and selling the actual commodities. Third, and most important, hedging cannot be practiced unless traders stand ready to buy or sell futures in large quantities; successful hedging demands a large group of speculators. For example, if the miller wishing to sell a contract for 10,000 bushels of December futures had to hunt up another man to buy it as a hedge against a cash sale, the advantage of speed and certainty would be gone. It might take considerable time to find a buyer, and then that buyer might not want exactly 10,000 bushels. The speculator fills this important gap.

The speculator stands ready to buy or sell futures in large or small amounts at a certain price. He does not hedge his purchases or sales, since his object is to make a profit, not on a manufacturing operation, but on a change in price. Frequently, the profit he has in mind is a very small one on a per-unit basis: "Floor traders" on the cotton futures markets will speculate when they see a profit even as small as 0.04 cents per pound, and "pit scalpers" usually attempt to make one-eighth cent per bushel of corn, oats, and wheat and one-quarter cent per bushel on soybeans. Speculators interested in such small margins seek a large volume of purchases and sales on a quick turnover basis. In contrast, other speculators—frequently referred to as "position traders"—look for larger unit profits on transactions which extend over a considerable period of time. In fact, such a trader may purchase grain and then not sell it for several months.

Unconsciously, the activities of speculators result in a valuable service to society. If they did not stand ready to accept the risks of price changes, these risks would fall on others engaged in marketing—such as millers and terminal elevator operators in the wheat trade.[10] If all the price risk devolved upon manufacturers and middlemen,

---

[9] Shepherd and Futrell, *Marketing Farm Products*, p. 171. By "short-time fluctuations" is meant the hour-to-hour or day-by-day price changes.

[10] And these risks are considerable! "A single cloud sighted over Manitoba two years ago was enough to cause a drop of $750 in flaxseed future contracts, which had been rising in the belief that a drought was destroying the crop." *Time*, September 27, 1963, p. 74.

a series of violent price changes might result in the failure of a number of millers, which, in turn, would lead to the disintegration of their production and marketing organizations. Such results would be far more serious to society than would the failure of a number of speculators.[11]

Moreover, it seems probable that successful speculators with a broad knowledge of the market are a price-stabilizing factor. When they see certain futures prices moving out of line with their forecast of what such prices should be, they immediately make the appropriate purchase or sale so as to make a profit if their judgment turns out to be correct. Such actions tend to prevent wide swings in prices which might result from ignorance of supply and demand conditions.

Spreading in commodity markets. One operation used by speculators which tends to keep even short-term prices in line is called spreading or arbitrage. A speculator puts on a spread when he observes the price difference between two futures contracts are out of line. He simultaneously buys one futures contract and sells another in the expectation that the price difference will widen or narrow back to normal, at which time he would liquidate his spread for a profit. Thus he is not concerned with upward or downward price movements but with abnormal differences in prices at one point in time. The four most common types of spread positions found in commodity exchanges are shown in Table B–2.

TABLE B–2
Usual forms of arbitrage (spreading) found on commodity exchanges

1. Interdelivery spread position—futures contracts for the same commodity on the same exchange spread between two different delivery months, e.g., December corn versus July corn on the Chicago Board of Trade.
2. Intermarket spread position—futures contracts for the same commodity deliverable in the same month spread between two different exchanges, e.g., July corn in Chicago versus Kansas City Board of Trade.
3. Intercommodity spread position—futures contracts negotiated on the same commodity exchange for the same delivery month spread between two different commodities which are substitutes for each other, e.g., July corn versus July oats in Chicago or soybeans versus cottonseed oil on the New York produce exchange.
4. Commodity-product spread position—futures contracts spread between a commodity and the products derived from it for the same or different delivery months on the same exchange, e.g., January soybeans versus soybean oil on the Chicago Board of Trade.

Source: *Commodity Trading Manual* (Chicago: Board of Trade of the City of Chicago, 1971), p. 43.

Summary

Futures markets are facilitating marketing institutions because they provide a vehicle for shifting unwanted price risk from marketing institutions to speculators. Thus speculators perform the risk-bearing function at a low price to the marketing system and make the total cost of marketing less than it would be if middlemen and manufacturers had to absorb inventory losses.

Speculators alone cannot make a market. Institutions in the business of marketing commodities must want to hedge in order for a futures market to be successful. Many examples may be cited.

---

[11] To minimize the risk of failure, speculators in commodity futures have developed various rules or guides. Some of these rules are discussed in Merrill Lynch, Pierce, Fenner & Smith, Inc., *Handbook for Commodity Speculators* (New York, 1970).

Marketing: Principles and methods

1. Following the floating of the U.S. dollar in 1971, the International Commercial Exchange and the Chicago Mercantile Exchange began trading futures contracts on small margins in foreign currencies so that multinational marketers could protect themselves against devaluation of the currencies they hold.
2. When government price-support programs set cotton prices at artificially high levels, the futures markets in cotton dried up, for the only price was the government support price. In January 1971 a new government cotton program which freed prices somewhat took effect and the number of open cotton contracts on the New York Cotton Exchange jumped from 4,200 in March to 15,000 in May.
3. A futures market in plywood became possible because lumber mills decided, after a rapid 1969 price decline, that they wanted to shift price risk.
4. Copper marketers, who are not vertically integrated, hedge their inventories against violent price changes, while iron and steel companies, which are vertically integrated, do not feel a need to protect their ore inventories against price changes.

Over the years, the exchanges have added and dropped commodities from the trading list. Some fail because of lack of interest by potential hedgers. Others fail because the commodity does not have the characteristics that meet the conditions for futures trading. A commodity must be storable, homogeneous, and capable of adequate standardization and grading. Both the supply and the demand for the commodity must be broad and uncertain.

Vertical integration, monopoly, collusion, and government price control are all alternative techniques producers and middlemen can employ to give protection techniques against price changes. While hedging is mainly practiced by middlemen and processors, farmers can, and sometimes do, hedge crops still in the ground. They can also engage in the marketing process by storing a harvested crop in bins at the farm rather than selling at local cash prices; it is becoming increasingly common for them to hedge this inventory and earn the carrying charges. Often, however, they can obtain better risk-shifting services from government price support programs or government crop insurance, which protects the farmer against storm loss. Because the advantages of hedging are not obtained without considerable skill, many family farmers are prevented from engaging in hedging activities. Finally, future markets also encourage wide dissemination of market prices and other information and facilitate equalization of prices among geographical markets.

REVIEW AND DISCUSSION QUESTIONS

1. Explain the major functions of a commodity exchange.
2. What factors determine whether some commodities are traded on commodity exchanges and others are not traded?
3. Distinguish clearly between "cash" contracts and "futures" contracts. Be sure to point out the purposes for which each is used.
4. States one economist: "It should not be surprising to economists that . . . some futures prices approach ideal behavior, perhaps more closely than any other prices, for after all these markets are designed to fit the competitive requirements better than other markets." Why are futures markets designed to fit competitive requirements better than other markets?

5. Consult the financial page of a newspaper and list the cash and futures closing prices of a particular day for wheat, cotton, corn, and soybeans. How do you account for the spread between the cash and futures prices for particular "futures" months for each of the commodities?

6. In your own words, explain the basic purpose of a hedge and how it operates.

7. On October 1 a country wheat elevator bought 10,000 bushels of wheat at $1.80 per bushel. On that day the Chicago cash price was $1.92, and December futures were selling at $1.96. The elevator operator figures that it would take eight days for his wheat to be transported to Chicago for sale, and he did not wish to speculate during this period. He estimated that it would cost 10 cents per bushel to get his wheat to Chicago. On October 9, when the wheat arrived in Chicago, cash wheat was selling at $1.88 and December futures at $1.92.

   a) Discuss the steps the elevator operator would take to minimize his risks from October 1 through October 9. What was his final profit on the transaction?

   b) How do you explain the "spread" between the Chicago cash price of October 1 and December futures? Is there any way of determining the maximum spread? The minimum spread? How would the prospects of a bumper wheat crop to reach the market in three months influence the spread between the present cash and futures on the third month from now?

8. Discuss the factors that tend to reduce the protection afforded by hedging.

9. "The commodity exchange is one of the world's greatest gambling devices. In addition, it tends to reduce the prices paid to farmers for their products. It should be abolished." Discuss.

SUPPLEMENTARY READINGS

Board of Trade of the City of Chicago   *Commodity Trading Manual.* Chicago, 1971. A complete explanation of exchange operations and a summary of statistics on commodities traded on that exchange.

Commodity Research Bureau, Inc.   *Commodity Yearbook.* New York, published annually. Provides statistical data on production, prices, and other important information on many raw materials.

Darrah, L. B.   *Food Marketing.* New York: Ronald Press Co., 1967. Futures trading and hedging are discussed in connection with protection against storage risks on pages 164–75.

Gold, G.   *Modern Commodity Future Trading.* 4th ed. New York: Commodity Research Bureau, Inc., 1966. Current policies and practices are outlined.

Hieronymus, T. A.   *Economics of Futures Trading.* New York: Commodity Research Bureau, Inc., 1972. A new, readable presentation of the basics of commodity futures trading which catches the excitement and importance of these institutions.

Kohls, R. L.   *Marketing of Agricultural Products,* chap. 21. "Risk and the Futures Exchanges." 3d ed. New York: Macmillan Co., 1967. A good treatment of commodity futures markets is afforded by this chapter.

Merrill Lynch, Pierce, Fenner & Smith, Inc.   *How to Hedge Commodities.* New York, 1963. Also see *How to Buy and Sell Commodities.* New York, 1970. The operation of commodity exchanges, terms used in exchange dealings, and hedging practices are treated in these two valuable pamphlets.

New York Coffee and Sugar Exchange   *The Story of the New York Coffee and Sugar Exchange.* New York, n.d. Also see *Active Coffee Futures Contracts.* New York, 1963. These publications of the Exchange provide a brief history of this organization, describe how trading takes place, and afford illustrations of contracts used and regulations applying to all contracts.

Shepherd, G. S. and Futrell, G. A. *Marketing Farm Products: Economic Analysis.* 5th ed. Ames: Iowa State University Press, 1969. Chapters 12 and 13 deal with "Hedging in Futures Contracts" and "Effect of Speculation in Futures Contracts upon Grain Prices."

Teweles, R. J.; Harlow, C. V.; and Stone, H. L. *The Commodity Futures Trading Guide.* New York: McGraw-Hill Book Co., 1969. A complete book designed for the trader.

U.S. Commodity Exchange Authority *Report of the Administrator.* Washington, D.C.: U.S. Department of Agriculture, published annually. Also see *Commodity Futures Statistics.* These publications are a valuable source of information on commodity exchanges and their regulation.

University of Illinois College of Agriculture in cooperation with **Chicago Board of Trade** *Marketing Grain through a Grain Exchange.* Rev. ed. Chicago, n.d. By text and pictures, this monograph answers such questions as: What is a grain exchange? How does the cash market operate? What is a hedge? What does the futures market mean to the farmer?

Indexes

Name index

Reynolds, W. H., 98
Rich, L., 518, 519
Ring, L. W., 80
Riordan, M. J., 519
Robertson, L. H., 521
Robertson, T. S., 117, 123
Robinson, P. J., 285, 289, 298, 512
Roebuck, A. C., 222
Rogers, E. M., 116, 123
Rosenberg, L. J., 64
Rosenburg, Arthur, 185

S

Salisbury, P., 521
Samuels, J. K., 344
Sandage, C. H., 547
Savage, A. H., 628
Savitt, R., 24, 36, 49
Scherer, F. M., 566, 586, 589, 600, 620, 640
Schiff, M., 655
Schlink, F. J., 137
Schoner, B., 407, 408, 411, 412, 415, 416, 428
Schramm, W., 503
Schreiber, G. R., 156
Schumpeter, J. A., 613
Schwartz, D. A., 553
Schwartz, G., 25
Scott, J. C., 640
Sears, R. W., 222
Sederberg, K., 302
Servan-Schreiber, J. J., 379
Sethi, S. P., 380
Sevin, C. H., 655
Shafer, E. L., Jr., 415
Shapiro, S. J., 24, 29, 70, 114, 576
Shaw, S. J., 512
Shepherd, G. S., 331, 342, 348, 352, 665, 667, 669, 673
Sheppard, E. J., 152
Sheth, J. N., 80, 81, 85, 86, 98, 415
Shuchman, A., 455, 501
Simon, J. L., 613
Simon, L. S., 299
Singer, E. M., 640
Skeock, L. A., 633
Skow, L., 219
Sloane, L., 174
Smith, A. B., 158
Smith, Adam, 78
Smith, L. G., 380
Smith, R. A., 607
Smith, S. V., 41, 402, 428
Smykay, E. W., 488, 498
Sommers, M. S., 501
Sosnick, S. H., 613
Spengler, J. J., 567
Sprague, J. R., 260
Stafford, J. E., 127, 370, 402, 428
Stanton, R. R., 90
Stanton, W. J., 473
Staudt, T. H., 316
Steiner, G. A., 75, 85, 97
Stern, L. W., 64, 67, 71, 420, 473
Stone, H. L., 668, 673
Sudman, S., 422

Summers, J. O., 547
Surface, F. M., 57

T

Taff, C. A., 499
Taggert, H. F., 628
Tarpey, L. X., Sr., 631
Taylor, L. D., 123
Teninga, W. H., 218
Teweles, R. J., 668, 673
Thorelli, H. B., 126
Tillman, R., Jr., 370, 374, 501
Tolley, B. S., 531
Tosi, H. L., 504
Toynbee, Arnold, 114
Travaglini, V., 387
Trump, R. M., 41
Tull, D. S., 427
Turner, D. F., 640
Turner, E. B., 368
Twain, Mark, 494
Twedt, D. W., 76, 218

U

Uhitto, C. M., 553
Uhl, K. P., 77, 403, 407, 408, 411, 412, 415, 416, 423, 428
Ule, M., 551
Urban, G. L., 404, 549

V

Vaile, R. S., 49
Vance, J. E., Jr., 239, 247
Vancil, R. F., 302, 324
VanDagens, M. L., 517
Vernon, J. M., 613
Vernon, R., 398
Vollbrecht, J., 519
Vredenburg, H. L., 391, 398

W

Wales, H. G., 79, 423, 501, 525
Walras, Leon, 78
Walsh, C. E., 287
Ward, W. H., 415
Warne, C., 500
Warshaw, M. R., 501, 526
Webster, F. E., Jr., 286, 298, 520
Weckstein, R. S., 134
Weeks, D. A., 520
Weiss, E. B., 357, 467, 519, 520
Wertis, J., 299, 519
Westfall, R., 422
Westing, J. H., 298, 310, 456, 526, 586
Wheaton, W. L. C., 167
Wheeler, J. T., 610, 613
Whittier, W. F., 182
Wieting, C. M., 195
Wilcox, C., 640
Wilemon, D. L., 71, 247, 475
Williams, B., 521
Williamson, O. W., 613
Wind, Yoram, 285, 287, 298, 380

Marketing: Principles and methods

Subject index

Marketing: Principles and methods

D

Dallas Apparel Mart, 258
Data Automation Co., 300
Decennial Census of the United States, 418
Decentralized markets, 334
Deceptive practices, 129–33
Defense Supply Agency, 320
Defensive advertising, 566
Demand characteristics, industrial products and serv-
    ices, 292–95
Demand estimation, 569
Demand schedule, advertising influence, 532
Department of Agriculture, 331, 344
Department of Defense, 319, 320, 322, 533
Department of Justice, 618
Department store, 154, 165, 215–18
    branches, 217–18
    chains, 216
    classifications, 215–17
    definition, 154, 215
    future, 218
    income groups, 216–17
    independents, 215
    ownership-group, 215
Departmentized specialty store, 165
Derived demand, 293–94
    marketing implications, 294
Des Moines Register, 547
Detail men, 515
Dick, A. B., Company, 230
Diebold Computer Leasing, Inc., 300
Differentiated oligopoly, 562–66
Diffusion theory, 116–21
    horizontal, 118
    marketing implications, 120–21
Direct export marketing, 387
Direct mail, 542
Direct private investments, 377–78
Direct sale
    industrial goods, 307–10
    problems, 307–10
Directory of Newspapers and Periodicals, 417
Discount house, 155, 164, 218–21
    channel of distribution problems, 220–21
    characteristics, 218–19
    future, 220
    importance, 220
Discounted cash flow model, 655
Discounts; *see* cash discounts; Promotional dis-
    counts; Quantity discounts; *and* Trade discounts
Discrepancy of assortments, 31–32, 149, 538
    definition, 31
Discriminatory restrictions, 617
Disenfranchised consumers, 131–33
Disney World, 571
Distribution centers, 486–87
Distribution cost analysis, 655–58
    channels of distribution, 655–58
    customers, 655–58
    model, 655–58
    order size, 655–58
    products, 655–58
    salesmen, 655–58
    territories, 655–58
Distributors' brands, 447
Diversification strategy, 437
Diversion in transit, 491

Dodge, F. W., Corporation, 305, 425
Doubleday & Company, Inc., 190
Drop shipper, 252
Dual distribution, 463
Dumping, 394
Dun and Bradstreet, 425
Dunkin' Donuts, 182
DuPont de Nemours & Co., 53, 295
Dynamic efficiency, 29–31, 609
    aggregate growth, 29
    availability of alternatives, 29
    measures, 29–31
    poor measures, 30
    progressiveness, 29

E

Eastman Kodak Company, 52, 190, 634
Economic order quantity, 233
Economic Research Service, 330
Economic systems, 20–22
    advertising's role, 538
    command based, 20–21
    marketing, 22
    marketplace, 20, 22
    tradition-based, 20–21
Economies of scale, 594–95
    marketing activities, 594
Effort information, 408
Effort share information, 408
Ego, 79
Elasticity of demand schedule, advertising influence,
    532–33
Electrolux Corporation, 52, 188, 189
El Paso Natural Gas Co. case, 623
Engel's laws, 112–14
Environment
    agricultural products, 327–30
    global marketing, 391–96
    industrial products and services, 273–96
Equalization process, 32–36, 42, 55–57, 149, 325
    advertising's role, 538
    allocation, 34, 36
    assembly, 33–34, 36
    assorting, 34–36
    definition, 32
    sorting out, 32, 36, 40
European Common Market, 396
European Free Trade Association, 396
Evoked set, 505; *see also* Consumer behavior
Evoked-set comprehension, 81
Exchange control systems, 395
Exclusive dealerships, 636
Exclusive distribution
    advantages, 471–72
    disadvantages, 471–72
    legality, 472
Exclusive selling versus exclusive dealing, 470
Exogenous variables, industrial buyers, 291–92
Experimental research designs, 423
Explanatory information, 409
Export and import agents, 356, 386
Export associations, 386–87
Export commission house, 386
Export duties, 394
Export marketing, 377–78
Exports and direct private investments, magnitude
    and expansion, 377–78

Marketing: Principles and methods

Goal and objective hierarchy, advertising, 543
Goal-objects, 80, 90, 507; *see also* Consumer behavior
Good Housekeeping, 138
Goodwill Industries, 530
Goodyear Tire & Rubber Company, 463
Government control, 637
Government control of agriculture, 347–50
  objectives, 347–48
Government market
  advertising vs. negotiated contract, 321
  audit and renegotiation, 321
  geographic concentration, 320
  implications, 322–23
  one buyer, few sellers, 320
  research and development, 320–21
  subcontracting, 321
Government marketing, 319–23
  implications, 322–23
  market segments, 319–20
Government regulation, 614–38
Grand Union Company, 211
Grange (Patrons of Husbandry), 344
Grant, W. T., 151, 155, 163, 204, 205, 206
Great Atlantic and Pacific Tea Company, 138, 155, 177, 201, 202, 203, 208, 224, 567, 572
Green Giant Company, 448, 572
Grolier Corporation, 45, 188, 189
Gross margin, 647, 656–57
Group activities
  drug and other fields, 186–87
  future outlook, 187
  grocery and supermarket, 185–86
Guarantee against price decline, 576–77
Gulf and Western Industries, 437
Gulf Publishing Company, 305

H

Hart, Schaffner & Marx, 190, 470
Hedging, 42, 336, 665–69
  actual practice, 667
  carrying charges, 667–68
  closing, falling market, 666–67
  closing, rising market, 667
  opening, 666
  short selling, 668
Heinz, H. J., Company, 486
Hershey Chocolate Company, 533
Hertz, 182
Hewlett-Packard Company, 318
Hibbard, Spencer, Bartlett & Company, 231
Hickok Manufacturing Company, 53
Hierarchy of effects model, 510
High Point Furniture Mart, 258
Holiday Inns of America, 171, 182
Homeostasis, 19
Homestead Act, 615
Homogeneous oligopoly, 561–62
Hoover Company, 376
Horizontal integration, 266
Horizontal merger, 562, 602, 622
House-to-house selling, 187–89
  importance, 188
  problems, 188
  reasons, 188

Howard-Sheth model, 80–93
  decision making process, 91–93
  exogenous variables, 86–91
  extensive problem solving, 91–92
  learning stages, 91–93
  learning variables, 80–83, 89
  limited problem solving, 92
  perception variables, 84–86
  real-world inputs, 83
  routinized response behavior, 92–93
Hunt-Wesson, Inc., 539
Hypotheses formulation, 413–14
Hystron Fibers, Inc., 540

I

Id, 69
Import quotas, 395
Incidental information, 412
Income statement analysis, 643–45
Independent grain merchants, 336
Independent Grocers Alliance of America, 181
In depth-crisis subsystem, 409, 411–12
Indirect export marketing, 385–87
Industrial distributors, 306, 307, 308–9, 313–16
  limitations, 316
  services, 315–16
Industrial marketing
  catalog use, 303–5
  information & promotion, 303–5
  leasing, 300–303
  product servicing, 299–300
  trade shows, 305
  unique functions, 299–305
Industrial products and services
  classification, 274–80
  definition, 273–74
  demand characteristics, 292–95
  derived demand, 293–94
  markets, 280–82
  user types, 281–82
Infant industries, 384, 394
Information
  analysis, 414–15
  buyers' side, 407–9
  collection, 416–24
  commercial sources, 424–25
  communication, 415
  continually collected, 406, 413
  cost/benefit ratio, 414
  custom, 424
  definition, 403
  direct testing, 422–23
  effort (cost), 408
  experimental research designs, 423
  external, 406
  internal, 406
  potential, 408
  sales, 407–8
  sellers' side, 407–8
  special problem, 406, 409, 413–14
  types, 407–9
Information function, 37, 42–43
  wholesalers, 263–64
Informative labeling, 127
Information sources, internal, 288
Inland waterways, 492–94
Institutions in marketing, 45–48

Marketing: Principles and methods